TRAVELER

FRANCE

NATIONAL
GEOGRAPHIC

TRAVELER

# FRANCE

by Rosemary Bailey
photography by Gilles Mingasson

National Geographic
Washington, D.C.

# CONTENTS

■ Pages 2–3: The Thiou canal reflects the charming town of Annecy in the Alps.
■ Opposite: At the 18th-century Louvre Museum in Paris, architect I. M. Pei's
pyramids offer a modern counterpoint.

# TRAVELING WITH EYES OPEN

Alert travelers go with a purpose and leave with a benefit. If you travel responsibly, you can help support wildlife conservation, historic preservation, and cultural enrichment in the places you visit. You can enrich your own travel experience as well.

To be a geo-savvy traveler:

- Recognize that your presence has an impact on the places you visit.

- Spend your time and money in ways that sustain local character. (Besides, it's more interesting that way.)

- Value the destination's natural and cultural heritage.

- Respect the local customs and traditions.

- Express appreciation to local people about things you find interesting and unique to the place: its nature and scenery, music and food, historic villages and buildings.

- Vote with your wallet: Support the people who support the place, patronizing businesses that make an effort to celebrate and protect what's special there. Seek out local shops, restaurants, and inns. Use tour operators who love their home place—who love taking care of it and showing it off. Avoid businesses that detract from the character of the place.

- Enrich yourself, taking home memories and stories to tell, knowing that you have contributed to the preservation and enhancement of the destination.

That is the type of travel now called geotourism, defined as "tourism that sustains or enhances the geographical character of a place—its environment, culture, aesthetics, heritage, and the well-being of its residents."

# FRANCE

## ▌ ABOUT THE AUTHOR & THE PHOTOGRAPHER

**Rosemary Bailey** fell in love with France when she stayed on a rose farm in Provence. Since then she has written and edited a number of guides to the country and its regions, including the Côte d'Azur, Burgundy, the Loire Valley, and southwest France. She has also written three travel memoirs, including *Love and War in the Pyrenees*. Her website is *rosemarybailey.com*.

Photographer **Gilles Mingasson** grew up in Grenoble, France, before moving to Paris to pursue a career in photojournalism. Today, Mingasson works on feature and travel stories for clients including *Newsweek, Fortune, Reader's Digest, Scholastic, Sky, Le Nouvel Observateur, L'Equipe, Reppublica Delle Donne, Espresso, Elle,* and *Le Figaro*. His website is *mingasson.com*.

## 5TH EDITION UPDATE

**Jack Kavanagh,** author of *National Geographic Complete National Parks of Europe* and *Always Ireland* and the upcoming *National Geographic Complete UNESCO World Heritage Sites*, has worked for National Geographic since 2001. He is a contributing editor to National Geographic International Editions, which publishes magazines and books in 25 languages worldwide.

With contributions by:

**Professor Colin Jones,** professor of history at London University

**Elizabeth Carter,** restaurant critic and author

**Dr. Julian Petley,** lecturer in sociology, Brunel University

**Jo Sturgis,** editor of travel guides, author of a *Guide to France for Children*

**Helen Varley,** travel writer and and author of *Weekends Across the Channel*

**Ginette Vincendeau,** professor of film studies, King's College London

# CHARTING YOUR TRIP

**Europe's third largest country (after Russia and Ukraine), France is the world's most popular travel destination. Layers of its long, dramatic history can be seen everywhere. Celebrated for its art, culture, fashion, and, of course, food and wine, France rewards the traveler on a wealth of levels. It could take a lifetime to discover it all, but even a short visit allows you to sample many of its riches.**

## How to Get Around

Traveling in France is easy. Between cities it is most expedient to travel by train *(raileurope.com)*. The TGV (Train à Grande Vitesse high-speed train) network means you can travel between most of the big cities in two or three hours. Smaller places will take a bit longer on an SNCF (Société Nationale des Chemins de Fer Français) train, which are frequent and comfortable. If you prefer to drive, the autoroutes are excellent, though car rentals are expensive. But if you want to explore the countryside, you will need a car. Buses are sometimes an option, though in really remote areas there may be only one or two buses a day. There are a few small scenic trains, especially in mountain regions, which offer a splendid way to view the scenery. Cyclists are well respected, and you can take bikes on most trains or rent them at your destination. In Paris and the provinces, cycle routes are increasingly common.

## How to Visit

France is not easily covered in a whistle-stop tour. It is best to be selective and focus on appreciating a few chosen places. If you have only a week or so, it would be best to concentrate on a city or two and add on a trip to the coast or countryside. No visitor to France can miss **Paris,** but even a day or two is enough to absorb the flavor of this very special capital city, which is really quite easy to walk around; Parisians do it all the time. The Métro is easy and safe, as are the buses. Taxis can be expensive, and you need to be at a taxi stand to get a cab.

If you base yourself in Paris, you can make day visits by train to the great cathedral of **Chartres,** the palace of **Versailles,** or the gardens at **Giverny,** painted by Impressionist artist Claude Monet. Or spend a day or two a little farther afield. Less than 100 miles (161 km) from Paris is **Reims,** known for the stained glass of its magnificent Gothic cathedral and its fine champagne. It's about 145 miles (234 km) north of Paris to **Normandy,** where highlights include the Bayeux Tapestry and the World War II landing beaches. **Mont St.-Michel** and its glorious abbey is 175 miles (283 km) west of Paris. Another option is the **Loire Valley:** Head for **Tours** (126 miles/202 km

■ **A towering symbol of Paris since 1889**

southwest of Paris) by train or car and take in the finest châteaus—Chambord, Amboise, and Chenonceau.

Alternatively, from Paris you could head south to **Avignon** by speedy TGV (2 hours and 45 minutes); from there it is 122 miles (196 km) south to **Nice** and 65 miles (104 km) to **Marseille.** Or go to the gastronomic paradise of **Lyon** (a two-hour train trip south from Paris). You can add in a trip to the **Alps,** about 60 miles (97 km) east.

## If You Have More Time...

... to appreciate some of the fine food and architecture—and the quality of life of which the French are so proud— explore the **Loire Valley** via a boat trip on the famous river. Or plan a stay in one of the many private châteaus (see pp. 211–212). Another option would be **Bordeaux** with its incomparable wines, fine restaurants, superb classical architecture, and excellent museums.

### NOT TO BE MISSED:

**The views of Paris from the top of the Tour Eiffel**  74–75

**The stained glass at Chartres**  110–111

**A champagne toast at the source**  140

**Normandy's World War II landing beaches**  166–167

**Iconic Mont St.-Michel**  169–170

**The Loire Valley's dramatic and historic castles**  191–193 & 196–208

**Fine dining in Lyon**  241–244

**St.-Paul de Vence's art and creative spirit**  338

**The lavender of Provence**  351

## Visitor Information

The official tourism website of the French Government (*france .fr*) always offers a wealth of information in English and in other languages on all aspects of travel to France, with photographs and comprehensive descriptions of all regions and cities. You'll find practical trip-planning advice on driving, trains, buses, shopping, food, entertainment, special events, outdoor activities, and weather updates.

For a mine of information on Paris, go to *paris.fr.* and *france way.com.* For train information,

schedules, and bookings, go to *raileurope.com.*

Given the enduring appeal of France as a tourism destination, a whole cornucopia of websites exists to assist travelers and also those considering making France their new home.

Good English-language sites include:

*anglophone-direct.com, france .angloinfo.com, frenchentree .com, informationfrance.com, francethisway.com, about-france .com, americansinfrance.net, and monuments-nationaux.fr.*

## When France Closes

The French lunch hour remains a hallowed tradition, especially in rural areas and the south, so expect most shops, banks, and offices to close between 12 and 1:30 or 2 p.m. Given that lunch usually starts at noon in traditional restaurants, you need to be fairly prompt to be sure of being fed. Evening meals are not usually served until 7:30 or 8 p.m.

Most towns have one closing day, often Monday, and shut down completely after midday on Sunday. Be aware of specific holidays (see Travelwise p. 397), during which shops, post offices, and sometimes museums will be closed.

Wine lovers should also consider **Burgundy,** including a visit to the elegant towns of **Dijon** and **Beaune** plus a trip to the **Côte-d'Or** to learn about and sample its legendary Pinot Noirs and Chardonnays. For a taste of the real *France profonde*—deep France—go to the southwest. Start in **Toulouse** (five hours by train from Paris), a lively city of brick mansions and Romanesque cathedrals, or the preserved medieval citadel of **Carcassonne** (also about five hours by train from Paris). Stay in a small château (see Travelwise pp. 439–451) and enjoy the myriad preparations of duck, goose, and foie gras. Don't miss the **Dordogne**—out of season, preferably, because it has become so popular—which offers beautiful landscapes, rich stews, and good wine. The river is flanked by splendid castles and important caves with prehistoric paintings.

For more dramatic countryside and especially for those with a taste for skiing, hiking, or horseback riding, head for the **Massif Central** (central France; about 200 miles/322 km south of Paris) and the nearby volcanic region of the **Auvergne** or

## Cultural Etiquette

The French can seem quite formal. They often kiss or shake hands on greeting. The numbers of kisses remains a vexed question even to the French, but generally speaking they will kiss twice (once on each cheek) in Paris and the north, and three or even four times in the south. However, Covid has cooled the ardor with which many now observe this ritual. When you enter a shop, it is normal to wish the other customers and shopkeeper *bonjour*—and *au revoir* when you leave. It is always polite to address older people as *madame* or *monsieur,* even if the French today are more casual.

While the French can often be passionately argumentative among themselves—a fiesty French argument is well worth observing—they are also quite discreet. It is rare in a French restaurant to be able to hear the conversation at a nearby table. There is, however, one area in which manners fall away: Be sure to stand your ground when you are in line for a taxi or in a busy market waiting to pay.

the dramatic canyons of the **Gorges du Tarn.** The **Alps** (some 100 miles/160 km east of the Massif Central) offer plenty of opportunities for the *sportif,* from winter skiing to summer hiking through flowery mountain meadows. In the southwest of the country, on the border with Spain, the **Pyrenees** can also be enjoyed at all seasons.

For a classic seaside holiday, go to the northwest. The coasts of **Normandy** and **Brittany** (roughly two hours by train from Paris) delight with their fishing ports and deserted rocky coves. Farther down the Atlantic coast are the **Île de Ré** and **La Rochelle,** favorite summer destinations for Parisians in the know. Even farther south is **Biarritz,** with its dramatic waves and popular surfing beaches.

■ **Just imagine the rich, aromatic fragrance of lavender flowers rising from this Provençal field.**

For many, **Provence** and the **Côte d'Azur** (the TGV train from Paris to **Nice** takes about six hours) remain the supreme pleasure of a visit to France, and it is true that the lavender-scented southern hinterland of olive groves and sleepy villages is completely beguiling. Roman sites here include the great amphitheaters of **Nîmes** and **Arles,** and the Pont du Gard, a bridge still standing after 2,000 years.

The Mediterranean coast, loved by Picasso and Matisse, is a treasure trove, with its palm-fringed beaches, azure sea, glitzy nightlife, and many fabulous art museums. A string of legendary hotels re-create the glamorous heyday of this land of vacations. To get from Paris to the popular resort of **Cannes,** via **Marseille,** takes about six hours—most of them quite scenic.

Geography aside, a great way to really appreciate France and its culture would be to attend one of the many festivals that take place throughout the year (see Travelwise pp. 471–476). You can sample Celtic culture in **Brittany,** theater in **Avignon,** photography in **Arles,** dance in **Montpellier,** jazz in **Nice,** and **Menton**'s annual celebration of the lemon. And of course, film buffs flock to **Cannes.**

Indeed, you could simply revel in one or more of the many local food festivals that take place year-round, celebrating wine, oysters, chestnuts, cherries, apples, honey—or any of the gastonomic glories produced in France. Or plan your travel based on market days. Wherever you plan to visit, first find out when and where markets are held (see Travelwise pp. 463–470).

There is nothing more authentically and enjoyably French than to wander around the stalls of local vegetables and fruit, regional products, and bric-a-brac, perhaps buying lunch and gifts, but most definitely observing the French in their habitat, going about their daily lives with that certain élan and joie de vivre.

# HISTORY & CULTURE

Opposite page: A procession follows Sunday Mass at Reims cathedral, in northern France.

# FRANCE TODAY

**The boundaries of France are largely natural: the English Channel and the Ardennes hills in the north; the Atlantic Ocean in the west; the Pyrenees in the southwest; the Mediterranean in the south; the Alps in the southeast; and the Jura and Vosges Mountains and the Rhine River in the east. To these striking features add the Massif Central and its extinct volcanoes.**

## The Land

France is the largest country in western Europe at 211,150 square miles (547,020 sq km) and the 37th largest in the world; at the same time, it is actually slightly smaller than the state of Texas. Although twice the size of the United Kingdom, it has roughly the same population—65 million. France is a largely rural country: 56 percent of the land is farmed and 25 percent forested. Agriculture, the country's largest industry, has been described as France's *pétrole vert* (green oil). France has by far the largest cultivatable area, and the biggest agricultural output, of any state in the European Union. Big cities are few and far between; Paris is the largest, with a population of 2.1 million, followed by Lyon (1.7 million) and Marseille (1.6 million)—all of them small cities by European standards.

> **For all the splendors of Paris, and of provincial cities such as Lille and Nice, France is predominantly a country of villages.**

## Regional Diversity

The first feature that strikes any visitor traveling through France, aside from its rurality, is its remarkable regional diversity. France is the only European country that extends into both the north and south of the continent. Significant regional differences in climate, geology, geography, and culture have given rise to the extremely varied and rich agriculture that contributes so strikingly to the diversity of the French landscape—and, of course, produces France's fabled cuisines and wines. Again, these are above all regional: The cuisine of Périgord is as unlike that of Normandy as the wines of Champagne differ from those of Bordeaux.

## Village Life

For all the splendors of Paris, and of provincial cities such as Lille and Nice, France is predominantly a country of villages. There are 33,000 communes (the smallest administrative unit in France), each embracing a number of villages. Again, these vary from region to region—from the gray, granite fishermen's cottages of Brittany shielded against the rolling Atlantic breakers, to the thatched and half-timbered Normandy hamlets nestling among apple orchards dotted with cows, to the flat, Roman-tiled, red roofs of Provençal hill villages clinging in terraces to steep slopes.

At first sight, many of these villages and their rural surroundings may appear to have changed little over the centuries. But changes there most certainly have been. In 1789, the population of France was 27 million, 22 million of whom lived in the countryside. Since the middle of the 19th century, there has been a steady flight from the land, and, since 1945, more than 6 million people have left for the towns and cities, driven away by dramatic changes in farming practice. In 1939, 35 percent of France's active population worked on the land; now the proportion is down to about 2.5 percent and expected to fall further. Hardest hit of all has been the smallest farmer, the *paysan* or peasant—unknown in America, already extinct in many European countries, and in almost certain terminal decline in France. In the brave new world of agribusiness and European Union farm

■ **Paris and its citizens have become more casual over the years, but romance and style remain hallmarks.**

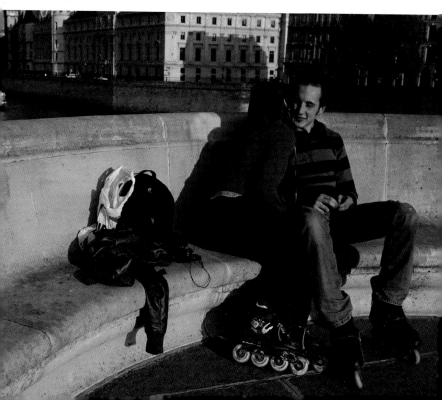

subsidies, the peasant farmer and his tiny, much-divided smallholding is simply being modernized out of existence. Subsidy farming and the remote, absentee landlord-businessperson have become unattractive but increasingly common features of the French countryside. The evidence can be seen in the vast, eerie prairies that now clothe parts of the north and center, unbroken by the outline of a single house, let alone a village. This is less an empty countryside than an emptied one. Traveling through France, and especially through poorer parts such as the Auvergne or the Ariège, it is hard not to be struck by the number of ruined houses left as the visible sign of this exodus.

But, while it is important to understand the forces that have made the French countryside what it is, one should also beware of romanticizing the peasant past—a considerable body of French literature exists to suggest that most of us would actually have loathed to have lived in those hard times. And in recent times French villages have undergone something of a revival, as French people and foreigners have bought rural vacation houses or even set up small businesses, thus bringing new forms of work and encouraging fresh types of rural economic activity.

## The People

As with the French landscape, the keynotes here are again diversity and regionality. Although the French are famously patriotic (Chauvin was a Frenchman, after all), a French person referring to *mon pays* may mean the area in which he or she lives rather than France as a whole. It can be quite disconcerting to discover just how little acquainted some French people are with parts of the country other than their own. In its most pronounced form, this identification with region over country has led to separatist demands—largely peaceful (albeit unconstitutional)—in Brittany, Corsica, and the Basque region of the Pyrenees. Language is also a symbol of regional independence—Breton in Brittany (see p. 173), and Occitan in Provence and Languedoc (as in "tongue of oc," see pp. 365–366), are both experiencing a revival.

 **Nothing illustrates so clearly the enormous diversity of France as the differences among its peoples.**

Nothing illustrates so clearly the enormous diversity of France as the differences among its peoples. The Celtic Bretons are culturally distinct not only from the Mediterranean people of Provence and Languedoc but also from their Norman neighbors—and so on all around France. A gulf still exists between Parisians and the rest of France. Parisians may think of themselves as urban sophisticates, but there are those outside the capital who regard them as arrogant. Parisians may enjoy having their *maisons secondaires* (second houses) deep in rural France, but for some the word "provincial" is still virtually a term of abuse. Even celebrated writers such as François Mauriac (Bordeaux) and Gustave Flaubert (Normandy) frequently seem

## À la Mode

Paris is still considered the fashion capital of the world, as it has been since the 17th century. Haute couture (a legally protected term in France) developed during the early 20th century with designers such as Elsa Schiaparelli, Paul Poiret, Madeleine Vionnet, and Coco Chanel and returned after the deprivations of World War II with Christian Dior's "new look" and the prêt-à-porter (ready-to-wear) line of Yves Saint Laurent.

Increasing competition is now challenging the French dominance of the industry, and many foreign designers have directed Paris fashion houses, including German Karl Lagerfeld at Chanel and British Phoebe Philo at Céline. Avenue Montaigne, the high-fashion street of the 16th arrondissement, now hosts designer Ralph Lauren's flagship store.

Nevertheless, the twice-yearly Paris fashion week in the Carrousel du Louvre are highlights of the fashionista's calendar, and many of the world's top designers have their headquarters in Paris.

In the end, there is still no better place in the world to sit than in a Paris café if you wish to observe the natural fashion chic of these most stylish of European citizens, the French.

to have harbored distinctly ambivalent feelings about their own provincial backgrounds. There can be few more poisonous portrayals of small-town bourgeois life than Flaubert's *Madame Bovary* (which makes it all the more surprising that various Normandy villages vie with each other in claiming to be the model for Flaubert's suffocating town of Yonville).

Not surprisingly, given its colonial past (in Algeria, Morocco, Indochina, French West Africa, and so on), France also has many communities of different ethnic origins. From the mid-1950s to the mid-1970s, furthermore, labor shortages led to massive recruitment campaigns not only in North Africa but also in several poorer European countries such as Greece, Spain, and southern Italy. Many of these foreign workers chose to settle permanently. In spite of that famous French saying, "*Vive la différence!*" France is not free of racism. It has been exploited by the overtly racist Front National political party, with considerable success in some areas. Tourists are unlikely to encounter this side of France, however, unless they visit the run-down housing projects on the fringes of cities.

France remains a deeply civilized country, nevertheless, and the liberal majority are disgusted by this particular blot on their nationhood. Indeed, no one can visit France and fail to notice the role that courtesy, decorum, and good manners play in everyday life (except, unfortunately, behind the wheel of a car).

It is impossible to visit France without immediately becoming aware of the importance of style. Looking good really matters. This is the case not only in super-fashionable Paris. Chairs outside French bars and cafés often face outward, not toward each other: You are there to watch the passersby. People don't spend all that money and time on their images simply to be ignored!

Immensely stylish, too, is the presentation of food. One of the many joys of walking down just about any French street is not simply the sheer variety of small shops but also the virtuoso window displays, particularly of food—mouthwatering works of art in their own right. And even in the simplest of restaurants, dishes are frequently presented with a style and flair—and taste—that completely belie the modest prices charged for them. France is a gourmand's wonderland.

The French are also extremely proud of their rich cultural heritage. Intellectuals and artists are listened to and even revered. A significant number of politicians are writers, too—and not simply of the usual turgid, self-serving memoirs.

> **Given the importance that the French accord to culture, it is hardly surprising that the country abounds in cultural festivals. Best known is the Cannes film festival.**

In this increasingly global era, the French do tend to feel that their very Frenchness is at risk, be it from American films and hamburgers, or the conditions for European monetary union, and they are quite prepared to take to the streets to defend it. In France, with its historical revolutionary tradition, direct action is seen not as inimical to democracy, but rather as an integral part of it. This is seen time and again in dramatic countrywide protests, whether it be against new youth employment laws, which were perceived to threaten the basis of French society, or to proposed changes to the pension entitlement, which threatened the relatively young retirement age in France.

In 21st-century France, there is also particular concern that French culture—be it food, fashion, film, or even the very language itself—is under threat from an Anglo-Saxon invasion induced by a globalized and digitized world. On the other hand, no European country has done more than France to celebrate the best of American culture: its jazz in the 1920s and '30s, "hard-boiled" crime writing in the 1940s, Hollywood in the 1950s, and so on. And it is France—not, as might be expected, English-speaking Great Britain—which plays host to the European Disneyland.

## Festivals

France has a large number of public holidays (for details see Travelwise p. 397) when everything is closed. Seven of these are religious days. As France has been a secular state since 1905, the existence of so many religious holidays may seem curious. Only about 14 percent of the French go regularly to Mass, and although this may rise to 80 percent in traditionalist rural areas, it drops to 10 percent in Paris and 4 to 5 percent in certain industrial centers. The flight from the land has contributed significantly to the decline of religious observance.

On the other hand, a majority of French people are still nominally Christian, and about half of all children are baptized. Furthermore, the organized church is still a formidable force. A socialist government discovered this to its cost when in 1984 it tried to integrate Catholic schools into the state system, thus sparking off one of the biggest demonstrations ever seen in postwar Paris.

Aside from the national holidays, there is a myriad of local religious festivities. Perhaps the most striking is the Romany pilgrimage held every year on May 24–25 at Stes.-Maries-de-la-Mer in the Camargue (see p. 358).

Given the importance that the French accord to culture, it is hardly surprising that the country abounds in cultural festivals. Best known is the Cannes film festival. But enlightened local, regional, and national attitudes to what the French call the *septième art* (the cinematographic art is the seventh classification of the arts) ensure funding for a whole host of smaller (and many would say better) film festivals.

Every form of art is catered to in France's myriad of festivals: You can hear classical music at Aix-en-Provence, Montpellier, Orange, and Prades; jazz at Juan-les-Pins and Marciac; or rock at Bordeaux and Rennes; you can see graphic art at Angoulême and St.-Malo; theater at Avignon. And these are but a fraction of the hundreds of festivals that take place each year, especially in summer. ■

■ **The annual pre-Lent carnival in Nice rocks with fun, food, and fabulous floats.**

# HISTORY OF FRANCE

**The distinctive style associated with France and Frenchness is rooted in an extraordinarily rich history that is full of contrasts. Contemporary France stands as an object lesson in state centralization, its carefully honed administrative procedures an example to the world. Yet it has always been a bastion of resistance to bureaucracy and of regional diversity, localism, and individualism.**

France's past has often seemed inextricably linked with the peasant, rural orientation of its society. Yet at the same time, this apparent rootedness belies the extent to which the country has been built up through a gradual accretion of other peoples. As much as other richly diverse states, such as the United States, France is a melting pot on whose history a dazzling succession of peoples have left their mark: Celts and Romans in earliest times, Germans

■ **Prehistoric artists used the contours of the Lascaux caves to make animals more lifelike.**

and Scandinavians in the Middle Ages, Africans and Asians in the 20th century, and spasmodically the English, the Spanish and Portuguese, the Jews, and many other groups have all affected the composition and temperament of French society.

Although France is sometimes seen as a supremely land-based state, its destiny linked intrinsically with that of continental Europe, it is in reality an amphibious power, as much at home at sea as on land. Its naval and commercial strengths have made it a crucial player in the fates of parts of North America, Africa, India, Southeast Asia, and the Pacific.

> **At every stage of its history, France's role in the development of Western civilization and culture has been crucial.**

## Prehistory

At every stage of its history, France's role in the development of Western civilization and culture has been crucial. The prehistoric cave art found in the Dordogne area and in the Pyrenees, dating back 20,000 years or so, is among the richest in Europe.

### The Romans

The Romans infused a sense of collective identity into the diverse and belligerent Celtic tribes who had developed a powerful Iron Age culture. The Roman Empire had brought the Mediterranean fringe of France under control in 125–121 B.C., but it was Julius Caesar who conquered the warlike Celts. Though the last resisting chieftain, Vercingétorix, defeated by Caesar at Alésia in Burgundy in 52 B.C., was to become something of a national hero, the establishment of the *pax romana* brought new wealth and prosperity to the region.

### The Franks

With the collapse of the Roman Empire in the fourth and fifth centuries, Roman Gaul gave way to Francia—the kingdom of the Franks. The Franks were originally just one among a tribal swarm of Germanic societies outside the Roman Empire whom the Romans dubbed "barbarians." They were well placed to benefit from the slow crumbling of imperial power. In the late fourth and fifth centuries, one Frankish group, the Merovingians, took over northern France and extended its power southward. Their ruler, Clovis, chose Paris as his capital, and in A.D. 496 became a Christian, thus assisting the spread of Frankish power over the Christian south.

Louis XII (*R.* 1489–1515) graces the pages of *Le Voyage de Gêby* by Jean Marot.

## Charlemagne

In the eighth century, the Frankish prince Charlemagne founded the Carolingian dynasty, building up a European power bloc centered on what would later be France and Germany. In 800, he was crowned emperor (the first since Roman times) by the pope. The centrifugal tendencies within feudalism, together with new incursions by Saracens from northern Italy, by Magyars from central Europe, and by Norsemen (or Vikings) from Scandinavia, cut short the life of the Carolingian Empire. In the Treaty of Verdun of 843, the empire was divided into three units: the Germanic kingdom of the East Franks; the kingdom of the West Franks, which was to become the historic core of France; and an intermediary state, Lotharingia.

In 987, West Francia, or simply Francia as it was increasingly called, passed into the hands of Hugh Capet, founder of the Capetian dynasty. Branches of this family provided the French ruling house to the 19th century. His authority was initially meager—he ruled over a tiny region in the Île-de-France around Paris, a power base dwarfed by the territory and war bands possessed by feudal lords throughout France. One of his vassals, William, Duke of Normandy, became King of England after a successful invasion in 1066. The English kings built an empire stretching from the Scottish border to the Pyrenees. But the Capetians gradually—through a combination of military force, diplomacy, skillful marriage alliances, and outright chicanery—rolled back the power of the English and their other overmighty subjects.

## The Crusades

From the 11th century to the 13th, French kings were in the forefront of the West's Crusades to convert the Holy Land to Christianity. One monarch, St. Louis (Louis IX), even died on a Crusade. The extension of Capetian power into southwest France into the 13th century came through an internal Crusade authorized by the pope against the so-called Albigensian heresy. Now the authority of kings of France was imposed, almost for the first time, in the Mediterranean as well as in the northern regions.

The increasing political power of the Capetian monarchy was accompanied by considerable economic prosperity. Much newfound wealth was channeled into cathedral building, and the Gothic style that Capetian rulers sponsored was widely copied throughout Europe. The towns also saw the emergence of the first universities. The university in Paris, where Pierre Abélard and Thomas Aquinas taught, soon achieved wide renown and respect.

## The Hundred Years' War

But by the early 14th century, there were already signs that the economy was failing, and the Black Death of 1348 came as a final hammer blow. The disease killed perhaps one-third of France's population, which in many regions took centuries to rise again to pre-plague levels. The epidemic caused unparalleled damage to the economy, though the ensuing labor shortage did lead to the erosion of feudalism, as lords were obliged to lessen the feudal burden on their serfs. At this critical moment, English claims to French lands triggered the Hundred Years' War (1337–1453), with the

> Despite sacrificing Jeanne d'Arc to the Anglo-Burgundians, Charles VII drove the English back to the Channel.

English forming an alliance with the dukes of Burgundy, who were then angling for autonomy from France.

The wars went badly for the French. English feats of arms—most famously at the Battle of Agincourt in 1415—humiliated the French kings. By the early 15th century, the power of the latter was negligible, and the country seemed on the verge of partition. With the charismatic Jeanne d'Arc (Joan of Arc) at the helm, though—notably in 1429–1430—the French king fought back. Despite sacrificing Jeanne d'Arc to the Anglo-Burgundians, Charles VII drove the English back to the Channel. He and his successors also brought Burgundy to heel. Its integration into the French kingdom in 1477 was complemented by that of Provence in 1481 and Brittany in 1491.

## The Renaissance

In 1494, Charles VIII invaded the Italian peninsula, thus inaugurating the Italian wars that would last to 1559. Though they were fought on Italian soil, the main targets of French aggression were the Habsburg rulers who held the title of Holy Roman Emperor in Germany and who also ruled Spain. The struggle, though a stalemate, marked a period of cultural and economic vitality as well as political recovery in France. Italian Renaissance masters such as Leonardo da Vinci and Benvenuto Cellini worked for the French king, François I, and the court culture that François developed gave rise to important building projects. The most outstanding of those were in the Loire Valley, resulting in a dazzling spread of both new châteaus such as Chambord, Chenonceau, and Azay-le-Rideau and up-to-date additions to older ones, like Blois.

## The Wars of Religion

The Renaissance was accompanied by religious reformation. France was split between two antagonistic camps, as Protestants and Catholics fought no fewer than eight Wars of Religion between 1562 and 1598. The struggle was marked by terrible bloodshed—most notoriously in the infamous St. Bartholomew's Eve Massacre of 1572. In Paris alone, 2,700 Protestants were slaughtered (more than the Revolutionary Tribunal was to manage in two years of the

■ **Behind the Apollo Basin stands the largest and most opulent palace in France: Versailles.**

Terror, between 1792 and 1794), with as many as 20,000 more deaths in other cities throughout France. Only the conversion from Protestantism to Catholicism of Henri IV—first of the Bourbons—accompanied by the military defeat of his ultra-Catholic enemies and his erstwhile Protestant allies, was to bring the religious struggles to a conclusion. The Edict of Nantes in 1598 established an uneasy truce between the two sides.

> **The Enlightenment fostered a widespread taste for freedom, which the monarchy did little to satisfy.**

By rallying his subjects around the notion of religious tolerance and social welfare after the horrors of civil war—his ideal of every peasant having a "chicken in the pot" was an enduring propaganda image—Henri IV sealed his reputation as Good King Henry. But from the 1620s on, the cardinal ministers, Richelieu and Mazarin, who successively wielded great power, sought to defeat the Austrian Habsburg monarchy in Europe and to establish a centralized absolutist state. This placed severe strains on French society—the tax burden rose threefold between 1630 and 1648—and the discontent of the poor, amplified by the grievances of nobles and religious dissidents, exploded in riots and rebellions.

### The Sun King

Despite these alarms, the groundwork for a strong centralized monarchy had been laid by 1661, when Louis XIV achieved his majority and began his personal rule. The reign of the "Sun King" was to be one of the longest in French history, mingling glory and ingloriousness in equal measure. The elaborate court society that Louis installed and led in his new palace at Versailles became the envy of Europe. It was also the base from which Louis pursued European power and a colonial empire, notably in Canada.

This was the period in which some of the greatest creative talents in French cultural history—Descartes, Corneille, Racine, Molière—flourished and lent luster to France's *Grand Siècle* (Great Age), when France was Europe's greatest power. From the 1680s on, however, Louis lurched into an increasingly desperate struggle against an alliance of his principal European foes, the English and the Dutch. He added to his problems by revoking the Edict of Nantes in 1685 and launching a repressive campaign against France's Protestants.

## The Enlightenment

If the cultural achievements of 17th-century France centered on the palace at Versailles, those of the 18th-century Enlightenment largely flowed through the network of organs and institutions that characterized the bourgeois society now emerging as trade and manufacturing increased. Salons, coffeehouses, academies, novels, periodicals and newspapers, masonic lodges, and political clubs all now proliferated. Thus developed an urbane and humane culture that did not shrink from criticism of hidebound court-based hierarchy. There was an international, pacifist flavor to the French Enlightenment, too—English and Scottish philosophers were honorary members, as were Americans Benjamin Franklin and Thomas Jefferson. In contrast, the dynastic wars of kings seemed primitive and cruel.

The Enlightenment fostered a widespread taste for freedom, which the monarchy did little to satisfy. The crown became increasingly indebted, even though for most of the century the economy boomed. Foreign policy was directed for the most part against France's commercial rival, England; this antagonism was to remain the fulcrum of European relations from the last wars of Louis XIV in 1688 to the overthrow of Napoleon in 1815. For most of the century, France was losing the struggle. The only significant success it managed—when French armed forces helped England's American colonies achieve independence (1775–1783)—bankrupted the state. Financial crisis, combined with a social crisis caused by several poor harvests in the late 1780s, drove the state toward something more drastic than reform: revolution.

### Off With Their Heads!

The guillotine remains the bloody emblem of the French Revolution, with the horror of heads rolling into baskets and enraptured mobs howling for blood. The executions took place at the Place de la Revolution in Paris, now Place de la Concorde; during the Reign of Terror, up to 40,000 people were executed in this fashion. However, the guillotine was actually devised as a more humane method of execution, a substitute for traditional beheadings, hangings, or burning at the stake. It remained the legal method of execution in France until 1981, when the death penalty was finally abolished.

## The French Revolution

The French Revolution was to provide the seeds of European liberal democratic traditions. The values of liberty, equality, and fraternity, enshrined in the Declaration of the Rights of Man of 1789, established an ideal both for political action and for the political culture within which most European states have evolved. The decade from 1789 to 1799 saw a kind of fast-forward scramble through five types of government: absolutist monarchy of the Ancien Régime type, constitutional monarchy, authoritarian republicanism (and the Terror), liberal republicanism, and finally—with the advent of Napoleon Bonaparte—military dictatorship.

It was probably asking too much of the well-meaning but ineffectual Louis XVI to mutate from an absolute monarch to a liberal ruler working within strict constitutional limits. His queen, the implacably antirevolutionary Austrian Marie-Antoinette, did not help, urging him to view his duty as lying more toward the old nobility than the new political nation. Her compromised worldview, applied to the reality of 18th-century France, would allow only one strata of society to have their cake and eat it, too.

The king's tireless efforts to sit on the political fence were doomed following the declaration of war against Austria. His failure to give his full support to the national war effort led to his overthrow in August 1792 (he was executed the following January) and to the establishment of a republic that became increasingly authoritarian as the war became more desperate.

By early 1793, France was fighting virtually the whole of Europe. The Enlightenment had put religious tolerance on the agenda, so it was perhaps surprising that religion became a major bone of contention, too, with the church supporting the Ancien Régime and the revolutionaries tempted into ever more anticlerical policies.

## The Terror

The Committee of Public Safety, with Maximilien de Robespierre as its mouthpiece, set out to assure the defense of the Republic against internal and external enemies through policies of internal terror (combined with radical social legislation aimed at eliciting support from peasants and urban workers) and national mobilization. The so-called *levée en masse* of August 1793 was the closest that any state came to total warfare prior to the 20th century.

However, Robespierre and his faction seemed to want to intensify the Terror even as the war threat receded. In July 1794, his fellow deputies in the National Assembly deposed him in order to move toward a more liberal republic, enshrined in the Constitution of 1795. The period known as the Directory failed to impose internal harmony on warring factions or to bring the external war to a successful conclusion. In November 1799, the regime fell to a coup d'état by the revolutionary Corsican general, Napoleon Bonaparte. A new constitution was organized, but within a couple of years Napoleon's de facto dictatorship had become a de jure imperial regime.

- **François Gérard painted Napoleon in the robes in which he crowned himself emperor in 1805.**

## The Napoleonic Empire

To a considerable degree, Napoleon only continued what the revolutionaries had already started. Through brilliant generalship and astute diplomacy, he built an empire encompassing a good deal of western and central Europe. He also famously redrew the map of Europe in order to provide sufficient new states for the members of his extensive family to rule.

The spread of French power under Napoleon was far from a victory for the Rights of Man. Though he accepted and consolidated some of the gains of the revolution—notably equality before the law, religious tolerance, economic freedom, and the abolition of feudalism—in many respects he represented an absolutism even more absolute than that of his Bourbon predecessor. The Napoleonic Civil Code was a signal achievement, though it showed that the emperor was concerned even less with the rights of women than with the Rights of Man.

As long as he could ensure that the costs of warfare fell on his enemies rather than on the people of France, Napoleon remained popular. After his disastrous Moscow campaign of 1811–1812, however, he was always on the run. The main European states combined forces against him and encouraged dissent within territories under French rule. By 1814, he had been deposed, and though he made a brief return from exile, he was defeated definitively by the Duke of Wellington at the Battle of Waterloo (in Belgium) in 1815.

## After Napoleon

The factionalism and acrimony of French politics in the revolutionary and Napoleonic periods did not simply fade away after 1815. The restoration of the Bourbon dynasty in 1815 failed to satisfy all but dyed-in-the-wool enthusiasts for "Throne and Altar" since they had learned nothing from the preceding 25 years and continued to strive for a return to a long-gone past. The revolution of 1830 brought a more liberal regime under an older Bourbon branch, the Orléanists. But this, too, failed to find general favor.

A further revolution in 1848 brought a flirtation with more radical policies, but the president of the new Second Republic—Louis Bonaparte—stayed true to his uncle's sympathies. He seized power in a coup d'état in 1851, and in 1852 installed the Second Empire. This, too, failed to put down strong enough roots to survive defeat by the Prussians in 1870–1871, along with the loss of Alsace and Lorraine, which were incorporated into the new Germany.

## Social & Political Change

A republican regime seemed to be the type of government that divided the country least, though in the early days of the Third Republic many believed that it would preface the restoration of the monarchy. Fearing this, the people of Paris seized power and set up the Commune to rule the city. Its brief rule ended in massive loss of life as the Communards fought government forces street by street for the city. The monarchy was not restored, but French political life remained venomously divided.

The emergence of organized working-class parties, some of which proudly laid claim to a revolutionary tradition, brought fresh lines of division.

> While politics oscillated wildly in the late 19th century, French society was rapidly changing under the impact of industrialization.

While politics oscillated wildly in the late 19th century, French society was rapidly changing under the impact of industrialization. The process was slower than in neighboring England, but less painful, too. The growth of towns and the development of industry neither spelled the end of peasant farming nor utterly transformed the countryside. By the last years of the century, moreover, industrialization was bearing fruit for a large proportion of the population. Writing on the eve of World War I, the writer Charles Péguy claimed—with a certain amount of accuracy—that the world had been transformed more radically since his own school days in the 1880s than it had been between then and the time of the Romans.

## Paris Renewed

Paris was the beacon of the new, with its Tour Eiffel constructed in 1889 for the international exhibition to commemorate the centenary of the revolution, towering over the city. The city enjoyed wide new boulevards and was famed for fashion houses, department stores, and glamorous sites of all imaginable pleasures. The elegant belle epoque had its dark side, however. As realist novelists such as Émile Zola showed, working-class conditions were appalling, and yet the Third Republic took little interest in social questions.

## Conflict With Germany

France had lost its colonial empire to England during the revolutionary and Napoleonic wars. In 1830, it conquered Algeria and began to amass a new one. The bulk of imperial acquisitions were made after the 1870s, amplifying tensions with other European powers, notably Britain. Nevertheless, the prime target for French aggression was now Germany, which in economic and military terms seemed to be outstripping France in the years before the outbreak of World War I in 1914.

■ **Gen. Charles de Gaulle, shown here in French Equatorial Africa in 1941, led the Free French forces during World War II.**

France benefited from being on the winning side of that war. Alsace and Lorraine were restored to the Third Republic with the Treaty of Versailles in 1919, but the victory was won at a massive price. France lost more men in the war—1.3 million—than any other nation. Much of the northern part of the country was devastated by the passage of the Allied and German armies, as first one side and then the other gained a few miles of country in the fruitless struggle of trench warfare. Modernization meant not only more consumer goods and more elegant lifestyles but also murderous new forms of mechanized and mass warfare.

French men and women still found it difficult to sleep soundly at night, moreover. The German call for revenge became ever more threatening in the interwar years, as Hitler and the Nazis came to power in Germany in 1933. France had its own Fascist movement, too, against which was pitted a revolutionary Communist movement linked to the Soviet regime established in Russia in 1917.

The Third Republic still had its charms: Foreigners such as writers Gertrude Stein, Ernest Hemingway, F. Scott Fitzgerald, and Ezra Pound; Black jazz musicians; and a variegated range of painters and sculptors found Paris in particular a welcoming center of cultural dynamism in the years between the World Wars. But the Third Republic's political compromise would not be sufficient to deal with the new challenge of war in 1939.

## Occupation & Decolonization

In the middle decades of the 20th century, France had to cope with two profound traumas: World War II and the process of decolonization. The French defeat at the hands of Nazi Germany in 1940 brought German occupation, at first in the northern half of the country and then, from 1942 on, throughout all of France. It also involved collaboration with the Nazis. Under Marshal Pétain, a World War I hero, Jews and Communists became the prime targets of the Vichy regime's collaborationist zeal.

Resistance was at first directed from London by the self-exiled Gen. Charles de Gaulle, and from the early 1940s was spearheaded by a wide range of political activists, with Communists to the fore. The Allied landings on the Normandy beaches in 1944 found Resistance movements coming out into the open to mop up the retreating German forces. After the war, France united around the new Fourth Republic (which granted women the vote for the first time). Yet painful memories of collaboration remained, rising spasmodically to haunt the national conscience.

> **Political scars should not blind us to the way in which France came to terms with some of its thorniest problems in the late 20th century.**

The process of decolonization had a similar effect. From the early 1950s, the liberation movements in North Africa and Indochina elicited a strong military response from the French. Their defeat at the battle of Dien Bien Phu in Indochina (which Vietnam was then part of) in 1954 by the Communist Viet Minh led to the withdrawal of the French from the Far East. Civil war flared up in Algeria and threatened political stability within France itself. Political crisis triggered by events in Algeria brought General de Gaulle to power as president of the new Fifth Republic. His solution to the crisis—granting complete independence to Algeria and offering repatriation to the colonists—left lasting rancor on both sides of the Mediterranean.

## The "May Events"

Political scars should not blind us to the way in which France came to terms with some of its thorniest problems in the late 20th century. Most notably, it has achieved an almost undreamed-of political stability. During de Gaulle's lifetime, many political thinkers suspected that the structure of the Fifth Republic was such that only a right-wing figure could operate effectively within it. The regime, however, has proved able to accommodate the death of its founder; the election of a Socialist president, François Mitterrand, in 1981; and since then an acceptance of the principle of alternation (*alternance*) between left- and right-wing governments and presidents. The only time the regime appeared to be in danger was during the "May Events" of 1968, when protests almost brought down de Gaulle's government. After almost 50 years, however, the

Fifth Republic has become the second-longest-enduring regime in French history since the 18th century, after the much-underestimated Third Republic.

## European Cooperation
Another specter exorcised from French political life since World War II was that of an aggressive Germany. From the 1860s to the 1940s, French foreign policy was constructed around hostility to Germany. But Germany's defeat in war led farsighted individuals in both countries to work toward cooperation. France and Germany have been at the forefront of every stage of European cooperation.

The end of World War II in 1945 initiated the Thirty Glorious Years, which saw the French economy modernizing and expanding at a faster rate than ever before. Impressive economic growth and an unparalleled baby boom combined with a shake-up in infrastructure and services, the widespread diffusion of consumer durables and other commodities, the growth of mass leisure, and a new affluence that put a question mark against hallowed customs and conventions.

France is one of the world's richest countries, though unemployment and taxes are high, and its general health and pension benefits are under threat. Despite international tensions, and the deadly ISIL attacks on Paris in 2015, France remains a popular tourist destination. More than 90 million visit annually. Paris, beneficiary of a policy of cultural grandeur (as exemplified by the Centre Pompidou, the Opéra National de Paris-Bastille, the Musée d'Orsay, and the Musée du Quai Branly), is still outstanding among cities. Equally striking has been the dynamism of provincial cities such as Lyon, Montpellier, Lille, Toulouse, Rennes, and Nantes. A growing concern for regionalism, multiculturalism, and gender issues is leading to a broadening of political and cultural options and greater respect for the country's heritage.

In 2017, Emmanuel Macron was elected president, France's youngest ever at 39. His administration has weathered yellow vest (populist) protests and pension reform strikes, with civil unrest in many areas. Nevertheless, despite rising racial tensions France remains one of the most tolerant countries in the world. ■

■ In an annual tradition, **May Day demonstrators in Paris speak out on critical social issues.**

# FOOD & DRINK—FRENCH WAYS

**Gastronomy—the art and science of good eating and drinking—is not just a French pastime: The population spends more of its income on gastronomical pleasures than on anything else. In 2010, UNESCO added French cuisine to its list of intangible cultural treasures. In 2022, French baguettes joined the list.**

France's gastronomic and regional diversity is probably greater than that of any other country. An exasperated Charles de Gaulle once famously remarked, "How can anyone be expected to govern a country that produces 265 different cheeses?" (The official tally is now closer to 400.) And a gastronomic pilgrim traveling the southwest coast from La Rochelle to the Spanish border (a distance of some 300 miles, or 480 km) could encounter more than 500 different seafood dishes.

The French pleasure in food is perhaps most apparent at the ubiquitous street markets. For the visitor, a tour of a French market is an education in

A diner's delight: Les Deux Magots café in the St.-Germain-des-Prés area of Paris the nature of Gallic society. Established food shops are also busiest on market days. French butchers and fishmongers are masters of their craft who can be counted on to dispense verbal recipes and banter with each purchase, while sellers of cheese, fruits, and vegetables will ask if your purchase is meant for that evening or for the next day, and then select accordingly.

Although daily shopping at local stores and markets is still the general rule in France, giant supermarkets filled with prepackaged bread, vegetables, diet cuisine, and frozen foods are hugely popular, and there is concern that individual shops will eventually find it hard to compete. *Boulangeries* (bakeries) are a case in point. The traditional French baguette goes stale in a matter of hours. As bakers become reluctant to bake twice a day (early morning and again in the afternoon), so the French have changed their habits, buying their bread once a day instead of, as was customary, twice. And so the baguette seems to get flabbier as preservatives are added. The faster-paced lifestyle of modern France is fueled by microwaveable meals and chains of fast-food restaurants (McDonalds is known as Macdo).

Curnonsky, the French gastronome and author of the 32-volume *La France gastronomique,* described four distinct types of French cookery: "la Haute Cuisine, la Cuisine Bourgeoise, la Cuisine Régionale, et la Cuisine Improvisée." Half a century later, these categories still stand.

Haute cuisine is professional cooking by chefs of the highest achievement. In current terms, it describes accurately the cooking of multi-Michelin-starred chefs such as Hélène Darroze and Alain Ducasse. Nouvelle cuisine is (or was) a modern interpretation of haute cuisine. Top chefs reconstructed classic French dishes in response to the demand for lighter dishes containing less butter

---

**INSIDER TIP:**

A major Burgundy event since the 19th century, the annual November Beaune wine auction is a gala three-day affair. The auction itself is traditionally candlelit.

—ROSEMARY BAILEY
*National Geographic author*

---

and cream and fewer heavily reduced sauces. In its original form, the style was short-lived, but nouvelle cuisine has left its mark on French haute cuisine; classic dishes are prepared in a much lighter vein than 20 years ago. By contrast, *cuisine improvisée* is peasant in origin. This cuisine comprises farmhouse dishes of hams, sausages, stews, and omelets.

But it is the two remaining categories that have most shaped the culinary map of France. *Cuisine bourgeoise* is the simple and unbeatable ordinary middle-class French cookery. *Cuisine régionale* consists of the great regional specialties of France in classic dishes such as bouillabaisse from Provence, coq au vin from Burgundy, and cassoulet from Toulouse.

Restaurants vary greatly. At their simplest, they are small, family-run affairs offering home-style cooking, with local

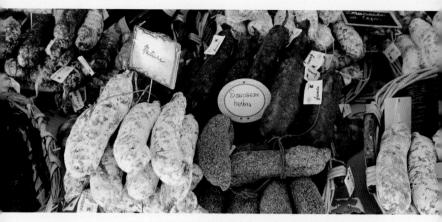

■ In the Alsatian town of Colmar, *saucissons* form a tempting still life in a shop window.

cheeses and desserts probably brought in from the local patisserie. Wine is offered by the carafe, with a small selection available by the bottle.

Then come brasseries, lively restaurants serving a limited menu at any time of day and often fairly late at night. Beer remains a feature (brasserie means "brewery"), with some brasseries offering an extensive selection. Typical dishes include *steak pommes frites* (frequently described as the national dish of France); *estouffade de boeuf*; and *blanquette de veau*, as well as cold meats and cheeses.

Most distinguished are topflight restaurants offering classic haute cuisine in a refined setting. Prices are higher, but often there will be a fixed-price menu representing surprisingly good value, especially at lunchtime. Some restaurants specialize in creative, modern cooking, others in seafood or regional classics, and all will offer an extensive wine list, possibly with a sommelier to give advice on what to order.

And then there are cafés, those picture windows for observing everyday life, as French as the baguette. No village is complete without one. To adopt the café lifestyle, just learn how to nurse a beer or coffee over the course of several hours, while watching passersby.

Regional differences are marked and defended vigorously with pride. In the cool north, where dairy produce is paramount, butter, cream, and cheese form the basis of a rich cuisine. Traveling south, the emphasis shifts, with chestnuts, walnuts, and truffles dominating dishes that rely on duck and goose fat. The market gardens of the Mediterranean provide the olive oil, garlic, tomatoes, and peppers for dishes reflecting the influence of Spain to the southwest and of Italy to the east.

## Wine

Climatic differences also distinguish French wine. Thousands of properties all over the country make wines of all complexions, though, in general, northern vineyards produce the stunning white wines, and those farther south make the great reds. In the United States, the names of a handful of grape varieties such as Chardonnay and Merlot are used as the ready reference for wine. But in France, more complex traditions prevail: Wine is usually known by its place of origin, rather than by the grape. Cahors, for example, produces delicious malbec.

## Cider & Beer

Not all French people drink wine with their meals. In Normandy and Brittany, farmers brew a sparkling range of ciders. Beer, too, is popular throughout northern France.

## EXPERIENCE: How to Eat Well in France

A favorite French pastime is strolling around a town or seaside resort, checking the menus of lots of restaurants before deciding—after a great deal of excited discussion—where to eat. Most restaurants display a list of variously priced menus outside. They are obliged to offer at least one set menu, and this is usually the cheapest option, particularly at lunch, when many French people have their main meal of the day. The menu will normally consist of a starter (hors d'oeuvres), main course (entrée), and dessert. Sometimes there is a lower price for just two of the courses. Usually a restaurant will offer one or two specials (the *plat du jour*—dish of the day), which may be based on whatever the chef has found in the market that morning. Wine or coffee may also be included in the price, and bread (usually sliced baguette) will be brought to the table at no extra charge.

You can ask for bottled water, but if you are happy to drink local water, simply ask for *l'eau du robinet* (tap water) or *une carafe d'eau*. The service charge is nearly always included (it will say *service compris* on your bill), but you can always leave a bit extra if you are pleased with the food and/or the service.

If you do not want a complete menu, you can order à la carte and simply choose what you want. If you can communicate in French, always ask the waiter or waitress for advice; servers are usually happy to tell you what looks good in the kitchen. (But address them as *monsieur, madame,* or *mademoiselle,* not *garçon.*) You can order wine by the bottle, but it is often offered in carafes and by the quarter or half liter. In a wine-producing area, this will be a good—and the best priced—option. If you order coffee—*café*—you will get simple black espresso. If you want coffee with milk, ask for café au lait, *café crème,* or a *noisette,* which is espresso with a bit of milk added. You may be offered herbal teas or tisanes, which can be delicious especially if made fresh. Classics include chamomile, vervain, mint, and linden *(tilleul),* the tea in which Proust dipped his famous madeleines.

# THE ARTS

**Hardly surprisingly, given all the riches, the French are extremely proud of their cultural heritage. Education is highly valued, and discussion of artistic and intellectual matters is taken for granted as part of everyday life.**

## Roman Era (56 B.C.–A.D. 476)

It was with the Romans that the first signs of "modern" civilization appeared in France. Their architecture symbolized the power of their empire, and it can still be seen to striking effect in the amphitheaters at Arles and Nîmes, the temples at Nîmes and Vienne, and the aqueduct of the Pont du Gard.

## Romanesque Period (11th–12th Centuries)

After the fall of the Roman Empire, France plunged into the Dark Ages until the coming of the Carolingian dynasty in the eighth century. This period has left few visible remains: For these one looks to the flowering of Romanesque ecclesiastical architecture in the 11th century. Here timber roofs give way to stone vaulting, buttresses take the increased weight, and the use of decoration grows.

The Romanesque style spread throughout France and developed regional features—especially in Burgundy, where you can appreciate an excellent example of the Romanesque at Vézelay (see p. 228).

■ **In Paris, visitors climb the floating staircase in I. M. Pei's glass pyramid at the Louvre.**

Fortresses were the other major buildings to survive from the Romanesque era, but most have been either reduced to ruins, modified, or rebuilt. Angers (see p. 208) retains its massive curtain wall, and Langeais still has a medieval exterior (see p. 213).

The predominant themes of this period's literature, which was mostly in verse, are faith and chivalry. Particularly important are the *chansons de geste* or heroic songs. A favorite theme was Charlemagne's wars against the enemy, as in the *Chanson de Roland* (circa 1098), which recounts the death of the Carolingian hero while defending the pass at Roncesvalles against the Saracens.

> **In 13th-century France, courtly romances were preoccupied with the Arthurian legend.**

The first courtly romances appeared in the 12th century—narrative poems concerned with idealized and chivalrous conceptions of love. The classical influence was strong, and the most famous romance writer, Chrétien de Troyes (died circa 1183), saw himself and his contemporaries as inheritors of the literary traditions of the Greeks and Romans. In 13th-century France, courtly romances were preoccupied with the Arthurian legend. The genre also produced the most influential work of the Middle Ages, the *Roman de la Rose*, a dream-allegory of courtly love. The same theme dominated the lyric poetry of the Provençal troubadours, who made a significant contribution to the development of French music.

## Gothic Period (12th–15th Centuries)

Gothic architecture had strong upward aspirations (see pp. 132–133). Gothic churches and cathedrals have high, pointed arches, flying buttresses, and large traceried windows filled with stained glass, which reach their apogee in the rose window, as at Chartres cathedral (see pp. 110–111). Interiors became more highly decorated and elaborate, with rood and choir screens, altarpieces, and statuary.

Book decoration and illustration, known as illumination and best represented by the books of hours, containing prayers to be said at the canonical hours, reached its zenith in the 14th century. At the same time, easel painting arrived. In its attention to detail and concern with representing space convincingly, French art of this period shows the influence of the more developed Italian and Flemish schools. The major figure is Jean Fouquet (circa 1420–1481), painter to Louis XI.

Medieval France's main contribution to music was through the monasteries, which preserved the tradition of the plainchant and elaborated it into polyphony. The Burgundian court also had a key musical role, employing a huge number of musicians, and composers such as Guillaume Dufay (circa 1400–1474) flourished under its patronage.

The 15th century saw France's most outstanding medieval lyric poet, François Villon, who used conventional verse forms but invested them with the spirit of the *fabliaux* (bawdy popular tales) to draw a vivid picture of low life in 15th-century Paris.

■ **Louis XV commissioned the construction of the Panthéon in Paris in the late 18th century.**

The most interesting prose writers of the time are the chroniclers, of whom the best known is Jean Froissart (circa 1337–circa 1405), the chief historian of the Hundred Years' War; he compiled a remarkable eyewitness account of the Battle of Crécy (1346).

## The Renaissance (16th–17th Centuries)

French campaigns in northern Italy at the end of the 15th century brought the aesthetics of the Italian Renaissance to the attention of French artists and architects and their patrons. This can be seen most clearly in the building of châteaus by the royal family and nobility that marked the final stages of the castle's progression from fortification to elaborate residence. Living quarters were extended, windows became larger, and moats, keeps, and turrets became purely decorative as opposed to defensive features. The castle descended from hilltop to riverside, where its watery reflection further enhanced its splendor. The château was supposed to harmonize with its natural surroundings, but formal grounds were integrated into the grand design more and more. The Renaissance influence made for increasingly regular and symmetrical architectural designs. Nonetheless, châteaus exhibit a number of different styles. Thus Cheverny, built in 1634, is classical in its purity of line, while Blois (see p. 191), built between the 13th and 17th centuries, reflects the development of secular French architecture from feudalism to classicism. Chambord (see pp. 192–193), the largest of the Loire châteaus, is a superb example of Italian Renaissance style.

The spirit of the Renaissance began to permeate literature in the 16th century, as scholars rediscovered the classical Greek and Latin writers. Under their renewed influence, a broader outlook began to challenge the rigid theological thinking of the late medieval period. The first printing press was established in Paris in 1470, and by 1515 some 100 operated in France. This had a huge impact on the development of vernacular literature. The work of François Rabelais is the supreme expression of this newfound freedom, vitality, and enthusiasm. His *Gargantua* and *Pantagruel* were parodies of chivalric romances, but also addressed serious philosophical issues.

Equally a Renaissance man, but far more methodical and rationalist, was Michel de Montaigne, whose three books of *essais* (literally "tryings out") gave the form its name. Montaigne's remark that "each man bears the complete stamp of the human condition" perfectly sums up the humanist spirit of Renaissance thought.

The key poet of the 16th century, and the leader of a group of writers known as the Pléiade, was Pierre de Ronsard (1524–1584). The Pléiade broke with medieval poetic forms and looked to Greece and Rome for models. The 12-syllable line—the Alexandrine—began its long dominance of French poetry.

> **The spirit of the Renaissance began to permeate literature in the 16th century, as scholars rediscovered the classical Greek and Latin writers.**

## Classicism (17th Century)

Classicism started during the reign of Louis XIII and reached its apogee with his successor, Louis XIV. The absolutism of the age is expressed in its architecture by grandiosity, stress on order and symmetry, and evocation of the glory of Greece and Rome. The zenith of the early Louis XIV style is undoubtedly the château of Vaux-le-Vicomte, built in 1656–1661 for Nicolas Fouquet, finance minister in Mazarin's time. Louis XIV was so envious that he hired the same design team (led by Louis le Vau) to build a château a hundred times bigger—Versailles.

In 1648, the Royal Academy of Painting and Sculpture, a key instrument for imposing "official" standards and principles of taste, was founded. It enshrined the classical idea that the practice and appreciation of art are rational activities that can be reduced to rules and precepts, and thus be taught and learned.

**Italian Influence:** In painting, Italy was the influential center of Europe. Especially important was Caravaggio for his rich colors, deep shadows, and dramatic compositions, and his introduction of a realism into conventional religious subjects as in his "Death of the Virgin" (in the Louvre). His influence is visible in the work of leading French 17th-century painters like Moïse Valentin, Georges de La Tour, and Simon Vouet. The two 17th-century French painters who best express the classical spirit are Claude Lorrain and Nicolas Poussin. Lorrain's landscapes are Arcadian, evoking the pastoral serenity of a golden age bathed in a glorious light. Poussin dealt with noble themes from classical mythology treated in a pastoral mood, but developed a more austere classicism in works that exude monumental simplicity, lucidity, and calm.

Elaborate ballets were the main form of musical entertainment at court, and a young Florentine, Jean-Baptiste Lully, became one of the principal dancers and composers. More popular than Italian opera were *tragédies lyriques* (a form of sung play with balletic elements). Lully composed a large number of these; he also greatly influenced church music and wrote solemn motets for the royal chapel, with soloists, chorus, and orchestra. This form was also developed by Gustave Charpentier, François Couperin, and Michel-Richard Delalande with strict counterpoint enriched by sonorous harmonies.

**Literature:** French classical literature was built on the foundations laid down by Montaigne. He saw literature as a part of the enlightened study of human nature, a search for its universal features, inseparable from what we would now think of as philosophy. Furthermore, Descartes's conception of man as essentially rational, endowed by the Creator with reason to be used in the pursuit of truth, had a massive impact on all forms of intellectual life. Their literary followers were preoccupied with the purity of language and style, and the dramatic unities of time and place. They divided literature into discrete genres such as comedy and tragedy and founded the Académie Française in 1634 to safeguard French language and literature. The century also saw the growth of salons, hosted by noblewomen such as the Marquise de Rambouillet, in which literary matters were discussed.

> " The two 17th-century French painters who best express the classical spirit are Claude Lorrain and Nicolas Poussin. "

Some of the most interesting writers of the age dealt in nonfiction. For example, La Rochefoucauld's *maximes*—such as "Hypocrisy is the homage which vice pays to virtue" and "We are all strong enough to bear other people's misfortunes"—give off a certain sense of cynicism and moral pessimism. Madame de Sévigné's *Lettres* paints a lively picture of daily happenings. Finally, the *Lettres Provinciales* and *Pensées* by Blaise Pascal provide a welcome antidote to the narrow and self-confident rationalism of much 17th-century thought. His famous saying, "The heart has its reasons of which Reason knows nothing," marks him as a precursor of Romanticism.

**Drama:** The chief poetry of the 17th century is in its drama (although one should not forget the sly and sometimes cynical *Fables* of Jean de La Fontaine, which borrows heavily from Greek fabulist Aesop's originals). The plays of Pierre Corneille and Jean Racine ensured that tragedy was the supreme genre. Corneille's tragedies such as *Le Cid* and *Polyeucte* are highly formal, concentrated dramas about passion versus moral duty, peopled by superhuman figures who are less three-dimensional, psychological characters than symbols of nobility and heroism. Racine took the theme of duty versus desire to even greater heights in *Andromaque, Phèdre,* and other classically inspired plays, but he was the greater poet; his characters are not just ciphers but passion-filled human beings, the language has an incantatory power, and the dramatic action has a remorseless intensity.

**Comedy:** Comedy flourished at the same time, thanks to Jean-Baptiste Molière (1622–1673). The first French playwright to use the genre for social commentary, he is, along with William Shakespeare and Ben Jonson, a key figure in the development of European comedy.

Molière's plays mingle farce, ballet, and the comedy of manners, and they have a satirical edge that sometimes caused trouble with the authorities. His attack on intellectual pretension, *Les Précieuses ridicules,* offended the habitués of the salons and earned him enemies there. *Tartuffe* attacked religious hypocrisy, but was taken as an attack on religion and banned for five years. But his masterpiece, *Le Misanthrope,* shows that Molière was not simply a deft satirist but also a master of the comedy of character who knew that the line between comedy and tragedy was indeed a fine one.

## French Rococo (18th Century)

Inevitably there was a reaction against the austere grandeur of the Louis XIV style. In architectural terms, interiors became smaller, more intimate, and highly decorated, with elaborate furniture to match. There was an abundance of curved lines, exotic woods, lacquered paneling, and gilt.

The paintings of Antoine Watteau, François Boucher, and Jean Honoré Fragonard best express the rococo spirit. Watteau may have been influenced by Rubens, but he is quintessentially 18th-century French. Painting in colors that are rich, yet also soft and light, he depicts an exquisitely delicate and artificial world of *fêtes galantes* in dreamy, pastoral settings. After this, Boucher (Madame de Pompadour's favorite artist—several of his most famous paintings are of Louis XV's mistress—and the epitome of the elegant superficiality of the mid-18th-century French court) seems rather frivolous. His pupil, Fragonard, painted lightly erotic works such as "The Progress of Love"—full of rococo verve, sparkle, color, and wit—for Madame du Barry, a later mistress of Louis XV.

## Neoclassicism & the Enlightenment (18th Century)

After the frivolity of the rococo, there was a return to the classical. In painting, the Académie Française insisted on seriousness, reviving heroic themes from antiquity. The most notable exponent of the new manner was Jacques-Louis David (1748–1825), whose subjects displayed self-sacrifice and moral duty in a suitably severe style. He had strong revolutionary sympathies, later becoming Napoleon's official painter and the main artist of the revolution. One of his best known works, "The Death of Marat" (1793), depicts the revolutionary hero assassinated in his bath.

In philosophy and literature, the spirit of free, rational inquiry was predominant, and there was a widespread belief in progress through enlightenment. This was the century of the philosophe, the progressive-minded individual involved in cultural and artistic activity as well as social and scientific thinking. In literary terms, the treatise and the essay were equally as important as the novel, play, or poem—marking the beginnings of a literature of thought.

**Philosophical Thought:** Montesquieu (1689–1755) epitomized the Enlightenment spirit. In his *Considérations sur les Causes de la Grandeur des Romains et de Leur Décadence* he laid down a rational approach to the study

■ **Molière posed for "La Mort de Pompée," painted by Pierre Mignard (1612–1695).**

of history, arguing that "it is not chance that dominates the world, but general causes, either moral or physical." Similarly *L'Esprit des Lois* attempts to explain why the laws of different countries vary; characteristically it enthrones reason as "the most noble, the most perfect, the most exquisite of our senses."

**Rousseau:** The 18th century also saw a reaction against rationalism and a foreshadowing of Romanticism. Nobody illustrates this better than the philosopher Jean-Jacques Rousseau (1712–1778), who proclaims the natural over the civilized, emotion over reason, the individual over society. Largely self-taught, Rousseau exerted an enormous influence on every field he entered. His *Discours sur les Sciences et les Arts* elaborated the theory of natural goodness, the *Discours sur l'Inégalité* the virtue of primitive society. The novel *La Nouvelle Héloïse* is the key work of the "sentimental revolution," which dethroned reason and reestablished the claims of the heart. It was the century's publishing sensation, going through 70 editions in its first 40 years. *Émile*, part novel, part treatise, and wholly a defense of nature as the greatest educator, was a key text of progressive education, as *Le Contrat Social* was of democracy. Finally, Rousseau's devastatingly intimate *Confessions* virtually defined the modern autobiography.

The sentimental revolution is also expressed in several novels concerned with libertinage. Typical is *Manon Lescaut* by the Abbé Prévost. The novel's ostensible purpose is to show "the disastrous effects of the passions," but it is so ambiguous and bizarre that it is almost a celebration of *l'amour fou*. Similarly, Pierre Choderlos de Laclos's much-adapted *Les Liaisons Dangereuses* poses as a moral lesson, but what emerges is the seductive fascination of evil. In the novels of the Marquis de Sade, the idea of presenting libertinage so as to deliver a moral message is taken to such pornographic extremes that it has the opposite result.

## Romanticism (19th Century)

French Romanticism was at its height from 1820 to 1850, but cultural movements are never neat. A reaction against the rationalism of the Enlightenment and its attendant classicism, French Romanticism proposed the primacy of unfettered, individual imagination. Romantics rejected external reality to seek solace and inspiration within themselves or in exotic or imaginary locales. Particularly via the writer Madame de Staël (1766–1817), who spent much time in Germany, interest grew in German writers such as Goethe, Schiller, and Novalis. Meanwhile, English influence ceased to be philosophical and rationalist and became lyrical and picturesque, thanks to such writers and artists as Byron, Scott, Constable, Turner, and the hitherto neglected Shakespeare.

■ **Empire dresses illustrated in the** *Journal des Dames et des Modes* **likely inspired many a dressmaker.**

**Painting:** Théodore Géricault (1791–1824) was the archetypal Romantic, dying young (at 33). His "Raft of the Medusa" is typical in its macabre subject (castaways dying), Romantic brio, movement, and energetic handling of paint. More important was Eugène Delacroix (1798–1863). Influenced by Rubens and the English painters Bonington, Gainsborough, and Constable, he specialized in emotionally charged and often exotic subjects; his technical virtuosity, freedom of brushwork, and richness of color were extraordinarily influential, way beyond the confines of Romanticism.

**Music & Opera:** The rigid institutionalization of music in France made it difficult for outsiders to break in, and the Romantics were outsiders by temperament. But German composer Christoff Gluck had helped to pave the way for Romanticism when he worked on his operas in Paris in the 1770s, and in the next century the French, no longer musically insular, welcomed the arch-Romantics Franz Liszt (1811–1886) and Frédéric Chopin (1810–1849).

France produced a key Romantic composer, indeed Romanticism personified, in the shape of Hector Berlioz (1803–1869). A composer with the grandest of ideas and a formidable sense of drama, his *Symphonie Fantastique*, with its evocations of a violent storm, a march to the scaffold, and a climactic witches' sabbath, broke all the bounds of what a symphony was "supposed" to be. Berlioz's *Mass* and *Te Deum* are works on a truly gargantuan scale, and had he completed *Les Troyens,* it would have been the equivalent of Richard Wagner's *Ring* cycle. His *Memoirs* is one of the great heroic expressions of the Romantic era, but it would be a mistake to regard its author simply as the archetypal Romantic rebel and outsider, disdaining all formal procedures. Berlioz also wrote one of the definitive treatises on orchestration and introduced the finest Romantic music to France. He was not only a key Romantic but also a pioneer of modern music.

Romanticism had a longer life in music than elsewhere. Charles Gounod's *Faust* was for many years the best loved French opera. Jules Massenet, the most popular opera composer of the second half of the century, specialized in grand but rather prettified and sentimental Romantic spectacles such as *Manon*. In orchestral music, the influence of Liszt was clearly felt in the symphonic poems of Camille Saint-Saëns and César Franck. For example, Saint-Saëns in *Danse Macabre* portrays Death playing his violin in a churchyard at midnight as skeletons dance around,

## In the Words of Voltaire and His Contemporaries

Voltaire (1694–1778) wrote *Lettres Philosophiques* based on two years' exile in England. These writings show an admiration (shared by Montesquieu) for tolerance and liberalism, as epitomized by English political and religious institutions. Voltaire's *Essai sur les moeurs,* a survey of world history, shows peoples' slow progress from superstition to rationality.

Voltaire is best known for his satirical philosophical tales. The most famous, *Candide,* hilariously satirizes the then influential philosopher Leibniz and his idea that what God had created was indeed the best of all possible worlds.

Voltaire made social thinking popular—even fashionable. The key product of the Enlightenment is the 17-volume *Encyclopédie,* edited by Denis Diderot and his assistant Jean d'Alembert. It laid out the latest positions in science and philosophy and aimed to "change the general manner of thinking."

In the theater, the *drame bourgeois,* with contemporary characters, began to replace the outmoded classical forms. This was first attempted by Beaumarchais, whose fame rests on the plays *Le Barbier de Séville* and *Le Mariage de Figaro,* the latter being the box office hit of the 18th century. These topical comedies, tinged with risqué democratic sentiment, restored a vitality to the genre that had been missing since Molière.

*Ohh-la-la!* Kitsch with a French accent: Montmartre's Moulin Rouge is pure Parisian entertainment.

while Franck's *Le Chasseur Maudit* paints a noisy picture of a huntsman doomed to be chased forever by the hounds of Hell as punishment for hunting on the Sabbath. After 1880, the German Romantic influence was further intensified by the seemingly irresistible lure of Wagner, which tends sometimes to make itself felt in a rather un-French grandiosity. However, French classical restraint, albeit tinged with Romantic feeling, reasserted itself in the work of Gabriel Fauré and Henri Duparc who, among other things, transformed the drawing room *mélodie* into an art song that can stand comparison with the great German lieder.

**Literature of Romanticism:** Some of the very finest expressions of French Romanticism can be found in the poetry of Lamartine, de Vigny, Hugo, and de Musset. Here, poetry is the expression of primarily personal feelings and emotions. Intensely lyrical and introspective, it allows the imagination full play, and uses the outside world, especially nature, as a reflection of inner feelings. This kind of Romantic poetry helped to establish the image of the poet as the tortured artist.

In the theater, Romanticism is best exemplified by the historical verse dramas of Victor Hugo. In prose, Alexandre Dumas *père* leads the way. Hugo rejected the classical unities of time and place, attacked the artificial separation of the tragic and the comic, and demanded more natural language and local color. His picturesque historical dramas *Hernani* and *Ruy Blas* feature noble characters battling against all odds.

The confessional tales of Chateaubriand, *Atala* and *René,* clearly prefigure the doomed Romantic hero, and Benjamin Constant's *Adolphe* is a bleakly Romantic story of *le mal du siècle.* But it is in the historical novel that the Romantic impulse is clearest: Alfred de Vigny's *Cinq Mars*, Hugo's *Notre-Dame de Paris*, and the colorfully exotic works of Prosper Mérimée, whose *Carmen* was the source of Georges Bizet's opera. However, it was Alexandre Dumas who developed the Romantic past into something really popular in his Musketeers trilogy and *The Count of Monte Cristo*.

> " In the theater, Romanticism is best exemplified by the historical verse dramas of Victor Hugo. "

Nineteenth-century French culture can be seen as a dialogue between Romanticism and realism, and the novels of Stendhal (Marie-Henri Beyle, 1783–1842) and Honoré de Balzac (1799–1850) straddle both. Stendhal was a Romantic in his fascination with Italy, his consistent championing of Shakespeare, his interest in the theme of love, and his novels' proud, young, egotistical heroes. The ambitious Julien Sorel in *Le Rouge et le Noir* enters the priesthood in order to climb the social ladder, and Fabrice in *La Chartreuse de Parme* becomes embroiled in the intrigues of the court at Parma. But society is portrayed with a profundity, irony, and sharpness that is more realist than Romantic. Meanwhile, Balzac's vast *Comédie Humaine*, which includes 80-odd novels and stories and covers French life from the revolution until 1840, has an extraordinary, even obsessive, realism of detail. At the same time, the novels often seem to be infused by a shadowy, Romantic aura.

## Realism (19th Century)

In art, an interest in unadorned nature and ordinary people began to appear in the middle of the century. There is still something of the Arcadian in Camille Corot's misty, soft-edged paintings, but he did attempt to represent nature without idealization or romanticization. Théodore Rousseau, Charles Daubigny, Jean-François Millet, and others painted direct from nature and formed the Barbizon school, named after the village in the Fontainebleau forest in which they painted. Millet's scenes from rural life emphasize its tough side, and he invested ordinary people with weight and dignity. His "Angélus" was the most frequently reproduced painting of the century, but because of the religious nature of its subject matter, his most famous piece also earned him an unjust reputation for pious sentimentality.

The chief realist painter is undoubtedly Gustave Courbet (1819–1877). A socialist who was imprisoned for his part in the 1871 Commune, he concentrated on the tangible reality of things and people. Conventional opinion regarded his pictures as crude and ugly, but his influence was tremendous, not least on the cubists.

The Impressionists also belong under the realist banner. They were not a unified school, but a loose association of artists with a certain community of outlook. They came together between 1860 and 1886 for the purposes of exhibiting in a largely hostile environment. Monet, Renoir, Sisley, Pissarro, Degas, Manet, and others, though often interested in different subject matter, shared the rejection of the

■ **Monet immortalized his gardens in Giverny in paintings now known the world over.**

Romantic ideal. In particular, they wanted to capture immediate, fleeting impressions of color and light rather than the permanent aspects of a subject. Thus, for example, Monet's series of paintings of poplars, haystacks, and the west front of the cathedral at Rouen, in which he tried to capture the impression of the same subject under different climatic conditions and times of day.

**Realist Literature:** Gustave Flaubert's (1821–1880) *Madame Bovary,* published in 1857, marks the arrival of the realist novel, although formally it also prefigures modernism. However, his notion that the author should be like God, omnipresent but invisible, is certainly realist. Flaubert's hostility to Romanticism is underlined in the novel by Madame Bovary immersing herself in escapist Romantic fantasies as compensation for the ghastliness of provincial life in Normandy. The Normandy countryside is also the setting for many of the best stories of Guy de Maupassant, the acknowledged master of the realist short story.

In Émile Zola (1840–1902), realism developed into naturalism. He believed that the novel should be an illustration of the laws of scientific determinism that govern human nature through heredity and the environment. He put this theory into practice in his *Rougon-Macquart* series of 20 novels—a vivid and imaginative panorama of the Second Empire.

In musical terms, Bizet's *Carmen,* based on a novel by Mérimée and, almost unbelievably, a flop at its first performance in 1875, is an interesting mix of realism and Romanticism. The Spanish setting may have exotic connotations, but its treatment of passionate (as opposed to simply romantic) feelings is realistic, as is the inclusion of speech between the music.

## Modern Times

In the first half of the 20th century, France became a hotbed of artistic modernism, and its culture was further enriched by the novelists, poets, artists, and composers who flocked there from across the world. These included Aaron Copland, Ernest Hemingway, Henry Miller, Ezra Pound, and Gertrude Stein. However, modernism's roots lie firmly in 19th-century France.

**Architecture:** During the Second Empire, Baron Haussmann laid the basis of modern Paris. He replaced the ancient narrow streets with wide boulevards, a move that went well beyond quality of life and aesthetics. Paris had seen three uprisings in 50 years; in any future trouble, the boulevards would facilitate rapid troop movements and provide clear fields for artillery fire. The year 1889 saw the opening of the Tour Eiffel, which demonstrated grandly the architectural potential of steel. It helped to usher in the modern era.

> **The year 1889 saw the opening of the Tour Eiffel, which demonstrated grandly the architectural potential of steel.**

Today we tend to blame modern architects for creating inhuman, alienating environments. But one of the founding figures of architectural modernism, the Swiss Le Corbusier, was almost utopian in his vision of the social benefits of a rationally planned urban environment, with skyscrapers, gridlike street systems, open spaces, and rings of satellite towns. That vision is exemplified by the Cité Radieuse in Marseille (see p. 348). Also worth visiting are La Roche Villa (now the Le Corbusier Foundation, *10 square du Docteur-Blanche*) in Paris and the extraordinary Chapelle de Notre-Dame-du-Haut in Ronchamp in the Jura (see p. 236), one of the few great modernist religious buildings.

Even in these supposedly postmodernist times, France has never shied away from promoting unapologetically modern architecture; nor has the country been afraid to use considerable public funds in doing so. Indeed, elected officials regard bold architectural commissions as an excellent means of leaving a mark and encouraging tourism. Consequently, no visitor to France can ignore its modern architecture.

**Modern Art:** In the early 20th century, Paris was considered the world center of contemporary art. The Impressionists and other painters of the time had begun to liberate art from the merely representational, and photography had made the straightforward copying of reality redundant. The founding figure of modern art is Paul Cézanne (1839–1906), who was concerned above all with the underlying structural forms of nature. His influence is incalculable, but can be seen clearly in the cubism of Picasso, Léger, Delaunay, and others. A key precursor of later abstract art, cubism abandoned traditional notions of perspective and tried to represent objects not as they appear from a particular angle, but analytically and from all sides at once, as if the eye could take in simultaneously every facet and plane.

Non- and indeed antinaturalism was the order of the day. Paul Gauguin and Vincent van Gogh (1853–1890) had been influential, in their different ways, in nonnaturalistic use of color. Further, van Gogh had taken to its extreme the use of the external world to express the inner; not only do his strong colors and bold lines communicate the artist's tortured state, but the thickly laid-on paint pushes ever closer toward abstract patterns and shapes. The influence of the way these artists used color is visible in the fauves (literally, "wild beasts"), including Henri Matisse, André Derain, Georges Braque, and Georges Rouault.

**Music:** Musical modernism also owes a great deal to France. In Paris in 1913, the émigré Igor Stravinsky's ballet *The Rite of Spring* caused one of modernism's great scandals. But just as important is Claude Debussy (1862–1918), and especially his *Prélude à l'Après-Midi d'un Faune* (1894). Though deceptively easy on the ear it marks the beginnings of modern music. The piece is by no means atonal, but already conventional harmonic relationships are giving way. Debussy does not take a clear-cut theme and develop it in consecutive, goal-directed fashion; rather the overall impression is improvisatory. There are fluctuating tempi and irregular rhythms, and orchestral color is no longer an ornament but increasingly an end in itself. Debussy was to develop these ideas further, but, without this seemingly innocuous piece,

In classic Renaissance style, the Hôtel de Ville—City Hall—in Paris is awash in statuary that blends art with architecture.

it would be hard to envisage the more obviously modern compositions of the great 20th-century French composers Olivier Messiaen and his pupil Pierre Boulez.

**Surrealism:** One modernist movement that spread across all the arts, and still has an influence on much contemporary culture, is surrealism. Again, this has its roots in the 19th century—in the extraordinary symbolist paintings of Odilon Redon and Gustave Moreau. It can also be seen in the hallucinatory, transgressive writings of Joris Karl Huysmans, Gérard de Nerval,

## Ten Classics of French Cinema (+1 New Epic)

French cinema provides us with one of the best windows through which to peer into the nation's psyche. This top ten list was compiled by Ginette Vincendeau, professor in film studies at King's College London.

—*La Grande Illusion/The Grand Illusion* (Jean Renoir, 1937). Poignant World War I POW drama starring Jean Gabin; voted one of the best films of all time.

—*Les Enfants du Paradis/The Children of Paradise* (Marcel Carné, 1945). An epic love story set in the Parisian theater of the 1830s; an allegory of France under German occupation.

—*Mon Oncle/My Uncle* (Jacques Tati, 1958). Tati's comic genius Monsieur Hulot disrupts the alienating modernity of France's new consumer society.

—*Les 400 Coups/The 400 Blows* (François Truffaut, 1959). The autobiographical tale of a rebellious adolescent boy in Paris; this was Truffaut's manifesto film for the French New Wave.

—*Cléo de 5 à 7/Cleo From 5 to 7* (Agnès Varda, 1962). Vivid prefeminist portrait of a woman's existential journey through Paris's Left Bank on a June afternoon; shot in real time.

—*Le Mépris/Contempt* (Jean-Luc Godard, 1963). An apt reflection on art cinema and sex goddess Brigitte Bardot, viewed through the breakdown of a marriage.

—*Le Samouraï/The Godson* (Jean-Pierre Melville, 1967). Alain Delon is the epitome of cool as a melancholy contract killer navigating Parisian nightclubs and dingy hotels.

—*Jean de Florette & Manon des Sources/Manon of the Spring* (Claude Berri, 1985). Two hugely successful adaptations of Marcel Pagnol's classics set against ravishing Provençal landscapes.

—*Au Revoir les Enfants/Goodbye, Children* (Louis Malle, 1987). The tragic, autobiographical tale of a child and his Jewish friend in a Catholic boarding school during World War II.

—*La Haine/Hatred* (Mathieu Kassovitz, 1995). Shot in black and white, the hard-hitting story of three young men in Paris's multicultural suburbs.

—*Napoleon* (Ridley Scott, 2023). A Hollywood take (the latest of many) on the rise and fall of France's most famous figure, played by Joaquin Phoenix.

and Lautréamont (the pseudonym of Isidore Ducasse) and especially in the intensely subjective, language-stretching poetry of Charles Baudelaire, Arthur Rimbaud, and Paul Verlaine.

Surrealists were fascinated by the unconscious, the bizarre, and the irrational. Clearly influenced by Freud, they wanted to challenge the dominance of reason and the conscious mind. Two of the key French poets of the 20th century—Louis Aragon and Paul Éluard—emerged from surrealism, and it also left a distinct mark on the scriptwriter Jacques Prévert and the films of Jean Cocteau, particularly *Le Sang d'un Poète*.

■ **Best known for his ground-breaking 1960 film *Breathless*, Jean-Luc Godard helped pioneer French New Wave cinema.**

**Cinema:** Cocteau brings us to cinema, the quintessentially modern medium, which the French have made their own. Pioneers Étienne Marey and Felix-Louis Regnault played key roles in cinematic prehistory, while the Lumière brothers laid the basis for the documentary and Georges Méliès for fantasy genres.

Film might have been regarded early as an art in France, but its commercial possibilities, too, were rapidly realized by Gaumont and Pathé. After World War I, however, France, like other European countries, felt the effects of Hollywood imports. Nevertheless, French cinema thrived, as evidenced by the immensely varied work of directors such as Marcel L'Herbier, Jean Epstein, René Clair, Jacques Feyder, Jean Renoir (the painter's son), and Marcel Carné, among many others.

After World War II, interesting new figures such as Henri-Georges Clouzot, Jean-Pierre Melville, Jacques Tati, and Georges Franju appeared. By the 1950s, several critics at the journal *Cahiers du Cinéma* argued for a more personal and contemporary form of cinema. They reexamined Hollywood cinema and argued that the works of Alfred Hitchcock, John Ford, and others, were *authored* movies, with strong personal content. Soon *Cahiers* critics such as Jean-Luc Godard, Claude Chabrol, and François Truffaut were putting their ideas into practice by making their own highly personal movies. This *Nouvelle Vague* (New Wave) became the new French art cinema, envied and imitated around the world. Indeed, by inspiring directors like Scorsese, Coppola, and De Palma, it later helped to revitalize the American cinema, which had helped to give birth to it in the first place. Today, thanks to its enlightened system of state support, France remains one of the key filmmaking countries. ■

The country's core—the Île-de-France—the heart of which is Paris, the pivot around which the fortunes of France have turned for 15 centuries

# PARIS & THE ÎLE-DE-FRANCE

# PARIS

Paris has a well-earned reputation for being one of the most beautiful, exciting, and romantic cities in the world. Often called the City of Dreams, Paris has been a mecca for aspiring artists, writers, thinkers, and adventurers since the earliest times. Stroll down almost any street in central Paris and you pass evidence of its past in the narrow, twisting medieval byways and awe-inspiring churches; in the ornate 17th-century Renaissance palaces that flaunt incredible wealth; in Napoleon's classically inspired monuments; and in the sweeping tree-lined boulevards of Baron Haussmann's 19th-century revamp of Paris.

Packed into the center of the grand, historic city on the Seine are some of the world's greatest museums, the most beautiful buildings in France, and all possible luxuries. Paris dazzles as a sophisticated, vibrant city, of course, but it is also a living capital city, and

## NOT TO BE MISSED:

continues to be the economic and cultural center of France.

The creativity of today is evident in the exciting new buildings and modern painting and sculpture that sit harmoniously alongside the treasures of the past. With dozens of museums and stylish galleries, a wealth of beautiful parks, stunning stores displaying the fashions of world-famous designers, unparalleled people-watching, and irresistible cafés and restaurants at every turn, the visitor can happily occupy each and every moment.

Over the centuries, the city has played host to a procession of performing artists. Kings and nobles acted as patrons to playwrights, musicians, and actors. Today, the capital still offers a vast choice of entertainment: theaters, rock venues, nightclubs, and bars—even beaches on the Seine in summer. Still, just wandering the streets of so lively a city can be entertainment enough. ∎

# ÎLE DE LA CITÉ

**The oldest and most celebrated part of Paris is the Île de la Cité, an island in the Seine, little more than half a mile (1 km) long. Here, on a sandbank at a crossing point on the river, the Parisii, or boat people, had built a fortified town by the third century B.C.**

■ **The jewel in the crown that is the Île de la Cité remains the high Gothic Cathédrale Notre-Dame. In the south tower is "Emmanuel," the only cathedral bell to escape destruction in the revolution.**

Under Roman rule, the settlement, called Lutetia Parisiorum, prospered, becoming the hub of a network of roads that crossed the northern portion of the Roman Empire. In the third century A.D. it was destroyed by barbarians, so when the Parisii restored it, they built a thick stone wall to create an island fortress.

By A.D. 508, Paris was the seat of the kings of the Franks. When Hugh Capet was declared King of France in 987 (see p. 22), Paris—as the capital city—became ever more important.

The Île de la Cité was the residence of the French kings from the 10th to the 14th centuries. In a display of wealth and power by the Church, the medieval streets were overshadowed by the new Gothic cathedral of Notre-Dame, built in the 12th and 13th centuries. Royal power was equally evident in the huge palace, so vast that it now forms the Conciergerie, the Palais de Justice, and Ste.-Chapelle. When the court left in the 14th century, the Île lost its significant place in French affairs.

The island, connected to the mainland by bridges that crossed the Seine, was later linked to the nearby Île St.-Louis. In the 16th and 17th centuries, the Île St.-Louis became a highly desirable locale and noblemen built their beautiful mansions here. ■

# NOTRE-DAME

**The Cathédrale Notre-Dame is the essence of Paris. The 2019 fire that destroyed Notre-Dame's roof and spire badly seared the French psyche. Yet the nation responded with an ambitious plan to faithfully restore the beloved landmark. More than 200 craftsmen labored tirelessly to save this masterpiece of Gothic architecture, thus honoring the work of the armies of craftsmen who had constructed the cathedral between 1163 and 1375.**

The first challenge was to stabilize the damaged structure; a skeleton of scaffolding was built up to the vaultings and the exposed roof, allowing the walls to be bolstered. This involved a vast project of limestone desalination and cleaning.

Lead decontamination was also a huge challenge, with teams exposed daily to materials that dated back centuries and were now newly exposed and airborne. Rigorous protocols were put in place to protect workers.

The central task was to replace "The Forest," the vast area of wood that had been the cathedral's roof. Some 850 perfect oaks were sourced throughout France; 1,200 other trees were raised up toward the heavens to re-create the 19th-century, 210-foot (64 m) spire.

Some $900 million was raised in donations worldwide for the restoration work, the latest chapter in the storied history of this remarkable edifice.

## Mysteries Revealed

**The Notre-Dame fire of 2019 cast a gloom over Paris for months. However, long-term reconstruction brought teams of experts into the medieval building, whose work revealed some secrets of the original builders. Damaged walls were shown to be held together by dozens of iron staples, which may have prevented a total collapse. The vast scaffolding erected to bolster the walls and vaulting allowed experts to examine the rose windows up close; carbon dating showed only glass from the 13th- and 19th-century had survived previous maintenance work and also that one circular window had been rotated, probably to ensure its stability.**

Changing fashions, neglect, and vandalism had previously taken their own toll on the cathedral, particularly in the 18th century. The revolution saw carvings removed

**Cathédrale Notre-Dame** 🗺 55 D2 ✉ place du Parvis Notre-Dame, Île de la Cité 💲 $$ To donate: **friendsofnotredameparis.org**
🚇 Métro: Cité **notredameparis.fr**

**NOTE:** Due to the 2019 fire, the cathedral will remain closed until at least 2024. Consult the website for more information.

and statues beheaded. By the time Napoleon crowned himself emperor here in 1804, the cathedral had fallen into a sorry state.

Victor Hugo's 1831 novel *Notre-Dame de Paris* prompted restoration plans, and work by historian-architect Eugène Viollet-le-Duc began in 1844, bringing back the cathedral's past splendor. Today, Notre-Dame remains a masterpiece of French Gothic style. It displays several phases in the development of Gothic cathedrals (see pp. 132–133).

## Place du Parvis Notre-Dame

Medieval houses and streets were swept away in a 19th-century scheme designed to enlarge the square overlooked by Notre-Dame's west front. People could stand here to see the facade's biblical carvings—a valuable introduction to Bible stories in an age when congregations were largely illiterate.

Clerestory

South tower

Rose window

Portals

Triforium

Nave

## West Facade

Crowned by two early Gothic towers, where nine new bells were installed in 2013, the west facade has three imposing portals. In the Middle Ages, the statues and sculptures here were brightly painted. The central portal depicts the Last Judgment, with Christ and the celestial court. The cathedral's oldest sculptures (1165–1175), on the right-hand portal, show the life of St. Anne, and include one of the Virgin Mary showing Jesus to a kneeling King Louis VII (who consecrated the cathedral in the 12th century) and to the founder, Bishop Sully. The Virgin's portal, on the left, depicts her coronation, resurrection, and assumption, surrounded by saints, angels, and zodiac signs.

Above the portals is the Galerie des Rois (Gallery of Kings). The 21 statues of Old Testament kings are reconstructions. The originals, damaged by revolutionaries who mistook them for French monarchs, were found in a 1977 excavation. Fragments are in the Musée de Cluny (see pp. 65–66). Higher still, above the rose window, is the Galerie des Chimères, a balustrade embellished with grotesque figures of demons, birds, and strange beasts. The gargoyles, together with Quasimodo, the hunchback of Notre-Dame, feature in Victor Hugo's *Notre-Dame de Paris*. Redesigned by Viollet-le-Duc, the gargoyles were intended to drain water from the roof (and, perhaps, to deter evil spirits).

## Towers

Designed to be surmounted by spires, the towers are 226 feet (69 m) high. Climbing the 238 steps to the north tower is hard work; a further 140 steps lead to the top of the south tower, but the views over the city make the climb well worthwhile. The 13-ton (11.8 t) bell in the south tower is famous for its pure tone.

## Flying Buttresses

The famous flying buttresses, so typical of a high Gothic cathedral, were built between 1220 and 1230. Each incorporates a channel to allow rainwater to run off. Those at the east

**Flying buttress**

## Notre-Dame
**before the 2019-fire**

end have a span of 49 feet (15 m). The chapels between the buttresses date from 1250 to 1325.

## Interior

The traditional Gothic layout consists of a nave of 10 bays flanked by double aisles continuing around the choir. The walls are lined with 37 chapels, added during the 13th and 14th centuries. Stand at the crossing of the transepts for the best view of the rose windows.

**Windows:** The cathedral has three magnificent rose windows. The north window measures an amazing 69 feet (21 m) across. Almost all its medieval glass remains. It depicts the Virgin encircled by figures from the Old Testament. The west window, above the main door, was completed in the 1490s, but restored in the 19th century. It also portrays the Virgin. The south rose window, with some original 13th-century glass, shows Christ surrounded by angels, saints, and the 12 Apostles.

The original stained glass of the nave windows survived until 1771, when Louis XV, declaring stained glass outmoded, had it replaced with clear panes. These were changed in 1965 to modern abstract stained glass by Jacques Le Chevallier.

**Great Organ:** With 110 stops and 6,000 pipes, this is the largest organ in France. Miraculously, it survived the 2019 fire, but is now being cleansed of toxic dust.

**Chancel & Choir:** At one time a carved 14th-century stone screen shut off the nave from the chancel; only parts survive, in front of the first three north and south bays. Inside the chancel are the choir stalls, with scenes from the life of the Virgin. Bishops lie in their tombs around the ambulatory and below the choir. The sacristy is located on the south side of the choir. ■

Cathédrale Notre-Dame undergoes a 21st-century reconstruction in the wake of the 2019 fire that destroyed its wooden roof and spire.

# STROLLING THE ISLANDS

**The Île de la Cité and the Île St.-Louis are the oldest parts of Paris. This walk takes you around both islands—past their most historically memorable features—and offers wonderful views up and down one of the world's great rivers.**

Begin at Place Louis-Lépine, whose colorful flower market (one of Paris's last remaining) makes way for the Marché aux Oiseaux (Bird Market) on Sundays. Walk along Rue de Lutèce to the ornate gates of the **Palais de Justice ❶** *(tel 01 44 32 52 52; ca-paris.justice.fr)*. Since the 16th century the palace has been the seat of the *parlement* (law court). After repeated fires and damage during the revolution, most of the palace was rebuilt in the 19th century.

Before turning left along Boulevard du Palais, look up for a glimpse of the spire of **Ste.-Chapelle** *(tel 01 53 40 60 80; sainte-chapelle.fr)*. This lovely Gothic chapel, built for Louis IX (St. Louis; R. 1226–1270) in 1248, is tucked away

> **NOT TO BE MISSED:**
> Ste.-Chapelle
> • Conciergerie
> • Notre-Dame

in a courtyard within the precincts of the Palais de Justice. The entrance is on Boulevard du Palais. Take binoculars for close-up views of the stained-glass windows, which depict more than 1,000 biblical scenes in an area of almost 7,000 square feet (620 sq m).

At Pont St.-Michel turn right along Quai des Orfèvres. Turn right again to cross quaint Place Dauphine, whose

## Boats on the Seine

Many of the most memorable views of Paris are from the river. Sightseeing trips in glass-roof boats take in the stretch of the Seine between the Tour Eiffel and Île St.-Louis, passing the Grand Palais, the Louvre, the Musée d'Orsay, Notre-Dame, and other top landmarks.

Most trips last about an hour, departing half-hourly in summer (hourly in winter) from 10 a.m. Some of the larger boats offer longer lunch or dinner trips.

Bateaux-Mouches *(tel 01 42 25 96 10, bateaux-mouches.fr)* vessels depart from Pont de l'Alma (Right Bank), while Bateaux Parisiens Tour Eiffel *(tel 01 76 64 14 45, bateauxparisiens.com)* uses the quay near the Tour Eiffel. Vedettes du Pont-Neuf *(tel 01 46 33 98 38, vedettesdupontneuf.com)* operates smaller boats, departing from the western tip of Île de la Cité near Pont Neuf. Vedettes de Paris *(tel 01 44 18 19 50, vedettesdeparis.fr)* offers one-hour cruises.

huge trees shade a *boules* (French bowls) area favored by Parisians. A narrow medieval street, Rue Henri Robert, leads to Pont Neuf, the center-stage setting for the cinematic classic *Les Amants du Pont Neuf* (*The Lovers of the New Bridge*). Beyond the bridge is a fine equestrian **statue of Henri IV.** Steps lead down to **Square du Vert-Galant ❷.** This little park, a peninsula in the Seine, offers marvelous views, especially at sunset. Picasso's 1943 painting of this view is in the Musée Picasso (see p. 82).

Walk east along Quai de l'Horloge, in the shadow of the turreted **Conciergerie ❸** *(tel 01 53 40 60 80, concierge rie.monuments-nationaux.fr).* The oldest part of the former royal palace, it was rebuilt in about 1300. The Salle des Gens d'Armes, the largest hall in medieval Europe, could hold the entire palace staff—some 2,000 people. In 1358 the palace was stormed and

> 🗺 See also area map pp. 54–55
> ▶ Place Louis-Lépine (Métro: Cité)
> ↔ 2.5 miles (4 km)
> 🕐 2 hours
> ▶ Place Louis-Lépine

the king was forced to move the royal residence. An important noble was appointed *concierge* (caretaker). From 1391 until 1914 the building was a prison. Prisoners here during the revolution included the queen, Marie-Antoinette. Her cell is one of several that have been reconstructed and can be visited. Mind your head!

At the far end of Quai de l'Horloge, notice the Conciergerie's famous clock tower; the clock dates from 1370 and still works today. Continue along Quai de la Corse and Quai aux Fleurs, where typical Parisian stalls, *bouquinistes*, sell books and artworks. Across the river is the 1882 neo-Renaissance **Hôtel de Ville** building.

Cross **Pont St.- Louis ④** to the Île St.-Louis. Follow Quai d'Orléans past magnificent 17th-century town houses; look for superb courtyards, wrought iron, and carved heads. The Île St.-Louis has long been a much sought-after residential area of Paris. Turn left onto Rue des Deux Ponts, then right onto Rue St.-Louis-en-l'Île. Pass the island's richly decorated church, **St.-Louis-en-l'Île ⑤**, and turn left on Quai d'Anjou. Continue along Quai de Bourbon then, at Pont Louis-Philippe, turn left and recross Pont St.-Louis to approach **Notre-Dame ⑥** (see pp. 57–60) through a small park.

Walk to **Place du Parvis Notre-Dame ⑦**, at the west end of the cathedral. Here a bronze star marks the official center of Paris, from where all distances on French roads are measured. Below the parvis, in the **Crypte Archéologique** (tel 01 55 42 50 10, crypte.paris.fr), lie the remains of 16th- and 18th-century houses, the church of St.-Étienne, and fragments from Lutetia, the Gallo-Roman city. From the parvis, take Rue de la Cité back to Place Louis-Lépine.

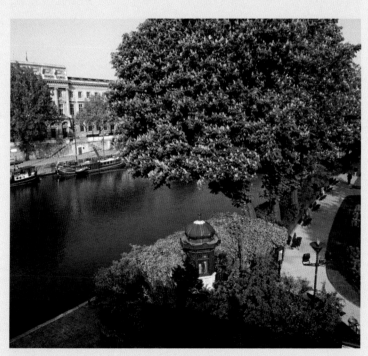

Bustling capital city or serene riverside? Yes, it's Paris—the Île de la Cité.

# LEFT BANK

The Left Bank—the famous Rive Gauche—is a lively area south of the Seine. Stretching from the Jardin des Plantes to the Champ de Mars, it encompasses the narrow streets of St.-Germain in the Latin Quarter (Quartier Latin)—until the revolution, teaching at the Sorbonne was in Latin—the quieter, grander areas around the Panthéon and the Palais du Luxembourg, the Musée d'Orsay, and the Assemblée Nationale.

■ With its mix of fashionable locals and wide-eyed visitors, charming old buildings, and worn-smooth cobblestone streets, the Latin Quarter is Paris at its most atmospheric.

For both visitors and local Parisians there is an endless attraction to the cozy, medieval streets of St.-Germain. The popular area possesses a wealth of little shops and cafés frequented by writers, artists, and students from the Sorbonne and the École des Beaux-Arts.

The Latin Quarter, right alongside the Île de la Cité, is where Paris first spilled onto the mainland. Scattered Roman remains show how extensive the city then became. The Latin Quarter also boasts several institutions of higher learning.

The Musée de Cluny houses a stunning collection of Roman and medieval artifacts, while the Roman-style Panthéon nearby serves as a mausoleum for many of France's most revered historical figures. Napoleon Bonaparte, perhaps the greatest, is close by; he was laid to rest a little farther west, in the magnificent Église du Dôme in Les Invalides.

Finally, soaring over central Paris, is la Tour Eiffel—the Eiffel Tower—a monument to the Parisian flair for innovation. The iron icon is flanked by the Musée du Quai Branly. ■

# MUSEUMS ON THE LEFT BANK

An embarrassment of riches, the Left Bank of Paris is home to several world-class museums. The Musée d'Orsay and the Musée Rodin, great destinations in their own right, showcase French art from the 19th and 20th centuries. Celebrated at Musée de Cluny is France's medieval history, while the Musée du Quai Branly spotlights ethnic art from many corners of the world.

## Musée de Cluny

Built for visiting Benedictine monks from Cluny, in Burgundy, in the late 15th century, the former Hôtel de Cluny stands beside the remains of Paris's oldest Roman baths, off Boulevard St.-Michel. The mansion, one of France's finest examples of Gothic domestic architecture, was owned after the revolution by art collector Alexandre de Sommerard. His acquisitions form the basis of the Musée National du Moyen Age et des Thermes de Cluny. Don't miss this unique combination of Gallo-Roman ruins, medieval mansion, and one of the world's finest collections of medieval art and crafts.

On display are medieval furniture, clothes, and accessories; textiles, including examples of Byzantine and Coptic work as well as European; and some magnificent tapestries. One series, "La Vie Seigneuriale," illustrates the life of a noble household in the Middle Ages. Also in the museum are the 21 mutilated stone heads of the kings of Judah, carved around 1220 for the west front of Notre-Dame but mistakenly defaced as French kings and then lost during the revolution. They were rediscovered in 1977—a major archaeological event.

## EXPERIENCE: Enjoy French Culture After Dark

For a truly romantic experience of Paris by night, take part with a loved one in the **Nuit Blanche** (White Night), on the first Saturday in October. From 7 p.m. until dawn, the city is illuminated with amazing creations, and you can spend the whole night immersing yourself in the whole series of creative, concerts, live shows, and contemporary design sites. The **Nuit des Musées**—Museum Night—is another event that takes place usually in May, with museums staying open until midnight, offering events and surprise guests at no extra charge. Details for both events: *parisinfo.com*.

**Musée de Cluny** 🄼 55 D2 ✉ 28 rue Du Sommerard ☎ 01 53 73 78 16 🕐 Closed Mon. 🅢 $$$ 🚇 Métro: Cluny, St.-Michel, Odéon **musee-moyenage.fr**

**Roman Baths:** On the ground floor are the remains of second-century baths: three stone chambers for steam, tepid, and cold baths, and a gymnasium. The vaulted ceiling of the cold bath *(frigidarium)* rises over 45 feet (14 m). The capitals of the supporting pillars are ships' prows, which suggests that the baths were originally built for the pleasure and recuperation of Nautae, the wealthy corporation of Paris boatmen.

**Hôtel de Cluny:** On the first floor is the abbot's chapel, with dramatic fan-vaulting radiating from a central pillar. One room has been restored as a medieval living room with wooden shutters, candelabra, armor, and tapestries. Also on this floor is a superb collection of goldwork and jewelry, including belts, bracelets, rare votive Visigoth crowns, and two 13th-century double gold crosses.

---

**INSIDER TIP:**

See more of the Roman baths' underground ruins on a guided tour, offered by the Musée de Cluny at 2 p.m. on Wednesdays.

—BARBARA NOE
*National Geographic Travel Books editor*

---

The most famous of the treasures are the six allegorical tapestries "La Dame à la Licorne" ("The Lady with the Unicorn"), splendidly displayed in a purpose-built room. Exquisitely woven, they are in 15th-century mille-fleurs style, noted for its graceful depiction of plants, animals, and people. Five of the tapestries show the lady acting out the five senses, while the enigmatic sixth presents her in front of the motto "À Mon Seul Désir" ("To My Only Desire").

## Musée d'Orsay

Opened in 1986, the Musée d'Orsay (about a 20-minute walk from Musée de Cluny along Boulevard St.-Germain) soon became one of Europe's top art museums. The unconventional building—a converted hotel and railroad station—lent itself to imaginative displays, winning wide acclaim. The collections cover the period from 1848 to 1914, an exciting time for the art world, with Paris very much at the helm. All the great names in European art are represented here.

**The Station:** The original hotel and station were built for the 1900 Universal Exhibition on the site of the Palais d'Orsay, burned down in the Commune uprising of 1871. Functional iron-and-glass railway architecture would have looked wrong in this elegant part of Paris, so a monumental stone facade was built, effectively concealing the building's purpose. The ornate belle epoque reception areas, restaurant, and ballroom are still intact.

*(continued on p. 70)*

---

**Musée d'Orsay** 🗺 55 C3 ✉ Esplanade Valéry Giscard d'Estaing ☎ 01 40 49 48 14 🕐 Closed Mon. 💲 $$$ 🚇 Métro: Solférino, Musée d'Orsay **musee-orsay.fr**

# LATIN QUARTER WALK

**Enjoy the special buzz of this enticing Paris neighborhood by strolling through its student-thronged streets and quiet backwaters.**

Stately, elegant, and serene, the Jardin du Luxembourg provides a perfect setting for strolling and relaxation.

Starting from the Pont au Double beside Notre-Dame, cross the Quai Montebello. Walk through the small garden facing you; a false acacia here is reputedly the oldest tree in Paris. Pass beside the little 13th-century church of **St.-Julien-le-Pauvre ❶**.

Turn right down Rue St.-Jacques and cross to Rue de la Huchette. Once the heart of the Latin Quarter, the street is now dominated by Greek restaurants but still retains the famous Caveau de la Huchette jazz club at No. 5. At the end of the street, turn left onto Rue de la Harpe, with its cafés and clubs. This area is at its most vibrant when crowded with students.

Cross Boulevard St.-Germain and climb the hill on Boulevard St.-Michel, past the remains of Roman baths. Turn left into Place Paul-Painlevé for the **Musée de Cluny ❷** (see p. 65).

From the museum, cross the small square and walk up to Rue des Écoles. Turn left past the buildings of the **Sorbonne,** Paris's world-famous university, founded in 1253.

## NOT TO BE MISSED:

**Musée de Cluny • St.-Étienne -du-Mont • Panthéon • Jardin du Luxembourg • Hôtel des Monnaies**

At the junction of Rue des Écoles and Rue de la Montagne de Ste.-Geneviève, turn right and walk up the steep hill. Named after the patron saint of Paris, the street was part of the Roman road that linked Lutetia (Paris) with Italy.

At the fork, take Rue Descartes. Turn right onto Rue Clovis, named after the king of the Franks who defeated the Romans and founded France. On your right is the charming church of **St.-Étienne-du-Mont 3**, well worth a brief visit to see the intricately carved 16th-century rood screen, flanked by spiral staircases.

Rue Clovis opens onto the Place du Panthéon. Walk around the square to enter the **Panthéon 4** (tel 01 44 32 18 04, pantheon.monuments-nationaux.fr), burial place of Voltaire, Rousseau, Hugo, and other French luminaries. Walk down

---

⛰ See also area map p. 55

➤ Pont au Double (Métro: Maubert-Mutualité)

↔ 3 miles (4.5 km)

🕐 2 hours

➤ Pont au Double

---

Rue Soufflot to the **Jardin du Lux-embourg** . The lovely 17th-century promenades offer relaxing strolls.

Leave the gardens to the right of the **Palais du Luxembourg** (seat of the French Senate) to reach the 18th-century Odéon-Théâtre de l'Europe. Continue downhill to Boulevard St.-Germain and cross to Rue de l'Ancienne Comédie. On the right is **Le Procope** (see p. 76; *13 rue de l'Ancienne Comédie*), Paris's first café, now a restaurant.

Turn left on Rue de Buci and right on Rue de Seine. The area is packed full of small stores, many selling antiques and art. Turn left on Rue Jacob and left again on Rue Furstemberg. In a corner of elegant Place Furstemberg is the **Musée National Eugène Delacroix**  (*tel 01 44 41 86 50, musee-delacroix.fr, closed Tues.*), based in the last home of the major Romantic artist, who died in 1836.

Turn right from Rue Furstemberg and continue to Place St.-Germain-des-Prés. Beside the old abbey church of **St.-Germain-des-Prés** , a little garden contains Picasso's sculpture "L'Hommage à Apollinaire."

Place St.-Germain-des-Prés offers the chance of a reviving drink at one of Paris's best known cafés, including the atmospheric **Les Deux Magots** and the **Café de Flore** (see p. 77). From the square, go down Rue Bonaparte, lined with interesting little stores and galleries. On the left you will see the École Nationale Supérieure des Beaux-Arts (School of Fine Art).

Having reached the Seine—and the splendid view of the enormous Louvre—turn right on Quai Malaquais and walk past the **Institut de France** . This is where the historic French academies, including the exclusive Académie Française, carry out their research.

Farther along, in the former mint—the 18th-century **Hôtel des Monnaies** —is the Musée de la Monnaie (*tel 01 40 46 55 00, monnaiedeparis.fr, closed Mon.*), which traces the history of coinage from 300 B.C. Limited-edition coins are still made here.

Go down the steps from Quai des Grands-Augustins to the lower embankment of the Seine, away from the busy road (but usually closed at night). Return to Pont au Double.

The Panthéon is an impressive 18th-century engineering feat and a site well worth a prolonged visit to ponder the scope of French history.

## INSIDER TIP:

An evocative museum to visit is the Maison de Victor Hugo [see pp. 93–94], especially on Nuit des Musées.

—JACK KAVANAGH
*National Geographic author*

Within 40 years, the station was obsolete, its platforms too short for modern trains. Temporary uses for the building have included a mailing center, film set, and hostel for prisoners of war. By the 1960s, demolition plans were well advanced when the present innovative conversion was proposed. This allowed various important art collections to be regrouped, including famous Impressionist works from the overcrowded Jeu de Paume across the Seine. The Musée d'Orsay thus filled a gap between the Louvre and the contemporary art of the Centre Georges Pompidou (Beaubourg).

**Ground Floor:** Visitors in a hurry may be tempted to head for the Impressionist works upstairs. Resist, if you have time: The ground floor, mostly covering the period 1848–1870, traces some of the developments that paved the way for 20th-century painting and sculpture. In the central gallery, devoted to sculpture, study the influential work of Jean-Baptiste Carpeaux (1827–1875), whose bronze group "Count Ugolino" gave Rodin ideas he used in "The Thinker."

Mid-19th-century paintings occupy the side galleries on this floor. To the

## EXPERIENCE: Get Artistic in Paris

Paris has always been the city of creativity, so what better place to try to express your own artistic talents? **Paris Loisirs Culturels** *(11 rue St.-Maur, tel 01 81 29 25 76, p.dizian.free.fr)* offers painting classes at every level. Lessons, available in French and English, concentrate on various painting techniques, composition, and pictorial construction. The great French masters are studied, notably Matisse, and once a month you can join the group expedition to the Musée d'Orsay or the Louvre. Personalized courses allow you to develop and advance at your own rhythm—in your own choice of subject matter and materials.

For weeklong courses or just to enjoy an outdoor Sunday class in drawing, painting, or watercolors, consider registering for **Atelier Alupi** *(tel 06 78 26 82 94, atelieralupi.com)*.

For art classes en plein air, learn to paint in Monet's garden and in his beloved village of Giverny. Engaging and educational artistic retreats in English are run by **ArtStudy/Giverny** *(tel 02 32 21 96 83, giverny.org/artists /schools/artstudy/index.htm)*, with hands-on workshops taught by professional artists.

■ Ethereal works of art can't mask the Musée d'Orsay's rail terminal past.

right (as you enter) you will encounter later works by the conservative Ingres, devotee of classical ideas and technical precision, and the Romantic Delacroix, for whom imagination and the use of color became more important.

Highlights of the galleries on the opposite (north) side include several pictures by realists Millet and Courbet. Note Millet's deliberately mundane portrayal of three peasant women, "The Gleaners," and Courbet's "Burial at Ornans," considered vulgar when it was first shown. The passage of time has allowed a broader sweep of subject matters to take their place on French canvases.

Many such paintings illustrate the important move away from heroic, stylized subject matter toward depictions of ordinary people and everyday themes in French art. Equally revolutionary approaches to color and light characterize the pre-1870 works of art by painters such as Monet, Pissarro, Manet, and Renoir that can be found toward the northeastern end of this floor of the museum.

**Upper Level:** The core of the museum's world-famous Impressionist collection is on the upper level. Familiar images include Manet's "Déjeuner sur l'Herbe," Monet's

"Poppies," and Whistler's portrait of his mother. All the great artists of the period are well represented; there are works by Renoir, Cézanne, Pissarro, and Degas. Some fine van Gogh paintings are also here, including "Bedroom at Arles," "Church at Auvers," and several self-portraits. Van Gogh was in Paris from 1886 to 1888, meeting and exchanging ideas with all the major artists.

Some of the rooms at the western end of this floor show pictures by the Pont-Aven school, a breakaway group led by Gauguin. They emphasized two-dimensional patterns from memory rather than nature. A nearby room is devoted to the *nabis,* another genre of late 19th-century painters including Bonnard and Vuillard, named for the Hebrew word *nabi* (prophet). Their flat, linear forms and arbitrary use of color paved the way for early 20th-century abstract art.

**Middle Level:** Make time, if you can, to visit the varied collections here. Some—such as the early photographs, the art nouveau glass and ceramics, and the sumptuous ballroom of the former hotel—offer a complete contrast with exhibits on other levels.

Other galleries return to artistic themes explored elsewhere in the museum: There are larger works by the nabis (such as Bonnard's "The Croquet Party"), some sculptures by Rodin, and rooms of naturalist and symbolist paintings.

## Musée du Quai Branly

The Musée du Quai Branly, located on the Seine near the Tour Eiffel, opened in June 2006. Its vast collection, comprising 3,500 pieces from the Musée de l'Homme and the Musée National des Arts d'Afrique et d'Océanie, showcases ethnic art from all over the world.

Jean Nouvel designed the glass-fronted structure, which echoes the shadow of the neighboring Tour Eiffel and is surrounded by a park of paths, a pool, and trees. One of its most curious features is a *mur végétal,* a wall with 150 species of plants.

## Musée Rodin

Sculptor Auguste Rodin (1840–1917) spent his last nine years in the Hôtel Biron, an elegant rococo mansion near Les Invalides. Built in 1730, the house and its beautiful garden were previously owned by a horticulturist, Maréchal de Biron, who died on the guillotine.

The house became artists' studios in 1908. Rodin stayed here from then until his death, paying the rent with his art. After he died, the house became a museum for the collection he left to

---

**Musée du Quai Branly** 🄼 54 B3 ✉ Entrances on rue de l'Université *&* quai Branly ☎ 01 56 61 70 00 🕒 Closed Mon. 🅢 $$$ 🚇 Métro: Iéna, Alma-Marceau. Or take the river shuttle. **quaibranly.fr • Musée Rodin** 🄼 54 B3 ✉ 77 rue de Varenne ☎ 01 44 18 61 10 🕒 Closed Mon. 🅢 $$-$$$ 🚇 Métro: Varenne, Invalides **musee-rodin.fr**

the nation. Rodin gained fame late in life, only gaining widespread recognition in his forties. Yet his output was prolific, and the museum possesses several thousand sculptures and fragments as well as many of the artist's impressive drawings.

Works from Rodin's youth include a bust of his father and the charming terra-cotta "Young Woman in a Flowered Hat" (circa 1865). The sculptor's first major commission, in 1880, was "The Gates of Hell." Intended as a bronze door for the planned Musée des Arts Décoratifs, the work was not cast until 1929, after Rodin's death, but many of the figures that he made for this project developed into independent sculptures; this remarkable artistic artifact acts as a sketched page of his future career.

Alongside Rodin's own works in the museum are several works by his contemporaries, notably his talented but tragic mistress, Camille Claudel. She never recovered from Rodin's rejection in 1898, spending her last years in a mental institution.

With their roses, well-placed seats, and summer café, the gardens make an agreeable end to your visit to the Musée Rodin. ∎

◾ The gardens of the Musée Rodin offer a restful space for thinkers.

# TOUR EIFFEL

Rising from the green expanse of the Champ de Mars, a former military parade ground established 140 years before its construction, the Tour Eiffel (Eiffel Tower) is Paris's most enduring symbol. Built for the centenary of the revolution in 1889, it was feted by half a million people at its own centenary celebrations in 1989.

When plans for the Tour Eiffel won first prize in a competition organized for the 1889 Universal Exhibition, Gustave Eiffel pronounced that France would be the only nation with a 300-meter (984 ft) flagpole. The precision of his plans, with exact measurements for more than 15,000 metallic parts, enabled 300 workers to complete the tallest structure in the world in just over two years (January 1887 to March 1889). A staggering 2.5 million rivets were used. Eiffel's towering achievement remained the world's tallest building for 41 years until the Chrysler Building in New York City was finished in 1930.

An immediate success, it was visited by almost two million people during the exhibition. Within a year it had recouped most of its building cost. The tower was due to be pulled down in 1909, but by then

The grand tower is the spot for bird's-eye-view Paris photos.

## Paris Icon: Facts & Stats

- **Height (including antenna): 1,051 feet (319 m)**
- **Height increase on hot days from metal expansion: up to 6 inches (15 cm)**
- **First platform at 187 feet (57 m)**
- **Second platform at 377 feet (115 m)**
- **Top platform at 905 feet (276 m)**
- **1,585 steps**
- **7 million visitors per year**
- **Made of puddle iron**

its role in the first transatlantic radio telephone service.

The tower's first platform has been completely renovated with new pavilions, an educational museum, and a stunning glass floor that is not for those with vertigo; but all others will be walking on air. It also has access for the disabled. The panorama from the top platform is breathtaking. On a clear day, the horizon can extend to 45 miles (72 km). Directly below flows the Seine and, on the opposite bank, the Palais de Chaillot. At night the tower is lit from within for ten minutes every hour, making a glittering spectacle, so evocative of Paris's romantic image. Few cities are as recognizable by one such iconic site. ■

it had become indispensable to the fast-changing world of telecommunications, gaining global acclaim for

**Tour Eiffel** ⛰ 54 A3 ✉ Champ de Mars ☎ 08 92 70 12 39 💲 $$$-$$$$ 🚇 Métro: Bir-Hakeim **tour-eiffel.fr**

■ **The unmistakable profile of the Eiffel Tower.**

# CAFÉ LIFE

For Parisians, the café has a special place in their lives: It is here that they meet friends, discuss the affairs of the day, and watch the world go by. For some, the café is virtually a second home. Many Parisian cafés have famous histories as melting pots for artists and intellectuals to exchange and develop ideas. Traditional café culture remains strong, though the number of cafés in Paris has dropped significantly in recent years.

Paris café culture: Lingering, reading, chatting, laughing, stealing glances . . . same again *s'il vous plaît!*

## Historic Haunts

The first café to open its doors in Paris, in 1686, was **Le Procope,** on the Left Bank. It soon became the meeting place of actors from the Comédie-Française and later of philosophers Voltaire and Rousseau, revolutionaries Danton, Robespierre, and Marat, and 19th-century writers, including Balzac and Hugo. Le Procope still exists, but as a classic restaurant with mirrors, chandeliers, and several rooms.

The broad, sweeping *grands boulevards* of the 19th century moved café life onto the sidewalks. One of the first of these places was **Café de la Paix** *(5 Place de l'Opéra, tel 01 40 07 36 36, cafedelapaix.fr),* which retains much of its Second Empire glory. Parisians delight in sitting outside where they can watch the passing street life. In the summer, as would be expected, the streets buzz with people crowded at outdoor café tables.

By the 1920s, café society had moved to Montparnasse, where the likes of revolutionary photographer Man Ray and controversial novelist Henry Miller—both American expatriates—frequented a trio of neighborhood spots. **La Rotonde** *(105 boulevard du Montparnasse, tel 01 43 26 48 26, larotonde-montparnasse.fr)* remains a traditional brasserie with a huge terrace, velvet banquettes, and perfect service. Starring on the menu are steak tartare and fresh oysters. **Le Dôme,** another Paris institution, has a famous glass-fronted terrace. The third legendary hangout of Lost Generation Americans is **Le Select** *(99 boulevard du Montparnasse, tel 01 45 48 38 24),* perfect for brunch.

In 1939, Picasso was a regular at **Café de Flore** *(172 boulevard St.-Germain, tel 01 45 48 55 26 cafedeflore.fr)*, likely setting the pace for Jean-Paul Sartre and Simone de Beauvoir. Sartre developed the philosophy of existentialism during the many hours he and de Beauvoir spent here—from 9 a.m. until well into the night. It's still a popular hangout, with plays performed upstairs.

Nearby is **Les Deux Magots** *(6 place St.-Germain, tel 01 45 48 55 25, lesdeux magots.fr)*, named for its two statues of Chinese mandarins, *magots,* which sit inside on a pillar—a reminder of the café's original function, selling silks. Les Deux Magots attracted the key figures of a whole postwar generation of philosophers and writers, including Ernest Hemingway, André Breton, and André Gide. It is still a favorite among Parisians.

### The New Crop
Modern cafés are keeping tradition alive. Many of the new spots still attract an artistic clientele while acting as a showcase for superb design. **Café Beaubourg** *(100 rue de St.-Martin, tel 01 48 87 63 96, cafebeaubourg.com)*, on the square outside the Centre Pompidou, was designed by Christian de Pontzamparc and is a fashionable rendezvous for artists, critics, and gallery owners.

On the Left Bank, **La Palette** *(43 rue de Seine, tel 01 43 26 63 15, cafelapaletteparis .com)* is very popular with students from the École des Beaux-Arts. Retired Parisians and the fashionable elite also go there—La Palette is *the* place in Paris to "be seen." The café's pretty tree-shaded terrace is a wonderful refuge in summer.

One very popular café is **Café Marly** *(93 rue de Rivoli, tel 01 49 26 06 60)*, with its arcaded courtyard terrace overlooking the famous pyramid of the Louvre. It's

expensive but delightful. Note: It must boast the most stylish restrooms ever seen in a café.

At the other end of the spectrum are the local cafés. Fashionable for its cafés and nightlife is the Rue Oberkampf, leading up to Belleville. Try the belle epoque **Café Charbon** *(109 rue Oberkampf, tel 01 43 57 55 13)* or the popular **Cannibale Café** *(93 rue Jean Pierre Timbaud, tel 01 49 29 95 59)*.

### Café Nuts & Bolts
Some cafés are low-profile local places where working people eat a quick snack at lunchtime and neighborhood residents meet in the evening. You can find plenty of these around Montmartre and Pigalle.

In general, cafés open early in the morning, in time to serve the traditional *grand crème* (large cup of coffee with milk) with croissants to commuters.

Throughout the day they also serve wine, beer, pastis—a strong aniseed spirit diluted with water—and, of course, espresso coffee. Drinks are cheaper *au bar* (standing at the bar) than *en salle* (sitting at a table inside). They are even pricier if you sit at a table outside, but this never seems to worry anyone who is intent on soaking up the atmosphere and lingering a while. This archetypal Paris experience is worth every euro.

# HÔTEL DES INVALIDES

Monumental even by the standards of the Sun King, the Hôtel des Invalides was founded by Louis XIV to care for his veteran soldiers, many of them sick or disabled and desperately poor. The impressive classical building, with its huge severe facade, was completed in 1676. The Église du Dôme, whose commanding gilded and painted cupola stands directly over Napoleon's tomb, was added in 1706.

The huge **Cour d'Honneur** is lined with two-story arcades. "The Little Corporal," a statue of Napoleon I, stands above the south side. Trophies, flags, guns, and heraldic symbols adorn four pavilions, and, at roof level, carved horses trample emblems of war. At the end is the entrance to the soldiers' church, **St.-Louis-des-Invalides,** its interior hung with captured regimental standards.

■ In Paris a military hospital gets grand architectural treatment.

The **Église du Dôme** alongside is a mausoleum to the military heroes of France. Directly under the dome is the centerpiece, the **tomb of Napoleon I.** At its center, a red porphyry sarcophagus stands on a green granite base, with Napoleon's ashes inside.

The complex includes **Musée de l'Armée** (*musee-armee.org*), one of the world's largest military collections. The **Musée des Plans-Reliefs** displays scale models of fortified towns and fortresses. Also visit the **Musée de l'Ordre de la Libération,** devoted to World War II (*ordredelaliberation.fr*). ■

---

**INSIDER TIP:**

Nearby Cour du Commerce St.-André, still a cobblestone passageway, is café/restaurant Le Procope [see p. 69 & 76]. Marat and others who planned the revolution met here in the 1700s.

—EMILIE C. HARTING
*Intelligent Travel blog writer*

---

**Hôtel des Invalides**  🗺 54 B3  ✉ esplanade des Invalides  ☎ 08 25 05 44 05  💲 $$  🚇 Métro: Varenne, La Tour-Maubourg

## Les Catacombes

More than six million skeletons in many miles of former Montparnasse quarry tunnels. *catacombes .paris.fr* 🅰 55 C1 ✉ 1 avenue Colonel Rol Tanguy ☎ 01 43 22 47 63 🕐 Closed Mon. 💲 $ 🚇 Métro: Denfert-Rochereau

## Cimetière du Montparnasse

Montparnasse in its heyday drew literary and artistic figures. Baudelaire, Saint-Saëns, Sartre, Ionesco, and others are buried here. 🅰 55 C1 ✉ 3 boulevard E. Quinet ☎ 01 44 10 86 50 🚇 Métro: Edgar Quinet, Raspail

## Docks en Seine

The old warehouses of the Quai d'Austerlitz, next to the Bibliotheque François Mitterrand, have been transformed. Between Charles de Gaulle and Bercy bridges is the Cité de la Mode et du Design (dubbed Docks en Seine), housing the Institut Français fashion college. The green steel and glass structure, with a terrace overlooking the Seine, houses shops, restaurants, and a recently added cultural center. *citemodedesign .fr* 🅰 55 E1 ✉ 34 quai d'Austerlitz ☎ 01 76 77 25 30 🚇 Métro: Gare d'Austerlitz

## Les Égouts (Paris Sewers)

Haussmann's vast 1850 network of sewers has become a popular tourist attraction. 🅰 54 B3 ✉ opposite 93 quai d'Orsay ☎ 01 53 68 127 81 🕐 Closed Thurs.–Fri. & Jan. 💲 $ 🚇 Métro: Alma-Marceau

## Institut du Monde Arabe

An innovative 1987 building, with light-sensitive windows and transparent elevators; museum displays Islamic metalwork, ceramics, and carpets. *imarabe.org* 🅰 55 E2 ✉ 1 rue des Fossés St.-Bernard ☎ 01 40 51 38 38 🕐 Closed Mon. 💲 $ 🚇 Métro: Jussieu, Cardinal Lemoine

## Jardin des Plantes

The splendidly restored botanical garden, with avenues of trees, a zoo, and grand greenhouses, includes the Natural History Museum *(mnhn.fr, closed Tues.)* with its Grand Galerie of Evolution in a 19th-century glass domed building. 🅰 55 E2 ✉ 57 rue Cuvier ☎ 01 40 79 56 01 💲 $ 🚇 Métro: Place Monge, Gare d'Austerlitz

## Jardin Tino-Rossi

Relax among trees, lawns, and sculpture in this peaceful area by the Seine, with views across to Île St.-Louis. Avoid after dark. 🅰 55 E2 ✉ quai St.-Bernard 🚇 Métro: Gare d'Austerlitz

## Grande Mosquée de Paris

France's largest mosque, inspired by the Alhambra. *mosqueedeparis.net* 🅰 55 D2–E2 ✉ 2 place du Puits-de-l'Ermite 🕐 Closed Fri. 🚇 Métro: Place Monge

## Tour Montparnasse

The 688-foot (210 m) tower offers panoramic views from its 58th floor. 🅰 55 C2 ✉ Place Rault-Dautry ☎ 01 45 38 52 56 💲 $$ 🚇 Métro: Montparnasse-Bienvenüe

# RIGHT BANK

The wealthy have favored this area north of the Seine ever since Charles V moved the royal residence here in the late 14th century. Palaces, elegant squares and gardens, sweeping boulevards, and grand town houses are their legacy. Recent decades have brought imaginative rejuvenation schemes to areas such as Les Halles, Beaubourg, and the Marais. Cultural life on the Right Bank (Rive Droite) ranges from the Opéra Garnier to a series of museums, including the Louvre, the largest museum in the world.

■ At the Palais-Royal, conceptual artist Daniel Buren's striped columns set the stage for fun.

As Paris grew in grandeur, so did its buildings—such as the Tuileries, built for Catherine de Médicis but destroyed by fire in 1871, and the Palais-Royal, which began life as the residence of Cardinal Richelieu. Napoleon encouraged neoclassical schemes such as La Madeleine and the imposing Arc de Triomphe to glorify his growing empire.

The *grands projets* of the 19th century swept away earlier housing to create broad vistas along the *grands boulevards* in Baron Haussmann's major exercise in town planning. The Champs-Élysées excels as a powerful setting for state occasions, from General de Gaulle's 1944 return to Paris, to the procession celebrating the 1989 bicentennial.

Among the Right Bank's art enclaves, dominated by the imposing Louvre, the much smaller Musée Picasso stands out. The ornate elegance of the Hôtel Salé, built for a salt tax collector in 1656, makes a perfect backdrop for the works of the great 20th-century master. The modern Beaubourg is another fine museum.

For up-to-the-minute elegance and style, look no further than the designer shops, jewelers, and galleries that line Rue St.-Honoré and Place Vendôme. This remains the hallowed center of the world of high fashion. Indeed, the Right Bank can be seriously chic. ■

# CHAMPS-ÉLYSÉES & THE ARC DE TRIOMPHE

From an unpaved, swampy track, the Champs-Élysées has evolved into one of the world's grandest and best known avenues. In civic planner Baron Haussmann's 19th-century modernizing transformation of the city, the monumental Arc de Triomphe became the central point of 12 radiating avenues.

## Champs-Élysées

Marie de Médicis began creating a sophisticated byway in 1616, and by the time landscape designer André Le Nôtre planted trees to frame the westward vista from the Louvre, her avenue was a soigné carriage drive.

---

**INSIDER TIP:**

Try classic Guerlain fragrances (including Shalimar) at the company's 68 Champs-Élysées flagship shop.

—SHEILA BUCKMASTER
*National Geographic writer*

---

By 1836, when the view was crowned by the Arc de Triomphe, the Champs-Élysées was firmly established as one of Europe's most elegant promenades.

After years of overcommercialization, the Champs-Élysées was revamped, with stylish restaurants, several dramatic architectural projects, and the restored

Publicis Drugstore, long a Paris landmark and now home to a bookstore, wine shop, brasserie, fancy food market, cigar store, boutiques, and two movie theaters.

## Arc de Triomphe

This Paris landmark dominates the axis leading east down the Champs-Élysées and west down the Avenue de la Grande Armée. It is now known as the Place Charles-de-Gaulle.

Napoleon I commissioned the triumphal arch in 1806 to honor his Grande Armée. It was finally completed in 1836, and Napoleon's remains passed under the arch on their way to Les Invalides in 1840.

The arch is 164 feet (50 m) high and has four massive sculptures carved on its main facades. These portray victories achieved during the 1789 revolution and the First Empire. Inside the arch, an elevator and stairs lead up to the panoramic viewing platform. A small museum in the crosspiece has video displays about the arch. The Unknown Soldier was buried beneath the arch in 1920. A flame is relit daily at 6:30 p.m. ■

**Champs-Élysées** 🅰 54 B4 🚇 Métro: Champs-Élysées Clemenceau, Franklin D. Roosevelt, George V • **Arc de Triomphe** 🅰 54 A4–B4 ✉ Place Charles de Gaulle ☎ 01 55 37 73 77 💲 $$ 🚇 Métro: Charles de Gaulle Étoile

# MUSÉE PICASSO

**The Hotel Salé, a fine 17th-century town house in the Marais, is the impressive showcase of the world's largest Picasso collection. The paintings, collages, sculptures, drawings, and ceramics are complemented by letters, photographs, and archival material. Picasso's collection of works by his contemporaries, including Cézanne and Matisse, is also on show here.**

Though Picasso (1881–1973) was born in Spain, his adult life was spent almost entirely in France. During his long career he had kept many of his own works, resulting in a huge inheritance tax liability when he died. The French state claimed this in the form of works of art amounting to a quarter of the artist's collection, and then undertook a lavish refurbishment of the Hôtel Salé as a museum for them. It opened in 1985, and has since been extended. With more than 250 paintings, 3,000 drawings, and 100,000 archival items, the collection is rotated regularly to highlight periods of Picasso's hugely varied output over some 70 years. The sequence of presentation is broadly chronological.

The collection, now spread over five floors, begins with works produced after Picasso's first visit to Paris from Spain in 1900, among them the bleak "Self Portrait" (1901), a masterpiece of his famous Blue Period, and "Celestine" (1904). Poignant sadness continued to pervade Picasso's work in his so-called Rose Period (1904–1906).

The rapid developments in Picasso's work during his twenties and thirties were influenced by key events in his life. In Paris, artists of the day such as Matisse, Cézanne, Braque, and Rousseau made a powerful impression on him. His travels, notably to Rome, Spain, and the Mediterranean, brought new themes. Primitive art from French colonies in Africa and the South Seas became the object of serious interest.

---

**INSIDER TIP:**

**Don't miss the joyful, experimental ceramics Picasso made in Provence. He crafted thousands of pots, jugs, plates, and figures.**

—ROSEMARY BAILEY
*National Geographic author*

---

In his mid-twenties, Picasso, with Georges Braque and Juan Gris, developed cubism, a style that aimed to depict the structure of an object from different angles by breaking it down into geometrical units. The artist's progression from traditional techniques to ever bolder artistic experiments can now be studied in the educational multimedia room. ∎

**Musée Picasso** 🅼 55 E3 ✉ Hotel Salé, 5 rue de Thorigny ☎ 01 85 56 00 36 🕐 Closed Mon. 💲 $$$ 🚇 Métro: Chemin Vert **museepicassoparis.fr**

# BEAUBOURG

**"This will cause a stir," said President Georges Pompidou about the museum and cultural center that officially bears his name. When the project was completed by architects Renzo Piano and Richard Rogers in 1977, its design was compared to a factory.**

 Getting from one floor to another at the Beaubourg is a great-views experience.

Today, the Centre Georges-Pompidou—called the Beaubourg by locals—is a familiar and much loved part of the Paris landscape. With its external glass-walled escalators, colored pipes, and massive steel struts, this icon of high-tech industrial style seems to fit into the center of historic (and evolving) Paris.

A revamp has given the center more room to display the fine contemporary art collection of the Musée Nationale d'Art Moderne—the largest modern art museum in Europe, with works by artists including Picasso, Braque, Ernst, Magritte, Chagall, Matisse, Delaunay,

Kandinsky, and Klee. Other parts of the building are devoted to temporary exhibitions, industrial design, the performing arts, film, and a vast reference library. There are also several restaurants, children's facilities, and a panoramic terrace with a view over the rooftops of Paris.

Next to the museum is the Place Igor Stravinsky, famous for its colorful mobile water-fountain sculptures by Swiss sculptor Jean Tinguely and French artist Nikki de Saint Phalle, and a 25-foot-high (7.6 m) Alexander Calder mobile. It is now a favorite gathering place, where you can listen to music, watch the jugglers and mimes, and visit the Brancusi workshop. ∎

**Beaubourg** 🅰 55 D3 ✉ rue St.-Martin ☎ 01 44 78 12 33
🕐 Closed Tues. 💲 $$-$$$ 🚇 Métro: Rambuteau **centrepompidou.fr**

# AN ART, PARK & PALACE WALK

**To see Paris at its most supremely elegant, follow this walk from the Opéra to the Champs-Élysées, then through the Jardin des Tuileries to return past the Palais-Royal.**

Equally lavish inside and out, Paris's legendary **Opéra Garnier ❶** (splendidly restored), opened in 1875, is now devoted to ballet. From the Place de l'Opéra, take Rue de la Paix past glittering jewelry stores to the classy Place Vendôme, dominated by the Ritz Hotel.

Cross the square to Rue de Castiglione and turn right on Rue St.-Honoré, celebrated for its designer shops. Fork right on Rue Duphot to Place de la Madeleine. **La Madeleine ❷**, with its 52 Corinthian pillars, commands a stunning vista down Rue Royale to Place de la Concorde.

From Rue Royale, turn right on Rue du Faubourg St.-Honoré, past the **Palais de l'Élysée ❸**, the French president's official residence since 1873 (not open to the public). Turn left on Avenue de Marigny and walk across the Champs-Élysées to Avenue Winston Churchill, between the **Grand Palais ❹** (tel 01 44 13 17 17, grandpalais.fr) and the **Petit Palais** (tel 01 53 43 40 00, petitpalais.paris .fr, closed Mon.), both built for the 1900 Universal Exhibition in the French capital.

The Petit Palais houses the art collections of the City of Paris in a fine, renovated building. In the west wing of the Grand Palais is the **Palais de la Découverte** (tel 01 56 43 20 20, closed Mon.), a science museum and planetarium.

## NOT TO BE MISSED:

**La Madeleine • Place de la Concorde • Jardin des Tuileries • Musée de l'Orangerie**

Cross Cours la Reine to view the Seine from the elaborate Pont Alexandre III. Turn left along the embankment to **Place de la Concorde ❺**, which witnessed thousands of executions during the Reign of Terror (1793–1794). The ancient Egyptian obelisk in the center overlooks eight statues representing the major French cities.

Go through the iron gates into the **Jardin des Tuileries,** originally landscaped for Catherine de Médicis's

palace here in 1564. The palace was destroyed by the Communards in 1871, but its gardens have changed little since.

⛰ See also area map p. 55

► Place de l'Opéra (Métro: Opéra)

↔ 3.25 miles (5 km)

🕑 2.5 hours

► Place de l'Opéra

The octagonal pond is flanked by two art galleries. The **Galerie Nationale du Jeu de Paume ❻** *(tel 01 47 03 12 50, jeudepaume.org, closed Mon.)*, built in 1878 as a tennis court, is now a center for photography.

The **Musée de l'Orangerie ❼** *(tel 01 44 77 80 07, musee-orangerie.fr, closed Tues.)*, built in 1852, has reopened to exhibit Monet's beautiful "Water Lilies" in a superbly lit space. Standing in this room gazing at this masterpiece is an experience no visitor to Paris should miss.

Continue through the gardens toward the Arc de Triomphe du Carrousel, built to commemorate Napoleon's victories of 1805. Cross the gardens and go through the arch beneath the Louvre's north gallery to Rue de Rivoli.

Turn right to Place du Palais-Royal, then left into Place des Pyramides, home of the **Comédie-Française,** still the venue for classic French theater. Walk beneath the theater's arcades to reach the **Palais-Royal ❽.** Cardinal Richelieu's palace (now used as government offices) is not open to the public, but the gardens are splendid and well worth a wander through. Walk past the shops to the left of the gardens, turn right and then left on Rue Vivienne, passing the former **Bibliothèque Nationale de France Richelieu,** whose 12 million books are now at the BNF Mitterrand (known as the TGB, or Très Grand Bibliothèque), in Bercy. At Rue du Quatre Septembre, opposite **La Bourse ❾** (Stock Exchange), turn left to return to the Opéra.

For a moment of rest during this walk, there is nothing better than stopping in front of the fountain in the Jardin des Tuileries.

# THE LOUVRE

Once the largest palace in the world, the Louvre was first a showcase for art during the reign of François I, who was eager to display his Italian paintings. Subsequent rulers acquired new works of art, and the Louvre in the end became one of the world's largest museums, with exhibits spanning more than seven millennia.

▪ Controversial when unveiled in 1989, I. M. Pei's glass pyramids are now a Louvre centerpiece.

The palace began as a fortress in the medieval city walls. Philippe-Auguste enlarged this tower about 1200, creating a keep encircled by a moat. Already called the Louvre, his building served as a prison and arsenal. Excavations beneath the Cour Carrée in 1984–1985 revealed some of its foundations, now on exhibit in the Sully Wing.

The Louvre's transformation into a palace began in 1385, when Charles V began to turn it into an elegant royal residence with large windows, a grand entrance, and luxurious apartments. The result was a Gothic palace fit for a king.

Succeeding monarchs preferred more fashionable residences in the Marais or on the Loire River. Not until the reign of François I (R. 1515–1547) did the Louvre regain royal favor. The cultured François had begun to collect paintings and sculptures on his travels in Italy, and he encouraged Renaissance artists such as Leonardo da Vinci and

**Musée du Louvre** 🅰 55 C3–D3 ✉ Palais du Louvre ☎ 01 40 20 53 17 🕐 Closed Tues. 💲 $$$ Free: Fri. 6 p.m.–9:45 p.m. for under-26s. Free: 1st Sun. Oct.–March 🚇 Métro: Palais-Royal–Musée du Louvre **louvre.fr**

Benvenuto Cellini to come to France. Toward the end of his life, he began to plan a rebuilding of the Louvre, in Renaissance style, as a fitting home for his collection, which included Leonardo's "Mona Lisa."

François's project was continued by Henri II. After his death in 1559, his widow, Catherine de Médicis, moved the official royal residence from the Hôtel des Tournelles to the Louvre. Between 1595 and 1607, Henri IV realized Catherine's plans for a long gallery beside the Seine, to join the Louvre to the neighboring Tuileries.

Building work in the 17th century included much of the Cour Carrée and the Colonnade at the eastern end. Progress slowed after Louis XIV moved his court to Versailles in 1682, but a great benefit of the Sun King's reign was a tenfold increase in the size of the royal art collections. Many of the Louvre's key works by major artists such as Raphael, Titian, Rubens, and Holbein were acquired during this period.

The 18th century saw the Louvre neglected and lacking a focus. Its apartments were put to various uses, from sheltering homeless artists to housing the French academies. Eventually, in 1793, the Musée Central des Arts was inaugurated at the Louvre, which soon became the home of many treasures acquired by Napoleon I from his victories in Europe. (A large proportion of them were returned after his defeat.) Napoleon III finally completed the museum's symmetrical "grand design" and created state apartments. The Louvre continues its tradition of change in a radical reorganization and expansion program known as the "Grand Louvre" project. The Salle des États now has an entire room dedicated to the "Mona Lisa."

Recent museum initiatives included the openings of extensions in Lens, northern France, and in Abu Dhabi. The Islamic Art gallery opened in 2012 in the Cour Visconti, an interior pavilion topped by a golden undulating roof that seems to float within the courtyard.

## Paris Icon: Facts & Stats

- **40 percent of visitors are under 26.**
- **80 percent of people only come to see the "Mona Lisa," "Venus de Milo," or "Winged Victory."**
- **The Louvre's director estimates it would take a month to see everything in the whole museum.**
- **The correct pronunciation of Louvre is LOOV-ruh.**
- **The Louvre is the world's most visited museum, welcoming more than ten million visitors a year.**

# The Louvre

SECOND FLOOR

FIRST FLOOR

GROUND FLOOR

Arc de Triomphe du Carrousel

Cour Marly

Cour Puget

Richelieu Wing

Cour Khorsabad

Cour Napoléon

Pyramid entrance

Denon Wing

Cour Visconti (Islamic Art gallery)

To Métro

Sully Wing

ENTRESOL

Paintings/drawings

Sculpture

Entrance hall (Hall Napoléon)

Objets d'art

Antiquities

Medieval Louvre history

Medieval Louvre

## Finding Your Way

The Louvre's main entrance, in the Cour Napoléon, is through I. M. Pei's ingenious 793-panel glass pyramid. Visitors go down into the gleaming marble underworld of the reception area, known as the Hall Napoléon.

The museum's three wings are Sully (enclosing the Cour Carrée), Denon (alongside the Seine), and Richelieu (beside the Rue de Rivoli). Each wing has four levels: entresol, ground floor, first floor, and second floor. Another entrance welcomes visitors in from the Carrousel du Louvre, a huge underground shopping complex, and the Métro.

With up to 35,000 fine artworks to choose from, you should plan for what you want to see on your visit to the Louvre. You will also need a floor plan, available from the information desk in the Hall Napoléon. Audio guides and guided tours are also offered.

The museum has eight departments: Oriental Antiquities; Egyptian Antiquities; Greek, Etruscan, and Roman Antiquities; Islamic Art; Objets d'Art; Sculptures; Paintings; and Graphic Arts. Within each of these individual departments you'll find several collections.

The Sully Wing is a good place to start. Here at the entresol level are the impressive remains of Philippe-Auguste's medieval fortress. The dungeons, the base of the towers, and the support for the moat drawbridge can be seen, together with displays of pottery and royal artifacts found during the excavations.

## Ancient World

The recently expanded galleries of the Egyptian Antiquities department, on the lower floors of the Sully Wing, are easily reached from the Medieval Louvre exhibition through the Crypt of the Sphinx. The collection has two parts: the ground floor, arranged by theme (The Nile; Writing and Scribes; Music and Games), and the first floor, arranged by date. This starts with a 5,000-year-old ceremonial dagger with an intricately carved ivory handle. Room upon room of mummies, friezes, exquisite fabrics, papyrus texts, jewels, and statues make up the largest Egyptian collection outside Cairo.

The main collections representing ancient Greece and Rome are also in the Sully Wing, where you will find the instantly recognizable "Venus de Milo," elegant as ever, on the ground floor. Don't miss the huge collection of Greek terra-cotta vases in the Galerie Campana (first floor) and the Greek and Roman glassware in the Salle des Verres. Not far away, in Napoleon III's

■ **The marble "Winged Victory of Samothrace"**

former stables (Denon Wing, entresol), is an exciting gallery devoted to pre-Hellenic Greece. Don't miss the Cycladic sculptures, whose simple shapes belie their early date (2,000–3,000 B.C.). Two floors up is the Louvre's second world-famous Greek statue, the graceful "Winged Victory of Samothrace" (circa 190 B.C.).

## Paintings

The Louvre's enormous collection of paintings spreads into all three wings. The second floor of the Richelieu Wing may be the best place to start. It can be reached by Pei's imaginative escalator—a 1990s answer to the grand staircase of bygone days.

The northern European paintings, occupying the western part of the wing, include works by important Dutch and Flemish masters such as van Eyck, Rembrandt, the Brueghels, and Vermeer. The large Médici Gallery is a fine setting for the most ambitious work here, Rubens's epic 24-panel sequence depicting scenes from the life of Marie de Médicis, designed to adorn the Palais du Luxembourg.

A broadly chronological sequence of French pictures, from the 14th to 19th centuries, starts at the eastern end of this area and continues clockwise around the entire second floor of the Sully Wing. Worth seeking out are Watteau's enigmatic "Pierrot" (1718–1719), Fragonard's "The Bathers" (1764), and several paintings by Ingres, including the technically brilliant portrait of the publisher Louis-François Bertin (1832) and the well-known "Turkish Bath" (1862). A number of pictures by Corot, including "The Church at Marissel" (1866), demonstrate revolutionary developments in subject matter and light, foreshadowing the Impressionist movement.

The Italian collection is based in and around the Grande Galerie on the first floor of the Denon Wing. Be sure to see Botticelli's delicate 15th-century frescoes and Raphael's portrait of his friend Baldassare Castiglione. Titian and Tintoretto are represented not only through their own paintings but also by Veronese, who is said to have depicted his fellow artists among the musicians in "The Wedding Feast at Cana" (1563). Close by is the world's most famous enigmatic smile—that of the "Mona Lisa" (1503–1506), known in France as "La Joconde."

## Celebrating Design

To gain a deeper understanding of French interior decor, visit the **Musée des Arts Décoratifs** (107 rue de Rivoli, tel 01 44 55 57 50, lesartsdecoratifs.fr), part of the Louvre. It offers a glorious overview of furniture and ornament from the Middle Ages to the present day. Each of its superb rooms is decorated in period style. Notable are the art nouveau and art deco rooms. Also worthy of some time are the exquisite jewelry and glass collections, a reconstruction of novelist Marcel Proust's cork-lined bedroom, and the fabulous marble and bronze bathroom of couturier Jeanne Lanvin.

## Sculpture

French sculpture is found on the lower floors of the Richelieu Wing, where three new glass-roofed courts were laid out during the conversion of the wing from government offices into a setting for fine sculpture.

The Cour Marly is named after the grand château and park that Louis XIV created just outside Paris. Perhaps not surprisingly, the Sun King commissioned many fine statues for his country retreat, including "Fame Riding Pegasus" (1699–1702) by Antoine Coysevox. Exhibits in the nearby Cour Puget include several sculptures by Pierre Puget. His most famous work, the dynamic "Milon of Croton" (1671–1682), was commissioned by Louis XIV for Versailles.

Foreign sculpture is displayed on the lower two floors of the Denon Wing. Michelangelo's two powerful (though unfinished) "Slaves" (1513–1515) are the most popular exhibits. Gaze at these and let your imagination figure out what his genius might have added.

## Decorative Arts

The Galerie d'Apollon, on the Denon Wing's first floor, is the site of a glittering display—the crown jewels of France, including the golden scepter made for Charles V in the late 14th century and the coronation crowns of Louis XV and Napoleon. Also here is one of the word's purest diamonds, the Regent, worn by Louis XV at his coronation in 1722.

For insight into Second Empire style at its peak, visit the sumptuously decorated and lavishly furnished state apartments of Napoleon III, at the west end of the Richelieu Wing's first floor.

Multimedia guides are now available at the Louvre, with commentaries from conservators on the history of the art.

## Beyond the Louvre

Three other nearby museums, accessible from the Rue de Rivoli, are the **Musée de la Mode et du Textile,** the **Musée des Arts Décoratifs** (see sidebar p. 91), and the **Musée de la Publicité,** devoted to advertising. ∎

▪ **The glass roof over the Islamic Art gallery in the Cour Visconti resembles a Bedouin tent.**

# A WALK AROUND THE MARAIS

**Architectural gems of the 17th and 18th centuries—several of them now museums—highlight this stroll through a rejuvenated area of the city.**

The Marais ("marsh"), a swampy area on the Right Bank, was enclosed by King Philippe-Auguste's great wall. In the 1200s, the marsh was drained and building began. Today the area is a medley of narrow medieval streets, grand 17th-century *hôtels,* and chic little shops, galleries, and bars.

Begin at the **Place de la Bastille ❶**, famous as the site where the Bastille fort was stormed on July 14, 1789, marking the start of the French Revolution. In the 1980s, the **Opéra National de Paris-Bastille** was built in the southeast corner. Its appearance and its cost provoked much criticism. The 164-foot (50 m) column towering above the square commemorates the 1830 revolution.

> **NOT TO BE MISSED:**
>
> **Place des Vosges • Musée Carnavalet • Musée Cognacq-Jay • Musée Picasso • Hôtel de Sens**

Walk west along busy Rue St.-Antoine and turn right on Rue de Birague for the spectacular Square Louis XIII, better known as **Place des Vosges ❷**. Commissioned by Henri IV, with two royal pavilions, the square was completed in 1612. It quickly attracted residents such as Cardinal Richelieu and the playwright Molière. **Maison de**

Pretty Place des Vosges has seen pedestrian traffic for some 400 years.

**Victor Hugo ❸** at No. 6 is a museum in memory of the writer who lived here from 1832 to 1848 *(tel 01 42 72 10 16, maisonsvictorhugo.paris.fr, closed Mon.).* On the southwest corner is an entrance to the **Hôtel de Sully,** a magnificent private palace dating from about 1630; its courtyards are open to the public. Stroll farther around the square to admire its symmetry, perhaps stopping to browse in galleries or shops, or to have lunch or a drink under the arcades of Ma Bourgogne (No. 19).

Leave the square on Rue des Francs-Bourgeois. Turn right on Rue de Sévigné for the **Musée Carnavalet ❹** *(tel 01 44 59 58 58, carnavalet.paris.fr, closed Mon.).* Part of the museum occupies

▲ See also area map p. 55
► Place de la Bastille (Métro: Bastille)
↔ 2.25 miles (3.5 km)
⏱ 2 hours
► Quai des Célestins (Métro: Pont Marie)

the Hôtel Carnavalet, a 16th-century mansion that was the home of aristocratic writer Madame de Sévigné (1626–1696), who penned vivid accounts of life in the era of Louis XIV. The museum brings to life the history of Paris, from Roman times to the 20th century. The extravagant decor of the 17th and 18th centuries can be seen in the renovated interiors. Some were rescued from buildings demolished by Baron Haussmann in his 19th-century remodeling of Paris.

Continue north up Rue de Sévigné. Turn left on Rue du Parc Royal and take the second left, on Rue Elzévir, to visit the remarkable **Musée Cognacq-Jay** ❺ *(tel 01 40 27 07 21, museecognacqjay. paris.fr, closed Mon.).* Here, in the Hôtel Denon, is a superb collection of 18th-century paintings, furniture, and decorative items. Retrace your steps to Rue de Thorigny and the Hôtel Salé, now the **Musée Picasso** ❻ (see p. 82).

Turn left onto Rue des Coutures-St.-Gervais and left again down Rue Vieille-du-Temple. Pass the gates of the Hôtel de Rohan and, on the corner of Rue des Francs-Bourgeois, the pretty turret of the Maison de Jean Hérouët (private).

Turn right onto Rue des Francs-Bourgeois, known for its eclectic shops, elegant mansions, and the Crédit Municipal ("municipal pawnshop") at No. 55. Across the street is the impressive courtyard of the **Hôtel de Soubise** ❼. This sumptuous building houses the Musée de l'Histoire de France and the National Archives *(tel 01 40 27 60 96, closed Tues.).* Rebuilt in 1709 from a 14th-century manor for the Princesse de Soubise, the interiors were decorated by the most talented artists of the day. On Rue du Temple, you'll find the **Musée d'Art et d'Histoire du Judaïsme** *(71 rue du Temple, tel 01 53 01 86 53, mahj .org/fr, closed Mon.),* which commemorates Jewish culture.

Turn left down Rue des Archives, then left on Rue des Blancs-Manteaux to the covered market. On the far side

of the market, take Rue des Rosiers. This is the city's central Jewish quarter, full of specialist shops as far as Rue Pavée. Walk past the **Synagogue** ❽ designed in 1913 by Hector-Germain Guimard, known for his art nouveau Métro stations, then turn right at Rue Pavée. Cross Rue St.-Antoine and follow Rue du Figuier to the 15th-century **Hôtel de Sens** ❾ near the Pont Marie, which houses the **Bibliothèque Forney** *(tel 01 42 78 14 60, closed Sun.–Mon.),* a decorative arts library. Nearby, on Rue Geoffroy l'Asnier, is the **Holocaust Memorial** *(tel 01 42 77 44 72, memorialdelashoah .org, closed Sat.),* a moving testimony to the fate of the Jews in World War II, with its Wall of Names, photographs, private letters, and documentary films.

## Paris-Plages

**Grab your sunscreen and head to the beach—not far from Notre-Dame. For a month, from mid-July to mid-August, Paris-Plages help define summer in the city for Parisians. The quaysides of the Seine, closed to car traffic, sport free beaches with all the trimmings: sand, parasols, deck chairs, and palm trees. You'll find all sorts of leisure activities, sports, and concerts here. The beaches stretch on the right bank from the Louvre to Pont de Sully, and on the left bank from Pont du Tolbiac to the Simone de Beauvoir footbridge as well as beaches around Bassin de la Villette.**

# MONTMARTRE & SACRÉ-COEUR

Thirty windmills once dotted the Montmartre skyline. The steep hill that Parisians call "La Butte" now has an even more distinctive landmark: the great white Basilique du Sacré-Coeur. Although tourists flock to Montmartre today, it is still possible to stroll in quiet backwaters where streets and squares have retained a village atmosphere.

■ Above it all in bustling Montmartre is the stately white dome of Sacré-Coeur.

Its commanding position overlooking Paris ensured Montmartre's importance from early times. The Roman temple here probably gave the district its name (from Mons Martis, "Hill of Mars"). The 12th-century Benedictine abbey church **St.-Pierre-de-Montmartre,** one of Paris's oldest, still overlooks the Place du Tertre.

Quarries and vineyards supported Montmartre, and it remained a separate village until the quarries (and their windmills) had to close because of collapsing tunnels. By 1860, the Montmartre area had become the 18th arrondissement of the city of Paris.

The late 19th century saw Montmartre as it is most often pictured now—a focus of the exciting, if lurid, bohemian life, enjoyed by resident poets and painters. Many great names from this period can be seen on the gravestones in the **Cimetière de Montmartre** on Avenue Rachel. They include composers Hector Berlioz and Jacques Offenbach (who wrote the famous cancan), writers Stendhal and Émile Zola, and painter Edgar Degas. Film director François Truffaut and Russian dancer Vaslav Nijinsky are also buried here.

Today the creative ferment of the belle epoque has been replaced by the engaging street artists at work on the **Place du Tertre.**

Visible from anywhere in Paris, the white **Basilique du Sacré-Coeur** was started in 1876 by the French govern-ment to honor the 58,000 killed in the Franco-Prussian War and to atone for the "crimes" of the Commune. Pillars had to be driven deep into unstable rock to support the huge church, which was finally consecrated in 1919. Inside the basilica, the chancel vaulting is deco-rated with a colossal square mosaic (1912–1922) by Luc-Olivier Merson. It depicts the French nation worshipping the Sacred Heart of Christ. Steep spiral stairs lead to the dome, where an exter-ior gallery offers a spectacular panorama of Paris. Given the elevation, views at street level are almost as stunning. ∎

## Artists in Montmartre

Paris has long been an inspira-tional magnet for artists, both French and foreign, who have come here and made it their home. With its picturesque streets, bohemian ways, and cheap lodging houses, Montmar-tre began to attract impoverished artists in the 19th century. Leg-endary cafés and clubs—Le Chat Noir, Au Lapin Agile, La Nouvelle Athènes—became known as liter-ary and artistic meeting places.

The Moulin Rouge, the famous night spot on Boule-vard de Clichy, opened its doors in 1889. Henri de Toulouse-Lautrec was a regular visitor, often sketching and painting as he sat in the dance hall. Dancers and cabaret *artistes* of the louche Montmartre world, such as Aristide Bruant, Jane Avril, and Yvette Guilbert, were immor-talized in his posters. Another Montmartre dance hall, the Moulin de la Galette, was the subject of paintings by Renoir, Bonnard, and others.

Montmartre's streets are peppered with memories of famous artists. Boulevard de Clichy, painted by van Gogh and Renoir, was a focal point. Seurat, Signac, and, later, Picasso all had studios here. Degas died at No. 6 in 1917. The squalid Bateau-Lavoir building, where Picasso lived from 1904 to 1909, was shared by 30 other residents, many of them artists. The building (at No. 13 Place Émile-Goudeau) is gone now—but the clowns and harlequins of the Montmartre circus world live on in Picasso's paintings.

**Basilique du Sacré-Coeur** 🅰 55 D5 ✉ place du Parvis du Sacré-Coeur
☎ 01 53 41 89 00 💲 $ (crypt & dome) 🚇 Métro: Abbesses, Anver, Caulaincourt **sacre-coeur-montmartre.com**

# LA DÉFENSE

**Paris has frequently hit the headlines for its daring new architectural exploits, such as the Opéra-Bastille and the Beaubourg (see p. 83). But of all of these *grands travaux*, none has been more ambitious than the controversial space-age development at La Défense, dominated by the truly monumental Grande Arche.**

■ **The Grande Arche dominates the modern cityscape of La Défense.**

The modern district of La Défense, to the west of Paris across the Pont de Neuilly, takes its name from a statue in the central square, symbolizing the defense of Paris in the 1870 Franco-Prussian War.

A broad pedestrian avenue, the Esplanade du Général de Gaulle, rises in steps from the Pont de Neuilly to give access to office towers, apartment blocks, the vast shopping complex of Les Quatre-Temps, and the CNIT. The oldest building on the site (1958), the triangular CNIT building is now a conference center. Roads and railroads run beneath the buildings, leaving the main areas traffic free. More than 70 works of contemporary sculpture punctuate the concrete landscape.

The focal point of La Défense is the colossal **Grande Arche.** Designed by Johann Otto von Spreckilsen, it was completed for the bicentennial of the revolution in 1989. Shaped like a huge hollow cube and faced with glass and white marble, this "window on the world" is so vast that the whole cathedral of Notre-Dame would easily fit beneath it. The walls of the arch contain government and company offices. External glass elevators can take visitors up to the roof to admire the views over Paris from a height of more than 300 feet (100 m). Be sure to look to the southeast, where a dramatic corridor cuts a swath straight across the city. Stretching to the Arc de Triomphe and beyond, it continues along the same axis to the Place de la Concorde and the Bastille. The Grande Arche was deliberately aligned on this historic "Triumphal Way."

At the base of the arch, fountains and cafés enliven the square of La Défense. An open-air museum of fountains and sculptures includes work by artists such as Miró, Serra, Calder, César, Takis, and Emily Young. ■

**La Défense & Grande Arche** 🅰 54 A4 ✉ esplanade de La Défense ☎ 01 49 07 27 16 💲 $$$ 🚇 Métro: Grande Arche de La Défense **grandearche.com**

# PARC DE LA VILLETTE & CITÉ DES SCIENCES

**A truly astonishing transformation has taken place in northeast Paris. The former livestock market and slaughterhouses of La Villette are now a futuristic cultural park and interactive science museum. Allow a full day to make the most of a visit—there is lots to see and do.**

Adults and children alike will be enthralled by the Parc de la Villette's star attraction, **Cité des Sciences et de l'Industrie.** This vast science museum occupies a former cattle auction hall, innovatively converted by Adrien Fainsilber. Notice how his designs play with the light reflected off water, steel, and glass.

---

### INSIDER TIP:

**To get to this part of Paris, rent a bicycle [see sidebar p. 116] and follow the canal de l'Ourcq. Enjoy the views!**

—CHRISTEL CHERQAOUI
*National Geographic Books
promotion director*

---

**Explora,** the main exhibition, invites visitors to find out about the universe, from space to volcanoes and the oceans, through its range of interactive presentations.

To see the stars, make your way up to the **Planétarium** on the second floor.

Its 10,000-lens astronomical projector throws images of some 5,000 stars onto the impressive 68-foot (21 m) hemispherical dome.

Children will love the robots and rockets, the sound bubble, and the room of optical illusions. **Cité des Enfants** (ages 3–12) encourages children to experiment with scientific theories and techniques.

Reflecting sky and water in front of the building is the shiny steel of **La Géode,** which contains an enormous curved IMAX cinema screen. Next to La Géode lies the submarine *Argonaute*, built in 1957, and the Cinaxe, a mobile projection room simulating high-speed flight.

Themed gardens such as the Garden of Dragons and the Bamboo Garden make playful use of space.

A portion of the original cattle market, the Grande Halle, is now an exhibition and concert hall, while the Zénith is a venue for rock concerts. **Cité de la Musique** *(tel 01 44 84 45 00)* is a center for music and dance. The Philharmonie de Paris is a massive new symphony hall designed by Jean Nouvel. ∎

---

**Parc de la Villette** 🗺 55 E5 ☎ 01 40 03 75 75 🖪 Métro: Porte de la Villette **lavillette.com** • **Cité des Sciences et de l'Industrie** ✉ 30 avenue Corentin Cariou ☎ 01 85 53 99 74 🕐 Closed Mon. 💲 $$$ 🖪 Métro: Porte de la Villette **cite-sciences.fr** • **La Géode** ☎ 08 92 70 08 40 🕐 Closed Mon. **lageode.fr**

# A SHOPPERS' PARADISE

From tiny boutiques in medieval streets to elegant department stores, Paris is a shoppers' paradise. Whatever you wish for is here in this Aladdin's cave of a city—at a price! If your purse does not stretch to haute couture or diamond necklaces, it is still fun to browse through arcades and hunt for bargains in markets or stalls along the Seine.

■ The giant glass dome of Galeries Lafayette lights three glorious floors of enticing merchandise.

## Specialty Shopping

Some streets and areas have particular specialties. On Île St.-Louis you will find unusual boutiques and restaurants (and the capital's best ice cream, at Berthillon). The *bouquinistes*, booksellers, with their ramshackle stalls along Quai de Montebello, are a particular Parisian delight. Flowers, birds, and animals are for sale in Place Louis-Lépine and on Quai de la Mégisserie.

The area around the chic Boulevard St.-Germain brims with galleries and antiques, especially on Rue Bonaparte and Rue des Sts.-Pères. Collectors of first editions head for Rue Jacob.

In the Marais, the Rue du Temple and the parallel Rue des Archives are known for leather goods and jewelry, while the arcaded shops of Place des Vosges sell antiques, art, and fashions.

## Fashion Capital

Paris is still a mecca for the design-conscious. Serious haute-couture seekers head for Avenue Montaigne, where nearly all the top names have their premises. Chanel, Givenchy, Dior, Cartier, Vuitton, Bulgari, and Ralph Lauren are here. Rue du Faubourg St.-Honoré is ultra-fashionable and high end. Expensive antiques gal-

## EXPERIENCE: Browsing the Flea Markets

The *puces* or flea markets located at the gates *(portes)* of Paris are a treasure trove for anyone who likes bargain hunting, searching out antiques or vintage clothing, or just savoring the ever changing panorama of a Parisian market. Most famous is the **Saint Ouen** *(avenue de la Porte-de-Clignancourt, tel 01 40 11 77 36, Sat.–Mon. 10 a.m.–5 p.m.)*, with thousands of exhibitors offering clothing, quality antiques, and objets d'art. While the main drag tends to be full of tourists and T-shirts, the warren of narrow passages around the market retains all the intrigue of a Moroccan souk.

**Montreuil** *(avenue de la Porte de Montreuil, Sat.–Sun. 7 a.m.–8 p.m.)* is the place to pick up knick-knacks, secondhand bikes, furniture, and clothes. **Vanves** *(Porte de Vanves & avenue Georges-Lafenestre, tel 06 86 89 99 96, Sat.–Sun. 7 a.m.–5 p.m.)* is essentially a secondhand market overflowing with a huge variety of stuff, from old toys to paintings and much much more.

Carry cash, and exercise your bargaining skills—it's all part of the fun! You can also visit the city's vintage boutiques with the help of Ooh La La Vintage or online guides such as *bonjourparis.com*.

leries, furriers, perfumeries, crystal and caviar shops, and designers Gucci, Hermès, Lagerfeld, and Lacroix all attract the well-heeled. Exclusive jewelers, such as Van Cleef et Arpels, line Rue de la Paix and Place Vendôme. Less expensive are the dress shops on Rue de Rivoli.

### Galleries & Arcades

In the 19th century, fashionable Parisians shopped in the 140 covered galleries of the Right Bank. Fewer than 30 remain. Hardly changed since they were built, the Galerie Véro-Dodat, Galerie Colbert, and Galerie Vivienne make harmonious settings for restaurants, galleries, and antiques and contemporary design shops. The area between Rue de Rivoli and Boulevard de Sébastopol is crisscrossed with glass-roofed walkways, such as the Passages Molière, des Princes, des Panoramas, and du Claire. Also relics of a veritable warren of 19th-century arcades, they now shelter a host of specialty shops.

### Department Stores & Shopping Centers

Paris's famed department stores offer clothes, accessories, and household goods. Printemps and the Galeries Lafayette are near the Opéra district, aka the *quartier des grands magasins*. Bazar de l'Hôtel de Ville (BHV), good for fashion and jewelry items, is on Rue de Rivoli. Au Bon Marché, on the Left Bank, has a fine food section. The Galeries des Champs-Élysées are worth exploring for their elegant boutiques, while Les Quatre-Temps at La Défense is one of the largest shopping centers in Europe.

# More Places to Visit on the Right Bank

## Bois de Boulogne

This huge expanse of parkland, lakes, and forest offers boating, fishing, cycling, horseback riding, horse racing, and a children's playground, the Jardin d'Acclimatation. If you're more accustomed to rural or even suburban surrounds, this is the ideal place to take a long walk, relax, and de-stress from the hectic whirl of the Parisian streets.

🚇 54 A4 🚉 Métro: Porte d'Auteuil (south), Les Sablons, Porte Maillot (north)

## Cimetière du Père-Lachaise

Beyond the city center but worth the trip, this vast, much visited cemetery is full of fantastic tomb designs and memorials to a host of *celebrés* (including Héloïse and Abélard, Chopin, Molière, Victor Hugo, Édith Piaf, Oscar Wilde, and Jim Morrison). *pere-lachaise.com* 🚇 55 F3 ✉ boulevard de Ménilmontant 💲 $ 🚉 Métro: Père Lachaise

## Musée Marmottan Monet

This museum housed in an elegant 19th-century mansion has a fabulous Monet collection; among the artworks are some of the "Water Lilies" paintings. Renoir, Sisley, and Gauguin are also represented. *marmottan.fr* 🚇 54 A3 ✉ 2 rue Louis-Boilly 🕿 01 44 96 50 33 🕐 Closed Mon. 💲 $$ 🚉 Métro: La Muette

## Palais de Chaillot

The curved wings and vast terrace of this 1937 edifice form the back-drop of many photos of the Tour Eiffel. Inside, museums include the **Musée de l'Homme**; the **Musée de la Marine** *(tel 01 53 65 69 69),* a maritime museum; and **Cité de l'Architecture et du Patrimoine,** the space devoted to the history of architecture. *citechaillot.fr* 🚇 54 A3 ✉ 1 place du Trocadéro 🕿 01 58 51 52 00 🕐 Closed Tues. 💲 $$ 🚉 Métro: Trocadéro

## Palais de Tokyo

In the east wing is the **Musée d'Art Moderne de la Ville de Paris,** a showcase for living artists. This collection also covers earlier 20th-century art movements, including the École de Paris, cubism, and pop art. Artists represented include Bonnard, Picasso, Gris, Matisse, Dufy, and Utrillo. The refurbished west wing shows contemporary art. *palaisdetokyo.com* 🚇 54 A3 ✉ 13 avenue du Président Wilson 🕿 01 81 97 35 88 🕐 Closed Tues. 💲 $-$$ 🚉 Métro: Iéna, Alma Marceau

## Parc Zoologique de Paris

After six years of major renovation, the former Zoo de Vincennes has reopened in the Bois de Vincennes. This celebrated landmark is designed around the animals with 2.5 miles (4 km) of walkways and 180 species grouped and cohabiting by region, in "a journey round the planet." *parc zoologiquedeparis.fr* 🚇 53 F2 🕿 01 44 96 50 53 💲 $$$ 🚉 Métro: Porte Dorée

# ÎLE-DE-FRANCE

Not literally an island, though largely bounded by rivers, the Île-de-France comprises the region ruled over by Hugh Capet when he was declared King of France in 987. Although his kingdom nominally extended over western and southern Gaul, he only controlled an area of 60 by 120 miles (100 by 200 km). Well populated even then, it is an area rich in art and architecture. St.-Denis, a royal burial place, was the site of the first French cathedral. Sèvres is famous for its 18th-century porcelain factory, and Meudon has a museum with works of Rodin. The elegance of Meaux and the charm of medieval Provins underscore the area's cultural richness.

With roots as far back as Roman times, the Île-de-France represents France's royal heartland. The district is littered with sumptuous châteaus and gardens that transport visitors back in time to prerevolutionary times. The most grandiose of all, of course, is the 17th-century palace of Versailles, a UNESCO World Heritage site. In terms of grandeur and impressive architecture, the palace at Versailles is closely followed by its precursor, the magnificent château of Vaux-le-Vicomte, a baroque French masterpiece.

A great number of smaller châteaus testify to the popularity of the area as a country retreat over the centuries. The intimate Malmaison was home to Empress Josephine in her last years, while Champs-sur-Marne belonged to Madame de Pompadour, stylish mistress of Louis XV. The forest and château of Fontainebleau have inspired generations of painters.

Just beyond the Île-de-France is the town of Chartres, best known for the stained-glass windows in its exquisite cathedral. ■

■ **The baroque Château de Vaux-le-Vicomte and its forbidding moat**

# CHÂTEAU DE VERSAILLES

In 1661, Louis XIV decided to build the ultimate royal residence at Versailles, 12 miles (19 km) from Paris. For nearly 50 years, the greatest artists of the time worked on the château: Louis Le Vau and then Jules Hardouin-Mansart were the architects; André Le Brun supervised the interior decoration; and André Le Nôtre designed the gardens.

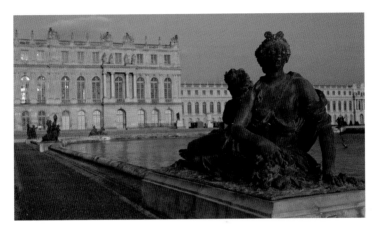

Versailles remains a grand testament to wealth, power, and artistic achievement.

The king and his vast court—some 5,000 people, rising later to 20,000—moved in during 1682. Versailles was the political heart of France until October 1789, when the enraged revolutionary mob invaded the palace and carried Louis XVI and Queen Marie-Antoinette off to captivity in Paris. During the revolution, the furniture was sold off, the paintings sent to the Louvre to be enjoyed by future generations of Frenchmen and women, and the buildings abandoned. In 1837, Louis-Philippe converted the palace into a museum of French history; in 1919, the Treaty of Versailles, bringing to an end World War I, was signed in the Hall of Mirrors. Only after that did any serious restoration begin.

The château was built around Louis XIII's small hunting lodge, whose brick

**Versailles** 103 B2 • **Château de Versailles** ✉ 12 miles (19 km) SW of Paris ☎ 01 30 83 78 00 🕐 Closed Mon.; palace gardens open daily 💲 $$-$$$$ 🚇 RER line C: Château de Versailles. Or SNCF train from Paris Montparnasse or Paris St.-Lazare **chateauversailles.fr**

front is still visible within the Marble Courtyard. Le Vau constructed the first enlargement in the 1660s, a series of wings that expanded into a courtyard. Columns were added to the west facade, and a great terrace was created on the first floor. In 1678, the huge north and south wings and the Hall of Mirrors were created. Ostentation on a royal scale was becoming a theme.

The private apartments of the king and queen are arranged around the Marble Courtyard. In the north wing the Great Staircase leads visitors up to the Grands Appartements, extravaganzas of colored marble, gilt bronze,

# Château de Versailles

Grand Canal

Apollo Basin

Latona Basin

Chapel

Statue of Louis XIV

Theater

silk and velvet drapes, trompe l'oeil murals, and paintings and sculptures. Each state room is dedicated to an Olympian deity. The Salon de Diane, its decor based on the themes of Diana and hunting, once served as a billiard room, a game at which Louis XIV excelled. The Salon de Mars displays the first of a series of beautiful Savonnerie carpets woven in the reign of Louis XVI for the Great Gallery in the Louvre. The Throne Room of Louis XIV, the Sun King, is dedicated (needless to say) to Apollo, god of the sun.

---

**INSIDER TIP:**

Beyond the city is the Cimetière des Chiens *[Métro: Mairie de Clichy]*, where beloved pets are given exquisite tributes.

—SHEILA BUCKMASTER
*National Geographic editor*

---

A two-decade, multimillion-dollar renovation began in 2003 with the cleaning of the Hall of Mirrors. It is

## The Palace Gardens

Landscaping work on some 2,000 acres (815 ha) created an extensive series of formal gardens with statues, fountains, a kitchen garden, a vast artificial lake, and even a zoo. Laid out by André Le Nôtre, 247 acres (100 ha) of gardens radiate from the west facade of the château. The apotheosis of 17th-century French formal style, their rigid symmetry and tamed version of nature reflect the classical ideals of the period.

The Grand Canal serves as the landscape's focal point, with ponds, fountains, sculptures, flower beds, lawns, groves, and shady retreats placed around it. Exquisitely gilded gondolas once plied the waters of the canal; today, handsome white-and-red rowboats can be rented.

The most impressive of Versailles's 300 statues grace the Water Garden, the Pyramid Fountain in the North Garden, and the Apollo Fountain in the Apollo Basin at the end of the Royal Avenue and start of the Grand Canal. Le Nôtre's water theater has been reimagined with woodland, lake, fountains, and glass sculptures. Allegorical references to the sun god Apollo pervade the palace's decorative scheme—above all, the superb figure of Apollo rising triumphantly in the Chariot of the Sun.

Beyond the North Garden, the Water Avenue leads to the Basin of Neptune, the central figure bordered by 22 fountains, each with a marble basin supported by charming bronze statues of children.

Within the garden's design are a variety of architectural follies, and one grove—decorated with shells, rock gardens, and ornamental lamps. Here, the court danced in the summer months. A marble colonnade provided an elegant setting for palace festivities.

supported by the American Friends of Versailles, a nonprofit organization based in Chicago.

## Hall of Mirrors

In 1678, Louis XIV built the Galerie des Glaces, Hall of Mirrors, to enhance the palace and glorify his stature. Flanked by the ornate salons of "War" and "Peace," this vast, restored room, 230 feet (70 m) long, has 17 huge mirrors—an ostentatious display of wealth in the days when mirrors were staggeringly expensive. Further embellishments include crystal chandeliers and silver furniture.

## Bedchambers & Beyond

From 1701, Louis XIV granted private audiences and dined informally in the royal bedchamber. The ceremonies of the king's *levée* (rising) and *couchée* (retiring) were held here, and it was here that Louis XIV died in September 1715 after reigning for 72 years. The bed alcove is lined with velvet, gold, silver, and brocade; most paintings were chosen by Louis XIV.

The Queen's State Bedchamber, with its balustrade, canopied bed, and silk hangings, has been restored to look as it did when Marie-Antoinette left in 1789, never to return. In this room, in full view of members of the court, various queens of France gave birth to 19 royal children.

The two-story baroque chapel, dedicated to St. Louis and finished in 1710, was Louis XIV's final addition to Versailles. Here, Masses were said for military victories and the baptisms and weddings of princes were celebrated, the royal family and members of the highest nobility sitting on the upper floor with the courtiers below. The interior of the chapel is gloriously decorated in marble, gilding, and baroque murals.

The Theater was inaugurated in 1770 for the wedding of Marie-Antoinette to Louis XVI. It seated 1,000 and doubled as a ballroom.

Louis-Philippe's museum, with 8,000 paintings and sculptures devoted to the history of France in the 17th and 18th centuries, is housed in the north wing.

## Grand & Petit Trianon

The Italianate Grand Trianon was built for Louis XIV in 1687 as a retreat. The Petit Trianon was for Louis XV's mistress Madame du Barry. Louis XVI gave the neoclassical jewel to Marie-Antoinette. She turned its grounds into an English-style park and built her famous hamlet, complete with a farm, in which she and her court play-acted an idealized form of rural life. ∎

**NOTE:** The musical fountains show can be seen weekends & some holidays in summer. Consult website for tickets: en.chateauversailles.fr

■ **The opulent Hall of Mirrors reflects the closed-world ostentation of the French royals.**

# CHARTRES

The modest town of Chartres, located about 45 miles (75 km) southwest of Paris just outside the Île-de-France, boasts a magnificent cathedral considered one of the greatest surviving examples of 13th-century Gothic architecture. Its asymmetrical spires rise majestically above the town and the surrounding countryside, a perfect monument to the medieval fervor for building to the glory of God.

▪ The Chartres cathedral, with its 13th-century stained-glass rose window, is a popular Paris day trip.

## Cathedral

Dedicated to the Virgin Mary, the first cathedral here was built (reputedly on the site of a Druid temple) to house a precious relic of her veil donated by Charles the Bald in the late ninth century. It is still displayed in the treasury. Chartres immediately became an important center of pilgrimage, which it remains to this day. Fire destroyed the first shrine and four successive churches, the last in 1194, but contributions to the rebuilding poured in from every side. Completed in a record 30 years, the new cathedral preserves the Romanesque west front and the south tower of the earlier building. The rest of this impressive cathedral, with its flying buttresses, is pure Gothic. The triple portal of the west front and its recessed statues, devoted to the glory of Christ, are superb examples of Romanesque carving. The sculp-

**Chartres** ⚐ 103 B2 Visitor Information ✉ 8 rue de la Poissonerie
☎ 02 37 18 26 26 **chartres-tourisme.com** • **Cathedrale de Chartres**
✉ place de la Cathédrale ☎ 02 37 21 59 08 **cathedrale-chartres.org**

tures on the north portal (circa 1230) are devoted to the Old Testament, and those on the south (1225–1250) to the New Testament.

The **Clocher Vieux,** standing at 345 feet (105 m), is the tallest Romanesque steeple in existence; the **Clocher Neuf** has a slightly taller Gothic spire, added after lightning damage in the 16th century. A strenuous 378-step climb up the tower leads to tremendous views from the top.

**Inside:** The breathtaking interior is illuminated by 176 incomparable stained-glass windows, covering a total area of 27,000 square feet (2,500 sq m). Most date from the 13th century, though the west facade contains three that survived the fire of 1194. The rose windows depict the events of the Apocalypse, the life of the Virgin, and the Last Judgment.

The floor of the nave features a circular **labyrinth** representing good and evil, with paradise at its center. Medieval pilgrims would crawl the 920-foot-long (280 m) path. The broad choir is surrounded by a stone wall sculpted with a filigree pattern and with scenes from the life of Christ and the Virgin arranged in 41 groups of about 200 figures. Behind the choir, in the Chapelle St.-Piat, is the **treasury.** The 11th-century crypt, entered via the Maisons des Clercs, is the largest in France and encloses another crypt dating from the ninth century.

**INSIDER TIP:**

**As you gaze at the cathedral's stained glass, think of how technologically advanced it must have seemed to pilgrims in the Middle Ages—the storytelling giant plasma screen of its era.**

—DIANA PARSELL
*National Geographic contributor*

## The Town

The Eure River creates a picturesque backdrop to the quiet town, with old washhouses and drying lofts along its banks. Some fine architectural features can be found in the medieval district, particularly on Rue du Cheval Blanc and also at 35 Rue des Ecuyers and 12 Rue des Grenets. The former bishop's palace, which still has some state rooms, now houses the **Musée des Beaux-Arts,** with collections including enamels; tapestries; 18th-century French paintings, notably by Chardin and Fragonard; and contemporary works, including a room of Vlamincks. Lovers of the truly bizarre will relish **Maison Picassiette,** where Raymond Isidore devoted his life to decorating every surface and object with fragments of china and glass. ■

**Musée des Beaux-Arts** ✉ Cloître Notre-Dame ☎ 02 37 90 45 80 🕐 Closed Sun. a.m. & all Tues. 💲 $ • **Maison Picassiette** ✉ 22 rue du Repos ☎ 02 37 90 45 95 🕐 Closed Tues. & Sun. a.m. & Nov.–March 💲 $

# CHÂTEAU DE FONTAINEBLEAU

This lovely château, situated 37 miles (60 km) south of Paris, started life in the tenth century as a hunting lodge in the huge forest of Fontainebleau and quickly became a favorite retreat of the kings of France. Beginning in 1527, François I rebuilt it as a château, importing Italian artists to design the interior. Within a few years, their mannerist style became known as the school of Fontainebleau, subsequently exerting a major influence on French painting.

■ Once a hunting lodge, Fontainebleau is one of France's largest châteaus.

Many French monarchs were born at Fontainebleau and several died here. The château also witnessed the fateful revocation of the Edict of Nantes in 1685 (see p. 25) and Napoleon's abdication as emperor of the French in 1814.

The interior is magnificently decorated with paneling, stucco, and frescoes—most famously in the Galerie François I.

Other highlights at the château include the 98-foot-long (30 m) Salle de Bal, the Galerie Henri II, and the salon of Marie de Médicis. The apartments of Napoleon I are in pure Empire style.

The beautiful forest of deciduous woodland offers opportunities for walking, cycling, horseback riding, and rock climbing. ■

## Barbizon School

The mid-1800s saw a move toward greater realism in landscape painting, pioneered by Jean-Baptiste Corot and Gustave Courbet in France, and British artist John Constable. Influenced by their ideas, a group of painters, led by Théodore Rousseau, settled in the village of Barbizon in Fontainebleau forest. Working outdoors and taking scenes from peasant life, they produced shimmering landscapes and touching tableaus.

The charming village features several house museums devoted to the artists, including Jean-François Millet's house *(27 Grande Rue, tel 01 60 66 21 55),* which is packed with his paintings. The Office de Tourisme *(barbizon-tourisme.fr, tel 01 60 66 41 87)* is in Rousseau's former house.

**Fontainebleau**  103 C2 Château de Fontainebleau 🕿 01 60 71 50 70 🕐 Closed Tues. (except gardens) 💲 $$ **chateaudefontainebleau.fr**

Jean-Baptiste Corot's painting of the Chartres Cathedral

# Short Excursions From Paris

## Cathédrale St.-Denis

According to French legend, Saint Denis was beheaded on the hill of Montmartre in A.D. 262. He then picked up his head and walked 6,000 paces north before expiring.

There the abbey church of St.-Denis was subsequently built, his tomb becoming a shrine. Clovis, king of the Franks, was buried here in 511 to be joined the following year by Ste. Geneviève, the patron saint of Paris.

By 1143, a great Gothic cathedral stood here, the first example of the new style in Europe. Massively damaged during the revolution, the cathedral was partially restored in the 19th century.

Today only the choir and west front authentically reflect the original. Reconstruction of the north tower and spire began in 2015.

The cathedral is the mausoleum of the French monarchy, with some 60 funeral monuments carved by the greatest sculptors from the 13th century onward. Louis IX commissioned monuments for his predecessors, the most remarkable being King Dagobert's tomb. The later graves are extremely elaborate, particularly the Renaissance monument of Henri II and Catherine de Médicis. The crypt contains the collective grave of the Bourbon dynasty; the bones of several centuries of French aristocracy resting in peace, presumably, or at least in a less bellicose atmosphere than enveloped many of their lives.

🅰 103  C3  ✉ rue de la Légion d'Honneur, St. Denis ☎ 01 48 09 83 54 💲 $$

## Chantilly

The Chantilly châteaus (see p. 134) make a very pleasant day's outing from Paris. Trains in France are timely, comfortable, and a relaxing way to see any of the destinations in this list, getting you back to the capital without any of the stress of driving on unfamiliar roads.

## Château de Malmaison

Empress Joséphine, first wife of Napoleon Bonaparte, bought this elegant château in 1799 and died there in 1814. It houses an extensive collection of Empire paintings and decorative arts. The Château Bois-Préau, located next door, is devoted to souvenirs of the life and military career of Napoleon. *chateau-malmaison.fr*  🅰 103  B2 ✉ avenue du Château, Rueil-Malmaison ☎ 01 41 29 05 55 🕐 Closed Tues. 💲 $$

## Château de Rambouillet

Since 1897, the château of Rambouillet has been the presidential summer residence, but it is open to the public when the president is not there. Only the round tower of the original 1375 fortress remains. The rest was rebuilt in 1706 for Louis XIV's illegitimate son, the Count of Toulouse. Here Louis XVI bred the noted Rambouillet sheep, known for their resistance to heat and drought, and built a grotto for his wife, Marie-Antoinette. 🅰 103 B2 ☎ 01 34 83 00 25 🕐 Closed Tues. 💲 $

## Resistance Celebrated

A 19th-century villa on the banks of the Marne River houses the Musée de la Résistance Nationale *(Parc Vercors, 88 avenue Marx-Dormoy, Champigney-sur-Marne, tel 01 48 81 00 80, musee-resistance.com, closed Mon., Sat. & Sun. a.m., & Sept., $)*, devoted to the history of the French Resistance. It offers a comprehensive and fascinating overview of France during World War II. A vast array of photographs, films, personal testimonies, and memorabilia, including a railway saboteur's kit, document the story. The exhibitions take you from the prewar political background to the fall of France, Nazi occupation and Vichy collaboration, the concentration camps, and the gradual development of internal resistance. Treasures include several clandestine publications, the photographs of Robert Doisneau, and the original manuscript of Paul Eluard's famous poem "Liberté."

## Château de Vaux-le-Vicomte

The original inspiration for Versailles, this outstanding baroque château built by Nicholas Fouquet, one of Louis XIV's ministers, was the first project on which the formidable team of architect Louis Le Vau, painter Charles Le Brun, and landscape gardener André Le Nôtre worked together. On the château's completion in 1661, Fouquet held a lavish party and banquet, to which he invited Louis XIV. Supper was served on 432 gold plates and 6,000 silver plates; 1,200 fountains framed the entertainment, written and performed by Molière and his troupe; and the evening culminated with spectacular fireworks. Unfortunately, just before the feast, Louis was told that Fouquet had embezzled state funds. Fouquet was arrested and Vaux-le-Vicomte confiscated.

The candlelight tours and dinners *(May–Oct.)*, lit by more than a thousand flickering candle flames, are breathtaking. Fountain displays are given on the second and last Saturday, April–Oct. *(3–6 p.m.) vaux -le-vicomte.com* 🅜 103 C2 ✉ Maincy ☎ 01 64 14 41 90 🕐 Closed Dec.–Feb. 🅢 $$–$$$

## Disneyland Paris

The vast theme park and resort of Disneyland Paris covers nearly 5,000 acres (2,000 ha) at Marne-la-Vallée. RER line A4 whisks visitors from the Gare de Lyon in central Paris directly into the park. The Magic Kingdom offers more than 50 rides in Fantasyland, Adventureland, Discoveryland, and Frontierland. Pirates, a haunted house, and a giant treehouse add to the fun. Walt Disney Studios takes you behind the scenes. There are also seven themed hotels, campsites, restaurants, stores, golf, tennis, and nighttime entertainment. *disneyland paris.com* 🅜 103 C2 ✉ Marne-la-Vallée, about 20 miles (32 km) E of Paris ☎ 08 25 30 05 00 🅢 $$$$$ (entrance fee includes all rides)

## Giverny & Monet

The village of Giverny, in the Seine Valley between Paris and Rouen, contains the house where Claude Monet lived from 1883 until his death in 1926. Gardens (including the famous water garden), studios, and house have all been lovingly restored as Monet himself designed them, and are a delight to wander through: the house with its yellow walls and tile floors, Monet's own furniture and Japanese prints, the shutters and garden furniture still painted in that exact Monet green. Maintained by **Fondation Claude Monet** (*84 rue Claude Monet, Giverny, tel 02 32 51 28 21, fondation-monet .com, $$$$-$$$$$*)

While in Giverny, you should also take time to visit the **Musée des Impressionnismes** (*tel 02 32 51 94 65, mdig.fr, $$, closed Nov.–March*)—formerly called the Musée d'Art Americain—devoted to the colony of Impressionist artists who came here, including Americans Winslow Homer and Mary Cassatt, and to the global impact of Impressionism on the world of art.

## MAC/VAL Musée d'Art Contemporain du Val-de-Marne

This museum just outside Paris is devoted to French art of the past 60 years, with works by Picasso, Miró, Tinguely, César, and others, in a stunning glass building in a huge park. *macval.fr* 103 C2 ✉ Place de la Libération, Vitry-sur-Seine ☎ 01 43 91 64 20 🕐 Closed Mon. $ $$

## St.-Germain-en-Laye

Just west of Paris lies this pleasant residential town, where you'll find the fortress of St.-Germain-en-Laye, home of French kings from François I to Louis XIV. Napoleon III restored the Renaissance castle, establishing the **Musée d'Archéologie** (*tel 01 39 10 13 00, closed Tues.*).

The tremendous **Grande Terrasse** provides a sweeping overview of the Seine Valley. Also of interest is **Ste.-Chapelle,** a Gothic masterpiece similar to the chapel of the same name in Paris (see p. 61). Nearby, the **Musée du Prieuré** (*rue Maurice Denis, tel 01 39 73 77 87, closed Mon.*) contains a trove of Postimpressionist art. You can also visit and attend concerts at the 17th-century residence of the beloved French musician Claude Debussy (*38 rue au Pain, tel 01 30 87 20 63, open 2–6 p.m., closed Mon. & Sat.*). 103 B2

## EXPERIENCE:
# See Paris by Bike

**Vélib'** (*www.velib-metropole.fr*), a hugely successful self-service bike-rental company, offers more than 19,000 bikes at more than 1,460 locations in Paris. There are 231 miles (371 km) of bicycle routes to enjoy, with more planned outside the city. Prices start from €1 for 30 minutes plus a refundable deposit. You will need a credit card to make the deposit. Electric bikes are now also available.

A land of great Gothic cathedrals, important wine regions (Champagne and Alsace), and, from Flanders to the Marne, sobering mementos of war

# NORTHERN FRANCE

# NORTHERN FRANCE

Some of France's greatest wines, earliest and most magnificent Gothic cathedrals, and most valued art collections are found in the five northern regions: Nord-Pas-de-Calais, Picardie, Champagne-Ardennes, Alsace, and Lorraine. These are France's borderlands with Germany, Switzerland, Luxembourg, and Belgium, and—mediated by the narrow Manche or English Channel—with Britain.

A myriad of languages, cultures, and traditions testifies to the historic impermanence of France's frontiers. Calais, for example, was once English; Alsace and most of Lorraine have intermittently been part of Germany; and Flandre (Flanders), now in the Nord-Pas-de-Calais region, was part of a medieval state that included much of Belgium. For travelers to the green fields and pleasant beaches of northern France, it seems scarcely credible that these frontiers were being fought over just 70-odd years ago. The great wars of the 20th century drew soldiers from many of the world's greatest nations to key battles in this northernmost part of France.

## Wine Country

Stained-glass windows in Reims's cathedral depict scenes of vine cultivation and wine production, for Reims is capital of the Champagne region, where wine has been made since Roman times. It was here that the renowned sparkling wine is thought to have been developed about 300 years ago. Champagne is France's most northerly wine-growing district, and the cool climate is a factor in the success of its great wine. Global warming, however, now threatens this crop.

The main area of production centers on the vineyards around Reims and Épernay, where the major maisons de champagne are located. Most invite you to tour their caves—the labyrinthine cellars where the wine is fermented, blended, and stored—and taste the champagne before buying.

Another delightful part of a visit to the Champagne region is touring the villages, abbeys, churches, and castles of the area along the signposted Route Touristique du Champagne.

Wine has also been made since Roman times in picturesque Alsace. You can follow the signposted Route du Vin for about 130 miles (200 km) along a scenic route that winds through the foothills of the Vosges Mountains, passing tidy vineyards and charming old towns and villages with fine eateries, churches, and castles.

## Cradle of the Gothic Style

Gothic architecture grew up here: Picardie alone has six major cathedrals. The former bishop's palace and medieval abbeys and churches cluster around Strasbourg cathedral and the early Gothic Cathédrale de Notre-Dame in Laon. The treasuries of these ancient cathedrals preserve centuries-old relics, gold and silverware, art, and church ornaments. The magnificent cathedral of Reims was the coronation cathedral of the kings of France, and its treasury includes an array of sacred vessels and coronation regalia. ∎

■ **One of the few remaining working mills in the Créquoise Valley is located just outside Montreuil.**

# NORD & PICARDIE

The rolling, wooded Nord area includes the French part of what was historically Flanders (the rest is now in Belgium). Flanders resembles the Low Countries, with canals and windmills, and towns with cobbled squares and gabled houses. North from Lille, capital of the region, are the medieval Flemish walled towns of Bergues and Wormhout, surrounded by canals. Fortified towns are a feature. Cambrai, for example, still has its old gatehouse, citadel, and keep. Farther south, Picardie has splendid cathedrals and notable Gothic churches, including the 16th-century abbey church of St.-Riquier, near Abbeville.

Picardie is the larger of the two northern regions, encompassing three *départements.* Of these, the peaceful Aisne in the east is a region of open plain crossed by rivers and interspersed with pockets of pastureland, villages, churches, and châteaus. Aisne's capital is the cathedral town of Laon, once a royal city.

The western département, Oise, is heavily wooded, and many of these fine forests were favorite hunting grounds of the French kings, whose summer palace was situated at Compiègne. Oise is home to a wealth of architectural gems, chief among them the Château de Chantilly and the beautifully preserved cathedral town of Senlis.

The Somme to the north will always be associated with the battles of World War I. However, venture a little off the many battlefields scattered around there and into the forest, and you'll find a place of peace and hope. A clearing in the Forêt de Laigue, 4 miles (6 km) east of Compiègne off the N31, is the site of the **Musée de l'Armistice** *(tel 03 44 85 14 18, $, musee-armistice-14-18.fr).* The museum is housed in a reconstruction of the railroad car in which the armistice that ended World War I was signed.

The Somme's capital, Amiens, is graced by one of the greatest Gothic cathedrals in the country.

The entire area, straddling the border between France and Belgium, is known globally for its historic church belfries. Some 23 belfries in Northern France have been awarded UNESCO World Heritage site status. ∎

## Lens Louvre

The impressive extension of the Louvre in the old mining city of Lens *(rue Paul Bert, Lens, tel 03 21 18 62 62, louvrelens .fr, closed Tues., $-$$)* has attracted huge crowds since opening in 2012. The stunning transparent structure of curved glass and aluminium pavilions is set in a park preserving the vestiges of the mining site. Treasures from the Louvre are presented chronologically, and mixed with works from regional museums and temporary exhibitions.

# LILLE

Lille is a frontier town (though France's border with its European Union partner Belgium is scarcely noticeable) and a major transport hub. During its thousand-year history, Lille has belonged variously to Flanders, Burgundy, the Spanish Netherlands, France, and Germany. One of its best-preserved buildings is the star-shaped Citadelle, a great fort designed by Louis XIV's military engineer Vauban in 1667, for protection against the Spanish Netherlands when Lille became part of France.

■ The Chamber of Commerce in Lille, previously known as the Stock Exchange Palace.

From the visitors gallery high up in the 345-foot (105 m) belfry of the 1930s **Hôtel de Ville,** a UNESCO World Heritage site, you get a notion of the scale of the largest industrial city in northern France.

**INSIDER TIP:**

For a fond and funny look at how the rest of France views the North, see *Bienvenue Chez les Ch'tis [Welcome to the Sticks]*, the hit 2008 movie.

—ROSEMARY BAILEY
*National Geographic author*

Lille's spreading suburbs embrace surrounding towns all the way to the Belgian border, situated some 6 miles (10 km) away.

The charming **Place Général de Gaulle** in the heart of the city, surrounded by old, steep-gabled Flemish houses, comes as a pleasant surprise. One of its most attractive buildings, the **Vieille Bourse** (Old Stock Exchange) was built in 1652–1653 in Flemish Renaissance style. The nearby

Lille's Palais des Beaux-Arts museum showcases fine European paintings.

**Palais des Beaux-Arts** displays artworks by Flemish, French, Dutch, Italian, and Spanish masters from the 15th century to the 20th, including a renowned collection of works by Goya.

Along with its cultural fluidity, Lille also offers the visitor a lively regional center with excellent shopping, theater, music, and cinema. It brightened its image with renovations and a major cleanup upon being designated the European City of Culture back in 2004; the Opéra reopened, and many buildings became art and performance spaces. Lille has become known for art, with an art fair held in the spring.

**Villeneuve-d'Ascq,** a suburb northeast of Lille, is home to the **Musée d'Art Moderne** *(1 allée de Musée, closed Tues.),* with a respected cubist collection, and in **Roubaix,** the **Musée d'Art et d'Industrie** provides a historic overview of the importance of industrial design and innovation throughout the region. The museum is aptly set in a converted art deco swimming pool. ∎

**Lille** 🗺 118 B4 Visitor Information ✉ 42 Palais Rihour, place Rihour ☎ 03 59 57 94 00 Ask for a permit to visit the Citadelle at the tourist office. **lilletourisme.com • Hôtel de Ville** ✉ place Roger Salergro ☎ 03 20 49 50 00 🕐 Closed Mon. Apply to tourist office for guided tours. • **Palais des Beaux-Arts** ✉ place de la République ☎ 03 20 06 78 00 🕐 Closed Mon. a.m. & Tues. 💲 $$ **pba-lille.fr • Musée d'Art et d'Industrie** ✉ 24 rue de l'Espérance, Roubaix ☎ 03 20 69 23 60 🕐 Closed Mon.

# BATTLEFIELDS

The map of northern France, from Dunkerque to Verdun and from Cambrai to beyond the Somme River, is a map of battlefields now buried beneath towns and villages, woods and fields. The most recent saw action within the last 100 years—it was only in 1940 that hundreds of thousands of retreating British troops evacuated the beaches of Dunkerque. Six centuries earlier in 1346, Edward III's soldiers vanquished Philippe VI's army at Crécy-en-Ponthieu. Memorials, cemeteries, and museums all over the region explain the actions in these wars, recent and long gone.

A multitude of monuments, some of great artistic distinction—Edwin Lutyens's British monument at Thiepval in the Somme, Walter Seymour Allward's **Canadian War Memorial on Vimy Ridge** near Vimy—mark the battle sites where more than a million young soldiers were killed from 1914–1918. The First World War laid waste to the entire region, from Amiens to Alsace and Reims to Belgium, and it is scattered with trenches, cemeteries, and memorials to French, British, Australian, New Zealand, American, Moroccan, Indian, Nepalese, and Chinese troops.

Many visitors make the journey to see the site of a particular battle, or to visit a certain graveyard or a memorial to a division.

Map Key
× Battle
† Cemetery
Ⓜ Memorial

Alternatively, you might follow one of the signposted memorial routes that trace the line of a front or the battles in a campaign, or visit one of several very moving museums of the wars. Here are some of the fields and wartime sites most worth visiting:

## Arras

Beneath the Grand'Place in Arras (see p. 128) are **Les Boves,** a network of caves thought to have been dug out more than 1,000 years ago. They have provided a refuge for locals during the region's many conflicts. During World War I, British troops were sheltered and their wounds dressed in Les Boves, now a memorial with guided tours.

## Musée de la Grande Guerre

This major 21st-century museum tells the story of World War I, based on its collection of uniforms, artillery, and vehicles, and including a reconstruction of a battlefield.

## La Coupole

The Nazis built their first factory and launch base for V2 missiles aimed at London during World War II in the Forêt d'Éperlecques located northwest of **St.-Omer.** The bunker, now a museum called La Coupole, shows everything from the liquid

---

## EXPERIENCE: Visit the Wilfred Owen Memorial

Follow in the footsteps of revered World War I poet Wilfred Owen in his last hours. Visit the **Forester's House** outside Ors, near Cambrai. Here he hid out in the cellar and wrote his last letter to his mother. The house is now transformed into a venue for poetry readings and performances. See the **Bois Leveque forest,** the canal where he was killed on November 4, 1918—a day commemorated every year—and the village of **Ors,** where the library bears his name. He is buried in the cemetery in Ors. For details, see *wilfredowen.org.uk.*

---

**Canadian War Memorial, Vimy Ridge** ☎ 03 21 50 68 68 (museum) 🕐 Open daily. Guided tours: May–Nov. **veterans.gc.ca** • **Musée de la Grande Guerre** ✉ rue Lazare Ponticelli, Meaux ☎ 01 60 32 14 18 🕐 Closed Tues. **museedelagrandeguerre.com** • **St.-Omer** 🅼 118 B5 • **La Coupole** ✉ Forêt d'Éperlecques ☎ 03 21 12 27 27 💲 $$ **lacoupole-france.com**

---

---

oxygen factory to the launchpad, accompanied by audiovisual displays and a 3-D planetarium.

## Hundred Years' War

The lookout tower at the site of the Battle of **Crécy** in 1346 displays an orientation table showing the battle plan. A small museum *(closed Wed.)* focuses on the Battle of Agincourt in **Azincourt** village. An orientation table and model archers and horsemen on the battlefield itself enable visitors to follow the battle of 1415, in which the English soldiers of Henry V overcame the French.

## The Somme

A moving Tour of Remembrance follows the front lines of the two World War I battles of the Somme *(information from the Somme tourist office; see also somme-battlefields .com)*. Among the signposted sights

are two blockhouses at **Pozières** taken by Australian divisions, the British memorial at **Thiepval,** the French cemetery at **Rancourt,** and the memorial at **Bellicourt** to U.S. soldiers. The tour encompasses trenches, shelters, and the rail supply line. The **Historial de la Grande Guerre** is a museum beside Péronne's medieval fort.

## Mémorial de Verdun

The 17th-century citadel holds a museum commemorating the 1916 German attack that destroyed this barracks town. Ask at the tourist office about battlefield tours. ■

### The End of the Fighting

On May 7, 1945, the Germans surrendered to the Allies in Reims (see pp. 136–137), in the schoolroom headquarters of Gen. Eisenhower. The **Musée de Reddition** *(12 rue Franklin Roosevelt, Reims, tel 03 26 47 84 19, closed Tues.)* preserves the space as it was at that dramatic moment, with the table, chairs, and huge wall maps detailing the progress of the war.

---

**Somme Regional Tourism** ✉ 21 rue Ernest Cauvin, Amiens
☎ 03 22 71 22 71 **somme-tourisme.com • Historial de la Grande Guerre** ✉ place du Château ☎ 03 22 83 14 18 🕐 Closed Wed. in winter & mid-Dec.–Feb. **historial.org • Mémorial de Verdun** 🗺 119 D3 Visitor Information ✉ 1 avenue du Corps Européen Fleury devant Douaumont, Verdun ☎ 03 29 84 35 34 💲 $$ **memorialdeverdun.fr**

# EXPERIENCE: Take to the Water (and Sand)

The Channel coast between Calais and the Somme estuary is called the Côte d'Opale due to the misty horizon of sea and sky visible from the white chalk cliffs stretching down to Boulogne-sur-Mer, the other side of the Channel from the White Cliffs of Dover. It was from this coast that Julius Caesar launched his invasion of England and that the rescue of the French and British troops by little boats from Britain took place after the fall of France. Today, the Côte d'Opale is the best place in northern France for water sports.

From Cap Blanc Nez and Cap Gris Nez coastal strollers and aquatic sports enthusiasts can enjoy terrific views of the Channel. On a clear day, you might be able to see all the way to England. The northern coastline of France offers numerous opportunities to experience the beach and sea by taking part in a host of outdoor adventure sports. Several of these are dependent on the winds that blow this way.

At low tide, the sea retreats so far that vast swaths of pale sandy beach are left exposed, making it an ideal location for sand yachting, also known as land sailing, a racing sport that's actually been around since the 1950s.

You can also sign up for kiteboarding, a sailing outing in a catamaran or small dinghy, kayaking, and sea fishing on board a former trawler. Beginners' group lessons and private courses are available. Waterproof clothing and helmets can be provided by most clubs, but having your own rubber-sole footwear is advisable.

If you are looking for more of a spectator water experience, head to the **Nausicaá Aquarium** (9 parvis de Nausicaä, Boulogne-sur-Mer, tel 03 21 30 98 98, nausicaa.fr).

### Kayaking
**Boulogne Canoë Kayak**
(7 Boulevard Chanzy, Boulogne-sur-Mer, tel 03 21 31 98 60, boulogneck.fr)

### Kiteboarding
**WimKite** (boulevard Thiriez, Wimereux, tel 06 81 76 82 05, wimkite.com)

### Sailing
**Club Nautique Wimereux** (Centre Régionale de Voile, Boulevard Alfred Thiriez, Wimereux, tel 03 21 83 18 54, club-nautique-wimereux.com)

**Dunkerque Plaisance**
(Centre Regional de Voile, quai d'Armement Nord, Dunkerque, tel 03 28 24 59 99, lesdunesdeflandre.fr)

### Sand Yachting
**Char à Voile Club de la Côte d'Opale** (272 boulevard Ste.-Beuve, Boulogne-sur-Mer, tel 03 21 83 25 48, cvcco.com)

**École de Char à Voile** (boulevard Pouget Base Nautique Sud, Le Touquet-Paris-Plage, tel 03 21 06 72 00, letouquet.com)

### Sea Fishing
**Étaples Tourist Office** (boulevard Bigot Descelers, Étaples, tel 03 21 09 56 94, etaples-tourisme.com)

# FROM ARRAS TO THE COAST

West of Arras, the Picardie plain slopes gently to the coast. The countryside is patched with woodland and threaded by rivers: the picturesque Authie, the majestic Somme, and the Canche, overlooked by the medieval hill town of Montreuil. Le Touquet on the Canche estuary is the most sophisticated of the resorts clustering along the sandy north-coast beaches.

Quaint Montreuil was once Europe's wealthiest port town.

With its underground shelters (see p. 125) and moving memorial to the many French Resistance members who were mercilessly executed here during World War II for acts of patriotism, **Arras** is an important site on any battlefield tour of northern France and Belgium.

The late Gothic **Hôtel de Ville** overlooks the **Place des Héros,** one

**Arras** 118 B4 Visitor Information ✉ Hôtel de Ville, place des Héros ☎ 03 21 51 26 95 **explorearras.com** • **Le Touquet** 118 A4 Visitor Information ✉ Palais de l'Europe ☎ 03 21 06 72 00 **letouquet.com**

of Arras's two great central squares. You can look down on it from the town hall's 250-foot (80 m) belfry, but you get a better sense of its scale from within. So take the time to stroll around the square, observe carefully the architecture, and enjoy good conversation and maybe a sweet treat in one of its cafés: The freedom to mix freely and express one's opinion, after all, are some of the democratic rights that so many young soldiers gave their lives and limbs fighting for in the killing fields of this corner of Europe.

During the 1914–1918 fighting, bombardments destroyed the Hôtel de Ville and many of the 16th-century houses surrounding the squares. After the war, these were faithfully reconstructed and the historic character of Arras was preserved for future generations to appreciate, at least in form.

Halfway between Arras and Lille is the location for the ancient university town of **Douai** *(visitor information, place d'Armes, tel 03 27 88 26 79, ville-douai.fr)*, with its 18th-century houses, narrow streets, and a famous 62-bell carillon in the belfry above the town hall.

Don't miss the **Musée Matisse Cateau Cambresis** *(tel 03 59 73 38 06, museematisse.lenord.fr, closed Tues.)*, near Cambrai. In the artist's birthplace, more than 170 paintings and sculptures cover Matisse's entire career; art lovers will delight in tracing the trajectory of his creative development.

A trip to **Le Touquet,** an elegant resort town, makes a pleasant morning's drive from Arras. Take the N39 via the pretty town of **Hesdin** (near the site of the Battle of Agincourt, see p. 126) and the D340 along the Canche River to the hill town of **Montreuil** with its well-preserved ramparts.

Le Touquet was fashionable in Edwardian times when England's Prince of Wales (later King Edward VIII) brought his guests there for royal rest and recreation.

Today it is an attractive and well preserved art nouveau and art deco period piece, albeit one with a casino, horse racing, golf, hotels, fine restaurants, boutiques, nightlife, great beaches, and, nearby, Bagatelle, an amusement park. Le Touquet, like many northern French coastal towns, offers travelers a chance to take the salt air and relish fine seafood in a relaxed and unpretentious atmosphere. ■

■ **Enjoy the coast without even getting wet. The sport of sand yachting has a wealth of practitioners along the English Channel.**

# AMIENS

Amiens, on the Somme River, was heavily bombed in 1918, and shelling in 1940 destroyed much of its ancient heart. But the grand cathedral has survived centuries of war and revolution. A classic model of the French Gothic style, it is the main reason to visit Amiens.

The **Cathédrale de Notre-Dame** (*place Notre-Dame, tel 03 22 71 60 50*) is France's tallest cathedral. Its nave, built between 1220 and 1236, was then the highest in France, at 139 feet (42 m). Stand at the west end of the nave and look toward the altar. Instantly, the soaring piers and pointed arches sweep your gaze heavenward, fulfilling one of the ideals of Gothic architecture.

The dramatic interior of this vast church is illuminated by windows that seem to replace the upper walls of the nave, choir, and chapels of the apse. The rose window in the west front still has its 16th-century glass, but much of the ancient glass was shattered during World War II. In the 16th century, local woodcarvers decorated the 110 oak choir stalls with more than 400 scenes. The west front's three great portals are masterpieces of stone carving. The "weeping angel," a hugely popular putto crying on a tomb, is by local sculptor Nicolas Blasset.

The streets around the cathedral contain painstakingly restored build-

---

**EXPERIENCE:** Look for Birds in the Somme

Exploring the bay of the Somme is a fine way to discover the birdlife in **Parc Regional du Nord-Pas-de-Calais** (*Maison de la Baie de Somme et de l'Oiseau, Carrefour du Hourdel, Lanchères, tel 03 22 26 93 93, baiedesomme.fr*). You can walk the coastal path that stretches from the Belgian border to south of Le Touquet to glimpse various migrating birds such as divers, grebes, ducks, and herons (best in spring or autumn), or make your way to the **Marquenterre Bird Park** located on the edge of the bay at St.-Quentin-en-Tourmont.

Hire a boat or take a guided open boat trip around the salt marshes. Another means of exploration is by bike. You can rent one and explore for yourself. In spring, a festival of birds and nature (*festival-oiseau-nature.com*) in Abbeville offers guided nature trips on foot, bike, horseback, and boat, plus photographic exhibitions and events for kids.

---

**Amiens** ⓜ 118 B4 Visitor Information ✉ 6 bis rue Dusevel ☎ 03 22 71 60 50 🕐 Closed Sun. **www.visit-amiens.com**

Amiens Cathedral, a classic Gothic construction that has weathered history

ings, such as the medieval belfry; the **Musée de Picardie** *(48 rue de la République, tel 03 22 97 14 00, closed Mon.);* the 17th-century **Hôtel de Berny** *(36 rue Victor Hugo, tel 03 22 97 14 00, closed Mon.),* now a museum with local decorative arts; and the restored **Maison à la Tour** *(2 rue Charles Dubois, tel 03 22 45 45 75),* the home of author Jules Verne.

Waterways flow around the city's St.-Leu district, and strolling the towpaths and bridges here lets you exchange a friendly *bonjour* with locals as they tend their gardens; professional *hortillons* (market gardeners) cultivate the dark and fertile soil of the district's Hortillonnage. On Saturdays they sell their produce at a water market. On the third Sunday of each month the

**INSIDER TIP:**

Take an evening boat ride around the myriad waterways of Amien's St.-Leu district *(visit-amiens.com/river-tourism).* Watch the son & lumière light show on the water—a great end to a day in Amiens.

—ROSEMARY BAILEY
*National Geographic author*

hortillons dress in traditional costume and travel down the Somme in *barques à cornet* (boats with an elevated stern). At the Quai Bélu they sell their vegetables on the Place Parmentier, stocking the many eateries along the quays. ■

# GOTHIC CATHEDRALS

The towers and spires of the Gothic cathedrals of northern France rise high above its spreading plains and cities, like spiritual land-marks. This is the birthplace of Gothic architecture—the style dates from circa 1140–1144, when the choir of the abbey church of St.-Denis, north of Paris (see p. 114), was built.

■ The Cathédrale St.-Étienne went up in the 13th century, when Metz was an important frontier city.

Notre-Dame in Paris, begun in 1163, was the next monumental church to be built in the new style, with a nave 109 feet (33 m) high. In a burst of cathedral building within a 100-mile (160 km) radius of Paris, the style evolved from the simplicity of Laon (see p. 133) to the dramatic verti-cal lines of the mature Gothic style at Amiens (see p. 131) and Chartres (see pp. 110–111) to the late or high Gothic style of Reims (see pp. 136–137), with its complex system of flying buttresses. Strasbourg cathedral (see p. 143), begun in the 13th century and finished in the 15th, reflects this evolu-tion from the Romanesque style (see pp. 374–375) all the way through to the Flamboyant, the ornate late form of high Gothic.

## Cathedral Tour

A round-trip of 240 miles (380 km) will take you to six of France's most magnificent Gothic cathe-drals. Begin at the cathedral of **Amiens,** whose interior is the supreme example of the mature French Gothic style. Follow the D934 southeast to **Noyon,** whose beautiful cathedral, begun around 1150, is transitional in style between Romanesque and Gothic. Take the N32 and N44 across the Aisne *département* to **Laon,** once the royal city of the Carolingian kings. Here the 12th-century cathedral of Notre-Dame, begun in the 1160s and completed in 1230, is a fine example of early Gothic style. It has beautiful rose windows and captivating sculptures of exotic animals—a hippopotamus gargoyle, for instance—on its facade. Clustered around it are the bishop's palace and the Dauphin's court,

medieval abbeys, and streets of charming old town houses.

From Laon, it is a 37-mile (60 km) journey southeast along the N44 (or the A26) to **Reims,** with its high Gothic cathedral. Then take the N31 west to **Soissons** to admire its cathedral, restored after shelling in 1918. Started in the 12th and not finished until the 14th century, it shows the evolution of the Gothic style.

Continue westward along the N31 via Compiègne to **Beauvais,** whose cathedral was a daring attempt to build the tallest such edifice ever. In 1284, 12 years after its completion, the choir collapsed and had to be rebuilt with reinforcing buttresses. However, this grand project overstretched the town's resources, and the cathedral was never finished; today you see the choir and transepts built onto the tiny, early 11th-century Romanesque nave, which the new cathedral was intended to replace. From Beauvais the A16 returns you to your start point of Amiens.

## Anatomy of a Gothic Cathedral

They are works of great beauty, and they follow simple rules: The classic, three-stage structural system of the Gothic cathedral consists of a nave arcade at ground level, a triforium (arcaded passage) above it, and a clerestory (upper wall zone, pierced by windows) above that. The high walls are buttressed for stability. In order to raise the nave roof to unprecedented heights, the builders constructed flying buttresses to transmit the thrust of the brick or stone vaults down to the main vertical buttresses.

The pointed arches characteristic of Gothic architecture take the thrust from the vaults downward, so buildings could have thin walls pierced by large windows. These windows were divided by a tracery of delicate stonework, which reached astonishing heights of complexity in the round rose windows.

# ROYAL FORESTS

The forests still surviving in the south of Picardie are just remnants of those that originally covered much of northern France. Kings and nobles came here from Paris and built hunting lodges, palaces, and châteaus in and around the forests.

## Chantilly

Once famous for lace, Chantilly is now known for its châteaus set on a lake island and surrounded by handsome gardens. The Petit Château and adjoining Grand Château form the **Musée Condé,** a collection of fine and decorative arts, and a priceless library, all assembled by the Duc d'Aumale in the 19th century. Treasures include *Très Riches Heures du Duc de Berry,* a 15th-century book of hours, and paintings by Raphael and French masters. The 18th-century stables house the restored **Musée du Cheval** (Museum of the Horse).

## Senlis

One of the most ancient towns in France, Senlis was founded before the Romans conquered Gaul. Its Gallo-Roman walls thread through the town; 16 of the 28 towers still stand, though hidden by houses.

**Cathédrale Notre-Dame,** begun in 1155, is a modestly scaled Gothic edifice. It has a 13th-century spire and, inside, superb sculptures of the Virgin.

From the cathedral, it is easy to explore the old town, castle remains, and ancient walls. The 18th-century **Château de Raray** nearby so enraptured Jean Cocteau that he set his film *La Belle et la Bête* (1945) in it.

---

**INSIDER TIP:**

In Senlis, have a nice lunch at Le Scaramouche *[4 place Notre-Dame, tel 03 44 53 01 26],* facing the cathedral. The seafood is a good choice here.

—SHEILA BUCKMASTER
*National Geographic editor at large*

---

## Compiègne

Located on the edge of the forest, the town of Compiègne is dominated by the palace built in 1754 for Louis XV. Inside are the apartments of Napoleon I and his wife Marie-Louise and the Hunting Gallery decked with its fine Gobelins tapestries. ∎

**Chantilly** 🏔 118 B3 Visitor Information ✉ 60 avenue du Maréchal Joffre ☎ 03 44 67 37 37 **chantilly-tourisme.com** • **Musée Condé** ✉ Route National 924A ☎ 03 44 27 31 80 🕐 Closed Tues. 💲 $$ **chateaudechantilly.com** • **Senlis** 🏔 118 B3 Visitor Information ✉ parvis Notre-Dame ☎ 03 44 53 06 40 **senlis-tourisme.fr** • **Compiègne** 🏔 118 B3 Visitor Information ✉ place Hôtel de Ville ☎ 03 44 40 01 00 🕐 Closed Mon. a.m. Oct.–March **compiegne-tourisme.fr**

# CHAMPAGNE

**The vineyards of the Champagne region carpet the wide river valleys and climb gentle slopes to wooded escarpments that overlook some of the most beautiful countryside in northern France. Venerable villages with Romanesque churches and medieval market towns dot the countryside. Reims, the northern, and Troyes, the southern capital of Champagne, have superb Gothic cathedrals and splendid museums. Both are little more than an hour's drive or train ride from Paris.**

The size and splendor of the half-timbered medieval merchants' houses that survive in the old towns testify to Champagne's past prosperity. During the Middle Ages, it lay at the crossroads of northern Europe's key trade routes. From the 14th to 16th centuries, cloth from Italy, Flanders, and the German states, furs from Scandinavia, leather from Catalonia, and costly woods, spices, and gold from the Mediterranean were traded in festive six-week-long summer fairs in Troyes, Lagny, Bar-sur-Aube, and Provins.

History has left a legacy of castles and fortifications, built in strong defensive positions high on the edges of escarpments right across the region. From the fifth century, when Attila the Hun's army was routed near Châlons-en-Champagne, to the Nazi invasions of 1940, this part of France has been chosen as an entry point for armies marching on Paris.

Grapes have been cultivated in the chalky soils of Champagne for some 2,000 years. In the late 17th century, Pierre Pérignon, cellarer at the Benedictine abbey of Hautvillers near Épernay, is said to have discovered how to make wine sparkle. Wine historians debunk this myth, but they recognize the part played by Dom Pérignon in the evolution of champagne. He learned to control the wine's fermentation, and he blended wines from different vineyards for richer, more subtle wines. ∎

∎ **In Épernay—champagne central—many a shop window is dressed for a sparkling celebration.**

# REIMS

In 498, in Reims's first cathedral, St. Rémi baptized Clovis, king of the conquering Frankish tribe from the upper Rhine. Subsequently, almost every king of France was crowned here. Reims has always been an important French city and is now only 45 minutes away from Paris by TGV.

The fittingly majestic **Cathédrale de Notre-Dame,** begun in 1211 after a fire destroyed the previous cathedral, was designed for

■ **The Cathédrale de Notre-Dame** showcases Gothic detailing.

coronations. To create room for the ceremonies, the nave and choir were broadened to embrace the transepts, so that the interior appears luxuriously spacious, and the nave, with its avenues of piers, seems to soar. Reims was intended to surpass in concept and ornament even the great cathedrals at Chartres and Amiens. Much of its old glass was lost as a result of World War II bombing; the modern windows of the Lady Chapel are by Marc Chagall.

Although built in stages between the 13th and 15th centuries, Reims has a unity of style representing the pinnacle of mature French Gothic. Its flying buttresses are daringly thin and light, an expression of the confidence medieval architects had achieved by the 13th century. It boasts a wealth of sculpture on its facade, though some are copies of originals damaged beyond repair. The central doorway is devoted to the Virgin. The statue of the coronation of the Virgin that used to grace the central gable is now in the

**Reims** 🅰 119 C3 Visitor Information ✉ 2 rue Guillaume de Machault ☎ 03 26 77 45 00 **reims-tourisme.com** • **Cathédrale de Notre-Dame** ✉ place du Cardinal Luçon ☎ 03 26 47 55 34 🕐 Mass at 9:30 a.m. & 11 a.m. Sun., 8 a.m. daily **cathedrale-reims.com** • **Palais du Tau** ✉ place du Cardinal Luçon ☎ 03 26 47 81 79 🕐 Closed Mon. 💲 $$ **palais-tau.monuments -nationaux.fr**

Palais du Tau. Above the rose window on the west front, look for the statues of the kings of France.

The bishop's palace next to the cathedral, the **Palais du Tau,** displays coronation regalia, carvings and statues rescued from the war-damaged cathedral, and several tapestries.

**Musée-Chapelle Foujita** *(33 rue de Champs de Mars, tel 03 26 40 06 96)* was created in 1966 by Japanese artist Leonard Foujita to express his gratitude for the mystical enlightenment he experienced in Reims cathedral. His designs for ironwork, sculptures, frescoes, and stained glass are exquisite, and this is his chosen burial place.

At the south end of town, the **Basilique St.-Rémi** *(place du Chanoine Ladaine),* founded in the 11th century, is the largest Romanesque church in northern France, though with later additions. It was built over the chapel of St. Christophe, where St. Rémi was buried.

Beneath the streets of Reims are the foundations of Durocorter, the metropolis of a Gaulish tribe called the Remes that in 55 B.C. made an alliance with Julius Caesar. You can visit the **Cryptoporticus** *(place du Forum, tel 03 77 75 28 74, closed a.m. mid-June–mid-Sept., & all day mid-Sept.–mid-June)*—vaulted galleries—and the **Porte de Mars,** the largest triumphal arch in the Roman world. Limestone for these edifices and for aqueducts, roads, and homes was cut from beneath the city. Centuries later, these subterranean quarries make ideal storage cellars for maturing wine.  ■

## Charles de Gaulle Museum

The Charles de Gaulle Memorial Museum *(tel 03 25 30 90 80, memorial-charlesdegaulle.fr, $$)* is located in Colombey-les-Deux-Églises, a small village in Haute Marne, where de Gaulle lived for much of his life. The museum nestles into the hillside, already dominated by a vast marble cross of Lorraine, and was designed by architects Jacques Millet and Jean-Côme Chilou, also responsible for the Memorial Museum of Caen. Almost a third is tucked into the mountainside, part of it with an eco-conscious grass roof. A grand staircase leads up to the cross, and a broad terrace offers an almost 180-degree view of the misty countryside de Gaulle revered. Using photographs, films, and reconstructions (including a World War I trench), the museum is a fascinating journey through 20th-century history. All the texts are in German, French, and English, and though it is an unstinting tribute to one patriotic Frenchman, it offers a moving sense of the deep necessity for European unity. You can also visit La Boisserie, de Gaulle's family home in the village. Stroll the gardens and see the splendid library de Gaulle designed for himself with three windows opening to grand views.

# CHAMPAGNE COUNTRY

Minor roads crisscrossing the Champagne region connect the many pretty wine villages. A leisurely drive is the best way to experience Champagne, with stops here and there to stroll the villages and to visit the *vignerons*—small independent wine producers—to taste their distinctive, often excellent champagnes.

■ Lush vineyards and charming villages catch the traveler's attention at every turn and act as lures to spend an hour or two celebrating life at leisure.

## Exploring the Champagne Countryside

Meandering east from Reims around Parc Naturel de la Montagne de Reims, the 40-mile (70 km) Route Touristique weaves through the heart of the Champagne countryside. Road-trippers can pause at vineyards and historical villages filled with architectural marvels and charming outposts of everyday life. The vines you see along the way primarily bear the Pinot Noir grape, the viticultural mainstay of Champagne.

Begin by taking the D380 southwest out of Reims and follow the signposts; soon you'll be driving east along the D26. The route rises to magnificent viewpoints at the St.-Lie chapel beyond Jouy-lès-Reims. Farther east, climb the woodsy path above Verzy

**Épernay** 🅜 119 C3 Visitor Information ✉ 7 avenue de Champagne ☎ 03 26 53 33 00 🕐 Closed Sun. in winter • **Centre Inter-professionel des Vins de Champagne, Épernay** ☎ 03 26 51 19 30 **champagne.fr**

to an observation point at **Mont Sinai** for a marvelous view of the vineyards. The road drops down to the Vallée de la Marne in the southwest corner of the Champagne region. Here the grapes are Pinot Meunier, which impart a certain spiciness to the wine.

Soon you'll come to the quiet town of **Épernay,** the capital of champagne country. The prestigious **Avenue de Champagne** is lined with sumptuous champagne houses, including industry giant **Moët & Chandon** (see Travelwise p. 472), founded in 1743. Opposite is the **Trianon Palace**—two pavilions and a lovely orangery surrounded by typically French formal gardens—built in the early 1800s by Jean-Rémy Moët to entertain his friend Napoleon Bonaparte.

The impressive **Château Perrier,** built in the 19th century by Charles Perrier, a former mayor of Épernay, is under restoration. The **Maison de Castellane** (castellane.com), identifiable by its ornate tower, houses a museum. The **Maison Pol Roger** (polroger.com) is headquarters of the eponymous firm founded in 1849; its champagne was Winston Churchill's favorite.

## Other Routes

West from Épernay, you can follow another "route touristique" along the Marne River, flanked on both sides with Meunier grapevines. On the way to Dormans, a peaceful riverside town, it passes through Hautvillers; here you can visit the abbey where Dom Pérignon was a monk. Another town en route is Boursault, with its 19th-century castle built for the enterprising Madame Clicquot, who sold her champagne to the Russian court.

A different tourist route heads south of Épernay to Vertus, through a region called the **Côte des Blancs** for the white Chardonnay grapes that are almost exclusively planted here. ∎

## How Champagne Is Made

After the grapes are pressed, the juice, or "must," is put in vats until the following spring, when the wine is blended and bottled. Blending makes champagne the drink it is; there are many sparkling wines made by the champagne method (méthode champenoise), but the blenders of champagne marry wines from the current vintage with reserve wines from other vintages. Once blended, sugar and yeast mixed with reserve wine are added to each bottle, which is then corked and stored in a V-shaped rack called a pupitre. The yeast converts the sugar into carbon dioxide, which dissolves in the wine, forming tiny bubbles. Bottles are turned daily and gradually tilted, a process known as remuage. When the cork is removed, escaping gas expels the residue and a small amount of wine, to be replaced by a mix of champagne and sugar. Champagne must be aged for at least a year, and a fine vintage may be aged for a decade or more.

# More Places to Visit in Champagne

## Châlons-en-Champagne

Châlons is the third, with Reims and Épernay, in Champagne's famous triangle of wine towns. Châlons is the quintessential regional settlement with its picturesque canals and half-timbered houses. The town gate, the Porte Ste. Croix, was erected in 1770 for Marie-Antoinette to pass through on her way to marry Louis XVI. In 1791, during the revolution, the royal couple were recognized and arrested in Ste. Ménéhould, 15 miles (25 km) east, on their flight from Paris. Their dreadful fate was now in the hands of God, and the queen's prayer book is displayed now in Châlons's public library.

*chalons-tourisme.com* 🅼 119 C3 **Visitor Information** ✉ 3 quai des Arts ☎ 03 26 65 17 89 🕐 Closed Sun.

## Langres

You enter the town through 17th-century gateways. Like many towns throughout France in medieval times, Langres was built on a hill. It was the first town fortified by the Romans and has a triumphal arch embedded in its curtain wall. The old town has several beautiful stone Renaissance mansions with courtyards open to the public. *bienvenue-hautemarne.fr*
🅼 119 D2 **Visitor Information** ✉ place O. Lahalle ☎ 03 25 87 67 67 🕐 Closed Sun. Oct.–April

---

## EXPERIENCE: Going to the Champagne Houses

Among the Reims champagne houses offering tours and tastings are **Veuve Clicquot** (*1 Place des Droits-de-l'Homme, tel 03 26 89 53 90, veuve-cliquot.com*), whose *chef de caves*, Antoine Müller, perfected the technique of re-*muage* (see sidebar p. 139) in 1818; **Charles Heidsieck** (*4 boulevard Henry Vasnier, tel 03 26 84 43 00, charlesheidsieck.com*), which first exported champagne to the United States of America in 1851; **Vranken-Pommery** (*5 place du Général Gouraud, vrankenpommery .com*), producer of the first brut or dry champagne, which would prove so popular in England;

**Louis Roederer** (*21 boulevard Lundy, louis-roederer.com*), maker of Cristal; and **Ruinart** (*4 rue des Crayères, tel 03 26 77 51 51, ruinart .com*), Champagne's oldest *maison*. **Maison Mumm** (*34 rue du Champ de Mars, tel 03 26 49 59 70, ghmumm.com*), founded in 1827 by two Protestant winemakers from the Rheingau region, runs guided tours of its cellars, followed by tastings, and has a small museum and an impressive archive of vintages, with bottles dating back to the late 19th century. Ask at the Reims tourist office (see p. 136) for details of tour times, duration, and charges.

## Sedan

The very impressive **Château Fort** *(1 Place du Château, tel 03 24 29 98 80, chateau-fort-sedan.fr)*, was built in 1424 on the site of 11th-century fortifications, and it still dominates the border town of Sedan. Vast and towering, it is one of the largest castles in Europe, still containing its sinister *oubliette* dungeons (the name comes from the French *oublier*, to forget; as in, lock them up, throw away the key and forget about whatever prisoners are down there). The lord's living quarters are also well worth a good look around. Situated southeast of Sedan is **Fort La-Ferté**, the northernmost fort on the Maginot Line, which was overrun in 1940. *sedan.fr* 🗺 119 D3

## Troyes

Half-timbered 16th-century houses overlook cobbled streets that glisten in the rain and shine in the sun within Troyes' atmospheric St.-Jean district. The European Center of Hebraic Study commemorates a medieval center of Jewish learning that once thrived here. The **Cathédrale St.-Pierre-et-St.-Paul** contains prime examples of beautifully preserved stained glass, some originating from the 13th century. Among the town's other attractions worth visiting is the **Musée d'Art Moderne** with an engaging collection of fauvist artworks. *tourisme-troyes.com* 🗺 118 C2 **Visitor Information** ✉ 16 boulevard Carnot ☎ 08 92 22 46 09

■ **The basilica of St.-Urbain: construction began in the 13th century, but due to economic difficulties, it was not completely finished until the 20th century.**

# ALSACE & LORRAINE

**Half plateau and half forested mountain range, half French and half German, Alsace and Lorraine share a history, landscape, and cultural identity that are unique in France. Along their eastern edge, they follow the German border, marked by the Rhine River, from Lauterbourg in the northwest to Basel in the southeast, where France, Germany, and Switzerland meet.**

These regions have a common history, having been part of a German state since the ninth century, entering the kingdom of France only in the 17th and 18th centuries, respectively. Several times since then, they have been conquered by Germany and later returned to France, making for an interesting mix in architecture, culture, and food.

Lorraine's southern *département* is the mountainous, forested Vosges, an ancient, low massif that spreads eastward into Alsace. In winter there is skiing at St.-Maurice-sur-Moselle, la Bresse-le-Hohneck, Bussang, and Gérardmer.

The highest peak of the Vosges, the 4,672-foot (1,424 m) Grand Ballon, is in Alsace, with vineyards blanketing the foothills of the massif. Few visitors can resist following the Route du Vin through wine villages that are among the prettiest in France, and most visitors take time to explore Colmar and other towns.

Strasbourg, one of the largest ports on the Rhine, has a world-class cathedral. And, like Brussels, it holds many European institutions, including the European Parliament.

■ **Among the peaks and valleys of Alsace, glacial Lac des Truites is the highest lake in the Vosges.**

Stretching between the region's two great capitals, Metz and Nancy, Parc Naturel Régional de Lorraine, a quiet countryside crossed by rivers, is dotted by ancient fortifications and sites associated with past wars. Growing numbers of visitors now come to follow the traces of these conflicts. ■

# STRASBOURG

**Strasbourg is France's biggest river port and its sixth largest city, yet it has extraordinary charm and beauty. Founded more than 2,000 years ago, the city grew on marshy ground around branches of the Ill River, which threads through its picturesque old quarter. The Rhine port and outlying districts are busily industrial, but the city has all the vitality of a student town—its university, founded in 1566, is one of the oldest in France. Strasbourg faces Germany, just a bus ride away across the Rhine, and has some of Europe's most powerful institutions in its northeast quarter.**

"I have seen many magnificent buildings in Switzerland, France, Italy and Greece. But the most beautiful thing of all is the interior of the Strasbourg cathedral with its great jewels, the miracle of its stained-glass windows." Thus wrote sculptor Hans Jean Arp (1887–1966), who was born in a house near the **Cathédrale Notre-Dame.** The glass, dating from the 12th to 13th centuries and set in two rose windows with beautiful tracery, was removed and hidden for safekeeping during World War II.

In the 1220s, when construction of the cathedral began, Strasbourg was an independent city. The cathedral's transept was built first in Romanesque style. Little more than a decade later, the nave was rebuilt in the French Gothic style. The plans show that the architect modeled the building on Notre-Dame in Paris, but because it was built in stages until the 15th century, it perfectly reflects the progression from Romanesque to high Gothic styles. It is worth climbing to the platform on top of the tower to admire the spire statuary.

The west front is remarkable for its medieval sculptures, especially the figures of the Wise and Foolish Virgins in the right portal. Many, however, are copies of those disfigured during the revolution: The originals are displayed in the **Musée de l'Oeuvre Notre-Dame** (*tel 03 88 52 50 00, closed Mon.*), opposite the cathedral.

In the cathedral transept is an astronomical clock. Made in the 16th century, it was given a new movement in the 19th. Its crowd of figures can be seen in action every day at 12:30 p.m.

Notre-Dame and the medieval streets around it survived terrible bombardments in 1944. Across the Place du Château next to the cathedral, the 18th-century **Palais Rohan** (*tel 03 88 52 50 00*), once the archbishop's palace, now houses the city's main museums (*musees.strasbourg.eu*), the Musée des Beaux-Arts and the Musée des Arts Décoratifs et d'Archéologie. Close by is

**Strasbourg** 🅰 119 F2 Visitor Information ✉ 17 place de la Cathédrale ☎ 03 88 52 28 28 **ot-strasbourg.fr • Cathédrale Notre-Dame** ✉ place de la Cathédrale 🆂 $; Astronomical clock $ **cathedrale-strasbourg.fr**

## EXPERIENCE: Tradition-Rich Holiday Shopping

The famous Christmas market in the streets of Strasbourg, held November 29 to December 24, is filled with holiday magic. This is one of the biggest Christmas markets in France, centered around the magnificent cathedral. It has been a local tradition since 1570, with hundreds of stalls offering an array of festive products and crafts. The warming food on offer is hard to resist and includes dense and spicy gingerbread, mulled wine, and Bredle cakes—delicious little morsels traditionally prepared during the Advent period. There is also a skating rink and merry Christmas music performed at locations around the city.

the 13th-century **Pharmacie du Cerf** (now a cultural center) in the Place de la Cathédrale. West of the city center in Place Hans Jean Arp is the **Musée d'Art Moderne et Contemporain** (*tel 03 88 23 31 31*), with works by Arp among others. The **Musée Alsacien** (*tel 03 88 52 50 01*), on Quai St.-Nicolas, has a fascinating collection of regional costumes and furniture. Take time to stroll around Strasbourg's old quarter built around canals once used by tanners and fishermen. The Ponts Couverts (the name means "covered bridges," but they lost their tops in the 18th century) cross the canals under the restored 14th-century city wall. Tall houses line the quays, and the area is full of restaurants and bars. ∎

# DRIVE ALONG THE ALSACE WINE ROUTE

**The Route du Vin winds through the Vosges foothills, threading between the valley floor and the fringes of woods blanketing higher slopes.**

The Alsace vineyards stretch for more than 130 miles (200 km) across the foothills of the wooded Vosges Mountains from Marlenheim in the north to Thann in the south. Alsace wines were not widely known before World War II and were sold mainly as *vin ordinaire*; today, these dry, full-bodied wines have a reputation for quality, and Alsace now boasts 51 *grands crus* vineyards that are sold around the globe.

Mainly white wines are produced in Alsace, varying from bone-dry Rieslings to the sweet dessert wines labeled Vendanges Tardives, made from very late harvested grapes. Most independent producers (who sell wines made from grapes grown in their own vine-

> **NOT TO BE MISSED:**
> **Turckheim • Riquewihr • Ribeauvillé • Château du Haut-Koenigsbourg • Rosheim**

yards) offer wine tastings and vineyard tours; their cellars and wineries are signposted along the way. You can also try wines at the many wine fairs and festivals (*visit.alsace, alsace-wine-route .com*).

The Route du Vin passes ancient castles such as Eguisheim in the south, and abbeys farther north such as Andlau, whose ninth-century church was part of a convent. Towns and villages have cobbled streets, overhanging

## Grapes of the Region

Alsace wines are varietal (pressed from one grape variety) and are identified by grape and the maker's name. Most are made from one of four "noble" grapes. However, rosé and red wines are also produced from the **Pinot Noir** grape in a few vineyards around Ottrott in the north of Alsace and Herrenweg in the south. Crémant d'Alsace is a sparkling wine made by the champagne method (see sidebar p. 139) from a blend of different wines. The following are the white wine grapes and the characteristics of the wine they make:

**Gewurztraminer**—powerful, aromatic, with a fruity, spicy bouquet
**Muscat**—citrusy, slightly aromatic, and essentially dry
**Pinot Blanc**—fresh, harmonious
**Pinot Gris**—richly flavored with complex aromas
**Riesling**—fruity, floral, but delicate
**Sylvaner**—light, refreshing

eaves, fountains, wells, and hanging baskets of flowers. The whole route takes days to enjoy, but the section between Colmar and Rosheim makes a fine day trip. Stopping off at any of the world famous vineyards you'll see signposted on this route to taste their celebrated wines must be among the great pleasurable experiences to be had by any visitor to France.

From Colmar (see pp. 150–151), take the D417 west to **Wintzenheim** ❶ and turn north onto the minor road that leads across the pretty Fecht River to **Turckheim,** with its three medieval gateways. From here, follow the Route du Vin signposts

🅰 See also area map pp. 118–119
➤ Colmar
🔁 52 miles (85 km)
🕐 One day
➤ Rosheim

along mountain roads, climbing through vineyards to the flower-decked village of **Niedermorschwihr;** then go east and back west to Katzenthal, known for its Rieslings; and north to the village of **Ammerschwihr.**

From here, follow the N415 north to **Kaysersberg ❷**—birthplace of the missionary doctor and Nobel Prize winner Albert Schweitzer—set among the woods.

Turn eastward through vineyards along the D28 and then left onto the D1B. A detour along the D3 takes you to the popular walled village of **Riquewihr ❸** (see p. 154).

Then follow the D1B north through medieval **Ribeauvillé ❹**. Still on the D1B, continue to Bergheim, where a Wednesday market is held in the cobbled square, and **St.-Hippolyte**

**❺**, whose medieval ramparts are overlooked by the spectacular towers of **Château du Haut-Koenigsbourg** (see p. 154).

From St.-Hippolyte, the D35 then meanders north through a string of wine villages—**Orschwiller,** with a small wine museum; Riesling-producing **Scherwiller ❻**; the old commune of **Dambach-la-Ville ❼**; **Ottrott ❽**, which makes red wine from its Pinot Noir grapes; and finally to **Rosheim ❾**, whose Maison des Païens may be the oldest domestic dwelling in Alsace (circa 1170).

The region of Alsace and Lorraine may have been historically divided by border disputes and contested cultural narratives, but wherever you stop along this route, the welcome will be warm and embracing.

The picturesque village of Niedermorschwihr, nestled among vineyards in the hills of Alsace.

# METZ

The immense scale of the defenses of Metz conveys something of the importance of this city, once one of the great frontier fortresses of France. A fortified bridge connects the Porte des Allemands, with its crenellations and 13th-century towers, to the two huge bastions on the opposite bank of the Seille River.

When the Romans invaded Gaul, Metz was the capital of the Frankish Merovingian dynasty before becoming a free city under the Holy Roman Empire. Water was brought in via an aqueduct whose remains can be seen at Jouy-aux-Arches, some 4 miles (7 km) southwest on the N57.

Set at the strategic confluence of the Seille and Moselle Rivers, the city center is crisscrossed by old bridges. **St.-Pierre-aux-Nonnains,** built on the site of a fourth-century Roman basilica, is thought to be France's earliest Christian church. The **Cathédrale St.-Étienne** was built between the 13th and 16th centuries. At 138 feet (42 m), its nave is the third highest of any French cathedral, lit by great windows with their original medieval glass.

The Petits-Carmes convent, between the cathedral and the Moselle River, became a museum in 1839. During a 1930s expansion, remains of the city's Roman baths were found. You can see them at the **Musée de la Cour d'Or.** The beaux arts collection here includes works by Rembrandt and Titian. ∎

## Pompidou Metz

The Centre Pompidou-Metz (1 parvis des Droits-de-l'Homme, tel 03 87 15 39 39, centrepompidou-metz .fr, $$) opened in 2010 as the first regional outpost of the Paris Pompidou (Beaubourg). Only 80 minutes from Paris with a new TGV rail connection, the museum has become one of the most visited cultural centers outside Paris. The extraordinary modern building, designed by Japanese architect Shigeru Ban and his French colleague Jean de Gastines, is a light and airy structure, with an exposed wooden frame and undulating fiberglass roof, rather like a Chinese hat, with a large atrium and adjoining public garden. There is no permanent collection; major works are borrowed from the vast collection of the Paris Pompidou. The inaugural exhibition featured masterpiece artworks by Pablo Picasso, Jackson Pollock, Wassily Kandinsky, and Joan Miró.

**Metz** 🏔 119 E3 Visitor Information ✉ place d'Armes ☎ 03 87 39 00 00 **tourisme-metz.com/fr** • **St.-Pierre-aux-Nonnains** ✉ Just off boulevard Poincaré • **Cathédrale St.-Étienne** ✉ place d'Armes • **Musée de la Cour d'Or** ✉ 2 rue de Haut-Poirier ☎ 03 87 20 13 20 🕐 Closed Tues. 💲 $$ **musee.metzmetropole.fr**

# NANCY

The capital of Lorraine, on the Meurthe River, may be a modern manufacturing city, but its historic heart is still caught in the 18th century. Nancy grew up in the 12th century around the stronghold of the dukes of Lorraine, but it was transformed in the 18th, when it was elegantly replanned and rebuilt under Stanislas Leszczynski, the Duke of Lorraine and dethroned king of Poland.

**Place Stanislas** is the focus of the 18th-century town planning and a UNESCO World Heritage site. In the middle, a statue of Stanislas is flanked by two ornate fountains and enclosed by magnificent gilded wrought-iron railings. Surrounding the square are several 18th-century palaces and the Hôtel de Ville by Emmanuel Héré, a student of Gabriel Boffrand, leading architect of French rococo style.

A hotel occupies the palace on one side of the square; the **Musée des Beaux-Arts,** the other. The 18th-century facade remains, but the building has been extended to accommodate its collection of works by 19th- and 20th-century artists as well as decorative arts.

The 16th-century ducal palace, west of Parc de la Pepinière, now holds the **Musée Lorrain,** featuring jewelry, arms, armor, and illuminated manuscripts, and a section devoted to the furniture, textiles, and even tombstones of the city's Jewish community.

Walking is the best way to appreciate the vistas from Place Stanislas along

■ **The gates of Place Stanislas are masterful works by Lamour.**

the tree-lined Place de la Carrière, flanked by 18th-century residences, to the Palais du Gouvernement.

Artists led by glass craftsman Émile Gallé helped found the school of art nouveau in Nancy. Look for the artists' work on the west side of town. The **Musée de l'École de Nancy** *(36–38 rue du Sergent-Blandan, tel 03 83 40 14 86, ecole-de-nancy.com, closed Mon.–Tues., $)* displays the art nouveau style. ■

**Nancy** 🗺 119 E2 Visitor Information ✉ 1 place Stanislas ☎ 03 83 35 80 10 **nancy-tourisme.fr** • **Musée des Beaux-Arts** ✉ 3 place Stanislas ☎ 03 83 85 30 01 🕐 Closed Tues. 💲 $ **mban.nancy.fr** • **Musée Lorrain** ✉ 64 Grande Rue ☎ 03 83 32 18 74 🕐 Closed Mon. 💲 $$

# COLMAR

An important fortified town in the Middle Ages, Colmar has kept many of its ancient churches and much of its medieval center. Half-timbered houses sport colored roof tiles and, in the Petite Venise quarter of the town, winding streets cross the canals that link to the Ill River, which in turn joins Colmar to the Rhine.

■ The second driest city in France, Colmar has long since perfected the art of outdoor dining.

## Isenheim Altarpiece

One of France's most visited buildings is the former Dominican convent of Unterlinden (named for its linden trees), founded in the 13th century and still retaining its arcaded cloister. Converted into the **Musée Unterlinden** in 1849, it became the repository for art from surrounding religious institutions. The most celebrated exhibit is the altarpiece originally painted for the convent at Isenheim, 14 miles (22 km) south of Colmar. This inspirational work is one of the few extant paintings by the 16th-century artist Mathias Grünewald, court painter at Mainz. An ambitious modern extension to the building is under way, and the altarpiece is temporarily housed in the nearby Dominican church.

## Around the Town

Southwest of the Unterlinden Museum, the 13th- to 14th-century **Basilique St.-Martin** contains some beautiful 14th-century stained glass. The Dominican church nearby boasts

**Colmar** 🗺 119 E2 Visitor Information ✉ rue d'Unterlinden ☎ 03 89 20 68 92 **tourisme-colmar.com** • **Musée Unterlinden** ✉ 1 rue d'Unterlinden ☎ 03 89 20 15 50 🕐 Closed Tues. 💲 $$ **musee-unterlinden.com**

the exquisite "Virgin in the Rose Bower," painted by the 16th-century Colmar artist Martin Schongauer.

Cars are banned in old Colmar, so you can stroll between ancient Colmar's superb buildings. The **Maison Adolphe,** built around 1350, and the former **Corps de Garde,** with a Renaissance balcony, are on Rue Mercerie, close to the St. Martin Basilica. The **Maison des Têtes** on Rue des Têtes, near the Unterlinden Museum, has a carved oriel window. The **Ancienne Douane** (Old Customs House) is 15th century and stands on the Grand Rue, by a canal. La Petite Venise is the former leather-tanners' district, where the Lauch River and its canals are overlooked by old town houses, hung with flower baskets in summer.

The birthplace of sculptor Frédéric-

Auguste Bartholdi is now the **Musée Bartholdi** (*30 rue des Marchands, tel 03 89 41 90 60, musee-bartholdi.fr, closed Tues.*), a local history museum displaying his studies for the Statue of Liberty. The **Fontaine du Vigneron,** a fountain dedicated to vineyard owners, adorns the town. To the west, vineyards climb the slopes of the Vosges. As the capital of the Alsace wine district, Colmar hosts its August wine fair. ■

## Routes des Crêtes

The most spectacular drive in northern France scales the Route des Crêtes (*massif-des-vosges.com*), literally the "road of the crests," a strategic route cut across the peaks of the Vosges by French army engineers during World War I. On a clear day, vistas from the summit of the 4,672-foot (1,424 m) Grand Ballon embrace the entire Vosges range—all the way to the Black Forest in Germany, south to the Jura, and across the Alps to Mont Blanc. Check the weather forecast before setting out; low clouds, not unusual, will obscure views.

The Route des Crêtes begins at Cernay, about 5 miles (9 km) west of Mulhouse. Take the D5 north to Uffholtz and turn west on the D431. The road twists and turns up the steep sides of the Grand Ballon, the highest peak in the Vosges, its name said to be a corruption of *bois long* (long forest—the mountaintops were once clothed with trees).

Past the Grand Ballon the road forks: Follow the D430 to Le Hohneck (4,467 feet/1,362 m), where the grassy summit affords lovely views across wooded mountainsides. Continue on the D430 to its junction with the D417, then take the D61 northward past Lac Noir and Lac Blanc, mountain lakes in extinct volcanic craters, surrounded by woods.

# FOOD & DRINK—RICH & TASTY

Alsace and Lorraine are the gastronomic giants of the north, home of quiche Lorraine, foie gras, suckling pig, and free-range goose. Alsatian cooks bring French elegance to such German staples as sauerkraut, dumplings, and stews—try the traditional *baeckenoffe*, a stew with beef and lamb. Lorraine has wonderful preserves and fruit tarts, such as bilberry, mirabelle plum, and red currant, and *jambon d'Ardennes* is one of the world's great cured hams.

■ Food with a sense of place: traditional *kugelhof,* sweet and rich

Along the northern coast of France and in Flanders, along the Belgian border, you find delicious winter stews: *hochepot* (meat and root vegetable stew), *waterzooi* (fish stew), and *carbonnade de boeuf à la flamande* (beef stewed in beer). In summer there are light fish dishes to search out, such as herring around Boulogne (look for *craquelot*—a dish using grilled, smoked herring). Marvelous vegetables come from the market gardens of the marshy Somme and Flanders, including endive and the raw ingredients for *flamiches* (leek, onion, or pumpkin tarts made with a pizza crust). Champagne offers extraordinarily imaginative cabbage dishes, and the Ardennes and the forests of the Vosges Mountains yield an equally astonishing array of mushrooms.

Amiens is famous for duck pie and pastry-encased pâtés; Arras and Troyes for *andouillettes*—spicy chitterling sausages. Pork is a specialty of Troyes; Ste. Ménéhould is celebrated for pig's trotters slow-cooked for 48 hours. Expect to find rabbit, hare, partridge, venison, wild boar, and truffles on menus in the Ardennes, as well as in the Vosges Mountains.

Travelers touring the Champagne vineyards may be surprised to find still wines produced there, too. Bouzy, for example, is a still red made from the Pinot Noir grapes grown on the Montagne de Reims; Rosé des Riceys is a still rosé from Les Riceys in the southern vineyard area.

France's reputation for great wines overshadows its tradition of beer (see sidebar below) and cider. Cider, though typically a Norman and Breton drink, is also produced in Champagne and by the Cidrerie Georges Maeyaert in Milly-sur-Thérain by Beauvais.

The globally loved quiche Lorraine, savory and rich

## The Other Bubbly

Northern France and Belgium share a long-established tradition of beer brewing, but only about three dozen non-industrialized breweries still operate in France. A French pressure group for traditional beer, Les Amis de la Bière, works hard to support these enterprises.

Although Strasbourg is still northern France's great brewing city, the best beer is actually brewed around Lille in the heart of Flanders. You could make a satisfying brasserie (brew-ery) tour of Nord and Picardie, including the brasseries of St.-Sylvestre, near Steenvoorde; Lepers at Annoeullin and Castelain at Bénifontaine, both near Lens; the Brasserie Duyck at Jenlain, near Valenciennes; and Les Enfants de Guyant in Douai.

Alsace still has a few independent breweries, notably Fischer in Schiltigheim, which also produces Adelscott beer, flavored with malt whiskey, and Meteor, which makes a rustic, unpasteurized pilsner beer.

# More Places to Visit in Alsace & Lorraine

## Alsace-Moselle Memorial Museum

This dramatic modern museum sits on the site of the Schirmeck internment camp and reveals the history of the region, which has changed nationalities four times since 1870. Also visible is the site of Struthof, the only concentration camp on French soil. *memorial-alsace-moselle .com* ✉ Schirmeck ☎ 03 88 47 45 50 🕐 Closed Mon. & Jan. 💲 $$

## Château du Haut-Koenigsbourg

The D159 loops its way up from St.-Hippolyte toward this castle, giving startling vistas across the Alsace plain, 2,500 feet (750 m) below. The present castle is a 19th-century restoration of 15th-century fortifications around a 12th-century keep. *haut-koenigsbourg.fr* 🗺 119 E2 ☎ 03 69 33 25 00 🚌 Shuttle bus from train station in Selestat 💲 $$

## Domrémy-la-Pucelle

This Vosges village about 45 miles (74 km) southwest of Nancy boasts the modest house where Jeanne d'Arc was born in 1412. In the surrounding fields, she heard the voices of saints who urged her to deliver France from English domination and restore the Dauphin Charles to the French throne. In the chapel of **Notre-Dame de Bermont** *(1 mile/1.5 km N in Brixey, open first Sat. of month, tel 03 29 34 31 73, nd-bermont.fr),* where she prayed, a fresco has been dated to the 15th century. It shows a teenage girl with blond hair and blue eyes in peasant dress and may be a portrait of the warrior saint.

## Mulhouse

A medieval town that was once a free city attached to the Swiss Confederation, Mulhouse saw some action in World War II. The 16th-century Hôtel de Ville survived and is now a museum of local history. The **Cité de l'Automobile** *(avenue de Colmar, tel 03 89 33 23 23, citedelautomobile.com)* displays the Schlumpf collection, including Juan Fangio's Maserati and Charlie Chaplin's 1937 Rolls-Royce Phantom III. *tourisme-mulhouse.com* 🗺 119 E1 **Visitor Information** ✉ 9 Hôtel de Ville, place de la Reunion ☎ 03 89 35 48 48

## Riquewihr

Layers of fortifications protect the 16th-century houses and courtyards of this picturesque wine town. The main street is defended by a medieval fortified gate, now a museum of archaeology. The Cour des Bergers is the original town gate, complete with portcullis and a prison with torture chamber. *ribeauville-riquewihr.com* 🗺 119 E2 **Visitor Information** ✉ rue 1ère Armée ☎ 03 89 73 23 23 🕐 Closed Sun.

Culturally distinctive Northern European provinces, historically more influenced by Norsemen and Celts than by Romans—and by the artists drawn here

# NORMANDY & BRITTANY

# NORMANDY & BRITTANY

Normandy and Brittany together form the northwestern corner of France and combine a largely agricultural hinterland with a coast that has long been popular with both French and foreign vacationers. Both regions are major agricultural producers: Normandy is particularly famous for its dairy products and apples and Brittany for its vegetables, though both now also produce substantial quantities of meat and grains.

The extensive northern coastline has made fishing an important industry, along with the cultivation of mussels and oysters. The shoreline of northern Normandy and northern Brittany is edged by the English Channel (la Manche), while to the south, Brittany's coast juts out into the Atlantic Ocean.

All along the coast, fishing harbors and ferry ports see constant traffic between France and Britain. The entire shoreline offers a wonderful variety of landscape: rugged granite headlands or chalky cliffs interspersed with sandy beaches.

The climate is relatively gentle, affected by the Gulf Stream and warmed by west winds that bring humidity and mild winters. However, harsher winds from the northwest and west can lower the temperatures and create sudden storms, especially along the coast. Brittany has some of the highest tides in the world around the bay of Mont St.-Michel.

Southern Normandy and Brittany cover what is known as the Armorican Massif, ancient granite mountains that have eroded into gently rolling hills. In the west, the hard granite produces the dramatic coastline of Brittany. To the east the granite gives way to the limestone of the Paris basin, the source of the pale, easily carved Caen stone used to build many cathedrals and churches, and

the chalk cliffs of the upper Normandy Channel coast.

The Seine is the main river of the region, looping its way through Normandy from Paris to Le Havre, a major communications route that has carried trade (and occasionally invading armies) for thousands of years. The main cities of the area are Rouen and Caen, both of which are regional capitals of Normandy, and Rennes, the capital of Brittany. Brest is a great naval port, while Nantes and Le Havre are important commercial ports.

Despite their proximity, the histories of Normandy and Brittany have diverged widely, resulting in very distinct regional and cultural identities.

Normandy, on the Seine River and on the way to Paris, has always been an easy target for invaders. The Vikings began their raids up the Seine in the ninth century and eventually settled and colonized the land that took its name from these Norsemen. Traffic with Britain, and the success of William the Conqueror's 1066 invasion, meant significant cultural exchange, exemplified in the many churches in the Romanesque style (referred to as Norman style in England) on both sides of the English Channel.

British Celts colonized the Armorican Peninsula in the sixth century, and it became known as "la Petite Bretagne" (Little Britain), a designation eventually shortened to Bretagne (Brittany is the anglicized version of Bretagne). They established a culture and spoke a language utterly different from those of the rest of France and these differences endure to this day. ∎

## NOT TO BE MISSED:

Rouen cathedral's west front 159

A drive on the Route des Abbayes 160–161

The Bayeux tapestry's stunning details 162–163

Sipping cider in the pays d'Auge 165

Sea-lashed Mont St.-Michel 169–170

The parish closes of Finistère 181

Carnac's superb Neolithic remains 183–185

# NORMANDY

Sheer variety of landscape is Normandy's most striking feature. The craggy grandeur of the coastline on the Cotentin Peninsula in the west gives way to the sands of the Calvados area, the elegance of Deauville and Trouville-sur-Mer, and the cliffs of the Côte d'Albâtre. Inland are rich rural landscapes with cheese producers, Calvados distilleries, and small restaurants. And everywhere, pretty stone villages, manors, and farmhouses evince an architectural heritage that has managed to survive even the devastation of World War II.

■ Normandy's steep chalk cliffs are being steadily eroded by the sea.

The peaceful scenes of picturesque rural contentment that typify Normandy today belie the region's momentous and often somber history. Conflicts of many ages are made tangible in the great cathedral city of Rouen and in the majestically ruined medieval abbeys studded along the meandering course of the Seine River.

Most awe inspiring of all is the Abbaye de Mont St.-Michel, a place of pilgrimage for ten centuries on its perilous rocky island above the sea. Bayeux still treasures its astonishing tapestry, a priceless record of William the Conqueror's invasion of Britain from these shores in 1066. Nearby, the Allied landing beaches mark a more recent story of invasion, serving as a permanent reminder of a period of heroism and extreme suffering.

Other, gentler, images of Normandy are owed to the Impressionist artists who sought inspiration in its seascapes and watery skies. Eugène Boudin's wind-blown dresses on the beach at Trouville and Raoul Dufy's gaily bobbing yachts at Le Havre elegantly capture these aspects of Normandy. Above them all, however, towers Claude Monet, who, in his exquisite gardens at Giverny (see p. 116), created compositions of light, reflections, and color that no visitor to Normandy should willingly miss. ■

# ROUEN

The ancient capital of the duchy of Normandy, founded as a Roman settlement on the Seine, Rouen today is a huge industrial city and port. The old city to the north of the river has been sensitively restored after the widespread destruction of World War II, and a stroll here will reveal a mass of museums, fine churches, and half-timbered Norman houses.

Start as Monet did, at the **Cathédrale Notre-Dame,** the glorious Gothic west front of which he painted in many different lights. Springing from 12th-century foundations are soaring Gothic arches, intricate Flamboyant carving, and two mismatched towers flanking the facade. Above the doorways, delicate openwork gables top rows of statues. The interior is a cool retreat of tall columns, luminous stained glass, and ancient tombs, including that of Rollo, first Duke of Normandy.

To find the heart of old Rouen, walk the pedestrians-only Rue du Gros Horloge; note its fine half-timbered buildings and pass under the medieval clock set in a Renaissance arch. At the western end is **Place du Vieux-Marché,** where Jeanne d'Arc was burned at the stake in 1431. At the site of her pyre is a modern church built in her honor. The **Historial Jeanne d'Arc** (Joan of Arc Museum), located in the Archbishop's palace, presents the saint's life and death in an engaging, multimedia experience.

Back toward the cathedral, the **Palais de Justice** is a remarkable example of 16th-century Gothic Flamboyant architecture, delicate and exuberant. West of Place du Vieux-Marché lies

**INSIDER TIP:**

Rouen's soaring Cathédrale Notre-Dame is magnificently detailed. Bring along binoculars to see the architectural elements way up high.

—JANE SUNDERLAND
*National Geographic contributor*

the **Hôtel-Dieu,** Rouen's old hospital, where novelist Gustave Flaubert was born in 1821. It is now the **Musée Flaubert et Histoire de la Médecine** (tel 02 35 15 59 95, closed Sun.–Mon.), devoted to his life and to medical history. Flaubert often visited the **Natural History Museum** (rue Beauvoisine, tel 02 35 71 41 50, closed Mon.), now refurbished.

To the north on Square Verdrel, the **Musée des Beaux-Arts** (tel 02 35 71 28 40, mbarouen.fr, closed Tues.) houses an excellent collection of European paintings, including one of Monet's Rouen cathedral series.

Beyond the cathedral are the beautifully restored **Église de St.-Ouen** and another Flamboyant Gothic masterpiece, the **Église de St.-Maclou.** ∎

**Rouen** 🅼 157 E3 Visitor Information ✉ 25 place de la Cathédrale ☎ 02 32 08 32 40 **rouentourisme.com** • **Cathédrale Notre-Dame** ✉ place de la Cathédrale

# SEINE VALLEY: ROUEN TO THE COAST

Beyond Rouen, the Seine River snakes its way slowly to the sea past wooded valleys, chalk cliffs, and apple orchards. This lovely drive along the north bank is also known as the Route des Abbayes, after the string of abbeys, which would become powerful centers of learning, were founded on the banks of the river in the seventh century.

Follow the D982 west from Rouen to the village of **St.-Martin-de-Boscherville** ❶, whose **Abbaye de St.-Georges** (tel 02 35 32 10 82, abbaye-saint-georges.com) is on the site of Roman temples. Begun in 1050, it escaped destruction during the revolution because the villagers adopted it as their parish church. Today it is one of the best preserved examples of Norman or Romanesque architecture.

Continue on the D982 to **Duclair,** with fine views of the river. Fork left to detour along the D65, following a great meander of the Seine past the or-

**NOT TO BE MISSED:**

Abbaye de St.-Georges
• Abbaye de Jumièges •
Abbaye St.-Wandrille •
Musée Victor-Hugo • Pont
de Tancarville

chards around Le Mesnil-sous-Jumièges. After the village, the white towers of the **Abbaye de Jumièges** ❷ (tel 02 35 37 24 02, abbayedejumieges.fr) soon loom into sight above the distant trees. These ruins, the most majestic in Normandy, bear witness to a turbulent past. Founded in 654, the abbey was sacked in the ninth century by Vikings, then refounded in 1067 in the presence of William the Conqueror. At its height, in the 13th and 14th centuries, it housed more than 2,000 monks and lay brothers. Only small portions of the abbey survived the revolution.

Proceed along the D143 back to the D982, and go northwest to the Fontenelle Valley and the **Abbaye St.-Wandrille ❸** *(tel 02 35 96 23 11, st-wandrille.com)*, a Benedictine community revived in 1931. Founded in the seventh century, then sacked by the Vikings, the abbey was refounded in the tenth century and flourished until the revolution. The church, dating from the 13th and 14th centuries, remains in ruins, but the 14th-century cloister has been restored. The monks founded a new church in the 1960s in an ancient barn. Try to time

your visit to attend a sung Mass of Gregorian chant *(weekdays 9:25 a.m., Sun. 10 a.m.)*.

Drive on to Caudebec-en-Caux on the D982, then take the D81 to **Villequier ❹**, where the **Musée Victor-Hugo** *(quai Victor-Hugo, tel 02 35 56 78 31, closed Tues., museevictorhugo.fr)* tells of the drowning of the writer's daughter, which inspired some of his most poignant poetry. **Lillebonne ❺**, farther west along the D81 and D173, has impressive Roman remains. Return to the D982 and cross the Seine on the **Pont de Tancarville ❻**, a stunning feat of engineering offering great views of the estuary.

From here, take the A131 to the D139 turnoff to Bourneville. Follow the D139 and D131 to La Mailleraye-sur-Seine, and then take the D65 south through the Forêt de Brotonne to Jumièges via the ferry *(free, leaves every 20 minutes)* and return to Rouen.

🅰 See also area map p. 157
🅿 Rouen
⬆ 90 miles (145 km)
🕐 4 hours
🅿 Rouen

# BAYEUX

Aside from its famous tapestry, Bayeux has a beautifully preserved medieval center and impressive cathedral. But it is, of course, the magnificent tapestry (actually an embroidery on linen) that makes Bayeux so irresistible.

■ The tower of the mainly 13th-century Gothic Cathédrale Notre-Dame in Bayeux was a late 15th-century addition. Within the cathedral are fine 15th-century frescoes.

Recounting the 1066 Norman invasion of England by the forces of William the Conqueror, the 230-foot-long (70 m) **Tapisserie de la Reine Mathilde** is an extraordinary historical document as well as a staggering work of art. Age has dimmed some of the dyes (green in particular), but the wit and vigor of its execution are still vivid. Panel by panel (58 in all), it tells a dramatic story rich in incident and amusing detail, from the original meeting of Harold and William, to the blessing of William's invasion fleet, the appearance of Halley's comet, and the fatal arrow that felled King Harold of England, ensuring victory for the Normans. The minutiae of medieval and military life are graphically detailed: Suits of chain mail are carried on portable hangers; soldiers picnic off their shields, while dukes dine at a table on roast chicken and kabobs.

**Bayeux** ⚐ 157 D3 Visitor Information ✉ Pont St.-Jean
☎ 02 31 51 28 28 **bayeux-bessin-tourisme.com**

Protected behind bulletproof glass in the **Centre Guillaume-le-Conquérant,** this medieval forerunner of the comic strip was probably commissioned by William's half brother, Bishop Odo of Bayeux, for the consecration of the cathedral in 1077—certainly Odo himself figures large in the story. The tapestry may have been the work of French or English embroiderers, but is usually attributed to Saxon weavers or English nuns. Allow at least 90 minutes for a visit in order to enjoy not only the tapestry itself but also the illuminating audiovisual displays that precede it and set it in context.

Emerging from the exhibition, stroll into the heart of medieval Bayeux. The town was particularly fortunate in being the first to be liberated by the Allies in 1944, thus escaping the devastation suffered by many others.

---

**INSIDER TIP:**

Walk along the ancient park-edged canal in the center of Bayeux; keep an eye out for the old mill works.

—BARBARA NOE
*National Geographic editor*

---

Overlooking the town are the Gothic spires of the **Cathédrale Notre-Dame** *(rue du Bienvenu, tel 02 31 92 01 85, notredamedubessin.org),* with its beautiful 11th-century crypt and towers remaining from Bishop Odo's original Romanesque church. The chapels and

## Normandie Pass

If you're planning to see the Bayeux Tapestry as well as visit several of the D-Day sights, it is worth buying a Normandie Pass *(normandie pass.com).* This gives a range of discounts for more than three dozen A-list museums and sights in the Normandy area.

Here's how it works: You simply pay an extra 1 euro on top of your first admission charge to cover all the other sights you might visit.

crypt showcase delightful 15th-century frescoes, and the 12th-century chapter house has a maze depicted in its 15th-century tiled floor. The cobbled streets around the south of Rue St.-Martin contain many fine stone and timber-framed houses dating from the 15th to the 17th centuries. The Aure River runs through the garden-filled town, spanned by a humpbacked bridge.

Saturday is market day in **Place St.-Patrice,** a huge bustling outdoor event recalling something of the flavor of medieval Bayeux. You can find all kinds of local fruits and vegetables, along with flowers and meat and regional specialties. Traditional Bayeux lace is still made in the town and is worth seeking out.

On the southern edge of the town is the **Musée Mémorial de la Bataille de Normandie** (see p. 166), with a poignant British war cemetery almost opposite it. ∎

---

**Centre Guillaume-le-Conquérant** ✉ rue de Nesmond
☎ 02 31 51 25 50 💲 $$ **bayeuxmuseum.com**

# FOOD & DRINK—OYSTERS & SHELLFISH

Both Normandy and Brittany rejoice in a long coastline that yields an abundance of fish and shellfish. Combined with the produce of the lush dairy farms and orchards of Normandy and the vegetable farms of Brittany, this rich trawl of seafood has shaped the gastronomy of the region.

## Cuisine in Normandy

Along the coast you can dine sumptuously on all manner of seafood, especially mussels, oysters, and lobster. Fish, particularly sole, is often served with *sauce normande,* containing cream, mussels, shrimps, and mushrooms.

Pork and pork products are also popular, especially the wide range of *andouille* (chitterling) sausages made locally. The lamb here is excellent, acquiring a delicate salty flavor from grazing on the coastal salt marshes *(prés-salés).* A favorite dish is *tripes à la mode de Caen,* a rich stew of tripe and root vegetables cooked slowly with cider and traditionally enjoyed as a mid-morning snack. Other hearty main courses of the region include Rouen duck in a blood-thickened sauce and *pieds de cochon farcis,* stuffed pig's trotters.

Normandy is famous for its dairy products and for the apples that go into its cider, traditionally drunk with meals instead of wine, and Calvados (apple brandy). Apples come sliced, caramelized, in almond cream, fried in fritters, or doused in Calvados. Apples and cream are often combined with Calvados to make delicious sauces for meat. The rich milk of Normandy cows produces France's finest butter and some of its best and most popular cheeses, including Camembert, Livarot, and Pont l'Éveque.

Calvados (or affectionately, Calva) is widely used in the cuisine of Normandy, enhancing the flavor and cutting the richness of the ubiquitous cream sauces that flavor so many meals. It is often drunk mid-meal as a *digestif* known as *le trou Normand* (literally "Norman hole," clearly intended to be filled with more deliciously rich food). Another regional specialty is Benedictine liqueur, made to an old herbal recipe developed by monks.

## Breton Food

The harsher landscapes of Brittany yield a gastronomy that is, not surprisingly, less rich. The sea dominates local menus: Among the bewildering variety of fish available, sole, turbot, and whiting come together in the spectacular *cotriade,* a fish soup, often with potatoes or, occasionally, cream.

*Moulade*—mussel soup—is a local favorite, as is *moules marinières*—mussels cooked in white wine, shallots, onions, and fresh parsley. *Palourdes farcies,* grilled

■ **A Normandy success story: cheese, bread, wine, friends, a pet dog, and the great outdoors**

clams on the half shell stuffed with shallots and herbs, is another popular dish.

Most impressive of all Breton dishes is the handsome *plateau de fruits de mer,* a giant spread of seafood, including oysters, crabs, langoustines, prawns, clams, and winkles. (This grand still life is a mainstay in Paris brasseries.)

Cancale is the center of the Breton oyster industry and worth a visit to sample its fresh-from-the-sea bivalves, usually served raw with a dip of shallot vinegar or a squeeze of lemon.

In the "turf," category, *gigot d'agneau à la bretonne*–roast lamb with white haricot beans–shows up on many menus.

Breton food is not all fish, pork, and pré-salé lamb. Brittany produces vast quantities of vegetables. Artichokes have now become the symbol of the region (not least when they are used to block the roads to protest EU agricultural policy).

■ **Order mussels as a starter that conveys the taste of the sea.**

Crepes *(galettes),* both sweet and savory, are mainstays of the Breton diet, served as a main course—usually with ham or cheese fillings, or with eggs on top—or lacily thin as exquisite desserts, known appropriately as *crêpes dentelles.* And, yes, *crêpes Suzette*–those thin sweet pancakes with orange juice and Grand Marnier—is authentic to the area. Another don't-miss dessert is *Kouign-Amann:* pastry topped with caramelized sugar.

## EXPERIENCE: Taking the Circular Cider Route

Enjoy the full flavor of the apples of Normandy by following the famous Cider Route *(calvados-tourisme.com)* through the pays d'Auge. A 25-mile (40 km) well-signposted circular route takes you to cider and Calvados (apple brandy) producers in traditional half-timbered houses. The route passes through tiny villages, cornfields, and, of course, apple orchards. Apples have been grown here since the ninth century; today, some 40 varieties are cultivated. The trees are in bloom from April to May, and are harvested from September to December.

Start at the village of **Cambremer,** where you could have lunch with a glass of cider, then head to **Calvados Pierre Huet** (*5 avenue des Tilleuls, tel 02 31 63 01 09, calvados-huet.com*) for a guided tour and tastings of cider, Calvados, and *pommeau* (a mixture of apple juice and apple brandy).

Next, visit the little village of **Beuvron-en-Auge,** the caves and cemetery at **Beaufour-Druval,** and the pretty little hamlet of **La Roque-Baignard.**

At **Le Domaine de Canon** (*14270 Mezidon-Canon, tel 02 31 90 94 49, coupdecanon.fr*), you can help with the harvest of apples and honey and explore the farm with its sheep, cows, pigs, and llamas. You can even spend the night in a tree house.

# NORMANDY LANDING BEACHES

Early on June 6, 1944—D-Day—a huge invasion force landed on the beaches of Normandy. This was Operation Overlord, the meticulously planned and desperately fought Allied offensive to reclaim Normandy and ultimately Europe from its German occupiers. Many of the towns and villages lay in ruins, but the Battle of Normandy was won, and the tide of the war turned in the Allies' favor. Several new memorials opened to commemorate the 70th anniversary in 2014.

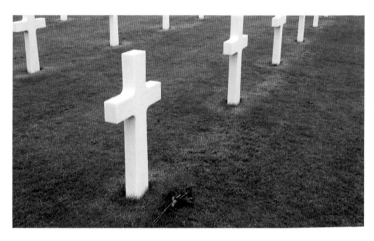

Among those buried in the Colleville-sur-Mer cemetery are 9,386 American war casualties.

Today, the debris of war can still be seen. To make sense of the deserted bunkers, tangles of barbed wire, and rusting hulks, begin by visiting one of the museums devoted to the subject. Almost every town in the area has its own small museum with a poignant display of mementos, but a useful overview—complete with a wealth of photographs and contemporary uniforms, weapons, and documents—is presented in the **Musée Mémorial de la Bataille de Normandie** in Bayeux.

All along the beaches, the remains of German bunkers have been converted into memorials, providing a terrifying intimation of the challenge faced by Allied

**Musée Mémorial de la Bataille de Normandie** ✉ boulevard Fabian-Ware, Bayeux ☎ 02 31 51 25 50 💲 $$. Free for World War II veterans
**bayeuxmuseum.com/musee-memorial-de-la-bataille-de-normandie**

troops. The vast expanses of sand—at low tide, in particular—make it chillingly clear why it was so critical to time the landing to coincide with high tide.

## Battles & Aftermath

Tales of heroism abound. At the west end of **Omaha Beach** rises **Pointe du Hoc,** with a visitors' center, where an advance force of U.S. Rangers scaled the cliffs at dawn to knock out the German batteries. They were fiercely fought and by the end only 65 Rangers, out of the initial 225, survived. **St.-Laurent-sur-Mer** has an Omaha museum *(rue de la Mer, tel 02 31 21 97 44, closed mid-Nov.–mid-Feb.).*

Overlooking Omaha Beach, where nearly 10,000 Americans perished in the face of the most effective German resistance of the battle, is the largest American military cemetery in Normandy at **Colleville-sur-Mer,** where the **Overlord Museum** *(tel 02 31 51 62 00, overlordmuseum.com)* includes restored military vehicles.

The town of **Arromanches** (near the beach code-named Gold) preserves part of the Mulberry harbors, striking remains of the hardware of war. The **Musée du Débarquement** *(place du 6 Juin, tel 02 31 22 34 31, musee-arromanches.fr, closed Jan.)* tells the incredible story of these artificial harbors, towed stealthily across the channel to land 135,000 men, 20,000 vehicles, mountains of ammunition, and stores to support the troops.

## Battlefield Routes

Eight routes signposted **Normandie Terre-Liberté** *(norman diepourlapaix.fr)* trace some of the key battle sites of 1944, starting from the famous Pegasus Bridge near Caen, the site of the first airborne assault. The itineraries, in chronological sequence, put the D-Day battle into a geographic perspective, showing how it unfolded in the penultimate year of World War II.

## After D-Day

In the days and weeks after D-Day, land was gained inch by inch across Normandy by dint of bitter fighting. Tanks struggled in the narrow sunken lanes and the thick hedges of Normandy's *bocage* country, and villages caught in the cross fire were pulverized, many of them suffering heavy civilian casualties.

Two months of fierce fighting left historic Norman towns in smoking ruins. St.-Lô and Falaise were the epicenters of the battle and suffered massive damage, but **Caen** (see p. 171) was also ravaged. Its rebuilding, like that of many other ports and towns in Normandy, took years. The town center has been completely reconstructed, and the castle, churches, and two great Romanesque abbeys have been restored. ∎

**Arromanches** 157 D3 Visitor Information ✉ 2 rue du Maréchal Joffre ☎ 02 31 22 36 45 **normandie-tourisme.fr** • **Le Mémorial (Musée pour la Paix)** ✉ esplanade Eisenhower, Caen ☎ 02 31 06 06 44 🕒 Closed Jan. 💲 $$. Free for World War II veterans **memorial-caen.fr**

# LEST WE FORGET

With each passing year, the D-Day landings and the ensuing battles on the beaches and fields of Normandy fade further into history. Fewer and fewer veterans who fought to free the western world from Nazi tyranny are alive to mark the day. Just a handful now, all in their nineties, recall their leap from landing crafts into cold seas to battle up the beaches toward a lethal line of German snipers and machine guns, while navigating mines, bodies, and barbed wire in the sand.

D-Day, June 6, 1944: American soldiers leaving a landing craft to invade Omaha Beach, Normandy.

Most of the French soldiers who died now lie in their hometowns, but the cemeteries for the American, British, Canadian, Polish, and German casualties dot the landscape.

Heartrending rows of crosses and Stars of David stretch to the horizon. Each marker represents a life cut short and collectively they remind all visitors that we must *never forget* the reason they died here. As authoritarianism rears its ugly head again, in Europe and the Americas, all who pass through these memorials should pause and vow to honor the memories of the fallen.

Caen's **Le Mémorial** (see p. 167), a museum for peace, is located where the German headquarters was sited in June 1944. It tells the story of D-Day through archive film and audiovisual displays. With its thoughtful tone and emphasis on the sacrifice rather than the glory of war, it is a fitting place to end a tour of the landing beaches.

# MONT ST.-MICHEL

Buffeted by ferocious tides and winds, ringed by treacherous quicksand–the greatest tidal range in continental Europe–the Abbaye de Mont St.-Michel rises magnificently from its pinnacle of rock. Symbol of Normandy and now a UNESCO World Heritage site, described by Guy de Maupassant as a "gigantic granite jewel, delicate as lace, thronged with towers and slender belfries," the abbey has been a place of pilgrimage for well over a thousand years.

First settled in the eighth century, Mont St.-Michel now receives more than three million visitors a year.

In the eighth century, this was a simple rock in the sea, a Celtic funeral mount covered in woods. Then in 708, according to legend, Aubert, Bishop of Avranches, had a vision of the Archangel Michael who instructed him to build an oratory on this rock, accessible only at low tide. In the church of St. Gervais in Avranches you can see Aubert's skull with a dent where the archangel is said to have tapped him on the head.

Richard I, Duke of Normandy, founded a Benedictine abbey here in the tenth century. Gradually the island became encased in monastic buildings. Through the centuries, these structures have been altered, have expanded, or have fallen down.

Over the original oratory, the monks built the church of Notre-Dame-sous-Terre, which is now the crypt of the Romanesque abbey church, begun in the 11th century. As the monastery

**Mont St.-Michel** 157 D2 Visitor Information ✉ boulevard de l'Avancée ☎ 02 33 60 14 30 $ $$ (1-hour guided tour) **abbaye-mont-saint-michel**

increased in importance, the French monarchy took a greater interest in its strategic potential, and more monastic buildings, known as La Merveille, were added in the new Gothic style. This soaring Gothic masterpiece encompasses three levels. At the top, the monks remained enclosed in the abbey church with its exquisite marble cloisters and the superbly lit refectory. On this level, a terrace on the seaward side gives superb views of the bay. The second story accommodated the abbot, noble guests, and knights: The rib vaulting and capitals of the knights' room are particularly magnificent. Humble pilgrims found succor on the lower level.

Even though medieval pilgrims risked being sucked into the quicksand surrounding the rock or overtaken by the

---

**INSIDER TIP:**

Experience Mont St.-Michel via horseback or by taking a micro-flight. Contact the visitor information office for details.

—ROSEMARY BAILEY
*National Geographic author*

---

incoming tide, Mont St.-Michel steadily prospered to become one of the most prominent sites of pilgrimage in France. In the 12th century, the influence of the great abbey was ensured when it hosted peace negotiations between Louis VII of France and Henry II of England.

The **Porte de l'Avancée** gives access to the **Grande Rue,** lined by 15th-

## Visiting the Abbey

Access to Mont St.-Michel (abbaye-mont-saint-michel.fr, lemontsaintmichel.info) is now by footbridge or by shuttle bus or horse and carriage that take you from the visitor's center to the entrance of the mount. Buses and cars are obliged to park in the designated lot. Every 18 years or so, a supertide covers the causeway road that links Mont St.-Michel with the mainland and turns the abbey fortress into an island again. If you go in spring, pack a bag, just in case.

and 16th-century houses. This primary access road leads steeply up to the abbey's stairway, the **Grand Degré.**

During the revolution, the abbey buildings were turned into a prison, and it was not until the mid-19th century, after a public outcry led by Victor Hugo, that restoration began. In addition to repair work, a spire was added to the church. The architect moved in, along with his maid, Mère Poulard, who married the baker's son and established a hotel. Her restaurant on the lower slopes of the mount remains to this day.

In 1966, monks returned and Mont St.-Michel is once more a Benedictine foundation: Monastic life continues despite the tourists. Visit early or late, or attend the daily lunchtime Mass.

The **Scriptorial** in Avranches, completed in 2007, exhibits thousands of Mont St.-Michel books and medieval manuscripts, most on view for the first time since the French Revolution. ■

# More Places to Visit in Normandy

## Caen

Heavily restored after World War II, Caen nevertheless retains magnificent vestiges of its past. This was the site chosen by William the Conqueror for his castle in the 11th century. As penance for their consanguineous marriage, he and his wife, Matilda, endowed the city with two Romanesque jewels, the **Abbaye aux Hommes** and the **Abbaye aux Dames.** The great church of St.-Étienne, in the Abbaye aux Hommes, sheltered hundreds of citizens during the 1944 bombardment; today the abbey houses the fine **Musée des Beaux-Arts.** Also worth visiting is the D-Day museum, **Le Mémorial** (see p. 167). *caenlamer-tourisme.fr* 157 D3 **Visitor Information** place St.-Pierre 02 31 27 14 14

## Cherbourg-Octeville

The great port of Cherbourg, on the tip of the Cotentin Peninsula, is famed chiefly for its harbor—and justly so: The building of its great breakwater, 2 miles (3 km) out to sea, was a heroic achievement, a feat of engineering that spanned two centuries. **Fort du Roule,** overlooking the town, offers panoramic views of the harbor. Cherbourg saw ferocious German resistance in 1944 and now houses the **Musée de la Guerre et de la Libération.** The **Musée Thomas-Henry** *(tel 02 33 23 39 30)* contains works by painter Jean-François Millet, who was born in the nearby village of Gruchy. The biggest attraction is the **Cité de La Mer,** where you can learn about the sea and explore a missile submarine. *cherbourgtourisme.com* 157 D3 **Visitor Information** 3 quai Alexandre III 02 33 93 52 02

## Côte Fleurie

The string of sandy beaches and fashionable resorts west of Honfleur, known as the "flowery coast," was popularized in the 19th century by artists and writers. In the 1860s, Napoleon III started bringing his court for summer visits to **Trouville-sur-Mer** *(map 139 E3, visitor information, boulevard F. Moureaux, tel 02 31 14 60 70, trouvillesurmer.org).* Fashionable Paris flocked in his wake, the journey facilitated by the new railroad.

   Even grander is **Deauville** *(map 157 E3, visitor information, place de la Mairie, tel 02 31 14 40 00, indeauville.fr),* the 19th-century creation of one of Napoleon's dukes, who also built its racecourse. The casino followed, along with the famous esplanade, Les Planches. Both Trouville-sur-Mer and Deauville boast exuberant villas and some very grand hotels.

   Farther west is **Cabourg** *(map 157 E3, visitor information, place Bruno Coquatrix, tel 02 31 28 88 88, cabourg.net),* immortalized in all its belle epoque elegance by Marcel Proust in *À la Recherche du Temps Perdu (Remembrance of Things Past),* under the pen name Balbec. The glorious beach is still there, as is the astonishing seaside architecture, including the Grand Hôtel, where Proust stayed (and where madeleines are served for breakfast, naturally).

## Dieppe

Dieppe, one of the deepest harbors on the English Channel, prospered through trade in the 16th and 17th centuries, but its heyday was as a 19th-century beach resort, the nearest geographically to Paris and very fashionable. Today, visitors enjoy the seafront esplanade, casino, amusement parks, seawater pools, and busy port. *dieppetourisme.com* ⚑ 157 E3 **Visitor Information** ✉ Pont Jehan-Ango ☎ 02 32 14 40 60

## Granville

Visit the childhood home of Christian Dior *(rue d'Estouteville, tel 02 33 61 48 21, musee-dior-granville.com),* a superb pink-and-white belle epoque villa on a cliff overlooking the sea, surrounded by beautiful gardens originally planned by the fashion designer's mother. The collection includes costumes, hats, and many accessories and artifacts. In summer you can take tea in the garden and enjoy the splendid views of the sea. ⚑ 157 D2

## Honfleur

This delightful harbor town at the mouth of the Seine has retained much of the charm that attracted artists in the 19th century, among them Boudin and Pissarro. It remains a magnet for artists: Painters perch on the quaysides, and exhibitions of contemporary art are held in the converted 17th-century warehouses around the Vieux Bassin, the old fishing port. The **Musée Eugène-Boudin** tells the compelling story of Honfleur's artistic past, with works by Boudin, Dufy, and Monet. One of Monet's many subjects was the 15th-century **Église Ste.-Catherine,** a structure built of wood and a rare surviving example of the medieval shipwright's craft. *ot-honfleur .fr* ⚑ 157 E3 **Visitor Information** ✉ quai le Paulmier ☎ 02 31 89 23 30

## Le Havre & the Côte d'Albâtre

Aside from the St. François quarter around the old docks, Le Havre has little to show for its long history as a major port. But the new town built by architect Auguste Perret on the ruins left by World War II is an example of bold 20th-century urban planning and was designated a UNESCO World Heritage site in 2005. The glass-and-steel **Musée Malraux** *(closed Tues.)* is an outstanding example of modern design, with works by Boudin, Dufy, and others. North of Le Havre and across the estuary now spanned by the vast Pont de Normandie stretch the dazzling white cliffs of the Côte d'Albâtre (Alabaster Coast). The chic little town of **Étretat,** nestling between huge cliffs, is famous for its rock formations. *lehavretourisme.com* ⚑ 157 E3 **Visitor Information** ✉ 186 boulevard Clemenceau, Le Havre ☎ 02 32 74 04 04

# BRITTANY

**Wave-lashed and windswept, Brittany's breathtaking coastline stretches for more than 700 miles (1,100 km), a world of rocky peninsulas and headlands, mist-wreathed islands and tiny harbors, secret coves and hidden inlets. Its strength is in fortified towns such as St.-Malo and Vitré, and its wealth in the ports that shelter its fishing fleet and the old fishing villages that now double as resorts. Its drama lies in the towering cliffs of Finistère and the fantastic—and treacherous—rock formations of the Côte de Granit Rose.**

Here the sea is a force to be treated with respect. But the mild climate, sheltered bays, and magnificent beaches also make Brittany a perfect place for family vacations, and a paradise for bird-watchers. Its clear skies and wild beauty have inspired generations of artists, including Turner, Monet, Picasso, and perhaps most famously Gauguin, who exulted: "I love Brittany. There is something wild and primitive about it. When my wooden clogs strike this granite, I hear the dull, muffled, powerful tone I seek in my painting."

Inland from the Armor, the Celtic name meaning land of the sea, lies the Argoat, or land of forests, the mysterious interior that was the legendary haunt of King Arthur. This is the heart of rural Brittany, a landscape of wild woodland, remote moorland, and fertile fields, threaded by rivers and studded with historic towns and villages. In Brittany, the rich legacy of the past is everywhere apparent, in great Gothic cathedrals and medieval castles, Renaissance manors and solid granite farmhouses, frescoed churches and Finistère's unique parish closes.

Far older in geological terms than the "mainland" of France, Brittany has a timeless quality. Nowhere else in Europe has such a wealth of megalithic monuments, including the mysterious alignments at Carnac. The Celtic legacy of Cornish settlers in the fifth century B.C. still permeates Brittany's language and culture. Independent of France until the 16th century, the province retains a fierce pride in its local traditions: The Breton language is still alive among the old, who remember it, and the young, who are taught it. Visitors may enjoy a taste of Breton culture in the many summer festivals and *pardons* (religious processions). ∎

■ **The fine sand beaches along the old summer resort of Val-André are made for walking.**

# RENNES

The capital of Brittany since 1561, Rennes today is a lively university town and telecommunications research center. Although few of its inhabitants actually speak Breton, it is the focal point for the revival of academic interest in Breton culture. The town is at its most spectacular in early July, when it erupts into a street festival (Les Tombées de la Nuit), celebrating music, poetry, and dance.

Although Rennes flourished in the Middle Ages, it lost most of its medieval buildings in a disastrous fire in 1720. This disastrous conflagration razed much of the town and the townspeople were forced to begin again with their urban *tabula rasa*.

In rebuilding, its citizens redesigned as well, and the result is a city of superb 18th-century buildings that wraps itself around a small medieval nucleus. Most of the old streets, with charmingly crooked half-timbered houses, are located in a relatively small area around the **Place des Lices.** Used for medieval jousting events, this square now hosts an excellent market on Saturday mornings. Look particularly for the medieval houses around Place Ste.-Anne, Rue de la Psalette, Rue St.-Georges, and Rue du Chapitre.

Sadly, the magnificent 17th-century **Palais de Justice** *(place du Palais),* the parliament building and survivor of the 1720 fire, was almost completely burned during fishermen's riots in 1994, but it is now reopened

## Les Tombées de la Nuit

Brittany exists on Europe's Celtic fringe, alongside coastal lands including Wales, Scotland, Ireland, and the Isle of Man.

To celebrate this heritage, the townsfolk of Rennes come out to make merry during the first three weekends in July. Les Tombées de la Nuit *(tel 02 99 32 56 56; lestombeesdelanuit.com)* is a lively festival of Celtic music, dance, and theater performances, staged in the streets of the town and in various churches. This "Nightfalls" Festival offers a feast of Breton culture, ranging from ancient instrumentation *(telen* or Breton harp to local bagpipes called *biniou)* to choral singing to dance and poetry.

after major renovation. The **Cathédrale St.-Pierre** *(tel 02 99 67 11 11 for guided tours),* in the center of old

**Rennes** ⚠ 157 C1 Visitor Information ✉ 11 rue St.-Yves ☎ 02 99 67 11 11 **tourisme-rennes.com**

Rennes, dates from 1844 but has a 16th-century Flemish altarpiece.

The stately public buildings and grand town houses of Rennes are laid out in a geometric arrangement around the Place de l'Hôtel de Ville. Worth noting are the Hôtel de Ville itself, the superb arcading of the Théâtre, and the Palais du Commerce. To the east lies the **Jardin du Thabor,** a delightful botanical and rose garden.

South of the river is the **Musée des Beaux-Arts** *(20 quai Émile Zola, tel 02 23 62 17 45, mbar.org, closed Mon.),* noted for its Georges de La Tour "Virgin and Child" and works from the Pont-Aven school. The **Musée de Bretagne** *(10 cours des Allies, tel 02 23 40 66 00, musee-bretagne.fr, closed Mon.)* offers an excellent overview of Breton history and culture. ■

**INSIDER TIP:**

The big idea of Les Tombées de la Nuit is "to find new ways of occupying public space and imagining the relationship with the spectator," according to its organizers. Don't be afraid to bring a picnic and some *calva*, seek out your best vantage point on the streets of Rennes, and then join in the singing and the dancing.

—JACK KAVANAGH
*National Geographic author*

■ **Front view of the facade of the Palais de Justice, which houses the court of appeal of Rennes.**

# ST.-MALO

This virtually impregnable port was known for centuries as the city of pirates. Its privateers plundered ships in the English Channel, building fine houses with the proceeds. More law-abiding corsairs from St.-Malo explored the distant Falkland Islands, and Jacques Cartier, who began the colonization of Canada in the 16th century, also sailed from here. Novelist Gustave Flaubert described St.-Malo's gray granite walls as a "crown of stone above the waves."

The first community here was founded on the neighboring island of Aleth (now part of St.-Servan), by the Welsh monk Maclou or Malo in the sixth century. Two centuries later, attacks by Franks drove the population onto the island of St.-Malo, linked to the mainland by a causeway. Behind their fortifications, the townspeople gained a livelihood from the sea.

The narrow streets of the old walled city (the citadel), grouped around the partly 12th-century **Cathédrale St.-Vincent,** are lined with the tall 17th- and 18th-century houses of wealthy shipowners. It is all so authentic that it is hard to believe that they were largely rebuilt, stone by stone, after the bombardments of World War II. Place Chateaubriand has some fine houses and good cafés, and the elegant dwellings on Rue Chateaubriand include the turreted **Maison de la Duchesse Anne.** The same duchess was responsible for the building of the late 15th-century **Château,** which houses the town museum. A walk around the ramparts provides exhilarating views out to sea and inland across the harbor. At low tide, you can walk out from the beach below the ramparts to the island of Grand-Bé, last resting place of the 19th-century writer Chateaubriand, and to the Fort National, built by Vauban. ∎

■ Hiking is nice, but the most impressive view of St.-Malo is undoubtedly from the sea.

**St.-Malo** 🅰 157 C2 Visitor Information ✉ esplanade St.-Vincent ☎ 08 25 13 52 00 **saint-malo-tourisme.com** • **Musée d'Histoire de la Ville et du Pays Malouin** ✉ Château's Great Keep & main tower ☎ 02 99 40 71 57 🕐 Closed Mon. in winter 💲 $$

# CÔTE D'ÉMERAUDE &
# CÔTE DE GRANIT ROSE

The Emerald Coast extends from Pointe de Grouin, west of St.-Malo and north of the oyster port of Cancale, to Val-André to the west, via a string of good beaches, pretty resorts, and headlands with spectacular views. The Côte de Granit Rose is characterized by pink rocks weathered into fantastic shapes.

Rothéneuf, just east of St.-Malo, has a rock face of bizarre sculptures, carved by an eccentric 19th-century cleric. Facing St.-Malo across the Rance Estuary is **Dinard,** described at the beginning of the 20th century as "the most aristocratic and elegant seaside resort in northern Europe." In the mid-19th century, this fishing village was adopted by wealthy British and American visitors. They proceeded to make it their own by lining its cliffs and shore with an extravaganza of villas, with turrets, cupolas, verandas, and other belle epoque embellishments. Dinard and St.-Malo are now linked by a road across the **Rance Barrage** *(tel 02 99 16 37 14),* the dam of the world's first and largest tidal power station, which is open to visitors.

To the west, some splendid beaches and attractive small resorts include **St.-Briac-sur-Mer** with its delightful little coves, the small fishing port of **St.-Jacut-de-la-Mer,** and the sands of **Sables-d'Or-les-Pins** and **Erquy.** The medieval **Fort la Latte** (with two drawbridges) overlooks the bay of La Frenaye, and **Cap Fréhel** offers won-

**INSIDER TIP:**

As a rule, the *sentiers des douaniers* [customs agents' trails] along the Emerald Coast offer great hiking above the sea. The trail near the town of Val-André is particularly scenic.

—GILLES MINGASSON
*National Geographic photographer*

derful views along the coast and over to **Île de Bréhat.** The island is accessible by ferry from Pointe de l'Arcouest. The cliffs here are a bird sanctuary: Keep an eye out for cormorants, razorbills, and guillemots.

Farther west, running from Pointe de l'Arcouest to Trégastel, is the **Côte de Granit Rose,** where winds and tides erode the pink granite rocks into the most extraordinary shapes. The most dramatic section is around the resort of **Perros-Guirec.** From here the **Sentier des Douaniers** ("path of customs officers") leads over cliffs to Ploumanac'h, giving excellent views of **Les Sept-Îles,** a wildlife sanctuary. ■

**Rothéneuf** 🗺 157 C2 Dinard 🗺 157 C2 Visitor Information ✉ 2 boulevard Féart ☎ 02 99 46 94 12 • **Perros-Guirec** 🗺 138 B2 Visitor Information ✉ 21 place Hôtel de Ville ☎ 02 96 23 21 15 **perros-guirec.fr**

# BRETON CUSTOMS

The key to the character and traditions of Brittany—so markedly distinct from anything else in France—lies not only in the rugged nature of the land but also, and more significantly, in the influence of the Celts. The Celtic colonizers who came from Britain during the sixth century B.C. were Druidic nature-worshippers. Their beliefs embraced a world of mystical beings and sorcery. Their monuments were adapted by the Roman invaders who subjugated them, and again by the second wave of British Celts who arrived in the fifth and sixth centuries A.D., bringing Christianity with them.

A traditionally garbed woman and man—a priest—share laughs in a festival performance in Locronan.

From this mix of influences, a distinctive culture developed with its own customs, a strong tradition of music and dance, and a separate language. The Breton language spoken today (by upwards of a quarter of a million people) bears no resemblance whatever to French, but has close links with Welsh, Gaelic, and Cornish.

Against heavy odds, Brittany retained its independence until the 16th century. Only with the death of the formidable Anne, Duchess of Brittany, in 1532 did King François I of France take possession of her daughter and her lands. The province then officially became French, and the Breton language, culture, and customs were suppressed.

## Celtic Spirit

The indomitable Breton spirit has survived through the centuries, nevertheless, and the 20th century has seen a great revival of all things Breton (though advocating independence from France remains a criminal offense). The Breton language is taught in schools, and Celtic music has experienced a tremendous upsurge in interest.

To experience Breton fervor at its most intense, you can attend one of several major festivals of Celtic culture. These celebrations of music, theater, dance, and poetry are held every year, but the biggest of them all is the Interceltic Festival in Lorient (see sidebar below). Other festivals of note are held in Rennes (Les Tombées de la Nuit, the first three weekends of July [see pp. 174–175]) and Quimper (the festival de Cornouaille, in the week up to the fourth Sunday in July).

The *telen,* or Breton harp, was a forerunner of today's modern harps.

### Pardons

Celtic Christians had a particular reverence for nature, and they were content to integrate their faith with other beliefs and religious customs, adopting local saints and holy wells and springs. The pagan figure of Ankou, a grim reaper figure representing death, made unique and

## A Celebration of Brittany's Celtic Past and Present

The Interceltic Festival in Lorient *(tel 02 97 21 24 29, festival-interceltique.bzh)* is the biggest Celtic event in Brittany, attracting revelers from all seven Celtic countries. The Celts were once the most powerful people in Europe and they still like a party. Distinctive Celtic crosses and symbols survive in many places. Hundreds of names of places, including Paris, have Celtic roots. The Celts were artistic and skilled and had a strong oral tradition of song and storytelling. But they left no written history and have traditionally been relegated to the role of pre-Roman barbarians. Today the countries of the seven Celtic nations around the Bay of Biscay—Asturias and Galicia in Spain, Cornwall, Wales, Scotland, Ireland, and Brittany—all claim their Celtic roots. In a popular celebration of cultural solidarity, well over a quarter of a million people come to Brittany in August and attend more than a hundred different shows, while Scotch whisky, Irish whiskey, and Guinness flow with French and Spanish wines and ciders.

vivid appearances in Breton religious imagery, as witnessed in the *danse macabre* in the 13th-century chapel of Kermaria, located just off the D786 between St.-Brieuc and Paimpol. The early Christian missionaries were soon elevated from being dragon-slaying miracle workers to the status of saints, revered within Brittany but largely unknown to the the powerbrokers of the Vatican on its canonization committees.

The Breton passion for music and dance, ritual, and religion come together in the *pardons:* annual processions to the shrines of local saints to make a vow or seek forgiveness. A Mass is followed by a procession; participants carry statues and relics and sing hymns, and some still wear traditional costume.

These pardons offer an opportunity to admire the men's intricately embroidered vests and the women's headdresses: magnificent confections of lace and starched linen, sometimes with holes to let the wind pass through. Each village has a traditional shape and style of headdress. After the procession, the whole village celebrates with traditional music and dancing.

Of the many pardons, some of the most impressive are those of St.-Yves, the patron saint of Brittany, an ecclesiastical lawyer who helped poor clients, at Tréguier *(third Sun. in May);* of Ste.-Anne at Ste.-Anne-d'Auray *(July 25–26);* and of the Petite Troménie at Locronan *(second Sun. in July),* when the procession climbs a hill, a place of spiritual retreat (Tro Minihy—Tour of the Retreat—Troménie in French). The Grande Troménie, when the procession goes right around the hill, takes place every six years; the next will be in July of 2025.

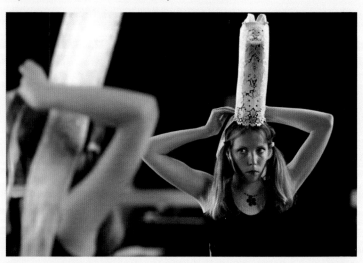

◼ **In Lorient, a teenager dons a traditional tall Breton cap crafted of lace.**

# PARISH CLOSES OF FINISTÈRE

The *enclos paroissiaux,* or parish closes, of Finistère are a phenomenon unique to Brittany, enshrining in this remotest part of a far-flung region not only the devoutness of traditional Breton Catholicism but also its somber preoccupation with death.

Dating mainly from the 15th century to the 17th, these walled church-yards typically contain, alongside the church and graveyard, a triumphal arch symbolizing entry into paradise, an ossuary, and, most importantly, a calvary. Stone carvings—intricate, sometimes primitive, and often very moving—frequently digress to include local legends, with figures clearly based on local characters. This was a prosperous period in Breton history, and villages made rich by the linen trade vied with each other in the extravagance of their parish closes. Two of the most flamboyant are located close together south of Morlaix, at St.-Thégonnec and Guimiliau.

The close of **St.-Thégonnec** *(map 157 B2)* spared no expense in attempting to outdo Guimiliau, its rival, in splendor, employing the finest craftsmen from as far away as England. The result is a rather indigestible but undeniably impressive interior to its vast church, with an especially fine pulpit. The calvary contains a wealth of detail and intriguing figures, including St. Thégonnec himself, shown with the wolves he harnessed to his plow after they consumed his horses. The events surrounding the Crucifixion appear slightly muddled. This is because many of the elements of the

■ **The 16th-century** *enclos paroissal* **of the Guehénno, which has been restored, depicts the Crucifixion.**

calvary, hidden for safekeeping before the revolution, were put back afterward in the wrong order.

The even more fabulous calvary at **Guimiliau** *(map 157 B2)*, a few miles away, teems with more than 200 figures depicting scenes from the life of Christ. A riot of other figures includes Kate Gollet (Katharine the Damned), who suffered a variety of deaths according to different calvaries. Here she is shown being torn apart at the gates of hell for stealing a holy wafer.

Other fine—and sometimes refreshingly simple—parish closes are to be seen nearby at Sizun, Commana, Ploudiry, La Martyre, and Guehénno near Josselin. ■

**Finistère** 🅰 156 B3  Visitor Information ✉ 14 avenue Foch, Landivisiau
☎ 02 98 68 33 33 **roscoff-tourisme.com**

# QUIMPER

Brittany's oldest city and capital of the ancient duchy of Cornouaille, Quimper has a history that begins in legend. King Gradlon founded Quimper after the flooding of his fabulous city of Ys, off Douarnenez. The spot he chose lay at the confluence (*kemper* in Breton) of the Odet and Steir Rivers, and the Odet threads through the cobbled streets of the medieval quarter, crossed by low, flower-decked bridges.

The delightful old town is dominated by the huge 13th-century Gothic **Cathédrale St.-Corentin,** its nave strangely set at an angle to the choir. The **Musée des Beaux-Arts** *(40 place St.-Corentin, tel 02 98 95 45 20, mbaq .fr)* has an outstanding collection of 19th- and 20th-century works, including some from the school of nearby Pont-Aven, where Paul Gauguin painted his colorful works.

Quimper is also famous for its very pretty faience, a local industry since the 17th century. Check out the **Musée de la Faïence** and the shops in Quimper, where you can buy the folk art porcelain, and visit the factory of the oldest of the *faienceries,* **HB-Henriot** *(place Berardir, tel 02 98 90 09 52 36, henriot-quimper .com, closed Dec.–Feb.),* to observe the manufacturing process. ∎

## Concarneau

A major fishing port located some 13 miles (22 km) southeast of Quimper and now also a resort, Concarneau's chief attraction is its **Ville Close,** the walled old town on an island in the bay. This rocky perch had been inhabited for centuries before its fortifications were started in the 13th century. The Hundred Years' War increased its strategic importance, and the defenses were strengthened again in the 17th century by Louis XIV's military architect Vauban. There are wonderful views to be enjoyed from the ramparts, and the tiny streets are full of restaurants and souvenir shops. The old barracks now house the **Musée de la Pêche** *(3 rue Vauban, tel 02 98 97 10 20, musee-peche.fr),* devoted to the local fishing industry. In the second half of August, the Ville Close comes alive with the Fête des Filets Bleus ("blue nets"), a festival of Breton music and dancing that developed from the tradition of blessing the fishing nets.

**Quimper** 🅰 156 B1 Visitor Information ✉ place de la Résistance
☏ 02 98 53 04 05 **quimper-tourisme.com** • **Musée de la Faïence**
✉ 14 rue Jean Baptiste Bourqe ☏ 02 98 90 012 72 **musee-faience**
**-quimper.com** • **Concarneau** 🅰 156 B1 Visitor Information
✉ quai d'Aiguillon ☏ 02 98 97 01 44 **tourismeconcarneau.fr**

# CARNAC & ITS MENHIRS

Brittany is strewn with megaliths—menhirs, cairns, passage graves, and dolmens—hewn from solid granite and put in place by a shadowy Neolithic civilization. How or why, no one knows for certain. Of them all, the stone circles and alignments at Carnac, which means "the place where there are piles of stones," are the most staggering in their sheer size, number, and complexity. Possibly dating back as far as 5000 B.C., making them far older than Stonehenge, they are now recognized as the most important prehistoric site in Europe.

Some of the lines of stones may originally have stretched as much as 2.5 miles (4 km) in length, each containing thousands of menhirs. A construction on this scale, and of this degree of difficulty, was clearly of enormous significance to the civilization that built it. Modern-day archaeologists generally favor the theory that this entire site formed a vast astronomical observatory.

Visit in the early morning or at dusk to avoid the crowds. To make the leap back in time necessary to

■ Menhirs that date back some 5,000 years continue to weather the elements at Le Ménec.

## Menhirs

Marching silently over the land, row after row and mile after mile, Brittany's many thousands of megaliths manage to impress us with a sense of deep significance while remaining unfathomably mysterious. As archaeologist R. P. Giot remarked: "We may conclude, simply, that they are religious monuments, and in resorting to this vague, easy description we may attempt to conceal our ignorance."

According to legend, the megaliths were Roman soldiers turned to stone by St. Cornély as they pursued him to the sea. Earlier centuries thought they were part of Roman or Celtic burial rites or that they were intended to help sailors find their bearings. Not until the late 18th century was the astronomical significance of the alignments first noted, and no other theory since has dislodged this one.

Was Carnac an observatory for following the motions of the stars, with a view to predicting the days of the summer solstice and the equinoxes? This would have enabled the designers to establish a calendar for sowing and harvesting.

The gigantic menhir at nearby Locmariaquer—a coastal commune known for oysters—was probably part of the same huge complex. Toppled by an earthquake in the 18th century and now lying in four pieces, this colossus once stood some 65 feet (20 m) high. Near it stands the dolmen known as the Table des Marchands, decorated with graceful spirals and curves.

The same ancient designs cover the burial chamber on Île de Gavrinis in the Golfe du Morbihan, where many of these mysterious stones are now half engulfed by the waves.

set the stones in context, start out your visit at the **Musée de Préhistoire** in Carnac.

The stones are set in three main locations: The largest, at **Le Ménec,** just north of Carnac beyond the D196, consists of two oval-shaped enclosures, one of which has a medieval village built on top. Here 12 lines of menhirs (with

more than a thousand stones in the principal alignment) extend for nearly a mile (1.6 km).

Access is restricted in order to protect the site from erosion, and plans are well under way for long-term protection. The **Maison des Megaliths** provides a viewing platform and informative audiovisual displays.

**Carnac** ⚐ 156 B1 Visitor Information ✉ 74 avenue des Druides ☎ 02 97 52 13 52 **ot-carnac.fr** • **Musée de Préhistoire** ✉ Place Christian Bonnet ☎ 02 97 52 22 04 🕐 Closed Dec.–Feb. & Tues. except in July & Aug. 💲 $$ **museedecarnac.com** • **Maison des Megaliths (Alignements du Ménec)** ✉ Carnac ☎ 02 97 52 29 81

The best preserved alignments are to be found at **Kermario.** Here, more than a thousand menhirs are arranged in ten lines, with the giant of Le Manio, at 21 feet (6.5 m) the largest menhir still standing at this site, surrounded by smaller stones. **Kerlescan** is home to another 594 stones, arranged in 13 lines, featuring a covered passageway that may be indicative of an ancient burial site.

Just to the east of Carnac rises the **Tumulus St.-Michel,** a tremendously ancient burial ground probably laid out around 4000 B.C. At the summit, the little chapel of St.-Michel has an orientation table overlooking the entire area. **Carnac-Ville** itself is a pretty town with many gardens and avenues and a 17th-century church. It is located just inland from the popular resort of Carnac-Plage.

A good way to savor the landscape and sea views is on a **Golfe du Morbihan** boat trip *(tel 02 97 57 19 38).* You can glimpse many of the stones from the sea and visit the tiny island of **Gavrinis**—only accessible by boat and guided tour—with its burial chamber and extraordinary carvings. Trips can be made from Vannes, Locmariaquer, Port Navalo, La Trinité-sur-Mer, or Auray.

As you step from the boat, you may experience similar reactions to many who visit the various ancient sites around Carnac: A sense of being spirited back to a time when the

**GLOSSARY**
*alignment:* row of upright stones
*dolmen:* two uprights roofed with a third; probably the supports of a burial chamber originally covered with earth
*menhir:* upright stone

**INSIDER TIP:**

**Windsurfers (and other sporting human amphibians) all adore St.-Colomban beach in nearby Carnac-Plage. It's a resort town also loved for its delicious oysters.**

—JAYNE WISE
*National Geographic senior editor*

sky above our heads and the ground beneath our feet were all that humans had to guide our passage, through this life and the next. ∎

■ The entrance to the burial mound of Gavrinis.

# More Places to Visit in Brittany

## Brest

Brest, one of France's key naval ports, suffered heavy damage during World War II. You can still see the remains of the 11th-century château and tour the naval town. Explore the marine world at **Océanopolis** (*Port de Plaisance du Moulin Blanc, tel 02 98 34 40 40, oceanopolis.com, closed Mon. Sept.–March, $$$*), an important research center with three pavilions that showcase the polar, tropical, and temperate marine ecosystems. Discover the flora and fauna of the underwater world in beautiful settings. The huge variety of exhibits includes a colony of 40 penguins and France's biggest seaweed forest. *brest-metropole-tourisme.fr* ⛰ 156 B2 **Visitor Information** ✉ place de la Liberté ☎ 02 98 44 24 96

## Crozon Peninsula & Pointe du Raz

The most magnificent spots on the coastline of southern Finistère are the rocky fingers of the Crozon Peninsula and the Pointe du Raz. Cliff paths lead out to the westernmost points: to Pointe du Raz from Lescoff, and to Pointe de Pen-Hir on the Crozon Peninsula from Veryach beyond Camaret. ⛰ 156 A2–B2

## Dinan

A lovely walled citadel, Dinan has been tactfully restored. Medieval cobbled streets, two fine churches, and a 14th-century keep lie within its 13th-century defenses. *dinan-capfrehel.com* ⛰ 157 C2 **Visitor Information** ✉ 9 rue du Château ☎ 02 96 87 69 76

## Fougères & Vitré

These two fortified frontier towns guarded the old border between Brittany and France. In its spectacular position on a loop of the Nançon River, the stronghold at **Fougères** (*map 157 D2, visitor information, 2 rue Nationale, tel 02 99 79 59, chateau-fougeres.com*) is a feudal fortress par excellence. A rocky moat surrounding the 11th-century core was later reinforced by 13 splendid towers.

Standing guard over the Vilaine Valley, the fairy-tale turrets and drawbridge of the castle at **Vitré** (*map 157 D1, visitor information, place du Général-de-Gaulle, tel 02 99 74 58 59*) were also begun in the 11th century. The ramparts offer fine views over a maze of half-timbered houses to the 15th-century Flamboyant Gothic church.

## Josselin

The three slate-roofed turrets of Josselin's mighty castle, rising from a wall of granite dropping down into the Oust River, make one of the most famous Breton silhouettes. Built by the powerful Rohan family in the 14th century, it is their home to this day but is open to the public. *chateaudejosselin.com* ⛰ 157 C1 **Visitor Information** ✉ place de la Congrégation ☎ 02 97 22 36 45

## Tréguier

The spire of a 14th-century cathedral dedicated to dragon-slaying St. Tugdual dominates the hill town of Tréguier. The *pardon* of St. Yves occurs here on the third Sunday in May. **Visitor Information** ✉ 67 rue Ernest Renan ☎ 02 96 92 22 33

Often considered to be the most quintessentially French region of this multifaceted country, with mild climate, delicate light, and gentle landscapes

# LOIRE VALLEY

# LOIRE VALLEY

The chief glory of the Loire Valley—now a UNESCO World Heritage site—lies in the magnificent châteaus studding the banks of the river and its tributaries like jewels. The playground of medieval kings and nobles, the valley was to become the cradle of the artistic explosion of the French Renaissance. Today these sumptuous palaces and castles and their noble gardens are among France's chief attractions.

The Loire is France's longest river, flowing some 600 miles (1,000 km) from its source in the Ardèche to its estuary at St.-Nazaire on the Atlantic coast. Most of the time, the river is a wide, slow stream, but sometimes it floods and breaks its banks. Raised embankments, *levées*, have been built up to contain it, but controversy rages over proposals to control it further with barrages and dams. Although the Loire was a crucial trade and communications route for centuries, today much of this beloved river is so silted up and shallow that it is barely navigable.

The Loire region is divided into two administrative areas, Centre and Pays de la Loire. Centre has the great city of Orléans as its capital, and includes Tours in the west and Bourges to the south. Its landscapes

## NOT TO BE MISSED:

encompass vast wheatfields in the Beauce, the area north of the Loire, and the lakes and forests of the Sologne south of the river, historically a favored royal hunting ground. Farther south still, the rolling hills of the Berry region are one of the most rural parts of France.

Touraine, the old name for the area around Tours, is the heart of the Loire Valley, its rich soils producing melons, asparagus, plums, strawberries, and some of the Loire's best wines. Many of the ravishing châteaus are in Touraine.

The Pays de la Loire starts just west of Tours and includes Angers, Le Mans, Nantes (the capital), and the Vendée to the south. Anjou, the old name for the region around Angers, was once a powerful duchy, with lands as far afield as Provence and Sicily. It was in the Loire Valley that the English were memorably defeated by Jeanne d'Arc at Orléans, and her memory is still cherished throughout the region. ■

# ORLÉANS

Because of its strategic but vulnerable position on a great bend of the Loire, Orléans has suffered greatly over the centuries, culminating in the devastation of the city center in World War II. Nevertheless, it now has fine restaurants, excellent shopping (especially on Rue Royale), and beautiful parks.

Start in Place du Martroi, with its statue of Jeanne d'Arc, and explore the rebuilt medieval streets of the old quarter. On Place du Général-de-Gaulle is the **Maison Jeanne d'Arc,** where the saint rested in 1429 after defeating the English. **Hôtel Groslot** on Place d'Étape is a fine Renaissance building. **Cathédrale Ste.-Croix** *(place Ste.-Croix)*, built in Gothic style, has long aroused controversy (Proust considered it the ugliest building in France), but it is interesting for its wedding-cake towers, grand nave, and huge rose window. Museums include the **Musée des Beaux-Arts** *(place Ste.-Croix, tel 02 38 79 21 55, closed Mon.)*, with works by Tintoretto and Velázquez, and the **Musée Historique et Archéologique** *(place de l'Abbé Desnoyers, tel 02 38 79 25 60, closed Mon.)*, whose exhibits include Celtic bronze statues. Outside Orléans, head south for Olivet, where you can visit the glorious **Parc Floral de la Source,** a 245-acre (100 ha) nature reserve surrounding a delightful 17th-century château. ■

## Jeanne d'Arc

The Maid of Orléans is honored annually in Orléans on May 7 and 8, the anniversary of the days in 1429 when she liberated the city from the besieging English forces, thus becoming one of French history's most potent heroines.

This young peasant girl from Lorraine (see p. 154) was first noticed when she came to Chinon and recognized the Dauphin, Charles VII, among a crowd of courtiers. She claimed that heavenly voices had instructed her to save him. She succeeded in rallying the French troops and relieving Orléans. The English were driven away, and she led Charles to Reims to be crowned. But a series of disasters led to her capture by the English, who tried her as a witch and burned her at the stake in Rouen on May 30, 1431. She was canonized a saint in 1920.

**Orléans** ▲ 189 E3 Visitor Information ✉ 2 place de l'Étape ☎ 02 38 68 32 63 **tourisme-orleans.com** • **Maison Jeanne d'Arc** ✉ 3 place du Général-de-Gaulle ☎ 02 38 52 99 89 🕘 Closed Mon. & a.m. Nov.–April 💲 $ • **Parc Floral de la Source** ✉ Orléans-la-Source ☎ 02 38 49 30 00 💲 $ (park), $$ (park & greenhouse) **parcfloraldelasource.com**

# BLOIS

Clinging prettily to hills overlooking the Loire, Blois makes a perfect touring base, small enough to be accessible and situated for exploring both up- and downriver. Its steeply winding streets, lined with half-timbered buildings, alleys, and hidden courtyards, have preserved both the architecture and the atmosphere of the town's illustrious past. The surrounding farmland and the game forests of the nearby Sologne area keep restaurants supplied with fine ingredients.

■ The Château de Blois underscores the power of royal taste and budget.

Blois is still dominated by its magnificent **château** *(place du Château, tel 02 54 90 33 33, chateaude blois.fr, $$)*. The great 13th-century Gothic hall and tower remain from the original fortress. Subsequent additions present an extraordinary mix of architectural styles. Louis XII *(R. 1498–1515)* transformed it into an opulent palace (his emblem, the porcupine, is everywhere). His son, François I *(R. 1515–1547)*, created its greatest feature, the octagonal open spiral staircase that forms part of the dazzling François I wing.

The cabinet of Catherine de Médicis is intriguing for its secret closets in which she reputedly hid her poisons. The château is also notorious for the murder of the Catholic Duc de Guise at the instigation of his Protestant brother, Henri III *(R. 1574–1589)*, fearful of the growing power of the Catholics. Henri was himself murdered only six months later.

The Louis XII wing of the château houses the **Musée des Beaux-Arts Décoratifs** and **Musée Archéologique;** the terrace gardens offer a view of the town, the Loire, the 18th-century bridge, and the 12th-century church of St.-Nicolas. A fine restaurant is set in the Orangerie (see Travelwise p. 427). ■

**Blois** 189 D3–E3 Visitor Information ✉ Pavillon Anne de Bretagne, 23 place du Château ☎ 02 54 90 41 41 **bloischambord.com** • **Musée des Beaux-Arts Décoratifs & Musée Archéologique** ✉ place du Château ☎ 02 54 70 33 33 $ Entrance included with château ticket

# CHAMBORD

The largest of the Loire châteaus, Chambord is a Renaissance masterpiece on an enormous scale, with 440 rooms, 85 staircases, and 365 chimneys—a fireplace for every day of the year. It was a simple hunting lodge until 1519, when François I decided to build himself the ultimate château. He was greatly inspired by Italian architecture and had invited Leonardo da Vinci to live at Amboise. It seems more than likely that Leonardo may have drawn the first plans for the château, including a scheme to divert the Loire to flow past it.

Chapel

Central staircase

Main courtyard

Royal gate

For 25 years almost 2,000 craftsmen and masons labored to build the Château de Chambord. Designed in the shape of a cross, the central keep is flanked by four towers and enclosed by a courtyard. The **Grand Staircase** rises through the keep to a lantern tower that was originally open, though glass was later added. This famous double spiral staircase was designed so that two people—one going up and one going down—could always see each other but would meet only at the top and bottom.

Apartments flank the staircase on four sides, and everywhere you see the image of the salamander, emblem of François I. Grandest of the rooms are the state apartments; in particular, the **bedchamber** hung with richly embroidered velvet, added by Louis XIV, who finished the château in 1685 while he waited for Versailles to be built.

Most extraordinary of all is the roof, a riot of gables, turrets, and spires, likened by Vivian Rowe to "the skyline of Constantinople on a single building." The roof terraces were designed for the court to watch summer spectacles or herald the king on his return from the hunt. They make a splendid vantage point to survey the vast estate of 13,600 acres (5,550 ha) that surrounds this magnificent château. ■

François I tower

Roof terrace

Keep

Chambord

**Chambord** 🗺 167
E3 Visitor Information
✉ 78–82 rue Bernard-Palissy ☎ 02 54 50 40 00 🕐 Closed Dec. 25, Jan. 1, & May 1 💲 $$$
**chambord.org**

# FOOD & DRINK—GEMS OF THE SOIL

**Vineyards flank the Loire along much of its length, though the Loire wines do not rank with those of Burgundy or Bordeaux. But for relaxation between visiting the châteaus and hearing the history of noble pleasures, try the excellent wines and regional dishes so graciously offered today.**

*"Artichokes and salad greens, asparagus, parsnips and the melons of Touraine, all are more tempting than great mounds of royal meats."*
—Pierre de Ronsard (1524–1585)

Vines were first planted in the Loire Valley by the Romans, then grown assiduously by the monks who established important abbeys throughout the region. Their wines were drunk enthusiastically by the kings, queens, and courtiers who made the fertile Loire Valley their playground. In recent years, the Loire vineyards have made great efforts to improve the quality of their wines and to promote those that have always been revered.

Restaurants in the Loire area will have a good list of local wines, and

there are signs everywhere for *dégustation*, or wine tasting (and buying, of course), at the vineyards themselves. Ask at a town's *syndicat d'initiative* or tourist office for a list of the nearby vineyards that welcome visitors.

Loire Valley wines are light, fresh, and sometimes relatively low in alcohol. White wines predominate, based on the Chenin Blanc, Muscadet, and Sauvignon Blanc grapes, perfect with shellfish, to fine Vouvrays and Sancerres farther east. Of the rosé wines, Rosé d'Anjou is the best known, and the Cabernet Franc grape grown here makes a number of good reds. Seek out the fruity reds of Chinon and Bourgeuil. In Saumur, look for the *méthode champenoise* (champagne method) sparkling wines. Most voluptuous of all are the sweet dessert wines of the Coteaux du Layon.

These local wines go perfectly with the regional cuisine, which, like the climate of the Loire, is gentle, agreeable, and never extreme. The key is simplicity: Local game, fish, vegetables, and fruit are so good they need only a subtle sauce to bring out the flavor.

The Loire Valley is the garden of France: young white asparagus tips in season, salad crops, squash, mushrooms (grown in caves along the riverside cliffs near Saumur), and tiny potatoes. Rasp-

**Sumptuously simple: Farm-fresh salads and fruity red and white wine are Loire Valley staples.**

berries and strawberries flourish in the market gardens, while orchards yield apples, pears, and quinces as well as plums, especially greengages *(reines claudes)*.

Fish from the river, spotlighted on many menus, include carp and pike, often served with a sauce of shallots, butter, and vinegar *(beurre blanc)*; salmon is delicious with sorrel sauce; and eel is often made into a succulent red wine stew. Tiny fish, impeccably fresh, are served simply fried, and great platters of seafood are available in profusion near the coast. A popular first course having nothing to do with the sea is the exquisitely rich *rillettes du Mans* (shredded pork or rabbit conserved in its own fat).

In Tours, pork is cooked with prunes, game comes from primarily from the Sologne region south of the Loire, and chicken and fat capons are the basis for fricassees and casseroles. Among the traditional local main dishes are duck

■ **Tarte tatin, a buttery caramel apple treat, sets the bar high when it comes to desserts.**

with turnips and chunks of pork cooked until crispy and golden.

Keep an eye out for fresh cheeses, especially the local goat cheese. You can't go wrong with Valençay, Crottin de Chavignol, Sainte-Maure de Touraine, or Crémet de Nantes. Crisp white wines are the best accompaniment for any of these great goat cheeses.

Traditional desserts abound around here, including open tarts of apples and plums, fritters flavored with eau-de-vie, puff pastry almond cake, and tarte tatin (see sidebar below).

## Upside Down & Irresistible

**Tarte tatin** is a famous French dessert, an upside-down apple tart in which the apples are caramelized in butter and sugar before the tart is baked. The story goes that tarte tatin was created by accident at the Hotel Tatin in Lamotte-Beuvron in 1898 by sisters Stéphanie and Caroline Tatin. Stéphanie, who did most of the cooking, was overworked one day. She started to make a more traditional apple dessert but left the apples cooking in butter and sugar for too long. Smelling the burning, she tried to rescue the dish by putting the pastry base on top of the pan of caramelized apples, then quickly finishing the cooking by putting the whole pan in the oven. After turning out the upside-down tart, she served it up and was surprised to find how much the hotel guests liked it.

The tart would become the signature dish at the Hotel Tatin, and the recipe spread through the Sologne region. It gained further fame thanks to the restaurateur Louis Vaudable, who tasted the tart on a visit to Sologne and then decided to make the dessert a permanent fixture on the menu at his world-famous Maxim's in Paris.

# AMBOISE

Although only a fraction now remains of the original Château d'Amboise, its creamy walls and slate roof turrets still make a lovely sight, dominating the Loire River and the charming narrow streets of the old town. For much of the 15th and 16th centuries, Amboise was a favorite residence of French kings, and it was here that the art of the Renaissance first came to France from Italy.

■ The medieval town of Amboise sits on the Loire River.

**INSIDER TIP:**

Amboise is a great château to visit with kids; many royal children grew up here, and there's a tour geared to youngsters.

—SYLVIE BIGAR
*National Geographic writer*

François I established a glittering court life at Amboise, enlivened by tournaments, masked balls, and fireworks designed by none other than Leonardo da Vinci. But in 1560, a Protestant conspiracy to murder the young François II (married to Mary, Queen of Scots) was put down with appalling ferocity, and many hundreds of corpses hung from the battlements.

Nowadays, after a great deal of demolition and a period as a jail, this elegant château is again in royal hands, administered by the Comte de Paris, heir to the French throne. Enjoy the view of the Loire Valley from the terrace, visit the royal apartments in the 15th-century **Gothic Logis du Roi,** and climb the **Tour des Minimes** with its extraordinary spiral ramp designed for carriages. The jewel of Amboise is the 15th-century **Chapelle St.-Hubert,** a dazzling example of Flamboyant Gothic that allegedly contains the tomb of Leonardo da Vinci.

In 1516, Leonardo came to Amboise as painter, engineer, and architect to the king, bringing some favored paintings, including the "Mona Lisa." François I installed Leonardo in the elegant **Château du Clos Lucé** *(2 rue du Clos Lucé, vinci-clos luce.com, tel 02 47 57 00 73, $$$),* just outside Amboise, where you can visit his restored rooms. A museum dedicated to his technical drawings and experiments offers computer-generated models of some of his astonishing inventions. ■

**Amboise** 🅜 189 D2 Visitor Information ✉ quai du Général de Gaulle ☎ 02 47 57 09 28 **amboise-valdeloire.com** • **Château Royal d'Amboise** ☎ 02 47 57 00 98 💲 $$$ **chateau-amboise.com**

# TOURS

**Louis XI's capital, Tours today is a big, prosperous city, well worth exploring for its museums, stores, restaurants, and handsomely restored old buildings.**

An important city even in Gallo-Roman times, Tours enjoyed great wealth and celebrity in the Middle Ages thanks to the tomb of its famous bishop, St. Martin (now in the crypt of the New Basilica). The town flourished during the Renaissance, becoming famous for its silks, jewels, and arms. But several centuries of decline followed, culminating in the devastation of World War II. In 1959, the city began the process of regeneration that has made it a model of modern urban development.

The **Quartier St.-Julien,** bordered by the river, is today all trendy restaurants and antique shops. Start with lively Place Plumereau, lined with cafés and restored half-timbered buildings. Nearby is the Hôtel Gouin, a lavishly sculptured Renaissance building that houses the **Musée de l'Hôtel de Gouin**.

On the other side of Rue Nationale (running across the Pont Wilson, a faithful 1978 reconstruction of an 18th-century stone bridge partly washed away by the river), in the former abbey of St.-Julien, is the **Musée des Vins de Touraine.** Equally fascinating is the **Musée du Compagnonnage** next door, devoted to the history of craft guilds and trades.

**Cathédrale St.-Gatien** *(place de la Cathédrale)* was built from the 13th to the 16th centuries. It is a superb example of the development of the Gothic style. Especially impressive are the Gothic facade, the richly colored medieval stained-glass windows, and a 14th-century fresco of St. Martin and the beggar.

Next door, in the 17th- and 18th-century former Bishop's Palace, is the **Musée des Beaux-Arts** *(18 place François-Sicard, tel 02 47 05 68 73, closed Tues.),* which has two parts of a triptych by Andrea Mantegna (1431–1506). ∎

■ **Cathédrale St.-Gatien boasts Flamboyant Gothic intricacies.**

**Tours** 🅰 189 D2 Visitor Information ✉ 78–82 rue Bernard-Palissy ☎ 02 47 70 37 37 **tours-tourisme.fr • Musée des Vins de Touraine &
Musée du Compagnonnage** ✉ Cloître St. Julien, 16 rue Nationale ☎ 02 47 21 62 20 🕒 Closed Tues. 💲 $

# CHENONCEAU & VILLANDRY

Built by women for women, Chenonceau is perhaps the most romantic château in France. Designed by Catherine Briçonnet in the early 16th century on the foundations of a manor house and watermill, this gem of Renaissance architecture was given by Henri II to his mistress Diane de Poitiers. It was she who in 1556 called in the great architect Philibert Delorme to build a bridge. The glory of the Château de Villandry, another star on the château circuit, is its 16th-century-style garden, faithfully re-created in Renaissance style.

■ Chenonceau spans the gentle water of the broad Cher River on a series of graceful arches.

## Chenonceau

When Henri II died, Diane de Poitiers was ousted by his jealous wife, Catherine de Médicis, who commissioned Delorme to build a two-story gallery on top of the bridge. These remarkable women were succeeded by the widow of Henri III, Louise, who retired here for an 11-year vigil, hanging her bedchamber with black velvet decorated with symbols of death.

Today, an avenue of plane trees leads to the château's forecourt. To the right is the 13th-century keep with a carved Renaissance doorway. Within the château, the lavish rooms have painted ceilings, monumental stone fireplaces, gorgeous Flemish tapestries, and fine paintings.

The Cabinet Vert, Catherine de Médicis's delightful study overlooking the river, was originally hung with green velvet and is still sumptuously

**Château de Chenonceau** 🅰 189 D2 ☎ 02 47 23 44 06 🆂 $$$
chenonceau.com

decorated in fine brocade, while the tragic Queen Louise's bedchamber has been refurbished in funereal black. There is also a little private chapel with stained-glass windows. Do not miss the extraordinary kitchens, deep in the hollow piers supporting the house.

In the 17th century the château fell into oblivion, re-surfacing in the 18th century, when philosopher Jean-Jacques Rousseau stayed here. It escaped damage in the revolution and became a military hospital during World War I.

Since 1913, Chenonceau has been owned by the Menier family, chocolate manufacturers. Try to visit early in the day or, even better, out of high season. Try to spend a day here, viewing the château, boating on the river, strolling in the gardens, and perhaps attending a son et lumière performance.

## Villandry

Less than a hundred years ago, the Château de Villandry was closed in by woodland. It was rescued by a Spanish doctor, Joachim Carvallo, and his wife, Ann, a steel heiress from Philadelphia. After restoring the château, with its moat on three sides, they furnished it in Renaissance style. Then they replanted the gardens as they would have been in the 16th century.

The gardens are on three levels, linked by shady pergolas and fountains. On the upper terrace is the **Jardin d'Eau,** where a huge basin feeds water to the moat and fountains. A linden tree avenue forms the main axis of the gardens. Below is the **Jardin Potager,** or vegetable garden, laid out in geometric patterns, with a variety of fruit trees and herbs.

On the south terrace is the **Jardin d'Ornement,** a love-themed garden with geometric box parterres shaped in flames, butterflies, hearts, and daggers, symbolizing the different manifestations of love. The **Sun Garden** is a cloister of greenery around a sun-shaped fountain, with a garden for children. ■

## French Gardens

The French Renaissance garden—a mix of broad avenues and geometrical patterns, terraces and clipped hedges, statues and water gardens, fountains and pools—was heavily influenced by Italian ideas. André Le Nôtre (1613–1700) was the master of this style, creating château gardens all over France, most famously at **Vaux-le-Vicomte** and **Versailles**. In the 18th century, Marie-Antoinette was largely responsible for the vogue for picturesque and informal gardens à l'anglaise, green spaces loosely inspired by the English landscape tradition. Examples of this style can be seen at the Grand Trianon at Versailles and the **Jardin de Bagatelle** at the Bois de Boulogne. An international garden festival takes place at Chaumont-sur-Loire every August, and Blois has a school of landscape gardening.

**Château de Villandry** ◬ 189 D2 ☎ 02 47 50 02 09 ⏱ Château closed seasonally; check website $ $$$ **chateauvillandry.com**

# A DRIVE ALONG THE INDRE RIVER

This route takes you along the Indre River from Rigny-Ussé as far as Loches. Start at Ussé, picturesquely located to the south of the Indre near its junction with the Loire, between Tours and Saumur.

The beautiful **Château d'Ussé** ❶ *(tel 02 47 95 54 05, chateaudusse .fr, closed mid-Nov.–mid-Feb.; $$)* located on the D7 is a treat: a truly fairy-tale castle of romantic turrets silhouetted against a dark forest. This was the setting of the original *Sleeping Beauty (La Belle au Bois Dormant),* a 17th-century tale by Charles Perrault.

From Rigny-Ussé, the D7 runs parallel to the Indre River, and its great sister the Loire is visible across a fertile floodplain. Flanking the other side of the road is the forest of Chinon. Se-

**NOT TO BE MISSED:**

Château d'Azay-le-Rideau
• Villaines-les-Rochers
basket weavers • Cormery
• Loches

veral turnings into the forest offer a chance for further exploration of its little hamlets.

Just past the village of Rivarennes, turn right on the D17, which follows the Indre and soon passes the little town of **Azay-le-Rideau** ❷ across the water; don't miss the lovely **château** here (see p. 203). Turn south off the D17, to the D57 and the village of **Villaines-les-Rochers** ❸, famous for its baskets made from rushes that grow beside the Indre. You can buy anything here from a bread basket to a baby's crib, and also watch the basket weavers at work.

Return to the river on the D217 and stay south until you reach **Saché** ❹, a small village with a 16th-century manor house set among chestnut trees. In 1835, Balzac wrote *Le Père Goriot* here, having fled from his creditors. It is now a museum *(Château de Saché, tel 02 47 26 86 50, musee-balzac .fr)*, with his rooms perfectly preserved (particularly his bedroom: the bed made up, his coffeepot ready, and his inkwell and quill pen set up for

a day's work atop the little wooden desk). Exhibits include first editions of his works and even his own carefully annotated proofs.

From here to **Montbazon** ❺, both banks of the river are equally rewarding. This is a gentle landscape of little wooded valleys and waterside villages with the river curving past orchards, châteaus, and mills. At Montbazon, the huge 11th-century stone keep now lies in ruins but is well worth climbing for the view. You might also stop at **Château d'Artigny** just outside the town, to indulge in the hospitality afforded by this luxury hotel and restaurant set within an early 20th-century mansion.

The D17 proceeds north of the river to the charming little town of **Cormery** ❻, where the remains of a medieval Benedictine abbey stretch along Rue de l'Abbaye. You can also explore the 12th-century Église de Notre-Dame with its wealth of frescoes, statues, and carvings. Cormery is also famed for its macarons, offering the sweet-toothed traveler one more good reason to stop here.

At Azay-sur-Indre, the Indrois River joins the Indre, and a delightful detour on the D10 takes you up beside the Indrois to **Montrésor ❼**, a peaceful little town beside an ancient château *(tel 02 47 19 27 50, closed Nov.–March except weekends, chateaudemontresor.fr)*. The walls and towers of the 11th-century fortress enclose a much-restored 16th-century residence overlooking the river.

From Azay-sur-Indre, the main route follows the D17; at Chambourg-sur-Indre cross the river and take the D25 along the valley past the forest of Loches, fronted by orchards and meadows. **Loches ❽** *(visitor information, place de la Marne, tel 02 47 19 18 08, citeroyaleloches.fr)* itself is a splendid town, its medieval core set high on a rock overlooking the river. Stroll around the old ramparts, admire the town's fine Renaissance doorways, and explore the 11th-century keep, the dungeons, the manor, and the royal apartments in the **château**. Here Agnès Sorel (1422–1450), the mistress of Charles VII, lived in great luxury; look out for her tomb and Jean Fouquet's painting of the Virgin, whose face was said to be that of Agnès.

From Loches, you can continue up the river and then return down the D25 to explore the forest, or take the N143 straight back to Tours.

**The interiors of Montrésor Castle**

# AZAY-LE-RIDEAU

Azay-le-Rideau is one of the loveliest of the Loire châteaus, famously described by Balzac as "a many-faceted diamond set in the Indre." With its delicate turrets and purely decorative fortifications reflected in the peaceful river moat against a background of trees, this is a château unquestionably built for pleasure rather than defense. While the building remains Gothic in its outlines, the delicate decorative work is of Italianate Renaissance inspiration.

Building at Azay started in 1518 for a wealthy financier, Gilles Berthelot (a relation of Catherine Briçonnet, who built Chenonceau), whose wife, Philippa Lesbahy, oversaw the work. It entered royal hands when it was confiscated by François I still unfinished (it did not receive its final touches until the 19th century).

Perhaps the most striking feature of Azay is the harmony achieved between the château and its setting, a virtuoso composition of pale stone, lush greenery, and limpid water. Set on an island between two arms of the Indre River, the château is almost surrounded by water. Azay is also noted for its grand staircase, a major innovation at that time, consisting of three zigzag flights of stairs, with open loggia windows in Italianate style on each landing.

The interior, though luxuriously appointed, has an authentic, somewhat domestic feel. It has been furnished with period pieces, hung with sumptuous brocades, and some fine tapestries. The impressive kitchen is equipped with huge stone fireplaces, oak doors, and an intriguing selection of antique cooking equipment. A son et lumière show tells the château's story every night from May to September.

The little town of Azay-le-Rideau is delightful, too. Look for the decorative Renaissance stone carving on a number of doors and windows in the old streets. The 11th-century **Église de St.-Symphorien,** close to the château, has a double-gabled front with fragments of a sixth-century facade and a row of little statues over the door. ∎

■ **Azay-le-Rideau: a gem on the Indre**

**Château d'Azay-le-Rideau** 🗺 189 D2 ✉ rue de Pineau ☎ 02 47 45 42 04 💲 $$ **azay-le-rideau.monuments-nationaux.fr**

# CHINON

**The best view of Chinon—a small town steeped in history and still dominated by the sprawling ruins of its great fortress—is from the opposite bank of the Vienne River. The formidable fortifications tell their own tale. Always a site of major strategic importance, the château played a key role in Anglo-French skirmishes throughout the Middle Ages.**

English king Henry II lived in the most ancient part of the Chinon stronghold—the Fort St.-Georges, now demolished, east of the Château du Milieu and the Vieux Logis—and died here in 1189. The French Crown took possession of the castle, and a keep and other fortifications were added in the following century. The best preserved parts of the château date from the 14th century.

Deteriorated as it is, the castle's massive walls, lofty ramparts, and tall towers make it a dramatic place to explore. Portions were recently reconstructed.

On the walls of the Château du Coudray, you can still see the melancholy graffiti carved in 1308 by imprisoned Knights Templar awaiting death by burning.

But Chinon is most famous as the place where Jeanne d'Arc had her fateful interview with the Dauphin, Charles VII, when she recognized him hidden amid a crowd of courtiers and recounted her dream that he would be crowned king. Her memory is evoked at every turn.

The cobbled streets of the old town are charming; the main street, Rue Voltaire, is lined with half-timbered houses, their carved windows and doorways fine

■ Jeanne d'Arc is commemorated at the venerable Château de Chinon, which dates back to the 14th century.

examples of Renaissance work. Off this street are the Caves Peintes (Painted Cellars), old quarries below the castle, where the local wine confraternity holds meetings. They are also the scene of fictional character Pantagruel's carousings in Rabelais's *Gargantua and Pantagruel.*

Rabelais, whose name has entered the language as a synonym for bucolic excess, was born in the late 15th century 3 miles (5 km) southwest of Chinon. His birthplace at La Devinière, a modest manor house in the heart of vineyard country, is now the **Musée Rabelais.** The dwelling has been restored and furnished in 15th-century vernacular style.

Chinon is also known far and wide for its well-priced wines. ■

**Chinon** 🗺 189 D2 Visitor Information ✉ place Hofheim ☎ 02 47 93 17 85 **azay-chinon-valdeloire.com** • **Château de Chinon** ✉ route de Tours ☎ 02 47 93 13 45 🅂 $ **forteressechinon.fr** • **Musée Rabelais** ✉ La Devinière, D117, Seuilly ☎ 02 47 95 91 18 🅂 $ **musee-rabelais.fr**

# FONTEVRAUD

Allow plenty of time to see Fontevraud, one of the most complete surviving (though heavily restored) collections of medieval monastic buildings anywhere. The church, cloisters, kitchens, refectory, and gardens provide an unrivaled picture of monastic life over 600 years from the 12th century to the 18th.

■ The abbey of Fontevraud is a portal into an ancient monastic life.

Founded in 1099 by a devout hermit, Robert d'Arbrissel, who embraced the ascetic and silent rule of St. Benedict, Fontevraud consisted of five separate religious establishments. It was unusual in including both monks and nuns in the community, and unique in being governed by a woman. The abbesses were women of considerable influence, often of royal blood, and Fontevraud became a favorite royal sanctuary.

The **Abbaye Royale de Fontevraud** was the spiritual retreat chosen by

**INSIDER TIP:**

Fontevraud has become the cultural center of western France, with concerts, theater, and exhibits.

—ROSEMARY BAILEY
*National Geographic author*

Eleanor of Aquitaine, one-time queen first of France and then of England. The abbey church later became the

**Abbaye Royale de Fontevraud** 🅰 189 C2 ✉ place des Plantagenêts
☎ 02 41 51 73 52 💲 $ **fontevraud.fr**

burial place of the Plantagenets, a royal heritage that would ensure its constant maintenance for centuries to come.

The royal lineage is also manifest in a peculiar type of artwork: The painted 13th-century effigies of Eleanor, her husband Henry II, their son Richard the Lion-Hearted, and their daughter Isabelle of Angoulême are preserved here within the abbey church.

The church is a superb Romanesque building. The simple lines of the nave are superb, and the great columns are topped by intricately and mysteriously carved capitals (binoculars are useful). After the revolution, parts of the monastery were destroyed, and it was used as a prison from 1804 until 1963. It has been restored, and excavation work continues. Visitors may wander outside the abbey buildings through the medieval gardens, the orangery, and the stables.

The magnificent Renaissance chapter house has fine vaulting, carved doorways, and 16th-century wall paintings. The lovely cloisters also date from the Renaissance, and the vast refectory has Romanesque walls and a Gothic vaulted ceiling. The most intriguing building is the perfectly (some say over-) restored Romanesque kitchen. Octagonal in shape, it has a large central tower and a cluster of chimneys with pepperpot roofs. Inside are no fewer than six hearths, over which meals were once prepared for several hundred members of the community.

Fontevraud is one of Europe's most important centers of medieval archaeology. The **Musée Ephémère** explores its history. ∎

## Unusual Domestic Architecture

The Loire region has the highest concentration of troglodyte dwellings in Europe. For centuries, cave houses were cut out of cliff faces. **Turquant** has several troglodyte dwellings, and the Loire River cliffs are riddled with houses. At **Deneze-sous-Doue** (tel 02 41 59 15 40) see an extraordinary cave of mysterious 16th- and 17th-century sculptures. Some houses, such as those in **Trôo**, were built around ancient burial mounds. **Rochemenier** has a well-preserved troglodyte village museum, the fascinating **Village Troglodyte** (tel 02 41 59 18 15, troglodyte.fr). Its alluring honeycomb of caves includes barns, wine cellars, stables, and dwelling places in use until the 1930s. There is an underground room where the entire village would congregate on long winter evenings to spin flax, shell walnuts, sing, and dance. Troglodyte restaurants are cozy spots. Try **Les Caves de Marson** (tel 02 41 50 50 05, caves demarson.com; see Travelwise p. 433) in Rou Marson or **Les Nobles Fouées** (tel 02 41 83 20 27) in St.-Hilaire-St.-Florent. Sleep in a cave at the **Hotel Bussy** (tel 02 41 38 18 10) in Montsoreau or the **Hotel Demeure de la Vignole** (tel 02 41 53 67 00, demeure-vignole .com) in Turquant, with a swimming pool dug out of the rock.

# SAUMUR

One of the most charming towns of the Loire Valley, Saumur is renowned for its sparkling wine, its château, and its crack cavalry school. The graceful white turrets of the 14th-century château rise over the town and river today, just as they do in the luminous illustration to the *Très Riches Heures du Duc de Berry,* a book of hours now in one of the châteaus at Chantilly (see p. 134), painted shortly after the château was built.

Once under the control of the kings of England, Saumur became the property of France in the 12th century.

While in the area, make sure to visit **Château de Saumur.** After considerable renovations, some museums are now open, and you can visit the courtyard and terrace, with fine views of the town and river. A survivor of heavy bombing in 1940, the château is surrounded by elegantly restored stone houses. The winding streets of the town are lined with half-timbered dwellings, among which Balzac set his novel *Eugène Grandet.* On Place St.-Pierre stands the medieval **Église de St.-Pierre,** with its fine 16th-century tapestries.

The **École Nationale d'Équitation** (National Riding School), in St.-Hilaire-St.-Florent just west of Saumur, stages riding displays given by the French army's skilled horseback riders. Guided tours of the school's grounds, stables, tack room, and arenas are offered.

In the village you can sample local sparkling wine in tufa caves near the river. Mushrooms are grown in caves,

■ The terrace of the Château de Saumur commands views of the old town and the Loire.

too; learn more about the French fungi at the **Musée du Champignon** *(St.-Hilaire-St.-Florent, tel 02 41 50 31 55, musee-du-champignon.com).* ■

**Saumur** 🅰 189 C2 Visitor Information ✉ place de la Bilange ☎ 02 41 40 20 60 **ot-saumur.fr** • **Château de Saumur** ☎ 02 41 40 24 40 🕐 Closed Mon. Nov.–March 💲 $$ **chateau-saumur.fr** • **École Nationale d'Équitation** ✉ St.-Hilaire-St.-Florent ☎ 02 41 53 50 50 🕐 Closed Sun.–Mon. **cadrenoir.fr**

# ANGERS

Anjou's ancient capital is the gateway to the western Loire Valley. With an old quarter rich in museums, cafés, and elegant shops, Angers is dominated by the impressive walls and 17 towers of its formidable 13th-century château. Built by Louis IX (St. Louis, R. 1226–1270) within the space of 20 years, this colossus of granite and black schist is approached by a drawbridge across a broad dry moat, now bright with formal plantings of flowers.

■ The battlements of the Château d'Angers were cut down to hold cannon.

Inside the **Château d'Angers** is the town's premier treasure, the almost surreal 14th-century Apocalypse Tapestry. The **Cathédrale St.-Maurice** *(4 rue St.-Christophe)* has 12th-century stained-glass windows. Nearby is the half-timbered 15th-century **Maison d'Adam**. Two Renaissance palaces in the old quarter house museums: **Hôtel Pincé** *(32 bis rue Lenepveu)* and the fine art **Musée des Beaux-Arts** *(14 rue du Musée, tel 02 41 05 38 00, closed Mon. except June–Sept.).* The 13th-century **Abbaye de Toussaint** *(33 bis rue Toussaint, tel 02 41 05 38 90, closed Mon.)* displays work by 18th-century sculptor David d'Angers.

Across the river, the medieval **Hôpital St.-Jean** *(4 boulevard Arago, tel 02 41 24 18 45, closed Mon. Nov.– May)* is one of the oldest hospital buildings in France and houses Jean Lurat's magnificent tapestry "Le Chant du Monde." ■

**Angers** ⛰ 189 C2–C3 Visitor Information ✉ place Kennedy ☎ 02 41 23 50 00 **tourisme.destination-angers.com • Château d'Angers** ✉ promenade du Bout-du-Monde ☎ 02 41 86 48 77 💲 $$

# LE LOIR & VENDÔME

To the north of the great Loire is the river Loir, which runs from Illiers-Combray to just above Angers. Vendôme, on a network of islands formed by the Loir, is one of France's most attractive towns. In the Middle Ages, it was famed for its tanneries, mills, and kid gloves. Now the old houses and mills provide second homes for Parisians.

Jean-Baptiste de Rochambeau (1725–1807), the military adventurer who led the French soldiers throughout the American Revolution, was born in Vendôme. His statue dominates the Place St.-Martin. The finest sight in town is undoubtedly the **Abbaye de la Trinité,** with its Gothic facade and some of the oldest stained glass anywhere in Europe.

Downriver from Vendôme is the small town of **Lavardin,** with medieval houses, a Romanesque church, and a fortress. **Trôo** contains troglodyte houses built around an ancient burial mound.

Just across the river, the church in **St.-Jacques-des-Guérets** is home to several Romanesque wall paintings. From Trôo, follow the signs to **La Possonnière,** where the poet Pierre de Ronsard—also known as the "prince of poets"—was born in 1524.

Downstream stands the 15th-century **Château du Lude** (tel 02 43 94 60 09, lelude.com, closed Wed. May–Sept.,). From here, proceed to the charming town of **La Flèche,** or southwest

to **Baugé** and the **Hospice de la Girouardière,** where you can view the Vraie Croix d'Anjou, a cross brought back from the Crusades; during World War II, it was the symbol of the Free French forces.

Horticulturalists should note the annual garden festival at Château du Lude, held on the first weekend of June. Plant collectors and gardeners share their knowledge and enthusiasm with visitors. Workshops on all kinds of gardening subjects are offered. ∎

## EXPERIENCE:
## Go Green

Outside Angers, **Terra Botanica** (route de Cantenay Epinard, tel 02 41 25 00 00, terrabotanica.fr, closed Dec.–March) is Europe's first horticultural theme park, devoted entirely to the understanding and discovery of plant life, combining gardens, water features, exotic trees, and greenhouses. Themed adventures take you on boat trips and treetop rides, battling through the jungle, and investigating the world of medicinal plants.

**Vendôme** 🅜 189 D3 Visitor Information ✉ Hôtel du Saillant, Parc Ronsard ☎ 02 54 77 05 07 **vendome-tourisme.fr** • **Hospice de la Girouardière** ✉ 8 rue de la Girouardière, Baugé ☎ 02 41 89 75 49 🕐 Open 3–4 p.m. except Tues.

# BOURGES

In the heart of rural Berry, the region south of the Loire Valley, lies the historic town of Bourges, with its many architectural treasures. Its celebrated Gothic Cathédrale St.-Étienne (a UNESCO World Heritage site since 1993) is one of the most outstanding examples of Gothic architecture in France.

Built mostly between 1195 and 1260, the cathedral has no transepts, so the interior seems unusually spacious. The facade has five beautifully carved doorways, three towers, and a gorgeous rose window from the 15th century. Within, the cathedral glows with stained glass; especially notable are the windows telling the story of the Annunciation in the chapel of Jacques Coeur.

■ Cathédrale St.-Etienne

Jacques Coeur was one of the most powerful men in 15th-century France. Having sailed to the East, trading in silks, spices, and precious metals, he returned to build a superb mansion. His **Palais Jacques Coeur** *(rue Jacques Coeur, tel 02 48 24 79 42)* incorporates some of the Roman wall of Bourges. Inside are elegantly patterned-tile floors, stone fireplaces, and fine painted ceilings.

The medieval and Renaissance quarter around the cathedral includes a 17th-century garden designed by Le Nôtre, a medieval tithe barn, and half-timbered, cantilevered houses. Among the town houses *(hôtels)*, look for the Hôtel des Échevins and the Hôtel Lallemant, which now houses the **Musée des Arts Décoratifs** *(6 rue Bourbonnoux, tel 02 48 70 23 57, closed Mon.)*.

The Hôtel Cujas, built in 1515 for a Florentine merchant, has the **Musée du Berry** *(4 rue des Arènes, tel 02 48 70 41 92, closed Sun. a.m. & Tues.)*, devoted to the history of the Berry region. ■

**Bourges** ⛰ 189 E2 Visitor Information ✉ 21 rue Victor-Hugo
☎ 02 48 23 02 60 **bourges-tourisme.com** • **Cathédrale St.-Étienne**
☎ 02 48 23 02 60

# EXPERIENCE: Live *La Vie en Château*

Take a step into history by sampling the traditional luxury of château life. The château experience is more and more popular, and all over France there are châteaus, grand and small, luxurious and more modest, offering a variety of facilities and experiences. You can become a guest in a stately manor, a Renaissance château, a medieval castle, or an aristocratic family home for one or more nights; most offer bed and breakfast, and often dinner, and some are available to rent completely for a week.

■ Guests at Château de la Barre are treated to live entertainment appropriate to an elegant centuries-old home.

Poets have for centuries hymned *la douce vie*, the gentle life, of this great valley straddling the heart of France, neatly dividing the north from the south. The region's fertile alluvial soil and an exceptionally mild climate combine to yield fine wines and a cornucopia of fruits and vegetables, so it's little wonder that the rich built their castles in the Loire Valley.

Most of the great châteaus lie close to the banks of the Loire or its tributaries and they make great bases for driving tours. Crisscrossing the great river in order to be on the right side at the right time is an art requiring careful planning, especially as the levées sometimes obscure the river from the road. Be prepared to forsake the Loire from time to time to explore its quiet backwaters and tributaries.

Some of the smaller Loire châteaus now offer accommodations

to travelers, presenting a great opportunity for travelers to experience firsthand la vie en château.

Small, elegant **Château de la Barre** (*Conflans-sur-Anille, tel 02 43 35 00 17, chateaudelabarre.com*) in the Loire region is surrounded by tranquil parkland. The Count and Countess de Vanssay (he is the 20th-generation count and she is Anglo-American) welcome you into their home, where you can spend two or more nights, listening to chamber music in the Grand Salon (surrounded by ancestor portraits), dining on family silver and porcelain in the vast 17th-century dining room, and sleeping in a sumptuous bedroom.

In the Lorraine region, near Nancy, **Château d'Hattonchâtel** (*au-chateau.com*) dates back in part to the ninth century. After destruction during World War I, it was restored by American Belle Skinner. Indeed, this is a fine base for exploring World War I sites. You can prepare meals yourself in the château tower or arrange for dinner to be made for you.

**Château Robert** (*au-chateau .com*), in the Landes in southwest France, is a classic 19th-century château with huge grounds, a saltwater swimming pool, tennis, and trout fishing in the pond. Horseback riding and golf are close by. Weeklong cooking classes and wine tastings are also offered.

**Château Juvenal** (*au-chateau .com*), a retreat in the Vaucluse area of Provence, is surrounded by vineyards and olive groves. Enjoy regional cuisine and the château's own wine. You can join painting and cooking classes; cheese, wine and truffle tastings; and even take tango lessons.

Comte and Comtesse des Monstiers Mérinville welcome guests to their Limousin **Château du Fraisse** (*au-chateau.com*), which goes back eight centuries. Approached by a long driveway with a marble columned entrance, this chateau is furnished with fine antiques and also offers tennis, French billiards, a dance floor, a bandstand, and a private chapel.

## The Vendée

South of Nantes is the Vendée area of the western Loire, a place notorious in the late 18th century for counterrevolutionary uprisings and guerrilla warfare. This unrest culminated in the massacre of 1794, in which more than 80,000 royalists died. Memorials and museums detailing the uprising are found in Cholet and Challans.

The Atlantic coast is dotted with small resorts. A bridge links Fromentine to the island of Noirmoutier, a haven of secluded beaches. Inland, canals thread the Marais Poitevin, a marshy landscape that hosts bird sanctuaries.

Near Les Epesses, the Château de Puy du Fou (*tel 08 20 09 10 10, puydufou.com, check for closings*) is famed for its open-air history pageants starring hundreds of actors.

# More Places to Visit in the Loire Valley

## Lesser Châteaus

**Montreuil-Bellay** *(map 189 C2, visitor information, place de la Concorde, tel 02 41 52 37 70, chateau -de-montreuil-bellay.fr)*, a river town south of Saumur, is the location of an 11th-century fortress enclosing an elegant and beautifully furnished 15th-century mansion.

The construction of the **Château de Serrant** *(map 189 C2, tel 02 41 39 13 01, chateau-serrant.net, closed Tues. & Nov.–March)* near Angers, surrounded by a moat and an attendant bevy of swans, took place over two centuries— though you would never guess from the harmony of the design. Inside the opulent château is an enormous library and a bedroom designed for Napoleon Bonaparte himself. The romantically prone emperor would have appreci- ated having the swans hereabouts—this creature being one of nature's more recognizable mourning birds; the col- lective noun even changes to a "lam- entation" of swans when one or more of their partners for life is no longer among the group.

A drawbridge leads to the small **Château du Plessis-Bourré** *(map 167 C3, tel 02 41 32 06 72, plessis-bourre.com)*, encircled by a moat that reflects its white walls, blue slate roof, and spires. The Renaissance interior is designed for elegance.

Medieval fortress on the out- side—with moat, drawbridge, towers, crenellations, and arrow-slit windows— Renaissance palace on the inside, 15th- century **Langeais** *(map 189 D2, tel 02 47 96 72 60, chateau-de-langeais.com)* contains fine tapestries.

The **Château de Cheverny** *(map 167 E3, tel 02 54 79 96 29, chateau -cheverny.fr)*, built between 1620 and 1634, has a classically regular facade and a lavishly painted interior.

The 19th-century novelist George Sand lived in **Nohant** *(map 189 E1, tel 02 54 31 07 37)*. Here she enter- tained her many lovers, Chopin among them, and wrote novels. Her house and garden, much as she left them, are open to the public.

---

**INSIDER TIP:**

Take a mad ride on the gigantic mechanical elephant at Les Machines de L'Île *(lesmachines-nantes .fr)*, which allows you and your fellow riders to control some of the metal beast's movements.

—JACK KAVANAGH
*National Geographic author*

---

## Nantes

The River Loire meets the sea just beyond the great estuary city of Nantes, whose wealth was derived from maritime activity. Now one of the most popular places to live in France, Nantes is undergoing a 21st-century renaissance. The huge 15th-century **Château des Ducs de Bretagne** *(chateau-nantes.fr)* has been extensively renovated, its dra- matic granite walls now housing a museum dedicated to the history of the city and its shipbuilding past.

The 19th-century neo-Gothic **Palais Dobrée** houses a rich private collection of art, furniture, tapestries, and manuscripts, which makes for a rewarding visit.

The 19th-century **Quartier Graslin** is a feast of neoclassical facades, wrought-iron balconies, belle epoque shopping arcades, and art nouveau cafés. Don't miss the celebrated brasserie La Cigale.

On a completely different note, for a truly entertaining and original experience take a gallery tour of the workshops of **Les Machines de l'Île** *(lesmachines-nantes.fr, $$)*, a partnership of artist-engineers François Delaroziere and Pierre Orefice, whose creative spaces occupy former warehouses on the Île de Nantes. *nantes-tourisme .com*  188 B2 **Visitor Information** ✉ 7 rue du Valmy ☎ 08 92 46 40 44

> # EXPERIENCE: Drive Le Mans Race Circuit
>
> You can drive the famous Le Mans 24-hour race circuit *(tel 02 43 40 24 30, lemansdriver.fr)*. You can do laps in cars or on motorbikes on the Bugatti course and the Maison Blanche circuit, or try out the endurance car simulator for the full experience of changing drivers and more. Later, the old town of **Le Mans** *(map 189 D3)* warrants a circuit—on foot.

## Sancerre

Far up the Loire, this red-roofed town of old streets winding up a hill, is ringed by vineyards and produces fine dry white wine. 189 F2 **Visitor Information** ✉ rue de la Croix de Bois ☎ 08 92 46 40 44

■ **The 24 Hours of Le Mans is still a much followed and appreciated race: born in 1923, it lasts 24 hours straight, as the name suggests, and each team alternates three drivers at the wheel.**

A variety of grand landscapes: from the Auvergne down to the rich lands around the Rhône and Saône Rivers, and up to the Alps

# CENTRAL FRANCE & THE ALPS

# CENTRAL FRANCE & THE ALPS

This region includes the province of Burgundy, primarily an agricultural region, and the quiet mountains of the Jura in the north. To the south, the Rhône Valley has been an important trade route for millennia. The rugged heights, deep gorges, clear lakes, and open spaces of the Alps in the east attract walkers and skiers, while in the west lie the mountains at the heart of France, the Massif Central.

## NOT TO BE MISSED:

Helping build a medieval castle at Guédelon  222

Tasting Burgundy vintages along the Côte-d'Or wine route  224–225

The serene Abbaye de Fontenay  229

A meal in Lyon  241–244

The marvelous view of Mont Blanc from Chamonix  246–247

Hiking to the summit of Puy de Dôme in the Auvergne  255–257

Driving through the spectacular Gorges du Tarn  258–260

0    60 kilometers
0    30 miles

AUBE
p. 105

HAUTE-MARNE
p. 105

VOSGES
p. 105

HAUT-RHIN
P. 105

Armançon

Tonnerre

Châtillon-sur-Seine

Luxeuil-les-Bains

Chablis

Cravant

Fontenay

Lure   Ronchamp

Montbard

Semur-en-Auxois

Vesoul

Belfort

Avallon

HAUTE-SAÔNE

Montbéliard

Vézelay

CÔTE-D'OR

Gray

Seine

TERRITOIRE-DE-BELFORT

Pouilly-en-Auxois

Dijon

Pesmes

Besançon

Maîche

Saulieu

Clos de Vougeot

Auxonne

Doubs

DOUBS

Château-Chinon

Nuits-St-Georges

Cîteaux

Dole

Ornans

Arc-et-Senans

Meursault   Beaune

Seurre

Salins-les-Bains

SWITZERLAND

Autun

Chagny

Arbois

Pontarlier

Le Creusot

Chalon-sur-Saône

Poligny

JURA

Champagnole

Montceau-les-Mines

SAÔNE-ET-LOIRE

Cirque de Baume

Lons-le-Saunier

Doucier

Cascades du Hérisson

Bourbon-Lancy

Louhans

Morez

Digoin

Charolles

Tournus

St.-Claude

Lac Léman (Lake Geneva)

Paray-le-Monial

Cluny

A39

1689m
Mont Colomby de Gex

Evian-les-Bains

Thonon-les-Bains

Lapalisse

Mâcon

Oyonnax

Chablais

Morzine

Juliénas

481m ▲ Mt. Brouilly

Bellegarde

Annemasse

Monts de la Madeleine

Beaujeu   Fleurie

Bourg-en-Bresse

AIN

St-Julien-en-Genevois

Cluses

HAUTE-SAVOIE

Roanne

Villefranche-sur-Saône

Oingt

Pérouges

Rumilly

Annecy

Megève

Chamonix

3842m
Aiguille du Midi

Lyonnais

Tarare

RHÔNE

Lac du Bourget

Lac d'Annecy

4810m
Mont Blanc

LOIRE

Feurs

LYON

Aix-les-Bains

Le Châtelard

Albertville

Monts du Forez

1634m

Montbrison

Monts du Lyonnais

La-Tour-du-Pin

Chambéry

3747m
Grande Sassière

Les Arcs

Ambert

St.-Chamond

Bourgoin-Jallieu

Vienne

Moutiers

La Plagne

SAVOIE

ST-ETIENNE

ISÈRE

Méribel

Courchevel

Tignes

Pélussin

Voiron

St-Pierre-de-Chartreuse

3676m
Ciamarella

Firminy

HAUTE-LOIRE

Hauterives

Valloire

Modane
Tunnel du Fréjus

ITALY

Annonay

Yssingeaux

Romans-sur-Isère

PARC NAT. RÉGIONAL

Grenoble

3983m
Le Meije

Le Puy-en-Velay

Lamastre

Lans-en-Vercors

Vizille

Le-Bourg-d'Oisans

3946m
Massif des Écrins

Briançon

Le Monastier-sur-Gazeille

1753m
Mt. Mezenc

Valence

DU VERCORS

La Mure

Mt. Pelvoux

Vallouise

Vercors

2086m
Mont Aiguille

Die

St.-Véran

Langogne

Monts du Vivarais

Privas

Drôme

HAUTES-ALPES

Gap

Embrun

Aubenas

Crest

DRÔME

Guillestre

Ste.-Enimie

1699m
Mt. Lozère

Largentière

Vallon-Pont-d'Arc

Montélimar

Serres

Durance

ALPES-DE-HAUTE-PROVENCE
p. 277

Florac

Gorges du Tarn

Pont d'Arc

Gorges de l'Ardèche

Aven de Marzal

St.-Martin-d'Ardèche

Nyons

Aven d'Orgnac

GARD
p. 277

VAUCLUSE
p. 277

The Romans left many surviving remains in Central France, and Burgundy is rich with religious and architectural sights. The power of the medieval duchy of Burgundy rivaled that of the kingdom of France.

Burgundy is one of the richest regions of France, its historic towns and cities the product of many centuries of civilization. The region is best known for producing some of the world's finest wines. A tour of the Côte-d'Or—and a visit to the wine town of Beaune in particular—are opportunities for any wine lover to savor.

The region's most important river, the Rhône, flows from Lake Geneva in Switzerland. A major producer of silk fabrics for centuries, Lyon, at the confluence of the Rhône and Saône Rivers, is the second largest city in France.

The Rhône Valley is also known for fine wines. A critically important trade route, the mighty Rhône River connects north and south. The Alps provide a dramatic backdrop, a skyline of peaks dominated by Mont Blanc, the highest mountain in Europe at 15,780 feet (4,810 m). The mountains of the Jura along the Swiss border are formed of limestone plateaus cut by deep valleys.

Mountains also dominate central France. Of the Massif Central's many faces, the most spectacular are its great volcanoes, their summits offering stellar views of a crater-pitted lunar landscape. The rugged river gorges of the Tarn and the Jonte thrill countless visitors, whether they hike and climb, drive through the canyons, or navigate the rivers by kayak.

At the heart of the Massif Central are the rocks produced by volcanoes—the *puys* that form the highest points of the massif. ■

■ Semur-en-Auxois, in Burgundy, is a medieval village.

# BURGUNDY & THE JURA

For much of its history, Burgundy was a powerful independent state, and it retains a strong pride in its regional identity. There is also misty-eyed nostalgia for its glorious past—for tales of Vercingétorix and the last stand of the Gauls. The vanquishing Romans founded several of Burgundy's cities and left remains in places such as Autun.

■ The small town of Irancy, near Chablis, is known for its vineyards and wine.

Austere abbeys and superb Romanesque churches testify to the importance of Christianity here throughout the Middle Ages. The Basilique de Ste.-Madeleine in Vézelay was a starting point for pilgrimages to Santiago de Compostela (see pp. 304–305).

Benedictine rule reached its greatest influence at Cluny between the 10th and 12th centuries. Dissatisfaction with the increasing luxury and slackening discipline among the Benedictines led St. Bernard to found a new order in the 12th century, the Cistercians.

The Abbaye de Fontenay stands as a tribute to the industry and austerity of Cistercian monastic life. In Burgundy you can see the architectural development in church building from the Romanesque barrel vault to the Gothic naves of the cathedrals of Sens and Auxerre.

The 13th and 14th centuries saw the rise of the dukes of Burgundy, a golden age evoked in the magnificent palaces, noble mansions, and art collections of Dijon. The magnificent châteaus that dot the countryside tell of the wealth of the rulers of Burgundy and their nobles.

Outside its towns and cities, Burgundy is full of wonderful landscapes, from the regional park of the Morvan to the pastures of the Brionnais. To the east, the mountainous region of the Jura is a tranquil land of deep valleys and waterfalls.

Burgundy spans a watershed. The Saône River runs south to the Rhône Valley; the Yonne flows north to join the Seine. In addition, canals link the main towns. A boat ride along Burgundy's waterways makes a truly delightful way to float through history. ■

# DIJON

Bourgeois, comfortable Dijon has for the best part of 2,000 years been a busy merchant city on an international trade route. Medieval trade in Eastern spices brought the ingredients for its two most noted gastronomic specialties: mustard and *pain d'épices*. What makes Dijon so pleasurable to visit is its balance of splendid architecture with a serious attitude toward food—and lots of good restaurants.

During the 14th century, Dijon was the capital of the grand dukes of Burgundy, and it is their palace, the **Palais des Ducs,** that dominates the city. The oldest parts remaining are the 14th-century Tour de Bar and the 15th-century vaulted ducal kitchens.

The Tour Philippe-le-Bon, also 15th century, affords the visitor terrific views over the city. In the 17th century, the States General of Burgundy extended the palace as their parliament house. Part of this vast building, a mini-Versailles, now houses the newly renovated **Musée des Beaux-Arts** *(beaux-arts.dijon.fr),* noted for its Dutch and Flemish masters.

Walk around old Dijon to view its many dignified buildings enlivened with statuary and carvings. Rue Verrerie stands out for its 15th-century half-timbered houses with stained-glass windows. Rue des Forges, north of the Palais des Ducs, is equally historic: The **Hôtel de Chambellan** (now the tourist office) has a Gothic courtyard and stone spiral staircase and dates from

## Kir, S'il Vous Plaît

Dijon is the place to sample *kir,* a popular drink usually served as an aperitif. It was named after Canon Félix Kir, a longtime mayor of Dijon, who first mixed Bourgogne Aligoté wine with cassis (black currant liqueur).

An enthusiastic pioneer of the town-twinning movement after World War II, Canon Kir offered the drink at receptions. A similar drink had been made with red wine, but according to Kir he had to make it with white because the Germans had imbibed all the red Burgundy.

Kir is now served all over the world in many versions, including *kir royale* (using sparkling wine) and *kir Breton* (using cider).

the 15th century. The arcaded facade of the **Hôtel Aubriot** dates from the 13th century. But it was in the 17th and 18th centuries, when Dijon flour-

**Dijon** ⚑ 217 D5 Visitor Information ✉ 11 rue des Forges ☎ 03 80 44 11 44 **visitdijon.com** • **Palais des Ducs et des États de Bourgogne** ✉ place de la Libération ☎ 03 80 74 52 09 🕐 Closed Tues. 💲 $$ • **Église de Notre-Dame** ✉ place Notre-Dame **notre-dame-dijon.blogspot.com**

ished as a strong regional power, that most of its grand mansions were constructed. The **Hôtel de Vogüé** features distinctive Burgundian polychrome roof tiles and a pink marble courtyard; the **Maison des Cariatides** has stone caryatids around its windows.

The many fine churches to be found in Dijon include the cathedral and the former **Abbaye St.-Bénigne,** which has the added attraction of a beautiful, 11th-century Romanesque crypt beneath it. The superb Gothic **Église de Notre-Dame** has a medieval Jacquemart clock on the facade.

Gourmands visiting Dijon will find an interesting array of local produce on a visit to the food market held every Tuesday, Friday, and Saturday in **Les Halles.** ∎

## EXPERIENCE: Try Escargots à la Bourguignonne

Burgundy is the place in France to eat snails, fattened on the vine and greatly esteemed. Plump, delicious, and smothered in garlic and butter, **snails** are traditional-ly served piping hot in a dish with hollows for the shells. You should use a thin-tined fork to extract them from their shells. **Chablis** pairs well with snails.

▪ Dijon's owl is the town mascot; sculpted into a buttress of Église de Notre-Dame, it is believed to bestow good luck on those who touch it.

# EXPERIENCE: Build a Medieval Castle

Deep in the forest of Puisaye in northern Burgundy lies Guédelon, a medieval castle under construction. Using the same methods, tools, and materials of 800 years ago, a dedicated team of 50 people, along with a host of eager volunteers, is building the castle entirely from scratch. Here you can completely immerse yourself in the 13th century—to the sounds of metal on stone, the sawing of wood, the hammer striking the anvil, and horses' hooves pounding on bare earth.

**Guédelon** *(Chantier Médiéval de Guédelon, Treigny, tel 03 86 45 66 66, guedelon.fr, $$)* is the brainchild of Michel Guyot, who began the project in the mid-1990s. Back then, Guyot already had one medieval castle under his belt, neighboring St.-Fargeau, which he had restored from a state of near dereliction. Eager to understand medieval construction, Guyot decided to build his own castle. Construction began in 1998.

The plan is for a traditional castle of four towers surrounding an inner courtyard; work on the domed vault is under way, and mural painting has begun. The Great Hall is now completed.

In the woods around the building site, carpenters, masons, weavers, potters, and blacksmiths all labor away busily. They quarry and hew stones, weave baskets, construct carts, mix mortar, and forge nails just as their forebears did in the 13th century. All transport is by horse and cart, and there is no electricity or modern machinery. The dedicated team of workers even wear medieval costumes.

Unlike most other building sites, Guédelon is open to the public. In fact, one of the project's main objectives is to explain and demonstrate medieval craftsmanship to as many people as possible. Visitors can sample medieval food and drink at the tavern on-site. Guided tours are available, but be aware that what you see will depend on whatever work happens to be going on at the time.

The castle is due for completion in about 10 years, so there is plenty of time for you to pitch in and help. Volunteers are welcome from three days up to one week. The site is located in the middle of the woods, so a car, or at least a bicycle, is essential, as is a grasp of basic French.

For other hands-on projects, **Rempart** *(rempart.com/en)* is dedicated to cultural restoration, from medieval gardens to historic trains. **Apare** *(apare-gec .org)* organizes volunteer groups in southern France to help rebuild ramparts and restore various châteaus in need of repair. **La Sabranenque** *(sabranenque.com)* runs volunteer programs, such as the restoration of the village of St. Victor la Coste near Avignon, to help maintain the rural Mediterranean habitat and preserve traditional building techniques.

# BEAUNE

A small town with a big reputation, Beaune is the nerve center of the wine business in Burgundy. Set among some of the world's most distinguished vineyards, it is the place to go to sample a variety of wines from the region. It is also home to one of Burgundy's most celebrated sights, the Hôtel-Dieu.

Enter through the 18th-century triumphal arch of **Porte St.-Nicolas.** Walk around the remains of the 11th- to 15th-century ramparts and explore narrow lanes and cobbled courtyards, peering up at fine Gothic and Renaissance houses. Head for Place Monge, with its 15th-century bell tower and houses such as the 16th-century Hôtel de la Rochepot. North from Place Monge runs Rue de Lorraine, lined with mansions richly embellished with Renaissance carving, elaborate ironwork, and stone staircases. The Hôtel de Ville, a former 17th-century convent, houses the **Musée des Beaux-Arts,** featuring a collection of works by Félix Ziem, born in Beaune in 1821.

The much-altered **Église de Notre-Dame** was built in the 12th century in Cluny Romanesque style, with Gothic and Renaissance decorations added later.

At the heart of Beaune is **Place de la Halle,** site of the medieval corn market. On Saturdays the market hall and stalls around it are laden with the gastronomic bounty of Burgundy. To learn about the mysteries of wine, make for the **Musée du Vin de Bourgogne,** housed in the mansion that was once a private residence of the dukes of Burgundy. The entire history of winemaking is recounted, with a fascinating exhibition of old equipment and presses. ∎

## Hôtel-Dieu

A splendid building with polychrome roof and turret tiles, the Hôtel-Dieu *(rue de l'Hôtel-Dieu, tel 03 80 24 45 00, $$)* was founded as a hospital as the Hundred Years' War ended, in 1443. The last patient left in 1971. Rooms open to the public include the linen room, pharmacy, and a kitchen, with a great fireplace and spit. Among the many fine paintings and tapestries, the most famous is the 15th-century altarpiece, the "Last Judgment" by Rogier van der Weyden.

**Beaune** 🅰 217 D5 Visitor Information ✉ 6 boulevard Perpreuil ☎ 03 80 26 21 30 **ot-beaune.fr** • **Musée des Beaux-Arts** ✉ rue de l'Hôtel de Ville ☎ 03 80 24 96 52 🕓 Closed a.m. & Tues. Dec.–March 💲 $ • **Musée du Vin de Bourgogne** ✉ Hôtel des Ducs de Bourgogne ☎ 03 80 22 08 19 💲 $

# DRIVE DOWN THE CÔTE-D'OR

The Côte-d'Or, now a UNESCO World Heritage site, is a 30-mile (48 km) strip of land that produces Burgundy's most venerated wines. Often the wine is blended, but a few are so distinguished they are bottled and sold individually; here the winemaker is as important as the *domaine* (similar to the Bordeaux château).

## Côte de Nuits

Start at **Chenôve ❶**, on the D122. This is the beginning of the Côte de Nuits region, starring the finest red wines, produced from the temperamental Pinot Noir grape. Next is **Gevrey-Chambertin ❷**, with more *grands crus* than any other village in Burgundy. The **Clos de Bèze** is the oldest vineyard in Burgundy, planted by the Abbey of Bèze in the sixth century. Continue to Chambolle-Musigny on the D122. Just south of here is **Clos de Vougeot ❸** *(tel 03 80 62 86 09, closdevougeot.fr)*, founded in the 12th century by the monks of Cîteaux. The 16th-century **Château du Clos de Vougeot** is the HQ of the Confrérie des Chevaliers du Tastevin *(tastevin -bourgogne.com)*, the wine brotherhood founded to promote Burgundy. Join the N74 and continue south to **Vosne-Romanée,** which claims six grands crus, including the Romanée-Conti—a little stone cross marks its treasured patch of soil. **Nuits-St.-Georges ❹** *(tel 03 80 62 11 17, ot-nuits-st-georges .fr)* has numerous cellars to visit and a 13th-century church; the town gives its name to this section of the Côte-d'Or: the Côte de Nuits. South of Nuits-St.-Georges on the N74 is the Côte de Beaune, where the soil is lighter and

### NOT TO BE MISSED:

Château du Clos de Vougeot
• Château Corton-André •
Château de Meursault

chalkier, perfect for the Chardonnay grape. Head for **Aloxe-Corton ❺** on the D2, home of distinguished red and white wines. Look for signs to **Château Corton-André.** Then continue north up the D18 to **Pernand-Vergelesses.** Go back down the D18, and continue on the D2 to **Savigny-lès-Beaune.** After the wine town of **Beaune ❻** (see p. 223), take the D973 southward. The Côte de Beaune continues with some of Burgundy's best white wines. Taste them in **Meursault ❼**, at **Château de Meursault** *(tel 03 80 26 22 75, meursault.com)* in 14th-century cellars. **Puligny-Montrachet ❽**, down the D113, is a quiet village with distinguished wines. The vineyard of Montrachet produces what is regarded by many as the finest dry white wine in the world. The D113 continues south to **Santenay.** Return to Beaune via the Hautes-Côtes. Take the D33 up via St.-Aubin to **Château de la Rochepot ❾** *(tel 03 80 21 71 37)*, then take the D17 to **Orches.**

DIJON

CHENÔVE

**START** ❶

600m ▲

Marsannay-la-Côte

Couchey

Fixin

Brochon

Gevrey-Chambertin ❷

Morey St.-Denis

Chambolle-Musigny

Vougeot

Clos de Vougeot ◇

❸

Vosne-
Romanée

❹

NUITS-ST.-GEORGES

CÔTE     432m ▲

D'OR

Prémeaux-
Prissey

Comblanchiên

Pernand-
Vergelesses     Corgoloin

❺

Savigny-lès-Beaune     Aloxe-
Corton

❻

BEAUNE

Pommard

Monthelie

Orches

Baubigny

Château de
la Rochepot ◇

❾

St.-
Aubin

Meursault

❼

Puligny-
Montrachet

❽

Santenay

521m ▲

CHAGNY

0 ——— 6 kilometers
0 ——— 3 miles

A38
D122
N74
A31-E17-E21
Meuzin
Rhoin
D2
D18
A6
D17
D973
D17
D113
N6
D33
N74
Dheune
A6-E15-E21
N6
D974

🔺 See also area map p. 217
▶ Chenôve
⬌ 38 miles (60 km)
🕐 1 day
▶ Beaune

# SENS

**If you arrive in Burgundy from the north, the first major town you come to is Sens, always an important crossroads. Its period of greatest influence was the 12th century, when it was an archbishopric with control over most of northern France, including Paris and Chartres.**

The **Cathédrale St.-Étienne,** one of the first of France's great Gothic cathedrals, shows Sens's medieval importance. Building began in 1130; and the influence of Cistercian austerity is clearly apparent in the simplicity of the structure.

The proportions of the cathedral are mathematically calculated (the width of the nave being twice that of the side aisles), but the overall effect is one of harmonious space. Stained glass fills the tall windows, some of which survive from the 12th century. The west portal is particularly beautiful, despite having lost one of its towers. In the central doorway, look for the 12th-century Gothic statue of St. Étienne.

The adjoining archbishop's palace is now the **Musée de Sens,** with one of the richest treasuries in France: a glittering collection of religious art, Byzantine silks, shrouds, altar cloths, reliquaries, and vestments. ∎

## Chablis

Chablis is home to the northernmost of the great Burgundian vineyards, an ancient stone village with one overwhelming interest—the fragrant white wine, pale and dry, to which it has given its name. In spring there is a scent of laburnum and a cool freshness in the air, reminiscent of the wine itself. There are good restaurants and hotels here, and several *domaines* open their cellars for tastings.

To drive around the vineyards (which have been planted with the Chardonnay grape, locally known as "Beaunois"), follow the course of the Serein River on the D91 north toward Maligny. To your right you will see the *grand cru* vineyards, facing south and southeast. Return on the D131 heading for Milly, from where there is an excellent view of the surprisingly few Chablis vineyards.

**Sens** ◪ 216 B6 Visitor Information ✉ place Jean-Jaurès ☎ 03 86 65 19 49 🕓 Closed Sun. Nov.–Apr. **tourisme-sens.com • Cathédrale St.-Étienne** ✉ place de la République • **Musée de Sens** ✉ place de la République ☎ 03 86 64 46 22 🕓 Closed Tues. 🔲 $ • **Chablis** ◪ 217 C6 Visitor Information ✉ 1 rue du Maréchal de Lattre de Tassigny ☎ 03 86 42 80 80 **chablis.fr**

# AUXERRE

Auxerre is a sleepy little town on the banks of the Yonne River, a perfect starting point for trips on the waterways of Burgundy. From across the river, you can see the steep roofs of the old town and of the churches for which it is famous.

The Abbatiale de St.-Germain, in Auxerre, stands reflected in the Yonne River.

**Cathédrale St.-Étienne** dominates the town. In 1215, Bishop Guillaume de Seignelay decided to rebuild the existing Romanesque cathedral in the new Gothic style. Two centuries later, the main body of the building was complete, but the cathedral wasn't finished until 1560. The columns and rib vaulting are so subtly arranged they seem to be carrying no weight at all. The airy lightness is increased by the jewel-like colors of the stained glass. The Romanesque crypt stands in complete contrast, its barrel vault and sturdy pillars intact. The apse still has remarkable 12th-century frescoes of Christ on horseback surrounded by angels, vestiges of a scheme that once covered the entire church.

A short walk up Rue Cauchois leads to the **Abbatiale de St.-Germain** *(tel 03 86 18 02 90, closed Tues.)* and the Musée d'Art et d'Histoire. Hidden beneath the neo-Gothic church is a dim, vaulted Carolingian crypt with ancient stone sarcophagi of long-forgotten bishops and the tomb of St. Germain. The ninth-century frescoes of the stoning of St. Étienne are among France's oldest religious wall paintings.

The 17th-century town gate, the **Tour de l'Horloge,** has a moondial as well as a sundial in its 15th-century clock face. ∎

**Auxerre** ⛰ 216 B5 Visitor Information ✉ 1–2 quai de la République ☎ 03 86 52 06 19 **ot-auxerre.fr** • **Cathédrale St.-Étienne** ✉ rue Fouriet ☎ 03 86 51 29 20 💲 $ (crypt & treasury) **ot-auxerre.com**

# VÉZELAY

**The great Basilique de Ste.-Madeleine in Vézelay rises on a rock from a deep valley. The best way to approach it is to climb the steep main street, following in the steps of the medieval pilgrims who flocked here to worship the (supposed) relics of St. Mary Magdalene.**

Vézelay's spiritual reputation still draws crowds, and the medieval streets of the town are crammed with bookstores, antique shops, and art galleries. Its ramparts give lovely views of the lush, rolling hills of the surrounding countryside.

Founded in 864, the **Basilique de Ste.-Madeleine** *(place de la Basilique, tel 03 86 33 39 50),* a UNESCO World Heritage site, thrived until 1280, when it emerged that the (supposed) bones of Mary Magdalene were still at St.-Maximin in Provence and that the relics at Vézelay were fakes. Virtually

■ **Beautifully evocative Romanesque sculptures decorate the Basilique de Ste.-Madeleine in Vézelay.**

abandoned, damaged by Protestants in the 16th century, and neglected during the revolution, the basilica was in a ruinous state when architectural historian Viollet-le-Duc began restoration in the 19th century.

Walk around the outside of the basilica to view the appealing apse with its radiating chapels; the chapter house, which is all that remains from the 12th-century monastery; and the west facade, with its restored 13th-century window and tower.

Then enter the vast narthex, added to accommodate the crowds of pilgrims in the 12th century. The famous tympanum over the inner door is the pièce de résistance of Burgundian Romanesque. With tremendous movement and feeling, it depicts the events of Pentecost: Rays of light streak from the fingers of Christ to the Apostles.

Looking through the door and straight down the aisle, the round Romanesque arches of the nave with alternating light and dark stones lead your eye to the soaring Gothic points of the choir. The carvings of the capitals dwell heavily on the torment awaiting unbelievers. For an insight into the medieval mindset, go down to the crypt to see the discredited relics. ■

**Vézelay** 🄰 217 C5 Visitor Information ✉ rue St.-Étienne ☎ 03 86 33 23 69 **vezelaytourisme.com**

# ABBAYE DE FONTENAY

The oldest Cistercian monastery still surviving, Fontenay has been superbly restored to give an intriguing picture of monastic life. Beautifully set in a quiet wooded valley, it was founded by St. Bernard of Clairvaux in 1118 and named after the spring there.

Serenity reigns in the Romanesque cloister at the Abbaye de Fontenay.

Aside from the 17th-century abbot's lodging at the western end of the church, all the buildings are original 12th-century structures, albeit restored. Many of the brown Burgundian roof tiles are original, too. The architecture embodies beauty at its most austere, in accordance with St. Bernard's belief that any superfluous decoration distracted from a building's spiritual purpose (see p. 231).

At the heart of the ancient abbey lies the **cloister,** a square of open galleries arcaded with double columns of golden stone. The **church** abuts the north gallery. Inside, aisles flank the long nave. A subtle glow from the windows enhances the spartan beauty. In the north transept stands a 13th-century statue of the Virgin and Child.

The **chapter house** has exquisite rib vaulting and columns. The monks slept on straw pallets in the **dormitory** above and copied manuscripts in the **scriptorium;** the **warming room** next to it kept the inks (and the monks' hands) from freezing in winter. The **forge,** where the monks worked the iron they dug from the hills, stands near the little river.

Fontenay thrived until the turmoil of the 16th-century religious wars. During the revolution the abbey was sold and became a paper mill. In 1906, new owners, a branch of the Montgolfier ballooning family, restored it to its original Cistercian form. ■

**Abbaye de Fontenay** ⚠ 217 C5 ✉ Fontenay, Marmagne
☎ 03 80 92 15 00 ⊕ Open year-round. Guided tours in French only.
💲 $$ abbayedefontenay.com

# MONASTERIES

The spread of Christianity, and in particular the development of the monasteries, was central to the growth and stability of the kingdom of France in the Middle Ages. Burgundy played a key role in the development of the monasteries in the ninth and tenth centuries. Two of the greatest medieval foundations were at Cluny and Cîteaux.

## Benedictines

The Benedictine order, founded in Italy by St. Benedict in 529, spread rapidly across Europe. "To work is to pray" was their motto. The monks were to do six to eight hours of work daily plus four hours each of prayer and reading. They had no private property other than the habit they wore, a rope and scapular (cloak), a belt, and a knife.

In contrast to the hermetic principles of earlier monasteries, the Benedictines emphasized community—sleeping, praying, reading, and eating together according to a precise daily routine of work and worship. The first monks built their

church and dwellings on virgin territory and then supported themselves by farming, planting vineyards, and raising livestock.

Oases of order in a time of chaos, the monasteries quickly became influential throughout Europe. Large (an important monastery might have a thousand or more people attached to it), prosperous, secure, and disciplined, they were often centers of learning and culture.

Prison

Forge

Infirmary

Scriptorium

Dormitory

Traditional Cistercian Monastery

## Cluny

By the tenth century, the Benedictine abbots were increasingly corrupt, and monks neglected their vows. In response, Cluny was founded in 910, reforming the order and spreading its influence over much of Europe. Eventually Cluny established some 1,450 daughter houses, and the original monastery grew so large that it required 40 farms to support it.

## Cistercians

But Cluny, too, fell into decadent ways. In reaction, the Cistercian order was founded at Cîteaux, near Dijon, in 1098. Its austerity attracted a nobleman named Bernard, who established his own monastery at Clairvaux in northern Burgundy. His passionate oratory attracted thousands and launched the Second Crusade from Vézelay. The Cistercian movement grew rapidly, founding hundreds of new monasteries, including Pontigny and Fontenay in Burgundy. Bernard revived the Rule of St. Benedict, stressing the importance of manual work, poverty, and simplicity. His veto on superfluous decoration had a profound effect upon Cistercian architecture. By the late 1700s, however, even these great abbeys had become corrupt, exploiting the people and abusing their influence. Deep popular resentment led to destruction of many buildings during and after the revolution. Cluny was destroyed; Cîteaux is still a monastery, but has few old buildings. Pontigny and Fontenay, both restored, offer a vision of monastic life as it was intended to be.

Church

Cloisters

Chapter house

# AUTUN

From a hill just south of the city, there is a glorious view of Autun, one of the key cities of Roman Gaul. Founded by Emperor Augustus in the first century B.C., Autun is also a gateway to the Morvan, rolling country ideal for walking.

■ **Cathédrale St.-Lazare sits at the heart of medieval Autun.**

The substantial legacies of the Roman period include the sanctuary of the **Temple of Janus,** the **Porte d'Arroux** with its sculpted arcades and columns, and the **Porte St.-André,** designed with separate arches for chariots and pedestrians. The remains of the Roman theater come to life every August with an evocative spectacle of Gallo-Roman life, complete with chariot races.

But this is also a medieval city, still partly cinched by ramparts. Its greatest treasure, the 12th-century Romanesque **Cathédrale St.-Lazare,** is famed for its incomparable sculpture. Gislebertus d'Autun was one of the greatest sculptors of an age that yields the names of few individual artists, and the tympanum over the

west portal was his masterpiece. It was saved from destruction during the revolution because it had been plastered over earlier in the 18th century. His vivid rendering of the Last Judgment, carved between 1130 and 1135, prompted André Malraux to describe him as "a Romanesque Cézanne." The chapter house contains more of his work, including capitals depicting the suicide of Judas and the dream of three kings.

The **Musée Rolin** is housed in the adjacent 15th-century mansion, built by Nicolas Rolin, who founded the Hôtel-Dieu in Beaune (see sidebar p. 223). It contains Gallo-Roman antiquities, as well as Romanesque and Gothic works. The jewel of the collection is by Gislebertus, a carved fragment taken from the cathedral and found built into a wall in 1856. This "Temptation of Eve" depicts Eve with sensuality and subtlety.

On the summit of Mont Beuvray, southwest of Autun, is **Bibracte,** a Gallic *oppidum* (army camp). Here Vercingétorix called a council of war of the Gallic tribes in 52 B.C. in an attempt to defeat the Romans. The **Musée Bibracte** documents this key site. ■

**Autun** 🅜 217 C4 Visitor Information ✉ 13 rue General Demetz ☎ 03 85 86 80 38 **autun-tourisme.com** • **Musée Rolin** ✉ 5 rue des Bancs ☎ 03 85 52 09 76 🕐 Closed Tues. & Dec.–Feb. • **Musée Bibracte** ✉ St.-Léger-sous-Beuvray ☎ 03 85 86 52 40 🕐 Closed mid-Nov.–mid.-March **bibracte.fr**

# CLUNY

Founded in 910, Cluny was for hundreds of years the most influential power in Christendom, described by Pope Urban II as the "light of the world." But the Romanesque abbey buildings were torn down after the revolution.

Of the original abbey, only the south transept and tower still stand. The town of Cluny covers much of the rest; excavations show the west end of the nave. The church was 600 feet (180 m) long with two towers, the interior painted For centuries it resounded to the strains of Gregorian chant, and as if to emphasize the role of music here, some surviving capitals are carved with scenes of musicians. The work of an unknown "master of Cluny," these carvings are on view at the **Musée Ochier** in the 15th-century abbey palace *(Palais Jean de Bourbon, 03 85 59 12 79).*

To set Cluny in context, visit the Burgundian churches that were influenced by it. The architecture of the older abbey church of **Tournus** *(place de l'Abbaye, tel 03 85 27 00 20),* 20 miles (33 km) to the northeast, is powerful and confident, with perfect round arches and attenuated columns. The 11th-century basilica of **Paray-le-Monial** to the west gives an idea of what Cluny actually looked like, on a reduced scale. Soaring to a daring 71 feet (22 m), the nave is crowned by austere, graceful vaulting. Clerestory windows provide the only clue as to how Cluny was lit.

The **Chapelle des Moines,** part of a Cluniac foundation at **Berzé-la-Ville,** southeast of Cluny, hints at how magnificently the abbey was decorated. The **Circuit des Églises Romanes** *(information: Mâcon tourist office or tourisme charolaisbrionnais.fr)* is a self-guided driving tour that takes in ancient churches including the priory of Anzy-le-Duc, Iguerande, and St.-Hilaire at Semur-en-Brionnais, with its octagonal belfry. ■

### Taizé

Famous for its meditative chanting and Bible readings in many languages, the village of Taizé *(taize.fr)* is a vibrant religious community and place of pilgrimage 4 miles (6.5 km) north of Cluny. Founded in 1940 by a Swiss pastor, Brother Roger, Taizé includes brothers from all denominations and draws thousands of visitors every year to share in simple candlelit worship and the daily life of the community.

**Cluny** 217 C4 Visitor Information 6 rue Mercière 03 85 59 05 34 **cluny-tourisme.com • Paray-le-Monial** 217 C4 Visitor Information avenue Jean-Paul II 03 85 81 10 92 **paraylemonial.fr • Berzé-la-Ville** Chapelle des Moines 03 85 36 66 52 Closed Nov.–March **chapelledesmoines.fr**

# FOOD & DRINK—TRULY ROBUST FARE

**Burgundians and the Lyonnais both lay claim to occupying the epicenter of French food. Their attitude to eating is summed up in the saying "Better a good meal than fine clothes." It is a robust cuisine, varying from the acme of sophistication to peasant dishes made according to the produce and resources available.**

■ On cold days in the mountains, cheese fondue is a group-pleasing must.

This is a protein-rich cuisine, with much meat and cheese, and sauces of wine and cream. Fine produce is plentiful: Bresse is famous for its *appellation contrôlée* chickens, Charollais for its beef. The Burgundian snail must be the plumpest in France, served with a rich emollient of butter and garlic. The Morvan produces one of France's best raw hams. Fish is plentiful, too, and cooked imaginatively: *Pochouse* is a kind of freshwater bouillabaisse, made with white wine; *quenelles de brochet* are delicate balls of pike.

Lyon is celebrated for its starred restaurants and superstar chefs. Its traditional cuisine is famous for its charcuterie, the sausages and other pork products that go so well with Beaujolais Nouveau. Dijon is famous for mustard and for spices that flavor *pain d'épices*, a spice-and-honey cake.

Once you reach the mountains, the food gets robust, with warming stews, soups, and gratins. *Gratin dauphinois* is a substantial dish of potatoes cooked with eggs, butter, milk, and cheese. Fondue is justly famous, and if you get the chance, try lesser known raclette and participate in a cozy ritual involving melting pieces of cheese. The mountains produce fine butter and cheese: The Jura is the home of Vacherin, the Savoie makes indispensible Gruyère, and the Massif Central produces Cantal, and of course there's the incomparable ewe's milk Roquefort.

The Auvergne volcanic center of the Massif Central also has a strong peasant cuisine. The staples are potatoes and cabbage; try *potée Auvergnate* (pork with stuffed cabbage). The Auvergne is also noted for its salted hams and dried sausages, and Le Puy is famous for its superior green lentils.

Cherries, raspberries, plums, and apricots feature on menus. Black currants, with their intense flavor, come deliciously in tarts and preserves, and are distilled into the rich liqueur cassis, a component of local aperitifs.

No visit to this rich agricultural region would be complete without

Baked snails are one of Burgundy's many tasty delicacies.

sampling the aristocratic wines of Burgundy: The fragrant whites of Chablis and Meursault, for example and the velvety reds of Gevrey-Chambertin or Nuits-St.-Georges.

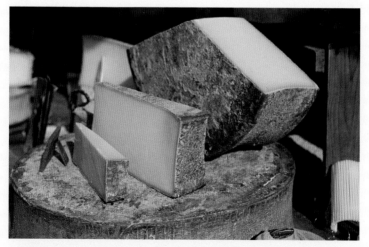

Perfectly aged cheese awaits takers at the Sunday market in Beaune.

# THE JURA

The mountainous region of the Jura, on the Swiss border, covers much of the old region of Franche-Comté, once ruled by the great duchy of Burgundy and part of the nation of France only since the 17th century. The Jura's ancient mountains, which give their name to the Jurassic period, have yielded several important dinosaur remains. Deep valleys with rushing torrents divide the rolling plateaus: The lakes and rivers teem with trout, carp, and pike, and forests of black spruce, pine, and broad-leaved trees cover the slopes.

Visitors to the Jura come to enjoy nature, walking on lower slopes, canoeing on the rivers, and, in the winter months, skiing. This is also France's wettest region, though a dry period in midsummer provides relief. Although it is no longer as inaccessible as it used to be, the Jura still is home to plenty of wildlife, including the lynx, otter, and mountain hare. The high rainfall waters peat bogs, which provide a habitat for rare birds, butterflies, and mosses. **Cirque-de-Baumes,** near Lons-le-Saunier, curiously, shelters a pocket of Mediterranean flora and fauna amid its limestone cliffs. Throughout the region, wildflowers carpet the roadsides and meadows in spring and summer.

Dotting the valleys are the Jura's distinctive wooden houses, with enormous chimneys serving as rooms, smokehouses, or even escape hatches when snow buries the house.

The Jura yields some of France's favorite cheeses, such as Morbier and dense, creamy Vacherin. The region also produces its own wine, mostly from a small region around the town of **Arbois,** a favorite haunt of wine lovers. You should try *vin jaune,* a sherrylike wine from Château-Chalon. You may also find the increasingly rare dessert wine known as *vin de paille,* made from grapes left out in the sun on straw mats before they are pressed. Arbois is also famed as the birthplace of Louis Pasteur, the inventor of pasteurization, whose house and laboratory are preserved in the **Maison de Pasteur** (83 *rue de Courcelles, tel 03 84 66 11 72).*

## Loue Valley

For a brief visit to the Jura, follow the course of the Loue Valley. Start from **Arc-et-Senans,** with its ambitious 18th-century new town, the **Saline Royale** *(tel 03 81 54 45 00, salineroyale.com).* Built to exploit the local salt mines, Arc-et-Senans now houses two museums featuring exhibitions on art and architecture. Take the D17 north to Quingey. Now follow the D101 east, changing to the D102 and D103 successively to follow

**Comité Départemental du Jura** 🅰 217 D4–D5 Visitor Information ✉ 8 rue Louis-Rousseau, Lons-le-Saunier ☎ 08 20 39 39 00 **jura-tourism.com**

the river upstream to **Ornans** with its flower-decked balconies overhanging the river. Famous as the birthplace of the great realist painter Gustave Courbet, the town boasts several of his paintings, displayed in his childhood home, now the **Musée Courbet**.

Continue up the valley on the D67, which provides stopping places for admiring the view. Two miles (3 km) past Mouthier, you reach the dramatic source of the Loue, springing in a great torrent from a cavern in the rock, only a short walk from the road. East of Salins-les-Bains, at the source of the Lison River, a waterfall plunges into a deep green pool.

To the west is **Lons-le-Saunier** *(place du 11 Novembre, tel 03 84 24 65 01, lons-jura.fr),* a town central for many of the region's sights. It was built over a thermal spring used by the Romans and now supplying its thermal baths and its swimming pool. ◼

---

## EXPERIENCE: Walk to Cascades du Hérisson

Get a feel for the rugged beauty of the Jura with a walk to explore the spectacular waterfalls of the **Cascades du Hérisson** *(cascades-du-herisson.fr),* the most glorious sight in the Region des Lacs, a magical landscape of villages and waterfalls, mountains and forests.

To reach the waterfalls, walk (or drive) from the village of Doucier to the **Maison des Cascades** *(tel 03 84 25 77 36)* at the foot of the Cascade d'Eventail, where there is a visitor center. Here you will find information about the history of the valley and the development of the landscape, including the industries dependent on water power.

You can see the dramatic cascades that tumble down the river by following the 4.3-mile (7 km) path along the Hérisson River. The three-hour hike culminates at the top in a magnificent cascade, the Grand Saut, which plunges 200 feet (60 m) to the pool beneath. For the most spectacular views, go after abundant rain, or in winter when the waterfalls are frozen. Wear suitable footgear.

---

**Arbois** 🅰 217 D4 • Visitor Information ✉ rue de l'Hôtel de Ville ☎ 03 84 66 55 50 **arbois.fr** • **Arc-et-Senans** 🅰 218 D5 • Visitor Information ✉ porche de la Saline Royale ☎ 03 81 57 43 21 **destinationlouelison.com** • **Ornans** 🅰 218 E5 • Visitor Information ✉ 7 rue Pierre-Vernier ☎ 03 81 62 21 50 **destinationlouelison.com** • **Musée Courbet** ✉ Maison Natale de l'Artiste, place Robert-Fernier, Ornans ☎ 03 81 86 22 88 🕐 Closed Tue **musee-courbet.fr**

# More Places to Visit in Burgundy & the Jura

## Besançon

The ancient fortress town of Besançon is the capital of Franche-Comté. It now specializes in watchmaking. Appropriately, a 19th-century astronomical clock adorns the 12th-century Gothic **Cathédrale St.-Jean.** The 17th-century citadel houses museums on local and natural history, Vauban *(tel 03 81 87 83 33),* and the his-

### The Swallow Train Line

**La Ligne des Hirondelles** *(lignedeshirondelles.fr)* crosses the Jura from one side to the other, linking Dole to St.-Claude. Originally constructed to transport goods, such as stone, marble, cheese, and crafts, this amazing piece of engineering follows 75 miles (120 km) of track through the wonderful scenery of the Haut Jura regional park, traveling through 36 dramatic tunnels and along 22 viaducts.

tory of the Resistance. A museum in Victor Hugo's birthplace *(140 Grande Rue, tel 03 81 41 53 65, citadelle.com)* opened in 2013. The **Musée des Beaux-Arts** has works by Courbet, Ingres, and Boucher. *besancon-tourisme .com* 217 E5 **Visitor Information** 2 place de la 1ère Armée Française 03 81 80 92 55

## Châtillon-sur-Seine

Châtillon-sur-Seine, which is located near the source of the Seine River, is the site of the Treasure of Vix, shown in the **Musée Archéologique** *(14 rue de la Libération du Pays Chatillonnais, tel 03 80 91 24 67).* This Gaulish cache was unearthed in 1953 in Vix, 4 miles (6 km) northwest of Châtillon. A sixth-century B.C. Celtic princess was buried here in a chariot, decked in jewels and gold, and surrounded by artifacts, notably the great Krater of Vix, the largest bronze vessel from antiquity. 217 C6 **Visitor Information** rue du Bourg 03 80 91 13 19

## Mâcon

Mâcon gives its name to the Mâconnais wine region, which produces many fine red, rosé, and white wines, most notably Pouilly-Fuissé and St.-Véran. Visit the **Maison des Vins** *(484 avenue le-Lattre-de-Tassigny, tel 03 85 22 91 11, maison-des-vins .com)* for information and tastings. The pleasant **Place des Herbes** has an elaborately carved 15th-century timber-framed building. The nearby **Roche de Solutré,** a huge limestone outcrop where the bones of thousands of prehistoric reindeer and horses have been found, has an excellent museum. *macon-tourism .com* 217 D4 **Visitor Information** place St.-Pierre 03 85 21 07 07

## Nevers

Famous for its faience, Nevers boasts an extensive collection displayed in the **Musée Municipal Frederic Blandin** *(16 rue St.-Genest, tel 03 86 68 44 60)*. The visitor can purchase the glazed ceramic ware from the 17th-century Faïencerie Montagnon *(rue de la Porte du Croux, tel 03 86 71 96 90, faience-montagnon.fr)*. Architectural highlights of the town include 12th-century ramparts, the 15th-century Palais Ducal, the Romanesque Église St.-Étienne, and **Cathédrale St.-Cyr,** where you will find the remains of a sixth-century baptistry and a 13th-century nave.

🗺 216  B4  **Visitor Information** ✉ Palais Ducal, rue Sabatier ☎ 03 86 68 46 00

## Ronchamp

The chapel of **Notre-Dame-du-Haut** at Ronchamp is significant as one of the works of Le Corbusier; the chapel is one of many such works scattered across Europe, Argentina, Japan, and India that make it a UNESCO World Heritage site under the designation of The Architectural Work of Le Corbusier, an Outstanding Contribution to the Modern Movement. Le Corbusier built the church in 1950–1954. The most revolutionary work of his sculptural, anti-rationalist period is now controversial due to neglect of the original building, and developments including a new access route and modern monastery.

🗺 217  E5  **Visitor Information** ✉ 13 rue de la Chapelle ☎ 03 84 20 73 26

◾ **Notre-Dame-du-Haut, Le Corbusier's chapel in Ronchamp**

# RHÔNE VALLEY & THE ALPS

**From the snowfields of the Alps to the olive groves of the Drôme Valley, from the starred restaurants of Lyon to remote mountain refuges, the Rhône-Alpes region embraces a huge variety of landscapes and activities. Wine lovers, skiers, walkers, and culture vultures will all feel at home here.**

The region's main hub is Lyon, France's second city, an important industrial metropolis with a lively cultural life and a fine arts museum second only to the Louvre in Paris. Justly famed for its cuisine, Lyon is a gourmand's paradise and boasts a wealth of exceptional bistros, cafés and restaurants, many of them coming with the imprimatur of Michelin stars.

The Romans colonized the area in the second century B.C., and substantial Roman remains can be found in Lyon as well as at Vienne and St.-Romain-en-Gal.

The Alps hereabouts boast some of the world's top-flight ski resorts, such as Chamonix and Courchevel. But many travelers can easily forget that the mountains also make a beguiling summer retreat, with limpid blue lakes and gracious spa towns. Several major nature reserves protect the rare wild flora and fauna that abound in some of the higher reaches of these glorious mountains.

The peasant life of the mountain farmers and shepherds is not as hard as it was for their forebears, but their large timber or stone farmhouses still have the wide balconies essential for winter stores. Imaginative regional museums pay tribute to centuries of traditional life.

To the north lies the rich farmland of the Bresse province. To the south is Nyons, famous for its huge variety of olives. The Beaujolais and Côtes du Rhône vineyards yield excellent drinking wines as well as many coveted appellations like Côte-Rotie and Hermitage. Farther south, the region meets Provence in the gorges of the Ardèche and the lavender fields, olive groves, and sunflower fields of the picturesque Drôme Valley. ∎

■ **Climbers head down the Aguille du Midi before venturing onto Mont Blanc.**

# LYON

A few days in Lyon, the second largest city in France, is a treat, not least because it has every right to call itself the gastronomic capital of France. Its key position at the confluence of the Rhône and Saône Rivers has historically made it a major hub on a vital trade route.

Old Lyon brims with charming places to eat and chat.

Lyon was founded by the Romans as Lugdunum in 43 B.C., and their great amphitheater on the hill of **Fourvière** is a good place to start a visit. To get there, walk up the winding Chemin du Rosaire, or take the funicular railroad from opposite the cathedral. The view from the top reveals the city on its peninsula (*presqu'île*) between the two rivers.

On a clear day, you can see the Alps. Many a Roman soldier must have looked eastward, too, and longed for home.

Lyon's ruins constitute the earliest Roman site outside Italy. The **Musée Gallo-Romaine**—a modern building cleverly tucked into the hillside, with vast windows overlooking the amphitheater—does a splendid job

**Lyon** 217 D3 Visitor Information ✉ place Bellecour ☎ 04 72 77 69 69 **lyon-france.com** • **Musée Gallo-Romaine** ✉ 17 rue Cléberg ☎ 04 72 38 49 30 🕐 Closed Mon. 💲 $ **lugdunum.grandlyon.com**

of evoking every-day Roman life. Its superb collection includes mosaics (most notably a wonderful depiction of a chariot race), inscriptions, statues, and ancient coins. Since Roman times, Fourvière has been a site of sanctuar-ies, the most recent one being the 19th-century **Basilique Notre-Dame-de-Fourvière** (place Fourvière, fourviere .org), with its turrets, marble, and stained glass.

## Old Lyon

At the bottom of the Fourvière hill, on the west bank of the Saône, lies Old Lyon. One of the largest ensembles of Renaissance build-ings in Europe, it is now a UNESCO World Heritage site. In the 15th century, Louis XI granted Lyon the right to hold fairs that attracted merchants from all over Europe. Magnificent *hôtels particuliers*, or town houses, were built, and since many of the merchants were Italian, there is a distinct Florentine quality

to the architecture of the old town. Each mansion had a courtyard with a well and often a turret with a spi-ral staircase. The 16th-century Hôtel Gadagne houses the **Musée His-torique de Lyon** and the restored

Musée de la Marionnette, devoted to the storied history of puppets in Lyon. At the heart of the old quarter is the **Cathédrale St.-Jean,** a synthesis of Romanesque and Gothic styles, built between 1180 and 1480.

**Musée Historique de Lyon & Musée de la Marionnette** ☒ Hôtel Gadagne, 1 place du Petit-Collège ☎ 04 78 42 03 61 🕘 Closed Mon.– Tues. 💲 $ **gadagne-lyon.fr**

---

## EXPERIENCE: Getting a Taste of Gastronomic Lyon

Long renowned for its food, the city of Lyon is home to some of the most sophisticated restaurants in France, and indeed in all of Europe. But the city's food story has much humbler origins. In fact, it begins with a group of women known as the *mères Lyonnaises,* or "Lyon mothers."

During the 19th century, in the wake of the revolution, these women left their positions as domestic servants and chefs in the great aristocratic houses of Lyon to set up restaurants. Although their establishments may have been rough, simple places, the food they offered was an innovative combination of bourgeois cuisine and authentic home cooking.

Mère Brazier, one of the best loved of the Lyon mothers, was the first woman to receive three Michelin stars. It was at her restaurant, **Mère Brazier** *(12 rue Royale, tel 04 78 23 17 20, lamerebrazier .fr),* that Paul Bocuse, the chef who was affectionately dubbed "the pope of gastronomy" served his apprenticeship.

You can also still sample some of the equally legendary *bouchons* of Lyon, traditional little bistros serving hearty fare like sausages, tripe, *oeufs en meurette* in a rich wine sauce, or black pudding with apples, usually washed down with Beaujolais wine.

To shop for food in Lyon, or to simply feast your eyes on the wonderful displays, head for the **Halles de Lyon–Paul Bocuse** *(102 cours Lafayette, tel 04 78 62 39 33, halles-de-lyon-paulbocuse.com, closed Mon.),* the traditional covered market halls, now restored and named in honor of the legendary chef who liked to do his shopping there. You will also discover many restaurants and seafood bars.

Alternatively, check out the **St.-Antoine Food Market** *(closed Mon.),* on Quai St.-Antoine on the banks of the Saône close to the Place Bellecour, or the **Croix-Rousse Food Market** *(place de la Croix-Rousse, closed Mon.),* in the center of the old silk weavers quarter overlooking the city.

## Modern Lyon

The Presqu'île is the center of modern Lyon, where much of the city's cultural and commerical life revolves around Place Bellecour. The best shops are here, especially around Rue de la République, Rue Émile-Zola, Rue Gasparin, and Rue du Président Herriot. Silk scarves make excellent souvenirs and very lightweight presents to take home.

To the north of the city, the hill of La Croix-Rousse is stacked with the houses of the silk workers *(canuts)* who made Lyon's fortune in the early 19th century. Their houses had to be tall to accommodate the huge Jacquard looms that transformed the industry from 1804 onward. Many of the houses have now been converted into fashionable lofts, but the area is still riddled with *traboules.* These passages played a key part in sheltering members of the Resistance during World War II, and it was here that their leader Jean Moulin was captured by the Nazis. The **Centre d'Histoire de la Résistance et de la Déportation** is housed partly in the cells in which the Gestapo tortured its prisoners, and tells the stories of the many safe houses, French underground railroad routes, and spy networks that kept Resistance volunteers out of the hands of the Germans.

Set in an 18th-century town house, the **Musée Historique des Tissus** recounts the history of Lyon's silk industry and fabrics in general. This is a fascinating museum in terms of science and history; whether you have an interest in fabrics is immaterial. Next door is the home of the **Musée des Arts Décoratifs,** filled with furniture, tapestries, and porcelain.

The city's artistic life revolves around Place des Terreaux. Here the **Musée des Beaux-Arts,** in a former Benedictine convent, displays works by Veronese, Tintoretto, Rubens, El Greco, and many modern French masters. Jean Nouvel's glass-and-steel dome for the neoclassical opera house towers over the Place des Terreaux, embellished by the modern sculpture of Daniel Buren. The Musée **d'Art Contemporain** is located in the Cité Internationale, a modern development on the east bank of the Rhône. ∎

**Centre d'Histoire de la Résistance et de la Déportation** ✉ 14 avenue Berthelot ☎ 04 78 72 23 11 🕐 Closed Mon.–Tues. 💲 $ **chrd.lyon.fr** • **Musée Historique des Tissus & Musée des Arts Décoratifs** ✉ 34 rue de la Charité ☎ 04 78 38 42 00 🕐 Closed Mon. 💲 $ **museedestissus .fr** • **Musée des Beaux-Arts** ✉ 20 place des Terreaux ☎ 04 72 10 17 40 🕐 Closed Tues. 💲 $ **mba-lyon.fr** • **Musée d'Art Contemporain** ✉ Cité Internationale, 81 quai Charles-de-Gaulle ☎ 04 72 69 17 17 🕐 Closed Mon.–Tues. & bet. exhibitions 💲 $ **mac-lyon.com**

# BEAUJOLAIS COUNTRY

Beaujolais is one wine region where the landscape doesn't play second fiddle to the vines: Rolling, wooded hills are punctuated by golden-stone châteaus and vignerons' houses with wine cellars on the ground floor, external staircases, and verandas.

The best wine comes from the north, where a day's drive could take in most of the ten Beaujolais *crus*, allowing time for leisurely *dégustations*.

**Villefranche-sur-Saône,** 20 miles (32 km) north of Lyon, is the main town of Beaujolais, a miniature version of Lyon with its Italianate mansions, elegant courtyards, and small cafés serving fresh Beaujolais with delicious *saucissons*. In **Beaujeu,** northeast of Villefranche, the Hospices de Beaujeu have held wine auctions since the 12th century. You can taste local wine in the **Place de l'Hôtel de Ville,** which hosts a museum outlining the many local traditions.

Quiet winding roads (D26 and D18 northeast from Beaujeu) lead to the **Terrasse de Chiroubles,** where you have wide views of the vineyards. Continuing north on the D26 you come to **Juliénas,** where every building appears to be a wine cellar, even the church. Next stop might be the eponymous windmill of **Moulin-à-Vent** (to the south of Juliénas on the D266), for wide-ranging views of the Saône Valley and a chance to taste the

oldest cru in Beaujolais. **Romanèche-Thorins,** nearby, is home to enthusiast Georges Duboeuf, whose Hameau du Vin offers a wide variety of wines. In **Fleurie,** west on the D32, look for the Chapelle de la Madone in the vineyards, and try the local specialty, *andouillettes au Fleurie*—chitterling sausages cooked in Fleurie wine, a truly mouthwatering experience.

**Villié-Morgon,** south on the D68, offers wine tastings in the cellar of an 18th-century mansion. Nearby you'll find **Château de Pizay,** with its splendid topiary gardens, and the Renaissance **Château de Corcelles,** painted by Maurice Utrillo.

Farther south you'll come to the village of **Brouilly** and the **Côte de Brouilly,** vineyards on the slopes of Mont Brouilly, followed by **La Chaise,** a fine 17th-century château with gardens designed by Le Nôtre.

With so much wine flowing, why not stay overnight? For delightful château accommodations combined with good Beaujolais wine, try **Château de Bagnols** (see Travelwise p. 436), southwest of Villefranche. ∎

**Beaujolais Country** beaujolais.com • **Villefranche-sur-Saône** 🅰 217 C3
Visitor Information ✉ 96 rue de la Sous-Préfecture ☎ 04 74 07 27 40
**villefranche.net** • **Beaujeu** 🅰 191 C3 Visitor Information ✉ place du
l'Hôtel de Ville ☎ 04 74 69 22 88 **aucoeurdubeaujolais.fr**

# MONT BLANC & THE MOUNTAINS

From Lake Geneva almost to the Mediterranean, the majestic snowy peaks of the French Alps offer awe-inspiring mountain landscapes. Most dramatic of all is Mont Blanc, Europe's highest peak at 15,780 feet (4,810 m).

■ A crisp, clear day offers a clear view of the Alps from the Aiguille du Midi near Mont Blanc.

At the foot of magnificent Mont Blanc sits **Chamonix,** the world capital of mountaineering. Its **Musée Alpin** presents a history of Mont Blanc and its early explorers. Nonclimbers can make the spectacular ascent of neighboring summits by cable car: 12,609 feet (3,842 m) up the **Aiguille du Midi,** or 8,408 feet (2,526 m) up **Le Brevent,** both of which give fabu-lous views of Mont Blanc. Go early to avoid the crowds and midday mists, and take warm clothes. If you have no head for heights, take the rack railroad up to the glacier of the **Mer de Glace.** Chamonix today is a year-round resort, with swimming, golf, and tennis, as well as winter skiing.

You do not have to be a winter-loving aficionado of snow to enjoy

**Chamonix–Mont Blanc** ◩ 217 E3 Visitor Information ✉ 85 place Triangle-de-l'Amitié ☎ 04 50 53 00 24 **chamonix.com** • **Parc National de la Vanoise** ✉ 135 rue du Docteur-Julliand, Chambéry ☎ 04 79 62 30 54 **vanoise-parcnational.fr** • **Val-d'Isère** ✉ **Maison de Val-d'Isère** ☎ 04 79 06 06 60 **valdisere.com**

## Ski Resorts

With high altitudes, reliable snow, the very latest in lifts and snowmaking systems, and a wide variety of *pistes* (trails), France offers some of the best skiing in the world for all levels of expertise. Connections between the valleys and pistes are good, enabling you to ski long distances from one valley to the next and to really explore and appreciate the mountains.

Accommodations range from four-star hotels to self-catering chalets. Most of the resorts are within a three-hour drive of the airports at Chambéry, Geneva, or Lyon. **Chamonix, Mégève** *(70 rue Monseigneur Conseil, tel 04 50 21 27 28, megeve.com)*, and **Morzine** *(place du Baraty, tel 04 50 74 72 72, morzine-avoriaz.com)* are located just one hour away from Geneva.

the Alps. In summer, the air up here is fresh and clear and the light sharp, the high mountain passes are open, and drifts of alpine flowers cover the pastures. The best way to experience the beauty of the region is by hiking *(see Travelwise p. 474 for various sources of information, or ask at the Chamonix tourist office).*

---

**INSIDER TIP:**

You, too, can get the world famous spring water straight from the "source" in Évian. Join the locals and fill your water bottles at the public fountain.

—CAROLINE HICKEY
*National Geographic editor*

---

Never forget, though, that these are major mountains and always take the usual precautions since, even in summer, the weather here can change quickly. Make sure you have warm clothing, good boots, a whistle, food, and a map, and tell someone where you are heading and when you should arrive.

The mountain region east of the Rhône formed the independent principality of Savoie until it was ceded to France in 1860. It remained poor and remote until first alpinism and then skiing transformed its economy. Now the mountains and crystalline lakes attract visitors year-round.

### Nature Reserves

The Alps remain a haven for a rich variety of flora and fauna. Savoie contains five major nature reserves, most notably **Parc National de la Vanoise** *(vanoise-parcnational.fr)* France's first **national park**. In this high mountain habitat between Courchevel and **Val-d'Isère,** hikers might spot any variety of wildlife including chamois, ibex, and golden eagles. The more remote pastures in this beloved national park support countless wildflower species, including crocuses, blue and yellow gentians, numerous lilies and orchids, tulips, and alpine anemones.

## Lakes

Ringed by snowy mountains, the lakes hereabouts are an unforgettable sight. **Thonon-les-Bains** and **Évian-les-Bains** are both charming spa towns located on the banks of Lac Léman (Lake Geneva); from both towns, passenger boats cross the lake to Switzerland. **Aix-les-Bains,** on the banks of Lac du Bourget, is another popular spa town; a boat trip on the lake can include a visit to the Benedictine **Abbaye d'Hautecombe.** Rebuilt in 19th-century neo-Gothic, the abbey church contains the tombs of the Savoie kings.

**Annecy,** situated on the banks of Lac d'Annecy, makes an ideal base for touring the region. The town rejoices in a charming old quarter with pastel facades, a château dating from the 12th century, canals and bridges, lakeside cafés to warm to in winter, and beaches to idle away summer days. ■

■ **The snow-capped panorama of the Alps, covered in pine trees, which can be admired in Évian-les-Bains.**

**Thonon-les-Bains** 217 E4 ✉ Château de Sonnaz, 2 rue Michaud ☎ 04 50 71 55 55 **thononlesbains.com** • **Évian-les-Bains** 219 E4 ✉ place de la Porte d'Allinges ☎ 04 50 75 04 26 🕐 Closed Sun. from Oct. to Apr. **evian-tourisme.com** • **Aix-les-Bains** 217 E3 ✉ 8 rue du Casino, Allée du Grand Passage ☎ 04 79 88 68 00 **aixlesbains-rivieradesalpes.com** • **Annecy** 217 E3 • Visitor Information ✉ Bonlieu, 1 rue Jean-Jaurès ☎ 04 50 45 00 33 🕐 Closed Sun. Hours vary seasonally; check website **lac-annecy.com**

# GRENOBLE

**Capital of the old province of Dauphiné, Grenoble, handsomely set at the confluence of the Isère and Drac Rivers, is the only large city in the Alps.**

Grenoble prospered from the 19th-century discovery of hydroelectricity and rapidly developed into a center of chemical and nuclear research. The pace of change accelerated even further after it hosted the Winter Olympics in 1968. The city also has a lively cultural life, animated by its large student population.

Take the cable car to the **Fort de la Bastille,** where orientation tables help interpret the views. Walk down from the fort through the Jardin des Dauphins to the **Musée Dauphinois,** an excellent regional museum in a 17th-century convent building. The **Musée de la Résistance** *(14 rue Hébert, tel 04 76 42 38 53)* is nearby.

To see the old quarter, with its 13th-century buildings and church, head for Place St.-André. The cathedral and the bishops' palace are on Place Notre-Dame. Place Grenette and Place Victor-Hugo are both lively squares, good for cafés and shopping. The former Hôtel de Ville houses the **Musée Stendhal** *(20 Grande Rue, tel 04 76 86 52 08, closed Sun.–Mon. & Thurs.),* devoted to the Grenoble-born writer. The arts are well supported by the huge **Musée de Grenoble** *(5 place de Lavalette, tel 04 76 63 44 44, museedegrenoble.fr, closed Tues.)* and **Maison de la Culture MC2** *(4 rue Paul Claudel, tel 04 76 00 79 79, mc2greno ble.fr),* for dance, music, and theater. ∎

■ *"Les bulles"* (the bubbles), a cable car, transports people up to the Fort de la Bastille.

**Grenoble** 🅰 217 D2 Visitor Information ✉ 14 rue de la République ☎ 04 56 52 38 39 **grenoble-tourisme.com** • **Musée Dauphinois** ✉ 30 rue Maurice-Gignoux ☎ 04 57 58 89 01 🕐 Closed Tues. 💲 $ **musees.isere.fr/musee/musee-dauphinois**

# CHAMBÉRY

**The historic capital of once Italian Savoie, Chambéry is another good base for a visit to the Alps. Its dignified old quarter is full of Italianate mansions and little covered passages.**

The extraordinary **Fontaine des Éléphants** on the Boulevard de la Colonneis is a monument to the Comte de Boigne, who amassed a fortune in India in the 18th century and left much of it to the municipality. The fountain has become the symbol of the town.

---

**INSIDER TIP:**

From Renaissance architecture to local pasta specialties on restaurant menus, Chambéry retains a delightful Italian accent.

—SYLVIE BIGAR
*National Geographic writer*

---

For a hundred years or so in the 15th and 16th centuries, the Holy Shroud was kept here in the Chapelle des Ducs de Savoie, and Chambéry became a pilgrimage town. But in 1578, the shroud was taken to Turin when that city became the administrative capital of the House of Savoie. Just southeast of Chambéry is **Les Charmettes,** the country retreat of philosopher Jean-Jacques Rousseau, now faithfully restored just as he described it in his *Confessions.* ∎

## Lac de Bourguet

Near the elegant spa resort of Aix-les-Bains (see p. 248) and just a few miles north of Chambéry, you will find Lac de Bourguet, its blue water set beautifully in the mountains. All kinds of water sports are available here, including canoeing and kayaking. For sailing, check with **Club Nautique Chambéry** (*tel 04 79 25 26 98*), and for water skiing, try **Club Ski Nautique** (*ycbl.fr*). **Bateaux du Lac** (*bateaux-aixlesbains.com*) offers cruises across the lake and to the abbey of Hautecombe on the western bank.

■ Chambéry's icon is the fun, famous Fontaine des Éléphants.

**Chambéry** 🅜 217 E3 Visitor Information ✉ place de Palais de Justice ☎ 04 79 33 42 47 **chambery-tourisme.com** • **Musée Jean-Jacques** Rousseau ✉ 890 chemin des Charmettes ☎ 04 79 33 39 44 🕒 Closed Tues. 💲 $

# GORGES DE L'ARDÈCHE

The Gorges de l'Ardèche, in the far south of the Rhône Valley and the Alps region, make a truly stunning tour. For some 20 miles (32 km) between Vallon-Pont-d'Arc and St.-Martin-d'Ardèche, the D290 twists along the rim of the gorge above the river.

The Gorges de l'Ardèche attract kayakers and climbers during the summer months.

Before heading out, take a good look at **Pont d'Arc** itself, a natural limestone bridge hollowed out by the fast-flowing waters of the Ardèche River. Along this thrilling route, there are heart-stopping views at every turn, especially on the Haute Corniche, perched dizzyingly high above the river.

Adventurous alternatives to driving include kayaking and white-water rafting: You can rent kayaks in Vallon-Pont-d'Arc and find transportation back at St.-Martin-d'Ardèche *(visitor information at Vallon-Pont-d'Arc)*. The Ardèche is one of France's fastest, and potentially most treacherous, rivers; early summer is the safest time for tackling its waters.

The limestone plateau around the gorge is riddled with caves. The huge **Grotte de la Madeleine,** just off the D290, bristles with stalagmites and stalactites; **Aven d'Orgnac** (*aven* means "pothole"), just to the west, has spectacular rock formations, colored red by iron oxides and sparkling with crystals. The museum here includes a reconstruction of a Stone Age settlement. The interior of **Aven de Marzal,** a little to the north, also glitters with colored crystals. A museum of speleology includes centuries-old equipment used to explore the cave when it was first discovered.

Pretty villages upstream of the gorge include 12th-century **Balazuc,** on a cliff above the Ardèche River, and **Vogüé,** tucked between cliff and river, with a 12th-century château. ∎

**Gorges de l'Ardèche** 217 C1 Visitor Information ✉ 1 place de la Gare, Vallon-Pont-d'Arc ☎ 04 75 88 04 01 **vallon-pont-darc.com**

# More Places to Visit in the Rhône Valley & Alps

## Bourg-en-Bresse

The market town of Bourg-en-Bresse is famous for chickens and for the Flamboyant Gothic **Monastère Royale de Brou.** Built between 1505 and 1536 by Margaret of Austria, it has a superbly carved facade, choir stalls, and rood screen. Most gorgeous of all are the tombs, sculpted in exquisite detail from Carrara marble. *monastere-de-brou.fr* 🅰 217 D3 **Visitor Information** ✉ 6 avenue Alsace-Lorraine ☎ 04 74 22 49 40

## Briançon

The highest town in Europe, at 4,300 feet (1,310 m), Briançon was heavily fortified by Vauban, Louis XIV's military architect. He also designed the solid **Église de Notre-Dame** set high on the defensive hill chosen for the citadel. The views over the surrounding mountains are superb. *ot-briancon.fr* 🅰 217 E2 **Visitor Information** ✉ place du Temple ☎ 04 92 21 08 50

## Hauterives

Located about 15 miles (24 km) north of Romans-sur-Isère on the D538, the **Palais Idéal** *(tel 04 75 68 81 19, facteurcheval.com)* at Hauterives was built by postman Ferdinand Cheval using stones collected on his route. It mixes Asian architectural styles. 🅰 217 D2

## Nyons

Charming Nyons is famous for its olives. The **Musée de l'Olivier** tells the story of olive cultivation. Visit on market day (Thursday), when you can buy a huge variety of olives, olive oil products, and olive-based delicacies. *maisondeshuilesetolives.fr* 🅰 217 D1 **Visitor Information** ✉ place de la Libération ☎ 04 75 26 10 35

## Parc Naturel du Vercors

Protected here are the pine forests, waterfalls, and gorges of the Vercors Massif. This quiet area was a center of the Resistance during World War II, and poignant cemeteries and memorials (in villages such as **Nizier** and **Vassieux**) mark the tragic events that took place here. *parc-du-vercors.fr* 🅰 217 D2 **Visitor Information** ✉ Maison du Parc, Lans en Vercors ☎ 04 76 94 38 26

## Pérouges

Some 19 miles (30 km) northeast of Lyon, the ancient town of Pérouges perches on a hill with fortifications, town gates, cobbled streets, and the marketplace shaded by a linden tree. *perouges.org* 🅰 217 D3 **Visitor Information** ✉ Office de Tourisme, Entrée de la Cité ☎ 04 74 46 70 84

## Vienne

Vienne is home to **Temple d'Auguste et Livie,** built in 25 B.C.; the remains of **Théâtre de Cybèle;** and **Théâtre Antique.** The **Musée des Beaux-Arts et d'Archéologie** covers the Roman city. *tourisme-vienne.com* 🅰 217 D3 **Visitor Information** ✉ 33 Pl. Charles de Gaulle ☎ 05 17 84 23 23

# MASSIF CENTRAL

At the very center of France lies the mountainous region of the Massif Central. Its ancient core is the Auvergne, settled by humans probably longer than anywhere else in France. The influence of the Auvergnats throughout France is considerable, from the many Auvergnat-run Paris cafés to the positions of power occupied by such Auvergnat politicians as Valery Giscard-d'Estaing, Georges Pompidou, and Jacques Chirac.

■ The Massif Central is a hikers' (and bikers') paradise, with multiple trails worth following.

South of the Auvergne, the wild uplands of the Cévennes plateau make a haven for wildflowers and rare birds. Such natural beauty and open countryside make this an ideal region for walking, hiking, river rafting, and hang gliding. Those who prefer gentler occupations can choose from a host of scenic drives or indulge in one of several elegant spas.

The history of the Massif Central, which is so ancient that it can be appreciated only on a geological timescale, is explained in a number of museums, including a major new museum of volcanology near Clermont-Ferrand. Regional museums evoke a firmly rooted traditional life, dependent on industries such as silkworm cultivation, knife production, and cheesemaking—the blue cheese of Roquefort (from sheep's milk) is an undisputed classic.

Distinctive local architecture features granite farms, heavy schist-tiled roofs with dormer windows, and open wooden verandas for drying winter stores. ■

# LE PUY-EN-VELAY

Don't rush into the town of Le Puy: Take time to gaze upon its extraordinary setting. The town sits in the middle of a high-rimmed plateau from which erupts a forest of volcanic cones. Perhaps its bizarre surroundings contributed to Le Puy's importance as an early place of worship. For centuries, pilgrims sought it out, and it was the starting point for the first recorded pilgrimage to Santiago de Compostela (see pp. 304–305), led by its bishop in 951.

Start by climbing the **Rocher Corneille** *(tel 04 71 04 11 33, closed mid-Nov.–Jan., $)* for its panoramic view over the old town. Topping this volcanic cone is the massive statue of **Notre-Dame-de-France,** which you can climb up inside.

The old town clusters around the Rocher in a maze of narrow streets. Dominating them is the **Cathédrale Notre-Dame-du-Puy** *(tel 04 71 05 45 52, cathedraledupuy.org, $),* built on another volcanic pinnacle with a dramatic approach up the stone steps of Rue des Tables. Recently restored, this 12th-century edifice demonstrates the Muslim influence that filtered along the pilgrim route. Inside, it has lovely 13th-century frescoes and a copy of the Black Madonna, brought back from the Crusades and burned during the revolution.

Just to the north of the Rocher Corneille, the 11th-century Romanesque chapel of **St.-Michel-d'Aiguilhe** perches on the steepest of the volcanic cones. The graceful curves and diamond patterns of the facade display a distinctive Eastern influence.

Lacemaking is a traditional craft in Le Puy, and the **Musée Crozatier** *(Jardin Henri Vinay, tel 04 71 06 62 40, closed Tues. Oct.–April)* has a collection of handmade lace. ∎

■ St.-Michel-d'Aiguilhe sits poised atop one of the volcanic cones that dominate Le Puy-en-Velay.

**Le Puy-en-Velay** ⚐ 217 C2 Visitor Information ✉ place de Clauzel ☎ 04 71 09 38 41 **lepuyenvelay-tourisme.fr** • **St.-Michel-d'Aiguilhe** ✉ Aiguilhe ☎ 04 71 09 50 03 🕐 Closed mid-Nov.–mid-Feb. (except for school holidays) 💲 $ **rochersaintmichel.fr**

# VOLCANOES OF THE AUVERGNE

An extraordinary lunar landscape of purple cones and craters lies in the middle of France. Most of these *puys* (or peaks) are included in the nature reserve of the Parc Régional des Volcans d'Auvergne, based in the Puy-de-Dôme *département* to the west of Clermont-Ferrand. Today they are all extinct, but three million years ago regular eruptions spewed out the lava that has created this strange and desolate terrain.

■ Reaching for the sky, the rugged Puy de Sancy is the highest point in the Massif Central.

The volcanoes fall into three groups: The Monts Dôme became extinct only some 4,000 years ago and are still dramatically volcanic in shape. The Monts Dore stopped erupting much longer ago, and their cones have a smoother silhouette. The Cantal volcano, originally huge, has mostly eroded, leaving lava plugs in a system of radiating valleys.

**Parc Régional des Volcans d'Auvergne** ✉ Centre d'Information et de Découverte Montlosier, 1.6 miles (2 km) from Pic de La Vache et de Lassolas ☎ 04 73 65 64 00 **parcdesvolcans.fr • Parc Régional Livradois** ✉ Forez Centre d'Information, St.-Gervais-sous-Meymont ☎ 04 73 95 57 57 **parc-livradois-forez.org • Vulcania** ✉ St.-Ours-les-Roches ☎ 04 73 19 70 70 🕐 Open daily mid-March–mid-Oct.; closed Mon.–Tues. Sept. **vulcania.com**

## INSIDER TIP:

The entire Massif Central makes magnificent walking country, but the most spectacular excursion is undoubtedly to the summit of Puy de Dôme. You can't cycle it any longer, alas, but after a 35-year hiatus, this climb is featured again in the Tour de France.

—JACK KAVANAGH
*National Geographic author*

This is great hiking and biking countryside, and the peak that attracts most enthusiasts is **Puy de Dôme.** This is the oldest and highest volcano, at 4,805 feet (1,464 m), of the Monts Dôme chain.

To the Celts, Puy de Dôme was a royal mountain, on which they worshipped their god of war. The Romans subsequently built a huge temple of lava stones and marble, dedicated to the god Mercury. Not until the mid-18th century was it confirmed that these strange formations were actually volcanoes. Until that time, people believed that the Romans had constructed them. The Auvergne is still reputed to be a place of sorcery and enchantment; some people believe that witches and sorcerers meet at the summit of Puy de Dôme to perform magic rituals.

You can drive to the summit up a spiraling road *($ toll)*, or walk up the original zigzagging Roman track *(park at Ceyssat Pass)*. Before choosing to walk up, bear in mind that this is considered one of the toughest legs on the grueling Tour de France bicycle race. At the top are an information center, observation tables, a restaurant, and a geology museum. The ruins of the Roman temple to Mercury lie just below the summit *(no access for visitors)*.

The summit of Puy de Dôme is a place of great silence and emptiness and the reward for a difficult climb is the feeling that one stands

## Robert Louis Stevenson in the Cévennes

The most celebrated account of a walk in the ancient landscape of the Massif Central is Robert Louis Stevenson's *Travels with a Donkey in the Cévennes*. In 1878, the Scottish writer walked 137 miles (220 km) with his truculent donkey Modestine from Le Monastier-sur-Gazeille, south of Le Puy, to Langogne. His journey took him over the granite massif of Mont Lozère to Florac, and then on to St.-Jean-du-Gard and along the Cévennes Corniche. On the way, he slept under the stars or in rudimentary inns. With warmth and humor, he describes his encounters with a colorful cast of characters. Walkers can follow a similar path today, with numerous *gîtes*, *auberges*, refuges, and camping grounds available along the route.

## Cross the Viaduc de Millau

**Millau** *(Office de Tourisme, 1 place du Beffroi, tel 05 65 60 02 42, ot -millau.fr)* was long notorious as a traffic bottleneck, as vehicles struggled up and down the steep sides of the Gorges du Tarn. Today, however, a magnificent bridge has reduced the crossing to a matter of minutes.

The **Viaduc de Millau** *(levia ducdemillau.com, $)* spans the gorge on a series of delicately soaring concrete pillars, over a distance of 1.5 miles (2.5 km)– a work of art of truly astonishing beauty visible from miles around.

Even before it was finished, the bridge lured visitors from near and far who came to marvel at the inspired engineering responsible for creating one of the world's highest bridges; the tallest pier is 1,115 feet (340 m)– higher than the Tour Eiffel.

Designed and built by British architect Sir Norman Foster and the French engineering company Eiffage, the bridge can be admired from below or from several viewing points around town. A detailed map of the top views is available from the tourist office. Best of all, head for the motorway parking area, just before the bridge coming from the north, where there is a high-level view, an exhibition space, and a restaurant.

The bridge is a five-minute drive north of Millau on the D911, following signs to Paris. Head toward Albi (junction 45) on the A75, and follow directions to Aire du Viaduc. Foster calls crossing the bridge itself "flying by car."

at the very center of France with fine views of this magnificent country in every direction. This is just one of 80 volcanoes in the Chaîne des Puys, a UNESCO World Heritage Site. For the 2023 Tour de France, there were no spectators allowed within the final four kilometres of this leg to help preserve the local flora and fauna.

From the top of Puy de Dôme, the view can, on a clear day, encompasse a chain of more than a hundred volcanic puys–although often their peaks wore down or were blown off long ago. Many of the resulting craters filled with lakes. The view changes by the minute according to the weather and time of day; it's at its most awe inspiring at sunset, starring a stunning palette of colors and dramatic shadows.

Topping the Monts Dore chain to the south is **Puy de Sancy,** the highest point in central France at 6,185 feet (1,885 m) and source of the Dordogne River. You can reach the peak by cable car from the town of Le Mont-Dore, followed by a walk.

The **Vulcania** theme park is devoted to vulcanology, with dramatic spectacles and interactive technology, and now balloon rides over the volcanoes. ∎

# DRIVE ALONG THE GORGES DU TARN

**South of the Massif Central, the Tarn and the Jonte Rivers have cut deep into the limestone plateaus, known as *causses*, creating spectacular canyons and gorges.**

A long, leisurely drive along the Gorges du Tarn is a wonderful way to experience some of the distinctive landscapes of the Massif Central. It's also a stunning lesson in geology and geography taken from the comfort of your car. Do what the French do, and take along a picnic and a bottle of table wine, and stop off at 1 p.m. at the nearest park or motorway rest stop (many have green spaces and outdoor tables hereabouts).

Heading north from **Millau** ❶ (see sidebar p. 257) on the N9-E11, take the D907 northeast along the Tarn River. Near **Les Vignes** ❷, about halfway along the canyon, zigzag up the D995 and then take the D46 to **Point Sublime** ❸ for a terrific view. The most spectacular part of the gorge, Les Détroits, comes between Les Vignes and the little village of **La Malène** ❹, an excellent place from which to take a boat trip downriver (*tel 04 66 48 51 10, gorgesdutarn.com*).

Farther on, the 15th-century **Château de la Caze** (*tel 04 66 48 51 10*)

## NOT TO BE MISSED:

Point Sublime • La Malène • Corniche des Cévennes • Grotte de Dargilan has a fine restaurant, and is a good place to stop off for lunch. If you can get there before midday you might beat the crowds and enjoy a ramble around the grounds.

Once you arrive at **Ste.-Énimie** ❺ *(Office de Tourisme Gorges du Tarn, route du Mende, tel 04 66 48 53 44),* you have a choice of routes. Take the D907 east to just beyond Ispagnac,

🗺 See also area map p. 217
▶ Millau
↔ 60 miles (90 km)
🕐 Half a day
▶ Millau

go right on the N106 to **Florac** ❻, then follow the D907 south into the Parc National des Cévennes. At the junction of the D996 and D983, you can follow the D983, D9, and D260 along the **Corniche des Cévennes** for 31 miles (50 km) to **St.-Jean-du-Gard** ❼ (tel 04 66 85 32 11, cevennes-tourisme.fr, which has a good museum outlining the historical rhythms of local life in this region, the **Musée des Vallées Cévenoles** (95 Grande Rue, tel 04 66 85 10 48).

Alternatively, you can head south from Ste.-Énimie on the D986 to

Roquefort cheese and the distinctive rooftops of Roquefort-sur-Soulzon, where it is produced.

Meyrueis across the glorious **Causse Méjean.** From **Meyrueis** ❽ (tel 04 66 45 60 33), the D996 follows the **Gorges de la Jonte** back toward Millau, passing some famous caves on the way: **Aven Armand,** a vast grotto full of colored stalactites, and **Grotte de Dargilan**, where staircases take you down into a series of caves and lakes. Southeast of Meyrueis off the D986 is the **Abîme de Bramabiau,** an abyss with an underground river.

Another drive from Millau takes you along the **Gorges de la Dourbie** ❾ on the D991. To the north is the rock formation **Montpellier-le-Vieux,** which looks like a ruined town. South of Millau, via the D992 and D23, is **Roquefort-sur-Soulzon,** where you can visit caves in which Roquefort cheese matures.

If you're a photography enthusiast and you want to add some images of the Viaduc de Millau to the album of your France road trip, try to time your drive across the great bridge for around twilight. The setting sun can catch the stretched multispan cables to dramatic effect; and, if you're lucky enough to get a red sunset, the play of light on the River Tarn and the valley below can be quite spectacular. A foggy day is also great for memorable photos, with car lights seeming to soar above the clouds.

Even if the weather is uncooperative you'll still have the thrill of driving across the bridge that is consistently ranked as one of the greatest engineering achievements of modern times.

# More Places to Visit in the Massif Central

## Clermont-Ferrand

A bustling commercial town, Clermont-Ferrand was once two towns. Clermont, the older half, has a daily market in Place St.-Pierre and the **Cathédrale Notre-Dame-de-l'Assomption,** with exquisite 12th- to 15th-century stained glass. Farther east is the **Basilique Notre-Dame-du-Port,** a superb example of the Auvergnat Romanesque style. Montferrand, annexed by its neighbor in 1731, is a quieter enclave of restored Renaissance houses. The much altered old palace was imaginatively modernized around a courtyard, in the style of the Solomon R. Guggenheim Museum in New York, to display the collection of the **Musée des Beaux-Arts.** *clermont-fd.com* 🅰 216 B3 **Visitor Information** ✉ place de la Victoire ☎ 04 73 98 65 00

---

**INSIDER TIP:**

**Around the Gothic cathedral in Clermont-Ferrand's old town are shops with reasonably priced antiques.**

—SYLVIE BIGAR
*National Geographic writer*

---

## Thiers

A visit to Thiers is worthwhile for the views alone. From its perch on the side of the ravine made by the Dorelle River, you can see the volcanic peaks of the Monts Dôme and Monts Dore. The river waters made Thiers's fortune, powering the grinding wheels of the knifemakers and making the town the most important center of cutlery-making in France. You can investigate

## Pulpits in the Desert

Located at Mas Soubeyran in the tiny town of Mialet, not far from St.-Jean-du-Gard, the **Musée du Désert** *(tel 04 66 85 02 72, musee dudesert.com, closed Dec.–Feb.)* is a somber, inspiring memorial to the oppression of the Huguenots (French Protestants) during the religious wars of the 17th and 18th centuries. The hills of the Cévennes provided sanctuary for the rebellious Camisards ("white shirts"), who held religious services among the caves, rocks, and woods—the wilderness or "desert."

At the remote hamlet of Mas Soubeyran, home of the Camisard chief Rolland, you can see the pulpits made from barrels (thus easily disguised), miniature Bibles and other forbidden texts, paintings, and documents that vividly evoke brutal massacres and torture.

From Mas Soubeyran, continue on to the **Grotte de Trabuc** *(guided visits Feb.–Nov.)* and its extraordinary rock formations. Here you can explore the caves where the Huguenots once hid and worshipped.

the history of cutlery at the **Musée de la Coutellerie,** as well as shop for a huge variety of utensils and knives. *thiers-tourisme.fr*  216 B3 **Visitor Information** ✉ Maison du Pirou ☎ 04 73 80 65 65

---

**INSIDER TIP:**

**Thiers is a great place to shop for sturdy, well-made cutlery, available at reasonable prices in ordinary supermarkets and department stores.**

—MARGARET ROBERTS
*Rotary Scholar*

---

## Vichy

Long famous as a spa, Vichy reached its fashionable heyday in the 19th century. You can still stroll around the **Parc des Sources** and take the waters, drink in the Grand Café, see the art nouveau Casino and cast-iron arcades, and seek out the **Source des Célestins** and other springs of Vichy water. Luxury hotels, fine restaurants, and glamorous stores abound, contributing to a seductive fin de siècle charm. Between 1940 and 1944, Vichy found notoriety as the headquarters of the collaborationist French government, close to the border between occupied and unoccupied France. *vichy-tourisme.com* 216 B3 **Visitor Information** ✉ 5 rue du Casino ☎ 04 70 98 71 94

■ The town hall in the city of Vichy, built in the early 1920s and inaugurated in 1928.

Combining handsome riverside towns, beautiful countryside scenery, exquisite fare, and a rich historical and cultural legacy

# SOUTHWEST FRANCE

★ Paris

Area of map detail

6▷ MAINE-ET-LOIRE p. 165    INDRE-ET-LOIRE p. 165

Thouars    Loudun
N149    Bressuire    **Châtellerault**
Parthenay    **Futuroscope** N10
**DEUX-**    **Poitiers**
**SÈVRES** A10
5▷    Chauvigny    St.-Savin
    **VIENNE**    Montmorillon    INDRE p. 165    CHER p. 165
**Niort**    Crozant    Boussac
Île de Ré    Melle    Marche    N145    Gouzon
St.-Martin-de-Ré    N11    Bellac la Souterraine    ALLIER p. 189
**La Rochelle**    A20    CREUSE
Surgères    Ruffec    Confolens    **HAUTE-**    Aubusson
Fouras    St.-Jean-    **VIENNE**    N141
**Rochefort**    d'Angély    Plateau    St.-Léonard-    PUY-DE-DÔME p. 189
Île d'Oléron    **CHARENTE-**    **Limoges**    de-Noblat
Marennes    **MARITIME**    du Limousin    Plateau de
**Saintes**    Cognac    La Rochefoucauld    Millevaches    Ussel
**CHARENTE**    Jarnac    A89    Bort-
**Royan**    N10    **Angoulême**    **CORRÈZE**    les-Orgues
Pointe de Grave    Barbezieux-St.-Hilaire    m    Massif    Central
Soulac-sur-Mer    **Puyguilhem**    o    Hautefort    **Tulle**
4▷    Aubeterre-sur-    St.-Jean-de-Côle    s    Collonges-
Lesparre-Médoc    Dronne    Brantôme    **Brive-la-**    la-Rouge
Étang d'Hourtin    Mirambeau    **Périgueux**    **Gaillarde**    Argentat    Dordogne
Carcans    Pauillac    A89    Lascaux    Gouffre de    CANTAL p. 189
Étang de    Blaye    **DORDOGNE**    N89    Sarlat-    Padirac    St.-Céré
Lacanau    Grotte de Rouffignac    la-Canéda    Rocamadour    Entraygues-
Lacanau-Océan    Libourne    A89    **Les Eyzies-de-Tayac**    Gramat    sur-Truyère
**GIRONDE**    St.-Émilion    **Beynac-et-Cazenac**    Domme    **LOT**    Espagnac-    Figeac
**BORDEAUX**    **Bergerac**    **Cadouin**    Ste.-Eulalie    Decazeville    Conques
3▷    A63    **Castelnaud**    Grotte de    Cajarc    **Larroque-**    **Rodez**
Andernos-les-Bains    La Réole    **Biron**    Monpazier    **Pech-Merle**    **Toirac**
Arcachon    Bassin    Monflanquin    **Bonaguil**    **Cahors**    Cénevières    Aveyron
**Dune du Pilat**    d'Arcachon    A62    **Cènevières**    St.-Cirq Lapopie    **AVEYRON**
Étang de Cazaux    Langon    Lot    Villeneuve-sur-Lot    A20    Causse
et de Sanguinet    Castaljaloux    **LOT-ET-**
Étang de Biscarrosse    Parentis-en-Born    **GARONNE**    **Agen**    **TARN-ET-**
et de Parentis    **Marquèze**    Nérac    **GARONNE**    Caussade    Cordes
Mimizan    Sabres    Condom    Moissac    **Montauban**    Carmaux    N88
2▷    Roquefort    Castelsarrasin    Gaillac    **Albi**
**LANDES**    **Mont-de-Marsan**    Eauze    A62    Gimone    **TARN**
Castets    Tartas    **GERS**    **HAUTE-**    A68    Lavaur    Monts de Lacaune
Hossegor    Aire-sur-l'Adour    **Auch**    **GARONNE**    **Castres**
**Dax**    N124    Mirande    **TOULOUSE**    Mazamet
**Biarritz**    **Bayonne**    A64    Orthez    Muret    A64    AUDE p. 277
St.-Jean-de-Luz    Sauveterre-de-Béarn    N117    A66
Espelette    **PYRÉNÉES-**    **Pau**    A64    **HAUTE-**    Grotte du    Mirepoix
**ATLANTIQUES**    Gave de Pau    **Tarbes**    St.-    **Mas-d'Azil**    Roquefixade
1▷    Oloron-Ste.-Marie    **Lourdes** Lannemezan    Gaudens    **Foix**
St.-Jean-    Laruns    **Grotte de**    Argelès-    St.-Lizier    **ARIÈGE**    Montségur
Pied-de-Port    **Bétharram**    Gazost    **PYRÉNÉES**    **St.-Bertrand-**    Massif del'Arize    Bédeilhac
A▷    Lescun    2877m    Cauterets    **de-Comminges**    **Niaux**    Tarascon-
Pic du    St.-Sauveur    3298m    **Lombrives**    sur-Ariège
Midi d'Ossau    Vignemale    **Parc Nat.**    3115m    Montaillou
SPAIN    **Cirque de**    **des Pyrénées**    Pic d'Estats    PYRÉNÉES-
Gavarnie    **Occidentales**    ANDORRA    ORIENTALES p. 277

0    60 kilometers
0    30 miles

A    B    C    D

# SOUTHWEST FRANCE

Travel through the southwest of France and you cross some of the country's richest agricultural land before climbing to the high Pyrenees. For centuries, the rivers hereabouts—the Garonne, fed by the Tarn and the Lot flowing down from the Massif Central, and the Dordogne—were the region's main arteries of communication and trade, with produce such as fine wines shipped to and from the port of Bordeaux. Today these great waterways are used more for pleasure than trade.

Until a century or so ago, the flat, sandy Atlantic coast was wild and inhospitable, and the sands were steadily encroaching inland. To stabilize the land, grasses were sown, followed by the pine trees that now form the great forest of the Landes, the largest pine forest in Europe. The once-threatening sands of the coast provide wide beaches, constantly pounded by rolling Atlantic breakers.

To the south, the great Pyrenees mountain range stretches from the Mediterranean all the way across to the Atlantic, forming a natural frontier between France and Spain. The southwest's biggest cities are Bordeaux and Toulouse. Bordeaux was capital of the ancient duchy of Aquitaine, which in the Middle Ages included Gascony, Périgord, Poitou, and Limousin as well as Aquitaine. Toulouse was the seat of the powerful counts of Toulouse and the heart of the glittering

troubadour culture. It was the capital of Languedoc, broadly embracing the whole of southern France from Aquitaine to Provence.

By the 12th century, southwest France, ruled autonomously but

## NOT TO BE MISSED:

**Tasting unmatched vintages along the Bordeaux wine trail** 276–277

**Surfing the waves in Biarritz** 278

**Travel through the dramatic Dordogne Valley** 286–289

**Glimpsing prehistoric paintings in the Lascaux caves** 291–293

**A pilgrimage to the Abbaye de Ste.-Foy in Conques** 298

**The stunning Romanesque carvings of Moissac** 306

**The cirque and waterfall of Gavarnie in the Pyrenees** 312

owing allegiance to the French Crown, was thriving both economically and culturally. But with the dynastic marriages of Eleanor of Aquitaine, and the spread of the Cathar heresy in Languedoc, the stage was set for trouble. Eleanor married the French king, Louis VII, in 1137, but the marriage was annulled, and in 1152, she married Henry Plantagenet, Count of Anjou and Duke of Normandy, who inherited the English Crown. Between them,

■ **One of the main streets of Cognac, where the famous spirit is produced**

**INSIDER TIP:**

Southwest France produces an abundance of fine red wines, from the Bordeaux region and beyond. A real gem is the deliciously dark and herb-tinged Malbec (known locally as both Côt and Auxerrois) produced around the town of Cahors.

—JACK KAVANAGH
*National Geographic author*

they ruled most of Britain and western France from Normandy to Aquitaine. Centuries of claims and counterclaims inevitably ensued, with the territorial ambitions of the rival French and English kingdoms finally erupting into the Hundred Years' War, a conflagration that would have long-lasting ramifications for Europe.

In Languedoc, the Albigensian Crusade against the Cathar heresy enabled the power-hungry French Crown to put an end to the autonomy of the counts of Toulouse.

You can still see solid evidence of these conflicts in the fortified *bastide* towns set high upon hill-tops, the castles that pepper the banks of the Dordogne and the Lot, the gaunt Cathar fortresses of the Pyrenean foothills, and the fortified churches of Toulouse and Albi. Paradoxically, these relics of a strife-torn past are now some of the loveliest features of this diverse region. ■

# AQUITAINE & THE ATLANTIC COAST

**France's southern Atlantic coast is a revelation: one great sweep of beach unfolding from the tip of the Gironde Peninsula to the Spanish border, its dazzling light and pounding white waves earning it the poetic name of the Côte d'Argent, or Silver Coast.**

Beaches, dunes, and massive lakes interspersed with small resorts and fishing ports make this coast perfect for family vacations. For more sophisticated tastes, Biarritz offers classic belle epoque hotels, luxury shops, casinos, and golf clubs. Inland stretches the tremendous wooded expanse of the Landes, Europe's largest pine forest, planted in the 19th century to contain the shifting sands of the coast and now a peaceful green retreat.

In the north of the region lies the quiet city of Poitiers, with a magnificent heritage of Romanesque churches, and now perhaps best known for its 21st-century cinematic theme park, Futuroscope. World famous for its exquisite porcelain and enamels, Limoges to the south has several fine museums devoted to the decorative arts.

North of the great Gironde estuary lies the irresistibly unspoiled resort of La Rochelle, an ancient port that now contains more yachts than anywhere else on the coast.

Always an important port, the metropolis of Bordeaux today offers a gracious 18th-century center, excellent museums and restaurants, and, of course, world-famous wines. No wine lover should miss the chance to visit the surrounding wine country, with its litany of magical names such as Château Mouton-Rothschild, Haut-Brion, St.-Émilion, and Margaux.

Finally, rising into the Pyrenees in the south is the French Basque country, a land apart, with its own language, ethnic identity, cuisine, and customs, and which offers an intriguing glimpse into an ancient but still thriving culture with a piquant flavor all its own. ■

■ **The sands of the Aquitaine coast formed the magnificent Dune du Pilat, Europe's highest sand dune.**

# POITIERS

**Poised between northern and southern France, Poitiers is an ancient city now reclaiming its heritage after years of decline. Its riches include a great concentration of Romanesque architecture. The city's position on a rocky promontory in a bend of the Clain River is best appreciated from the opposite bank, a view that also shows a cluster of church towers. Battles around this strategic stronghold changed the course of French history, most famously in 732 when Charles Martel, founder of the Carolingian dynasty, turned the tide on the invading Saracens.**

Echoes of history are everywhere in Poitiers' architecture. The 12th-century **Église de Notre-Dame-la-Grande** *(Grande Rue)* exemplifies the Poitevin Romanesque style. The west front is a mesmerizing gallery of idiosyncratic medieval sculpture flanked by a pair of pinecone pinnacles. The **Palais de Justice** *(rue Gambetta)* nearby contains magnificent vestiges of the 12th-century palace of the dukes of Aquitaine.

The 11th-century church of **St.-Hilaire-le-Grand** *(rue Doyenné)* is unique in Europe in having seven aisles, supported by an extraordinary forest of columns, many of them with fascinating carved capitals. The fourth-century **Baptistère de St.-Jean,** said to be the oldest Christian building in France, contains Roman marble columns, frescoes, and a full-immersion baptismal pool. ∎

## Parc de Futuroscope

The 21st-century design of Futuroscope (the European Park of the Moving Image) could not be in greater contrast to the stately Romanesque buildings of nearby Poitiers: Half-buried white cubes, white spheres, and mirrored crystalline shapes erupt out of the flat landscape. Every imaginable kind of visual technology is exploited here: screens seven stories high; a "magic carpet" with a screen below as well as in front of you; auditoriums with chairs simulating the movement on screen; 3-D projections; an interactive robot zoo; and the Gyrotour at the top of a rotating tower. Since it opened in 1987, Futuroscope *(tel 05 49 49 11 12, futuroscope.com, $$$–$$$$$ depending on length of visit & season)* has become a huge success, attracting several million visitors annually. It is located in Jaunay-Clan, about 4 miles (6 km) north of Poitiers via the N10.

**Poitiers** 🗺 264 C5 Visitor Information ✉ 45 place Charles-de-Gaulle ☎ 05 49 41 21 24 **ot-poitiers.fr • Baptistère de St.-Jean** ✉ rue Jean-Jaurés 🕐 Closed Tues. 💲 $

# LA ROCHELLE

**With its lovely old harbor, splendid towers, and pedestrians-only medieval streets, La Rochelle is one of the prettiest ports anywhere on the French Atlantic coast. Now also the biggest yachting center in western France, it is a lively place for vacations, buzzing with restaurants and cafés.**

This key port was a hotbed of Protestantism thanks to its trading links with northern Europe. Its most tragic—and heroic—moment came in 1627, when it was besieged by the Catholic forces of Cardinal Richelieu for 15 months. Only 5,000 of the population of 25,000 survived.

The town walls were razed, but the harbor entrance is still guarded by two 14th-century towers, the **Tour de la Chaîne** and the **Tour St.-Nicolas.** A third tower, the **Tour de la Lanterne,** west of the Tour de la Chaîne, was originally a lighthouse. You can climb to the top for a good view of the port. From the old harbor, the Porte de la Grosse Horloge leads into the town, a feast of Renaissance and 18th-century architecture in distinctive Rochelais style.

A grand 18th-century mansion built by wealthy shipowners now houses the **Musée du Nouveau Monde** (Museum of the New World). Exhibitions concentrate on the links between La Rochelle and the Americas, and its influence on Louisiana, Canada, and the West Indies. The **Muséum d'Histoire Naturelle,** located in a mansion with splendid gardens, houses an anthropological collection drawing on the travels of La Rochelle traders since the 17th century.

Just off the coast of La Rochelle, reached by a 2-mile-long (3.2 km) road bridge, is **Île de Ré.** A peaceful retreat of salt marshes, vineyards, and shallow lagoons, the island attracts all manner of birdlife, including curlews, teals, and geese. The capital, **St.-Martin-de-Ré,** is a fishing port of cobbled streets and white-washed cottages protected by 17th-century ramparts. ■

## Francofolies

**For five or six days every July, La Rochelle plays host to Francofolies (*francofolies.fr*), the biggest pop music festival in France. Begun in 1985, Francofolies has become the premier showcase for French and Francophone music, attracting as many as 100,000 spectators every year. Recent star appearances have included Charlotte Gainsbourg, Vanessa Paradis, and Sting.**

**La Rochelle** 🗺 264 B5 Visitor Information ✉ 2 quai Georges Simenon ☎ 05 46 41 14 68 **larochelle-tourisme.com • Musée du Nouveau Monde** ✉ 10 rue Fleuriau ☎ 05 46 41 46 50 🕒 Closed Tues., & a.m. Sat. & Sun. 💲 $ • **Muséum d'Histoire Naturelle** ✉ 28 rue Albert 1er ☎ 05 46 41 18 25 🕒 Closed Mon. **museum-larochelle.fr**

# FOOD & DRINK—TRUFFLES & TRIPE

From Périgord, the region north of the Dordogne River, to the Basque region along the Spanish border, southwest France glories in some of the finest produce and culinary skills that this gastronomically thrilling country has to offer.

■ Pigs are trained to seek out truffles in their underground hiding places.

The Aquitaine coast yields fish and fine seafood in abundance—mussels, scallops, prawns, and most of all oysters—and the Gironde even produces caviar. Périgord is synonymous with foie gras and truffles. The traditional cooking medium is goose or duck fat as opposed to butter or olive oil. Try the rich confits (duck or goose preserved in its own fat) and other delicious duck and goose dishes prepared hereabouts. Succulent local pork, beef, and lamb are enhanced with garlic, herbs, and truffles. *Tripons* (tripe) and *ris de veau* (calf's sweetbreads) are particularly prized.

Wild mushrooms such as morels, chanterelles, and ceps are served simply cooked in butter, as a filling for omelets, or in sauces. Truffles are traditionally savored in slivers, often to perfume an omelet. Walnuts are added to salads and sauces, crushed to make walnut oil, and distilled into eau-de-vie.

Bordeaux enjoys an enviable gastronomic reputation. Toulouse and farther south is cassoulet country, with many recipes for this slow-cooked casserole of white beans with sausages and meat, often duck, pork, or mutton, usually topped with bread crumbs. Farther south still, in the Basque country, the pimiento is king, combined most deliciously with egg in *piperade*. Bayonne ham is famous for its aromatic flavor.

Fruit here is superlative. The delicious plums of Agen make the best prunes in France. These are often combined with meat dishes, notably rabbit, or used to make jam.

Among the first-course specialties in southwest France are *chipirons* (squid, often cooked in its own ink), *garbure béarnaise* (thick soup made with cabbage, bacon, and confit of goose or pork), *sobronade* (bean and bacon soup), and *tourain bordelais* (soup of onions, tomatoes, bread, and egg yolks). Main courses include *boeuf à la sarladaise* (fillet of beef stuffed with pâté de foie gras), *canard aux cèpes* (duck with mushrooms), *cou farci* (stuffed goose neck), *coquilles St.-Jacques à la bordelaise* (scallops sautéed with shallots and parsley), *daube bordelaise* (beef stewed in red wine), *enchaud Périgourdin* (roast pork with garlic), *miques* (little dumplings of bread, boiled in stock), *poulet basquaise* (chicken with tomato, pimento, and Bayonne ham), and *zakiro* (mutton grilled on an open fire—a Basque dish). Dessert specialties of the region include *kanougas* (chocolate taffy) and *touron* (marzipan—almond paste—loaf with nuts).

## The French Paradox

With a diet rich in saturated fats, butter, cheese, and cream, why do the French have low rates of heart disease? This is the so-called French Paradox. Initial research suggested that the consumption of red wine might be the key. Subsequent research has challenged the evidence and suggested that the incidence of heart disease in France has been underestimated. Nevertheless, the correlation between wine and health is striking.

Red wine especially is a source of resveratrol, which has been linked to longevity and cancer prevention. Another constituent of red wine, procyanidins, is found in greatest concentration in European red wines and correlates with longevity in those regions. Some research suggests that procyanidins may also have an effect on cancer and diabetes. The highest concentration was found in the Tannat grape grown in the Gers area of southwest France. Clinical trials of grape seed extract showed that as little as 200–300 mg per day would lower blood pressure. Two small (4 oz/125 ml) glasses of a procyanidin-rich red wine, such as a Madiran wine made from Tannat, would provide this amount.

Comparison between French and American habits also suggests that the French eat less overall, serve smaller portions, and eat less processed food. The French eat three meals a day and do not snack. They drink plenty of liquids, including herbal teas; eat mindfully at the table, not in front of the TV; and emphasize freshness and pleasure in food.

# LIMOGES & AUBUSSON

For anyone with a passion for the decorative arts—and particularly for porcelain, enamels, and tapestry—Limoges and Aubusson offer rare delights. The discovery of a major deposit of kaolin nearby in 1768 made the name of Limoges synonymous with fine, white porcelain. Thus began a major industry that produced some of the finest china ever made. Aubusson has been the tapestry capital of the world since the 15th century and is now a UNESCO World Heritage site.

■ **Cathédrale St.-Etienne in Limoges contains a colorful surprise.**

## Limoges

The **Musée National Adrien-Dubouché** contains a superb collection of more than 11,000 items of porcelain, chinaware, and metalwork from earliest times to the present.

Centuries before the porcelain industry started, Limoges was already famed throughout Europe for its virtuoso enamels. An unrivaled collection from the 11th century onward is to be found in the **Musée des Beaux-Arts.** The museum also has paintings, including Renoir's "Portrait of Madame le Coeur," given by the artist to his native city.

Limoges's soaring Gothic **Cathédrale St.-Étienne** features some magnificent stone carving, especially its famous rood screen, and it's worth bringing a small pair of binoculars to study the details.

## Aubusson

In the mid-17th century, Aubusson's tapestry workshops received the royal warrant, but the revocation of the Edict of Nantes in 1685 caused Huguenot workers to flee. An 18th-century revival ended with the revolution. The **Musée Départemental de la Tapisserie** shows work from the 17th, 18th, and 20th centuries. A traditional workshop has been set up in the **Maison du Tapissier** (rue Vieille), a 16th-century weaver's house. At the **Manufacture St.-Jean** (3 rue St.-Jean, tel 05 55 66 10 08, manufacture-saint-jean.fr, closed Sat.–Sun. Oct.–June) you can watch tapestries and carpets being made. ■

**Limoges** 🅰 264 D4 Visitor Information ✉ 12 boulevard de Fleurus ☎ 05 55 34 46 87 **limoges-tourisme.com • Musée National Adrien-Dubouché** ✉ place Winston Churchill, Limoges ☎ 05 55 33 08 50 🕐 Closed Tues. 💲 $ **musee-adriendubouche.fr • Musée des Beaux-Arts** ✉ 1 place de l'Eveche, Limoges ☎ 05 55 45 98 10 🕐 Closed Tues. 💲 $ **museebal.fr • Aubusson** 🅰 264 E4 Visitor Information ✉ rue Vieille ☎ 05 55 66 32 12 **tourisme-creuse.com /aubusson-felletin/ • Musée Départemental de la Tapisserie** ✉ avenue des Lissiers, Aubusson ☎ 05 55 83 08 30 🕐 Closed Tues. 💲 $ **cite-tapisserie.fr**

# BORDEAUX

Bordeaux enjoys an illustrious reputation as the hub of a large region of vine-yards producing some of the finest wines in the world. Although it has been part of the wine trade since Roman times, it is the 18th-century city that you see today, the result of a massive civic rebuilding scheme marked by decades of restoration and cleaning. An urban renewal plan has created new parks, landscaped quays, pedestrian promenades, and a successful new tramway.

Start your visit on the waterfront. From the **Pont de Pierre,** a magnificent view takes in the classical facades lining the wharves fronting the St.-Pierre quarter. A stroll along the quays brings you to the stately **Hôtel de la Bourse,** the old maritime exchange, standing on one of the city's most impressive 18th-century squares. Farther along the waterfront, you reach the vast Esplanade des Quinconces. Towering above it is the **Monument aux Girondins,** erected in memory of local deputies sent to the guillotine by Robespierre.

Inland from the river, the broad tree-lined avenues of Cours de l'Intendance, Cours Georges Clemenceau, and Allées de Tourny, known as the Triangle, enclose the heart of Bordeaux life, full of fashionable shops and traditional cafés. A visit to the **Bar à Vin** (3 cours du 30 Juillet, tel 05 56 00 43 47, baravin.bordeaux.com) is a perfect prelude to any wine tour or tasting. The Bar's street, cours de 30 Juillet, opens out into place de la Comédie, dominated by the **Grand Théâtre.** Built by Victor Lewis between 1773

Pont de Pierre, on the Garonne, lights the way into Bordeaux.

**Bordeaux** 264 B3 Visitor Information 12 cours du 30 Juillet
05 56 00 66 00 **bordeaux-tourisme.com**

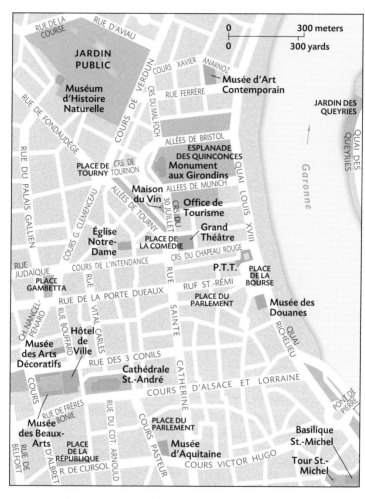

and 1780, it boasts a staircase taken by Charles Garnier as his inspiration for the Opéra Garnier in Paris, and a fabulously refurbished auditorium. To the north lies the old merchants' quarter, now a hip bustle of antique shops. Cours Xavier-Arnozan is resplendent with the great houses built by the wine merchants, their classical facades adorned with wrought-iron balco-

**Grand Théâtre** ✉ place de la Comédie 🕐 Guided visits by reservation. Information & reservations at the tourist office. Tour: 1 hr. ☎ 05 56 00 85 95 💲 $$ **opera-bordeaux.com**

■ **The Grand Théâtre of Bordeaux**

nies. Here, too, art lovers will want to carve out some time to spend at the **Musée d'Art Contemporain,** housed in a beautifully converted 19th-century spice warehouse.

The most interesting of the city's other museums cluster around the Cathédrale St.-André: The **Musée d'Aquitaine** provides an imaginative overview of local history, both rural and urban. The collection of the **Musée des Beaux-Arts** has Renaissance paintings; two famous Eugène Delacroix canvases, "Greece on the Ruins of Missolonghi" and "The Lion Hunt"; and a number of Impressionist works. The **Musée des Arts Décoratifs,** gives a sense of life inside the city's 18th-century mansions, with rooms displaying period furniture, porcelain,

glassware, and the wrought iron for which Bordeaux is famous.

The **Cathédrale St.-André** is a vast 11th-century foundation, with later additions including a soaring Flamboyant Gothic choir and transepts. The 13th-century Porte Royale, on the south facade, has a notable tympanum of the Last Judgment. The almost equally immense **Basilique St.-Michel,** off the waterfront to the south of the city, has a freestanding Gothic belfry that at 374 feet (114 m) is the highest tower in southwest France. The terrace halfway up affords a commanding city view.

To understand the complete story of this ancient city, visit **Bordeaux Monumental** *(28 rue des Argentiers, tel 05 56 48 04 24),* an exhibit of its history and buildings. ■

**Musée d'Art Contemporain** ✉ 7 rue Ferrère ☎ 05 56 00 81 50 ⏰ Closed Mon. $ Free for permanent collection **capc-bordeaux.fr** • **Musée d'Aquitaine** ✉ 20 cours Pasteur ☎ 05 56 01 51 00 ⏰ Closed Mon. $ Free for permanent collection **musee-aquitaine-bordeaux.fr** • **Musée des Beaux-Arts** ✉ 20 cours d'Albret ☎ 05 56 10 20 56 ⏰ Closed Tues. $ $$ **musba-bordeaux.fr** • **Musée des Arts Décoratifs** ✉ 39 rue Bouffard ☎ 05 56 10 14 00 ⏰ Closed a.m. & all Tues. $ Free for permanent collection

# DRIVE THROUGH THE HAUT-MÉDOC

**In a region that produces the noblest wines in the world, the Médoc—a formerly marshy area northwest of Bordeaux that was drained and planted in the 18th century—boasts the lion's share of the most aristocratic growths.**

Visit the Haut-Médoc (the upper Médoc) just before the harvest in mid-September, when the grapes hang tantalizingly heavy and luscious. The **Conseil des Vins du Médoc** *(cours du 30 Juillet, tel 05 56 48 18 62, medoc-wines.com)* in Bordeaux organizes bus tours and will provide all the information you need.

## The Tour

Take the D2 *(route du Vin)* north out of Bordeaux. Stop first at **Château Siran ❶** *(tel 05 57 88 34 04, chateausiran.com),* furnished with paintings including Caravaggio's "The Young Bacchus." **Château Margaux ❷** *(tel 05 57 88 83 83, chateau-margaux.com, closed Sat.–Sun. & Aug., by appt. only),* east of the D2 about 2 miles (3.5 km) farther on, is outstanding. Take a detour on the D5 to **Château Maucaillou ❸** *(tel 05 56 58 01 23, chateau -maucaillou.com)* and the **Musée des Arts et des Métiers de la Vigne et du Vin.** From Vauban's star-shaped 17th-century **Fort Médoc ❹** *(tel 05 57 88 85 00)* there is a view of the Gironde estuary and the vineyards of Blaye. Back on the D2, you come to **Château Beychevelle ❺** *(tel 05 56 73 20 70, beychevelle.com),* set in an 18th-century building.

> **NOT TO BE MISSED:**
>
> Château Siran • Château Margaux • Château Mouton-Rothschild • Château Cos d'Estournel

Farther on, **Château Latour ❻** *(tel 05 56 73 19 80, chateau-latour.com, reservations essential)* is named after the impressive old tower that stands next to the château.

At the old river port of **Pauillac,** look for signs that point to some of the most hallowed names in wines. At **Château Mouton-Rothschild ❼** *(tel 05 56 73 21 29, chateau-mouton -rothschild.com, by appt. only),* part of the cellars is now a museum. At **Château Lafite-Rothschild ❽** *(tel 05 56 59 26 83, lafite.com, by appt. only),* another fine château in a grand park, you can avail of guided tours. A little farther on the D2, **Château Cos d'Estournel ❾** *(tel 05 56 73 15 50, estournel.com, by appt. only),* an 18th-century palace with a modern warehouse designed by Spanish architect Ricardo Bofill, produces one of the five *crus classés* from St.-Estèphe. Retrace your steps, or take the fast route back to Bordeaux on the N215 and D1.

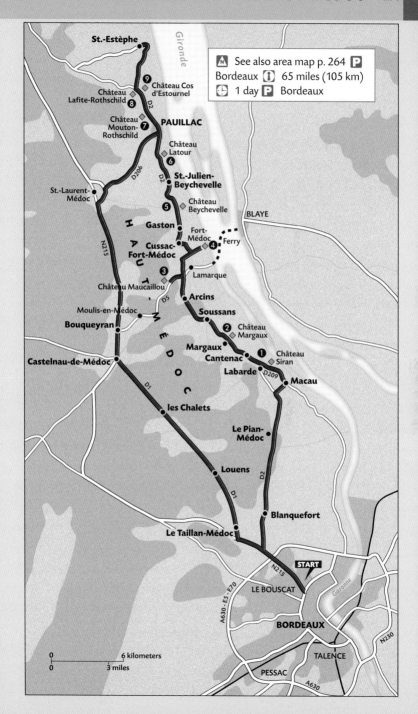

St.-Estèphe

Gironde

⚅ See also area map p. 264 🅿

Bordeaux ⓘ 65 miles (105 km)

🕐 1 day 🅿 Bordeaux

❾ Château Cos
d'Estournel

Château
Lafite-Rothschild ❽

Château
Mouton-
Rothschild ❼ PAUILLAC

D2

Château
Latour ❻

D206

St.-Julien-
Beychevelle

St.-Laurent-
Médoc

BLAYE

Château
Beychevelle

❺

Gaston

H
A
U
T

Fort-
Médoc

❹ Ferry

N215

Cussac-
Fort-Médoc

❸

Lamarque

Château Maucaillou

D5

Moulis-en-Médoc

Arcins

Soussans

Bouqueyran

M
É
D
O
C

❷ Château
Margaux

Margaux

Castelnau-de-Médoc

Cantenac

❶ Château
Siran

Labarde

D209

Macau

D1

les Chalets

Le Pian-
Médoc

D2

Louens

D1

Blanquefort

Le Taillan-Médoc

START

N215

LE BOUSCAT

Garonne

A630 · E5 · E70

BORDEAUX

N230

TALENCE

PESSAC

A630

0          6 kilometers
0      3 miles

# BIARRITZ

The swankiest and largest resort on the French Atlantic seaboard, Biarritz enjoys a mild climate, invigorated by its perfect position between the Pyrenees and the rugged coast.

■ Biarritz has drawn a wealth of beach lovers, including Empress Eugénie and Coco Chanel.

The famous little whaling village of Biarritz first attracted attention in the 19th century, when sea bathing became fashionable. Its fortunes were sealed when Empress Eugénie persuaded her husband, Napoleon III, to build the Villa Eugénie, now the **Hôtel du Palais.** Queen Victoria and so many other royals followed that the resort became known as the beach of kings. Coco Chanel added a note of chic, while the casino, now restored to its art deco magnificence, attracted the world's gamblers.

While these old-world splendors have faded slightly, the coastline is still gorgeous. The **Grande Plage** is the most fashionable stretch of beach. The **Vieux Port** shelters a gentler one, while great waves break on the **Plage de la Côte des Basques,** a place of annual pilgrimage for Basques. It all makes a perfect setting for nonchalant strolling, with cliff walks and promenades lush with tamarisk and purple and blue hydrangeas.

An alluring footbridge from the promontory at the south end of the Grande Plage takes you to the **Rocher de la Vièrge,** with its statue of the Virgin and an exhilarating view right down the coastline to Spain. If you have the energy for the climb, the top of the lighthouse north of the Grande Plage rewards with an even more thrilling panorama.

On the promontory above the Virgin stands the fascinating **Musée de la Mer,** which has displays on local fishing as well as pools of sharks and seals. At Thalmar (*Plage Marbella, tel 05 59 41 75 43, thalmar.com*) you can indulge yourself in a variety of aquatic indulgences including seawater baths and also enjoy a massage. ■

**Biarritz** 🅰 264 B2 Visitor Information ✉ 1 square d'Ixelles ☎ 05 59 22 37 10 **biarritz.fr** • **Musée de la Mer** ✉ esplanade de la Rocher de la Vièrge ☎ 05 59 22 75 40 🕐 Closed 2 weeks mid-Jan. 💲 $$$ **museedelamer.com**

# BAYONNE

Now the elegant capital of the French Basque country, Bayonne was for centuries disputed for its strategic frontier position between France and Spain.

Constantly besieged, and under English rule for almost 300 years, Bayonne found prosperity in privateering, shipbuilding, and arms manufacture (and gave its name to the bayonet). The narrow streets around the **Cathédrale Ste.-Marie** are a pleasure to explore. The cathedral, begun in the 13th century, is a monument to changing times and masters. Its soaring Gothic nave, built by the English in the 14th century, is in the northern Gothic style, while French fleurs-de-lis decorate the keystones. Nearby, the excellent **Musée Bonnat** includes works by Rubens, Poussin, and Goya. Located in a restored 16th-century Basque house, the **Musée Basque** *(quai des Corsaires, tel 05 59 59 08 98, musee -basque.com, closed Mon.)* offers a wide selection of Basque artifacts. ∎

**Bayonne** 264 B2 Visitor Information place des Basques 08 20 42 64 64 **bayonne-tourisme.com** • **Musée Bonnat** 5 rue J.-Lafitte 05 59 59 08 52 Closed Tues. **webmuseo.com/ws/musee-bonnat-helleu**

## EXPERIENCE: Catch a Wave in Surfer's Paradise

The great Atlantic waves of Biarritz have made this city the surf capital of Europe. Every April, board riders from all over the globe flock here to participate in the Biarritz Quiksilver surfing competition.

Biarritz owes its popularity as a surfing destination to Hollywood. During the 1950s, film stars like Gary Cooper and Rita Hayworth discovered the city's spectacular coast. Then, in 1957, Deborah Kerr and her screenwriting husband, Peter Viertel, arrived in Biarritz to film *The Sun Also Rises*. They began board-surfing and soon inspired the locals to take to the waves.

Plage de la Côte des Basques is now the great surfing beach where the annual surfing championships take place. Check out **Restaurant Le Surfing** *(9 bd Prince de Galles, tel 05 59 24 78 72, lesurfing .fr)*, a bar behind the beach, decked out with vintage surfboards.

You can learn to surf at a variety of local establishments, including **École de Surf Jo Moraiz** *(2, 3 place Bellevue, tel 06 62 76 17 24, jomoraiz.com)* and **École de Surf La Vague Basque** *(Plage de la Côte des Basques, tel 06 62 76 17 32, vaguebasque.fr)*. **Biarritz Paradise Surfschool** *(tel 06 14 76 01 18, biarritzparadisesurfschool.com)* offers packages tailored to suit all levels, from a single lesson to an entire week of surf camp. Lessons are given on Plage Marbella in July and August.

# More Places to Visit in Aquitaine & the Atlantic Coast

## Cognac

The port of Cognac on the Charente River is known for the fine brandy distilled from the wine of the local vineyards. The best producer is **Distillerie Otard** *(tel 05 45 36 88 88, baronotard.com)* in its 15th-century château. Look for the black fungus that grows on the warehouses, fed by brandy evaporates, called the "angels' share." Visit the **Musée des Arts du Cognac** *(place de la Salle Verte, tel 05 45 36 21 10, closed Mon.). tourism-cognac.com* 🅜 264 C4 **Visitor Information** ✉ rue du 14 Juillet ☎ 05 45 82 10 71

## Côte d'Argent

The Aquitaine coast has Europe's highest sand dune, **Dune du Pilat,** and ideal beaches for swimming and surfing. **Arcachon** *(visitor information, esplanade Georges-Pompidou, tel 05 57 52 97 97, arcachon.com)*, where oysters are cultivated, is a beguiling 19th-century town with a marina and whimsical vacation villas. Farther south are **Hossegor** *(hossegor .fr)*, on a saltwater lake, and **Cap-Breton,** with its ancient lighthouse. 🅜 264 B3

## Les Landes

In the 18th century at Les Landes, coastal dunes were stabilized and marshes drained by the planting of grass and pines. The

**Écomusée** *(tel 05 58 08 31 31, marqueze.fr)* at Marquèze shows the hard nature of traditional life in the Landes. *landes-tourisme.info* 🅜 264 B2

## St.-Émilion

With its medieval walls, the former citadel of St.-Émilion is now the very essence of a southwestern wine town. The handsome houses of golden limestone make it a picturesque base for day trips

### Angoulême

The town of Angoulême *(map 264 C4)* is the world center of comic books, a particular French passion. Every year at the end of January, the festival of **La Bande Dessinée** attracts thousands of enthusiasts. The BDs, as comics are popularly known, are fêted in a modern museum, **La Cité Internationale de la Bande Dessinée et de l'Image** *(121 rue de Bordeaux, tel 05 45 38 65 65, citebd.org)*, in the old wine warehouses on the banks of the Charente River. The museum's collection of more than 8,000 drawings traces the history of comics over 150 years, including Asterix, Peanuts, Tintin, and Popeye. There is also a browsable library of comic books.

■ The streets of Angoulême come alive in surprising ways each January for La Bande Dessinée, the annual celebration of comic books.

to surrounding wine country. *saint-emilion-tourisme.com* 264 C3 **Visitor Information** ✉ place des Creneaux ☎ 05 57 55 28 28

### Saintes

Saintes, located in the Charente Valley, boasts a rich heritage of Roman and medieval architecture. The **Arc de Germanicus** (now in Place Bassompierre) once stood on a Roman bridge, and there are also remains of baths and an amphitheater. The 12th-century **Abbaye aux Dames,** a Romanesque building, has finely carved portals. About 12.5 miles (20 km) outside Saintes is **Paléosite** *(Ste.-Césaire, tel 05 46 97 90 90, paleosite.fr),* a center dedicated to the prehistoric era that was built on the site where a Neanderthal woman was found.

*saintes-tourisme.fr* 264 B4 **Visitor Information** ✉ 62 cours National ☎ 05 46 74 23 82

## Wines & Spirits

The Bordeaux region produces some of the world's most exquisite wines. Visit a few of Bordeaux's many châteaus to try the aromatic reds, dry fruity whites, and sublime sweet white wines. Local wines usually represent the best value in restaurants. Aside from the châteaus of Bordeaux, look for the local wines from Bergerac, Buzet, Cahors, Gaillac, and Basque country Irouléguy. The unsurpassed local brandies include Cognac and Armagnac.

# THE DORDOGNE & MIDI-PYRÉNÉES

**The Dordogne touches the hearts and stirs the senses of visitors more than perhaps any other region of France. In the dark days following the outbreak of World War II, its meandering streams, rolling hills, and quiet villages prompted Henry Miller to write in a kind of optimism: "France may one day exist no more, but the Dordogne will live on just as dreams live on and nourish the souls of men."**

For many foreigners, the very name conjures up a large area of elegiac river country. The climate is gentle, the summer sun never as unrelenting as farther south. The Dordogne, Lot, and Tarn Rivers water the land, ensuring a rich variety of crops.

North of the Dordogne River is Périgord, some of France's richest agricultural land. South of the river are treasures of a different kind: underground chasms and grottoes, and some of the finest medieval religious architecture in France. The many castles and *bastides* (fortified towns) are relics of the bitter fighting throughout the Middle Ages.

Market towns such as Sarlat-la-Canéda, Cahors, and Périgueux have historic centers full of shady arcades and ornately carved buildings.

To the south lies the Midi-Pyrénées region. Its capital, Toulouse, is Latin in atmosphere and humming with life. To the east, pink-brick Albi, with its wonderful cathedral and lovely old streets, boasts an unrivaled collection of artworks by its famous son, Toulouse-Lautrec. West of Toulouse is the rolling farmland of Gascony, home of Armagnac brandy.

In addition to its impressive religious architecture, the region has some of the most enchanting rural architecture in France. Weathered farms of golden limestone beneath steep slate roofs bristle with dormer windows, little turrets, and elaborate dovecotes. Terracotta tiles and vine-shaded verandas herald the deep south. Restored, many of these fine old buildings are now vacation homes. ■

The Dordogne River winds its way slowly through rich farmland.

# AROUND PÉRIGORD

The ancient territory of Périgord (largely covered by the present *département* of Dordogne) matches the ideal image of provincial France: lush, gently rural, and dotted with farms and manor houses. The region is united by its rivers, the Dronne, Isle, Vézère, and Dordogne, all of which have provided routes for transporting goods and people since the Gallo-Roman era. Today they make ideal routes for exploring the countryside.

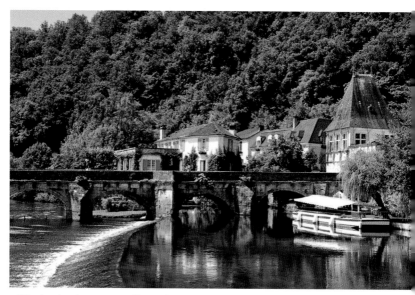

The lovely, picturesque village of Beynac is not far from Périgord.

Périgord—so green and tranquil—was once the epicenter of the ferociously fought Hundred Years' War and the front line between the kingdom of France and English-held Aquitaine. The fortified towns and châteaus that are such a delight to visit today testify to this history of belligerence, all built to keep the invader out rather than welcome the stranger in, the purpose many of them serve in the tourist-driven era of modern-day Dordogne.

Traditionally, this storied region has been divided into Périgord Blanc (so called for the white of its limestone), centered on Périgueux and the Isle River; and Périgord Noir (because of its dense woodland) around Sarlat-la-Canéda in the southeast.

■ *Truffe,* or truffle, is a rare and pricey delicacy found in the southwest and southeast.

## Truffles & Foie Gras: The Inside Story

Truffles and foie gras are the heavenly twins of epicurean indulgence in Périgord, unsurpassed anywhere. Capricious and mysterious, resistant to all attempts at cultivation or scientific analysis, truffles must be sniffed out from their hiding places among the roots of certain oak trees by specially trained pigs or dogs. Their incomparable flavor is not only exquisite but also highly pungent. Sold in specialist markets such as those at Périgueux and Sarlat, truffles fetch as much as $2,500 per pound for white and $700 for black. They may also be bought in cans, carefully graded.

A 19th-century essayist and wit, the Reverend Sydney Smith, defined heaven as "eating pâté de foie gras to the sound of trumpets." Foie gras is made by force-feeding geese or ducks with corn to enlarge their livers, resulting in a rich and deliciously smooth meat. Although many people regard the practice (known as *gavage*) as cruel, it has to be said that the geese *do* flock to be fed. Foie gras comes in many forms, in jars or cans; *foie gras d'oie entier* indicates the best goose liver, presented whole; *bloc de foie gras* describes pieces pressed together to form a block; *mi-cuit* denotes that the liver is cooked enough to keep for about a month. Finest of all is *foie gras truffé,* perfumed with black truffles.

More recently, the color scheme has been broadened to include Périgord Vert (the green pastureland of the north) and Périgord Pourpre (the vineyards around Bergerac).

## Périgueux

The regional capital, Périgueux, in a loop of the Isle River, makes an excellent base for touring Périgord. Dominating its skyline are the exotic domes and turrets of **Cathédrale St.-Front,** the largest cathedral in southwest France. Originally built in the 12th century, this fine edifice was restored in the 19th century by architect Paul Abadie, who used it as an inspiration for the Basilique de Sacré-Coeur in Paris. Its remarkable roof offers a view of the old town at its feet, a tangle of cobbled streets, mullioned windows, and hidden courtyards.

From the **Tour Mataguerre,** part of the medieval ramparts, you can enjoy another splendid view over the rooftops of the old town, encompassing the ruins of a Gaulish amphitheater and temple. Be sure to visit the **Musée Gallo-Roman** *(rue Claude Bernard, tel 05 53 53 00 92, closed Mon. Sept.–June, $),* which

reveals the excavated Roman villa of Vesunna and its precious wall paintings.

East of Périgueux, the magnificent 17th-century **Château de Hautefort** stands in wooded parkland embellished with topiary and mosaic parterres.

## Brantôme

North of Périgueux, in the tranquil valley of the Dronne River, lies Brantôme, one of the most charming towns in the whole of Périgord. Stroll along the riverbanks to admire its bridges and riverside garden, its ancient abbey church, and its exceptionally fine 11th-century bell tower. The first monks here simply carved their monastery out of the cliffs behind the abbey, in caves that are now open to the public: The **Cave of the Last Judgment** has stunning carvings of the Crucifixion and the "Triumph of Death." Pierre de Bourdeille, abbot here in the 16th century, was to earn much notoriety with his scurrilous tales of ladies at court, written under the pen name Brantôme.

A few miles northeast of Brantôme, you'll find the alluring **Château de Puyguilhem,** a gracious example of French Renaissance architecture. ∎

**Périgueux** ▲ 264 C4 Visitor Information ✉ 26 place Francheville ☎ 05 53 53 10 63 **tourisme-grandperigueux.fr • Château de Hautefort** ▲ 264 D4 ☎ 05 53 50 51 23 🕐 Closed Nov.–Mar. 🛟 $$ • **Brantôme** ▲ 230 C4 Visitor Information ✉ Pavillon Renaissance, boulevard Charlemagne ☎ 05 53 05 80 63 **ville-brantome.fr • Château de Puyguilhem** ▲ 264 D4 ✉ 05 53 54 82 18 🕐 Closed Mon.–Tues. Oct.–March 🛟 $$

"We supped and lay, having amongst other dainties, a dish of truffles, which is a certain earth nut, and found out by a hog trained to it . . . It is in truth an incomparable meat."
*—John Evelyn (1644)*

# DORDOGNE VALLEY DRIVE

**One of the most beautiful drives in the Dordogne is upstream along the river valley from Bergerac to Sarlat-la-Canéda, a comfortable two-day excursion of 80 miles (170 km) or so. Here the great river cuts a swath between wooded valleys, fertile farmland, and craggy limestone cliffs topped by picturesque villages and castles at every turn. With its outstanding reputation for fine food and wine, this lovely region provides a perfect combination of the pleasures of the table, the landscape, and history.**

Take this drive at a slow, leisurely pace, allowing for frequent stops and exploratory detours, contemplating views, and happily enjoying the moods of the river—brilliant in the sun, silvery in the diffuse light of dusk.

The Dordogne flows wide at **Bergerac ❶** (*visitor information, rue Neuve d'Argenson, tel 05 53 57 03 11, bergerac-tourisme.com*), forming a broad alluvial plain that is the main area of tobacco production in France. The old port, once a flourishing center of the wine trade, spans both sides

> ## NOT TO BE MISSED:
>
> **Château de Monbazillac • Cingle de Trémolat • abbey of Cadouin • Beynac-et-Cazenac • La Roque-Gageac**

of the river, and the town has winding streets of medieval half-timbered houses. The **Musée du Tabac** (*place du Feu, tel 05 53 63 04 13, closed Sun. a.m.*) in the elegant 17th-century Maison Peyrarède presents a fascinating survey of the evolution of tobacco

See also area map p. 264 🅿
Bergerac ℹ 80 miles (128 km)
🕓 2 days 🅿 Sarlat-la-Canéda

START
**BERGERAC** Creysse Mouleydier
❶ D660
Dordogne
Canadou

❷ St.-Capraise-de-Lalinde
Lalinde D31
D29
St.-Front-de-Colubri

D37 • Couze-et-
Château de St.-Front ❸
Lanquais

Mauzac
Trémolat
Cingle de Trémolat ❹

D933   D13   N21
✈

Château de
◇ Monbazillac

0 _____ 8 kilometers
0 _____ 4 miles

smoking, with a huge variety of snuff-boxes and pipes, including Native American peace pipes. The **Musée du Vin et de la Batellerie** (*5 rue des Conférences, tel 05 53 63 04 13, closed Sun. & Nov.–March*) celebrates local wines and boat-building. Wines may be tasted at the wine center in the medieval **Cloître des Récollets** (*place du Docteur-Cayla, tel 05 53 63 57 55*). The most celebrated of the local vintages is the sweet white wine of Monbazillac. The moated 16th-century **Château de Monbazillac** (*tel 05 53 63 65 00, closed Mon. Nov.–March, chateau-monbazillac.com*), on the crest of hills just south of Bergerac on the D13, has an interesting local craft museum and wine tasting.

Return and take the D660 along the north bank of the river from Bergerac. Cross the river at **St.-Capraise-de-Lalinde ❷** on the D37 to **Château de Lanquais** (*tel 05 53 61 24 24, closed Nov.–March & Tues. April–Oct., chateaudelanquais.fr*). Part medieval fortress, part Renais-sance palace, the castle occupies a magnificent site above the pretty old village of Lanquais. A reminder of the region's turbulent past can be seen in the damage inflicted by cannonballs during the Wars of Religion.

The little town of **Couze-et-St.-Front ❸**, just to the east, is famous for papermaking, once a major industry here; the traditional methods are still used at **Moulin de Larroque** (*tel 05 53 61 01 75, dordogne-perigord -tourisme.fr, closed Sat.–Sun.*). Farther along the south bank, the pictur-esque village of **St.-Front-de-Colubri** perches on a cliff, offering a superb view of the Dordogne and the Gra-tusse rapids upriver, the most dan-gerous stretch to navigate when riverboats traded upstream.

The river now executes one of its extraordinary horseshoe bends, known as *cingles*, at the **Cingle de Trémolat ❹**. Cross to the north bank of the river at St. Front to go around the cingle and enjoy a panoramic view of the rich pastureland contained in

**Free-range geese wander the grounds of a farm in the Dordogne.**

the loop. Trémolat itself is a charming little village, made famous by director Claude Chabrol as the setting for the film *Le Boucher* (1969). Between Trémolat and Limeuil, the D31 follows the cliff, overlooking the river.

**Limeuil** lies at the confluence of the Vézère and the Dordogne; here, rocky terraces frame the river, and the little village, with its Renaissance houses and 12th-century church, winds up the hill, providing glorious views. Follow the D51 beside the wide river, flanked by cliffs, then cross it to take a short detour on the D25, through a valley of chestnut woods, to **Cadouin ❺** *(tel 05 53 63 36 28, closed Tues. in winter)*. This austerely beautiful Cistercian abbey of golden stone has a fine Gothic cloister. From Cadouin, a tiny road loops east to **Urval,** with its vast 12th-century fortified church. From Urval go north to the D25 and

then east to **Siorac-en-Périgord ❻**, which has a 17th-century château and a little river beach.

Cross the river back to the north bank and follow the D703E upstream to the market town of **St.-Cyprien ❼** *(visitor information, tel 05 53 30 36 09)*, clustered around its 14th-century church and massive bell tower on a wooded hillside. Continue upstream on the D703; now the valley starts to narrow. Towering above it is the formidable château at **Beynac-et-Cazenac ❽** *(visitor information, tel 05 53 29 43 08)*, sitting like a stone crown on its rock, accessible by a steep footpath or via a detour inland through the pretty little village. Restoration work is gradually bringing this tremendous fortress back to its 13th-century appearance, with drawbridge, portcullis, and medieval kitchen. The vaulted great hall has lovely naive frescoes, and the views from the castle keep are not for the fainthearted.

Beynac was a French bastion during the Hundred Years' War, and glowering opposite it on the south bank is the fortress of **Castelnaud** (tel 05 53 31 30 00, castelnaud.com), intermittently an English stronghold. It now houses a museum of siege warfare, including primitive cannons and a reconstructed catapult. Cross the river from the D703 to the D53 under the Château de Castelnaud and make a short detour downstream on this road to visit the 15th-century **Château des Milandes** (tel 05 53 59 31 21, milandes .com, closed Nov.–March), once the much loved home of the remarkable Josephine Baker. Here the American jazz singer and cabaret artist planned to realize her dream of a "world village" with her "rainbow tribe" of 12 children adopted from all over the world. Financial difficulties and frail health forced her to abandon the idea in 1969.

Retrace your steps to Castelnaud, then cross the river and continue east along the D703 to **La Roque-Gageac.** This irresistible place to pause shelters beneath the great craggy cliffside. Relax at a riverside café, stroll around the village with its ocher houses and craft shops, or climb the steep narrow streets to the 12th-century church to admire the view.

Continue along the D703, then cross to the south of the river again on the D46. Just south of the river, take the D50 winding steeply up to **Domme** ❾ (visitor information, tel 05 53 31 71 00, ot-domme.com), the best

## River Trip by Gabarre

The *gabarres* are the traditional flat-bottomed boats of the Dordogne, once used to transport goods—from wine to salt to wood—between the upper reaches of the river and the sea. Today they make a perfect way to enjoy the slowly meandering river and get fine views of the castles and golden-hued houses of the riverside villages reflected serenely in the water. There are numerous boarding points in Roque-Gageac, Beynac, and Bergerac. For more information, contact **Gabarres de Beynac** (tel 05 53 28 51 15, gabarre-beynac.com) or inquire directly at the quais or the local tourist office.

preserved and possibly the loveliest of all the *bastide* towns (see p. 299). High up on a crag above the river, the narrow, flower-decked streets still shelter within its 12th-century walls. Beneath the 17th-century covered marketplace is a cavern (now reached by an elevator), where it is supposed that the citizens of Domme took refuge during the Hundred Years' War and the Wars of Religion. The **Belvédère de la Barre,** located at the end of the Grand-Rue, offers breathtaking panoramas of the river and the surrounding countryside. From Domme, the D50 and D46 take you to **Sarlat-la-Canéda** (see p. 290).

# SARLAT-LA-CANÉDA

**Nestling in a little wooded valley a few miles north of the Dordogne River, Sarlat is like a living architectural museum, with one of the best ensembles of medieval, Renaissance, and 17th-century buildings in France. Its narrow cobbled streets, surrounded by ramparts, are full of houses rich in carving, their steep roofs sometimes tiled with the traditional limestone slabs. In 1962, Sarlat became one of the first towns in France to be restored and protected as a whole under a national policy of restoration.**

Rue de la République (the unfortunate 19th-century boulevard that bisects the town) is lined on both sides with a warren of medieval streets and many handsome buildings. One of the most beautiful, on Place du Peyrou, is the pinnacled 16th-century **Maison de la Boétie,** house of poet Étienne de la Boétie, with graceful arches on the ground floor

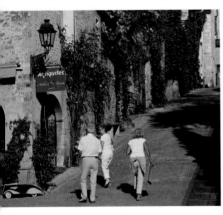

■ **Sarlat-la-Canéda is a treasure of history—a postcard-pretty home to more than a millennium of architectural notions.**

and delicately carved mullion windows. A relic of the town's powerful 12th-century abbey can still be seen in the **Chapelle des Pénitents Bleus** *(place du Peyrou).* The bizarre-looking conical tower of the **Lanterne des Morts,** in the abbey graveyard, was built to commemorate the sermons and miracles of St. Bernard in Sarlat in 1147.

**Place de la Liberté,** the lovely main square, has lots of cafés and is the focus of Sarlat's famous market on Wednesdays and Saturdays. The stalls offer truffles, walnuts, and foie gras, as well as everyday items for locals and souvenirs for visitors.

Not surprisingly, Sarlat is a tremendously popular tourist destination, and, if you can, it is best to visit out of season. Take time to wander its fascinating streets, poking into nooks and crannies; best of all, see it by night, when its history and atmosphere are enhanced by a modern system of gas lighting. For a good overall view, drive to the village of **Temniac,** which overlooks Sarlat from the north. ■

**Sarlat-la-Canéda** ⚠ 264 D3 Visitor Information ✉ rue Tourny ☎ 05 53 31 45 45 **sarlat-tourisme.com**

# LASCAUX & PREHISTORIC CAVE PAINTINGS

**The painted caves at Lascaux have been called the Sistine Chapel of prehistory for the powerful quality of the work. They can now be seen only in replica at Lascaux II and Lascaux IV. Though a visit there is still an amazing experience, the beautiful Vézère Valley is rich in original marvels, so there are other choices as well.**

■ **Prehistoric artists at Lascaux used the cave contours to bring their paintings of wild animals to life.**

The area's limestone caves create an underground network of tunnels and caverns protected from the light, with constant temperature and humidity.

Until about 17,000 years ago, people lived in dwellings of skin and turf, under rock overhangs, and sometimes in the cave entrances. Yet the paintings are usually buried deep within the caves' dark interiors, painted or engraved by the light of stone oil lamps or torches. These dark, hidden areas were probably religious sanctuaries devoted to the worship of the animals that sustained Cro-Magnon life. The range of animals depicted includes horses, bison, deer, boars, wolves, foxes, birds, and reptiles, with the occasional mammoth and rhinoceros representing big game, prehistoric-style. Very often the animals are shown pregnant, as if invoking fertility. Human figures appear only rarely; prehistoric man knew his place in the natural order.

These early artists used charcoal, ocher, and red and yellow pigments made from oxidized iron, applied with fingers or brushes or blown through tubes. They also scratched and carved with horn, stone, or bone.

Scientific excavations began in the mid-19th century, revealing entire periods of prehistory: The Mousterian, Magdalenian, and other cultures were named after the finds here. The first skeletons of Cro-Magnon man were discovered in 1868, during excavations for a railroad line at Cro-Magnon.

## Les Eyzies-de-Tayac

Les Eyzies-de-Tayac is now known as the prehistoric capital of the world. Here the **Musée National de Préhistoire** gives an excellent introduction to the subject (although all the information plaques are written in French).

A number of fascinating caves lie nearby. **Font-de-Gaume,** discovered in 1901, has some of the best art still

> ### Cave Talk
> The French word for a cave is *grotte; gouffre* is a chasm with a wide surface opening; *cave,* on the other hand, means "cellar" or "storeroom," often for wine. Signs pointing to a cave usually indicate wine for sale and tasting.

open to the public, with drawings of deer, horses, and mammoths and a frieze of bison. The **Grotte de Combarelles,** is situated in the Beune Valley east of Les-Eyzies-de-Tayac. It was discovered in 1910, and shelters more than 200 engravings and drawings of animals and magic symbols. Tickets for both sites are subject to a daily limit, so plan to arrive early.

The rock shelter of **Cap Blanc,** located farther up the Beune Valley, contains a frieze of horses sculpted in relief. At **Rouffignac** almost 5 miles (8 km) of caves and galleries can be toured by electric train to witness prehistoric drawings of ibex, rhinoceros, mammoths, and fighting stags.

The recently discovered **Grotte-de-Tourtoirac** boasts spectacular stalactites, explored by descending 82 feet (25 m) by elevator.

**Les Eyzies-de-Tayac** 🗺 264 D3 Visitor Information ✉ 19 avenue de la Préhistoire ☎ 05 53 06 97 05 **lascaux-dordogne.com** • **Musée National de Préhistoire** ☎ 05 53 06 45 45 🕐 Closed Tues. Sept.–June 💲 $ **musee-prehistoire-eyzies.fr** • **Grotte-de-Tourtoirac** ☎ 05 53 50 24 77 🕐 Closed Dec.–Feb. **grotte-de-tourtoirac.fr** • **Lascaux** 🗺 264 D3 ✉ On the D704E, Montignac ☎ 05 53 51 95 03 🕐 Lascaux II closed Jan. & Mon. Nov.–Easter 💲 $$

## Lascaux

Lascaux itself, located close to Montignac farther up the Vézère Valley, lay buried beneath a landslide for thousands of years before being accidentally discovered in 1940 (so the story goes) by children looking for their lost dog. What they found was a prehistoric art gallery of more than 150 paintings and 1,500 engravings, perfectly preserved by a fortuitous glaze of crystals.

Drawings of animals, executed in ocher and red pigments with strong lines of black charcoal, show an astonishingly sophisticated level of artistic skill. Opened to the public in 1948, the caves attracted huge numbers of visitors. In 1963, they were closed after green algae and white calcite were found to be spoiling the paintings.

A splendid replica was built nearby at **Lascaux II,** where the paintings were painstakingly copied over 11 years, using the same tools and pigments as the original artists. However, the replica itself is now degrading. Even more worrying, the original Lascaux caves have developed further problems following the installation of an air-conditioning system. **Lascaux III** is a series of five exact reproductions of the cave art that, since 2012, have been displayed around the world. **Lascaux IV** re-creates all painted areas of the cave at the Centre International de l'Art Pariétal. Since December 2016 this larger replica, integrating digital technology into the display, is presented in a new museum inside the hill overlooking Montignac. ■

■ Modern-day artists at Lascaux have used today's technology to re-create the paintings at a series of Lascaux museums of cave art.

# CAHORS

**The hills to the north and south of Cahors afford panoramic views of the handsome ensemble of towers, ramparts, and bridges that make up the town, encircled in a snug loop of the Lot River. Cahors was of significance in the Middle Ages as the capital of Quercy, the limestone area around the river.**

Prosperous and proud of its ancient university, medieval Cahors was an important center of trade, banking, and learning. But in 1360, during the Hundred Years' War, it was handed over to the English. The population fled, and the nearly deserted city never fully recovered.

One outstanding relic of its medieval grandeur survives: the famous 14th-century **Pont Valentré,** now a UNESCO World Heritage site, spanning the river on seven Gothic arches guarded by three fortified towers. According to local legend, the master builder made a pact with the Devil in order to finish the bridge, but by cunning managed to retain his eternal soul.

■ **Originally built to defend Cahors against invaders, the 14th-century Pont Valentré spans the Lot River.**

Lined with plane trees, the main street of Cahors is Boulevard Gambetta, named for the famous 19th-century radical politician Léon Gambetta, a native of the city. The shops here and the nearby covered market supply all manner of local delicacies, including the rich, plummy wine of Cahors known as *vin noir.* To the east of Boulevard Gambetta clusters the old quarter. Alleys crossed by bridges stripe the streets with shadows, and you can follow a marked path through secret gardens.

The light reveals the Renaissance windows, stone carvings, and finely worked wooden corbels of the old quarter's impressive mansions. One of the most entrancing is the **Hôtel Roaldès** *(quai Champollion),* with its south facade of timber and weathered redbrick, Italian-style loggia and tower, and carved north facade.

At the heart of the old town is the Romanesque **Cathédrale St.-Étienne** *(place Aristide-Briand).* The two great domes decorated with 14th-century frescoes give a spacious feel to the interior, and the Flamboyant Gothic cloister has beautiful carvings. But the cathedral's most splendid feature is the 16th-century tympanum over the north door, depicting the Ascension of Christ. ■

**Cahors** 🅜 264 D3 Visitor Information ✉ place François Mitterrand ☎ 05 65 53 20 65 **cahorsvalleedulot.com**

# ROCAMADOUR

In a cleft of the great gorge of the Alzou River, Rocamadour is one of the most impressive—and most visited—sites in France. In the 12th century, the village exploded into fame with the discovery of the body of a man, believed to be Zacchaeus, husband of St. Veronica, who was rechristened St. Amadour. Buried beneath an existing chapel dedicated to the Virgin, the remains were soon credited with miracles, and pilgrims came from far and wide.

The grand stairway leads from the village up to the shrine of the Black Virgin and the saint's tomb. The devout climbed the steps on their knees (some still do). Within the **Chapelle de Notre-Dame,** carved into the rock, stands the famous statue of the Black Virgin. Probably from the 12th century, the statue is crudely carved, but moving in its simplicity, the wood smoothed and darkened by time. Above it is a ninth-century bell, which is said to ring unaided to foretell a miracle. Down steps to the left of the chapel is the 12th-century crypt with the tomb of St. Amadour. The **Musée d'Art Sacré** *(parvis des Sanctuaires, tel 05 65 33 23 30)* displays sacred art. Above the chapel, the climb continues, either past the Stations of the Cross or up to the ramparts of the original fort. ■

The cliffside village of Rocamadour

**Rocamadour** 264 D3 • Visitor Information Maison de Tourisme l'Hospitalet 05 65 33 22 00 **vallee-dordogne.com**

## Gouffre de Padirac

The Gouffre de Padirac *(tel 05 65 33 64 56, gouffre-de-padirac.com, closed Nov.–March, $$ round-trip),* east of Rocamadour on the D673, is a vast limestone chasm, some 330 feet (100 m) wide and 800 feet (246 m) deep. It leads to a series of grottoes reaching at least 9 miles (15 km) underground. In the Middle Ages, it served as a refuge in turbulent times, but only in the 19th century did speleologists begin to discover its prehistoric significance. Elevators and stairs descend to the bottom of the chasm, and flat-bottomed boats ferry you along the subterranean river and into illuminated caves. After about 350 yards (315 m), you arrive at the Salle du Grand Dôme, a lofty cavern 295 feet (90 m) high.

# AROUND THE LOT VALLEY

As it flows toward Cahors, the Lot River cuts through *causses*—limestone plateaus. At one moment, it is overhung by creamy yellow or pink cliffs, with picture-postcard villages and turreted fortresses clinging to their flanks; the next moment, it meanders gently through bucolic meadows and vineyards. To the north, its tributary, the Célé, flows to meet it through a romantic valley studded with prehistoric caves and Renaissance castles.

Tourism has come in a gentle way here, with horseback riding, boating, several intriguing small museums, and caves in abundance: Everywhere you will see signs pointing to the *grottes*.

Leave Cahors on the D653, heading east on the D662 to reach **St.-Cirq-Lapopie,** justly designated one of the most beautiful villages in France. The winding cobbled streets, fortified church, and timber-framed houses have all been lovingly restored. Artists have colonized the place since the 1950s, most famously the surrealist writer André Breton (1896–1966). You can follow

■ **The perched village of St.-Cirq-Lapopie draws visitors year-round.**

the artists circuit around the village.

The Lot Valley bristles with castles. At **Cénevières** you can visit the 13th-century château *(tel 05 65 31 38 08, chateau-cenevieres.com, closed Nov.–Easter)* overlooking the river and admire its Renaissance additions, including the stone staircase, gallery, and coffered ceilings. You can also enjoy the views, which take in the trogolodyte village carved out of the opposite cliff.

The next major town is the pretty riverside resort of **Cajarc,** where the **Maison des Arts Georges Pompidou** (Georges Pompidou, president of France from 1969 to 1974, had a house here) stages exhibitions of contemporary European art. Continue up the valley to **Montbrun-les-Bains,** which has a spectacular ruined fortress. At **Larroque-Toirac,** the fairy-tale castle was rebuilt after the English burned it down in the 14th century.

A few miles farther on, the D662 cuts across the *causse* to reach **Figeac,** a beautiful old market town. Tanning was an important industry here, and many

**St.-Cirq-Lapopie** 🔼 264 D3 Visitor Information ☎ 05 65 31 31 31 **saint -cirqlapopie.com • Cajarc** 🔼 264 D3 Visitor Information ✉ place Françoise Sagan ☎ 05 65 40 72 89 **cajarc.fr • Maison des Arts Georges Pompidou** ✉ route de Gréalou, Cajarc ☎ 05 65 40 78 19 **magcp.fr**

## INSIDER TIP:

Cross-training sightseeing: After kayaking the Lot River, climb up to St.-Cirq-Lapopie and admire the medieval wooden houses.

—SYLVIE BIGAR
*National Geographic writer*

of the handsome medieval houses in the old town have octagonal chimneys and open *soleilhos*, drying rooms, on the top floor. The tourist office and local museum are housed in the 13th-century **Hôtel de la Monnaie,** the old mint.

Jean-François Champollion, the 19th-century Egyptologist who first deciphered Egyptian hieroglyphics, was born in Figeac. The restored **Musée Champollion** is devoted to the writing of the world. The Place des Écritures is floored with a copy of the Rosetta stone, created by American Joseph Kosuth.

Leave Figeac on the D13, then turn left on the D41 to follow the lovely valley of the Célé River. Stop to visit the beautiful village of **Espagnac-Ste.-Eulalie** and the atmospheric ruins of the aptly named 13th-century **Prieuré du Val-Paradis.** Continue past peach-colored cliffs and fortified caves to the Benedictine **Abbaye de Marcilhac.** About 3 miles (5 km) far-

ther on, stop at **Sauliac-sur-Célé** for its living museum of 19th-century farmwork, the **Musée de Plein Air de Quercy.** Two reconstructed farms illustrate traditional agriculture and crafts.

Beyond Cabrerets and its two commanding castles lie the incomparable treasures of the painted **Grotte de Pech-Merle,** which was discovered in 1922 by two local boys. This remarkable gallery of prehistoric paintings, a staggering 20,000 years old at the most conservative estimate, are still open to public view. You can explore almost a mile of spectacular caves and galleries decorated with glorious paintings of bison and mammoths, silhouettes of horses, female figures, and mysterious handprints.

### Bérenger's Folly

West of Cahors towers **Château de Bonaguil,** the ultimate military fantasy. In the late 15th century, Bérenger de Roquefeuil fortified and enlarged the existing 13th-century keep, determined to build an impregnable castle. Forty years later, he was the proud lord of a masterpiece of military engineering. Sadly, nobody ever attacked him, so Bérenger was never able to prove his point. ∎

*"St-Cirq has cast a spell on me, the one which lasts for ever. I have no desire to go anywhere else."*
—*André Breton (1951)*

**Figeac** 🅰 265 E3 Visitor Information ✉ place Vival ☎ 05 65 34 06 25 **tourisme-figeac.com • Musée Champollion** ✉ place Champollion, Figeac ☎ 05 65 50 31 08 🕐 Closed Mon. Sept.–June 💲 $$ **ville-figeac .fr • Musée de Plein Air de Quercy** ✉ Sauliac-sur-Célé ☎ 05 65 31 36 43 🕐 Closed Mon.–Tues. & Oct.–March 💲 $$ • **Grotte de Pech-Merle** ✉ Cabrerets ☎ 05 65 31 27 05 🕐 Closed Nov.–March 💲 $$, reservations recommended **pechmerle.com • Château de Bonaguil** ☎ 05 53 71 90 33 🕐 Closed Nov.–March 💲 $$ **chateau-bonaguil.com**

# CONQUES

**The little village of Conques is tucked away in the steep valley of the Dourdou River. This unlikely setting hides one of the great pilgrimage churches of France, the Abbaye de Ste.-Foy.**

The three great towers of the abbey rise above the village, tiled with the same local slate as the houses. Pilgrims began to come here in the 11th century, when the monks at Conques stole the relics of St. Foy, an early Christian martyr, from Agen. Soon the abbey became a stopping place on the way to Santiago de Compostela (see pp. 304–305) as well as a place of pilgrimage itself.

The 11th-century interior of the church is pure Romanesque, with a soaring nave, beautifully decorated capitals, and three chapels at the rounded east end, built to provide more altars for the pilgrims. The most celebrated feature of the church is the tympanum over the west door,

a masterpiece of 12th-century sculpture depicting the Last Judgment. Unusually, it still has traces of the original color. Note the stained-glass windows created in 1994 by artist Pierre Soulages.

The abbey's treasury, which survived the revolution intact, includes enamel work, vestments, and reliquaries, but the star of the collection is the ninth-century reliquary made to hold the bones of St. Foy herself. It is in the form of a statue, made of gold and studded with jewels, cameos, and intaglios, some of which may date from Roman times. The little village itself is sometimes overwhelmed by visitors to its church, but it has some charming old houses along its steep streets. ∎

∎ Conques is home to one of France's most famous pilgrimage churches, Abbaye de Ste.-Foy.

**Conques** ⚑ 265 E3 Visitor Information ☎ 05 65 72 85 00 **tourisme -conques.fr** • **Abbaye de Ste.-Foy** ✉ place de l'Abbaye ☎ 05 65 69 85 12 **abbaye-conques.org**

# *BASTIDE* TOWNS

Alongside its noble heritage of castles and abbeys, southwest France provides, through its *bastide* towns, insights into life in the war-torn Middle Ages.

■ Cordes is a quintessential *bastide* town, rising high on its fortified hill.

Built in the 13th and 14th centuries, *bastides* were new towns designed to protect the beleaguered rural population during the Hundred Years' War. Those settling the new towns were granted land to support a family, and benefited from privileges stated in a town charter, which included freedom from feudal service and the right to hold a market and to elect a council.

The basic design—always with an eye to defense—was a grid of streets around a central arcaded square. Built by both the English and French, they were fortified with massive walls. Since a bastide's inhabitants did not owe allegiance to an overlord, there was no castle for refuge, so churches were fortified as sanctuaries.

**Cordes,** 50 miles (90 km) southeast of Cahors, is one of the earliest bastides, founded by the Count of Toulouse in 1222. It retains perfectly preserved ramparts and town gates, and impeccably restored narrow cobbled streets lined with Gothic houses. Beside the covered marketplace is the well, bored 375 feet (114 m) deep for water during sieges.

**Monpazier,** southeast of Bergerac, retains its exquisitely arcaded central square, covered market hall, fortified church, a rectangular pattern of streets, and ancient walls.

**Monflanquin** *(visitor information, place des Arcades, tel 05 53 36 40 19, monflanquin-tourisme.com),* southeast of Bergerac, has a warren of medieval streets. Don't miss the arcade-edged square. Above the tourist office is the **Musée des Bastides,** which explains the history of these towns. ■

**Cordes** 264 D2 Visitor Information ✉ Maison Gaugiran ☎ 05 63 56 00 52 **cordessurciel.fr** • **Monpazier** 264 D3 Visitor Information ✉ place des Cornières ☎ 05 53 22 68 59 **pays-des-bastides.com**

**NOTE:** Other fine examples of *bastides* include **Domme** (see p. 289), **Toulouse** (see p. 300), **Montauban** (see p. 303), and **Mirepoix** (see p. 320).

# TOULOUSE

A cosmopolitan metropolis, regional capital, and thriving center of technology and aeronautical research, Toulouse—recently voted one of the most desirable places to live in France—still holds at its heart the lovely old *ville rose,* the pink-brick streets making up the old town. History may be powerfully tangible here, but this is still a lively city, with the biggest student population in France outside Paris. Visit the ancient city on foot, then for a change of pace take a trip on the state-of-the-art Métro, with each station credited to a different team of architect and artist.

Start in the **Place du Capitole,** the vast central square. This is dominated by the Capitole itself, the 18th-century **Hôtel de Ville** named after the city's medieval consuls, or *capitouls.* Beginning in the tenth century, Toulouse was the seat of the powerful counts of Toulouse. All this came to a brutal end with the Albigensian Crusade of the 13th century, when Toulouse lost its autonomy. In the 15th century, the city enjoyed another heyday, thanks to the *pastel* or woad plant cultivated here; it yielded a blue dye, to be supplanted by the arrival of indigo from the East in the 16th century. Merchants and *capitouls* grew rich, building themselves ever finer Italian Renaissance mansions.

■ The basilica of St.-Sernin, an architectural centerpiece of the city, dominates the square of the same name with its unmistakable tower.

**INSIDER TIP:**

Ever wanted to test out your moon-walking skills here on planet Earth? Now you can—at an astronaut training session in the popular Cité de l'Espace museum, just outside Toulouse.

—ROSEMARY BAILEY
*National Geographic author*

Look out for the **Hôtel d'Assézat** on Rue de Metz and **Hôtel Bernuy** on Rue Gambetta.

The **Basilique St.-Sernin** *(place St.-Sernin, tel 05 61 21 80 45, closed to visitors Sun. a.m.)* is the largest Romanesque church in Europe (consecrated in 1096, though the nave and tower both date from the 13th century) and was the most beautiful of all the pilgrim churches.

Follow in the pilgrims' footsteps: enter through the south portal with its tremendous carvings; down the nave, past glowing frescoes and tapestries, painted capitals, and carved choir stalls; then proceed to the 11th-century altar, ambulatory, and to the rich treasury below. The Gothic church of **Les Jacobins** *(rue Lakanal)* is also particularly fine.

Outstanding Romanesque sculptures from the city's churches and cloisters have been gathered together in the **Musée des Augustins.** The redesigned **Muséum de Toulouse** *(35 allée Jules Guesde, tel 05 67 73 84 84, museum .toulouse.fr, closed Mon.)* houses the first natural history museum in France. Don't miss the **Espace d'Art Moderne et Contemporain** in the old abbatoirs of St. Cyprien district, one of France's best contemporary art museums. ∎

## City of Canals and Music

Toulouse is a key point on one of the great engineering feats of the 17th century, the Canal du Midi. This 150-mile (240 km) waterway runs through Southern France, connecting the Atlantic with the Mediterranean. A UNESCO World Heritage Site, the canal draws boaters, bikers, and sightseers. Since 2023, Toulouse is also a UNESCO-designated City of Music, in recognition of its fine musical institutions, music education, and festivals that feature global acts. Music has a special place in Toulouse: its city hall is also home to the national theater and opera house.

**Toulouse** ⚑ 264 D2 Visitor Information ✉ Donjon du Capitole ☎ 08 92 18 01 80 **toulouse-tourisme.com** • **Musée des Augustins** ✉ 21 rue de Metz ☎ 05 61 22 21 82 **augustins.org** • **Espace d'Art Moderne et Contemporain** ✉ Les Abbatoires, 76 allées Charles-de-Fitte ☎ 05 34 51 10 60 ⊕ Closed a.m. & Mon. 🛇 $ **lesabattoirs.org** • **Cité de l'Espace** ✉ avenue Jean-Gonord ☎ 05 67 22 23 24 ⊕ Closed Mon. Sept.–March (except school vacations) 🛇 $$ **cite-espace.com**

# ALBI

Viewed from the 11th-century Pont Vieux over the Tarn River, Albi presents an unforgettable sight, its pink and ocher houses rising in tiers to the soaring bulk of its cathedral fortress.

■ **Cathédrale Ste.-Cécile** overlooks the Tarn River.

Like Toulouse, Albi is a *ville rose*, built of the same pink brick. Its single most breathtaking feature is the great **Cathédrale Ste.-Cécile.** The mighty brick walls, buttressed by tremendous piers, are as daunting as they are astonishing. In the spacious nave, built without pillars or transept, is a colorful world of 16th-century Italian wall paintings and ethereally delicate carving. Most remarkable are the filigree rood screen and the fresco of the Last Judgment that covers the west wall.

In the formal gardens of the 13th-century bishop's palace, the **Palais de la Berbie,** the ramparts offer ravishing views of the Tarn. Inside the palace lies an extensive collection of works by Henri de Toulouse-Lautrec, who was born in Albi (see sidebar below).

In the old town, you will find the **Maison Enjalbert** and **Hôtel de Reynes,** both built in the 16th century, as well as the Romanesque **Église de St.-Salvy** *(rue Mariès),* with a beautiful 13th-century cloister. ■

## Toulouse-Lautrec

**Born in the town of Albi in 1864, Henri de Toulouse-Lautrec was descended from the counts of Toulouse. Crippled and stunted in his youth by what may have been brittle bone disease, he sought solace in painting and freedom in the bohemian world of the Montmartre quarter of Paris. A superb draftsman with a wide technical range, he used just a few expressive strokes to convey the scenes that caught his eye. The renovated Musée Toulouse-Lautrec, in the Palais de la Berbie, has a collection of more than 600 of his works, ranging from early landscapes and portraits to sketches and book illustrations, drawings and paintings, lithographs and posters.**

**Albi** 🅰 264 E2 Visitor Information ✉ Palais de la Berbie, place Ste.-Cécile ☎ 05 63 36 36 00 **albi-tourisme.fr • Musée Toulouse-Lautrec** ✉ Palais de la Berbie, place Ste.-Cécile ☎ 05 63 49 48 70 🕐 Closed Tues. Oct.–March 💲 $$ **musee-toulouse-lautrec.com**

# MONTAUBAN

Another historic pink-brick town on the Tarn River, Montauban was founded in the 12th century by the Count of Toulouse. In the 16th century, the town became an important center of Protestantism and even resisted a siege by Louis XIII—despite the fact that the king had arranged a special lunch to view the assault.

An arcaded central square lies at the heart of Montauban, founded in the 12th century.

The focus of the old town is the **Place Nationale,** which owes its satisfying unity to the fact that it was rebuilt in the 17th century following a fire. Its brick buildings are handsome, and the square's shady arcades (site of a regular market) make it a fine place to shop or sit in a café.

The fortified **Église de St.-Jacques,** largely dating back to the 13th century, stands near the Pont Vieux, which is similar in style to the bridge at Albi and offers a fine view of the river. At the end of the bridge stands the former bishop's palace, now the **Musée Ingres.** On his death, Jean-

**INSIDER TIP:**

Stop at Guymare *[939 avenue de l'Europe],* for a scoop or two of artisanal ice cream.

—SHEILA BUCKMASTER
*National Geographic
editor at large*

Auguste-Dominique Ingres left his studio contents (including Greek vases and Roman sculpture), his violin, his paint box, and many of his drawings to his native town. Also at this museum you will find sculptures by another famous native of Montauban, Emile-Antoine Bourdelle. ∎

**Montauban** 264 D2 Visitor Information ✉ 4 rue du Collège ☎ 05 63 63 60 60 **montauban-tourisme.com** • **Musée Ingres** ✉ Palais Épiscopal, 19 rue de l'Hôtel de Ville 🕐 Closed Mon. (except July–Aug.) & Sun. a.m. Nov.–Mar. 💲 $$

# THE ROAD TO COMPOSTELA

**The symbol of the scallop shell marks stages on the pilgrim route to Santiago de Compostela in northwest Spain, one of the greatest shrines of medieval Christendom. Four main routes threaded across France: from Paris; from Vézelay in Burgundy; from Le Puy-en-Velay in the Auvergne; and from St.-Gilles, near Arles in Provence. All converged in the southwest to cross the Pyrenees and continue through Navarre on a single path.**

■ **Believers pray at the old town church in St.-Jean-Pied-de-Port.**

Thousands of pilgrims and travelers still follow the routes today, passing through the same towns as the original pilgrims. They, too, worship in the churches of Conques or Toulouse, wonder at the finely carved cloisters and tympanum of Moissac, pause to pray at wayside shrines and crosses, or seek shelter in tiny frescoed chapels. They may have different reasons for making this pilgrimage: Some may still walk the route for religious reasons, some to better understand their forebears, some just to enjoy the scenery. But, like the medieval pilgrims, they find satisfaction in the journey.

The object of the pilgrims' travels is the shrine of St. James (Santiago), the disciple who is believed to have brought Christianity to Spain, then part of the Roman Empire. On his return to Judea, he was executed by Herod, and his followers returned with his martyred body to Galicia in Spain. As they approached the shore, they saw a vision of a man covered in scallop shells rise out of the waves on horseback; the scallop shell then became the pilgrimage emblem. The body of St. James was buried, and subsequently most of Spain fell to the Moors. Then, in 814, a vision of stars (*compostela* means "field of stars") showed the way to the saint's tomb, and on July 25 (now the feast of Santiago) the body was discovered. Soon a church was built on the spot: The present building at Compostela is a vast Romanesque church with an elaborate baroque facade added later.

Pilgrims were lured with the promise of indulgences—forgiveness of their sins and remission of time in purgatory—and pilgrimages became enormously popular. The first recorded pilgrimage to Compostela was carried out by the bishop of Le Puy in 951.

Vital encouragement for the pilgrimage route was provided by the formidably powerful Benedictine abbey of Cluny in Burgundy, which established daughter houses, churches, and shrines along the way and donated relics to enhance their prestige and power. No shrine or place of pilgrimage was complete without a relic preserved in reliquaries of gold and silver embellished with jewels. Bones of saints were treasured, and pieces of the True Cross were considered especially valuable. Santiago de Compostela boasted the body of St. James, and many pilgrims would, en route, have prayed at shrines containing parts of no fewer than five Apostles and, at the Basilique St.-Sernin in Toulouse, a sliver of the True Cross. Intense and sometimes unseemly competition raged for the most potent relics. A monk from the abbey at Conques, for example, stole the relics of St. Foy from Agen.

Often pilgrims doggedly tramped the sacred path for years, suffering hardship and danger. Moved by their plight, at the end of the 12th century a monk from Poitou by the name of Amery Picaud penned the *Liber Sancti Jacobi*. This early guidebook gave pilgrims details of the best places to stop for sustenance, the most reliable

**INSIDER TIP:**
Along the old pilgrim route, spend the night in the tiny, charming town of St.-Bertand-de-Comminges, at the inexpensive Hôtel du Comminges. It's right near the cathedral and the Roman excavations.

—GILLES MINGASSON
*National Geographic photographer*

sources of water, and the most rewarding chapels or monasteries to visit on the way.

Pilgrims wore the sign of the scallop shell to denote their calling. Even today it still works its magic. In 1987, the European Community officially recognized a system of signposting that had been devised using the scallop shell (*santiago-compostela.net*). It described the pilgrim route to Compostela as "one of the oldest signs of European cooperation and enterprise . . . a key part of our European heritage."

■ **Details highlighting pilgrims and the ancient route can be found all along the way.**

# MOISSAC

The small town of Moissac on the north bank of the Tarn River is famed for the carvings on its abbey church, once one of the great abbeys of France. Wander the peaceful cloisters and admire the fine Romanesque sculpture.

In the 11th century, the **Abbaye de St.-Pierre** at Moissac became a daughter abbey of Cluny. The church—part Romanesque, part Gothic—is famed for the carvings on its south portal. A scalloped decoration frames the doorway, and a central column entwined with lions supports the tympanum. In minute and still perfect detail, it depicts St. John's vision of the Apocalypse from the Book of Revelation. In the middle sits Christ in Majesty surrounded by the Evangelists, the angels, and various symbolic beasts. The flowing figure of Jeremiah on the western door jamb has a melancholy beauty. On the east side, Avarice and Unchastity writhe in torment. Within the arcaded cloisters, the 76 slender columns support graceful arcades, their capitals carved with infinite delicacy. ∎

## Romanesque Sculpture

Look closely at the fine Romanesque sculpture that adorns so many chapels and churches in France, and you are in fact peering directly into the medieval mind. The figures and stories portrayed in these vigorous decorations offer us a picture of a period and its people of which we have very little record otherwise.

Figurative sculpture became popular during the 11th and 12th centuries, when craftsmen and artisans adorned column capitals, doorways, and tympana with glorious carvings. The carvings are full of detail—some of it endearing, though often quite frightening.

The narratives are usually biblical, from the familiar story of the Nativity to the Last Judgment, with the hanging of Judas a particular favorite. Fearsome demons and dragons abound. All were motifs designed to instruct the faithful on the realities of hell and the promise of paradise.

The sculptors themselves were usually anonymous, and they often used local characters as their models. The average medieval churchgoer would have recognized and possibly even chuckled at the portraits of their friends and neighbors, depicted jokingly as people with toothaches, boils, and squints.

**Moissac** 🅜 264 D2 Visitor Information ✉ 1 Boulevard de Brienne ☎ 05 32 09 69 36 **tourisme-moissac-terresdesconfluences.fr** • **Abbaye de St.-Pierre** ✉ place St.-Pierre ☎ 05 63 04 03 08 💲 $

# More Places to Visit in the Dordogne & Midi-Pyrénées

## Château de Biron

Just south of the *bastide* town of Monpazier (see p. 299), the gargantuan Château de Biron dominates a great swath of countryside as it has since the 12th century. Restoration is still in progress, and the château serves as an arts center during the summer. **M** 264 D3 **☎** 05 53 63 13 39 **⊕** Closed Jan. & Mon.

## Collonges-la-Rouge

The lords of Turenne built this red village, its delightful mansions, towers, turrets, market hall, and château forming an almost bizarre homogeneity. The white limestone tympanum of the otherwise red church (constructed in the 11th–12th centuries) comes almost as a relief. Stroll along Rue Noire in the oldest quarter to gain a good sense of the whole. **M** 264 D3

## Rodez

This small Aveyron agricultural town boasts a Gothic cathedral, an archaeological museum of menhirs, and now a new museum devoted to the work of locally born artist Pierre Soulages *(tel 05 65 75 76 77, musee -soulages.grand-rodez.com, closed Mon. Sept.–June),* which displays his paintings, engravings and work for the stained-glass windows of Conques. *tourisme.grand-rodez.com* **M** 264 E3

## St.-Céré

St.-Céré is a charming little market town, well situated for excursions to the Lot Valley. The Bave River ripples past its handsome streets, market square, and 15th-century balconied mansions. Above it to the north loom the two keeps (12th and 15th centuries) of the castle of **St.-Laurent-les-Tours,** home of the artist Jean Lurçat from 1945 to his death in 1966. Now it houses a museum of his work, and galleries in the town sell both original works and prints. **M** 264 D3 Visitor Information **✉** 13 avenue François de Maynard **☎** 05 65 33 22 00

■ Collonges-la-Rouge gets its name from its wealth of red buildings.

# THE PYRENEES

**Visible from the Plain of Aquitaine and—on a clear day—from the fringes of the Massif Central, the Pyrenees fill the horizon with unsurpassed grandeur. Here you will find majesty and solitude, combined with lush, green valleys, rushing waterfalls, and rare flora and fauna. In spring and summer, the alpine meadows are embroidered with flowers, while in winter the mountains offer a variety of ski slopes. But perhaps the best time of all is the *arrière-saison,* the golden days of autumn when wisps of wood smoke scent the air.**

Spanning the frontier between Spain and France, the Pyrenees really belong to neither. For many centuries, the main part of the Pyrenees consisted of a patchwork of tiny republics. The region still retains a sense of independent little states, each proud of its history and traditions.

There are few better ways of experiencing the mountains at close hand than by walking. These soaring mountains are a paradise for hikers: The GR10, one of France's most famous long-distance footpaths, crosses the entire range from the Mediterranean to the Atlantic. Any serious walk in the mountains takes time, so consider

■ Fabulous views of the Pyrenees from Col du Somport, a pass between France and Spain, abound.

camping out or staying overnight in refuges, undoubtedly the best way to immerse yourself in the natural wilderness of the Pyrenees.

Public transportation is erratic, with the delightful exception of some mountain trains and cable cars, so a car is essential for any foray. The roads are usually good and well signposted, though gas stations are few and far between and snow closes many higher roads from October to May. Remember your passport if you plan to cross to Spain. ■

**INSIDER TIP:**

Hikers should always be aware that the Pyrenees constitute a major mountain range. Always check the weather forecast before setting out, and go properly equipped with good boots, water, and maps. Don't rely on cell phone coverage.

—JACK KAVANAGH
*National Geographic author*

## Pyrenean Wildlife

The glorious wilderness of mountain lakes, valleys, and spectacuar peaks between France and Spain is protected under the umbrella of the Pyrenees National Park (see pp. 310–312). The French flock here year round to hike, ski, and climb, and to enjoy the vistas and the wildlife. The park is home to more than 400 species of flowers, 160 of which are found nowhere else in the world—including Pyrenean ramonda and saxifrage, separate species of columbines and lilies, tiny purple crocuses, and pink androsace. This diverse and rich flora supports a number of unique butterflies, such as the Gavarnie blue and the Gavarnie ringlet. On the upper mountain slopes, large raptors breed relatively undisturbed. The magnificent birds circling high in the sky are the griffon vulture, lammergeyer, and Egyptian vulture.

Mammals here include the isard, or Pyrenean antelope. The symbol of the park, the isard has horns that curve distinctively back at the tip. Its numbers are now increasing; it can be spotted on rocky outcrops high in the mountains. Other rare mammal species include the snow partridge, the marmot, and the Pyrenean desman, a tiny aquatic mammal.

A handful of brown bears also live in the Pyrenees, but these are threatened with extinction as they are driven farther away from their natural habitat in the lower stretches of the park and into the high reaches of the mountains. Efforts to reintroduce bears have met with bitter opposition from farmers.

# PARC NATIONAL DES PYRÉNÉES OCCIDENTALES

Established in 1967 and covering 113,000 acres (45,700 ha), the Western Pyrenees National Park encompasses some of the most spectacular scenery in the Pyrenees, including the breathtaking Cirque de Gavarnie. It is home to a number of rare and endangered species, including golden eagles, griffon vultures, lynx, ibex, and a few Pyrenean brown bears. Hunting and flower picking are strictly prohibited, and camping in the wild is permitted only at distances equivalent to more than an hour's trek from the road (and you must be off by sunrise).

■ Clouds shroud the mountain near a hiking trail in the Cirque de Gavarnie.

A number of magnificent valley roads climb up into the park, following the courses of the many rivers flowing from the mountains. The surrounding towns and villages are well equipped with hotels, restaurants, campsites, and mountain guides. Maisons du Parc are official information centers advising about walks, weather, wildlife, and the rich flora of the region.

## Vallée d'Aspe

To the west of the park, the N134 follows a Roman road along the valley of the Aspe from Oloron-Ste.-Marie, climbing to 5,354 feet (1,632 m) to enter Spain at the **Col du Somport.** This was the crossing place of the Saracen army on its way to defeat by Charles Martel in 732 and was trodden for centuries by pilgrims on their journey

**Parc National des Pyrénées Occidentales** 264 C1  Vallée d'Aspe
Visitor Information ✉ place François Saraille, Bedous ☎ 05 59 34 57 57
**tourisme-aspe.com**

to Compostela (see pp. 304–305). In 2003, a controversial 5-mile (8 km) road tunnel was finally pierced through the *col* (pass). This has relieved the traffic bottlenecks of the coastal routes, but it also threatens the peace of the valley and the last habitat of the Pyrenean brown bear. The village of **Lescun,** about halfway up the valley, offers views of the rock amphitheater and pinnacles of the Cirque de Lescun.

## Vallée d'Ossau

Just to the east, the D934 heads up the valley of the Ossau, leaving Pau behind to climb through spa towns perched between river and mountainside. Look for the golden

## EXPERIENCE: Spend the Night on Pic du Midi

At 9,439 feet (2,877 m), Pic du Midi was one of the great challenges for 19th-century tourists to the Pyrenees. Today it is the most accessible of the high peaks, with two cable cars making the 15-minute trip to the summit, weather permitting. At the top, you will enjoy one of the most sublime views in the Pyrenees: On a clear day, it is possible to see as far as the Atlantic Ocean, a distance of nearly 100 miles (160 km).

At the summit you will also find an observatory and a star museum. The observatory was built in 1880, a staggering achievement because most of the building material had to be brought up on the backs of porters and mules. For a long time, it was the highest observatory in Europe, and even now it is exceeded only by three others, one in Spain and the others in the Canary Islands.

Threatened with closure in 1983, the observatory nearly fell victim to scientific developments and budget restrictions. Instead, it was relaunched with a new role. It still operates as a meteorological station, supplying Météo-France with data, and as a stellar observatory, but now it also offers a museum devoted to the stars. Furthermore it allows all visitors to enjoy an unrivaled experience of a high-mountain summit without requiring a demanding climb. Accommodations *(tel 08 25 00 28 77 or 05 62 56 70 00, picdumidi .com)* once reserved for observatory staff are now open to the public, so anyone can stay overnight at the summit to stargaze and then see the sun rise the following morning.

The observatory is open year-round but is closed on Tuesdays in the off-season. To get there, drive to La Mongie or take the shuttle bus from Argelès-Gazost, Lourdes, or Bagnères-de-Bigorre. Cable cars depart for the summit every 15 minutes. Check the weather before leaving, and take warm clothing, good boots, sunglasses, and sunscreen.

eagles, goshawks, peregrines, and bearded vultures for which this valley is famous.

Continue through Laruns and Gabas, then turn southwest on the D231 to reach the artificial **Lac de Bious-Artigues,** part of the great Pyrenean hydroelectric network. From here, a marked footpath takes you on a spectacular four-hour walk around the **Lacs d'Ayous.** The path passes through forests and mountain pastures covered with spring wildflowers. Above you towers the extinct volcano of the **Pic du Midi d'Ossau.** Herds of *isars*, a wild goat, graze its slopes. A cable car runs from Gabas to Pic de la Sagette, at 7,550 feet (2,134 m), giving marvelous views.

Retrace your steps to Laruns to head east on the D198, a superb drive that swoops over two dramatic cols to reach Argelès-Gazost. Heading south on the D921 to Gavarnie, you pass the tiny village of **St.-Savin,** the site of an 11th-century abbey that once controlled the entire valley; the 12th-century church and chapter house survive. Opposite rise the ruins of Château de Beaucens, which is now a bird sanctuary.

## Cauterets & Gavarnie

From Pierrefitte-Nestalas, you have the choice of two fine valleys. The D920 runs along the narrow gorge to the grand old spa town of **Cauterets.** From here, a great walk leads you past waterfalls to the **Pont d'Espagne,** where three cataracts converge. Farther up lies **Lac de Gaube** at 5,660 feet (1,725 m), dominated by the snowy peak of Vignemale, the highest of the frontier peaks at 10,814 feet (3,298 m).

The D921, the other route from Pierrefitte-Nestalas, runs up the Gorge de Luz to **St.-Sauveur,** once an important frontier post and a fashionable 19th-century spa. The gorge allows a glimpse of the Pyrenees' most famous sight: the **Cirque de Gavarnie.**

From Gavarnie village you must walk or ride by donkey or horse to the cirque itself, a breathtaking rocky amphitheater rimmed by peaks up to 10,000 feet (3,048 m) high. Waterfalls cascade down the cirque, the most spectacular of all being the **Grande Cascade de Gavarnie.** Plunging 1,385 feet (422 m), it is Europe's highest waterfall and a UNESCO World Heritage site. To the right is the Brèche de Roland, where, in the medieval epic poem *La Chanson de Roland*, the hero tried to break his enchanted sword rather than relinquish it to the Saracens, and instead hacked a crevasse 400 feet (120 m) deep.

From Luz-St.-Sauveur follow the D918 via Barèges to the **Col de Tourmalet.** This pass, at 6,941 feet (2,115 m), is the highest in the mountains accessible by car. ■

**Vallée d'Ossau** Visitor Information ✉ Maison du Parc, Laruns ☎ 05 59 05 31 41 **ossau-pyrenees.com** • **Cauterets** 🅼 264 C1 Visitor Information ✉ place du Maréchal Foch ☎ 05 62 92 50 50 **cauterets.com** • **Cirque de Gavarnie** 🅼 264 C1 ☎ 05 62 92 49 10 **gavarnie.com**

# PAU

Pau is a fine place to start a visit to the Pyrenees. Boulevard des Pyrenees, below the château, offers a glorious panorama of the mountains encompassing no fewer than 83 peaks on a clear day. The city owes much of its elegance, curiously, to the British. The original British residents were retired officers of Wellington's army who decided to stay on after the Peninsula Campaign (1807–1814). They were joined later by compatriots attracted by the healthy air.

Elegant and relaxed, Pau invites you to saunter down its leafy boulevards, past elegant mansions and art nouveau villas, and along the narrow cobbled streets lined with half-timbered houses. Don't miss a walk along Boulevard des Pyrenees, where on a clear day you can see a vast panorama of the mountains. At the western end, overlooking the Gave de Pau River, rises **Château de Pau.** Originally a hunting lodge built by the counts of Foix, it has a great redbrick keep that was added in the 14th century by Gaston Fébus, defender of the duchy of Foix from all comers.

In the 16th century, Margaret of Angoulême, also known as Margaret of Navarre, transformed the château into a Renaissance palace, with finely carved doorways, windows, and archways. This was the birthplace of her grandson, Henri of Navarre, who ascended to the throne of France in 1859 as Henri IV. A tour of the château includes the fine Gobelins tapestries in the state rooms, the magnificent Second Empire apartments of Empress Eugénie, the 16th-century kitchens,

■ **A bouquet of French flags graces Château de Pau.**

and a giant tortoise shell that reputedly served as the infant Henri's cradle.

The impressive **Musée des Beaux-Arts** *(rue Mathieu-Lalanne, tel 05 59 27 33 02, closed Tues., $),* northeast of the château, includes artworks by El Greco, Rubens, and Degas, plus those of several painters of the Pyrenees.

**Jurançon** lies just across the Gave de Pau River. A wine route is signposted to guide you through the vineyards. Ask at the Pau tourist office for information on the route and about vineyards that welcome visitors. ■

**Pau** ⚠ 264 C2 Visitor Information ✉ place Royale ☎ 05 59 27 27 08 **pau-pyrenees.com • Musée National du Château de Pau** ✉ rue du Château ☎ 05 59 82 38 00 💲 $. Guided visits only **musee-chateau-pau.fr**

# LOURDES

The most popular Christian shrine in the world, Lourdes is also the gateway to the valleys of the Arrens, Cauterets, Ossau, and Gavarnie Rivers. Five million pilgrims flock to Lourdes annually, and the town has more hotels than anywhere else in France outside Paris. The faithful come in search of miracle cures for sickness and disability, many making the trip of a lifetime. Despite its formidable commercial trappings, Lourdes does not disappoint them.

JE NE VOUS PROMETS PAS DE VOUS RENDRE

■ The shrine of St. Bernadette in Lourdes remains the most popular Christian shrine in the world.

It all began in January 1858, when a 14-year-old girl called Bernadette Soubirous claimed to have seen visions of the Virgin Mary. Divine directions led her to the spring in the Grotte de Massabielle, and ever since her last vision in 1862, pilgrims have come to the tiny cave to fill their bottles with miraculous waters and abandon their crutches. Some visit the humble little house on Rue des Petits-Fossés where she lived with her family.

A church was built over the miraculous grotto, where a statue of the

Virgin stands in the apparition niche. In addition to the **Basilique du Rosaire,** built in honor of Bernadette in 1889, a vast underground church, the **Basilique St.-Pie X,** was consecrated in 1958, the centenary of the visions. It holds nearly 30,000 people.

The range of entertainment offered in the town includes a waxworks museum depicting the life of Christ and the life of Bernadette, and a miniature stone model of Lourdes as it was in the time of Bernadette.

The older part of Lourdes, by the castle on the other side of the Gave de Pau River, contains the **Musée Pyrénéen d'Art et de Traditions Populaires.** Devoted in part to the *pyrénéistes,* pioneer climbers in these mountains, the museum displays early equipment, maps, and drawings alongside exhibits devoted to local crafts and costumes, and Pyrenean wildlife. A funicular railway will take you to the top of the nearby Pic du Jer for some fine views.

Some 9 miles (15 km) southwest of Lourdes you can visit the truly spectacular **Bétharram caves** *(tel 05 62 41 80 04, closed Feb.–March).* Here, a miniature railroad and barges ferry visitors on an underground river through a subterranean landscape of fantastic limestone formations. ∎

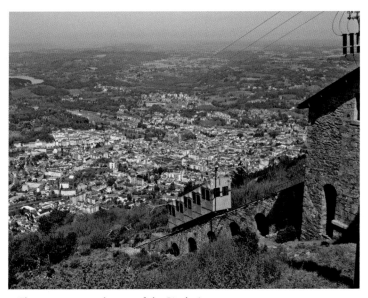

The panorama at the top of the Pic du Jer

**Lourdes** 🅜 264 C1 Visitor Information ✉ place Peyramale ☏ 05 62 42 77 40 **lourdes-infotourisme.com • Musée Pyrénéen d'Art et de Traditions Populaires** ✉ Le Château Fort ☏ 05 62 42 37 37 💲 $

# ST.-BERTRAND-DE-COMMINGES

Once an important Roman town, St.-Bertrand-de-Comminges still contains vestiges of this former glory. These include traces of thermal baths, a theater, and a temple, together with the ruins of a broad arcaded market square and a Christian basilica added in the fifth century. Barbarian invasions from the north and the plague combined to destroy the town, which lay in ruins until the 11th century. It was at this point that a local count, later to be canonized as St. Bertrand, embarked on the building of a cathedral.

Dubbed the Mont St.-Michel of the Pyrenees, the **Cathédrale Ste.-Marie** completely overwhelms the tiny 15th- and 16th-century village that clusters beneath it. The stunning natural beauty of its setting, the grandeur of its architecture, and the artistic treasures the cathedral contains make it one of the most outstanding buildings in the Pyrenees.

The church is Romanesque in style with several later Gothic additions, notably in the exquisite cloister. The superb carvings of its capitals frame sublime views of the mountains beyond: These vistas of God's grandeur were adroitly incorporated into the architectural planning of this magnificent place of worship.

Within, the cathedral contains a virtuoso feast of 16th-century wood carving in its organ loft, and most particularly in its choir stalls and misericords. Here the medieval craftsmen depicted in riotously entertaining detail a gallery of devout, humorous, and even satirical figures and scenes. No doubt these were based on local characters known to one and all in the locality.

## Beware of Hunters

French country folk love hunting with shotguns, and they go after everything from deer and wild boar to small birds. So beware if you are walking in the country, especially during hunting season *(Aug.–Nov.)* and on Sundays. Wear bright colors, keep an ear out for the barking of hunting dogs, and avoid anywhere signposted for *la chasse.*

Look for the resulting produce in the restaurants and markets: partridge, quail, wild boar sausage, and venison.

In the shadow of this awe-inspiring monument are the streets of the little village, its stone and timber-framed houses painstakingly restored. A couple of miles down the valley, you'll find the lovely 12th-century Romanesque **Église de St.-Just-de-Valcabrère.** This incorporates a patchwork of Roman masonry, from capitals to marble sarcophagi, that has been recycled from the ruins of the Roman city. ■

**St.-Bertrand-de-Comminges** 🗺 264 C1 Visitor Information ✉ Les Olivetains, parvis de la Cathédrale ☎ 05 61 89 04 91 🕐 Closed Jan. 💲 $

# AROUND THE ARIÈGE VALLEY

Rich with interest—from Cathar castles to painted prehistoric caves—and easily accessible (about an hour's drive) from Toulouse, the Ariège Valley is one of the best areas of the Pyrenees for a short visit. It has been designated a regional park to protect and revitalize the region.

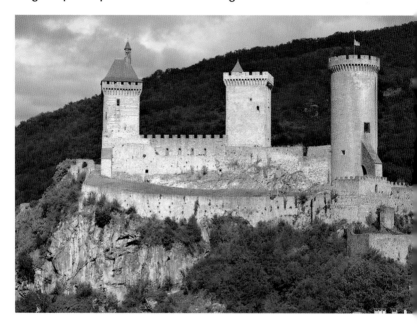

■ Like something from a storybook, Foix's 11th-century castle looms over Ariège's capital.

Driving from Toulouse, approach the Ariège along the beautiful valley of the Lèze River. Though the wild mountain scenery is dramatic hereabouts, the driving is not too hair-raising, and nervous passengers with vertigo can breathe easy on these well-maintained roads. At Pailhès, make a pretty detour west along the D119 to **Grotte du Mas d'Azil,** a spectacular cave with a vast tunnel. Leading off the main cave are smaller ones inhabited by prehistoric people for some 20,000 years.

**St.-Lizier** 264 D1  Visitor Information ✉ place de l'Église ☎ 05 61 96 77 77  **tourisme-couserans-pyrenees.com • Foix** 264 D1 Visitor Information ✉ 29 rue Delcassé ☎ 05 61 65 12 12  **foix-tourisme.com**

A guided tour takes in some of the prehistoric artifacts discovered here. More recently, the caves have served as sanctuary for Protestants, Cathars, and even earlier religious refugees: A little chapel found here dates back to the third century.

## St.-Lizier

Head along the D119 and turn right onto the D117 to reach St.-Lizier, a fortified medieval hilltop village with two cathedrals. The **Cathédrale St.-Lizier,** in the lower town, has Romanesque frescoes and a delightful two-story cloister. Its exquisite pink-brick Gothic bell tower, modeled on St.-Sernin in Toulouse (see pp. 300–301), makes a stunning sight against the distant peaks. The **Cathédrale de la Sède** dates from the 12th century.

## Foix

Farther east, Foix, capital of the Ariège, was the power base of the turbulent counts of Foix in the Middle Ages. Four times Simon de Montfort besieged the castle before finally capturing this bastion of the Cathar faith in 1211. Nowadays Foix is a pleasant town of winding old streets, dominated by the three keeps of its castle, the earliest dating from the 11th century; it's worth climbing to the top for the commanding views over the town and foothills of the Pyrenees.

## Prehistoric Caves

A little way to the south on the N20, **Tarascon-sur-Ariège** is in the middle of a number of prehistoric caves. **Bédeilhac** *(map 264 D1, tel 05 61 05 95 06, grotte-de-bedeilhac.org, closed Jan.–March),* northwest of Tarascon-sur-Ariège, is a gigantic cave bristling with stalagmites, its walls covered with paleolithic images of animals painted some 15,000 years ago. **Lombrives** *(map 264 D1, tel 05 61 05 98 40, grotte delombrives.com),* to the southeast, is the location of a vast 380-foot-high

### Niaux Caves

Located south of Tarascon-sur-Ariège, the caves at Niaux boast some of the finest prehistoric cave paintings in Europe: vigorous drawings of bison, horses, and deer, with delicately rendered details. Unlike the caves at Lascaux in the Dordogne (see pp. 291–292), the Niaux caves *(tel 05 61 05 10 10, sites-touristiques-ariege.fr, closed Mon.)* are still open to the public. So far no deterioration has been detected, but entrance is strictly controlled. It is essential that you book ahead, either by phone or in person at the caves. Ensure you have sturdy footwear, because the cave floor can be uneven and slippery, and light is kept to a minimum. Claustrophobics beware.

**Parc de la Préhistoire** ☎ 05 61 05 10 10 🕒 Closed Mon. Sept.–Oct.
💲 $$ • **Château de Montségur** 🗺 264 D1 ☎ 05 61 01 06 94
🕒 Closed Jan. 💲 $ **montsegur.fr**

(117 m) cavern known locally as La Cathédrale, where a little train takes you right through the caves.

Most impressive of all the caves, however, are those at **Niaux** (see sidebar p. 318).

The village of Niaux has the **Musée Pyrénéen** *(tel 05 61 05 88 36)*, which is devoted to crafts, costumes, and traditional life in the Ariège. For a taste of prehistory, visit the **Parc de la Préhistoire** in Tarascon.

## Montségur

Heading back northward on the N20, turn right just before Foix onto the twisting D9. The road passes under the walls of two Cathar fortresses, Montgaillard and Roquefixade, before reaching **Montségur,** the tragic last bastion of Catharism.

After the Treaty of Meaux gave legal backing to the Albigensian Crusade (see pp. 372–373), this region became the center of Cathar resistance. As fortress after fortress fell, the lord of Montségur turned this bleak, comfortless castle into a refuge for all Cathar heretics. In 1244, however, after a ten-month siege and despairing of relief, the Cathars surrendered. Under the truce, those who recanted their faith would go free. More than 200 Cathars—men, women, and children—who refused to recant were burned alive on a vast pyre. A monument in their memory stands at the foot of the château. ∎

The interior of the caves of Tarascon-sur-Ariège

**PREHISTORIC CAVES**
The caves described in the text open at varying times throughout the year, and some may be seen only by appointment, as numbers are limited. Before visiting, check times with the tourist office in Foix, or phone the site directly for information.

# More Places to Visit in the Pyrenees

## Mirepoix

The 13th-century *bastide* town of Mirepoix, northeast of Foix, is celebrated for the beautiful half-timbered arcading of its main square and for the huge Gothic nave and graceful spire of its cathedral. Visit on market day *(Thurs. or Sat.)* or during the twice-monthly cattle market. *tourisme-mirepoix.com* 264 D1 Visitor Information ✉ place du Maréchal Leclerc ☎ 05 61 68 83 76

## Oloron-Ste.-Marie

This little market town, on the N134 at the junction of the Ossau and Aspe Valleys, is distinguished by the **Cathédrale Ste.-Marie,** with its Romanesque doorway of carved marble, and the **Église Ste.-Croix,** with its 13th-century Spanish stonework. *tourisme-oloron.com* 264 ✉ Visitor Information ✉ allée du Comte de Tréville ☎ 05 59 39 98 00

■ **The ancient bridge of St.-Jean-Pied-de-Port leads to the whitewashed facades of the old town.**

## St.-Jean-Pied-de-Port

On the D933 at the foot of the Roncesvalles Pass, St.-Jean-Pied-de-Port was on one of the pilgrim roads to Santiago de Compostela. It is also the site where Roland was defeated by the Basques, immortalized in the medieval poem *La Chanson de Roland.* The cobbled old town and the new town on the opposite bank of the Nive River are both enclosed by 15th- to 17th-century fortifications. *saintjeanpieddeport-paysbasque-tourisme.com* 264 ✉ Visitor Information ✉ place Charles de Gaulle ☎ 05 59 37 03 57

## Sauveterre-de-Béarn

A lovely town on the N124 with fine river views, a 13th-century church, castle ruins, and the remains of a fortified bridge, Sauveterre is also the venue for the annual world salmon-fishing championships in July. *tourisme-bearn-gaves.com* 264 ✉ Visitor Information ✉ place Royale ☎ 05 59 38 58 65

## Tarbes

Tarbes stands on the west bank of the Adour River east of Pau and just off the east–west motorway, La Pyrénéenne. In the center of town lies the **Musée Massey,** devoted mainly to the Hussars. The birthplace of World War I commander Maréchal Foch now houses a museum. The stud farm **Le Haras** stages displays of horsemanship. *tarbes-tourisme.fr* 264 ☎ Visitor Information ✉ 3 cours Gambetta ☎ 05 62 51 30 31

Roman monuments, medieval villages, sandy beaches, and endless lavender against a backdrop of sweet sunshine

# SOUTH OF FRANCE

# SOUTH OF FRANCE

The South of France is a hugely popular vacation region and a highly desirable place to live. It remains warm for much of the year, with pockets of the Côte d'Azur, sheltered by mountains, being particularly mild. Summers are very hot and dry. The only blight is the cold wind of the mistral, which howls down from the north in winter. Millions come to the South of France: to the Côte d'Azur, the villages of Provence, and the vacation lands of Languedoc-Roussillon.

## NOT TO BE MISSED:

**A walk on Nice's Promenade des Anglais**   329

**The beautiful beaches of St. Tropez**   345

**A visit to Avignon's Palais des Papes**   352

**The ramparts of the medieval fortress at Carcassonne**   370–371

**Driving the Cathar Trail**   372–373

The Massif Central and the Alps divide the Mediterranean coast geographically from the rest of France. This coast's main connection with the north is the great Rhône River. To the east, the mountains drop almost to the sea, and much of the

Côte d'Azur is rocky. Beyond the Rhône delta to the west, the coast sweeps in a great arc, fringed with beach resorts and washed by clear waters.

The plain of Languedoc-Roussillon is intensively cultivated, producing a wide range of fruit and particularly wine, which has rapidly improved in quality in recent years. Shellfish are cultivated in the lagoons that edge the coast. To the north are the foothills of the Cévennes, and farther south, the Pyrenees form a natural frontier with Spain.

Marseille, a Mediterranean melting pot, is the biggest city in the south of the country, and France's largest port. Sète, located to the east along the coast, is another important port. Nîmes and Montpellier are both highly attractive cities, centers of high-tech industry and key links in the developing Mediterranean sunbelt.

Historically, the Romans played a key role throughout the region. The whole of the south coast was their Provincia, with Narbonne as its capital. Many of their buildings survive, notably the Pont du Gard, the impressive amphitheaters of Arles and Nîmes, and the theater at Orange.

Throughout the Middle Ages, Provence and Languedoc were famous for the "courts of love" and the poetry of the troubadours, and in the 19th century local enthusiasts made efforts to revive the Provençal language and identity.

Like much of the rest of France, the region suffered during the 16th-century Wars of Religion, when towns and cities were seriously damaged. In the 18th and 19th centuries, the English came to the South of France for health cures and winter holidays. By the 1920s, sunbathing had become fashionable and the Côte d'Azur the land of summer vacations. In the 1960s, the Languedoc-Roussillon coast was developed as a vacation playground with areas set aside as nature reserves and animal parks.

The light and color that are so characteristic of the South of France have always attracted artists and have given rise to such important artistic movements as cubism and fauvism. The legacy of the creative spirit is clearly evident in the many fine art museums that dot the region.

But the paradise that is Provence is constantly under threat from forest fires, pollution, and mysterious algae. Assiduous efforts are being made to preserve the environment with scrupulously protected beaches and new regional parks. ■

## Protecting the Mediterranean

According to a 2010 census of marine life, the Mediterranean is the "world's most threatened sea," seriously at risk from overfishing, as well as the pressure of increasing human population and pollution. Great efforts are being made to protect the Mediterranean, including the establishment of marine protected areas. The French Mediterranean coast now has several protected marine parks: **Parc National de Port-Cros** *(portcros-parcnational .fr; see p. 326)*, along the coast of Hyères and the Île de Porquerolles; the **Banyuls marine reserve;** the **Parc National de Calanques** *(calanques-parcnational .fr)* near Marseille; and **Réserve Naturelle de Scandola** in Corsica *(ecase-pnrc.fr/reserve-naturelle -de-scandola)*. The Blue Flag classification of beaches, now a global measure of environmental quality, was originally conceived in France as le Pavillon Bleu. According to the most recent assessment published in 2023, the French coastline is now able to boast of a total of 405 Blue Flag beaches and 105 marinas.

# CÔTE D'AZUR

Breathtaking beauty, clear blue waters, and a superb climate have earned the French Riviera, or Azure Coast, a premier position among the world's stylish vacation playgrounds. Despite the crowds, the coast retains its glamour and its place in the social calendars of the world's elite. The harbors are full of megayachts; superb restaurants, nightclubs, and casinos cater to serious eating, partying, and playing; and the exclusive beaches gleam with oiled bodies.

■ On the waterfront: Exclusivity in Monaco's Monte Carlo doesn't necessarily mean "singularly unique," as these docked yachts would suggest.

The Romans built their spas and villas designed to catch the cooling sea breezes along this lovely coastline, but only in the 19th century, with the arrival of the English aristocracy in search of health cures and botanical specimens, did the Côte d'Azur as we know it today come into being. Wealthy visitors from America and Europe soon followed, building villas and playing the tables at Monte Carlo's casino.

In the 1920s, Coco Chanel popularized sunbathing and F. Scott Fitzgerald wrote the jazz age into existence. After World War II, Brigitte Bardot launched St.-Tropez as a symbol of the new Côte d'Azur.

But the coast offers more. Its museums are filled with modern art (much of it created here), and world-class jazz musicians play in Roman amphi-theaters on starry nights. The simplest delights are perhaps the most potent and enduring: the brilliant blue sea, pine-shaded beaches, and cliff-top views; the scent of herbs and lavender, mimosa and pine; and terra-cotta villages perched among spectacular rocky landscapes a few miles inland. ∎

▪ The picturesque port of Île de Port-Cros is dotted with palms.

**INSIDER TIP:**

Divers should beware of the black scorpionfish, which deftly camouflages itself on the seafloor. Its dorsal fin spines are poisonous.

—JACK KAVANAGH
*National Geographic writer*

## EXPERIENCE: Dive into Port-Cros National Park

Hidden away on the glorious Côte D'Azur, the islands of Port-Cros and Porquerolles and the deep-blue waters of the Mediterranean around them constitute France's least known nature reserve, **Parc National de Port-Cros** (*portcros-parcnational.fr*).

Both islands can be reached by boat from the mainland at Hyères; both have fine sand beaches; and both carry the scent of their pine and eucalyptus forests on the sea breezes. But while Port-Cros is a mountainous island, Porquerolles is flatter, making it a cyclist's heaven; a variety of hiking and biking trails lead through pine vineyards, evergreen oak forests, and scrubland.

The park also offers a chance to get up close to Mediterranean marine life: From the beach at La Palud, you can follow an underwater trail for snorkelers and divers, which takes about 45 minutes and has six stops with informational panels. The Maison du Parc in the village rents diving gear.

Enjoy the sea grass meadows waving in the currents and look out for dolphins and whales, frequent passersby at Port-Cros.

# GARDENS OF THE CÔTE D'AZUR

Sheltered to the north by mountains, untouched by frost throughout the winter, and blessed with an early, balmy spring, the Côte d'Azur is a paradise for gardeners and garden lovers.

The opulent villas built along the coast in the 19th- and 20th-century were surrounded by glamorous gardens that revel in exotic plants.

## Menton

Cosseted Menton boasts a clutch of subtropical paradises, in which fountains and shady terraces, creative topiaries, and distant vistas combine irresistibly. For a variety of palms and subtropical species, the **Jardin Botanique du Val Rameh** is hard to equal. English landscape designer Lawrence Johnston made his only French garden at **Jardin de la Serre de la Madone,** where he grew plants collected from China, South Africa, and elsewhere.

## Cap Ferrat & Hyères

**Jardin & Musée Ephrussi-de-Rothschild** has inspired gardens—from Italian to Japanese, with grottoes, a temple of Diana, and a cactus collection. In Hyères, **Parc St.-Bernard** is a riot of Mediterranean flora. And **Parc Ste.-Claire** contains terraced gardens established by writer Edith Wharton. ∎

### Domaine du Rayol

The botanical gardens of Domaine du Rayol *(avenue des Belges, Rayol-Canadel-sur-Mer, tel 04 98 04 44 00, domainedurayol.org)* are in the Var, on the Corniches des Maures above Rayol-Canadel-sur-Mer. Designed as a botanical index of all the regions of the world with a Mediterranean climate, the 50-acre (20 ha) site features different areas dedicated to the plants of South Africa, California, Chile, the Canary Islands, and Australia.

Guided and themed walks are offered with commentaries in French, English, and German. Learn about aromatic plants and exotic winter flowers, or walk the mimosa trail. The gardens, open year-round, are at their best in springtime. There is a library, café, workshops, musical evenings in summer, and even a guided underwater tour.

**Menton** 🄰 323 G3 ✉ 8 avenue Boyer ☎ 04 83 93 70 20 **menton -riviera-merveilles.fr • Jardin Botanique du Val Rameh** ✉ avenue St.-Jacques, Menton ☎ 04 93 35 86 72 💲 $ • **Jardin & Musée Ephrussi-de-Rothschild** ✉ Cap Ferrat ☎ 04 93 01 33 09 💲 $ **villa-ephrussi.com**

# NICE

Combining a Provençal heart with a welcoming joie de vivre, the wonderful city of Nice raises life alfresco to an art form. It combines a wealth of fine museums with a profusion of gardens, fountains, and palm trees, and now the tramway is the focus for a permanent open-air art gallery.

■ Lined with grand hotels, Nice's Promenade des Anglais is the last word in overbuilt elegance.

## Old Nice

Once deliciously dangerous and seedy, old Nice is now a fashionable enclave of bistros, nightclubs, and galleries. But the authentic aroma of dried fish and garlic still hangs in the air, and its little shops remain the best place to buy local varieties of olive oil. The outdoor market on Cours Saleya is famous for its flowers and local produce. Lunch on delicious, inexpensive Niçois specialties in one of the cafés.

The tiny squares and lovely chapels of the old town are dominated by the huge cathedral with its dome of glazed tiles. Of the palaces and *hôtels particuliers* (mansions), the

**Nice** 🅼 323 G3 Visitor Information ✉ 5 promenade des Anglais ☎ 08 92 70 74 07 **nicetourisme.com**

## EXPERIENCE: Head for the Mountains by Rail

Two small tourist trains provide a great way to explore the hinterland of the Côte d'Azur without a car. Departing from Nice daily at 9 a.m., the **Train des Merveilles** (tel 08 91 70 30 00, beyond.fr/travel/railcuneo.html) will take you to Peillon, the Roya-Bévéra Valley, and Mercantour Park and the Vallée des Merveilles. It has an *espace rotonde* with panoramic windows. The **Train des Pignes** (tel 04 97 03 80 80, trainprovence.com), now a protected historic monument, offers a tour of the villages that sit perched between Nice and Digne. It climbs to more than 3,300 feet (1,000 m) through 50 tunnels, bridges, and viaducts. This steam train makes four round-trips daily from Nice.

grandest is the 17th-century **Palais Lascaris** (15 rue Droite, tel 04 93 62 72 40, closed Tues.), with frescoed ceilings and rococo silver inlaid doors. Take the elevator up to the park to enjoy the waterfall, café, and the great views.

Old Nice ends at the Paillon River, now the site of spacious gardens, squares, and fountains, as well as the striking glass-and-marble **Musée d'Art Moderne et d'Art Contemporain (MAMAC).** The collections focus on French and American avant-garde art.

### City Center

To the west of the old town stretches the **Promenade des Anglais.** This famous length of seafront is lined with grand hotels, including the magnificent Négresco (see Travelwise p. 454), with its huge Baccarat chandelier. The now restored Palais Masséna, a splendid belle epoque villa, houses the **Musée d'Art et d'Histoire** (65 rue de France, tel 04 93 91 19 10, closed Tues.).

Beyond the river lies 19th-century Nice, replete with its dignified arcaded squares, Italianate apartment buildings, fashionable shops, and an impressive array of art galleries. The **Musée International d'Art Naïf** (Château Sainte-Hélène, avenue de Fabron, tel 04 93 71 78 33, midan.org, closed Mon.) is located in a pink château, and the **Musée des Beaux-Arts** hosts works by Monet, Degas, and Sisley. Fine old frescoes and icons are displayed in the ornate Russian Orthodox cathedral, **Cathédrale-St.-Nicolas,** on Boulevard Tzaréwitch.

**Musée d'Art Moderne et d'ArtContemporain** ✉ promenade des Arts ☎ 04 97 13 42 01 🕐 Closed Mon. **mamac-nice.org** • **Musée des Beaux-Arts** ✉ 33 avenue des Baumettes ☎ 04 92 15 28 28 🕐 Closed Mon. 💲 $ **musee-beaux-arts-nice.org**

## Cimiez

Art treasures (and fine views) are plentiful in the wealthy suburb of Cimiez, a cradle of hills to the north of the town. Here you'll also see the remains of the original Roman settlement. Among the collection at the **Musée National Marc Chagall** (avenue du Dr. Ménard, tel 04 93 53 87 20, musee-chagall.fr, closed Tues.) are Chagall's "Biblical Message" canvases.

Farther up the hill is the 17th-century villa that houses the **Musée Matisse** (164 avenue des Arènes de Cimiez, tel 04 93 81 08 08, musee-matisse-nice.org, closed Tues., $). Works from Matisse's personal collection include still

lifes and sketches of Chapelle de la Rosaire, as well as the "Tempête à Nice." ∎

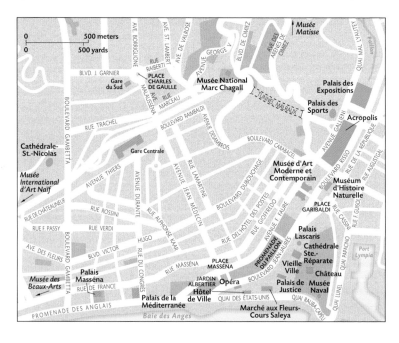

# MERCANTOUR NATIONAL PARK

Just inland from Nice lies a natural wilderness of towering mountainous terrain, azure blue lakes, and Alpine meadows that slope
down toward the coastline. This is a hiker's heaven, where forested
hills wrap around several gorgeous valleys, many of them laced with
trails. The park's biodiversity and climactic variety spring from its location as the last promontory of the Alpine range, before the land
rolls down to the Mediterranean Sea.

Mercantour National Park *(tel 04 93
16 78 88, mercantour-parcnational.fr)* has
370-odd miles (600 km) of marked
footpaths, including the mountain pass
of Col de la Cayolle. The human foot-
print stretches back millennia: Around
Mont Bégo, petroglyphs carved onto
schist and granite faces tell of early
inhabitants during the Late Neolithic
and Bronze Ages. More can be seen
at the Vallée des Merveilles (Valley of
Marvels). At the base of Mont Bégo,
hikers are mesmerized by some 37,000
Bronze Age petroglyphs representing
cattle, weapons, and humans.

Walkers will see plenty of wildlife
too, including chamois, the distinctive
goat-antelope native to these parts.
You might also hear the whistling of
marmots in summer as these large
ground squirrels fatten up in the meadows. Ermine are more furtive, and the
ibex and the mouflon (wild sheep) are
seen only on higher grounds. Watch
the skies for golden eagles and buz-
zards. Since the early 1990s, about 50
Italian wolves have taken up residence
here; the Alpha Park in Saint-Martin-
Vésubie educates visitors to the park
on all things lupine. ∎

# THE CORNICHES

In a region with such a wealth of spectacular beauty, the stretch of coast between Menton and Nice is particularly outstanding. The best way to drink in the glorious views of cliffs, sea, and extravagant villas set among palm trees is to take a corniche. Of the three, the Grande and Moyenne Corniches offer the most sweeping panoramas, while the Corniche Inférieure, closest to the sea, has the worst traffic and the best views of luxurious resorts. A round-trip takes two lower roads from Nice to Menton, returning mainly on the Grand Corniche.

■ The sixth-century Trophée des Alpes dominates the town of La Turbie.

## Corniche Inférieure

From Nice, the N98 circles the Cap de Nice and passes through the port to reach **Villefranche-sur-Mer.** Here, narrow streets rush steeply down to the deep natural harbor that has turned this small fishing village into an important naval port, lending it a more raffish flavor than most of this coast. Pretty, pastel-colored houses and lively cafés line the tiny harbor,

overlooked by the **Chapelle St.-Pierre,** a beguiling little church decorated by Jean Cocteau in 1957.

Jutting out into the sea just beyond Villefranche, the peninsula of **Cap Ferrat,** together with those of Cap d'Ail and Cap Martin farther along the coast, is famously the preserve of the seriously rich, its natural beauty embedded with fabulous villas and luxuriant gardens. Do not miss the **Musée Ephrussi-de-Rothschild,** a pink-and-white villa with marble floors and Tiepolo ceilings, housing a superb decorative arts collection and surrounded by magnificent gardens (see p. 327). At the end of the *cap,* the rocky end of the peninsula, is the **Grand Hôtel du Cap-Ferrat** (see Travelwise p. 455), featuring among other luxuries a funicular railroad to the beach. The little fishing and yachting village of **St.-Jean-Cap-Ferrat** makes a picturesque place for lunch; relatively quiet **Plage des Fossés** leads to a path around the peninsula with fantastic views.

A couple of miles farther east of Ville-

**Villefranche-sur-Mer** ▲ 323 G3 Visitor Information ✉ square François-Binon ☎ 04 93 01 73 68 **villefranche-sur-mer.fr**

franche on the N98, sheltered **Beaulieu-sur-Mer** has some extremely grand hotels. Its most bizarre and delightful offering is the remarkable **Villa Kérylos,** an authentic reproduction of an ancient Greek villa, in which the eccentric archaeologist Théodore Reinach lived in the manner of an Athenian citizen. One of his few concessions to the 20th century was glass in the windows.

## Moyenne Corniche

Continuing around the coast, the road threads past rocky bays and caps. As it nears **Monaco** (see pp. 336–337), you can avoid the traffic by diverting onto the Moyenne Corniche (N7) as far as Menton.

**Menton** (see p. 327), only a mile (1.5 km) from the Italian border, remains the grande dame of the littoral: genteel, cradled by mountains, with tropical gardens. The steep streets of old Menton drop down to the **Promenade du Soleil,** lined with cafés, restaurants, and palm trees. See the **Musée Jean Cocteau** (*2 quai de Monleon, tel 04 93 81 52 50, museecocteaumenton.fr, closed Tues., $*), a modernist glass maze on the seafront, housing a major collection of his drawings, paintings, photos, and ceramics, or visit the **Hôtel de Ville,** where he decorated the Salle des Mariages in his own inimitable fashion. The 17th-century **Église de St.-Michel** hosts a chamber music festival

**INSIDER TIP:**

Villefranche-sur-Mer's Port Darse harbors boats large and small. A beach and several cafés sit behind the harbor walls.

—AMY ALIPIO
*National Geographic editor*

in August. From Menton, head back on the N7 to Roquebrune-Cap-Martin.

## Grande Corniche

Turn inland onto the Grande Corniche (the D2564) to **Roquebrune,** a medieval village of steep streets and vaulted alleys, opening to magnificent sea views. Follow this spectacular road westward for about 4 miles (6 km) to **La Turbie** and the Trophée des Alpes. A little garden on the cliff edge offers fine views out to sea and a superb panorama of Monaco.

At Col d'Èze, 4 miles (6 km) farther, the D45 leads to the tiny village of **Èze,** perched dizzyingly over the Mediterranean. Visitors now throng its exquisitely restored streets, covered alleyways, and steep, twisting stairways.

Return to the winding Moyenne Corniche (N7) from Èze to Nice, stopping at the pull-offs to savor the many ravishing views. ■

**Beaulieu-sur-Mer** Visitor Information ✉ place Georges-Clemenceau ☎ 04 93 01 02 21 **beaulieusurmer.fr** • **Villa Kérylos** ✉ rue Gustave-Eiffel, Beaulieu-sur-Mer ☎ 04 93 01 01 44 **villa-kerylos.com** • **Hôtel de Ville** ✉ rue de la République, Menton • **Église de St.-Michel** ✉ place St.-Michel, Menton

# FOOD & DRINK—SUN-KISSED FARE

*Cuisine du soleil,* cuisine of the sun, is the name given to the food of this blessed region. It is a Mediterranean cuisine—luscious, aromatic, fresh, and, as it happens, healthy. Market stalls are laden with seasonal local produce such as peppers, tomatoes, figs, melons, peaches, and especially olives. It is the olive that is most central to southern cooking, its oil used almost exclusively instead of animal fat. More than 15 different olive varieties are grown in Provence, destined for olive oil or the table. Garlic is the other keynote, along with herbs like rosemary, thyme, and marjoram, which grow wild in the countryside.

■ **Olives galore for sale at the St.-Rémy-de-Provence farmers market**

To the east the cuisine of the South of France has a distinctly Italian accent, and local specialties include *socca* (chickpea flour) pancakes; *pissaladière,* a pizza with onions, anchovies, and black olives; *pistou,* vegetable soup with basil; stuffed zucchini flowers; and the ubiquitous *pan bagnat,* a large roll stuffed with *salade Niçoise.*

Farther west the influence is Spanish. In Roussillon, look for *cargolade,* a grill of snails and sausages served with

aioli, a rich golden mayonnaise made from olive oil, garlic, and egg yolk, served with raw vegetables, fish, or soup. Anchovies are another specialty, good with grilled red peppers.

All along the Mediterranean coast you'll find excellent fish and seafood. In Languedoc-Roussillon, the saltwater lagoons produce mussels, oysters, and more obscure marine delicacies such as sea urchins and crayfish. Bouillabaisse (a fish stew) is a key specialty (see sidebar opposite). A simple *soupe de poisson* is also delicious, served with croutons and *rouille,* a hot red pepper mayonnaise. *Bourride* is another fish stew, with aioli added at the last moment. Simple fish dishes like grilled sardines or red mullet are always good, as is *brandade,* a puree of salt cod and olive oil.

The south is certainly the best place in France to be a vegetarian, but there are plenty of good meat dishes, too. Lamb from the Sisteron area, grazed on fragrant herb-rich vegetation, is a great delicacy. Rich, slow-cooked *daubes* are serious affairs. Usually beef stewed in red wine (often with olives and tomatoes), they are also made with other ingredients, including calamari. In the Camargue, you should try *gardiane de taureau*, bull's meat stew, usually served with the delicious nutty rice grown locally.

Among the light menu items of note, for enjoying with a cocktail, starting a meal, or for a snack, there is *anchoade* (anchovy dip), *salade Niçoise* (tomatoes, anchovies, hard-boiled eggs, olives, and sometimes tuna and beans), and the local tapenade (a puree of olives and anchovies). Main course options include *aubergines farcies à la Provençale* (eggplant stuffed with meat, onions, and herbs, served with tomato sauce), *perdrix à la Catalane* (partridge with orange and pepper sauce), and *stockfish à la Niçoise* (dried cod stewed with onions, tomatoes, garlic, and herbs). Regional vegetarian courses include *artichauts à la barigoule* (small artichokes stewed in oil and white wine), *fleurs de courges farcies* (stuffed zucchini flowers), and ratatouille (a tasty stew of eggplant, zucchini, peppers, and tomatoes).

What to drink with your meal is never a problem in France. Languedoc-Roussillon produces most of France's table wine, and its wines are becoming increasingly respected. Drink the local *vin de pays* or sample slightly more expensive local wines from Corbières, Nîmes, Minervois, Fitou, and the Côtes de Roussillon. In Provence, look for Châteauneuf-du-Pape or Gigondas. Along the coast, the local selection of wines is more limited; try the Côtes de Provence rosé or Bandol.

Anise-flavored *pastis* is a very popular aperitif, and sweet dessert wines include Banyuls and various Muscats, especially from Beaumes-de-Venise and Rivesaltes.

For dessert, you can't go wrong with *calissons d'Aix* (almond cookies) or *crème Catalane* (caramelized egg custard).

## EXPERIENCE: Cooking Bouillabaisse in Marseille

Fierce argument continues to rage over the exact recipe for this magnificent fish stew, a specialty of the Mediterranean that the city of Marseille claims as its own. **Restaurant Miramar** (12 quai du Port, Marseille, tel 04 91 91 10 40, lemiramar.fr) has the reputation of serving one of the best versions in town, prepared by Marseillais chef Christian Buffa. Here you can also learn how to make the famous dish yourself.

The lesson (reserve at tourist office, tel 08 20 50 05 00) begins on every third Tuesday with a trip to the fish market in the Vieux Port to select the right fish (monkfish, eel, and red mullet). Then, it's back to the kitchen, where you spend four hours preparing and cooking the dish. Finally, you have a chance to savor the result. Traditionally the fish broth is served first and then the fish itself, accompanied by rouille, a peppery mayonnaise.

# MONACO

Smaller than New York's Central Park, the tiny independent state and tax haven of Monaco is a magnet for those in search of glamour. Visitors flock to Monaco for its glittering nightlife, luxurious hotels, and expensive restaurants. After his accession in 1949, Prince Rainier III transformed the principality, extending it vertically and horizontally with skyscrapers and landfill, and earning it the epithets "Hong Kong on the Mediterranean" and "Las Vegas *plage.*"

■ **The fairy-tale principality of Monaco is sometimes called Hong Kong on the Mediterranean.**

The old town of Monaco, out on the jagged promontory of the Rocher, is an immaculate affair of elegant mansions, charming squares and fountains. The **Palais Princier,** seat of the Grimaldi family (see sidebar opposite), has sections dating from every century since 1000. Packed with gorgeous furniture, paintings, and frescoes, it is open to visitors only when the prince is away. But the changing of the palace guard outside is a daily spectacle. The fabulous white 19th-century neo-Romanesque cathedral nearby contains the tomb of Princess Grace (originally from Philadelphia), perpetually strewn with roses. High on the cliff sits the world-class **Musée Océanographique.**

South of the Rocher lie the marina of **Fontvieille,** the **Princess Grace Rose Garden** (Roseraie Princesse Grace; *avenue des Guelfes*), and the port of **La Condamine,** a vast marina with promenades for yacht-ogling. On the cliffs behind rise the superbly situated **Jardin Exotique,** sheltering a huge range of exotic plants, as well as prehistoric caves and an anthropological museum. Located in two restored villas, the **Nouveau Musée National de Monaco** is dedicated to art and performance.

Monaco hosts a round of festivals, fireworks, and rallies, culminating in the Grand Prix every May, when the roads are closed to traffic and the entire port becomes a Formula One racetrack.

## Monte Carlo

Beyond the port is Monte Carlo, with its fabled casino and opera. To make sure visitors look the part, there's a

**Monaco** ▲ 323 G3 Visitor Information ✉ 2A boulevard des Moulins, Monte Carlo ☎ 377 92 16 61 16 **visitmonaco.com** • **Palais Princier** ✉ place du Palais ☎ 377 93 25 18 31 🕒 Closed Nov.–March 💲 $

dress code. Designed by Charles Garnier, who was also responsible for the Opéra Garnier in Paris, the interiors retain their extravagant belle epoque glamour.

The palm tree gardens around the casino and the wonderful terrace surrounding them afford beautiful views over the Mediterranean. More ostentatious opulence is provided by a string of Monte Carlo's sumptuous hotels, most notably the **Hôtel de Paris** *(hotelde parismontecarlo.com)* and the **Hôtel Hermitage** (see Travelwise p. 453) with its famous, elegant winter-garden foyer luxuriating under a fine glass roof designed by Gustave Eiffel. ◼

## The Grimaldis

The Grimaldi family has ruled the independent principality of Monaco since the 14th century, making it the longest reigning dynasty in Europe. In its heyday, Monaco stretched from Menton to Antibes, living off taxes levied on the lemons and olives of Menton. When Menton was ceded to France in 1860, financial disaster loomed, but the reigning prince, Charles III, had the inspired idea of opening a casino (gaming rooms were banned in France at this time) on the hill, named Monte Carlo in his honor. New railroad connections along the coast helped attract a dazzling clientele, and the venture proved so lucrative that Charles was able to waive taxation for his subjects.

Thus has Monaco prospered and, along with it, the Grimaldi family. The right touch of glamour was added in 1956, when Prince Rainier III married the American actress Grace Kelly. For years they were a fairy-tale couple, but since her death in a car accident in 1982, the family has been beset by problems: Princess Caroline's first husband was killed in a boat race, while Princess Stephanie was a source of scandal, leaving behind a trail of broken romances and abandoned careers. Prince Albert succeeded Rainier upon his death in 2005.

According to the CIA World Factbook, Monaco has the highest number of millionaires and billionaires in the world.

**Musée Océanographique** ✉ avenue St.-Martin ☎ 377 93 15 36 00 💲 $$ **oceano.mc** • **Jardin Exotique** ✉ boulevard du Jardin Exotique Moneghetti ☎ 377 93 15 29 80 💲 $$ **jardin-exotique.mc** • **Nouveau Musée National de Monaco** ✉ 8 rue Honoré Labande ☎ 377 98 98 19 62 **nmnm.mc** • **Monte Carlo** 🅼 323 G3 **visitmonaco.com**

# AROUND ST.-PAUL DE VENCE

Set in the hills behind the Baie des Anges, St.-Paul de Vence is a perfectly preserved hill village, encircled by 16th-century ramparts, overlooking terra-cotta roofs, cypresses, and azure swimming pools. Though tiny, St.-Paul de Vence has gained an international reputation, thanks in large measure to the illustrious catalog of artists and writers who have lived and worked here. Today its galleries and restaurants attract thousands of visitors.

■ **The cobbled streets and fountains of St.-Paul de Vence survive from medieval times.**

## St.-Paul de Vence

Entering the chic little village through the 13th-century gate, you follow Rue Grande past the fountain to the 12th-century Gothic church and the local history museum. The museum proudly displays photos of celebrities who have visited St.-Paul:

Simone de Beauvoir, Catherine Deneuve, F. Scott Fitzgerald, and many more.

But the village is famed for the **Fondation Maeght,** one of the world's most distinguished modern art museums, surrounded by a labyrinth of witty, colorful modern sculpture and tinkling fountains by Miró, Calder, and others. Attenuated Giacometti figures stroll across the courtyard, and the chapel is decorated by Braque. The founders, Aimé and Marguerite Maeght, commissioned the Spanish architect José-Luis Sert to design a building conceived in harmony with the works within, and the result is extremely impressive.

At the world-famous **Colombe d'Or** (see Travelwise p. 455) hotel-restaurant, you can dine on the terrace surrounded by a priceless collection of art, including works by Picasso, Dufy, Modigliani, and many others, all donated by impecunious artists in exchange for their keep.

**St.-Paul de Vence** 🅰 323 F3 Visitor Information ✉ Maison de la Tour, 2 rue Grande ☎ 04 93 32 86 95 **saint-pauldevence.com • Fondation Maeght** ✉ Montée des Trious, St.-Paul de Vence ☎ 04 93 32 81 63 💲 $$$ **fondation-maeght.com**

## Cagnes

The best part of nearby Cagnes is the original village of **Haut-de-Cagnes,** with its narrow medieval village streets and steep stairways, crowned by the 14th-century **Château Grimaldi** *(tel 04 92 02 47 35, closed Tues.).* Within its fortress walls is a spectacular Renaissance interior that now houses a museum devoted to the olive; a collection of modern Mediterranean art with works by Matisse, Chagall, and more; and the Suzy Solidor collection: 40 portraits of the 1930s nightclub singer by artists including Cocteau, Dufy, and Tamara de Lempicka.

Renoir spent the last 20 years of his life in Cagnes, at the Maison Les Collettes, where the heat helped to ease the pain of his arthritis. The fine old house, set among the ancient olive trees that fascinated him, is now the **Musée Renoir,** with one studio preserved just as he left it, complete with palette and easel (at which he painted with the brush strapped to his hand when moving his fingers was too painful).

## Vence

The town of Vence perches high, surrounded by several commercial rose gardens. Just outside is the **Chapelle du Rosaire** *(avenue Henri-Matisse, tel 04 93 58 03 26, closed*

## A Haven for the Creative

In a satisfying circular movement, the works of artists and writers that this region inspired now inform our image of it. Picasso's nymphs and sea urchins, Matisse's views of the sea, and Renoir's golden light and olive trees are constant presences. It was the intensity of the light that attracted the Impressionists. Now we see the luminous skies and seas through their eyes in galleries and museums amid the settings that inspired them.

Writers, too, have flocked here. Colette penned evocative portraits of Provençal life. Ford Madox Ford and Aldous Huxley worked here; and Katherine Mansfield and D. H. Lawrence died here. F. Scott Fitzgerald portrayed the beautiful people who partied here.

*mid-Nov.–mid-Dec.),* decorated by Matisse at the end of his life when he, too, was afflicted by arthritis. In an otherwise all white interior, the pared-down monochrome drawings of the Stations of the Cross and the aqueous greens, blues, and yellows of the stained glass are a fitting tribute to the artist's style. ■

**Cagnes** 🅰 323 F3 Visitor Information ✉ boulevard Maréchal Juin ☎ 04 93 20 61 64 **cagnes-tourisme.com • Musée Renoir (Maison Les Collettes)** ✉ 19 chemin des Colettes, Cagnes ☎ 04 93 20 61 07 🕐 Closed Tues. 💲 $ • **Vence** 🅰 279 F3 Visitor Information ✉ place du Grand-Jardin ☎ 04 93 58 06 38 **vence-tourisme.com**

# IN & AROUND GRASSE

Nestling in a cradle of hills behind Cannes lies the perfume capital of the world: charming, sleepy Grasse. The surrounding landscape is a fragrant sea of flowers: Golden mimosa clothes the hillsides in January and February, followed by summer roses and lavender and autumn jasmine, all heady with scent. The town itself is an intriguing warren of steep, arcaded streets, with Renaissance details betraying the influence of Italian merchants.

## Grasse

In the Middle Ages, tanning was the main industry practiced here, but the 16th-century vogue for scented gloves sparked the perfume industry. By the 18th century, Grasse had become the world center of scent.

Today every shop you enter in Grasse seems to sell a variety of perfumes and flower waters. While in this most fragrant of French towns, try to include a visit to the market in Place aux Aires, which sells a magnificent array of dried flowers and herbs.

■ Fragrant jasmine grows in abundance around Grasse, adding to the many alluring aromas that surround the visitor in Provence.

**Grasse** ▲ 323 F3 Visitor Information ✉ place de la Buanderie ☎ 04 93 36 66 66 **grasse.fr** • **Villa-Musée Fragonard** ✉ 23 boulevard Fragonard, Grasse ☎ 04 97 05 58 00 🕑 Closed for renovations

## EXPERIENCE: Inhale the Perfumes of Provence

Can't get enough of the heady scents of Provence? Learn to make your own customized fragrance at the **Musée International de la Parfumerie** (see below). Find out all about the music of perfume—the top note, the volatile smell you first notice that stays on the skin for 5 to 15 minutes; the flower-based "heart note" that stays for up to seven hours; and the base note, the strong heady smell of amber, musk, patchouli, or vanilla that can remain for a few days.

A wonderful time to visit the region is during the local **flower harvests.** The jasmine festival in Grasse takes place in August, or head for the lavender festival in Dignes-les-Bains in July. In winter follow the **Mimosa Route,** from Bormes-les-Mimosas to Grasse, to enjoy the symbol of the Riviera in winter, golden flowers with a scent that seems impossibly exotic. This aromatic 81-mile (130 km) journey is highly recommended anytime from January to March.

The Molinard and Fragonard perfume companies have museums and provide tours. The **Musée International de la Parfumerie** (8 place du Cours, tel 04 97 05 58 00, $, museesde grasse.com) provides a splendid introduction to the art of perfumery, with a beautiful collection of bottles from all over the world and its own rooftop garden of fragrant plants. There are few better places in France to–quite literally–stop and smell the flowers.

The artist and engraver Jean-Honoré Fragonard (1732–1806) was born in Grasse. The **Villa-Musée Fragonard,** where he lived, contains some of his drawings and copies of wall panels. A rare religious work by him hangs in the **Cathédrale Notre-Dame-du-Puy** (place du Petit-Puy), a building that was started in the 12th century, as well as three works by Rubens and a 16th-century triptych by Bréa.

### Gourdon

To the north of Grasse, a wonderful drive past the rocky ravines and rushing waterfalls of the **Gorges du Loup** takes you up to Gourdon. This beautiful little hamlet is pure Provence, and one of the most spectacular villages perchés (hill villages) in the region.

From the approach road, you can see the precipitous drop of several hundred feet below Gourdon's castle walls, and the view from the top is just as dramatic. The castle is perched right on the cliff edge with vertiginous views of the Loup valley. There are stunning gardens (tel 04 93 09 68 02, chateau-gourdon.com, closed Oct.–March). The main terrace, la Terrasse d'Honneur, has 17th-century formal gardens designed by André Le Nôtre, with an herb garden around an ancient sundial,

Italianate designs, and a rock garden of alpine plants.

## The Coast

The coast south of Grasse is primarily Picasso country. The artist spent much of his life in Juan-les-Pins, Antibes, and Cannes. He died in **Mougins,** now a chic hilltop village with splendid views and numerous art galleries. The **Musée de la Photographie** (*67 rue de l'Église, tel 04 93 75 85 67*) features a fine collection of photos of Picasso by Lartigue, Doisneau, and Villiers.

Mougins is also a place for serious eating. Most serious of all is **Le Moulin de Mougins** (see Travelwise p. 453), a mill that has been transformed into a paradise of French gastronomy and is a must for visiting foodies.

**Vallauris,** in the hinterland of Cannes, owes its fame to Picasso, who revived its fortunes as a pottery center by working in a ceramic studio there. The main street, Avenue Georges-Clemenceau, is packed with shops selling pottery. Galerie Madoura (*guided visits by reservation at Vallauris tourist office, madoura.com*), where Picasso worked, is still the place for high-quality pots. In 1952, the artist painted the Romanesque chapel of

the 16th-century Renaissance château with his tremendous "War and Peace" composition, and in the same year he gave the town his life-size bronze, "Man with Sheep," which stands in Place Paul-Isnard.

Just up the coast, the ancient village of **Biot** has a medieval quarter and a glass factory. The **Musée National Fernand-Léger** (*chemin du Val-de-Pome, tel 04 92 91 50 20, musee-fernandleger .fr, closed Tues.*), just outside the village, houses Fernand-Léger's own collection in a custom-built museum, its exterior adorned with ceramic panels and mosaics. Kids will enjoy **Marineland** (*Antibes, tel 04 93 33 49 49, marineland .fr, $*), a huge theme park full of whales and dolphins. ∎

---

**Gourdon** 🄰 323 F3 Visitor Information ✉ 24 rue de Majou
☏ 05 65 27 52 50 **tourisme-gourdon.com** • **Mougins** 🄰 323 F3 Visitor Information ✉ 39 place de Patriotes ☏ 04 92 92 14 00 • **Vallauris** 🄰 279 F3 Visitor Information ✉ square du 8 Mai 1945 ☏ 04 93 63 82 58 **vallauris-golfe-juan.fr** • **Biot** 🄰 279 F3 Visitor Information ✉ 46 rue St.-Sebastian ☏ 04 93 65 78 00 **biot-tourisme.com**

# ANTIBES

Cap d'Antibes remains one of the truly exclusive hideaways of the Côte d'Azur, its exotic belle epoque and modernist villas and fabulous hotels discreetly veiled by dense vegetation, through which paths lead to private beaches. But the public beaches here, though mostly rocky, are unspoiled; try Plage de la Sales, on the eastern shore, or tiny Plage de la Garoupe, where Picasso and F. Scott Fitzgerald frolicked in the 1920s.

An old Greek settlement (Antipolis) that later became a frontier town (neighboring Nice was in Savoie), Antibes had its fortress and port reconstructed by Vauban in the 17th century. The town faces Nice across the Baie des Anges. Above the harbor is the old town, a maze of narrow streets with one of the region's best markets every morning (and a great flea market twice a week).

On the ramparts, overlooking the sea, looms the 16th-century **Château Grimaldi.** Here, Picasso was given a studio after World War II; in gratitude, he gave the town paintings, drawings, and ceramics of the period, including "La Joie de Vivre," "Night Fishing at Antibes," and the "Antipolis Suite." The château is now the revamped **Musée Picasso,** and the works are beautifully displayed in the lustrous sea light pouring in through the windows. Paintings by Nicolas de Staël are also on show, along with works by artists of the school of Nice. The terrace garden

The attractive city of Antibes graces the French Riviera.

provides the perfect setting for sculptures silhouetted against the sea.

The **Musée d'Histoire et d'Archéologie,** farther along the ramparts, presents Greek, Roman, and other finds in two huge barrel-vaulted chambers. By day, **Juan-les-Pins** *(visitor information, tel 04 22 10 60 01, antibesjuan lespins.com),* west of Antibes, seems much like other resorts along the coast, but by night it comes alive, and the July jazz festival under the eponymous pines is hard to beat. ■

**Antibes** 323 F3 Visitor Information 42 avenue Robert Soleau 04 22 10 60 10 **antibesjuanlespins.com** • **Musée Picasso (Château Grimaldi)** place Mariejol 04 93 95 85 98 Closed Mon. $$ • **Musée d'Histoire et d'Archéologie** Bastion St.-André, avenue Adm. de Grasse 04 92 90 54 35 Closed Mon. $

# CANNES

**A perfect Riviera base and one of southern France's most glamorous cities, Cannes is big enough to have all the grand hotels, restaurants, beaches, and shopping you could ever want, and small enough to walk around. It also offers easy access to inland beauty spots such as Grasse and Mougins.**

In 1834, when Cannes was just a fishing village, the former British lord chancellor, Lord Brougham, was on his way to Nice when he was held up here by a cholera scare. Falling in love with the place, he built a summer villa; other foreigners soon followed, and Cannes blossomed.

Now Cannes is best known for the International Film Festival held every May. The action centers on **La Croisette,** lined with palm trees, grand boutiques, and world-famous hotels such as the Carlton (see Travelwise p. 452). The Carlton terrace is the place favored by movie moguls for cocktails during the film festival.

Cannes is expensive and chic and determined to stay that way. To the west of the new **Palais des Festivals,** the main venue for the film festival, lies the yacht-filled harbor of the old port, also the site of the morning flower market. The covered **Marché de Forville,** two blocks inland, offers an alluring array of local delicacies.

From the market, little lanes lead up to the old town of **Le Suquet,** a charming alternative to the ostentatious pleasures of the seafront, with lots of restaurants to choose from. If you climb as far as the 11th-century

**Tour du Mont Chevalier,** you will be rewarded by a fine view along the coast. Above Cannes the immodestly named and exclusive **Corniche du Paradis Terrestre** (Corniche of Earthly Paradise) also offers spectacular views, particularly of the Bastille Day (July 14) fireworks.

From Cannes take a boat *(tel 04 93 38 66 33 or 04 92 98 71 30, trans-cote -azur.com, $$$$$)* to the **Îles de Lérins** across the bay. The monastery on St.-Honorat once controlled much of the coast; now the monks cultivate lavender and grapes. In the 17th century, the prison on the island of Ste.-Marguerite held the Man in the Iron Mask. ∎

## EXPERIENCE:
## Go Grape Harvesting

While in southern France, consider taking part in the grape harvest at **Château de Berne** *(tel 04 94 60 48 88, chateauberne.com),* a 1,360-acre (550 ha) estate west of Cannes. The 18th-century château has a four-star hotel, as well as a food and wine school. Help pick grapes and learn about cultivating vines and making wine.

**Cannes** ⬛ 323 F3 Visitor Information ✉ Palais des Festivals ☎ 04 92 99 84 22 **cannes-destination.fr**

# ST.-TROPEZ

Until fairly recent times just a tiny fishing village more easily reached by sea than land, St.-Tropez has become one of the hot spots for which the Côte d'Azur is famous.

Summer is high season for celebrity-spotting around the mazy streets of St.-Tropez and the eternally chic Pampelonne beach.

Writer Guy de Maupassant moved here in the 1880s, followed by painter Paul Signac, whose villa was a haven for artists. Another bohemian influx came in the 1930s, led by Jean Cocteau and Colette. In the 1950s, Brigitte Bardot arrived as the ultimate crowd puller. Now celebrities moor their yachts or keep villas here. Rich bohemians rent restored village houses on the surrounding hills and spend their days on **Plage de Pampelonne** (the hippest by far) and other inviting beaches. And yet the little town remains charming: Visit the market on Place des Lices in the morning, and in the evening head for the cafés around the harbor. The 16th-century **citadel** *(rue de la Citadelle)* houses a maritime museum and offers evocative views. The same panoramas translated into paint are on view in the **Musée de l'Annonciade.** The old chapel of the Annunciation now houses the art collection given to St.-Tropez by Georges Grammont. Excellent examples of Postimpressionism include works by Derain, Signac, Seurat, Dufy, and Braque, many of whom were pilgrims to the quiet of old St.-Tropez. ■

**St.-Tropez** 323 F2 Visitor Information ✉ quai Jean-Jaurès, avenue Général de Gaulle ☎ 04 94 97 45 21 **sainttropeztourisme.com** • **Musée de l'Annonciade** ✉ 2 rue de l'Annonciade ☎ 04 94 17 84 10 🕐 Closed Tues. 💲 $

# HYÈRES & ÎLES D'HYÈRES

The most venerable and southerly of the Côte d'Azur's resorts is dignified and old-fashioned Hyères. In the 19th century, it was a favorite wintering place for Empress Eugénie, Queen Victoria, Robert Louis Stevenson, Edith Wharton, and members of the British aristocracy in search of health cures. But it never attracted the crowds that flocked to Nice and Cannes.

## Hyères

Despite wholesale development of its coastal suburbs, Hyères, with miles of sandy beach, has kept its slightly faded charm and is much in demand as a film set for belle epoque dramas.

Palm trees and Moorish architecture impart an exotic quality on the broad 19th-century boulevards. Through a medieval gatehouse is the old town, with streets climbing the slopes of Casteau hill, lovely gardens, and sea views. The 12th-century **Tour St.-Blaise** and **Église de St.-Paul** hint at Hyères's former status.

## Îles d'Hyères

The three exotically beautiful Îles d'Hyères, former haunt of pirates and now partly given over to the French armed forces, are remarkable, unspoiled, protected environments. Cars are restricted hereabouts, so these islands are ideal for bathing and gentle walks among the scented maquis.

On **Porquerolles,** the largest island, you can explore the rocky creeks of the north coast (not safe for swimming) and the sandy coves of the south. Watered with natural springs and rich in flora and fauna, **Port-Cros** (see sidebar p. 326), a national park since 1963, is strictly protected. Offshore is a marine nature reserve: From the beach at La Palud, you can dive along an underwater trail to see a fantastic range of sea creatures, including sponges, sea urchins, octopuses, and moray eels. And for real nature lovers, the **Île du Levant** contains the world's oldest nudist colony, Héliopolis. ∎

---

**INSIDER TIP:**

Rent a bicycle on the island of Porquerolles and pedal to the north coast for magnificent views of the Mediterranean Sea.

—ASHLEY THOMPSON
*National Geographic contributor*

---

**Hyères** 🗺 323 F2 Visitor Information ✉ avenue de Belgique
☎ 04 94 01 84 50 **hyeres-tourisme.com**

**FERRIES**
Ferries to the Îles d'Hyères *(tlv-tvm.com, vedettesilesdor.fr)* run from Hyères harbor (90 min.; tel 04 94 58 21 81); from Le Lavandou (35 min.; Gare Maritime, tel 04 94 71 01 02); and from Cavalaire-sur-Mer (45 min.; tel 04 94 64 08 04). Round-trip fare: $$$$.

# MARSEILLE

France's oldest and largest port is tough, raffish, cosmopolitan, and has recently experienced a cultural renaissance. Founded by the Greeks in the seventh century B.C., it remained independent of France until the 15th century, after which it made a specialty of its own Mediterranean brand of turbulence. The revolutionary hymn "The Marseillaise" owes its name to the fervor of the Marseillais rebels.

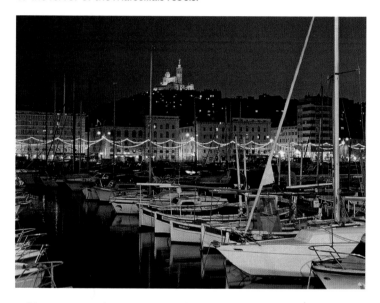

■ After centuries of grittiness, Marseille's Vieux Port (Old Port) sparkles with economic renewal.

France's gateway to the Middle East and North Africa, Marseille has always been a cultural melting pot. While their ships moored in the harbor, Western magnates and Eastern potentates once met along **La Canebière,** a bustling, slightly run-down thoroughfare. The **Vieux Port** remains the city's focus, its old forts now overlooking a fish market and some superb seafood restaurants.

To the north of the port, the old quarter of Le Panier was largely

**Marseille** 🗺 323 E2 Visitor Information ✉ 4 La Canebière
☎ 04 91 13 89 00 **marseille-tourisme.com**

Bassin de la
Grande Joliette

Musée
d'Archéologie
Méditerranéenne
Cathédrale
de la Major
Ancienne
Major
La Vieille
Charité
PL. FRANCIS
CHIRAT
RUE J. FR
LECCA
AVE R. SCHUMA
RUE DE LA JOUETTE
BOULEVARD DES DAMES
AVE C. PELLETAN
PLACE
J.GUESDE
Gare
PLACE
DE LA
MAJOR
R. DU PETIT
PUIT
R. DU PANIER
R. ST-ANTOINE
SPHOCEENS
RUE DE LA RÉPUBLIQUE
RUE ST-BARBE
RUE D'AIX
Musée des
Civilisations de
l'Europe et de
la Méditerranée
QUAI DE LA
TOURETTE
R. DE
REUGE
R. BELLES
ÉCUELLES
les Carmes
PLACE
S.CARNOT
RUE COLBERT
PL. DES
MOULINS
Clocher des
Accoules
Hôtel
Dieu
Fort
St-Jean
LE
PANIER
PL. DE
LENCHE
MONTÉE
DES ACCOULES
PL.
DAVIEL
St-Cannat
Musée
d'Histoire
de Marseille
Belvédère
St. Laurent
AVE. DE
ST-JEAN
RUE CAISSERIE
GRAND RUE
R.H BARBUSSE
Centre
Bourse
Musée des
Docks
Romains
RUE ST-LAURENT
RUE DE LA
LOGE
Musée du
Vieux Marseille
RUE
COUTELL
JARDIN
DES
VESTIGES
COURS BELSUNCE
PARC
DU
PHARO
ESP. DE LA TOURETTE
QUAI DU PORT
Hôtel
de Ville
RUE DE
BIR-HAKEIM
RUE DE
St-Ferréol
Musée de
la Marine
LA CANEBIÈRE
Bas Fort
St.-Nicolas
BLVD. CHARLES LIVON
TUNNEL ST-LAURENT
Vieux Port
Q. DES BELGES
Office de
Tourisme
Palais de
Longchamp
QUAI DE RIVE NEUVE
Fort
St.-Nicolas
Théâtre
de la Criée
PL.
REYER
CRS. J. BALLARD
RUE PARADIS
RUE ST-FERRÉOL
RUE DE
ROME
Basilique
St.-Victor
AVE. DE LA CORSE
RUE SAINTE
Opéra
RUE SAINTE
0          300 meters
0          300 yards
BLVD.
DE LA
CORDERIE
St.-Charles
RUE GRIGNAN
Musée
Cantini
Basilique Notre-
Dame-de-la-Garde/
Musée d'Art Contemporain
JARDIN
P. PUGET
COURS PIERRE
PUGET
Palais de
Justice
RUE
BRETEUIL
Cité Radieuse

dynamited by the Germans during World War II. A few historic buildings remain, including the 17th-century hospice of La Vieille Charité, which now houses the **Musée d'Archéologie Méditerranéenne.** Nearby, the 19th-century **Cathédrale de la Major** (*esplanade de la Tourette*) dwarfs the 12th-century **Ancienne Major,** the original cathedral that was partially destroyed to make space for the new one. The **Musée des Docks Romains** displays Roman finds.

East of the port, the 19th-century Palais de Longchamp now houses the **Musée des Beaux-Arts** (*2 rue Edward Stephan, tel 04 91 14 59 25*). To the south is the fifth-century **Basilique St.-Victor** (*quai de Rive Neuve*). Nearby is the dominating 19th-century **Basilique Notre-Dame-de-la-Garde** (*parvis de la Basilique de Notre-Dame-de-la-Garde*).

The city's long-term commitment to modern architecture is evident in Will Alsop's **Hôtel du Département** and in Le Corbusier's **Cité Radieuse** near the **Musée Cantini,** an attractive modern art gallery. The **Musée d'Art Contemporain,** located in a 17th-century mansion, has a fine collection of modern art.

Between Marseille and Cassis lie the *calanques,* a nature preserve of fjordlike inlets and azure Mediterranean waters loved by the locals. Everyone has a favorite calanque.

—TOM MUELLER
*National Geographic writer*

Marseille's corniche, Boulevard J. F. Kennedy, offers views to the island prison of **Château d'If** and paths to the Malmousque promontory. It ends at the city's main beach, **Plage du Prado.** The **Musée des Civilisations de l'Europe et de la Méditerranée** is the world's first museum entirely dedicated to Mediterranean culture. The building itself is a dramatic structure located at the entrance to Marseille's harbor, combining modern architecture with a footbridge suspended over the sea connected to the 12th-century Fort St.-Jean and its gardens.

Since being named as European Capital of Culture for 2013, Marseille has set its sights on a long-term program of comprehensive urban

The traditional Provençal fish stew, bouillabaisse, originated in the port city of Marseille.

revitalization. The EuroMéditerranée *(euromediterranee.fr)* urban renewal and development project is already transforming a large area along the coast, but the essence of the old port city remains in place. ∎

**Musée d'Archéologie Méditerranéenne** ✉ 2 rue de la Charité ☎ 04 91 14 58 59 🕐 Closed Mon. • **Musée des Docks Romains** ✉ place Vivaux ☎ 04 91 55 36 00 🕐 Closed Mon. 💲 $ • **Musée Cantini** ✉ 19 rue Grignan ☎ 04 91 54 77 75 🕐 Closed Mon. • **Musée d'Art Contemporain** ✉ 69 avenue d'Haifa ☎ 04 91 25 01 07 🕐 Closed Mon. • **Musée des Civilisations de l'Europe et de la Méditerranée** ✉ 1 esplanade du J4 ☎ 04 85 35 13 13 🕐 Closed Tues. 💲 $ **mucem.org**

# More Places to Visit in the Côte d'Azur

## Esterel Massif

The Esterel Massif boasts a rare stretch of unspoiled coastline along the Côte d'Azur. This constitutes a dramatic and inviting landscape of jagged cliffs and forested ravines. A spectacular corniche winds through pine forests, past porphyry cliffs and aquamarine *calanques*. Stop at **Pointe de l'Esquillon** for a grand view of the Mediterranean, the Esterel Massif, and the cliffs of Cap Roux. From **Agay** *(visitor information, place Gianetti, tel 04 94 82 01 85, agay.fr),* set in a beautiful bay, you can walk across the Cap du Dramont to Le Dramont, where American troops came ashore and established a beachhead in 1944. 🗺 323 F3

## Fréjus

A Roman port (Forum Julii) that was established by Julius Caesar, Fréjus is particularly rich in Roman and medieval remains. Though the port has silted up, a sizable amphitheater remains, along with parts of an aqueduct, a gateway, and a theater. Highlights of the medieval **Cité Épiscopale** include the Gothic and Renaissance cathedral with its elegant cloister, the 14th-century bishops' palace, and one of the oldest baptisteries in France, probably fifth century—an octagon of Corinthian columns pilfered from the forum. *frejus.fr* 🗺 323 F3 **Visitor Information** ✉ 325 rue de Jean-Jaurès ☎ 04 94 51 83 83

## Port-Grimaud

Port-Grimaud, across the bay from St.-Tropez, is an intriguing 1960s precursor of the return of vernacular architecture—a clever pastiche of a Provençal fishing village, built by architect François Spoerry in 1968. The Venetian-style lagoon village resembles an ancient village. *grimaud-provence.com* 🗺 323 F2

## Toulon

The naval port of Toulon lies on a deep natural harbor. The **Quai de Stalingrad** is lined with shops and cafés. The old town includes the 11th-century **Cathédrale Ste.-Marie-Majeure,** remodeled in the 17th century. The **Musée National de la Marine** *(place Monsenergue, tel 04 22 42 02 01, musee-marine .fr)* presents the city's maritime history. *toulontourisme.com* 🗺 323 E2 **Visitor Information** ✉ 12 place Louis Blanc ☎ 04 94 18 53 00

---

**INSIDER TIP:**

In Toulon, check out the morning market on Cours Lafayette *(closed Mon.; Cours Lafayette, Rue Paul Lendrin, Place Louis Blanc, Rue de Lorgues & Place Paul Comte),* a street bazaar of vegetables, fruit, flowers, and textiles.

—JACK KAVANAGH
*National Geographic author*

---

# PROVENCE

**Land of lavender fields and olive groves, scented hillsides and fertile valleys, dazzling colors and limpid light, Provence is lauded for all its ravishing natural gifts. Only the maddening winter mistral wind blights this garden of Eden: To withstand it, the traditional blue-shuttered farmhouses *(mas)* are built without windows in their north-facing walls.**

■ Sunshine-filled Provence's tiny patches of farmland are a Roman legacy.

Provence was colonized by the Greeks before the Romans called it Provincia and left behind great amphitheaters and monuments at Arles and Orange, among the finest in France. Medieval popes based themselves in Avignon, where the Palais des Papes remains, a testament to their power. Great Cistercian abbeys bear witness to the less worldly side of medieval Christianity. The strong regional identity is evident in the cosmopolitan city of Aix-en-Provence, with its long literary and cultural history, and in Arles, home to proud Provençal folklore.

The region's natural wonders range from the Gorges du Verdon to the mysterious Fontaine de Vaucluse. Mont Ventoux is the highest point of the region; its most distinctive part is the wide expanse of the Camargue.

Perhaps most delightful of all are the simple pleasures: a quiet pastis on a café terrace, a game of *boules* in a village square, produce-laden market stalls, local lavender and honey, and traditional Provençal fabrics. And no aspect of Provence is more evocative than the unspoiled *villages perchés* (hill villages) of areas such as the Lubéron. For a perfect day, you can explore one of these ancient terra-cotta-roofed villages, visit an art gallery, and stroll past fields of wildflowers or aromatic herbs.

In this land of sensual delights, fine restaurants abound. But a picnic is a perfect way to savor the fragrant melons, peaches, and cherries, goat cheeses, and the tomatoes and olives that are found here. Or simply take a nap in the shade of an olive tree and enjoy *la vie en plein air*. You will want to stay forever. ■

# AVIGNON

Secure within its great walls, Avignon retains the grand self-assurance of its 14th-century heyday, when a series of popes lived here. These days the city is a thriving cultural center, animated in summer by its music and drama festival. The focus at festival time is the Place de l'Horloge, with its Gothic clock tower and lively cafés.

■ The Palais des Papes in Avignon, early papal center of power

The magnificent **Palais des Papes** dominates the historic city. Begun in 1334, most of the interior of this great white edifice is empty after the depredations of the revolution, but six magnificent Gobelins tapestries and remarkable frescoes by Matteo Giovanetti reflect its former glory. The Chambre du Cerf, study of Clement VI, has beautiful ceramic tiles and frescoes.

The beautiful 14th-century **Petit Palais** (*tel 04 90 86 44 58, petit-palais .org, closed Tues.*) opposite contains distinguished medieval painting and sculpture—an impressive introduction to the International Gothic style pioneered in Avignon by 14th-century Italian artists.

Next to the palace stands the **Cathédrale Notre-Dame-des-Doms** and, behind it, the park of the **Rocher des Doms.** Below are the Rhône River and the celebrated remains of the Pont St.-Bénézet, known as the **Pont d'Avignon.** The 12th-century bridge was partly swept away by the Rhône in the 17th century. Only four spans of the original 22 remain.

To the south are the narrow streets of the old town, including **Rue des Teinturiers,** beside the Sorgue River. Here, dyers produced the Provençal patterned cottons known as Indiennes, inspired by Indian calicos brought back from the Crusades. Museums include the **Musée Calvet;** the **Musée Anglado n** (*rue Laboureur, tel 04 90 82 29 03, angladon.fr*), with the only van Gogh painting still in Provence, "Les Wagons de Chemin de Fer"; and the contemporary art of the growing **Collection Lambert** (*rue Violette, tel 04 90 16 56 20, collectionlambert.com*). ■

**Avignon** ⛰ 323 D3 Visitor Information ✉ 41 cours Jean-Jaurès ☎ 04 32 74 32 74 **avignon-tourisme.com** • **Palais des Papes** ✉ place du Palais ☎ 04 90 27 50 00 **palais-des-papes.com** • **Musée Calvet** ✉ 65 rue Joseph-Vernant ☎ 04 90 86 33 84 🕐 Closed Tues. **musee-calvet.org**

# IN & AROUND ORANGE

Visit Orange for its magnificent Roman heritage: Its triumphal arch and theater are among the finest Roman remains in the world. Lying in the Rhône Valley on the Roman Via Agrippa, Orange was the gateway between north and south. Under the emperor Augustus it was a thriving city, with temples, baths, and a stadium. In the 16th century, Orange was inherited by William, Prince of Nassau, of the Dutch royal family.

## Orange

Visitors enter the city from the north through the Roman-era **triumphal arch,** now beautifully restored. Built about 20 B.C. to commemorate Julius Caesar's victory over the Greeks at Massina (Marseille), this monumental masterpiece is encrusted with intricately carved battle scenes.

The arch is dwarfed by the **Théâtre Antique.** The best surviving example of a Roman theater anywhere, the Théâtre Antique still has most of its original seating (for 8,000), columns and arches, and its tremendous stage wall, dwarfing a huge statue of Emperor Augustus. The acoustics here are perfect, and the theater provides a superb setting for a music festival each July, with concerts and opera on offer. It now has a new discreet glass-and- steel roof.

To the south lies **Châteauneuf-du-Pape,** planted by popes, and the most distinguished of the Côtes du Rhône vineyards, making world-famous wines.

**INSIDER TIP:**

Don't miss the Musée d'Art et d'Histoire d'Orange, across the street from the ancient Roman theater.

—BARBARA NOE
*National Geographic senior editor*

## Vaison-la-Romaine

Northeast of Orange is Vaison-la-Romaine. Excavations revealed sections of a Roman city *(Fouilles de Puymin, place du Chanoine-Sautel, tel 04 90 36 50 48, closed Jan.–Feb.),* complete with a basilica, baths, and a theater. The excellent **archaeological museum** on the site has a number of finds, notably an exquisite peacock mosaic.

Over the river, across a Roman bridge, is the **Haute Ville;** little cobbled streets twist through a clutch of restored 14th-century houses before rising up to the ruins of the château. ∎

**Orange** 🗺 323 D4 Visitor Information ✉ 5 cours Aristide-Briand ☎ 04 90 34 70 88 otorange.fr • **Théâtre Antique** ✉ place des Frères-Mounet, Orange ☎ 04 90 51 17 60 💲 $ theatre-antique.com • **Châteauneuf-du-Pape** 🗺 323 D3 Visitor Information ✉ place du Portail ☎ 04 90 83 71 08 • **Vaison-la-Romaine** 🗺 323 D4 Visitor Information ✉ place du Chanoine-Sautel ☎ 04 90 36 02 11 🕐 Closed Sun. **vaison-la-romaine.com**

# AROUND THE LUBÉRON

The ridge of hills from Manosque to Cavaillon, and the valleys on either side, form the Lubéron. A tour of this haven of lavender fields, vineyards, and orchards offers *villages perchés*, majestic mountain views, and fine walking.

■ **Gordes might well be the most beautiful town in Provence.**

In the north of the region, steep ravines split the hills of the Lubéron Massif and oaks grow in the valleys. To the south, fertile land slopes to the Durance River. The Grand Lubéron has been designated **Parc Naturel Régional de Lubéron,** its HQ in the little town of **Apt.**

The Maison du Parc in Apt has videos and information about local walks, wildlife, and vegetation. The town's main square offers *boules* and fountains in the shade of linden trees. The 11th-century **Cathédrale Ste.-Anne** *(rue Ste.-Anne, tel 04 90 04 61 71)* shelters the saint's shroud, and a small archaeological museum documents the town's Roman past. Apt's Saturday market is a lively affair with specialties of local crystallized fruits, lavender oil, and handsome pottery.

Southeast of Apt, a strenuous walk from Auribeau leads up to the **Mourre Nègre,** the highest peak of the Montagne du Lubéron, with fine views in all directions. Before the days of synthetic dyes, ocher quarrying was a major industry in the Lubéron. North of the Mourre Nègre are the abandoned quarries of the **Colorado de Rustrel,** a towering landscape in every shade of red and orange.

The walls and archways of the pretty village of **Roussillon,** just northwest of Apt, range from brick red through rose to crimson. The **Falaises du Sang** (Cliffs of Blood) outside the village are spectacular in the setting sun.

Beyond the Vaucluse plateau to the north looms the great summit of **Mont Ventoux,** more than 6,000 feet (1,900 m) high. The walk (or cycle) to the top (from Brantes, Malaucène, or Bédoin) is a breezy but fabulous climb.

The western Lubéron—the Petit Lubéron—is studded with delightful villages. Tiny **Bonnieux** *(visitor information, place Carnot, tel 04 90 75 91 90, tourisme-en-luberon.com)* clings to a hilltop, offering a glorious view of the valley, and the **Musée de la Boulangerie** *(tel 04 90 75 88 34, closed Tues. & Nov.–March),* a bread museum; **Oppède-le-Vieux** has a ruined castle. The picturesque village of **Gordes** clusters below its splendid 16th-century château, which displays contemporary art. The nearby **Village des Bories** is a collection of ancient dwellings. Just north of Gordes is the Cistercian **Abbaye de Sénanque,** the pale stones of its chapel and cloister contrasting beautifully with the surrounding lavender.

**Fontaine-de-Vaucluse** sits along a gorge, at the foot of which lies the Sorgue River's source. In winter and spring, an underground torrent erupts into a dark green pool. The **Musée Pétrarque** (tel 04 90 20 37 20, oti-delasorgue.fr, closed Tues.) displays Petrarch's poems illustrated by Picasso, Miró, and others. The **Moulin à Papier Vallis Clausa** (tel 04 90 20 34 14) has made paper here since the 16th century. ∎

**Parc Naturel Régional de Lubéron** ✉ Maison du Parc, Apt ☎ 04 90 04 42 00 **parcduluberon.fr • Apt** 🅼 279 E3 Visitor Information ✉ 20 avenue Philippe-de-Girard ☎ 04 90 74 03 18 **luberon-apt.fr** • **Roussillon** 🅼 323 E3 Visitor Information ✉ place de la Poste ☎ 04 90 05 60 25 **roussillon-provence.com • Gordes** 🅼 323 E3 Visitor Information ✉ place du Château ☎ 04 90 72 02 08 **gordes-village.com** • **Abbaye de Sénanque** ☎ 04 90 72 18 24 🕐 Guided visits only; reservations recommended 💲 $ **senanque.fr • Fontaine-de-Vaucluse** 🅼 323 D3 Visitor Information ✉ chemin de la Fontaine ☎ 04 90 20 32 22

# ARLES

Climb to the top tier of the Roman arena for the best view of Arles, south of the Lubéron, looking across the terra-cotta roofs and ocher walls to the Rhône River.

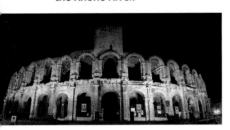

■ **Ancient majesty illuminated at the Roman arena in Arles**

Enough remains of this great Roman city to convey a powerful sense of history. Now used for bullfights and festival pageants, the vast first-century **Arènes Romaines** was once the scene of gladiatorial combat. Measuring 446 feet by 351 feet (136 m by 107 m) with two stories each made up of 60 arches, it could seat 25,000 spectators. As you walk around the lower arcade of the arena, look for the tunnels through which wild beasts charged into the arena.

Nearby is the slightly earlier Roman theater. The two great columns of the stage wall (formerly used to hang prisoners) today provide a backdrop for performances during the Arles Festival in late June and early July.

The town's Roman remains are rivaled by its medieval buildings, notably the **Église St.-Trophime** (place de la République). A masterpiece of Provençal Romanesque, this cathedral is famed for its glorious cloister and an elaborately carved 12th-century portal.

Not content with being, in Chateaubriand's words, a great "open-air museum," Arles has a number of great indoor museums. The modern **Musée de l'Arles Antique** on the riverbank covers the city's Roman history. The **Museon Arlaten** is devoted to Provençal folklore, crafts, and costumes, while the **Musée Réattu** includes 57 Picasso drawings donated by the artist, who reveled in Arles's bullfights.

**Arles** 🗺 323 D3 Visitor Information ✉ boulevard des Lices
☎ 04 90 18 41 20 **arlestourisme.com** • **Arènes Romaines**
✉ Rond-point des Arènes ☎ 04 90 49 36 74 💲 $ **arenes-arles.com**
• **Musée de l'Arles Antique** ✉ Presqu'île du cirque Romain
☎ 04 13 31 51 03 🕐 Closed Tues. 💲 $ **arles-antique.cg13.fr/root**
• **Museon Arlaten** ✉ 29 rue de la République ☎ 04.13.31.51.99
💲 $ **museonarlaten.fr** • **Musée Réattu** ✉ 10 rue du Grand Prieuré
☎ 04 90 49 37 58 🕐 Closed Mon. 💲 $ **museereattu.arles.fr**
• **Fondation Vincent van Gogh** ✉ 35 rue de Docteur Fanton
☎ 04 88 65 82 93 **fondation-vincentvangogh-arles.org**

But the artist most closely associated with Arles is without doubt Vincent van Gogh. It was in Arles that he fell in love with the south and its brilliant colors; here in 1888 that he painted some of his best known works, including "Sunflowers" and "Chair"; and here that shortly afterward he sliced off his ear in the depths of his depression. The **Fondation Vincent van Gogh** makes up for its lack of original van Gogh works with paintings inspired by him. The **Espace van Gogh** (place Docteur Felix Rey), once the hospital where the artist was committed, is now an exhibition space and library with a garden planted to look like a van Gogh painting.

Arles hosts a variety of festivals, including the Fête St.-Jean in June and the Easter bullfights, when Arlésiens

**INSIDER TIP:**

Fans of van Gogh: Follow the art trail around town with panels of his most famous artworks set up on the precise spots where he painted them.

—JACK KAVANAGH
*National Geographic author*

emerge in full costume, the men in cowboy outfits, the women in lace headdresses and embroidered shawls. Arles also hosts an annual photography festival, Les Rencontres des Arles.

Just outside Arles, the ancient burial ground of **Les Alyscamps** (tel 04 90 49 36 74), painted by van Gogh, is a serene avenue of tombs and sarcophagi. ∎

## EXPERIENCE: Bullfighting—Choose Your Style

Although bullfighting is held in high regard in southern France, its pros and cons are passionately debated. Animal rights activists are pitted against aficionados who consider bullfighting a noble art. In fact, there are two styles of bullfight.

In the Spanish *corrida*, which you can see at the Roman arena in Nîmes (*arenesdenimes.com;* see sidebar p. 368) the bull is killed after much fanfare. The best time to be there is in May, for the Feria festival.

More preferable perhaps is the Course Camarguaise, which you can see in Arles. Go in July for the Cocade d'Or festival. This style of bullfighting is more sport

than ritual, and the bull is more equally matched with his human opponents. Here the bull is not killed but spends only 15 minutes in the arena, where it is chased by the *raseteurs,* who gesture and run across the arena to attract the bull. Using a *crochet,* or metal comb, they try to snatch the *cocarde* and *ficelles* (rosette and tassels) attached to the bull's head. The bull chases the raseteur, who escapes behind the barrier, often just in the nick of time. The raseteurs are awarded points for their skill and courage; the bulls are applauded as they leave the ring and sometimes honored with statues in their memory.

# THE CAMARGUE

**Eerily beautiful, this vast wetland area formed by the Rhône delta is a world of infinite horizons, swaying grasses, and blue lagoons, all suffused with an extraordinary light.**

■ The *roussataio*—the releasing of horses and mares into the city streets—is a Camargue tradition.

The unique ecology of the Camargue includes abundant wildlife, most notably flamboyant flocks of flamingos. The glittering salt flats yield vast amounts of salt, and a tasty variety of rice grows here. The pastures are grazed by native white horses, ridden by the Camarguais herdsmen known as *gardians*. These hardy people cling passionately to their traditional way of life, herding their small black bulls destined for the arenas of Nîmes or Arles. The gardians still live in the low white cabins integral to the Camargue landscape.

The history and traditions of this extraordinary wilderness, now protected as a *parc régional,* are traced at the **Musée Camarguais** *(Mas du Pont de Rousty, tel 04 90 97 10 82, closed Tues.*

*& Oct.–March),* the park's main center. Located southwest of Arles on the D570, the museum explores different aspects of local life: agriculture, fishing, breeding stock, and domestic activities. It also has information on walking and riding, and on ranches converted into hotels and restaurants.

## Stes.-Maries-de-la-Mer

Stes.-Maries-de-la-Mer nestles cozily around its fortified church (climb up to the roof for excellent views) and is now surrounded by stores bursting with all things Provençal. The **Musée Baroncelli** *(rue Victor-Hugo, tel 04 90 97 87 60),* housed in the old town hall, has fascinating displays on Camargue traditions.

In a tradition dating back to the 16th century, every year on May 24 and 25, Romany pilgrims flock to the town to take part in a procession carrying the statue of St. Sarah, patron saint of the Romany, to the sea to be blessed. During the festival, the streets throb with flamenco, horse races, and a kaleidoscope of costumes. Carmaguais dishes available in the restaurants here include *boeuf gardian,* a rich stew of bull's meat, best enjoyed with nutty Camargue rice.

## St.-Gilles-du-Gard

To the north, travelers will come upon St.-Gilles-du-Gard, dubbed the "Gateway to the Camargue."

---

**INSIDER TIP:**

The local *fleur de sel de Camargue*—gourmet sea salt with just a hint of violets—makes an excellent gift for friends back home.

—BARBARA NOE
*National Geographic senior editor*

---

This tiny village is dominated by a church, where statues of the saints crowd around three carved 12th-century portals, and a spiral staircase winds up its bell tower.

## Aigues-Mortes

The Camargue's far western edge is guarded by the eerily haunting medieval walled town of Aigues-Mortes (Place of the Dead Waters). Once an important port, it is now silted up and marooned 3 miles (5 km) inland. The top of the old town walls, accessed via the **Musée Archéologique** *(tel 04 66 53 61 55),* offer great views. ■

## Nature Reserve

One of Europe's major wetlands, the Camargue is an important haven for a wide variety of animals, grasses, and flowers, which thrive in its huge flat marshlands dotted with shallow saltwater lagoons *(étangs).* The great central **Étang de Vaccarès,** covering 16,000 acres (6,500 ha), has been designated a zoological and botanical reserve. Access is severely restricted (this is, for example, the only breeding site in France for the slender-billed gull and the red-crested pochard). A walk along the **Digue de la Mer** from Stes.-Maries-de-la-Mer provides good views of the reserve, and various points on the D37 and C134 may offer sightings of herring gulls and black-headed gulls, herons, avocets, egrets, and—most memorable of all—the famous flamingos (their distinctive pink color comes from the tiny crustaceans on which they feed). The visitor center at **La Capelière** *(closed Sun.),* on the east side of the Étang de Vaccarès, provides information on the reserve, along with an exhibition following the Camargue through the seasons. The **Parc Ornithologique** *(tel 04 90 97 82 62, parcornithologique.com),* at Pont-de-Gau north of Stes.-Maries-de-la-Mer, displays a variety of birds, including Egyptian vultures, black kites, and eagle owls.

---

**Stes.-Maries-de-la-Mer** 🗺 323 D3 Visitor Information ✉ 5 avenue Van Gogh ☎ 04 90 97 82 55 **saintesmaries.com** • **St.-Gilles-du-Gard** 🗺 323 D3 Visitor Information ✉ place Mistral **tourisme.saint-gilles.fr** • **Aigues-Mortes** 🗺 323 D3 Visitor Information ✉ place St.-Louis ☎ 04 66 53 73 00 **ot-aiguesmortes.fr**

# LES BAUX-DE-PROVENCE

**Rising above the white limestone crags of Les Alpilles, the ruins of the feudal citadel of Les Baux meld into the rocky outcrop on which they stand.**

This was once the stronghold of the bloodthirsty lords of Baux. With ancestry dating back to the Magi king Balthazar, the lords placed the Star of Bethlehem on their coat of arms and terrorized the region in the Middle Ages. Most infamous was the psychopathically violent Raymond de Turenne, the "scourge

---

**INSIDER TIP:**

Christmas Eve in Les Baux is an experience of a lifetime with a candlelight procession that winds up at tiny St.-Vincent church for the Shepherds' Mass.

—SHEILA BUCKMASTER
*National Geographic editor at large*

---

of Provence." In the 14th century, he amused himself by forcing prisoners to leap to their deaths from the castle walls.

In the 13th century, by contrast, Les Baux was the embodiment of romance, the most famous of the Provençal courts of love that lured

troubadours from afar to serenade noble ladies. But the great citadel came to an ignominious end in 1632, when Cardinal Richelieu, finally tiring of the rebellious lords and inhabitants of Les Baux, ordered the entire edifice to be demolished. The result is the ruin visible today, strung out along a narrow and vertiginous spit.

Enter the **Ville Morte** (Dead City) through the 14th-century **Tour du Brau,** which houses the castle's museum. From here, you can climb over the ruins of the castle and early village. The edge of the escarpment offers tremendous views across the contorted rocks of the **Val d'Enfer,** the legendary haunt of witches and reputedly the inspiration for the setting of Dante's *Inferno*.

The village below the citadel dates mainly from the 16th and 17th centuries, with several Renaissance chapels and mansions now hosting museums. The **Fondation Louis Jou** in the Hôtel Jean de Brion displays the paraphernalia of a master typographer; the **Musée des Santons** in the Ancien Hôtel de Ville *(rue Porte Mage)* is devoted to the clay figures that decorate Provençal Christmas cribs. ∎

**Les Baux** ⬛ 323 D3 Visitor Information ✉ rue Porte Mage ☎ 04 90 54 34 39 **lesbauxdeprovence.com** • **Musée de l'Histoire de la Citadelle** ✉ Château des Baux de Provence ☎ 04 90 54 55 56 💲 $ • **Cathédrale d'Images** ✉ route Val d'Enfer ☎ 04 90 54 38 65 💲 $$ **cathedrale-images.com**

# AIX-EN-PROVENCE

"The most beautiful town in France after Paris," according to an 18th-century traveler, Aix is a chic and elegant city, with graceful boulevards, shady squares, and hundreds of beautifully carved stone fountains. Water is the raison d'être of the city, founded by the Roman consul Sextius, who was attracted by the hot springs that are still in use today.

■ Rotonde at the Place General-de-Gaulle at the entrance to the Cours Mirabeau, Aix-en-Provence

## Cours Mirabeau

At the heart of Aix lies the majestic Cours Mirabeau, the famous tree-shaded boulevard laid out on the site of the old ramparts, flanked by elegant 17th- and 18th-century houses and punctuated by beautiful fountains. Take time to watch the world go by from the terrace of one of the cafés here, such as Les Deux Garçons, a favorite haunt of artists and intellectuals since 1792.

## Old Town

To the north, the old town extends through a maze of squares. On Saturdays, when it is taken over by a market, this area is even more irresistible. Distinguished buildings include the 17th-century **Hôtel de Ville** and the old bishops' palace, or Ancien Archevêché, which now houses the **Musée des Tapisseries.** Next door is the lovely Gothic **Cathédrale St.-Sauveur,** unmistakable for its 16th-century carved

**Aix-en-Provence** 🗺 323 E3 Visitor Information ✉ 300 avenue Giuseppe Verdi ☎ 04 42 16 11 61 **aixenprovencetourism.com** • **Musée des Tapisseries** ✉ place de l'Ancien-Archevêché ☎ 04 42 23 09 91 🕐 Closed Tues. & Jan. 💲 $ • **Cathédrale St.-Sauveur** ✉ place de l'Université • **Musée Granet** ✉ place St.-Jean-de-Malte ☎ 04 42 52 88 32 **museegranet-aixenprovence.fr**

## In the Footsteps of Cézanne

Want to see Aix-en-Provence the way Cézanne did? Every Thursday in July, the **Atelier Paul Cézanne** offers artistic exchanges and a country picnic in the gardens of the artist's studio. Events begin at 7 p.m. Or consider taking a sketching trip to discover some of the beautiful spots around the city. If you would like to improve your artistic skills, the **Académie Libre** (academielibre.com) has courses available for artists of all levels, from beginners to experienced. The **Aix City Pass,** which is available at the tourist office, includes a guided tour of the city, a tour of Cézanne's studio, and a visit to Fondation Vasarely, the Cézanne family estate.

**INSIDER TIP:**

To really connect with the spirit of the place, find a small rural church and spend some time strolling through its cemetery, preferably in the spring.

—DIANA PARSELL
*National Geographic Books*
*contributor*

the artist worked from 1897 until he died in 1906. It has been re-created just as he might have left it. West of the city center, is the **Fondation Vasarely,** an extraordinary museum designed by the artist himself, with exterior walls that look like his paintings.

## Outside of Town

Less than 2 miles (3 km) north of the city is the location of **Oppidum d'Entremont** (entremont.culture.gouv .fr, closed Tues.), on the site of the original Gallic settlement of Aix. Excavations have revealed fortifications and residential buildings.

West of the city is the **Site Memorial Les Milles** (campdesmilles.org), a brick factory used as a concentration camp during World War II. Artists and intellectuals considered "undesirables" were sent here, including Max Ernst. Documents and photos tell the story; the refectory has fragments of caricatures and murals done by prisoners. ∎

doors, the cool columns of its 5th-century Merovingian baptistry, and its Romanesque cloisters. Among its treasures is Nicolas Froment's 15th-century triptych, "Burning Bush."

## Cézanne's City

South of Cours Mirabeau is the elegant Quartier Mazarin. The **Musée Granet** has eight works by Paul Cézanne, Aix's most famous son (see sidebar above). A Cézanne circuit leads you around town. Visit the **Atelier Paul Cézanne,** where

**Atelier Paul Cézanne** ✉ 9 avenue Paul Cézanne ☎ 04 42 21 06 53 **cezanne-en-provence.com** • •**Fondation Vasarely** ✉ 1 avenue Marcel Panol ☎ 04 42 20 01 09 **fondationvasarely.fr**

# GORGES DU VERDON

The deepest, widest gorge in Europe, this natural wonder and precious refuge is a *parc naturel régional* sheltering unusual flora and fauna. For a circular tour starting from Castellane, an ancient town of ruined ramparts and now a busy tourist center, you need to allow a day and plenty of gas. The route affords breathtaking views, but beware hairpin turns and precipices.

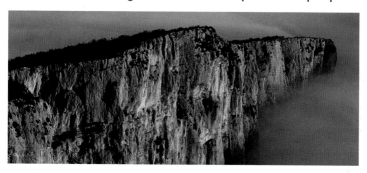

With plunging limestone walls and vertiginous views, the Gorges du Verdon does not disappoint.

Leave Castellane westward on the D952. At **Point Sublime,** on the north bank, hikers can walk down 590 feet (180 m) to the bottom of the gorge. The D23 then loops off to the south, providing spectacular views before rejoining the main D952 at **La Palad-sur-Verdon** to skirt the canyon.

Set in a deep ravine above the western end of the canyon is **Moustiers-Ste.-Marie,** a 15th-century settlement known for its pottery; see examples at the **Musée de la Faience** *(tel 04 92 74 61 64)*. From here head south on the D957 past the **Lac de Sainte-Croix,** an artificial lake of cobalt blue waters, then turn left along the south side of the canyon on the Corniche Sublime, the D71. Views abound, particularly at **Pont de l'Artuby,** spanning the gorge of the Artuby River, and at the **Balcons de la Mescla.** These "balconies" drop almost vertically to the churning waters far below. To return to Castellane, follow the D71 east, turn north on the D90 (a steep, narrow road), and north again on the D955 to rejoin the D952. For an easier route, take the D71 east to the D21 at Comps-sur-Artuby. Turn east on this road, then almost immediately left on the D955 and proceed north to the D952. ∎

**Castellane** 323 F3 ✉ rue Nationale ☎ 04 92 83 61 14 **verdontourisme.com** • **Moustiers-Ste.-Marie** 323 F3 ✉ place de l'Église ☎ 04 92 74 67 84 or 04 92 72 56 60 (sailing club) **moustiers.fr**

# More Places to Visit in Provence

## Haute-Provence

Located in Provence's northeast corner, the Haute-Provence is a mountainous region of remote villages, river gorges, pine forests, and sheep pastures. Discover the area by narrow-gauge railroad, the **Chemins de Fer de Provence** *(trainprovence.com)*, which runs from Nice to the spa town of **Digne-les-Bains** *(place du Tampinet, tel 04 92 36 62 62, ot-dignelesbains.fr)*, the regional capital as well as the processing center for the lavender crop. Near the Italian border, **Parc National du Mercantour** *(contact Bureau des Guides de Mercantour, tel 04 93 04 67 88, mercantour-roya.com or tel 04 93 16 78 88, mercantour.eu)* shelters ibex and chamois (see p. 331). At the **Musée des**

---

**EXPERIENCE:**
## Seek out Art Refuges

In the Hautes Alpes of Provence, acclaimed British land artist Andy Goldsworthy has decorated a series of mountain refuges in his inimitable style, reflecting and appreciating the many varied forms of nature. You can follow the entire 93-mile (150 km) route, staying in some of the refuges, or visit them individually. Start from the **Gassendi Museum** *(tel 04 92 31 45 29, musee-gassendi.org)* in Digne, where there is an introductory exhibition on the route. Ask at the museum for a key to the refuges or to arrange a guide.

---

**Merveilles** *(avenue 16 Septembre, tel 04 93 04 32 50, museedes merveilles.com)* in Tende, you'll find amazing carvings and interactive exhibits relating to the park's fascinating prehistory.

## St.-Rémy-de-Provence

On the fertile plain north of the Chaîne des Alpilles lies this market town. In 1889, Vincent van Gogh was a patient at **St.-Paul-de-Mausole** hospital. You can visit its 12th-century cloister and also the **Centre d'Art Présence van Gogh** in the 18th-century Hôtel Estrine. The **Musée des Arômes et des Parfums** is dedicated to herb growing. St.-Rémy is most celebrated for the ruins of a Greco-Roman town at nearby **Glanum,** which has baths, a forum, a theater, and a sacred spring. *saintremy-de-provence.com* ▲ 323 D3 **Visitor Information** ✉ place Jean-Jaurès ☎ 04 90 92 05 22

## Tarascon

Perched beside the Rhône, Tarascon is dominated by its 15th-century Gothic château, once a medieval cultural hub. The 12th-century **Église de Ste.-Marthe,** opposite, is dedicated to the saint who reputedly saved the town from an amphibious monster, the Tarasque, a feat celebrated on the last weekend in June. The **Musée Souleïado** *(souleiado .com)* displays antique and contemporary Provençal fabrics, with workshops and a shop. *tarascon.org* ▲ 323 D3 **Visitor Information** ✉ avenue de la Republique ☎ 04 90 91 03 52

# LANGUEDOC-ROUSSILLON

The "other" South of France, Languedoc-Roussillon, is every bit as dazzling as Provence and the Côte d'Azur, but flaunts itself less. Its two provinces extend from the Rhône to the Pyrenees, and from the coast to the highlands of the Cévennes, Corbières, and Minervois. Languedoc owes its name to the medieval language of the troubadours, *la langue d'oc*. In Spanish-flavored Roussillon, the Catalan language is still common, and on village squares you may well witness the national dance, the *sardaña*.

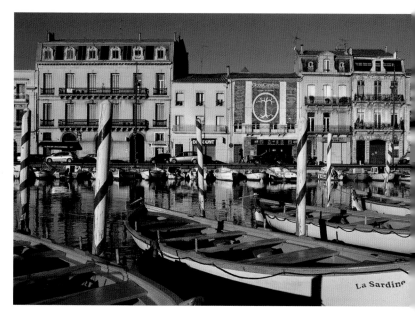

■ The busy port of Sète boasts a network of canals and bridges surrounded by old buildings.

No other region in the whole of France encompasses such a wide variety of landscapes. The wine villages of the coastal plain, surrounded by vineyards and thyme-scented *garrigue*, epitomize the sunbaked Midi; beneath the soaring, snowcapped Pyrenees, orchards of peach and plum, almond and cherry flourish among pastures rich with wildflowers in spring and threaded by hikers' paths. Walkers will relish the lonely Corbières hills and the uplands of the Haut-Languedoc. The fishing villages and saltwater lagoons are a paradise not only for wildlife (as well as birdspotters and other lovers of wildlife), but also for artists.

There is a rich legacy of Roman *(romain)* and Romanesque *(roman)* architecture, from the Roman monuments of Nîmes and the Pont du Gard to the Moorish-influenced Romanesque abbeys of Roussillon.

A romance language derived from Latin, the langue d'oc takes its name ultimately from the Latin formula for "yes," *hoc ille*. In the South of France this became *oc,* in the north *il*. Thus the language of the south became known as *langue d'oc* and that of the north as *langue d'oïl*–the language that now constitutes modern French.

The language of the troubadours and their lyric poetry, the langue d'oc survived determined efforts by the French to eradicate it. You can still hear it in the patois spoken by older people in markets and cafés, and in the Occitan (Provençal) language now taught in schools and universities. It's the poetic tongue of the defiant and undefeated. ∎

## Dancing the Sardana

When most people think of Catalan culture, it is in the context of northeastern Spain, and the region known as Catalonia. But that culture extends across the French border into the Roussillon region, where you might hear the Catalan language spoken in the streets or the markets of many towns. On those same streets you might well witness the dance that proves definitively that Catalans (in both Spain and France) dance to the beat of a completely different drum. The unkind observer of this strange communal dance of Catalonia would remark that the *sardana* reflects a somewhat chilly sobriety for which Catalans are known elsewhere, especially throughout Spain.

Sardana dancers hold hands in a circle and, accompanied by multiple musicians playing various kinds of flutes, proceed to bob about in a rather controlled fashion—they take a series of steps to the right, then one back, and then the same to the left.

When the dancers decide to get *really* crazy, they raise their arms in the air for a moment. Travelers who may have witnessed some of France's other traditional dance moves—say the can-can in Paris—may find themselves a little underwhelmed by this comparatively restful ritual. Even many Catalans will admit to finding the whole thing a little boring, yet others turn up for a twirl at 6 p.m. on Saturdays and noon on Sundays in many town squares, one of the best chances you will have to witness this unique traditional dance, whose origins lie in old folk dances of northeastern Catalonia.

# MONTPELLIER

**Founded in the tenth century, Montpellier is now one of the fastest growing cities in the South of France. Its ancient medical school and university still attract many students.**

Life in Montpellier revolves around **Place de la Comédie,** a square that bustles with cafés. At one end stand the 19th-century opera house that gives the *place* its name and a fountain topped by Étienne d'Antoine's statue of the three Graces. North and west of the place lie the car-free, winding medieval streets lined with stately 17th- and 18th-century mansions.

In the 16th and 17th centuries, Montpellier became a stronghold of Protestantism. Louis XIII subjected the city to a devastating eight-month siege in 1622, leaving little of its medieval fabric intact. But the city turned this to its advantage, building great mansions arranged around courtyards with stone staircases. Ones open to visitors include the **Hôtel de Manse** on Rue Embouque-d'Or and the **Hôtel des Trésoriers de la Bourse** on Rue Ancien-Courrier. The Hôtel Lunaret on Rue des Trésoriers-de-France, a masterpiece built by Jacques Coeur, Charles VII's treasurer, houses the **Musée Languedocien** *(entrance at 7 rue Jacques Coeur, tel 04 67 52 93 03, musee-languedocien.com, closed Sun.).*

The 17th-century former bishops' palace beside the cathedral, now the medical school, contains the French and Italian drawings of the **Musée**

■ **At the center of Montpellier, a lively university town founded in the tenth century, is the Place de la Comédie.**

**Atger.** The superb **Musée Fabre** *(39 boulevard Bonne Nouvelle, tel 04 67 14 83 00, museefabre.fr)* has works by Veronese, Courbet, Poussin, Delaunay, and others.

To savor Montpellier's setting between the Cévennes and the sea, stroll along the **Promenade du Peyrou,** formal 18th-century gardens dominated by a neoclassical *château d'eau,* an elaborate fountain, and the aqueduct that used to bring water to the city. North of the promenade is the **Jardin des Plantes,** one of the oldest botanical gardens in Europe.

Like its neighbor and rival, Nîmes, Montpellier prides itself on its modern architecture, including Ricardo Bofill's postmodern Antigone quarter (east of Esplanade Charles-de-Gaulle) and squares based on a reinterpretation of classical architecture. ■

**Montpellier** ⚇ 322 C3 Visitor Information ✉ allée Jean-de-Lattre de Tassigny ☎ 04 67 60 60 60 **ot-montpellier.fr**

# NÎMES

**Nîmes combines ancient history and modern life with tremendous brio and zest, at its most colorful during the Féria du Pentecôte, the annual bullfighting and folklore festival in May.**

The Romans settled Nîmes around the spring of Nemausus, building various fortifications. Emperor Augustus gave the city its walls and gates, as recorded on the **Porte d'Auguste.** Most impressive is **Les Arènes** (tel 04 66 21 82 56, arenesdenimes.com), an oval arena two stories high, engineered and constructed in the first century A.D. The seating was segregated according to rank and gender. The city's other Roman glory, the 2,000-year old temple known as the **Maison Carrée,** is now an exhibition space for archaeological research. Opposite stands the **Carrée d'Art,** a vast art gallery and library designed by British architect Norman Foster as a glass-and-aluminum tribute to the ancient temple. The old town is a jumble of narrow streets, shady squares, and fountains. Many of the 16th- and 17th-century houses are a legacy of the textile industry (this is the birthplace of the fabric called "de Nîmes"—denim), founded by enterprising Protestants. For a quiet retreat, head to the **Jardin de la Fontaine** (quai de la Fontaine), which has the springs and ruins of a Roman nymphaeum. The **Tour Magne** above, part of Augustus's city walls, offers good views of the city. ∎

---

**INSIDER TIP:**

A must-taste treat is the locally made *croquant villaret,* an almond cookie that is great with coffee.

—SHEILA BUCKMASTER
*National Geographic editor at large*

## Good Seats

Constructed around the year 70 A.D. to hold 20,000 people, the Roman amphitheater in Nîmes is one of the largest and best preserved in France. The original fighting spectacles featured animals and gladiators. Spectators, positioned according to social status, were shaded from the sun by a canopy supported by ropes attached to poles. Now you can see the Roman games staged as a historic pageant with several hundred participants in gladiatorial combat. You can also attend bullfights (see sidebar p. 357).

**Nîmes** 🗺 323 D3 Visitor Information ✉ 6 rue Auguste ☎ 04 66 58 38 00 nimes-tourisme.com • **Maison Carrée** ✉ place de la Maison Carrée ☎ 04 66 21 82 56 • **Carrée d'Art** ✉ place de la Maison Carrée ☎ 04 66 76 35 70 🕐 Closed Mon. 💲 $

# PONT DU GARD

As beautiful as it is functional, the Pont du Gard is an indication of the heroic scale on which the Romans built and thought. The problem was simple enough: The spring at Nîmes was not sufficient to supply the growing city with water. The solution was radical: Fresh water would be piped from springs at Uzès, some 30 miles (48 km) away, along a system of aqueducts, trenches, and tunnels carved out of the solid rock. The total drop was a mere 56 feet (17 m), and the engineering skills involved were immense.

The Pont du Gard is a tribute to Roman engineering skills.

Two millennia later, the aqueduct spans the Gardon River virtually unchanged, despite the depredations of time. Even the marks of the Roman builders can still be seen on some of the stones (the largest of which weighs 6 tons/5.4 t), along with graffiti left by young French *compagnons* or journeymen masons, for whom this used to be a place of pilgrimage.

You may wonder why it was necessary to build on such a monumental scale. In winter, the river may swell to become a rushing torrent, capable of destroying modern bridges. The Roman engineers designed the aqueduct with a slight curve that enabled it to withstand a great pressure of water; it was tested again in recent years, when floods devastated Nîmes. Other technical refinements are the almost imperceptible fall that carried the water along and the waterproof rendering that sealed the inside of the channel along the top.

The Pont du Gard is just outside the village of Remoulins. You can see it from the visitor centers on both banks of the Gardon River. For the right bank, turn off from the D981; for the left bank, take the D19. ■

**Pont du Gard** 🗻 323 D3 Visitor Information ✉ place des Grands Jours, Remoulins ☎ 04 66 37 50 99 💲 $$$ per vehicle **pontdugard.fr**

# CARCASSONNE

The turreted and machicolated double walls of Carcassonne crystallize our notions of the perfect medieval citadel. Sieges heroically resisted, knights in armor jousting in the lists, and troubadour romance spring to mind in this evocative setting.

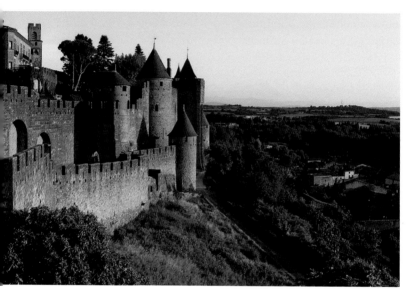

■ The medieval fortress of Carcassonne, overlooking southern France countryside, has seen its fair share of history.

The largest and most impressive medieval citadel in Europe, Carcassonne was known to the Celts and fortified by the Romans. Commanding the communication route between Toulouse and the Mediterranean, it was coveted by Visigoths, Saracens, and Charlemagne. In the 13th century, Simon de Montfort's army arrived at Carcassonne, by then a Cathar stronghold, and—fresh from their massacre of the Cathars of Béziers—besieged and captured it.

De Montfort made the citadel the headquarters for his murderous raids. The inhabitants rebelled, but Louis IX moved them to the new *bastide* he built below the city. Thus the twin sites of Carcassonne evolved. In the late 13th century, Philip the Bold massively strengthened the citadel's defenses, creating a bulwark against Spain.

But when the French annexed

Roussillon in 1659, the Spanish border shifted southward, and the citadel became redundant. The *ville basse* prospered and the *cité* declined so far that in the mid-19th century it was decided to demolish the remaining fortifications. Mercifully, the architect and medievalist Viollet-le-Duc stepped in to save this jewel. Thanks to him, we can now see a complete medieval city. Wander between the two sets of ramparts, then penetrate the twin sandstone towers of the **Narbonne Gate,** with its portcullis

and drawbridge. Inside is a warren of meticulously restored medieval houses (not to mention hotels, restaurants, and souvenir stores).

The core of the city is the 12th-century **Château Comtal.** Walk around the ramparts past medieval defenses: watchtowers, posterns, and machicolations for hurling boiling oil and stones on attackers. The Romanesque and Gothic **Cathédrale St.-Nazaire** boasts superb stained glass and the 13th-century "siege stone," perhaps depicting the siege of Carcassonne in 1209. ■

## EXPERIENCE: Drinking Pastis in a French Café

Sit in the quiet shade of a café terasse, order a pastis, an anise-flavored liqueur that's served ice-cold, and take part in an age-old tradition of the south of France.

The story goes that a monk in pursuit of the elixir of life invented this drink, which is now among France's most popular. (Others say it was the invention of a hermit who resided in the Luberon forest, but hermits are notoriously bad at self-promotion, so we'll never know). Whoever it was, the inventor stewed aromatic local herbs—thyme, star anise, fennel—in a giant pot. The resulting concoction, it was claimed, protected the imbiber from the plague and quenched his

thirst. In 1932, Paul Ricard commercialized the drink, and it's often referred to as Ricard. Its popularity may have coincided with the fact that dangerous absinthe had been outlawed just years before, and this lesser evil was a suitable substitute.

You'll be served the liqueur in a tall glass, accompanied by a bottle of cool water and a bowl of ice. As you add water into the amber-colored pastis, the mixture turns milky. It's up to you to decide the proportions of pastis and water, typically 1 to 5. Add the ice last. No matter what, it's the perfect refreshing drink to order at a French café on a hot, dusty afternoon. The French love it as an apéritif as well.

**Carcassonne** 🅰 323 B2 Visitor Information ✉ 28 rue de Verdun
☎ 04 68 10 24 30 **carcassonne-tourisme.com Château Comtal**
☎ 04 68 11 70 72 💲 $; guided tour obligatory

**THE CITY ABLAZE** The annual Festival de la Cité begins July 8 and culminates in the "Burning of the City" (L'embrasement de la Cité) on July 14—Bastille Day, the great French national holiday.

# DRIVE THE CATHAR TRAIL

**Follow this trail to the last strongholds of the Cathars, where they took refuge in perilously inaccessible castles and fortified hilltop villages, in the wild and inhospitable foothills of the Pyrenees. Though the route is mountainous, the driving isn't difficult.**

The golden era of Languedoc was cut short in the 13th century with the crusade against Cathar heretics. The Cathars (also known as Albigensians after the town of Albi) pursued a faith of high moral principles ("Cathar" is derived from the Greek *katharos*, meaning "pure") and were critical of Church corruption.

The key to their heresy lay in their Manichean belief in the dual powers of good and evil, and the resulting conviction that only the world of the spirit was good, while the material world was irredeemably evil. Their leaders, known as *perfecti*, traveled the countryside preaching in *langue d'oc*. In 1209, the pope and

> **NOT TO BE MISSED:**
>
> **Villerouge-Termenès •
> Château de Peyrepertuse •
> Château de Quéribus •Musée
> de Quercorb •Montségur**

the French king launched a crusade led by the ruthless Simon de Montfort. The heretics sought refuge in the castles of the Corbières, whose names are now forever linked with the memory of the doomed Cathars.

A mountain drive takes you to a number of Cathar castles (*payscathare.org*). Start from **Couiza** on the D118, 25 miles

See also area map p. 323
► Cuiza
115 miles (180 km)
1 day
► Montségur

(40 km) south of Carcassonne, and take the D613 east to **Arques ❶** *(tel 04 68 69 82 87)*, with its preserved 13th-century keep. Turn north on the D40 for a difficult climb to the ruins of **Termes ❷** *(tel 04 68 70 09 20)* and the **Château de Durfort ❸**, dramatically perched over a ravine. Montfort's capture of the apparently unassailable Termes in 1210 sent shudders of foreboding through all the other Cathar fortresses in the region.

Return to the D613 and go east to the village of **Villerouge-Termenès ❹** *(tel 04 68 70 09 11)*. This was the refuge of the last Cathar "perfect," who was finally burned at the stake in 1321. A banquet is held in the courtyard each year in his honor.

Double back on the D613 for 2 miles (3 km) to just beyond Félines-Termenès, then head south to Padern, through the rocky gorge of the Torgan River. Go west on the D14 to some mighty spectacular castles. **Château de Peyrepertuse ❺** *(tel 04 82 53 24 07, chateau-peyrepertuse.com, $)* is reached by a 30-minute drive up a long, winding road. The castle stretches out to fit its dizzy perch, with one narrow entrance. Inside is a Romanesque chapel, and beyond it another flight of exposed steps leads up to the final refuge.

Visible from Peyrepertuse is **Château de Quéribus ❻** *(tel 04 68 45 03 69, cucugnan.fr)*, its keep and chapel dominating the Roussillon plain. Backtrack on the D14 for 5 miles (8 km) and take the D123 to reach this last stronghold of the Cathars. It proved impregnable, finally surrendering peacefully in 1255. A single stairway is still the only access.

Proceed southwest on the D19 and D117 to **Puilaurens ❼** *(tel 04 68 20 65 26)*, bristling with machicolations, arrow-slit windows, and ramparts. The single stone stairway, zigzagging precariously to the top, ensured that no assailant went unnoticed. Take the D117 to Quillan, south of Couiza, and head west, still on the D117, to **Puivert ❽** *(tel 04 68 20 80 98, chateau-de-puivert .com)*, more palace than castle. You can also visit the **Musée de Quercorb** *(16 rue Bairy du Lion, tel 04 68 20 80 98, museequercorb.com, closed, Nov.–March)*, for exhibitions on local traditions and medieval music. Farther west (on the D117 and D9) rises the rock of **Montségur,** the Cathar headquarters and site of a terrible massacre (see p. 319).

# ROMANESQUE ABBEYS

Among the chief glories of Languedoc-Roussillon are its Romanesque abbeys. These lovely buildings, dating from the 10th to 12th centuries, combine simple, austere spaces with exquisitely carved stone capitals and panels. Some are set in remote places and preserve the peaceful monastic atmosphere. These abbeys have been beautifully restored, and you can see several in a tour of the Roussillon *département* around Perpignan.

## St.-Michel-de-Cuxa

Founded by the Benedictines in 878, the lovely monastery of St.-Michel-de-Cuxa outside Prades is actually pre-Romanesque. Its unusual keyhole-shaped arches are in the Mozarabic style, a legacy of the Moorish occupation of the region. The abbey's surviving great square tower is beautifully silhouetted against the dark massif of Mont Canigou. The finest of the capitals from the 12th-century pink marble cloister, looted after the revolution, was found in Prades in 1909 and sold to the Metropolitan Museum of Art in New York City.

## St.-Martin-du-Canigou

On a crag set high up on the remote

### Pablo Casals Festival: Celebrating a Local Star

As the Spanish Civil War drew to a close, the great Catalan cellist Pablo Casals took refuge in the little Pyrenean town of **Prades,** escaping from Franco. At the end of World War II, bitterly disappointed at the reluctance of the West to liberate Spain from the fascists, he protested by refusing to play in public, calling this "the greatest sacrifice of my life."

Attempts were made to persuade him to perform in the U.S. for large sums of money, but he always refused. Eventually the Americans decided to come to him and suggested a musical festival in Prades. This became the **Prades Bach festival** *(tel 04 68 96 33 07, prades-festival-casals .com, late July–early Aug.),* now a key date on the European music calendar. St.-Michel-de-Cuxa is the primary performing space, its high Romanesque vault providing sublime acoustics, with many other concerts in small area churches.

**St.-Michel-de-Cuxa** ⛰ 322 B1 Visitor Information ✉ rue de Taurinya ☎ 04 68 96 15 35 🕐 Closed a.m. Sun. & religious holidays 💲 $ **abbaye-cuxa.com • St.-Martin-du-Canigou** ☎ 04 68 05 50 03 🕐 Closed Mon. & Jan.; guided visits only 💲 $ **stmartinducanigou.org**

slopes of Mont Canigou, the silent, ascetic retreat of St.-Martin-du-Canigou is accessible only by jeep or a 40-minute climb from Castél on foot. But its beauty and setting more than repay the effort. A guided tour showcases the cloister, Romanesque chapel, and tombs of Guifred, Count of Cerdagne (who founded the monastery in the 11th century in penance for killing his wife and his son), and his second wife.

## Serrabone

The Augustinian priory of Serrabone also clings to the side of Mont Canigou, commanding a spectacular view of the surrounding peaks. It is set in a lovely garden of vines, shrubs, and fragrant herbs (where you may picnic). The beautifully simple 11th-century church houses a splendid tribune of pink marble columns and arches, carved with an astonishing array of mythical beasts, flowers, and human figures. The marble cloister arches frame the mountain views.

## Elne

Among the orchards and vines south of Perpignan is the ancient town of Elne, which every year hosts a music festival in its 11th-century cathedral. Elne's incomparable treasure is its cloister, where the marble capitals were vigorously carved; several feature monks peeking around doors.

The picturesque village of St.-Guilhem-le-Désert surrounds its ninth-century abbey.

The oldest (12th century) and finest tell the Creation story: The panel of Adam and Eve is a masterpiece.

## St.-Guilhem-le-Désert

Half hidden in the Hérault gorge, north of Montpellier, are the picturesque village and austere abbey of St.-Guilhem-le-Désert. Guilhem of Aquitaine, a lieutenant of Charlemagne, founded the abbey in the ninth century. His piety, coupled with a relic of the True Cross awarded him by Charlemagne, assured him a following.

You climb up to the abbey through the charming village below. The abbey church is a perfect example of the simplicity and strength of Romanesque building, with a great barrel-vaulted nave, massive pillars, and sturdy arches. Two galleries of the cloister are still here, but to see the rest you must go to the Cloisters, part of the Metropolitan Museum of Art in New York, where they join those from St.-Michel-de-Cuxa. ■

**Serrabone** 322 B1 Visitor Information ✉ Prieuré de Serrabone et Jardin Mediterranéen, Boule d'Amont ☎ 04 68 84 09 30 💲 $ • **Elne** 322 B1 Visitor Information ✉ 2bis Rue du Couvent ☎ 04 68 22 05 07 **tourisme -pyrenees-mediterranee.com** • **St.-Guilhem-le-Désert** 322 C3 ✉ St.-Guilhem-le-Désert ☎ 04 67 56 41 97 **saintguilhem-valleeherault.fr**

# COLLIOURE & THE CÔTE VERMEILLE

The Côte Vermeille, where the Pyrenees meet the Mediterranean, is the most beautiful stretch of the Languedoc coast. The jewel is the little port of Collioure. Its brilliant light, painted fishing boats, and stuccoed houses inspired Matisse and others to experiment with the violent eruptions of pure color that earned them the soubriquet fauvist (literally "wild beast").

Collioure's harbor is flanked by **Château Royal** *(tel 04 68 82 06 43)*, built by the Knights Templar in the 13th century. It now hosts art exhibitions. The 14th-century **Église de Notre-Dame-des-Anges** uses the former lighthouse as its bell tower. Three small sheltered beaches extend beneath harborside eateries with sunny terraces. South of Collioure, the road runs past the terraced vineyards of **Banyuls-sur-Mer.** Stop at **Cap Béar** for a fine panorama. Banyuls has palm-shaded cafés, a little beach, and wine *caves* along the ancient narrow streets. On its southern side is an oceanographic research institute with an aquarium of sea life. At the most southerly point of the French coast, **Cerbère** flies the red-and-gold Catalan flag. ∎

## Dynamite Beach

To appreciate the efforts made to conserve the beaches along the Mediterranean, visit **Paulilles** on the Côte Vermeille. A fine sandy beach, fringed by pines, sheltered by hills and vineyards, with safe swimming, Paulilles is close to the marine reserve of Banyuls. Until 1984, the beach was also the site of a dynamite factory.

Dynamite inventor (and Nobel Prize endower) Alfred Nobel founded the factory in 1870. He chose the site because it was far from the eastern front with Germany and close to Port Vendres *(Maison de site Paulilles, tel 04 68 95 23 40)*, which enabled easy shipping to French colonies.

After the site closed, it fell into neglect, and groups vied to pursue projects such as a nuclear power station and a pharaonic marina. Finally the Conservatoire de Littoral intervened, and now the site is a triumph: Paulilles includes a museum and preserved industrial buildings, a fine park of exotic trees and plants, and a public beach. The marine area around the beach is also a protected zone.

**Collioure** ⓜ 322 C1 Visitor Information ✉ place du 18 Juin ☎ 04 68 82 15 47 **collioure.com • Banyuls-sur-Mer** ⓜ 322 C1 Visitor Information ✉ avenue République ☎ 04 68 88 31 58 **banyuls-sur-mer.com**

# CÉRET & THE TECH VALLEY

A 14th-century single-span bridge across the Tech River, the Pont du Diable leads into the winding streets and shady squares of Spanish-style Céret, capital of the Vallespir (the Tech Valley). Catalan Céret is a lively center, with colorful Easter celebrations, an international festival in August, and bullfights in its arena.

## Céret

Céret's charms once attracted artists like Picasso and Braque. Here, they painted works such as "Landscape at Céret" (Picasso, 1911) and "Rooftops, Céret" (Braque, 1911). Their evenings at the **Grand Café** *(boulevard Maréchal-Joffre)* left tangible evidence: several Picasso drawings on café notepaper.

Céret has a fine **Musée d'Art Moderne** *(8 boulevard Maréchal-Joffre, tel 04 68 87 27 76, musee-ceret.com, closed Tues. Oct.–April)*. A modern building of ocher terraces and shady patios, the museum houses works by Catalan artists Capdeville and Tapiès, as well as canvases by Dufy and Chagall; a series of ceramic bowls from Vallauris by Picasso, depicting bullfighting; and an early Picasso, "Portrait of Corina Père Romeu" (1902).

## Tech Valley

The valley stretches westward from Céret to the Roman spa town of **Amélie-les-Bains.** A few miles farther on the D115 is **Arles-sur-Tech** *(ville-arles-sur-tech.fr)*, where a Benedictine abbey was founded in 900. The Romanesque church was rebuilt in the 12th century.

Farther up the valley is the **Gorges de la Fou,** allegedly the world's narrowest gorge. An iron walkway winds through the cliffs, accessible only on foot and with the mandatory protective headgear. ∎

■ **Pont du Diable (Bridge of the Devil), a favorite subject for artists**

**Céret** 🗺 322 B1 Visitor Information ✉ 1 avenue Georges-Clemenceau ☎ 04 68 87 00 53 **ot-ceret.fr • Amélie-les-Bains** 🗺 322 B1 Visitor Information ✉ 2 avenue de Vallespir ☎ 04 68 39 01 98 **amelie-les-bains.com**

# PERPIGNAN & FRENCH CATALONIA

With its historical roots in the county of Barcelona and the kingdoms of Aragon and Majorca, it is not surprising that Roussillon often feels more Spanish than French. It is proudly conscious of its distinct identity as French Catalonia: The red-and-yellow Catalan flag flutters everywhere, the national dance, the *sardaña*, is danced solemnly in village squares, and many people speak Catalan, sometimes still as a first language.

■ Winding streets and colorful facades make up the old quarter of Perpignan, the capital of French Catalonia.

The welcoming, sunny southern city of **Perpignan** is the capital of French Catalonia, with a strong Spanish influence underscored by the large population of émigrés from Franco's Spain.

The **Palais des Rois de Majorque** takes up virtually a quarter of the old town—in the 13th century, the city was the capital of the kings of Majorca. Within its 17th-century ram-

parts, the vast two-story palace and its arcaded courtyard, its beautifully frescoed and tiled royal chapels, and its great Gothic hall show unmistakable Spanish-Moorish influence.

The focus of the old town lies to the north, in **Place de la Loge.** Here, among pink marble-paved streets and narrow alleys, stands the **Loge de Mer.** Built in exquisite 14th-century Gothic style as the city's stock exchange and maritime court, it boasts carved wooden ceilings and sculpted windows. The ground floor houses a restaurant where you can inspect the glories up close. Its gargoyles and filigree balustrades, meanwhile, may be contemplated from one of the cafés on the square. Beside it stands the 14th-century **Hôtel de Ville,** with its superb 17th-century gates, and the 15th-century Roussillon parliament building, the **Palais de la Députation.**

**Le Castillet,** a 14th-century gateway, houses the **Musée Casa Païral,** a museum that documents the rich Catalan heritage of traditions and crafts. **Musée Rigaud** shows work by Perpignan-born Hyacinthe Rigaud, along with paintings by Dufy

## Perpignan's Good Friday Procession

The most dramatic time to be in Perpignan is Good Friday, when you can witness La Sanch procession to the cathedral. This walk has taken place since the Middle Ages, when the Red Penitents Brotherhood accompanied condemned prisoners to the gallows. Today the penitents wind slowly through the medieval streets of the old town, tolling bells, garbed in sinister pointed black hoods and red robes, some barefoot, carrying crucifixes and reliquaries. Young and old participate, and locals and visitors cram the streets to watch.

and Picasso and works by sculptor Aristide Maillol.

The 14th-century **Cathédrale de St.-Jean** dominates Place de Gambetta, a former parade ground lined with 16th-century houses. Built by the kings of Majorca, the cathedral is in the Roussillon style of red brick and pebbles and has a typical southern Gothic wrought-iron bell tower. Inside, candlelight illuminates frescoed walls, stained glass, and a glowing gilt altar. In a chapel on the south side hangs the harrowing 14th-century wooden statue of the Devôt Christ, which is carried through the streets on Good Friday by a brotherhood of penitents (see sidebar left). Beside the chapel is the huge **Campo Santo,** one of France's oldest cloistered cemeteries, which has been restored and is now used for atmospheric summer concerts.

## Around Perpignan

The beaches of **St.-Cyprien-Plage** and **Canet-Plage,** within convenient reach of Perpignan, are popular but otherwise unremarkable. The remains of Europe's oldest human being, dating back to about 450,000 B.C., were discovered in 1971 at **Tautavel.** The **Musée de la Préhistoire** tells the story and displays a reconstruction of the famous skull.

Dominating Perpignan is the snowy peak of **Mont Canigou** (9,138 feet/2,785 m), sacred and mystical mountain of the Catalans, with a great iron cross perched on its summit. The climb to the top from Vernet-les-Bains to Cortalets is a great experience. ∎

**Perpignan** 🗺 322 B2 Visitor Information ✉ place Armand Lanoux ☎ 04 68 66 30 30 **perpignantourisme.com** • **Palais des Rois de Majorque** ✉ 4 rue des Archers, Perpignan ☎ 04 68 35 42 05 💲 $ • **Musée Casa Païral (Le Castillet)** ✉ place Verdun, Perpignan ☎ 04 68 66 30 30 🕐 Closed Tues. 💲 $ • **Musée Rigaud** ✉ 16 rue de l'Ange, Perpignan ☎ 04 68 35 43 40 🕐 Closed Tues. 💲 $ • **Tautavel** 🗺 322 B2 • **Musée de la Préhistoire** ✉ avenue Leon-Jean-Gregory, Tautavel ☎ 04 68 29 07 76 💲 $$ **450000ans.com**

# More Places to Visit in Languedoc-Roussillon

## Béziers

This lively city climbs steeply up the left bank of the Orb River to the vast 14th-century **Cathédrale St.-Nazaire.** Southwest of Béziers stands **Oppidum d'Ensérune,** one of France's most important pre-Roman sites. *beziers-mediterranee.com* 322 C2 **Visitor Information** 1 boulevard Wilson 04 99 41 36 36

---

**INSIDER TIP:**

Salvador Dalí called Perpignan's train station the "center of the universe." It's certainly a great hub for day trips around the region, but the city's Catalan influence on food and festivities is the bigger draw.

—DAVE YODER
*National Geographic photographer*

---

## Canal du Midi

Stretching some 150 miles (241 km) from Toulouse down to the Mediterranean at Sète or Agde, the Canal du Midi is a magnificent feat of engineering and an architectural masterpiece (see sidebar p. 301). Today it attracts leisure boaters and hikers. 322 A2–C2

## Narbonne

Capital of the largest Roman province in Gaul and a great port until the Middle Ages, Narbonne is thriving again thanks to the surrounding wine region. At its heart looms the fortified **Palais des Archevêques,** the archbishops' palace, built in the 13th and 14th centuries. Beside it, the Gothic cathedral displays a fine cloister, 14th-century stained glass, and tapestries. Behind lies a vestige of Roman Narbo, underground warehouses known as the **Horreum.** *narbonne-tourisme.com* 322 B2 **Visitor Information** 31 rue Jean Jaurès 04 68 65 15 60

## Sète

Stroll along Sète's **Grand Canal** to discover a string of fine seafood eateries. Sète is liveliest in August during the water jousting tournaments. *ot-sete.fr* 322 C3 **Visitor Information** 60 Grand Rue Mario-Roustan 04 99 04 71 71

## Villefranche-de-Conflent

Founded in the 12th century, Villefranche has a fine medieval garrison. Its alterations date from the 17th century, when Vauban added massive ramparts, gates, and **Fort Libéria.** The fort is accessible by path or underground passage. *villefranchedeconflent.com* 322 B1 **Visitor Information** place de l'Église 04 68 96 22 96

An island in the Mediterranean 140 miles (225 km) from Nice and 90 miles (145 km) from Italy—part of France now but Italian for centuries

# CORSICA

# CORSICA

Perhaps the best way to soak up the flavor of Corsica is to sip an aperitif on a café terrace in the early evening and observe the *passeggiata*–locals on their nightly stroll. Like the local language, this custom is more Italian than French, but Corsica is far too independent to be described in terms of either. It has been a French province since 1769, after several centuries of Italian rule. In the 18th century, it enjoyed a brief (and nostalgically evoked) period of autonomy.

Bonifacio's fortified upper town blends into the limestone cliffs on which it sits.

The third largest island in all the Mediterranean, Corsica is a very wild and beautiful place, which has been aptly described as a mountain in the sea. The coastline is glorious, with rugged cliffs and wonderful beaches. Parts are now fully developed resorts with huge marinas, water sports of all kinds, and frenetic nightlife to match the mainland's. Coastal ports such as Ajaccio, Bastia, and Bonifacio are as colorful and lively as anywhere in the Mediterranean. But there are still lots of remote coves and deserted beaches to discover, and the mountains are a nature lover's paradise. Corsica also has a legacy of fine Romanesque churches and several important megalithic monuments, most notably the stone warriors of Filitosa.

The real Corsica lives on behind the coastal facade: Shepherds still move their flocks between lowlands and higher pastures every year, and religious festivals are celebrated with medieval passion. In the mountains and fortified citadels, Corsica's stormy past of bandits and vendettas never seems very far away. ∎

## NOT TO BE MISSED:

The *passeggiata*—evening stroll—in the old town of Bastia   382

Swimming in the sparkling clear water off Cap Corse   385

A boat trip around the Golfe de Porto   386

The curious ancient menhirs of Filitosa   386

Walking along the GR20 across the mountains   388

The all-pervasive scent of Corsica's wildflowers   388

A Corsican goat (also known as *Corse*) gazes toward Centuri village, on the Cap Corse peninsula.

# AROUND THE ISLAND

**The most romantic way to get to Corsica is by sea—by ferry either into Bastia in the north or Bonifacio or Ajaccio in the south. As you disembark, the fragrance of the herb-scented maquis, for which the island is famous, greets you.**

Bustling, vibrant, and colorful **Bastia** *(map C4)* is a good starting point. The town is dominated by a great 16th-century Genoese citadel sited above the old harbor. Life revolves around **Place St.-Nicolas** (the tourist office is located here; *tel 04 95 54 20 40, bastia-tourisme .com*), a charming square surrounded by a warren of Italianate streets.

The renovated 14th-century **Palais des Gouverneurs** *(tel 04 95 31 09 12, closed Mon., $)* houses the Musée d'Ethnographie, explaining the history of the island. The port itself has a lively waterfront with plenty of cafés and restaurants flanking the 17th-century **Église de St.-Jean-Baptiste.**

North of Bastia stretches the peninsula of **Cap Corse.** You can drive around it in a day, stopping off at beaches and fishing ports at your leisure.

Located along the eastern shore is **Erbalunga,** a fishing harbor much favored by artists. A rewarding detour might take in the villages of **Macinaggio, Rogliano,** and the castle of **San Colombano.** Down the west coast, the road is often precipitous, but the views are ample compensation. **Canari** boasts an excellent 12th-century Pisan-Romanesque church, with a fine view out to sea. The Genoese watchtower at **Nonza** also gives a magnificent view over the **Golfe de St.-Florent** to the south.

## Nebbio Valley & Monte Grosso

**St.-Florent** *(map 384 C4, visitor information, tel 04 95 37 06 04, corsica-saintflorent.com)* in the Nebbio Valley basin is positively chic, with a marina full of yachts. **L'Île Rousse,** a major resort named for its red cliffs, is best avoided in high summer. Charming **Calvi,** enclosed on its promontory and dominated by a baroque church, can also get very crowded.

A splendid drive leads inland from L'Île-Rousse to **Belgodère** and **Muro,** villages with superb sea views. **Calenzana** *(map 384 B4)* is a starting point for long-distance hiking trails and for the route up Monte Grosso.

■ Sailboats and fishing craft anchor in pretty Macinaggio, a small port town north of Bastia.

The **Golfe de Porto** is so beautiful that it is protected in its entirety; wonderful drives and boat trips go around the coast. The red cliffs at **Calanche,** dipping straight into the sea, are best seen by boat *(ask at the information office in Porto).* **Porto** is a pretty little harbor but very popular; a better bet is **Piana.**

## Ajaccio & Prehistoric Corsica

The capital of southern Corsica is **Ajaccio** *(map 384 A2–A3, visitor information, boulevard du Roi Jerome, tel 04 95 51 53 03, ajaccio-tourisme .com).* Cradled by mountains, this bustling town basks in Corsica's mildest climate. There is a distinctly Arab flavor to its white stucco houses, fountains, and palm trees. Napoleon Bonaparte was born here, and the evidence is everywhere. The **Maison Bonaparte** *(rue St.-Charles, tel 04 95 21 43 89, closed Mon.),* where he grew up, has family portraits and memorabilia. The **Palais Fesch,** built by Napoleon's uncle, houses a superb collection of Italian art plundered during Napoleon's Italian campaign. The **Chapelle Impériale** next door was built by Napoleon III as a Bonaparte family mausoleum. There is a splendid view of the town and the bay from the **Jetée de la Citadelle.** Ajaccio is as

close as you can get to the Côte d'Azur in Corsica, with good restaurants, cafés, a marina crowded with yachts, and a casino. At the bay's northern tip rise the **Îles Sanguinaires,** rocky islets so named as they glow bloodred at sunset.

To the south is **Filitosa** with 3,000-year-old menhirs carved to resemble armed warriors. Some of the best are displayed in the Musée de Préhistoire Corse in Sartène (see next page).

At the extreme south of Corsica is the port of **Bonifacio,** its upper town set on craggy limestone cliffs hollowed into caves by the sea. From here the views in clear weather stretch as far as Sardinia. The 12th-century citadel was once the headquarters of the French Foreign Legion.

## Porto-Vecchio & Inland

The **Golfe de Porto-Vecchio** *(map 384 C2)* offers splendid beaches. This is the beginning of the Côte

**Calvi** ⛰ 384 B4 Visitor Information ✉ Port de Plaisance ☎ 04 95 65 16 67 **balagne-corsica.com • Porto** ⛰ 384 A3 Visitor Information ✉ place de la Marine ☎ 04 95 26 10 55 **portovecchio-tourisme.corsica • Palais Fesch** ✉ 50 rue Fesch ☎ 04 95 26 26 26 🕐 Closed Tues. 💲 $ **musee-fesch.com**

des Nacres (Mother-of-Pearl Coast), with marinas, bars, and discos. Inland is **Solenzara** *(map 384 C2);* winding roads lead to the pass at Col de Bavella, dominated by the statue of Notre-Dame de Bavella.

## Sartène

An inland mountain town of granite walls and cobbled lanes above the Rizzanese Valle, Sartène has an old Genoese palace that is now a wine center with tastings of local Sartènais wine. The **Église de Ste.-Marie** houses the wooden cross and iron chain used for the local religious procession of U Catenacciu (The Chained One). On Good Friday, a citizen, disguised in red robes and hood, reenacts Christ's struggle to carry the cross to Calvary. A candlelit procession follows. The **Musée de Préhistoire Corse** *(rue Croce, tel 04 95 77 01 09, lacorsedesorigines.com)* in Sartène's old prison has archaeological finds from all over the island.

## Corte

Corte is the main university town. From 1755 to 1769, it was the capital of a briefly independent Corsica. The old town's steep streets and the citadel—housing the **Musée de la Corse** *(tel 04 95 45 25 45, museudiacorsica.corsica)*—sit on a rocky promontory. You can reach Corte by the narrow-gauge railroad that runs between Bastia and Ajaccio. ∎

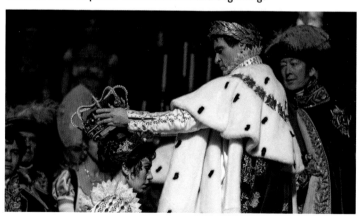

■ **Joaquin Phoenix as Napoleon in Ridley Scott's 2023 epic movie about the Corsican's rise to power from humble island beginnings**

**Filitosa** ◭ 384 B2 ☏ 04 95 74 00 91 **filitosa.fr** • **Bonifacio** ◭ 384 B1 Visitor Information ✉ 2 rue Fred. Scamaioni ☏ 04 95 73 11 88 **bonifacio.fr** • **Sartène** ◭ 331 B2 Visitor Information ✉ 14 cours Soeur Amelie ☏ 04 95 77 15 40 • **Corte** ◭ 384 B3 Visitor Information ✉ La Citadelle ☏ 04 95 46 26 70 **corte-tourisme.com**

# WALKING IN CORSICA

Experiencing Corsica by foot involves rugged landscapes and grand flora. A long-distance trail (GR20) crosses the mountainous center of the island from north to south through the Parc Naturel Régional de la Corse, a vast conservation area of mountains and coastline.

■ A 15-minute drive from bustling Calvi is the perched village of Montemaggiore, a quiet place that's a magnet for hikers.

Starting from Calenzana, just inland from Calvi, and ending at Conca on the Golfe de Porto-Vecchio, the GR20 is about 130 miles (210 km) long and can take up to 15 days to walk. Basic mountain refuges are set along the way (bring your own food). The first section between Calenzana and Vizzavona is the most difficult: Experience in mountain walking is essential, but the rewards are great.

An easier alternative is the **Mare e Monti Trail** between Calenzana and Cargese. You can take the train to Corte or Vizzavona from Ajaccio or Bastia. **Corte** (see p. 387) makes a good base for walking; suggestions are the **Gorges de la Restonica, Lac de Melo,** and the **Forêt de Vizzavona,** where several hiking trails are marked. ■

## Wildflowers

Corsica is famous for its maquis, the aromatic undergrowth of shrubs and herbs that covers most of the island. Once, the island was forested, mainly by oaks, like those at Porto-Vecchio. When the trees were felled, the vegetation became maquis, a spiny thicket of lentisk, Spanish broom and juniper, wild olive, rock rose, thyme, rosemary, and lavender. (In World War II, partisans hid in the maquis of southern France, giving the Resistance its other name, the Maquis.) In Corsica, spring is the best time to see the maquis in flower, with unique species such as the Corsican crocus and Corsican hellebore.

# TRAVELWISE

# TRAVELWISE

## PLANNING YOUR TRIP
### When to Go
Choosing when to go depends on what type of vacation you are looking for. The French Government Tourist Office (FGTO) has a number of offices outside France to advise you (see p. 399). Air France offices abroad also offer many vacation services beyond booking flights (see p. 392). Once you have decided which areas you want to visit, you can contact the region's Comité Departmental de Tourisme (CDT) or the local visitor information office for more information. Most big towns have an Office de Tourisme, while in smaller villages, the town hall (mairie) or the Syndicat D'initiative provides details.

    tourisme.fr
    rendezvousenfrance.com

There are several excellent English-language websites which are a mine of information:

    franceguide.com
    gofrance.com
    holidayfrance.org.uk
    francetourism.com
    paris.org
    visitmonaco.com
    anglophone-direct.com
    france.angloinfo.com
    frenchentree.com
    informationfrance.com
    francethisway.com

### Climate
Partly in both northern and southern Europe, France has three different climates: Atlantic, Mediterranean, and continental. Winter temperatures throughout the country may drop below freezing, with winds and storms lashing the Atlantic coastal regions. Southern Atlantic and Mediterranean France, though much warmer, nevertheless has a chilly winter. Snow is not unknown in the south. The continental climate of eastern France is generally cooler in both winter and summer, but is subject to the greatest extremes, with cold winters followed by hot and sometimes stormy summers.

Overall, winter temperatures in France vary from around 15° to 50°F (-10° to 10°C), and summer temperatures from around 65° to 85°F (18° to 30°C) in the hottest areas.

## Main Events
Throughout the year, France is alive with festivals, ranging from the major traditional fêtes, such as the flower festival in Nice to tiny village celebrations of the local harvest of, say, garlic or chestnuts. Others, such as the famous pardon processions in Brittany, celebrate individual saints' days.

More and more French towns and cities stage cultural events such as jazz, opera, and theater festivals, and these often take place in historic buildings, from Romanesque abbeys to Roman amphitheaters. Depending on the event, most tickets can be bought at the door, but for blockbuster concerts in summer months, reserve in advance online, over the phone, or at the FNAC chains in major towns.

Although most of the major festivals take place during the summer months, others are seasonal; wine festivals, for example, take place in October, after the vendange (grape harvest). Religious festivals are often celebrated with great ceremony, and Easter and Christmas both offer opportunities to see and participate in traditional local events. (See pp. 383–386 for more listings.)

**January** Paris fashion shows; Limoux Carnival.
**February** Menton Lemon Festival; Nice Carnival.

**March** Monte Carlo festival of contemporary film music.

**April** Lourdes Sacred Music Festival; Easter celebrations; Paris marathon; Le Mans motorcycle race.

**May** Cannes Film Festival; Grasse rose show; Mâcon wine fair; Stes.-Marie-de-la-Mer Romany pilgrimage; Monaco Grand Prix; Nîmes feria.

**June** Strasbourg Music Festival; Les Imaginaires at Mont St.-Michel; Chartres International Organ Festival; Noirlac Music Festival; Le Mans 24-hour car race; Chantilly Prix de Diane Hermès horse race.

**July** Tour de France; Aix-en-Provence Festival; Antibes Jazz Festival; Avignon Festival; Bastille Day, celebrated throughout France on the 14th; Nice Jazz Festival; Quimper Fêtes de Cornouailles.

**August** Antibes International fireworks festival; Lorient Celtic Festival; Marciac Jazz Festival; Menton International Chamber Music Festival; Dijon grape harvest and folk fair; Bagnères de Luchon flower festival.

**October** Dijon International Gastronomy Fair; Paris Motor Show; Paris Jazz Festival.

**November** Beaujolais Nouveau celebrations; Beaune wine auction; Dijon Gastronomic Fair.

**December** Paris Boat Show; Strasbourg Christmas market.

## What to Take

You can buy anything you need in France. Pharmacies offer a wide range of drugs and medical supplies, along with expert advice, but you should bring any prescription drugs you might need. If you wear them, a second pair of glasses or contact lenses are a legal requirement if you plan to drive. Sunscreen and anti-mosquito products are advisable in summer. Clothing will depend on your destination and when you travel. You will only need to really dress up for big-city restaurants or for casinos; don't be too casual, however. Sports equipment can be rented, but bring personal equipment like walking boots with you. In France, electricity is 220 volts, 50 Hz, and most plugs have two round pins. If you bring electrical equipment, you will need an adapter, and, for U.S. appliances, a transformer.

Lastly, don't forget the essentials: passport, driver's license, ATM card, and insurance documentation.

## Insurance

Always make sure you have adequate coverage for medical treatment and expenses, including repatriation and baggage and money loss.

## HOW TO GET TO FRANCE

### Passports

U.S. and Canadian citizens need only a passport to enter France for up to 90 days' stay. No visa is required. However, note that starting in 2025, American passport holders traveling to 30 EU countries will need travel authorization via the ETIAS for short term trips.

### Airlines

All the major airlines have flights to France, and many arrange package tours and budget-price flights. Most nonstop flights from North America go to Paris, though some fly to Strasbourg, Nice, and Lyon. You will arrive in Paris from abroad either at Roissy–Charles de Gaulle or Orly Sud airport. Package tours may fly into other airports.

**Air France,**
  airfrance.com
**American Airlines,**
  aa.com
**Continental**,
  continental.com
**Delta,**
  delta.com

**Easyjet,**
easyjet.com
**Ryanair,**
ryanair.com
**United,**
united.com

## Budget Airlines
The growth of budget airlines has created options for less expensive flights from Britain to regional airports in France. It is a volatile market, however, with frequent changes.

## Airports
### Roissy–Charles de Gaulle (CDG)
Tel 01 70 36 39 50 *aeroportsdeparis.fr*
Roissy–Charles de Gaulle is 15 miles (26 km) north of Paris near the A1 autoroute. From here you can get on the Paris *périphérique* (beltway). The airport bus from Roissy–CDG (lines 1 & 2) will take you as far as Rue Scribe; it runs daily 5:45 a.m.–11 p.m. An airport bus goes to the Gare de l'Est main-line railroad station. There is also a rail service (RER B every 15 minutes) with stops at Gare du Nord, Châtelet, St.-Michel, Notre-Dame, Luxembourg, Port Royal, Denfert-Rochereau, and Cité Universitaire. Taxis are very expensive.

### Orly Sud
aeroportsdeparis.fr
Orly is 10 miles (15 km) south of Paris. A shuttle bus links Orly Sud (international flights) to Orly Ouest (national flights) every 15 minutes between 6 a.m. and 11:30 p.m. The jetbus from the Orly airports runs to Denfert-Rochereau Métro station from 6 a.m. to 10:30 p.m. The railroad service from Orly to central Paris (RER C every 15 minutes) takes approximately 40 minutes. Tickets for rail services can be bought inside the airport terminals from a computerized ticket machine.

Buses to connect with rail services are within easy access. Besides renting a car,

the rail links are the easiest way to get into the city, and most railroad stations are close to a Métro station, or linked to one. An airport bus runs between Orly and Roissy–CDG every 20 minutes. The Orlyval bus links up with the RER B rail line, which goes out to Roissy–CDG.

## From the United Kingdom
Eurotunnel (or the Channel Tunnel) offers a fast, frequent rail service (**Eurostar;** *euro star.com*) between London, Lille, and Paris. The SNCF central reservation office is in Paris *(tel 08 36 35 35 35, raileurope.com).* **Le Shuttle** *(eurotunnel.com)* transports cars and passengers between Folkestone and Calais. The journey through the tunnel lasts about 35 minutes. Le Shuttle runs 24 hours a day year-round.

Several ferry and hovercraft services operate from the U.K. to the northern French ports (aferry.co.uk offers a wide choice). For information, contact **Brittany Ferries** (Portsmouth & Plymouth to St.-Malo, Caen, & Roscoff), Wharf Road, Portsmouth P02 8RU, brittany-ferries .com. **Norfolkline** (Dover to Dunkerque), norfolkline.com. **P&O** (Dover to Calais & Portsmouth to Le Havre, Cherbourg, & St.-Malo), Channel View Rd., Dover CT17 9TJ, poferries.com.

## GETTING AROUND
## By Airplane
Air France is the main domestic airline *(tel 08 20 82 08 20, airfrance.com).*

## By Train
The French national railroad, the **SNCF** (Société Nationale des Chemins de Fer), links Paris and all major cities. You can buy train tickets in advance online, from your travel agent or an SNCF office *(sncf-voyages.com),* or at a station or travel agency *(agence de voyage)* in France.

Some services require a seat reservation as well as a ticket, and stations often have separate ticket and reservation desks. You can travel to all major cities from Paris by

TGV (Train à Grande Vitesse), or by regular train. The Motorail service transports passengers together with their cars or motorbikes. Both the TGV and the Motorail service require reservations.

For long-distance journeys, you can travel overnight by *couchette* (shared sleeping car) or *voiture-lit* (private sleeping car). Both of these services must be reserved in advance.

If you buy your train ticket in France, you must punch it at the time-stamping machine *(composteur)* by the platform entrance before boarding. Once stamped, a ticket is valid for 24 hours.

Foreign visitors to France can buy a special vacation rail pass valid for up to one month. The pass costs less than individual tickets and often offers reduced rates on other transportation. Ask for details of La Carte "France Vacances Pass." North Americans have a wide choice of passes, including Eurailpass, Flexipass, and Saver Pass, which can only be purchased in the U.S. *(1-877-257-2887, raileurope.com)*. The France Rail 'n' Drive pass offers a flexible rail and car rental package, while the Fly, Rail, and Drive pass combines internal flights with train travel and car rental. Discounts are available for students and seniors.

## By Car

France has a good network of roads, from small and often picturesque C and D roads to autoroutes, often called *péages,* because a toll *(péage)* must be paid. Occasionally you pay a fixed fee upon entering a section of autoroute; more often you are given a ticket as you enter, and you pay as you leave according to the distance traveled. Credit cards are accepted in the pay booths. There are gas stations with 24-hour service approximately every 15 miles (20 km), but there are also, more frequently, parking and picnic places (called *Aires).* The main *routes nationales* between towns and cities (N on maps) are generally in excellent condition.

## Renting a Car

You can arrange a car rental with your local travel agent or book online before leaving home—it can be much cheaper. Otherwise there are desks in airports and major railroad stations in France. There are fly-drive options with most flights, and the SNCF offers a train/car rental package.

Central offices:
rentalscars.com
holidayautos.co.uk
**ADA,** ada.fr
**Avis,** avis.fr
**Budget,** budget.com
**Europcar,** europcar.com
**Hertz,** hertz.com

To rent a car, you must have a current driver's license (held for at least three years) and be at least 21 years old. Some companies will not rent to people under 26 or over 60.

## Age Limits & Licenses

The minimum age limit for driving in France is 18 years. Visitors from North America and the U.K. need only their home driver's license. Drivers who wear glasses or contacts must have a pair with them while driving.

## Breakdown Assistance

Autoroutes and routes nationales have emergency telephones every mile (2 km). Police stations *(gendarmeries)* have information about breakdown services or garages—dial 17. For accidents, see p. 400. You must set up a red warning triangle if you break down.

## Busy Periods

Roads will usually be busy from the beginning of July and especially around August 15, a major national holiday in France. In summer, watch for the small green BIS (Bison Futé) signs, which indicate alternative routes. A brochure in English on the Bison Futé routes is available from French government tourist offices.

## Children
Children under ten must travel in the rear seat.

## Drunk Driving
The French drunk-driving limit is 50 mg of alcohol per 100 ml of blood (.05%). This can mean that as little as one glass of beer can take you up to the limit.

## Gas
Fuel is sold by the liter (3.75 liters equals an American gallon). Most gas stations accept credit cards. Be aware that 24-hour self-service machines may take only Cartes Bancaires (French bank cards) and no other credit cards.

## Green Travel
Travel by train and local public transportation is the most eco-friendly way to go. Or put your car on the train and only drive when you get there. For information on carbon offsetting go to:
carbonfund.org
ecotourism.org
icrtourism.org
climatecare.org

## Headlights
Motorcycles must have headlights on when moving, and cars must use headlights in poor visibility. All vehicles must carry a spare set of lightbulbs.

## On-the-Spot Fines
On-the-spot fines may be levied by police for several offenses, including speeding, not wearing seat belts, and not having the car's documents with you. Speedcheck cameras are very common.

## Parking
Some French towns and cities have blue zones where parking is free for up to an hour. You need to display a parking disk *(disque de stationnement)*, which you obtain from garages, *tabacs*, and tourist offices. Otherwise, most towns have on-street parking machines *(horodateurs)*. Coins required vary from 20 cents to 2 euros. Multistory parking garages are common. Some close overnight and may shut by 8 p.m.

## Priorité à Droite
Traditionally, priority on French roads was given to vehicles approaching from the right, except where otherwise indicated. Nowadays, on main roads, the major road will normally have priority, with traffic being halted on minor approach roads with one of the following signs:
• *Cedez le passage:* yield
• *Vous n'avez pas la priorité:* you do not have right of way
• *Passage protégé:* no right of way
A yellow diamond sign indicates that you have priority; a diamond sign with a diagonal black line indicates that you do not.

Take care in small towns and rural areas without road markings, where you may be expected to yield to traffic coming from the right. If oncoming drivers flash their headlights, it is to indicate that they have priority, not the other way around. Priority is always given to emergency and public utility vehicles.

## Road Conditions
For current road conditions, telephone the Inter Service Route line or tune into the local radio frequency (often indicated on signs beside roads). Autoroute information: autoroutes.fr.

## Road Signs
• *Access interdit:* no entry
• *Allumez vos feux:* switch on lights
• *Interdiction de stationner:* no parking
• *Passage pour piétons:* pedestrian crossing
• *Sens unique:* one-way traffic
• *Virages sur...km:* curves for...km
• *Zone bleue:* parking disk required

## Seat Belts
The wearing of seat belts is mandatory in both the front and rear seats.

## Speed Limits
Note that there are different speed limits for normal weather and times of poor visibility (heavy rain or fog).

Autoroutes have limits of 75–85 mph (110–130 kph; slower limit applies in poor visibility); two-lane roads 60–75 mph (90–110 kph); other open roads 50–55 mph (80–90 kph); and towns 30 mph (50 kph).

## Traffic Circles
Vehicles already in a traffic circle have priority, except very occasionally in small towns where *priorité à droite* still applies.

## Traffic Lights
Signals are sometimes suspended high over the road and can easily be missed.

# Transportation in Paris
## Taxis
Taxis can be found outside every mainline train station and airport, and at taxi ranks throughout the city. You can also call a taxi *(tel 01 45 30 30 30, taxi -reservation.fr)*.
Taxi drivers in Paris operate on three tariffs:
• Tariff A, 7 a.m. to 7 p.m.
• Tariff B, 7 p.m. to 7 a.m.
• Tariff C, at night in the suburbs and during the day in the outer districts of Hauts-de-Seine, Seine St.-Denis, and Val-de-Marne, when the taxi has no client for a return trip.

Extra charges are added for pickups at train stations, luggage weighing more than 12 pounds/5 kg, a fourth passenger (the driver can refuse to take more than three passengers), and an animal (except for a seeing-eye dog). A 10 percent tip to taxi drivers is usual.

## Public Transportation
There are three kinds of public transportation in Paris: Métropolitan (Métro), Réseau Express Régional (RER)—high speed suburban rail lines—and Autocar (the bus, sometimes called "car"). A Carte Orange is good for unlimited trips on Métro, RER, and buses for one week, or for a month. You will need a passport-size photograph for a Carte Orange. A Paris Visite card is available at Métro stations and is good for one, two, three, or five days and entitles you to unlimited use of public transportation and discounts at some sights. The Formule 1 card, also available at the Métro ticket booths, is good for all transportation for one day only. For advice on bus, Métro, or rail travel, ask at a tourist office.

## Using the Métro
Maps are posted in every Métro station, or ask for a free *Plan du Métro* when you buy a ticket. Each line has a number and is identified by the station at the end of the line. A *carnet* (book) of ten tickets is a useful savings if you plan to use the Métro frequently. A Carte Orange is good for unlimited trips on Métro, RER, and buses for one week, or for a month. You will need a passport-size photograph for a Carte Orange. A Paris Visite card is available at Métro stations and is good for one, two, three, or five days and entitles you to unlimited use of public transportation and discounts at some sights. The Formule 1 card, also available at the Métro ticket booths, is good for all transportation for one day only. For advice on bus, Métro, or rail travel, ask at a tourist office.

## Vélib' Bikes
This is a self-service bike-rental system in Paris and several other cities *(www .velib-metropole.fr)*, including Nice and Perpignan. You will need a credit card for the deposit.

# PRACTICAL ADVICE
## Communications
### Post Offices
The PTT (pronounced *pay-tay-tay*) controls both the mail and telecommunication services. Offices are open from 9 a.m. to 5 p.m. on weekdays and from 9 a.m. to noon on Saturdays (in smaller towns, offices will close for lunch, and in villages, they may only be open for two or three hours on weekday mornings). Mail can be delivered to you at a post office if it is marked "Poste Restante" with the postal code of the Bureau de Poste at which you collect it; you will have to pay a fee for each item of mail *(laposte.fr)*.

### Mailboxes
Yellow *boîtes postales* (mailboxes) are located outside every PTT and on walls in larger towns. They may have separate compartments for local mail, *départemental* (mail within the département), and *autres départements/destinations* (elsewhere in France and foreign).

### Telephones
French telephone numbers have ten digits usually written divided into pairs, for example, 01 23 45 67 89. Numbers in Paris begin with 01, numbers in the northwest of the country begin with 02, in the northeast with 03, in the southeast with 04, and in the southwest with 05. Reach an operator by dialing 12.

To call a French number (e.g., 01 23 45 67 89) from abroad, dial the international code (011 from the U.S. and Canada, 00 from the U.K.), then the code for France (33), followed by the number, omitting the first 0: 011 33 1 23 45 67 89. Numbers beginning in 08 are accessible only in France. French mobile numbers begin with 06.

### Phone Booths
*Cabines téléphoniques* stand outside larger post offices, in railroad stations and airports, or near roads or parking garages in towns and villages. They take either phone cards or credit cards. Post offices may still contain telephones where you can make your call first and pay at the counter afterward. Phones in bars and cafés may still take cash, and proprietors will usually permit use of the phone in an emergency. Phone cards *(télécartes)* can be bought at post offices, newsagents, and any tobacconist *(bureau de tabac)*.

### International Calls
To make an international call from France, dial 00 followed by the country's international code. These can be found in the front of the Pages Jaunes section of the *annuaire* or posted in a telephone booth. Some useful ones are: Australia 61; Canada 1; Ireland 353; U.K. 44; U.S. 1. For international directory assistance, dial 32 12, followed by the country code. Additional information can be found at pagesjaunes.fr.

To dial toll-free numbers *(numéros verts)*, insert a card or money to make the connection (coins will be returned after the call, units will not be registered against cards). Reduced-rate calls in France and Europe are 7 p.m.–8 a.m. weekdays, noon Sat.–8 a.m. Mon.; for U.S. and Canada, 7 p.m.–1 p.m., Mon.–Fri., and all day Sat.–Sun. Reduced rates also apply on public holidays.

### Cell Phones
Many cell phones can be used in France, so long as there is network coverage. Don't rely on it in rural or mountainous regions. Making or receiving international calls can be very expensive. Of the U.S.-based cells, only those that are "tri-band" will work in France. Consult your provider before you travel to see if they have arrangements for making international calls.

If you need to make a lot of local calls, it may be worth buying a French SIM card and charge cards from French operators (Orange, SFR, and Bouyges), which have public shops. There are also many Web-based services, such as Skype and VOIP (Voice Over Internet Protocol) that will allow you to make free calls via your computer to other Skype users or cheaper calls to cell phones or landlines.

**Internet**
Wi-Fi is widely available in hotels, cafés, and bars. Broadband is also widely available. Libraries and tourist offices may provide access.

## Départements
France is divided into 96 administrative *départements,* each named after a principal river and identified by a number. When making any inquiries about a region, it is helpful to know the département name and numbers: for example 09 *(zero-neuf)* Ariège.

## Conversions
1 kilo = 2.2 lbs
1 liter = 0.26 U.S. gallons
1 mile = 1.6 km

## Etiquette & Local Customs
Etiquette is very important in France. Always be ready to shake hands when you are introduced, and when you meet friends and acquaintances. Kissing on both cheeks is also very common, but has lessened since the Covid-19 pandemic. When entering any establishment, it is polite to offer a general *"Bonjour, messieurs/dames."* Young women are addressed as *"Mademoiselle,"* a woman in her 20s or older as *"Madame."* Address a waiter as *"Monsieur"–"garçon"* (boy) is not acceptable—and call a waitress either *"Madame"* or *"Mademoiselle."*

When visiting churches and cathedrals, dress appropriately and respect the sensitivities of those who are there for devotional purposes. Visitors are requested not to walk around religious buildings during services. Even though in most cases no fee is charged to visit a church or cathedral, it is polite to contribute to one of the donation boxes.

## Holidays
All banks, post offices, and many museums, galleries, and stores close on these national holidays:
January 1 *(Jour de l'An)*
Easter Sunday *(Pâques)* and Monday
May 1 *(Fête du Travail)*
May 8 *(Victoire 1945)*
Ascension *(Ascension)*
Pentecost *(Pentecôte)*
July 14 *(Fête Nationale)*
August 15 *(Assomption)*
November 1 *(Toussaint)*
November 11 *(Armistice 1918)*
December 25 *(Noël)*

## Media
### American & British Newspapers
Newspapers and magazines are sold in Maisons de la Presse, many of which stock American or British newspapers (often the previous day's edition). International newspapers are available in airports, major railroad stations, and most large hotels.

Regional newspapers contain national and international as well as local news, and are often read more than the national press. The main national dailies are *Le Monde,* conservative *Le Figaro,* and left-wing *Libération* and *L'Humanité.* American and British dailies—the *International Herald Tribune, Times,* and *Daily Telegraph*—are widely available in major towns and cities.

### TV Channels
French television offers six TV channels: TF1, France 2, France 3, 5, and La Cinquième, which in the evening becomes Arte (a combined Franco-German transmission), and M6. TF1 occasionally shows undubbed American films with French subtitles; Arte more frequently shows subtitled international films and art programs. The main television news programs are at 1 p.m. and 8 p.m. You can also see cable and satellite channels such as Al Jazeera, CNN, MTV, and BBC World.

## Radio

The national radio station, France Inter (1892m long wave), broadcasts English-language news twice a day in summer (generally at 9 a.m. and 4 p.m.). During the peak holiday period, other local stations may have English broadcasts. On the Mediterranean, Riviera Radio (106.3 and 106.5 kHz) broadcasts 24 hours a day in English.

## Money Matters

The euro is available in 500, 200, 100, 50, 20, 10, and 5 euro notes, 2 and 1 euro coins, and 50, 20, 10, 5, and 1 cent coins.

Most banks have ATMs for bank (debit) cards and international credit cards with instructions in a choice of languages. You can withdraw money from your own account in euros, but you may be charged a fee. You will need a four-digit PIN: Arrange this with your bank before leaving home. Currency can be exchanged in banks and *bureaux de change* in train stations and airports.

Credit cards are widely accepted. Visa is by far the most common. MasterCard (Access/Eurocard) and Diners Club are also widely accepted, while American Express is less popular. Carte Bancaire (CB) is a French card encompassing both Visa and MasterCard.

## Opening Times

Nearly all stores and offices close for lunch from noon to 2 p.m., often to 3 p.m. or 4 p.m. in summer in the south. Many stores close for the morning or all day Monday or Wednesday.

**Banks** 9 a.m.–5 p.m. Mon.–Sat., closing for lunch

**Post offices** 9 a.m.–6 p.m. weekdays, closing for lunch; 9 a.m. to noon Sat.

**Stores** 9 a.m.–7 p.m. Mon.– Sat., closing for lunch; some food stores also open on Sun a.m.

**Grocery stores** 9 a.m.–7 p.m. Mon.–Sat., some closing for lunch often except Sat. & sometimes Fri.

**Bureaux de Tabac & Maisons de la Presse** 8 a.m.–7 p.m. Mon.–Sat., 8 a.m.–noon Sun.

**Gas stations** usually close at 9 p.m. except on autoroutes.

**Museums** close for lunch from noon to 2 p.m, except perhaps during the months of July and/or August. Municipal museums usually close on Mon., national museums on Tues.

## Pets

Animals under 3 months old are not allowed into France; older pets must have a certificate attesting that they have had a rabies vaccination within the last year, or an official declaration that they have been brought from a rabies-free area.

## Time Differences

France runs on CET (Central European Time), one hour ahead of Greenwich Mean Time, six hours ahead of Eastern Standard Time. France uses the 24-hour clock.

## Tipping

Most restaurant bills include a service charge, generally indicated at the bottom of the menu. If in doubt, ask: *Est-ce que le service est compris?* It is usual to leave a small additional tip for the waiter if the service has been good. It is customary to tip taxi drivers 10 percent, though this is not obligatory. Give porters, doormen, tour guides, and hairdressers a tip of 1–2 euros; usherettes and cloakroom attendants 5 euros. There is no need to leave a tip for hotel maids unless you have required out-of-the-ordinary service.

## Toilets

Self-cleaning toilet cabins can be found on the street (not wheelchair accessible). You can use the toilet in a bar or café, signposted *les toilettes* or *les WC* (pronounced *lay vay-say*). Public toilets vary; some, particularly in the south, are old-fashioned squat toilets. If there is an attendant, tip with small change.

## Tourist Offices
### U.S.A.
**East Coast**
Maison de la France
825 Third Ave.
New York, NY
Tel 212/838-7800
rendezvousenfrance.com
**West Coast**
9454 Wilshire Blvd., Suite 715
Beverly Hills, CA 90212
Tel 310/271-6665
**Midwest**
205 North Michigan Ave.
Chicago, IL 60611
Tel 514/288-1904

### CANADA
**Montréal**
1981 Ave. McGill College, #490
Montréal, Quebec H3A 2W9
Tel 514/288-2026
Fax 514/845-4868

### FRANCE
Maison de la France
79 rue de Clichy
75009 Paris
Tel 01 42 96 70 00
rendezvousenfrance.com

## TRAVELERS WITH DISABILITIES
France can be hard for disabled travelers, especially on the steep winding streets of old towns and villages. Parking spaces are provided (bring your international orange disc with you), and wheelchairs can be rented through pharmacies. Wheelchair access is often limited, though newer museums will offer facilities, and beaches try to provide access. SNCF has train carriages designed for wheelchairs, and taxi drivers are obliged to take disabled people and guide dogs. More hotels now have adapted rooms. For more information contact:

**Association des Paralysés de France,** tel 01 40 78 69 00, apf.asso.fr
**Access in Paris,** accessinparis.org
**Federation Française Handisport,** tel 01 40 31 45 00, handisport.org; information on sports and leisure facilities
**Le Guide Accessible Accommodation,** guide-accessible.com; restaurants, etc.
**Mobility International USA,** 132 E. Broadway, Ste. 343, Eugene, OR USA 97401, tel 541/343-1284, miusa.org

## EMERGENCIES
### Embassies in France
**U.S. Embassy** 2 avenue Gabriel, Paris 75008, tel 01 43 12 22 22; **Visas Information Service** (from U.S.): tel 011 338 10 26 46 26, france.usembassy. gov; **Consulate** Place Varian Fry, 13286 Marseille Cedaz 6, tel 04 91 54 92 00
**Canadian Embassy** 35 avenue Montaigne, Paris 75008, tel 01 44 43 29 00, canadainternational.gc.ca
**British Embassy** 35 rue du Faubourg St.-Honore, Paris 75008, tel 01 44 51 31 00, gov.uk or embassy-paris.com

### Emergency Phone Numbers
**15 SAMU** (Service d'Aide Medicale d'Urgence; ambulance)
**17 Police secours** (police rescue)
**18 Pompiers** (fire rescue)
Both police and fire rescue have medical backup and work in close contact with SAMU. For legal assistance in an emergency, contact your embassy or consulate for English-speaking lawyers.
**112** Standard European emergency number

### What to Do in the Event of a Car Accident
There is no need to involve the police if you have an accident in which no

one has been hurt. The official procedure is for each driver to fill out a *constat à l'amiable*, each signing the other's copy. Phone the rental company and explain what has happened.

If you are involved in a serious road accident, phone the police (17) or fire rescue (18). These numbers are free, but in a phone booth you need to insert a coin or card to make a connection (it is returned to you after the call). An address in the telephone booth will give your location. Alternatively, you may find the local *police secours* number posted in the phone booth. Call your insurance company on your cell phone if possible, as they may connect you to a local representative.

## Lost Property

If you lose something on a bus or the Métro, first try the terminal to see if it has been handed in. In Paris, after 48 hours, you can go to the Bureau des Objets Trouvés, 36 rue des Morillons, 75015 Paris, tel 08 21 00 25 25, where you have to pay 4% of the value of any item reclaimed. To report a theft or loss, go to a *gendarmerie* or *commissariat de police*. Their numbers are in local directories. If you lose your passport, report first to the police, then to the nearest embassy or consulate (see p. 399). If you are detained by the police for any reason, you are entitled to call the nearest consulate for a member of the staff to come to assist you.

### Lost credit cards

**American Express:** tel 01 47 77 72 00, americanexpress.com
**MasterCard:** tel 08 00 90 13 87, mastercard.com
**Visa:** tel 08 00 90 11 79, visaeurope.com

## Health

Check that your insurance covers visits to France. Pharmacies—recognizable by a green cross sign—are staffed by pharmacists who can recommend treatment and tell you where to find a doctor. The fee to see a doctor is 23 euros; for a doctor to come out to see you is at least 30 euros. For serious injury, go to a hospital emergency room *(urgences)*.

To renew a prescription, take your medicine in its package to a pharmacy. If they do not have that product, they will try to find its equivalent. If they can only sell it to you with a prescription, they will direct you to the nearest doctor.

**International Association for Medical Assistance to Travelers**
IAMAT *(iamat.org)* is a nonprofit organization that anyone can join free of charge. Members receive a directory of English-speaking IAMAT doctors on call 24 hours a day and are entitled to services at set rates.
**U.S.:** 1623 Military Rd., #279, Niagara Falls, NY 14304, tel 716/754-4883
**Canada:** 67 Mowat Ave., Toronto, M6K 3ER, tel 416/652-0137

## Medical Emergencies

For an ambulance, dial 15, Service d'Aide Médicale d'Urgence. French medical treatment is of a high standard, and facilities are generally excellent. In rural areas, the *pompiers* (fire brigades) are also trained paramedics and can be called in an emergency (dial 15). In major cities, a 24-hour doctor service *(médécin de garde)* is available. Emergency heart defibrillator kits are now available—usually outside the *mairie* (town hall) in many small villages where emergency services may take some time to get there. In Paris, the American Hospital is at 63 boulevard Victor-Hugo, Neuilly 92292, tel 01 46 41 25 25.

## FURTHER READING

*The Cathedral Builders,* Jean Gimpel (Harper & Row, 1984)

*Celestine: Voices From a French Village,* Gillian Tindall (Minerva, 1996)

*The Food Lovers Guide to France,* Patricia Wells (Workman Publishing, 1999)

*Footsteps,* Richard Holmes (Flamingo, 2004)

*Fragile Glory: A Portrait of France and the French,* Richard Bernstein (Plume, 1991)

*The French,* Theodore Zeldin (Kodansha, 1996)

*Life in a Postcard,* Rosemary Bailey (Bantam Books 2002)

*A Little Tour in France,* Henry James (Farrar, Straus and Giroux, 1983)

*Montaillou,* Emmanuel Le Roy Ladurie (Gallimard, 1978)

*On the Brink,* Jonathan Fenby (Abacus, 2002)

*Paris: Biography of a City,* Colin Jones (Allen Lane 2004)

*Paris: The Secret History,* Andrew Hussey (Penguin, 2006)

*Paris to the Moon,* Adam Gopnik (Random House, 2001)

*Two Towns in Provence,* M. F. K. Fisher (Vintage Books, 1983)

# HOTELS & RESTAURANTS

Excellent and varied accommodation is available all over France, ranging from grand hotels to cozy farmhouses. You can splurge on some of the finest hotels in the world or stay at cheap motel-style chains such as Formule 1 or Balladins, which will accommodate a family of four for less than 50 euros per night. You can stay in grand châteaus, or seek out small farmhouses (chambres d'hôte) for bed and breakfast and meals of homegrown produce. Obviously, facilities will be reflected in the price, and in cheaper hotels you may not have private baths.

## Hotels

Many French hotels offer pension or demi-pension accommodations. Demi-pension includes breakfast and dinner, while full pension includes lunch, as well.

## Grading System

French hotels are officially graded according to a star system, from four to one stars, indicating the minimum level of facilities. A few hotels in this selection, either restaurants with rooms or château hotels, are not star-rated.

✪✪✪✪✪ These hotels have exceptional characteristics in terms of geographical position, historical interest, architectural particularities and tailor-made services.

✪✪✪✪ Four stars indicate a hotel with a restaurant and all rooms with private bath/shower rooms.

✪✪✪ Three-star hotels have at least 80 percent of the rooms with bath/shower and offer breakfast in the room.

✪✪ Two-star establishments must have 40 percent of the rooms with bath/shower and a telephone in each room.

✪ One-star hotels offer plain but adequate accommodation.

## Organization

The following is a selection of good quality hotels throughout the country (listed by location and price, then in alphabetical order). Wherever possible, we have chosen hotels that are both individual and typical, perhaps with notable local or historic associations.

Please note that, unless otherwise stated:

1. Breakfast is not included in the price.
2. The hotel has a restaurant. If it is outstanding, the restaurant symbol is also given or reference is made to a separate entry for the restaurant.
3. All rooms have a telephone and television.

Room price categories are given only as guidance and do not take into account seasonal variations. Further taxes may be added to the price. Prices are per (double) room. In high season, always try to book in advance, if possible confirming by email. You may be asked for a deposit or credit card number.

## Credit & Debit Cards

Most hotels accept all major cards. Abbreviations used are: AE (American Express), CB (Carte Bancaire), DC (Diners Club), MC (MasterCard), V (Visa). American Express and Diners Club tend to be less popular.

## Hotel Chains & Groups

**Concorde Hotels,**
 concorde-hotels.com
**Hilton,** hilton.com

---

🏨 Hotel  🍴 Restaurant  🛏 No. of Guest Rooms  🪑 No. of Seats  🅿 Parking  Ⓜ Metro  🕐 Closed  🛗 Elevator

## PRICES

### HOTELS

An indication of the cost of a double room in the high season is given by $ signs.

| | |
|---|---|
| $$$$$ | Over $800 |
| $$$$ | $500–$800 |
| $$$ | $300–$500 |
| $$ | $150–$300 |
| $ | Under $150 |

### RESTAURANTS

An indication of the cost of a three-course meal without drinks is given by $ signs.

| | |
|---|---|
| $$$$$ | Over $300 |
| $$$$ | $200–$300 |
| $$$ | $100–$200 |
| $$ | $70–$100 |
| $ | Under $70 |

**Leading Hotels of the World,**
lhw.com
**Maisons des Gîtes de France,**
gites-de-france.com
**Relais & Châteaux,**
relaischateaux.com
**Châteaux and Hotels Collection,**
chateauxhotels.com.
airbnb.com
au.chateau.com
hotels.com
logishotels.com
tables-auberges.com

You can also book through local French tourist office departments. Most hotels have websites; it is better to book directly with them. Many *départements* have a Loisirs Acceuil booking service to reserve hotels, *gîtes,* and campsites; request a list at the French Tourist Office or the local tourist office, or visit rendezvousenfrance.com.

## Restaurants

Wherever you go, you will find a wide variety of restaurants, from humble auberges to the great classics. Many hotels have their own restaurants, and some restaurants also rent rooms.

Our selection (listed by location, price, then in alphabetical order) suggests good regional restaurants offering typical local dishes, as well as including some of the great stars of French cuisine. In the regions, it is always worth seeking out typical local restaurants and sampling the specialties of the area. See each regional food section for a guide to local cuisine and dishes, and the menu reader on p. 388.

L = lunch   D = dinner

The following websites are useful for booking restaurants:
idealgourmet.fr
lefooding.com
parisbymouth.com
parisinfo.com
resto.fr
restoaparis.com
www.restoenfrance.com

### Dining Hours in France

Lunch usually starts around midday and continues until 2 p.m. Dinner is eaten around 8 p.m. but may start about 7 p.m.; in smaller places or in the countryside, you may be too late after 9 p.m. Dinner tends to be earlier in the north of the country, later as you go south. At the height of the season, or if you have a particular place in mind, make a reservation.

Restaurants often have outdoor tables for good weather, and even in towns and cities you may find yourself sitting on the sidewalk or in a courtyard. Facilities for outside dining are mentioned here only where the view, or perhaps the garden, is of particular note.

---

🚭 Nonsmoking  ❄️ Air-conditioning  🛏 Indoor Pool  🏊 Outdoor Pool  🏋 Health Club  💳 Credit Cards

Menus must by law be displayed outside any establishment that is serving food, and studying and comparing these as you stroll along a French boulvard or street before making your choice is all part of the pleasure of dining out in one of the world's great culinary destinations.

Most restaurants offer one or more *prix-fixe* menus—set meals at a fixed price, sometimes including wine. Otherwise (and usually more expensively), you order individual items à la carte—from the menu.

The French usually eat a salad after the main course and sometimes with the cheese course, which comes before dessert. Bread and water are supplied free. (Note that French tap water is safe to drink.) Whichever way your food arrives, either in a French café or restaurant, or if you're lucky enough to be invited into a French home, you should do as the French do and savor each course slowly, enjoying the conversation as much as the food. In France, the two pleasures go together and are an essential part of the day.

Wine lists in the various regions are often dominated by local wines, and all restaurants offer a *vin de pays* by the carafe or demi-carafe. Although smoking is now forbidden by law in all public places in France, some hotels and restaurants have smoking terraces.

**Cafés**

Cafés remain a French institution, good for morning coffee, leisurely drinks, or modest meals. In small towns and villages, they are very much the center of local life. Note that drinking at the bar is cheaper than sitting at a table.

**Tipping**

A service charge is usually included in the bill. Only add more if the service has been particularly good.

▶ **PARIS**

**ÎLE DE LA CITÉ**

🏨 **DU JEU DE PAUME**
**$$$** ✪✪✪✪
54 Rue St.-Louis-en-l'île
Tel 01 43 26 14 18
FAX 01 40 46 02 76
jeudepaumehotel.com
In the 17th century, Court (Royal) tennis was played in this building, now creatively converted into an attractive hotel. Rooms are chic and modern. The garden offers a pleasant green escape after a day wandering busy Parisian streets.
🛏 30 🚇 Pont Marie �e �e
🃏 All major cards

🏨 **DE LUTÈCE**
**$$** ✪✪✪
65 Rue St.-Louis-en-l'Île
TEL 01 43 26 23 52
FAX 01 43 29 60 25
paris-hotel-lutece.com
A fire burns in the lobby's fireplace, and each modest room has an interesting detail, like exposed beams or a pretty mirror, making De Lutèce a welcoming home away from home while staying in the French capital.
🛏 23 �e 🚇 Pont Marie
�e 🃏 AE, MC, V

🍴 **LA TOUR D'ARGENT**
**$$$$$**
15 Quai de la Tournelle
TEL 01 43 54 23 31
FAX 01 44 07 12 04
latourdargent.com
Located on a quay just across the Seine from the Île de la Cité. Perhaps no longer the peak of excellence it once was, but it still has one Michelin star and is a favorite with visitors for its superb, succulent duckling, and its

entrancing view of the Seine River and Notre-Dame.

🚇 Pont Marie 🕐 Closed Sun.–Mon. & all of Aug. 🔁 🔆
🆑 All major cards

## LEFT BANK

### 🏨 RELAIS CHRISTINE
**$$$$$ ✪✪✪✪**
3 Rue Christine
TEL 01 40 51 60 80
FAX 01 40 51 60 81
relais-christine.com
Discreet luxury in a former convent. No restaurant, but breakfast is served in the vaulted, 13th-century kitchens. Includes a relaxing garden.
🛏 35 rooms + 16 duplex 🅿
🚇 Odéon 🔁 🔆
🆑 All major cards

### 🏨 DUC DE SAINT-SIMON
**$$$$ ✪✪✪**
14 Rue St.-Simon
TEL 01 44 39 20 20
FAX 01 45 48 68 25
hotelducdesaintsimon.com
A luxurious haven, with exquisite antique furnishings. There is a charming basement breakfast room and courtyard garden, but no restaurant.
🛏 29 + 5 suites 🚇 Rue du Bac
🔁 🆑 AE, DC, MC, V

### 🏨 HOTEL BANKE
**$$$$ ✪✪✪✪**
20 Rue La Fayette
TEL 01 55 33 22 22
hotelbanke.com
Located close to shopping and opera, this hotel, a converted belle epoque bank, is wildly opulent with an exotic glass ceiling lobby and stylish modern rooms.
🛏 94 🚇 Chaussée d'Antin
🔁 🔆 ♿ 🆑 All major cards

### 🏨 L'HÔTEL
**$$$$**
13 Rue des Beaux-arts
TEL 01 44 41 99 00
l-hotel.com
Beautifully renovated hotel with magnificent staircase and swimming pool. Famous for the room where Oscar Wilde died—now with its own terrace, and the wallpaper is not as bad as the Irish writer made out.
🚇 St.-Germain-des-Prés 🏊
🆑 All major cards

### 🏨 DE VIEUX PARIS
**$$$ ✪✪✪✪**
9 Rue Git le Coeur
TEL 01 44 32 15 90
FAX 01 43 26 00 15
vieuxparis.com
The famous Beat hotel that in the 1950s and 1960s accommodated American writer William Burroughs and poet Allen Ginsberg. The 15th-century building has been completely refurbished, but the rooms are small.
🛏 13 + 7 suites 🚇 St.-Michel
🆑 All major cards

### 🏨 MAMA SHELTER
**$ ✪✪✪**
109 Rue de Bagnolet
TEL 01 43 48 48 48
mamashelter.com
Located near the famous Père Lachaise cemetery, the most visited necropolis in the world. So if you're in Paris to pay your respects to Jim Morrison, Colette, Chopin, Édith Piaf, Marcel Proust, Sarah Bernhardt, or Oscar Wilde, this is a perfect destination hotel with small but perfect rooms designed by Philippe Starck, with funky restaurant and a fashionable bar.
🛏 171 🚇 Gambetta 🔆 ♿
🆑 All major cards

## 🍴 CLOSERIE DES LILAS
$$$$

171 Blvd. du Montparnasse
TEL 01 40 51 34 50
closeriedeslilas.fr

This bar/brasserie/restaurant was once upon a time a famous hangout of Picasso, Hemingway, Apollinaire, Lenin, and others. Closerie des Lilas is a good place to eat and drink amid the literary crowd, where you'll hear many a passionate post-prandial debate on the merits of publications past and present. Not a bad place to try your first pastis after you've landed in one of the chicest capital cities in the world.

🚇 Vavin
💳 All major cards

## 🍴 VIOLON D'INGRES
$$$$

135 Rue St.-Dominique
TEL 01 45 55 15 05
maisonconstant.com

Christian Constant, the former chef at Les Ambassadeurs in Hôtel de Crillon, provides the same high-quality cuisine at this excellent Michelin one-star restaurant, at more affordable prices.

🚇 Pont de l'Alma 🛗
💳 AE, CB, MC, V

## 🍴 LE DÔME
$$$

108 Blvd. du Montparnasse
TEL 01 43 35 25 81
restaurant-ledome.com

A famous Montparnasse brasserie. Fish and seafood are served up to perfection in this restaurant with a lively ambience.

🚇 Montparnasse-Bienvenüe
🕐 Closed Sun.–Mon. in July & Aug. 🛗 💳 All major cards

---

### PRICES

**HOTELS**
An indication of the cost of a double room in the high season is given by $ signs.

| | |
|---|---|
| $$$$$ | Over $800 |
| $$$$ | $500–$800 |
| $$$ | $300–$500 |
| $$ | $150–$300 |
| $ | Under $150 |

**RESTAURANTS**
An indication of the cost of a three-course meal without drinks is given by $ signs.

| | |
|---|---|
| $$$$$ | Over $300 |
| $$$$ | $200–$300 |
| $$$ | $100–$200 |
| $$ | $70–$100 |
| $ | Under $70 |

---

## 🍴 BRASSERIE LIPP
$$

151 Boulevard St.-Germain
TEL 01 45 48 53 91
brasserielipp.fr

Perhaps more noted for its historical and literary connections, and wonderful turn-of-the-century decor, than for the food, this is still a fun place to drink cocktails or enjoy a snack or supper while basking in the evocative atmosphere of Paris in times past.

🚇 St.-Germain-des-Prés
🛗 💳 AE, MC, V

## 🍴 LA CIEL DE PARIS
$$

Tour Maine Montparnasse
33 Avenue du Maine
TEL 01 40 64 77 64
cieldeparis.com

---

🏨 Hotel 🍴 Restaurant 🛏 No. of Guest Rooms 💺 No. of Seats 🅿 Parking 🚇 Metro 🕐 Closed 🛗 Elevator

On the 56th floor of the Tour Montparnasse, vast picture windows offer amazing views of the City of Light, fine cuisine, late night champagne bar—the works! If you're in Paris, you might as well dine with a view of one of the world's most beautiful cities. This place is top of the world!

🚇 Montparnasse-Bienvenüe
💳 All major cards

## 🍴 LA COUPOLE
$$
102 Blvd. du Montparnasse
TEL 01 43 20 14 20
lacoupole-paris.com
A legendary art deco brasserie—everyone who was anyone (including, of course, Ernest Hemingway and his gang of expats) came here in the 1920s. Good food and great service, too. Papa would still approve of this famous old Parisian joint.

🚇 Montparnasse-Bienvenüe
❄️ 💳 All major cards

## 🍴 L'OS À MOELLE
$$
3 Rue Vasco de Gama
TEL 01 45 57 27 27
Trained by Christian Constant, the young chef at L'Os à Moelle makes a serious effort to provide refined fine cuisine at low prices for an appreciative Parisian clientele. Fixed-price menus offer excellent value.

🕐 Closed Sun.–Mon. & Aug.
💳 All major cards

## 🍴 LE PROCOPE
$$
13 Rue de l'Ancienne Comédie
TEL 01 40 46 79 00
procope.com
Now restored to its 17th-century splendor, Le Procope (see Café Life p. 76) serves popular brasserie dishes.

Sorbets and ice creams are a specialty and a must-try for anyone with a sweet tooth.

🚇 Odéon ❄️ 💳 AE, MC

## 🍴 LE BISTRO PAUL BERT
$
18 Rue Paul Bert
TEL 01 43 72 24 01
bistrotpaulbert.fr
The wood panels, tiled floor, chalkboard menu—all make for a perfect French bistro. Enjoy the cozy banquettes and the outside terrrace as you choose from a range of classic French dishes.

🕐 Closed Sun.–Mon.
💳 MC, V

# RIGHT BANK

## 🏨 BRISTOL
$$$$$ ✦✦✦✦
112 Rue du Faubourg St.-Honoré
TEL 01 53 43 43 00
FAX 01 53 43 43 01
lebristolparis.com
Luxury and discretion for the rich and/or famous, with fine works of art, tapestries, and Persian carpets. Garden. The rooftop pool and restaurant let you look over the rooftops of the City of Light.

🛏️ 195 + suites 🚇 St.-Philippe du Roule 🍴 ❄️ 🏊 💪
💳 All major cards

## 🏨 DE CRILLON
## 🍴 $$$$$ ✦✦✦✦
10 Place de la Concorde
TEL 01 44 71 15 00
FAX 01 44 71 15 02
crillon.com
This is one of the great palace hotels in Paris (or anywhere in France for that matter), offering great views

over the Place de la Concorde. Guests have a choice of two restaurants and the chance to indulge a taste for the outdoors (or a taste for tobacco) in a winter garden.

🛈 163 + suites
🚇 Concorde 🛗 🔁 🚭
♦ All major cards

### 🏨 FOUR SEASONS GEORGE V
$$$$$ ○○○○○
31 Avenue George V
TEL 01 49 52 70 00
FAX 01 49 52 70 10
fourseasons.com/paris/
Recent refurbishment has brought this venerable palace hotel luxuriously up-to-date and the George V has built on its age-old credentials to establish itself as a vital destination hotel for the 21st century. The courtyard garden is a delightful repose from the heat of a summer in Paris.

🛈 260 🚇 George V
🛗 🔁 🔲 🔳
♦ All major cards

### 🏨 MARIGNAN–CHAMPS-ÉLYSÉES
$$$$$ ○○○○
12 Rue Marignan
TEL 01 40 76 34 56
FAX 01 40 76 34 34
hotelmarignanelyseesparis.com
A Beauvais tapestry in the salon, antique furnishings, and comfortable rooms make this a delightfully French classic in the heart of the capital.

🛈 73 rooms
🚇 Franklin D. Roosevelt 🛗 🔁
♦ All major cards

### 🏨 PAVILLON DE LA REINE
$$$$$ ○○○○
28 Place des Vosges
TEL 01 40 29 19 19
FAX 01 40 29 19 20

pavillon-de-la-reine.com
Elegant, antique-furnished rooms, some with four-poster beds. Pretty courtyard.

🛈 31 + 14 suites + 10 duplex
🚇 St.-Paul 🛗 🔁
♦ All major cards

### 🏨 PISCINE MOLITOR
🍴 $$$$$ ○○○○
8 Avenue de la Port Molitor
TEL 01 56 07 08 50
mltr.fr
The legendary 1930s open-air swimming pool (how Pi in *Life of Pi* got his name), is now a Monument Historique, and has been renovated and reopened as a luxury hotel, restaurant, and spa. The pools (winter and summer) are only open to hotel residents or club members but the rooftop and restaurant are open to

all comers (at a price) and are well worth a visit for a quintessential Parisian experience.

🛈 104 rooms 🚇 Michel Ange Molitor 💳 All major cards

# 🏨 VERNET
# 🍴 $$$$$ ○○○○

25 Rue Vernet
TEL 01 44 31 98 00
hotelvernet-paris.fr

Fireplace and piano in the lobby, Jacuzzis in rooms. The belle epoque restaurant **Le V** has great food in a fine ambiance.

🛈 42 + 9 suites
🚇 George V 🔲 ❄️
💳 All major cards

# 🏨 PERGOLÈSE
# $$$$ ○○○○

3 Rue Pergolèse
TEL 01 53 64 04 04
FAX 01 53 64 04 40
pergolese.com

Modern designer decor and marble bathrooms. Centrally located near the Arc de Triomphe.

🛈 40 🚇 Argentine
❄️ 💳 All major cards

# 🏨 LE RELAIS DU LOUVRE
# $$$ ○○○

19 Rue des Prêtres–St.-Germain-l'Auxerrois
TEL 01 40 41 96 42
FAX 01 40 41 96 44
relaisdulouvre.com

A cozy little hotel with a garden, conveniently positioned between the Louvre and St.-Germain-l'Auxerrois. Perfect for art lovers and city strollers who want a relaxing home base for days spent by the Seine.

🛈 20 🚇 Louvre-Rivoli or Pont-Neuf 🔲 💳 All major cards

# 🍴 PIERRE GAGNAIRE
# $$$$$

6 Rue Balzac
TEL 01 58 36 12 50
pierre-gagnaire.com

One of France's most innovative chefs. Three Michelin stars. Don't miss the "grand dessert." This is a small but superb restaurant, so book far ahead to avoid disappointment.

🚇 George V
🕐 Closed Sat.–Sun. & Aug.
❄️ 💳 All major cards

# 🍴 TAILLEVENT
# $$$$$

15 Rue Lamennais
TEL 01 44 95 15 01
taillevent.com

A long-standing leader in haute cuisine with two Michelin stars, Taillevent has beautiful dining rooms, perfect service, and a renowned wine cellar. Reservations are essential, because Parisians appreciate fine dining in comfortable surroundings when they find it.

🚇 George V 🕐 Closed Sat.– Sun., public holidays, & Aug. ❄️
💳 All major cards

# 🍴 MARSAN
# $$$$

4 Rue d'Assas
TEL 01 42 22 00 11
marsanhelenedarroze.com

Hélène Darroze is one of France's celebrated female chefs—from a family of cooks in the Landes, and trained by Alain Ducasse. At this Michelin two-star location, she adds an imaginative twist to the traditional cuisine and ingredients—from squid to foie gras—of the Southwest.

🚇 Sèvres-Babylone 🕐 Closed Sun.–Mon. 💳 All major cards

---

🚭 Nonsmoking  ❄️ Air-conditioning  🏊 Indoor Pool  🏊 Outdoor Pool  🏋️ Health Club  💳 Credit Cards

## 🍴 LA MASCOTTE MONTMARTRE
$$$

52 Rue des Abbesses
TEL 01 46 06 28 15
la-mascotte-montmartre.com

Old-time Paris the way everyone likes it in this lively brasserie, where the waiters still wear the traditional vest and long apron and like to joke with the customers while they sample their seafood and steaks. A good humor on leaving is always guaranteed.

🚇 Abbesses 💳 V

## 🍴 LE TRAIN BLEU
$$$

Gare de Lyon, 20 Boulevard Diderot
TEL 01 43 43 09 06
le-train-bleu.com

Enjoy the breathtaking belle epoque decoration in this railroad station restaurant; and relish the typical brasserie food of Paris on the go. The Gare de Lyon always evokes a bygone age when travel was a real pleasure and train stations were places where waiting was enjoyable.

🚇 Gare de Lyon 🕐 Closed Sun. 🛗 💳 All major cards

## 🍴 ANGÉLINA
$$

226 Rue de Rivoli
TEL 01 42 60 82 00
angelina-paris.fr

Why not get dressed up and join the Parisian fashion crowd for a café au lait or hot chocolate in this elegant tearoom? You may have to wait in line on the weekends, but you can have fun checking out the clothes of the clientele.

🚇 Tuileries 🕐 Closed D & Tues. in Aug. 🛗 💳 AE, V

---

### PRICES

**HOTELS**
An indication of the cost of a double room in the high season is given by $ signs.

| | |
|---|---|
| $$$$$ | Over $800 |
| $$$$ | $500–$800 |
| $$$ | $300–$500 |
| $$ | $150–$300 |
| $ | Under $150 |

**RESTAURANTS**
An indication of the cost of a three-course meal without drinks is given by $ signs.

| | |
|---|---|
| $$$$$ | Over $300 |
| $$$$ | $200–$300 |
| $$$ | $100–$200 |
| $$ | $70–$100 |
| $ | Under $70 |

---

## 🍴 AU PIED DE COCHON
$$

6 Rue Coquillière
TEL 01 40 13 77 00
pieddecochon.com

This is the place to go in the City of Light for night owls. A lively all-night restaurant serving the best of brasserie dishes; specialties include pig's feet and shellfish platters. The conversation may get more philosophical as the night rolls into the wee hours, but the food and the service will retain the same high standards.

🚇 Louvre-Rivoli or Les Halles 💳 All major cards

## 🍴 BOFINGER
$$

5 & 7 Rue de la Bastille
TEL 01 42 72 87 82
bofingerparis.com

The huge mirrors at this classic 19th-century brasserie make the room as spacious as a boulevard, while the fare is as tantalizing as the menu suggests. Try the *choucroute* (Alsatian sauerkraut with sausages and potatoes).

🚇 Bastille 🈂️
💳 All major cards

## 🍴 LES OMBRES
**$$**
**Musée du Quai Branly**
**TEL 01 47 53 68 00**
**lesombres-restaurant.com**
This is top of the world Paris: The roof of the museum hosts this glass-roofed restaurant offering panoramic views and light, as well as a delightful range of eclectic cuisine from Africa, Asia, and the Americas.

🚇 Alma-Marceau
💳 All major cards

## 🍴 FRENCHIE
**$ ☺☺☺**
**5–6 Rue du Nil**
**TEL 01 40 39 96 19**
**frenchie-restaurant.com**
Under the wooden beams of a 17th-century building is this cheeky addition to the French restaurant scene from Gregory Marchand, protégé of British chef Jamie Oliver; wine bar, Frenchie-to-go, and updated bistro classics like *boudin noir* with apple chutney offset by British cheese list. Reservations recommended.

🚇 Sentier 🕐 Closed Sat. L & Sun.
💳 All major cards.

## 🍴 HARRY'S NEW YORK BAR
**$**
**5 Rue Daunou**
**TEL 01 42 61 71 14**
**harrysbar.fr**
New York–style piano bar once popular with Hemingway and F. Scott Fitzgerald. Highly recommended: the Bloody Marys.

🚇 Opéra 💳 AE, CB, DC, V

# OUTER PARIS

## 🍴 LE PRÉ CATELAN
**$$$$**
**Route de Suresnes**
**TEL 01 44 14 41 14**
**precatelanparis.com**
Talented chef Frédéric Anton has completely livened up the cuisine of this lovely restaurant. Has kept three Michelin stars.

🚇 Porte Maillot, then Bus 144 (until 8 p.m.) 🕐 Closed Sun.–Mon. & all of Aug.
💳 All major cards

## 🍴 BRASSERIE FLODERER
**$$**
**7 Cour des Petites-Écuries**
**TEL 01 47 70 13 59**
**brasserieflo-paris.com**
A sparkling, 19th-century Alsatian brasserie where the menu has typical dishes, such as sauerkraut and snails. Friendly service.

🚇 Château d'Eau 🈂️ 🈂️ 💳 All major cards

## 🍴 PIZZERIA CESAR
**$–$$**
**8 Avenue du General de Gaulle, Place les Maneges, Versailles**
**TEL 01 39 53 02 29**
Just the place for an unpretentious, but utterly delicious, pizza or pasta lunch after walking through the decadence of the palace hereabouts. You can even eat cake!

🚇 RER C: Gare de Versailles Château Rive Gauche
💳 All major cards

---

🈂️ Nonsmoking 🈂️ Air-conditioning 🏊 Indoor Pool 🏊 Outdoor Pool 🏋️ Health Club 💳 Credit Cards

▶ **NORTHERN FRANCE**

## NORD & PICARDIE

## AIRE-SUR-LA-LYS

### 🏨 HOSTELLERIE DES TROIS MOUSQUETAIRES
**$–$$** ✪✪✪✪
Château du Fort de la Redoute
TEL 03 21 39 01 11
FAX 03 21 39 50 10
hostelleriedes3mousquetaires
.com

A family-run hotel located within a large wooded garden, the Three Musketeers is one for all. The interior is beautifully designed in grand, traditional French style; and the older, larger guest rooms are very elegant. The estate includes a golf course, if you have a couple of aficionados in your traveling party who like to shoot a round or two.

🛏 33 🅿 🕐 Closed mid-Dec.– mid-Jan. 🖬 AE, MC, V

## AMIENS

### 🏨 MAROTTE
**$$** ✪✪✪
3 Rue Marotte
TEL 03 60 12 50 00
hotel-marotte.com

This relatively new luxury hotel is situated in a beautifully renovated 19th-century bourgeois residence in the heart of the town of Amiens; it's cozy, welcoming, and includes all modern conveniences; a charming bar for breakfast. It has no restaurant, but front-desk staff will happily recommend good local dining that will suit any tastes or culinary requirements.

🛏 12 ⊖ 🅱 🖬 All major cards.

---

### PRICES

**HOTELS**
An indication of the cost of a double room in the high season is given by **$** signs.

| | |
|---|---|
| **$$$$$** | Over $800 |
| **$$$$** | $500–$800 |
| **$$$** | $300–$500 |
| **$$** | $150–$300 |
| **$** | Under $150 |

**RESTAURANTS**
An indication of the cost of a three-course meal without drinks is given by **$** signs.

| | |
|---|---|
| **$$$$$** | Over $300 |
| **$$$$** | $200–$300 |
| **$$$** | $100–$200 |
| **$$** | $70–$100 |
| **$** | Under $70 |

---

## BOULOGNE-SUR-MER

### 🏨 MÉTROPOLE
**$** ✪✪✪
51–53 Rue Thiers
TEL 03 21 31 54 30
FAX 03 21 30 45 72
hotel-metropole-boulogne.com

Between the ramparts and the sea, this quiet hotel has a delightful garden. No restaurant.

🛏 25 🅿 🕐 Closed late Dec.– early Jan. 🚇 🚇 🖬 AE, MC, V

## CALAIS

### 🏨 MEURICE
### 🍴 **$–$$$** ✪✪✪
5 Rue Edmond-Roche
TEL 03 21 34 57 03
FAX 03 21 96 28 12
hotel-meurice.fr
Until World War II, the Meurice was

---

one of France's luxury hotels. It was restored in 1953, and today offers comfortable hospitality to travelers. Restaurant **La Diligence** serves good standard French cuisine.

🅸 41 🅿 🕒 Restaurant closed Sat. L 🅰 All major cards

## HESDIN-L'ABBÉ

### 🏨 CLÉRY
### 🍴 $–$$$ ✪✪✪

11 Rue du Château
TEL 03 21 83 19 83
FAX 03 21 87 52 59
clery.najeti.fr

A dignified 18th-century house surrounded by parkland. Sitting room with log fire; contemporary decor. Tennis. Fine dining at **Restaurant Le Berthier**.

🅸 27 🅿 🕒 Restaurant closed L 🅰 🅰 🅰 All major cards

## LILLE

### 🏨 GRAND HÔTEL BELLEVUE
### $$$ ✪✪✪

5 Rue Jean-Roisin
TEL 03 20 57 45 64
FAX 03 20 40 07 93
grandhotelbellevue.com

Mozart once stayed in this 18th-century Bourbon hotel located close to the Opéra, the Palais de la Musique, and the Palais de Congrès. The building is a fine example of Lille architecture with classic decor. No restaurant on site, but there are plenty of options in Lille for lunch and supper.

🅸 61 🅰 🅰 🅰 All major cards

### 🍴 L'HUÎTRIÈRE
### $$$$–$$$$$

3 Rue des Chats-Bossus

TEL 03 20 55 43 41
lhuitriere.fr

L'Huîtrière is a well established and very fashionable establishment, with one Michelin star to its name, located in the old town of Lille. An art deco, blue-and-gold tiled entrance leads to a richly furnished dining room, where staff make you feel right at home. The service is good and the menu offers an excellent range of fresh seafood and regional cuisine.

🕒 Closed Sun. D, public holidays, & Aug. 🅰 🅰 All major cards

### 🍴 BRASSERIE DE LA PAIX
### $$

25 Place Rihour
TEL 03 20 54 70 41
brasserie-delapaix.fr

Typical northern brasserie with art deco furnishings and cozy banquettes serving classic fare.

🕒 Closed Sun. 🅰 AE, MC, V

## MONTREUIL-SUR-MER

### 🏨 CHÂTEAU DE
### 🍴 MONTREUIL
### $$$$ ✪✪✪✪

4 Chaussée de Capucins
TEL 03 21 81 53 04
FAX 03 21 81 36 43
chateaudemontreuil.com

Tastefully decorated bedrooms look out over the gardens of this secluded château situated on the edge of town. The one-star Michelin restaurant specializes in seafood.

🅸 13 🅿 🕒 Closed mid-Dec.– Feb. & Mon. except July & Aug. 🅰 All major cards

### 🍴 AUBERGE DE LA
### GRENOUILLÈRE
### $$$–$$$$

19 Rue de la Grenouillère,

**La Madeleine-sous-Montreuil**
TEL 03 21 06 07 22
lagrenouillere.fr
A charming Picardie farmhouse, particularly popular for lunch on the terrace. Try dishes like *pré-salé agneau de la baie de Somme,* or the house specialty, frogs' legs with garlic and fried parsley. One Michelin star.
🕐 Closed Tues.–Wed.
(except July & Aug.) & Dec.–Jan.
🚫 🅰 All major cards

## CHAMPAGNE

## REIMS

🏨 **LES CRAYÈRES**
🍴 **$$$$$ ○○○○○**
64 Boulevard Henry-Vasnier
TEL 03 26 24 90 00
lescrayeres.com
A beautiful turn-of-the-20th-century family château, home to master chef Gérard Boyer, this is the very epitome of French refinement and luxury. The restaurant offers a variety of dishes that includes lamb with truffles *en croûte* and pig's trotters stuffed with foie gras. There's a huge wine list and, of course, plenty of champagne. Reservations are essential in this perennially popular destination.
🛏 16 + 3 suites 🕐 Closed Jan.; restaurant closed Mon.–Tues.
🚫 🅿 🅰 All major cards

🏨 **DE LA PAIX**
**$–$$ ○○○**
9 Rue Buirette
TEL 03 26 40 04 08
FAX 03 26 47 75 04
bestwestern-lapaix-reims.com
Located in the heart of the car-free city center, this is a peaceful old hotel with an inviting garden. There is a

rich, warm interior decor throughout the hotel and the guest rooms are modern and comfortably furnished.
🛏 168 🅿 🚫 🕐 🏊
🅰 All major cards

## ALSACE & LORRAINE

## COLMAR

🏨 **HOSTELLERIE LE**
🍴 **MARÉCHAL**
**$$$ ○○○**
4 Place Six Montagnes Noires
TEL 03 89 41 60 32
FAX 03 89 24 59 40
le-marechal.com
This is a 16th-century half-timbered hotel and restaurant, beautifully situated canalside in Colmar's "Little Venice" district. The specialties here include *terrine de foie de canard à la gelée au muscat d'Alsace* and lobster

and monkfish salad served with a truffle vinaigrette.

 30 All major cards

### GRAND HÔTEL BRISTOL
**$–$$ ○○○**
7 Place de la Gare
TEL 03 89 23 59 59 OR
03 89 23 15 86 (RESTAURANTS)
grand-hotel-bristol.com

This beautifully decorated, centrally located hotel charms with its turn-of-the-20th-century elegance. It also hosts two excellent restaurants: the Michelin one-star **Rendezvous de Chasse** and the more informal **l'Auberge.**

70 All major cards

## KAYSERSBERG

### CHAMBARD MARÉCHAL
**$$$$ ○○○○**
9 Rue du Général-de-Gaulle
TEL 03 89 47 10 17
FAX 03 89 47 35 03
lechambard.fr

This stylish hotel boasts modern rooms, a spa, and a two-star Michelin restaurant, **Restaurant Gastronomique.** This elegant eatery is renowned for Alsace wine and regional cuisine; try the foie gras with *choucroute,* or the celebrated platter of three meats—pork, lamb, and beef.

32 + 5 suites + 6 deluxe suites
Closed mid-Nov.–Feb.; restaurant closed Mon., Tues. L, & Wed. L
AE, MC, V

## MARLENHEIM

### LE CERF
**$$–$$$**
30 Rue du Général-de-Gaulle
TEL 03 88 87 73 73

FAX 03 88 87 68 08
lecerf.com

This picturesque inn with a flowery courtyard, located in a village on the N4 21 miles (30 km) west of Strasbourg, contains a Michelin one-star restaurant specializing in Alsatian dishes such as *tête de veau* or sauerkraut with pork and foie gras.

18 Restaurant closed Tues.–Wed.
All major cards

## NANCY

### GRAND HÔTEL DE LA REINE
**$$ ○○○○**
2 Place Stanislas
TEL 03 83 35 03 01
FAX 03 83 32 86 04
hoteldelareine.com

This exquisite 18th-century palace, one of the historic buildings in the heart of Nancy, was once the home of Marie-Antoinette. The Grand Hotel of the Queen has luxurious guest rooms that are furnished in Louis XV style. The hotel's restaurant is called **Stanislas,** after the dethroned Polish king.

48 All major cards

## STRASBOURG

### MONOPOLE MÉTROPOLE
**$–$$$ ○○○**
16 Rue Kuhn
TEL 03 88 14 39 14
bw-monopole.com

Close to the historic Petite France district, this peaceful, grand hotel offers rooms either in contemporary mode or in traditional Alsatian style.

90 All major cards

 Nonsmoking  Air-conditioning  Indoor Pool  Outdoor Pool  Health Club  Credit Cards

## 🍴 AU CROCODILE
**$$$$–$$$$$**
10 Rue de l'Outre
TEL 03 88 32 13 02
au-crocodile.com
With luxurious surroundings, and boasting impeccable service along with one Michelin star, the Crocodile is probably still the most stylish restaurant in the city of Strasbourg. Favorite dishes here include roast monkfish with fennel confit and saffron tomatoes.
🕐 Closed Sun.–Mon. 🔆
🀫 All major cards

## 🍴 BUEREHIESEL
**$$$$–$$$$$**
4 Parc Orangerie
TEL 03 88 45 56 65
buerehiesel.fr
A reconstructed Alsatian farmhouse is now a Michelin one-star restaurant. Chef Eric Westermann offers seasonal delicacies such as Bresse chicken with potatoes and artichokes. Inventive desserts include brioche with pear and beer-flavored ice cream.
🅿 🕐 Closed Sun. & Mon.
🔆 🀫 All major cards

# VERDUN

## 🏨 LES JARDINS DU MESS
## 🍴 $$–$$$
22 Quai de la République
TEL 03 29 80 14 18
coq-hardi.com
This delightful hotel is located on the banks of the Meuse in the heart of Verdun. This magnificent 19th century building , once an officers' mess, has been tastefully converted into a luxury hotel with a fine restaurant and parklands that are ideal for walking and relaxing, and building up an appetite for the fine food on offer.

---

## PRICES

### HOTELS
An indication of the cost of a double room in the high season is given by **$** signs.

| | |
|---|---|
| **$$$$$** | Over $800 |
| **$$$$** | $500–$800 |
| **$$$** | $300–$500 |
| **$$** | $150–$300 |
| **$** | Under $150 |

### RESTAURANTS
An indication of the cost of a three-course meal without drinks is given by $ signs.

| | |
|---|---|
| **$$$$$** | Over $300 |
| **$$$$** | $200–$300 |
| **$$$** | $100–$200 |
| **$$** | $70–$100 |
| **$** | Under $70 |

---

🛈 50 + suites 🕐 Restaurant closed out of season 🔆 ♿
🀫 All major cards

## 🍴 CHEZ MAMIE
**$$**
52 Avenue 42ème Division
TEL 03 29 86 45 50
Classic French and European fare are served in a rustic setting replete with bookshelves and chequered tablecloths. This friendly local bistro is a Verdun treasure. Make reservations a day in advance as Chez Mamie is extremely popular with the locals; and when you sit down for the smoked salmon, or the "tournedos" steak (wrapped in ham, and cooked in a rich sauce) you'll soon discover why.
🕐 Closed Tues.
🀫 All major cards

---

🏨 Hotel  🍴 Restaurant  🛈 No. of Guest Rooms  🔆 No. of Seats  🅿 Parking  🚇 Metro  🕐 Closed  ♿ Elevator

## ▶ NORMANDY & BRITTANY

## NORMANDY

### AUDRIEU

#### 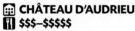 CHÂTEAU D'AUDRIEU
#### $$$–$$$$$
TEL 02 31 80 21 52
FAX 02 31 80 24 73
chateaudaudrieu.com

Located between Bayeux and Caen, this 18th-century château is surrounded by delightful parkland. Guests can enjoy long walks in the woodlands to whet the appetite for a visit to the elegant one-star Michelin restaurant. The comfortable and elegant rooms boast lovely period decoration.

🛈 23 + 6 suites 🕓 Restaurant closed Mon., L except Sat.–Sun.

🌊 🗞 All major cards

### BAYEUX

#### 🏨 D'ARGOUGES
#### $ ✪✪
21 Rue St.-Patrice
TEL 02 31 92 88 86
FAX 02 31 92 69 16
hotel-dargouges.com

Set in a peaceful garden, this old family mansion is conveniently situated within walking distance of the town's center. There is no restaurant in the building, but plenty of eateries to choose from in Bayeux, and the front desk will gladly recommend one to suit your gastronomic needs or to match your mood of the night.

🛈 28 🕓 Closed Dec.–Jan.
🅿 🚭
🗞 All major cards

#### 🏨 LION D'OR
#### 🍴 $ ✪✪✪
71 Rue St.-Jean
TEL 02 31 92 06 90
liondor-bayeux.fr

This most attractive 17th-century post house is set around a central courtyard and boasts a good-value restaurant serving dishes such as duck foie gras with honey and succulent sausages.

🛈 25 🅿 🕓 Restaurant closed D Sun.–Mon.; L Mon.–Tues., & Sat.; & Nov.–March
🗞 All major cards

### BEUVRON-EN-AUGE

#### 🍴 LE PAVÉ D'AUGE
#### $$
TEL 02 31 79 26 71
pavedauge.com

This Michelin one-star restaurant is located within the covered market hall, and serves simply cooked, local ingredients. Try the lobster with herb butter, and the local cheeses along with some Calvados. An excellent wine list is also available.

🕓 Closed Mon. 🗞 MC, V

### CABOURG

#### 🏨 GRAND HÔTEL
#### $$–$$$$ ✪✪✪✪
Promenade Marcel-Proust
TEL 02 31 91 01 79
FAX 02 31 24 03 20
mgallery.com

Cabourg's Grand Hôtel stylishly dominates the seafront just as it did in Marcel Proust's novel *Remembrance of Things Past.* Proust often stayed here, and the hotel restaurant still serves the memorable madeleine cakes.

🛈 70 🅿 🗞 All major cards

🗞 Nonsmoking 🌀 Air-conditioning 🏊 Indoor Pool 🏊 Outdoor Pool 🏋 Health Club 🗞 Credit Cards

## CAEN

### 🍴 LE CARLOTTA
$$
15 Quai Vendeuve
TEL 02 31 86 68 99
le-carlotta.fr
This art deco–style brasserie offers diners a veranda overlooking the busy port of Caen. No surprise then that the fish is a specialty and the seafood dishes are all routinely fresh and delicious.
🕐 Closed Sun.
🖾 AE, MC, V

## DEAUVILLE

### 🏨 NORMANDY-BARRIERE
### 🍴 $$$$$
TEL 02 31 98 66 22
FAX 02 31 98 66 23
38 Rue J. Mermoz
lucienbarriere.com
This classic belle epoque mansion is where the stars like to stay in this ever so chi-chi seaside town (Anouk Aimée likes a sea-facing window, apparently). There's a fine courtyard restaurant that's great for summer dining.
ℹ 290 + 28 suites + 8 apts.
🏊 🍽 🖾 All major cards

### 🍴 LE SPINNAKER
$$–$$$
52 Rue Mirabeau
TEL 02 31 88 24 40
spinnakerdeauville.com
A highly regarded seafood restaurant located on the promenade, serving traditional Norman cuisine with lots of cider and Calvados. The baked lobster in cider vinegar is a special treat.
🕐 Closed Mon.–Tues
🖾 All major cards

## PRICES

**HOTELS**
An indication of the cost of a double room in the high season is given by $ signs.

| | |
|---|---|
| $$$$$ | Over $800 |
| $$$$ | $500–$800 |
| $$$ | $300–$500 |
| $$ | $150–$300 |
| $ | Under $150 |

**RESTAURANTS**
An indication of the cost of a three-course meal without drinks is given by $ signs.

| | |
|---|---|
| $$$$$ | Over $300 |
| $$$$ | $200–$300 |
| $$$ | $100–$200 |
| $$ | $70–$100 |
| $ | Under $70 |

## DIEPPE

### 🍴 A LA MARMITE DIEPPOISE
$$$
8 Rue St.-Jean
TEL 02 35 84 24 26
marmitedieppoise.fr
This popular restaurant is situated close to the harbor named after its most famous local dish: fish and shellfish in a cream sauce. This delicious recipe includes lotte, turbot, local Saint Jacques (depending on the season) or sole, julienne, crayfish and mussels, accompanied by steamed potatoes. It's a veritable who's who of the maritime delicacies caught hereabouts.
🕐 Closed Sun. D & Mon.
🖾 MC, V

# DINARD

## 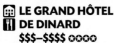 LE GRAND HÔTEL DE DINARD
### $$$–$$$$ ○○○○
46 Avenue George V
TEL 02 99 88 26 26
lucienbarriere.com

This is Dinard's classic grand hotel, located right on the promenade., where the beautiful people take their leisure. The restaurant and café tend to take center stage during the film festival, so reserving a table—if you can—is never a bad idea.

(1) 90 P ⊕ Closed Dec.–March
⊗ ⊠ 🖅 ⊗ All major cards

# HONFLEUR

## LA FERME SAINT-SIMÉON
### $$$–$$$$$ ○○○○
20 Rue Adolphe Marais
TEL 02 31 81 78 00
fermesaintsimeon.fr

This peaceful 17th-century farmhouse was a favorite place to stay and seek inspiration for the Impressionist painters. The restaurant serves specialties such as stuffed *pré-salé* lamb that will melt in your mouth. This bucolic hotel also has plenty of facilities that will satisfy the health-conscious modern-day wayfarer, including sauna, solarium, and hydrotherapy complex. Your impression of La Ferme Saint-Siméon will be long-lasting.

(1) 31 + 3 suites ⊠ 🖅
⊗ AE, MC, V

##  SA.QUA.NA
### $$$$
22 Place Hamelin
TEL 02 31 89 40 80

alexandre-bourdas.com

Sa.Qua.Na stands for Saveurs, Quality, Nature—or "fish" *(sakana)* in Japanese. Chef Alexandre Bourdas, with two Michelin stars, adds a touch of zen to local food—such as lobster with lime and coconut.

⊕ Closed Mon.–Wed. 🔆
⊗ AE, MC, V

# EGUISHEIM

## AUBERGE ALSACIENNE
### $
12 Grand-Rue
TEL 03 89 41 50 20
FAX 02 31 23 89 32
www.auberge-alsacienne.net

A traditional hotel situated in one of France's favorite villages with modern interior decor and restaurant serving Alsatian classics such as *choucroute,* knuckle of pork, and fabulous fruit tarts. This is regional cooking done superbly well, in a setting that is the essence of French hospitality.

⊕ Restaurant closed Sun. p.m., Mon.–Tues. L
⊗ All major cards

# LA BOUILLE

## LOGIS HÔTEL LE BELLEVUE
### $$ ○○
13 Quai Hector Malot
TEL 02 35 18 05 05
FAX 02 35 18 00 92
logishotels.com/fr

A good-value, renovated, small hotel located on the banks of the Seine River with a rustic, wooden-beamed restaurant. Your perfect night out in northern France.

⊗ AE, MC, V

# LE BEC-HELLOUIN

## 🏨 L'AUBERGE DE L'ABBAYE
### $ ⓪⓪⓪
12 Place Guillaume Le Conqueror
TEL 02 32 44 86 02
hotelbechellouin.com

This 18th-century inn with a terrace is situated close to the Bec-Hellouin monastery. The restaurant serves regional specialties based on cider and apples, a staple ingredient in many of the cuisines of Normandy and Brittany. Be sure to try the Calvados, a lovely apple-based drink that originated in this part of France.

🛈 11 🅿 🕐 Hotel closed mid-Nov.–mid-Feb.; restaurant closed Mon.–Tues. Nov.– Easter
💳 MC, V

# LES ANDELYS

## 🏨 LA CHAÎNE D'OR
### $–$$$ ⓪⓪⓪
27 Rue Grande
TEL 02 32 54 00 31
FAX 02 32 54 05 68
hotel-lachainedor.com

Overlooked by the ruins of the Château Gaillard, this 18th-century auberge stands beside the Seine. There are picturesque views from most rooms and from the restaurant. The hotel also has a good terrace where guests can enjoy the air.

🛈 12 🅿 🕐 Closed Sun. D, Mon Nov.–March, & Wed. April–Oct.
💳 AE, MC, V

# MONT ST.-MICHEL

### SOMETHING SPECIAL

## 🍴 LA MÈRE POULARD
### $$$ ⓪⓪⓪
Grande Rue

TEL 02 33 89 68 68
lamerepoulard.com

Visitors from Ernest Hemingway to Margaret Thatcher have sampled the famous "Omelette Mère Poulard", made from a secret recipe over an open fire and still as popular as ever at this long-established restaurant (opened by Annette Poulard in 1888). The Iron Lady's review is not recorded, but Papa Hemingway's surely is in some leather-bound notebook somewhere. Other specialties include grilled pink lobster and rack of lamb. Rooms are available should the desire for "just one more glass" from the wine list persuade you to linger long into the night and sample the breakfast too.

🛈 27
💳 All major cards

---

🏨 Hotel  🍴 Restaurant  🛈 No. of Guest Rooms  🪑 No. of Seats  🅿 Parking  🚇 Metro  🕐 Closed  🛗 Elevator

# PONT-AUDEMER

## ⊞ BELLE ISLE SUR RISLE
### $$$–$$$$ ✪✪✪✪

112 route de Rouen
TEL 02 32 56 96 22
FAX 02 32 42 88 96
bellile.com

Beautiful grounds with ancient trees surround this handsome mansion on an island in the Risle River. Elegantly furnished guest rooms encourage a lie-in and a read. For the more active among us, the facilities include a sauna and tennis courts.

ⓘ 24 🅿 🕐 Closed Jan.–mid-March; restaurant closed L Mon.–Wed. 🏊 🏊 🎽 🏦 All major cards

# PORT-EN-BESSIN

## ⊞ LA CHENEVIÈRE
## 🍴 $$$–$$$$ ✪✪✪✪

Escures-Commes (NW of Bayeux)
TEL 02 31 51 25 25
FAX 02 31 51 25 20
lacheneviere.com

A noble Normandy mansion dating from the 1800s, La Chenevière has an excellent restaurant. This elegant hotel is set in a tree-lined park a short distance from the sea and Omaha Beach golf course. Each room has its own little secret garden, which makes for an enchanting and memorable stay.

ⓘ 18 + 3 suites 🅿 🕐 Closed Dec.–Feb. 🏊 🏊 🏦 All major cards

# ROUEN

## ⊞ CATHÉDRALE
### $ ✪✪

12 rue St.-Romain
TEL 02 35 71 57 95
FAX 02 35 70 15 54
hotel-de-la-cathedrale.fr

This old, half-timbered town hotel has a flowery courtyard and a *salon du thé*. No restaurant.

ⓘ 24 🏦 AE, MC, V

## 🍴 GILL
### $$$$

9 quai de la Bourse
TEL 02 35 71 16 14
gill.fr

Modern and elegant, one of Rouen's top restaurants with two Michelin stars. Fresh produce is cooked with great style here. Sample such delicacies as langoustine ravioli and the Rouen specialty, pigeon stuffed with liver and cooked in a sauce of its own blood.

🕐 Closed Sun.–Mon. & Aug.

🏦 🏦 🏦 All major cards

# TROUVILLE-SUR-MER

## 🍴 LES VAPEURS
### $$

160 boulevard Fernand-Moreaux
TEL 02 31 88 15 24

A popular art deco brasserie located close to the fish market, with fresh dishes to suit late-nighters and early risers. The shrimp and the *moules frites* (mussels with french fries) are especially recommended.

🏦 AE, MC, V

# BRITTANY

# BREST

## ⊞ LOGIS HÔTEL DE LA CORNICHE
### $ ✪✪✪

1 rue Amiral Nicol
TEL 02 98 45 12 42
logishotels.com/fr

A modern hotel built in the old Breton style. On the coast road west of the town. Tennis courts available.

ⓘ 16 🏦 AE, MC, V

---

🚭 Nonsmoking  ❄ Air-conditioning  🏊 Indoor Pool  🏊 Outdoor Pool  🎽 Health Club  🏦 Credit Cards

# CONCARNEAU

## 🍴 COQUILLE
$$$
**Quai Moros**
**TEL 02 98 97 08 52**
This very attractive Breton-style restaurant situated in the old port serves a satisfying variety of fresh fish and seafood to suit most tastes and fine wines to wash all that nautical nutrition down.
🕐 Closed Sun. D & Mon.
🅢 🕭 AE, MC, V

## 🍴 CRÊPERIE DES REMPARTS
$
**31 Rue Théophile-Louarn**
**TEL 02 98 50 65 66**
Located in the Ville Close (walled town), this is a great place to sample the excellent crêpes and galettes that are so popular with the locals. Careful though, crêpes can become an obsession with first-time visitors to France and anywhere you visit will have a bewildering range of temptations from which to choose.
🕐 Closed Mon. except July–Aug.
🕭 MC, V

# LORIENT

## 🍴 L'AMPHITRYON
$$–$$$$
**127 Rue du Colonel Muller**
**TEL 02 97 83 34 04**
amphitryon-lorient.com
Looking for a friendly, local restaurant that serves fresh seafood with panache? Look no further than this excellent establishment with its two Michelin stars and its warmly inviting dining ambiance.
🕐 Closed Sun.–Mon. 🕭
🕭 AE, MC, V

---

## PRICES
**HOTELS**
An indication of the cost of a double room in the high season is given by $ signs.

| | |
|---|---|
| **$$$$$** | Over $800 |
| **$$$$** | $500–$800 |
| **$$$** | $300–$500 |
| **$$** | $150–$300 |
| **$** | Under $150 |

**RESTAURANTS**
An indication of the cost of a three-course meal without drinks is given by $ signs.

| | |
|---|---|
| **$$$$$** | Over $300 |
| **$$$$** | $200–$300 |
| **$$$** | $100–$200 |
| **$$** | $70–$100 |
| **$** | Under $70 |

# PONT-AVEN

## 🍴 ROSMADEC LE MOULIN
$$–$$$
**Venelle de Rosmadec**
**TEL 02 98 06 00 22**
rosmadec.com
This is a Michelin one-star restaurant located in an old millhouse near the bridge in the town center. The dining room is welcoming with its traditional Breton decor. The specialties here include grilled Breton lobster, *sauté de langoustines,* and beautifully prepared artichokes. Reservations are essential as this place is always popular with the locals. The people of Pont-Aven are perennially proud of fine cuisine made with fresh local produce and a large dash of imagination.
ⓘ 4 🕐 Closed Sun. D
🕭 AE, MC, V

---

## QUIMPER

### 🏨 CHÂTEAU DE GUILGUIFFIN
**$$$**

Landulec (on the D874 S of Quimper)
TEL 02 98 91 52 11
FAX 02 98 91 52 52

This large château is surrounded by wild and magnificent parkland that will make you feel like a lord or lady at leisure. There's no restaurant to work up an appetite for, but brunch and/or buffet supper can be served by prior arrangement. The accommodation price includes breakfast.

🛏 3 + 2 suites 🕐 In winter by reservation only 🔇 All major cards

### 🍴 L'AMBROISIE
**$$$**

49 Rue Elie-Fréron
TEL 02 98 95 00 02
ambroisie-quimper.com

Conveniently situated close to the cathedral and well known for its excellent fish and imaginative desserts. Now has one Michelin star.

🕐 Closed Sun. D & Mon.
🔇 MC, V

## RENNES

### 🍴 AUBERGE ST.-SAUVEUR
**$$**

6 Rue St.-Saveur
TEL 02 99 79 32 56

A handsome half-timbered building that survived the great fire of 1750. Inside, it retains the traditional atmosphere. Specialties include Breton lobster and other shellfish and fish dishes.

🕐 Closed Sun. & Mon. p.m.
🔇 AE, MC, V

## RIEC-SUR-BELON

### 🍴 CHEZ JACKY
**$$$**

Port de Belon
TEL 02 98 06 90 32
chez-jacky.com

The place to eat Belon oysters—a basic, authentic restaurant on the Belon River with oyster beds right next to the restaurant. The *plateau de fruits de mer* is a real treat. Reservations are essential. Chambres d'hôtes are also available.

🕐 Closed Oct.–Easter 🔇 MC, V

## ROSCOFF

### 🏨 BRITTANY
### 🍴 $$–$$$ ✪✪✪

Boulevard Ste.-Barbe
TEL 02 98 69 70 78
FAX 02 98 61 13 29
hotel-brittany.com

This lovely old stone manor house faces the old port of Roscoff and l'Île de Batz, and has its own spa and renowned restaurant serving excellent seafood, and a range of Breton culinary delights.

🛏 25 🅿 🕐 Closed Nov.–March; restaurant dinner only. 🏊
🔇 AE, MC, V

### 🏨 LE TEMPS DE VIVRE
**$$$**

Place Église
TEL 02 98 19 33 19
FAX 02 98 19 33 00

This granite Breton house with stylish interior is located on the shore with wonderful views of the ocean. The Michelin one-star restaurant next door offers imaginative local specialties as well as efficient and friendly service from the helpful wait staff. The time of your life (Le Temps de Vivre) will be well spent here.

🛏 15 🕐 Closed Sun.–Mon. in winter 💳 All major cards

## STE.-ANNE-LA-PALUD

### 🏨 DE LA PLAGE
🍽 $$$$ ◐◐◐◐
TEL 02 98 92 50 12
FAX 02 98 92 56 54
plage.com

A classic seaside hotel delightfully located on a tiny remote beach. Sea views and sunsets are always within sight from the excellent restaurant. Try the great local crab and the memorable Breton speciality, a *pot au feu* of lobster and vegetables. De la Plage is a memorable dining experience in an unforgettable setting.

🛏 26 + 4 suites 🅿 🕐 Restaurant closed Nov.–March; L Thurs., Sat., & Sun. only 🌊 💳 All major cards

## ST.-MALO

### 🏨 GRAND HÔTEL DES THERMES
$$$–$$$$$ ◐◐◐◐
100 Boulevard Hébert, Courtoisville
TEL 02 99 40 75 75
warwickhotels.com/le-grand-hotel-des-thermes

A hotel situated right on the seafront with plenty of facilities, including a garden, a sea-therapy center, six pools, and two restaurants.

🛏 168 + 7 suites 🅿 🕐 Closed 2 weeks in Jan. 🌊 💳 All major cards

### 🏨 LE NAUTILUS
$ ◐◐◐
9 Rue de la Corne-de-Cerf
TEL 02 99 40 42 27

## PRICES

**HOTELS**
An indication of the cost of a double room in the high season is given by $ signs.

| | |
|---|---|
| $$$$$ | Over $800 |
| $$$$ | $500–$800 |
| $$$ | $300–$500 |
| $$ | $150–$300 |
| $ | Under $150 |

**RESTAURANTS**
An indication of the cost of a three-course meal without drinks is given by $ signs.

| | |
|---|---|
| $$$$$ | Over $300 |
| $$$$ | $200–$300 |
| $$$ | $100–$200 |
| $$ | $70–$100 |
| $ | Under $70 |

FAX 02 99 82 23 89
hotel-lenautilus-saint-malo.com

This small charming hotel is located in a 17th-century building within the walls of the old town and guarantees a good night's sleep and a decent continental breakfast in the morning.

🛏 15 🕐 Closed Nov.–Dec. 💳 All major cards

### 🍽 LA DUCHESSE ANNE
$$$
5 Place Guy-la-Chambre
TEL 02 99 40 85 33
duchesse-anne.bzh

La Duchesse Anne is a veritable institution in this region with elegant decor and impeccable cuisine. Specialties include *foie gras de canard* and local grilled lobster, but you can't really go wrong with a chef this good and an ambiance this cheerful. Whatever appears on the plate before you will be well prepared and richly satisfying.

🕐 Closed Tues. D & Wed.

🔌 MC, V

### 🍴 HÔTEL DE L'UNIVERS SAINT-MALO

$$

Place Chateaubriand
TEL 02 99 40 89 52
hotel-univers-saintmalo.com

This popular restaurant located within the walls of the old town offers excellent seafood at reasonable prices.

🔌 All major cards

## ST.-THÉGONNEC

### 🏨 AUBERGE ST.-
### 🍴 THÉGONNEC

$–$$$

6 Place Marie
TEL 02 98 79 61 18
aubergesaintthegonnec.com

This is a traditional auberge in a village historically known for its parish close. The fare is good simple Breton cooking that is satisfying and served in an elegant dining room. Rooms are also available.

🛈 19 🕐 Closed Sun. Sept.–March

🔌 MC, V

## RÉBEURDEN

### 🏨 TI AL-LANNEC

$–$$$ ✪✪✪

14 Allée de Mezo-Guen
TEL 02 96 15 01 01
tiallannec.com

The Ti Al-Lannec is set within delightful wooded grounds overlooking the Bay of Lannion, with a path that leads down to the sea. This is a good place for some aim-

less rambling in a beautiful part of France that is less visited than the hot spots further south. Some rooms have terraces or verandas so enquire upon booking if you are seeking a view. And for those feeling engergetic there's a tennis court, while those who just wish to relax can enjoy the sauna. Whatever you want to do in Rebeurden, the Ti Al-Lannec is the perfect base camp for your activities. Or your intentional inactivity.

🛈 29 🕐 Closed Nov.–Feb. 🎽

🔌 CB, DC, MC, V

## VANNES

### 🏨 LA MARÉBAUDIÈRE

$ ✪✪✪

4 Rue Aristide-Briand
TEL 02 97 47 34 29
marebaudiere.com

A quiet, stylishly decorated hotel with a delightful garden, located near the old town of Vannes. There's no restaurant on site, but you can get dining recommendations from the front desk staff, who will happily direct you to the places that the locals frequent for a good supper in town.

🛈 41 🅿 🔌

🔌 All major cards

## ► LOIRE VALLEY

## AMBOISE

### 🏨 LE CHOISEUL
### 🍴 $$–$$$$ ✪✪✪✪

36 Quai Charles-Guinot
TEL 02 47 30 45 45
le-choiseul.com

This charming boutique hotel in an elegant, 18th-century mansion is situated close to the château, facing the Loire River. Le Choiseul has its own flower garden and restaurant.

**(i)** 29 + 3 suites **P** 🚫 🛗 🏊
🃏 All major cards

## 🍴 LE LION D'OR
**$$ ○○**

17 Quai Charles-Guinot
TEL 02 47 57 00 23
FAX 02 47 23 22 49
leliondor-amboise.eatbu.com
Located near to Clos Lucé, this stylish restaurant offers excellent cuisine and gives fresh local ingredients a contemporary flourish.

**(i)** 21 **P** 🕐 Closed Sun. p.m. & Mon. 🃏 All major cards

## ANGERS

### 🏨 ANJOU
🍴 **$–$$$ ○○○○**

1 Boulevard Maréchal Foch
TEL 02 41 21 12 11
hoteldanjou.fr
Large 19th-century hotel, beautifully renovated, close to the old town. The restaurant, **Salamandre**, has Renaissance decor as a backdrop to very good value food; try the ravioli stuffed with lobster or the excellent fish soups.

**(i)** 53 **P** 🕐 Restaurant closed Sun. 🛗 🃏 All major cards

### 🏨 FRANCE
**$ ○○○**

8 Place de la Gare
TEL 02 41 88 49 42
hoteldefrance-angers.com
A classic hotel conveniently situated near the railroad station and major sights. No restaurant.

**(i)** 56 🚫 🛗 🃏 All major cards

---

**PRICES**

**HOTELS**
An indication of the cost of a double room in the high season is given by **$** signs.

| | |
|---|---|
| **$$$$$** | Over $800 |
| **$$$$** | $500–$800 |
| **$$$** | $300–$500 |
| **$$** | $150–$300 |
| **$** | Under $150 |

**RESTAURANTS**
An indication of the cost of a three-course meal without drinks is given by **$** signs.

| | |
|---|---|
| **$$$$$** | Over $300 |
| **$$$$** | $200–$300 |
| **$$$** | $100–$200 |
| **$$** | $70–$100 |
| **$** | Under $70 |

---

## 🍴 LE RELAIS
**$$**

9 Rue de la Gare
TEL 02 41 88 42 51
le-relais-restaurant-angers.fr
Charming wine-themed restaurant with frescoed walls, classic cuisine, and fine selection of Loire wines.

🕐 Closed Sun.–Mon.
🃏 All major cards

## AZAY-LE-RIDEAU

### 🍴 GRAND MONARQUE
**$$–$$$**

Place de la République
TEL 02 47 45 40 08
legrandmonarque.com
A friendly hotel-restaurant with a shady terrace. Delicious local fare; salmon and goat's cheese, for example, complemented by local wine.

---

🏨 Hotel 🍴 Restaurant **(i)** No. of Guest Rooms 🛏 No. of Seats **P** Parking 🚇 Metro 🕐 Closed 🛗 Elevator

ⓘ 24 🕐 Closed Dec.–mid-Feb.
🛇 AE, MC, V

## BLOIS

### 🏨 LE MÉDICIS
**$–$$ ✦✦✦**
2 Allée François I
TEL 02 54 43 94 04
le-medicis.com
An elegant 19th-century hotel located within walking distance of the château and close to the railroad station. The restaurant serves classic French cuisine.
ⓘ 12 🕐 Closed Sun., Oct.–Easter, & Jan. 🅰 🛇 All major cards

### 🏨 ANNE DE BRETAGNE
**$ ✦✦**
31 Avenue Jean Laigret
TEL 02 54 78 05 38
FAX 02 54 74 37 79
hotelannedebretagne.com
Situated on a small square close to the château, this modest hotel is quiet and friendly. No restaurant.
ⓘ 28 🛇 MC, V

### 🍴 AU RENDEZVOUS DES PÊCHEURS
**$$$**
27 Rue foix
TEL 02 54 74 67 48
rendezvousdespecheurs.com
A simple little bistro now with one Michelin star serving excellent fish dishes; try the asparagus and langoustine. Reservations are suggested.
🕐 Closed L Sun.–Mon., & first 3 weeks in Aug. 🅰 🛇 MC, V

## SOMETHING SPECIAL

### 🍴 L'ORANGERIE DU CHÂTEAU
**$$–$$$$**
1 Avenue Jean Laigret

TEL 02 54 78 05 36
orangerie-du-chateau.fr
A lovely terrace restaurant with one Michelin star in the château orangery. Specialties include perch with asparagus (in season), *filet de pigeonneau à la Vendômoise,* and *panier de poudre d'ail.*
🕐 Closed Sun.–Mon. 🛇 AE, MC, V

## BOURGES

### 🍴 LE D'ANTAN SANCERROIS
**$$**
50 Rue Bourbonnoux
TEL 02 48 65 96 26
dantansancerrois.fr
A popular restaurant located in a venerable building, which offers excellent local cooking and has one Michelin star to its name.
🕐 Closed Sun.–Mon. 🛇 AE, MC, V

## CHAMBORD

### 🏨 LE GRAND SAINT-MICHEL
**$ ✦✦✦**
TEL 02 54 20 31 31
FAX 02 54 20 36 40
relaisdechambord.com
A quiet hotel located close to the château and on the edge of the forest. Reservations are required, so book ahead. The restaurant serves good traditional and regional cuisine on the terrace. Tennis is also available.
ⓘ 38 🅿 🛇 MC, V

## CHAMPIGNÉ

### 🏨🍴 CHÂTEAU DES BRIOTTIÈRES
**$$$**
Route de Marigne
TEL 02 41 42 00 02
briottieres.com

An intimate 18th-century family-owned château, full of antiques, with lovely gardens. Dine on traditional Anjou cuisine in the elegant dining room.

🛏 17 🅿 🕐 Closed Nov.–March ❧ AE, MC, V

## CHENONCEAUX

### 🏨 BON LABOUREUR DU 🍴 AUBERGE
**$$$ ✪✪✪**
6 Rue du Dr. Bretonneau
TEL 02 47 23 90 02
FAX 02 47 23 82 01
bonlaboureur.com
This village-center hotel has been family run for generations. Chintz-bedecked living rooms and pleasant bedrooms overlook a courtyard. Michelin one-star restaurant serves nouvelle cuisine.

🛏 22 + 5 suites 🅿 🕐 Closed Tues. L & Jan. 🏊 ♿ ❧ AE, MC, V

### 🏨 LA ROSERAIE
**$$ ✪✪✪**
7 Rue du Dr. Bretonneau
TEL 02 47 23 90 09
FAX 02 47 23 91 59
hotel-chenonceau.com
A charming hotel with a delightful garden, tastefully decorated rooms, and beamed dining room. There's also a terrace for outdoor dining when the weather is good.

🛏 17 🅿 🕐 Closed mid-Nov.–mid-Feb. 🔳 🏊 ❧ MC, V

## CHINON

### 🏨 CHÂTEAU DE MARÇAY
🍴 **$$–$$$$ ✪✪✪✪**
Marçay (4 miles/6 km S of Chinon via D749 & D116)

---

### PRICES

**HOTELS**
An indication of the cost of a double room in the high season is given by **$** signs.

| | |
|---|---|
| **$$$$$** | Over $800 |
| **$$$$** | $500–$800 |
| **$$$** | $300–$500 |
| **$$** | $150–$300 |
| **$** | Under $150 |

**RESTAURANTS**
An indication of the cost of a three-course meal without drinks is given by **$** signs.

| | |
|---|---|
| **$$$$$** | Over $300 |
| **$$$$** | $200–$300 |
| **$$$** | $100–$200 |
| **$$** | $70–$100 |
| **$** | Under $70 |

---

TEL 02 47 93 03 47
FAX 02 47 93 45 33
A medieval turreted château situated in its own parkland with a Michelin one-star restaurant (temporarily closed). Tennis is also available.

🛏 30 + 4 suites 🅿 🕐 Closed mid-Jan.–mid-March 🏊 ❧ All major cards

### 🏨 DIDEROT
**$ ✪✪**
4 Rue Buffon
TEL 02 47 93 18 87
hoteldiderot.com
A pretty, ivy-covered town house set in a quiet courtyard. Breakfast is served on the terrace or in the rustic dining room. No TV in rooms.

🛏 28 🅿 🔳 Rooms ❧ All major cards

---

## 🍴 HOSTELLERIE GARGANTUA
**$$**

73 Rue Voltaire
TEL 02 47 93 04 71
hostellerie-gargantua.loire-valley
-hotels.com

Popular restaurant in a Renaissance palace overlooking the river. Eight rooms are available.

🕐 Closed Wed. 🔳 MC, V

## FONTEVRAUD

### 🏨 LA CROIX BLANCHE
**$ ✪✪**

7 Place des Plantagenêts
TEL 02 41 51 71 11
FAX 02 41 38 15 38
hotel-croixblanche.com

A simple but agreeable hotel located close to the abbey with rooms overlooking the garden and restaurant.

🛏 21 🅿 🔳 AE, MC, V

### 🍴 LA LICORNE
**$$$$**

Allée Ste.-Catherine
TEL 02 41 51 72 49
lalicorne-restaurant-fontevraud.fr

A restaurant in an 18th-century building. Try the langoustine ravioli and roasted Loire salmon with vanilla butter and Loire wines. Reservations are required.

🕐 Closed Sun. D, Mon., & Wed. D
🔳 AE, MC, V

### 🍴 LA ROUTE D'OR
**$$**

Place de l'Église, Candes-St.-Martin
TEL 02 47 95 81 10
routedor.free.fr

A tiny restaurant situated in the village of Candes-St.-Martin east of Fontevraud. Your choice of tables is available either in a cellar dining room or on the cobbled square. Try the perch in foie gras or baby eels flavored with Roquefort.

🕐 Closed Tues.–Wed. Nov.–March 🔳 MC, V

## JOUÉ-LÈS-TOURS

### 🏨 CHÂTEAU DE BEAULIEU
**$$–$$$ ✪✪✪**

67 Rue de Beaulieu
TEL 02 47 53 20 26
FAX 02 47 53 84 20
chateaudebeaulieu37.com

A 17th-century manor house hotel set in quiet surroundings with a restful garden and beautiful rooms.

🛏 19 🅿 🔳 🔳 AE, MC, V

## SOMETHING SPECIAL

### 🏨 HOSTELLERIE PRIEURÉ ST.-LAZARE
**$ ✪✪✪**

Rue St.-Jean de l'Habite

This relatively new hotel is located in the old St.-Lazare priory, within Fontevraud Abbey. The 19th-century wing contains the guest rooms, and in summer the restaurant tables are spread out into the cloisters.

🛏 52 🅿 🔳 🔳 AE, MC, V

## LA FLÈCHE

### 🏨 LE MOULIN DES QUATRE SAISONS
**$–$$ ✪✪✪**

Rue Gallieni
TEL 02 43 45 12 12
moulindes4saisons.fr

This seventeenth-century mill with a terrace offers a fine view overlooking the Loire River. One-Michelin-star cuisine includes delicacies such as scallops, Limousin veal, and cherry soufflé, complemented by a varied wine list.

🕐 Closed D Wed. & Sun.
🏛 All major cards

## LAMOTTE-BEUVRON

🍴 **TATIN**
$$–$$$
5 Avenue de Vierzon
TEL 02 54 88 00 03
lamaisontatin.fr

A small hotel-restaurant serving simple local cuisine with excellent game and fish. It claims to be the originator of tarte tatin. The upside-down caramelized apple tart is always available here.

P 🕐 Closed Sun. D & all Mon.
🍴 🏛 All major cards

## LE MANS

🏨 **CHANTECLER**
$ ✪✪✪
50 Rue de la Pelouse
TEL 02 43 14 40 00
FAX 02 43 77 16 28
hotelchantecler.fr

A modern hotel close to the old town. No restaurant.

🛏 32 + 3 suites P
🏛 All major cards

## LOCHES

🏨 **LE GEORGE SAND**
$–$$ ✪✪
39 Rue Quintefol
TEL 02 47 59 39 74
FAX 02 47 91 55 75
hotel-restaurant-georgesand.fr

Former 17th-century coach inn beneath the castle ramparts with stone staircases and a medieval watchtower. Rooms overlook the castle or the river, and meals

---

are served on the terrace in fine weather.

🛏 20 🏛 AE, MC, V

## MONTBAZON

🏨 **CHÂTEAU**
🍴 **D'ARTIGNY**
$$$–$$$$$ ✪✪✪✪
TEL 02 47 34 30 30
FAX 02 47 34 30 39
chateauartigny.com

Beautiful white-stone château set in its own wooded parkland, overlooking the Indre Valley. This was built for the perfumer Coty, and now its sumptuous interior is sometimes a venue for musical evenings. Rooms in the château and the lodge by the river. Excellent cuisine, impressive wine cellar. Sauna, tennis, small golf course.

---

🏨 Hotel  🍴 Restaurant  🛏 No. of Guest Rooms  🪑 No. of Seats  P Parking  🚇 Metro  🕐 Closed  🛗 Elevator

**(i)** 65 + 4 duplex **P** 🔆 🏊 🛡
🅢 All major cards

## MONTLOUIS-SUR-LOIRE

### 🏨 CHÂTEAU
### DE LA BOURDAISIÈRE
**$$$–$$$$**

25 Rue de la Bourdaisière
TEL 02 47 45 16 31
FAX 02 47 45 09 11
labourdaisiere.com

Charming château set in park-
land, built for Marie Gaudin, the
mistress of François I. The beauti-
fully furnished rooms have period
pieces. Tennis, horseback riding.
Reservations only. Includes its own
restaurant.

**(i)** 10 **P** 🕓 Closed Jan.–March
🏊 🅢 MC, V

## NANTES

### 🏨 LA PÉROUSE
**$ ✪✪✪**

3 Allée Duquesne
TEL 02 40 89 75 00
FAX 02 40 89 76 00
hotel-laperouse.fr

Situated in the Cours des Cinquante
Otages, this modern building has
won awards for its minimalist
design.

**(i)** 47 🚭 🔆 🅢 All major cards

## SOMETHING SPECIAL

### 🍴 LA CIGALE
**$$**

4 place Graslin
TEL 02 51 84 94 94
lacigale.com

Famous belle epoque café/brasse-
rie in the center of Nantes serving
superb fish and seafood.

🅢 MC, V

## ORLÉANS

### 🏨 DES CÈDRES
**$ ✪✪✪**

17 Rue Maréchal Foch
TEL 02 38 62 22 92
hotelcedresorleans.com

A modern, well-run hotel located on
a quiet street, just outside the town
center. Large rooms and garden. No
restaurant.

**(i)** 34 🕓 Closed Dec. 24–Jan. 2
🚭 Rooms 🅢 AE, MC, V

### 🏨 LE RIVAGE
**$ ✪✪**

635 Rue Reine Blanche, Olivet
TEL 02 38 66 02 93
FAX 02 38 56 31 11
lerivage-olivet.com

Situated 3 miles (5 km) south of
Orléans beside the Loire, this modern hotel offers meals on the terrace
overlooking the river. Tennis.

**(i)** 17 **P** 🕓 Closed late Dec.–late
Jan.; restaurant closed D Sat. & Sun.
Nov.–March 🅢 All major cards

## ROMORANTIN-
## LANTHENAY

### 🏨 GRAND HÔTEL DU
### 🍴 LION D'OR
**$$–$$$$**

69 Rue Clemenceau
TEL 02 54 94 15 15
FAX 02 54 88 24 87
hotel-liondor.fr

Luxurious château with a garden and
Michelin one-star restaurant, thought
by some to be the best cooking in the
Loire Valley. Fine local produce such
as white asparagus and wild mush-
rooms in season; the frogs' legs and
caramelized brioche with angelica
sorbet are especially recommended.

**(i)** 13 + 3 suites 🕓 Closed mid-

---

🚭 Nonsmoking 🔆 Air-conditioning 🏊 Indoor Pool 🏊 Outdoor Pool 🛡 Health Club 🅢 Credit Cards

Feb.–mid-March; restaurant closed
Tues. L 🔄 🔲 All major cards

## SACHE

### 🍴 AUBERGE DU 12ÈME SIÈCLE
**$$–$$$**
**Rue Principale**
**TEL 02 47 26 88 77**
**auberge12emesiecle.fr**
Half-timbered inn with a medieval
interior, opposite the manor house
where Balzac used to write. Good-
value traditional cooking.
🕐 Closed Sun. D, Mon. & Tues. L
🔲 MC, V

## SAUMUR

### 🏨 ANNE D'ANJOU
**$$ 🔵🔵🔵**
**32 Quai Mayaud**
**TEL 02 41 67 30 30**
**hotel-anneanjou.com**
An 18th-century building overlooking
the Loire. There is a good affiliated
restaurant in the hotel gardens called
Les Ménestrels.
🛏 50 🅿 🔲 All major cards

## TOURS

### SOMETHING SPECIAL

### 🏨 LES HAUTES ROCHES
**$$$–$$$$ 🔵🔵🔵**
**86 Quai de la Loire**
**Rochecorbon**
**TEL 02 47 52 88 88**
**leshautesroches.com**
Four miles (6.5 km) upstream from
Tours, this elegant troglodyte hotel
on the north bank of the river has
rooms carved out of the rock. The
restaurant offers classic Michelin
one-star cooking; meals are served
on a delightful terrace overlooking
the river. Try the rabbit and foie gras

terrine, and the Grand Marnier souf-
flé. Simply *magnifique!*
🛏 14 🕐 Hotel closed Feb.–
March; restaurant closed Sun. &
Mon. D 🔲 All major cards

### 🏨 L'UNIVERS
### 🍴 $$$ 🔵🔵🔵
**5 Boulevard Heurteloup**
**TEL 02 47 05 37 12**
**FAX 02 47 61 51 80**
**oceaniahotels.com**
Situated in the town center, this
grand hotel in the classic style once
hosted Henry James. (He remarked
on the overwhelming politeness of
the staff.) Frescoes of famous visitors
from 1846 to the present day decorate the walls.
🛏 85 + 8 suites 🅿 🔲 Rooms
🔄 🔲 All major cards

### 🏨 CODU MANOIR
**$ 🔵🔵**
**2 Rue Traversière**
**TEL 02 47 05 37 37**
**hotel-du-manoir-tours.fr**
A small and charming hotel in a
19th-century building close to the
railroad station and the old town.
Prettily decorated rooms. No restaurant.
🛏 20 🅿
🔲 All major cards

### 🍴 LA ROCHE LE ROY
**$$$**
**55 Route de St.-Avertin**
**TEL 02 47 27 22 00**
**larocheleroy.com**
Beguiling town restaurant with one
Michelin star for classic local dishes
like asparagus with soft boiled egg,
or roasted pigeon.
🕐 Closed Sun.–Mon.
🔲 All major cards

## SOMETHING SPECIAL

### 🍴 LES CAVES DE MARSON
$

1 Rue Henri fricotelle
TEL 02 41 50 50 05
cavesdemarson.com

A delightful troglodyte eatery near Saumur with candlelit rooms quarried out of the tufa caves. Try the *fouaces,* stuffed wheat pancakes cooked in a traditional wood-fired oven.

🐾 AE, MC, V

---

▶ **CENTRAL FRANCE &
THE ALPS**

## BURGUNDY & THE JURA

## AUXERRE

### 🏨 PARC DES MARÉCHAUX
$–$$ ✪✪✪

6 Avenue Foch
TEL 03 86 51 43 77
FAX 03 86 51 31 72
leparcdesmarechaux.com

A large 19th-century house close to the town center, with traditionally decorated rooms, some looking out onto the park. No restaurant.

ⓘ 25 🅿 🌊 🐾 All major cards

## AVALLON

### 🏨 CHÂTEAU DE VAULT- DE-LUGNY
$$$–$$$$$ ✪✪✪✪

TEL 03 86 34 07 86
FAX 03 86 34 16 36
lugny.fr

A beautifully restored, 16th-century country mansion standing on its own grounds. Some guest rooms have four-poster or canopy beds. The restaurant serves traditional cuisine and is open only to hotel guests. Tennis and fishing are also available.

ⓘ 12 🅿 🕐 Closed mid-Nov.–late March 🐾 All major cards

## BEAUNE

### 🏨 LE CEP
$$$ ✪✪✪✪

27 Rue Maufoux
TEL 03 80 22 35 48
hotel-cep-beaune.com

A 16th-century hotel decorated in Renaissance style close to the Hôtel-Dieu.

ⓘ 56 🅿 🐾 🐾 All major cards

### 🍴 LA BOUZEROTTE
$–$$$

25 Bouze-lès-Beaune
TEL 03 80 26 01 37
labouzerotte.fr

A village restaurant with country-style food, including rich omelets with bacon and potatoes, delicious salads picked from the garden, and fruit tarts. Sunny terrace for outside dining or open fire indoors.

🕐 Closed Mon.–Tues. 🐾 AE, MC, V

## CHABLIS

### 🏨 HOSTELLERIE DES CLOS
### 🍴 $$ ✪✪✪

18 Rue Jules Rathier
TEL 03 86 42 10 63
fax 03 86 42 17 11
hostellerie-des-clos.fr

This stylishly comfortable hotel in a medieval hospice has individually furnished guest rooms. The restaurant serves dishes such as a *fricassée* of Burgundy snails and veal kidneys. A wide variety of local Chablis wines includes many by the glass.

---

🐾 Nonsmoking 🐾 Air-conditioning 🐾 Indoor Pool 🌊 Outdoor Pool 🐾 Health Club 🐾 Credit Cards

(i) 26 P ⊕ Closed late Dec.– mid-Jan.; restaurant closed Mon.– Thurs. L. ⬧ AE, MC, V

## CHAGNY

### ⊞ MAISON LAMELOISE
### ⦀ $$$$–$$$$$
Place d'Armes
TEL 03 85 87 65 65
FAX 03 85 87 03 57
lameloise.fr

A 15th-century hotel with traditional wood-beamed Burgundian decor contains one of the region's great restaurants—a Michelin three-star establishment, friendly and family run. Excellent local cheeses. Reservations are essential.

(i) 16 ⊕ Closed Tues.–Wed. & late Dec.–late Jan. ⬧ All major cards

## CLUNY

### ⊞ DE BOURGOGNE
### $–$$ ✪✪✪
Place de l'Abbaye
TEL 03 85 59 00 58
FAX 03 85 59 03 73
hotel-cluny.com

A 19th-century mansion built over part of the remains of Cluny abbey. The ancient ambiance here includes stone walls, period furniture, and objets d'art. The well-regarded restaurant serves Burgundian cuisine.

(i) 14 + 3 suites P ⊕ Closed Dec.–Jan.; restaurant closed Tues.–Wed. ⬧ ⬧ AE, MC, V

## DIJON

### ⊞ HÔTEL PHILIPPE LE BON
### ⦀ $$$
18 Rue Ste.-Anne
TEL 03 80 30 73 52
maisonphilippelebon.com/fr

The restaurant in this grand 15th-cen-

tury mansion, **Les Oenophiles,** serves fine traditional dishes like coq au vin, snails in Meursault sauce, and the Dijon specialty saddle of hare marinated in *marc de Bourgogne.* It is home to the Compagnie Bourguignonne des Oenophiles (Burgundian wine lovers) so you can expect a superb selection of the region's wines.

(i) 32 P ⊕ Closed Sun. & L mid-Aug. ▣ ⬧ All major cards

### ⊞ HOSTELLERIE CHAPEAU
### ⦀ ROUGE
### $$–$$$ ✪✪✪✪
5 Rue Michelet
TEL 03 80 50 88 88
FAX 03 80 50 88 89
chapeau-rouge.fr

This elegant historic hotel in the center of Dijon, with a Michelin two-star restaurant, offers Burgundian classics.

(1) 30 🔄 🕐 Closed Sun.–Mon.
🏔 All major cards

## GEX

### 🏨 AUBERGE DES CHASSEURS
**$–$$ ❖❖❖**
711, Route de Naz Dessus,
Echenevex
TEL 04 50 41 54 07
FAX 04 50 41 90 61
logishotels.com

Just south of Gex in the Jura Mountains, this delightful farmhouse has a well-tended garden and wonderful views.

(1) 15 🅿 🕐 Closed Nov.–Feb.
🏔 🏔 AE, MC, V

## LA BUSSIÈRE-SUR-OUCHE

### 🏨 ABBAYE DE LA BUSSIÈRE
**$$$**
19 Rue de Saint-Aubin
TEL 03 80 49 02 29
FAX 03 80 49 05 23
abbayedelabussiere.fr

Lovingly restored old abbey with ancient frescoes, surrounded by its own parkland. Restaurant offers local specialties like Charolais beef served with fine Burgundy wines.

(1) 16 🅿 🕐 Closed Mon.;
restaurant closed Mon.–Tues. & L
(except Sun.) 🏔 AE, MC, V

## SAULIEU

### 🏨 LE RELAIS BERNARD
### 🍴 LOISEAU
**$$$$$**
2 Rue Argentine
TEL 03 80 90 53 53
bernard-loiseau.com

Famed restaurant and hotel of the late chef Bernard Loiseau. Still the same imaginative *cuisine légère,* with three Michelin stars in a delightful

setting with a garden.

(1) 23 + 7 suites & 3 duplex
🕐 Restaurant closed Tues.–Wed. in winter 🏔 🏔 🏔
🏔 All major cards

## VÉZELAY

### 🏨 L'ESPÉRANCE
### 🍴 **$$$$$ ❖❖❖❖**
St.-Père de Vezelay
TEL 03 86 33 39 10
marc-meneau-esperance.com

In a village just south of Vézelay, this charming country hotel has an intimate restaurant in the hotel conservatory, the setting for the Michelin two-star cooking of chef Marc Meneau, who treats local ingredients with great imagination. Try potato pancakes with caviar, or turbot in a crust of salt with lobster butter, served with the wines of Vézelay and Chablis. Some rooms in the restored watermill are available for stays.

(1) 19 + 5 suites 🕐 Restaurant closed Mon. L, Tues., Wed. L, & Jan.–mid-March 🔄 Restaurant
🏔 All major cards

## RHÔNE VALLEY & THE ALPS

## BAGNOLS

### 🏨 CHÂTEAU DE BAGNOLS
**$$$$$ ❖❖❖❖**
TEL 04 74 71 40 00
FAX 04 74 71 40 49
chateaudebagnols.com

A beautifully restored moated castle of golden stone with exquisitely landscaped gardens. Antiques and silk draperies enhance the elegant interior. The Michelin one-star restaurant excels in regional dishes such as fillet of beef with *girolles* and a ravioli of fresh peas.

**(i)** 16 + 4 suites **P** **(c)** Closed early Jan.–March & Nov.–late Dec. **(S)** **(S)** Rooms **(≈)** **(S)** All major cards

## CHAMONIX-MONT-BLANC

### **(m)** GRAND HOTEL DES ALPES
**$$$**

75 Rue du Dr. Paccard
TEL 04 50 55 37 80
grandhoteldesalpes.com
A legendary grand hotel of the 19th century, now superbly restored to its original atmosphere with cozy bars and elegant salons.

**(i)** 30 **(c)** Closed Oct.–Dec. & mid-Apr.–mid-June **(S)** All major cards

## COURCHEVEL

### **(m)** LA SIVOLIÈRE
**$$$–$$$$$** ⓞⓞⓞⓞⓞ

Quartier des Chenus
TEL 04 79 08 08 33
hotel-la-sivoliere.com
A charming, tasteful chalet hotel at the foot of the Courchevel ski runs. Very comfortable and exquisitely decorated. Includes a very cozy restaurant and bar.

**(i)** 32 **P** **(c)** Closed May–Dec. **(≈)** **(Y)** **(S)** MC, V

## GRENOBLE

### **(m)** CHÂTEAU DE LA COM-MANDERIE
**$–$$** ⓞⓞⓞ

17 Avenue d'Échirolles
TEL 04 76 25 34 58
FAX 04 76 24 07 31
commanderie.fr
Just outside Grenoble and close to the ski slopes, this historic château has a walled garden, tapestry-hung rooms, and beautiful guest rooms.

**(i)** 25 **P** **(c)** Closed Sat. L,

Sun.–Mon., & late Dec.–early Jan. **(≈)** **(S)** All major cards

## JULIÉNAS

### **(ii)** LA COQ À JULIÉNAS
**$$**

Place du Marché
TEL 04 74 04 41 98
lecoqajulienas.com
A Beaujolais bistro in the wine village famous for its special recipe for coq au vin and other traditional favorites.

**(c)** Closed Wed.–Thurs. & late Dec.–early March **(S)** All major cards

## LA MALÈNE

### **(m)** CHÂTEAU DE LA CAZE
**$$–$$$$** ⓞⓞⓞⓞ

TEL 04 66 48 51 01

FAX 04 66 48 55 75
chateaudelacaze.com
A wonderfully romantic, 15th-century château on the banks of the Tarn, perfect for a meal or a stay while touring the Tarn Gorges.
🛏 13 🕐 Closed Wed. & Nov.–March 💳 All major cards

# LYON

## 🏨 VILLA FLORENTINE
## 🍽 $$$$–$$$$$ ❂❂❂❂
25 Montée St.-Barthélemy
TEL 04 72 56 56 56
villaflorentine.com
A romantic hotel with a wonderful view over the red roofs of old Lyon, a favorite with visiting heads of state. Michelin one-star restaurant, **Les Terrasses de Lyon;** try the lamb cooked in milk with anchovies.
🛏 16 + 3 suites 🅿 🕐 Restaurant closed Sun.–Mon. ❄ ⛲
💳 All major cards

## 🏨 COUR DES LOGES
## 🍽 $$$$ ❂❂❂❂
6 Rue Boeuf
TEL 04 72 77 44 44
courdesloges.com
A gorgeous hotel in the old town, with a contemporary interior created around 15th-century courtyard and galleries. Stylish restaurant.
🛏 52 🕐 Restaurant closed Aug.
💳 All major cards

## 🍽 LÉON DE LYON
## $$$$$
1 Rue Pleney
TEL 04 72 10 11 12
leondelyon.com
One of Lyon's great brasseries, long established on a narrow street off Quai St.-Antoine. The menu includes traditional Lyon favorites such as sau-

sages, lentils, and rich potato gratin, along with more modern lightweight fare. Superb cheese board and an excellent wine list.
🅿 ❄ 💳 AE, MC, V

## 🍽 PAUL BOCUSE
## $$$$$
40 Rue de la Plage
TEL 04 72 42 90 90
bocuse.fr
Paul Bocuse's restaurant is 9 miles (16 km) north of Lyon, but it is worth the pilgrimage, and plenty of people make it to this Michelin three-star restaurant. They find simple, perfect food—exquisite roast chicken, creamy potato gratin, and luxuries like truffle soup, grandly served.
🅿 ❄ 💳 All major cards

## 🍽 LA MÈRE BRAZIER
## $$$
12 Rue Royale
TEL 04 78 23 17 20
lamerebrazier.fr
A Lyon legend (Mère Brazier inspired generations of chefs) remains a fine restaurant, with two Michelin stars. Try the specialties of spider crabs and Bresse chicken.
🕐 Closed Sat.–Sun. and 3 weeks in Aug. 💳 AE, MC, V

# MÉGÈVE

## 🏨 CHALET DU MONTE
## 🍽 D'ARBOIS
## $$$–$$$$$ ❂❂❂❂
Route Mont d'Arbois
TEL/FAX 04 50 21 25 03
domainedumontdarbois.com
This magnificent hotel in a peaceful setting was once home to the Rothschild family. The restaurant serves choice meals accompanied by an excellent wine list.

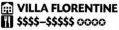

(i) 23 + 6 suites (L) Closed mid-April–mid-June & mid-Sept.–mid-Dec. ⬛ 🔲 All major cards

## MÉRIBEL

### ⊞ LE GRAND COEUR
**$$$$–$$$$$** ✪✪✪✪
TEL 04 79 08 60 03
legrandcoeur.com
One of Méribel's grand hotels, a luxury establishment with every comfort, located in the town center. Includes a spa and an excellent restaurant.
(i) 41 P (L) Closed mid- April–mid-Dec. 🔲 🔲
All major cards

## PÉROUGES

### ⊞ L'HOSTELLERIE DU VIEUX PÉROUGES
**$$$–$$$$** ✪✪✪–✪✪✪✪
Place du Tilleul
TEL 04 74 61 00 88
FAX 04 74 34 77 90
hostelleriedeperouges.com
An old Bresse inn in this restored medieval town. Guest rooms in the 14th-century parts of the building are decorated in the style of the original sleeping quarters.
(i) 15 P AE, MC, V

## MASSIF CENTRAL

## LAGUIOLE

### ⊞ HOTEL RESTAURANT 🍴 MICHEL BRAS
**$$$$$**
Route de l'Aubrac
TEL 05 65 51 18 20
FAX 05 65 48 47 02
bras.fr
On the remote plateau of Aubrac is a modern hotel and restaurant where Michelin three-star chef Michael Bras brings a touch of genius to local cuisine and ingredients; try the Bras take on *gargouillou*, a mix of herbs, vegetables and salads. Reservations are essential because the name Michael Bras is synonomous with excellent French cuisine in these parts.
P (L) Closed Mon. except July–Aug. 🔲 🔲 All major cards

## RODEZ

### ⊞ ISABELLE AUGUY
**$** ✪✪
154 Rue Pierre Carrère
TEL 05 65 47 77 51
restaurant-isabelle-auguy.business.
site
Try local specialities such as *aligot* (cheese potatoes), *filet de boeuf*, and porcini mushroom salad. Wine list and cheese selection recommended.
(L) Closed Sun.–Mon.
All major cards

## SALERS

### ⊞ LES REMPARTS
**$** ✪✪
Esplanade Barrouze
TEL 04 71 40 70 33
FAX 04 71 40 75 32
salers-hotel-remparts.com
Perched on the edge of the ancient fortifications of medieval Salers, this hotel has spectacular views and delicious local cooking.
(i) 18 (L) Closed mid-Oct.–mid-Dec. MC, V

## VICHY

### ⊞ PAVILLON D'ENGHIEN 🍴 **$** ✪✪✪
32 Rue Callou
TEL 04 70 98 33 30
pavillondenghien.com

---

⊞ Hotel 🍴 Restaurant (i) No. of Guest Rooms 🔲 No. of Seats P Parking 🚇 Metro (L) Closed 🔲 Elevator

A small, old-fashioned hotel near the Enghien gardens and Callou baths, with a restaurant, **Jardins d'Enghien.**
🛈 22 🕐 Restaurant closed Sun. D & Mon. (except public holidays)
🏨 🗝 All major cards

# ▶ SOUTHWEST FRANCE

## AQUITAINE & THE ATLANTIC COAST

## AINHOA

### 🏨 ITHURRIA
### 🍴 $$–$$$
Place du Fronton
TEL 05 59 29 92 11
ithurria.com
A charming hotel and Michelin one-star restaurant. Typical dishes include *foie gras des Landes,* roast pigeon, and Basque cassoulet with red beans.
🛈 28 🕐 Closed Dec.–March;
🏨 🗝 All major cards

## ARCACHON

### 🍴 CHEZ YVETTE
### $–$$
59 Boulevard du Général Leclerc
TEL 05 56 83 05 11
A seasonal table with produce fresh from the market or garden. Try the fricassée of octopus with Espelette peppers or *soupe de poisson d'Arcachon.*
🅲 🗝 All major cards

## BIARRITZ

### 🏨 HOTEL DU PALAIS
### 🍴 $$$$
1 Avenue de l'Imperatrice
TEL 05 59 41 64 00
hyatt.com/en-US/hotel/france/hotel-du-palais-biarritz

This palace has chandeliers, marble pillars, rotunda restaurant (best at sunset), two pools, fabulous luxury spa, and Michelin-star restaurant.
🛈 122 🅿 🅲 🏊 🗝 All major cards

### 🏨 CHÂTEAU DU CLAIR DE LUNE
### $$ ✪✪✪
48 avenue Alan-Seeger
TEL 05 59 41 53 20
hotelclairlune.fr
An elegant fin-de-siècle family house set in a quiet park south of Biarritz. Breakfast is served around one large table in a very French-family style.
🛈 15 🅿 🗝 MC, V

### 🍴 CAFÉ DE LA GRANDE PLAGE
### $$–$$$
1 Avenue edouard vii
TEL 05 59 22 77 88
casinosbarriere.com/fr/biarritz/le-cafe-de-la-grande-plage
The terrace of this classic art deco café, serving drinks and excellent food based on Basque cuisine, offers glorious views over the ocean. The sunsets can sometimes be as spectacular as the food and drinks.
🗝 All major cards

### 🍴 CHEZ ALBERT
### $$
51 bis all Port des Pecheurs
TEL 05 59 24 43 84
chezalbert.fr
Fresh fish straight from the sea with a stunning terrace view to match. Sample Basque style grilled sardines, red peppers stuffed with codfish, or squid in its own ink. Seafood to write home about.
🕐 Closed Wed. (except July–Aug.)
🗝 All major cards

---

🅲 Nonsmoking 🅲 Air-conditioning 🏨 Indoor Pool 🏊 Outdoor Pool 🏋 Health Club 🗝 Credit Cards

## BIDARRAY

### 🍽 OSTAPÉ
$$$$
Chahatoa
TEL 05 59 37 91 91
ostape.com
An estate of Basque villas surrounded by gardens and mountains, where you can sample stylish regional cuisine from a 17th-century farmhouse. Lovely outdoor pool with panoramic views.
🕐 Closed Dec.–Feb.
💳 All major cards

## BORDEAUX

### 🏨 GRAND HOTEL DE BORDEAUX
$$$$$
2 Place de la Comédie
TEL 05 57 30 44 44
ghbordeaux.com
An 18th-century building opposite the Grand Théâtre, now completely refurbished in last-word luxury, with glass domes, velvet drapes, and a lovely terrace. Also included are a spa and two restaurants.
🛏 150 💳 All major cards

### 🏨 BURDIGALA
$$$$ ○○○○○
115 Rue Georges-Bonnac
TEL 05 56 90 16 16
FAX 05 56 93 15 06
burdigala.com
A beautifully decorated hotel with every comfort, located just outside the city center.
🛏 68 + 15 suites 🅿 💳 Rooms 🏊 📺 💳 All major cards

### 🏨 HÔTEL DE NORMANDIE BORDEAUX CENTRE
$$ ○○○
7 Cours 30-Juillet

TEL 05 56 52 16 80 hotel-de-normandie-bordeaux.com
Opposite the Maison du Vin, this central hotel is comfortable and welcoming. Some rooms have balconies.
🛏 100 💳 All major cards

### 🍽 COMPTOIR CUISINE
$$$
2 Place de la Comedie
TEL 05 56 56 22 33
comptoircuisine.com
Casual bistro with an open kitchen, convivial bar, and a wonderful selection of wine by the glass.
💳 All major cards

### 🍽 LA TUPINA
$$$
6 Rue Porte de la Monnaie
TEL 05 56 91 56 37
latupina.com

Savor excellent regional cuisine, fine wines, and the ambience of this popular restaurant located close to the river.

All major cards

## BOULIAC

### LE ST.-JAMES
**$$$$**
Place C. Holstein
TEL 05 57 97 06 00
saintjames-bouliac.com
Original rustic buildings in a small village outside Bordeaux combine with the chic architectural design of Jean Nouvel in this unusual hotel. Home to the esteemed **St. James** restaurant, now with one Michelin star.

Restaurant closed Sun.–Mon. & 2 weeks in Jan. All major cards

## CAP-FERRET

### DES PINS
**$ ✪✪**
Rue de Fauvettes
TEL 05 56 60 60 11
hoteldespins.eu
A small hotel converted from a theater with a huge glassed-in terrace, located in a quiet part of town and set in gardens.
14 Closed Dec.–Feb.
MC, V

## CASTELNAU-DU-MÉDOC

### CHÂTEAU DU FOULON
**$$**
TEL 05 56 58 20 18
FAX 05 56 58 23 43
An elegant white château set in a large park just outside the village. Breakfast *en famille* at the magnificent grand table. No restaurant.
4 + 4 suites P Cash only

## ESPELETTE

### EUZKADI
**$$**
285 Karrika Nagusia
TEL 05 59 93 91 88
FAX 05 59 53 90 19
hotel-restaurant-euzkadi.com
This hotel and restaurant in a typical Basque house prepares excellent Basque specialties.
Closed Mon.–Tues. in winter & all Nov.–Dec. MC, V

## EUGÉNIE-LES-BAINS

### LES PRÉS D'EUGÉNIE
**$$$$ ✪✪✪✪**
TEL 05 58 05 06 07
michelguerard.com
The empire of the legendary chef Michel Guérard, inventor of *cuisine minceur* and holder of three Michelin stars, this complex encompasses two hotels: Les Prés d'Eugénie and Le Couvent des Herbes, an 18th-century former convent. Two health spas, La Maison Rose and La Ferme aux Grives, complete the four establishments. All are individually decorated in exquisite taste. Restaurants serve both traditional and minceur cuisine, and there are luxurious spa facilities. Go for your health, your tastebuds, or both. Anyone for tennis? That's covered too.
60 + 15 suites Opening times vary; call ahead
All major cards

## LA ROCHELLE

### HÔTEL LES BRISES
**$$ ✪✪✪**
Chemin Digue Richelieu
TEL 05 46 43 89 37
FAX 05 46 43 27 97
hotel-les-brises.com

Located close to the port with a fine terrace overlooking the sea, this is a fine modern accommodation with an airy, spacious feel. No restaurant.

🛏 50 🅿
🎴 AE, DC, MC, V

### 🏨 HOTEL RESIDENCE DE FRANCE
**$$ ✪✪✪✪**
43 Rue Minage
TEL 05 46 28 06 00
hotel-larochelle.com
This calm retreat in the center of old town offers a shady courtyard and a small pool. Stylish modern decor and artworks lift the spirits, while excellent local seafood dishes satisfy the appetite.

🛏 16 🅿 🎴 All major cards

## LIMOGES

### 🍴 LES PETITS VENTRES
**$–$$**
20 Rue de la Boucherie
TEL 05 55 34 22 90
les-petits-ventres.com
A 15th-century house with Old World charm and a terrace where you dine on the region's traditional cuisine. Try *tête de veau* (calf's head) or the *pot au feu.*

🕐 Closed Sun.–Mon.; weeks in Feb., May, & Sept. 🎴 AE, MC, V

## MARGAUX

### 🍴 AUBERGE DE SAVOIE
**$**
1 Place Trémoille
TEL 05 57 88 31 76
lesavoie.net
A good-value restaurant in this wine town, specializing in wine tastings and regional dishes such as a quiche of *foie de canard et jus de truffe.*

🕐 Closed Sun. 🎴 DC, MC, V

## PAUILLAC

### 🏨 CHÂTEAU 🍴 CORDEILLAN BAGES
**$$$$ ✪✪✪✪**
Route des Châteaux
TEL 05 56 59 24 24
cordeillanbages.com
An English country house–style hotel with a Michelin two-star restaurant. This is the home of the École de Bordeaux, which arranges wine courses for those interested in all aspects of the local viniculture.

🛏 25 🅿 🕐 Closed early Dec.– early Feb.; restaurant closed Mon.– Tues. 🎴 All major cards

## POITIERS

### 🏨 NOVOTEL FUTUROSCOPE
**$$ ✪✪✪**
Portes du Parc
TEL 05 49 49 91 91
FAX 05 49 49 91 90
novotel.com
A modern hotel convenient to the popular Futuroscope visual technology park.

🛏 110 + 18 studios
🅿 🚫 🛗 🎴 All major cards

## ST.-ÉTIENNE-DE-BAÏGORRY

### 🏨 ARCÉ
**$$ ✪✪✪**
TEL 05 59 37 40 14
FAX 05 59 37 40 27
hotel-arce.com
This mountain-village hotel has been in the same family for more than a hundred years. A veranda sits out over the river, and some rooms have their own balconies. Beamed sitting room, library, and dining room with picture windows. Tennis is available.

🛈 23 🕐 Closed mid-Nov.– mid-March 🏊 🅂 All major cards

## ST.-JEAN-DE-LUZ

### 🏨 PARC VICTORIA
### 🍴 LES LIERRES
**$$$$ ✪✪✪✪**
5 Rue Cépé
TEL 05 59 26 78 78
FAX 05 59 26 78 08
parcvictoria.com
A 19th-century villa with a formal park and gardens. Luxuriously appointed rooms have marble bathrooms, and some balconies. The restaurant, **Les Lierres,** has dining rooms in 1930s-style garden pavilions.
🛈 8 + 4 suites 🅿 🕐 Closed mid-Nov.–mid-March 🏊
🅂 All major cards

### 🍴 CHEZ MATTIN
**$$**
63 Rue Baignol, Ciboure
TEL 05 59 47 19 52
chezmattin.fr
Rustic decor, Basque specialties, and a warm family welcome. Sample the stuffed peppers or Basque gâteau.
🕐 Closed Sun.–Mon. & Jan.–Feb.
🅂 AE, MC, V

## ST.-JEAN-PIED-DE-PORT

### 🏨 LES PYRÉNÉES
### 🍴 $$$$ ✪✪✪✪
19 Place du Général-de-Gaulle
TEL 05 59 37 01 01
hotel-les-pyrenees.com
An excellent hotel with a terrace. The restaurant (Michelin one star) is well known for the quality of its Basque/Gascon cuisine. Excellent fish dishes include langoustine, and they do a fine gazpacho.

🛈 20 🅿 🕐 Restaurant closed Mon. D in Nov.–March, Tues. Oct.–June, 3 weeks in Jan. & late Nov. 🅂 🅂 🏊 🅂 All major cards

## THE DORDOGNE & MIDI-PYRÉNÉES

## ALBI

### 🏨 HOSTELLERIE ST.-ANTOINE
**$$–$$$ ✪✪✪✪**
17 Rue St.-Antoine
TEL 05 63 54 04 04
FAX 05 63 47 10 47
hotel-saint-antoine-albi.com
A charming 18th-century inn owned by the same family for five generations. Most rooms look out onto the garden. No restaurant.
🛈 44 🅿 🅂 🅂
🅂 All major cards

### 🍴 LE JARDIN DES QUATRE SAISONS
**$$**
5 Rue de la Pompe
TEL 05 63 60 77 76
le-jardin-des-quatre-saisons.fr
A restaurant of exceptional quality and good value. Try the terrine of escargots with pig's trotters and truffles, or the roast pigeon with charlotte of mushroom and rosemary.
🕐 Closed Mon. & Sun. D
🅂 AE, MC, V

## AUCH

### 🍴 FRANCE
**$$$–$$$$**
2 Place de la Libération
TEL 05 62 61 71 71
hoteldefrance-auch.com
Try the best of Gascon cooking in this hotel-restaurant, known for its pro-

motion of the region's cuisine and its key elements of duck, goose, garlic, and wine.

🚹 31 🕒 Closed Sat. L, Sun. D, & Mon. 💳 All major cards

## BERGERAC

### 🏨 CHÂTEAU LES MERLES
### 🍴 $$$

Tuilieres, Mouleydier
TEL 05 53 63 13 42
FAX 05 53 63 13 45
lesmerles.com

A small 18th-century château with stunning views, stylish modern interior, and casual but impeccable service from Dutch owners. Fine cooking includes on-site lessons.

🚹 12 + 2 suites + 1 apt. 🅿 🏊 💳 All major cards

## BRANTÔME

### 🏨 LE MOULIN DE
### 🍴 L'ABBAYE
### $$$

1 Route de Bourdeilles
TEL 05 53 05 80 22
moulinabbaye.com

Dine on the terrace of this lovely old mill, once the house of Abbé Pierre de Bourdeilles and now a hotel and restaurant. Watch the Dronne River roll by, and enjoy the excellent cuisine: pigeon with ceps, *foie gras de canard,* crème brûlée with strawberries.

🅿 🕒 Closed Nov.–April, Mon., & L (except weekends) 💳 All major cards

### 🍴 LES JARDINS DE
### BRANTÔME
### $$

33 Rue Pierre de Mareuil
TEL 05 53 05 88 16

---

## PRICES

**HOTELS**
An indication of the cost of a double room in the high season is given by $ signs.

| | |
|---|---|
| $$$$$ | Over $800 |
| $$$$ | $500–$800 |
| $$$ | $300–$500 |
| $$ | $150–$300 |
| $ | Under $150 |

**RESTAURANTS**
An indication of the cost of a three-course meal without drinks is given by $ signs.

| | |
|---|---|
| $$$$$ | Over $300 |
| $$$$ | $200–$300 |
| $$$ | $100–$200 |
| $$ | $70–$100 |
| $ | Under $70 |

---

Delightful rustic ambience for local and seasonal dishes. Try local Périgord pork with caramelized vegetables.

🕒 Closed L Mon., Wed., & Thurs. L. 💳 V, MC

## CORDES

### 🏨 HOSTELLERIE DU
### 🍴 VIEUX CORDES
### $$

Rue St.-Michel
TEL 05 63 53 79 20
FAX 05 63 56 02 47
hotelcordes.fr

Sit on the terrace in the relaxing shade of an ancient wisteria at this hotel-restaurant converted from a 13th-century monastery. Try authentic cassoulet or delicious fish dishes.

🕒 Closed Tues. L, Sun. D, & Mon. out of season 💳 AE, MC, V

---

🏨 Hotel  🍴 Restaurant  🚹 No. of Guest Rooms  🪑 No. of Seats  🅿 Parking  🚇 Metro  🕒 Closed  🛗 Elevator

## CUQ-TOULZA

### 🏨 CUQ EN TERRASSES
**$$–$$$**
TEL 05 63 82 54 00
FAX 05 63 82 54 11
cuqenterrasses.com
In a hilltop hamlet just outside Cuq-Toulza, this former presbytery is charmingly decorated and has several terraces. Meals by reservation only.

🛏 8 🅿 🕐 Closed Nov.–March; restaurant closed Wed. & L 🌊
🅰 All major cards

## DOMME

### 🏨 L'ESPLANADE
### 🍴 $$ ◌◌◌
TEL 05 53 28 31 41
FAX 05 53 28 49 92
esplanade-perigord.com
A quiet hotel within the fortifications of this historic *bastide* town, with a terrace and lovely views over the Dordogne Valley. The restaurant makes good use of local produce, particularly truffles.

🛏 25 🕐 Closed early Nov.–mid-Feb.; restaurant closed Mon. except D in season
🅰 All major cards

## FIGEAC

### 🍴 LA DÎNÉE DU VIGUIER
**$$**
4 Rue Boutaric
TEL 05 65 50 08 08
cite-hotels.com
Le Dinée is the restaurant of the hotel Viguier du Roy, a château spanning the 12th to 18th centuries. Try gigot of monkfish spiked with truffles, the Quercy tart with morels, or the warm shrimp omelet.

🕐 Closed Sat. L & Sun.–Mon. D in winter 🅰 All major cards

## CABRERETS

### 🏨 NOCT'EN BULLE
**$**
Lieu-dit Merlan
TEL 06 88 96 61 77
noct-enbulle.fr
High on a Lot plateau, stay in a bubble tent with a clear dome for stargazing, free of light pollution in a dark sky zone known as Triangle Noir de Quercy. The bubbles offer an uninterrupted view of the night sky; swimming pool; picnics and breakfast available in a restored barn.

🛏 4 🚭 🌊 🅰 All major cards

## LES EYZIES-DE-TAYAC

### 🍴 LES GLYCINES
**$$**
4 Avenue de Laugerie
TEL 05 53 06 97 07
les-glycines-dordogne.com
A little auberge among greenery with a rustic interior and a terrace beside the river. Rooms available.

🕐 Closed L 🅰 AE, MC, V

## PÉRIGUEUX

### 🍴 HERCULE POIREAU
**$$**
2 Rue Nation
TEL 05 53 08 90 76
restaurant-perigueux-hercule
-poireau.fr
It's no great mystery where to go to dine on the best of Périgord cuisine beneath the low vaulted ceiling of this fine Renaissance building.

🕐 Closed Wed. & Tues. in winter
🅰 MC, V

---

🚭 Nonsmoking 🌀 Air-conditioning 🌊 Indoor Pool 🌊 Outdoor Pool 🏋 Health Club 🅰 Credit Cards

## PUYMIROL

### MICHEL TRAMA
**$$$ ✪✪✪✪**
52 Rue Royale
TEL 05 53 95 31 46
aubergade.com
In the center of a fortified town, this 13th-century residence once belonged to the counts of Toulouse. The owner-chef, M. Trama, serves excellent cuisine that has won him two Michelin stars, and also offers a selection of cigars. Rooms have Jacuzzis or massage showers.
🛈 11 🅿 Ⓢ 🕐 Closed L Mon. & L Tues., & D Sun. & Mon. out of season All major cards

## ROCAMADOUR

### LES VIEILLES TOURS
**$ ✪✪**
Route de Payrac (2 miles/ 4 km W of Rocamadour)
TEL 05 65 33 68 01
vtrocamadour.com
This partly 13th-century manor house makes a comfortable and historic hotel. Good restaurant, too.
🛈 17 🕐 Closed mid-Nov.– April; restaurant closed L AE, MC, V

### SAINTE-MARIE
**$$**
Place de Senhals
TEL 05 65 33 63 07
A rustic restaurant with a terrace where you can dine on excellent local cuisine.
🕐 Closed Nov.–Easter MC, V

## ST.-CÉRÉ

### VILLA RIC
**$$$**
Route de Leyme

TEL 05 65 38 04 08
FAX 05 65 38 00 14
villaric.com
A small restaurant with a summer terrace, serving regional cuisine. Rooms are also available for overnighters.
🛈 5 🕐 Closed mid-Nov.–March MC, V

## ST.-CIRQ-LAPOPIE

### LA PELISSARIA
**$$ ✪✪✪**
Le Bourg
TEL 05 65 31 25 14
FAX 05 65 30 25 52
This popular hotel in a 13th-century building is perched on the edge of this dramatic hill village. Enjoy the wonderful views.
🛈 8 +2 suites 🕐 Only open July 23–Aug. 28 MC, V

🛏 Hotel 🍴 Restaurant 🛈 No. of Guest Rooms 🪑 No. of Seats 🅿 Parking 🚇 Metro 🕐 Closed 🛗 Elevator

## 🍴 AUBERGE DU SOMBRAL
### $$
TEL 05 65 31 26 08
FAX 05 65 30 26 37
lesombral.com
A peaceful old house and restaurant in the heart of this picturesque medieval village.
🕐 Closed Mon.–Thurs. D
🏧 MC, V

## ST.-CYPRIEN-EN-PÉRIGORD

## 🏨 LA GRANDE MARQUE
### $ ❀❀
Marnac
TEL 05 53 31 61 63
lagrandemarque.fr
This 18th-century house on a hill with remarkable country views has rooms and apartments in the renovated former tobacco drying sheds. Dine on the shady terrace.
🛏 5 🍴 🅿 🕐 Closed Nov.–Easter 🏊 🏧 MC, V

## SARLAT-LA-CANÉDA

## 🍴 LE GRAND BLEU
### $$
43 Avenue de la Gare
TEL 05 53 31 08 48
legrandbleu.eu
This one-Michelin-star restaurant in Sarlat, located in the capital of Périgord cuisine, is the domaine of the next-generation chef Maxime Lebrun; try the foie gras and don't miss the Grand Marnier soufflé.
🕐 Closed Mon., Tues.–Wed. L, & Sun. D 🏧 All major cards

## SOUILLAC

## 🏨 CHÂTEAU DE LA TREYNE
### $$$–$$$$ ❀❀❀❀
La Treyne
TEL 05 65 27 60 60
FAX 05 65 27 60 70
www.chateaudelatreyne.com
A charming white château surrounded by parkland above the Dordogne River, this is a beautiful place to spend a few days of rest and relaxation. The amenities and activities include a great restaurant, tennis, and canoeing.
🛏 14 + 2 suites 🅿 🕐 Closed mid-Nov.–Easter 🏊
🏧 All major cards

## TOULOUSE

## 🏨 BEAUX-ARTS
### $$$ ❀❀❀
1 Place du Pont Neuf
TEL 05 34 45 42 42
FAX 05 34 45 42 43
hoteldesbeauxarts.com
This 18th-century building beside the river has been a hotel for 100 years. It has no restaurant, but beneath the hotel is the very lively Brasserie des Beaux-Arts.
🛏 19 🚭 🌀
🏧 All major cards

## 🏨 HOTEL GARONNE
## 🍴 $$$ ❀❀❀❀
22 Descente de la Halle aux Poissons
TEL 05 34 31 94 80
FAX 05 34 31 94 81
hotelgaronne.net
A handsome hotel by the river offering Japanese-style chic at a price.
🏧 AE, V, MC

## 🏨 GRAND HÔTEL DE
## 🍴 L'OPÉRA
### $$–$$$ ❀❀❀❀
1 Place du Capitole
TEL 05 61 21 82 66
grand-hotel-opera.com

Centrally located, the hotel is situated in a courtyard hidden behind its two well-known restaurants. **Les Jardins de l'Opéra** has seasonal specialties on its inventive menus. The **Grand Café de l'Opéra** serves light meals.

🛈 45 + 5 suites 🅂 Rooms 📺 🅂 All major cards

## 🍽 LE CANTOU
**$$**
**98 Rue Velasquez St. Martin du Touch**
TEL 05 61 49 20 21
cantou.fr

A country restaurant where you can sample the best of regional cuisine, for example, fricassée of langoustines and scallops, or *civet de canard* with calf's foot.

🕓 Closed Sat.–Sun., 1 week in early Jan., & 1 week in mid-Aug.
🅂 All major cards

## 🍽 LE SAINT SAUVAGE
**$$**
**20 Rue des Salenques**
TEL 05 61 23 56 86

Reasonably priced modern restaurant located close to Basilique St.-Sernin which serves up authentic Southwest regional dishes that don't disappoint.

🕓 Closed Sat. L & Sun.
🅂 MC, V

## TRÉMOLAT

### 🏨 LE VIEUX LOGIS
🍽 **$$$–$$$$** ⚫⚫⚫
TEL 05 53 22 80 06
FAX 05 53 22 84 89
vieux-logis.com

This splendidly restored village hotel with its charming mix of buildings has been in the same family for 400 years. The Michelin one-

star restaurant serves versions of regional classics. The galleried dining room looks out onto the pretty garden, which is a delight to gaze upon no matter what the season.

🛈 18 🅿
🅂 All major cards

## THE PYRENEES

## ARREAU

### 🏨 HOTEL D'ANGLETERRE
🍽 **$$$**
**Route Luchon**
TEL 05 62 98 63 30
FAX 05 62 98 69 66
hotel-angleterre-arreau.com

A charming old post house in a tiny slate-roofed village. Its restaurant has existed since the 19th century, its *carré d'agneau* and river trout favored

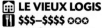

by the legendary mountaineer Sir Henry Russell.

🕐 Closed Mon., except July–Aug., Oct.–Dec., & April–May 🅿 🏊
🏠 All major cards

## AX-LES-THERMES

### 🏨 LE GRILLON
### 🍴 $$

Rue St.-Udaut
TEL 05 61 64 31 64
hotel-le-grillon.com
A hotel-restaurant situated high up in the mountains offering a terrace with truly wonderful views. The hotel is conveniently located close to thermal baths and ski resorts.

🛏 71 🕐 Closed Tues. D & Wed. (except holidays) 🏠 MC, V

## FOIX

### 🏨 LONS
$ ○○○

6 Place Georges-Duthil
TEL 05 34 09 28 00
FAX 05 61 02 68 18
hotel-lons-foix.com
Situated next to the Ariège River, this friendly hotel has a terrace, a brasserie, and a restaurant.

🛏 40 🕐 Closed late Dec.–mid-Jan. 🏠 All major cards

## FONTJONCOUS

### 🍴 AUBERGE DU VIEUX PUITS
$$$$

5 Avenue St.-victor
TEL 04 68 44 07 37
aubergeduvieuxpuits.fr
This is a celebrated three-Michelin-star restaurant located in an obscure Corbières village, featuring the best local produce treated with imaginative and elaborate flourish. Try duck with elderflower glaze.

🕐 Closed Jan.–March, Sun. D, & Mon. 🏠 🏠 All major cards

## GAVARNIE

### 🏨 HOTEL COMPOSTELLE
$

Rue de l'Église
TEL 05 62 92 49 43
compostellehotel.com
This small hotel on edge of the village of Gavarnie offers magnificient views of the cirque and the waterfall. Proprietor Yvan is also a mountain guide and can organize expeditions for individuals or groups.

🕐 Closed Oct.–Jan. 🏠 CB, V

## GÈDRE

### 🏨 LA BRÈCHE DE ROLAND
$ ○○

Gèdre
TEL 05 62 92 48 54
FAX 05 62 92 46 05
pyrenees-hotel-breche.com
An old mountain mansion, situated in a village 5 miles (8 km) north of Gavarnie. The hotel has a garden and a terrace where you can dine. The owner can also arrange trips up into the mountains and helicopter rides.

🛏 28 🕐 Closed mid-Nov.–Dec. 🏠 MC, V

## MIREPOIX

### 🏨 LA MAISON DES CONSULS
$$ ○○○

6 Place du Maréchal Leclerc
TEL 05 61 68 81 81
FAX 05 61 68 83 63
maisondesconsuls.com
Set in the central square of a *bastide* town, this renovated 14th-century house has historically themed

rooms overlooking the medieval streets. A delightful, step-back-in-time accommodation option in a hillside town that makes for a magical stay in this unique location.

🛈 8 🅿 🕸 All major cards

## ORION

### 🏨 CHÂTEAU D'ORION
**$$$**

Orion
TEL 05 59 65 07 74
FAX 05 59 65 08 21
chateau-orion.com

An exquisite small château overlooking rolling Béarn countryside, lovingly restored with original furniture, paintings, and meals served in candlelit dining room. A night at the Château d'Orion is not soon forgotten.

🅿 🕸 No cards

## PAU

### 🏨 HÔTEL DE GRAMONT
**$**

3 Place Gramont
TEL 05 59 27 84 04
FAX 05 59 27 62 23
hotelgramont.com

Centrally located traditional hotel, a 17th-century coaching inn, located close to Boulevard des Pyrenees. No restaurant, but generous breakfast buffet will set you up for a day hiking in the hills.

🕸 All major cards

### 🏨 PAU VILLA NAVARRE
**$**

59 Avenue Trespoey
TEL 05 59 14 65 65
FAX 05 59 14 65 64
villanavarre.fr

The atmosphere is "très British" in this superb villa, brought back

---

## PRICES

**HOTELS**

An indication of the cost of a double room in the high season is given by **$** signs.

| | |
|---|---|
| **$$$$$** | Over $800 |
| **$$$$** | $500–$800 |
| **$$$** | $300–$500 |
| **$$** | $150–$300 |
| **$** | Under $150 |

**RESTAURANTS**

An indication of the cost of a three-course meal without drinks is given by **$** signs.

| | |
|---|---|
| **$$$$$** | Over $300 |
| **$$$$** | $200–$300 |
| **$$$** | $100–$200 |
| **$$** | $70–$100 |
| **$** | Under $70 |

---

to 19th-century life with leather armchairs and wood paneling. Surrounded by a large park with a pool and excellent views of the Pyrenees looming in the distance.

🛈 26 🅿 🕒 Restaurant closed Sun. D 🚬 🕸 All major cards

## ST.-BERTRAND-DE-COMMINGES

### 🍴 LUGDUNUM
**$$**

Valcabrère
TEL 05 61 94 52 05
le-lugdunum-restaurant.com

Reservations are essential for this unique and historic culinary experience. The St.-Bertrand has quite the reputation and the cuisine always lives up to expectations. Sample recipes compiled by Apicius, a first-century Roman gastronome. Serves

---

dishes such as boar or partridge with authentically spiced wines.

🕐 Closed Mon. & Tues. D 🅳 🅼🅲, V

## ST.-GIRONS

### 🏨 EYCHENNE
### 🍴 $$$ ⓞⓞⓞ
8 Avenue Paul-Laffont
TEL 05 61 04 04 50
FAX 05 61 96 07 20
hoteleychenne.com

A beautiful old family-run hostelry with well-equipped rooms and a lovely garden to relax and read or just to ruminate on the joys of being in this most delightful part of the world. The restaurant serves traditional southwestern local cuisine; try monkfish with saffron or the *confit de canard* with ceps.

ⓘ 41 🕐 Closed Sun. D, Mon. Nov.–March (except public holidays), & late Dec.–end of Jan.
🅰 🅲 All major cards

## ▶ SOUTH OF FRANCE

## CÔTE D'AZUR

## BEAULIEU-SUR-MER

### 🏨 LA RÉSERVE DE BEAULIEU
### $$$$$ ⓞⓞⓞⓞ
5 Boulevard du Maréchal Leclerc
TEL 04 93 01 00 01
reservebeaulieu.com

La Réserve de Beaulieu is a truly fabulous Riviera hotel located right on the seafront. The establishment was originally founded, way back in the day, by the famous James Gordon Bennett, proprietor of the *New York Herald Tribune*. This is one of the iconic locations on the French Riviera. The excellent hotel restaurant, which has one Michelin star, specializes in fish.

ⓘ 33 🅿 🕐 Closed mid-Oct.– mid-Dec. 🅲 Rooms 🅰 🅷
🅲 All major cards

## BIOT

### 🍴 LES TERRAILLERS
### $$$–$$$$
11 Route du Chemin-Neuf
TEL 04 93 65 01 59
lesterraillers.com

A large farmhouse restaurant south of Biot, with imaginative cuisine that has gained it one Michelin star. Try baby rabbit with *fines herbes* or foie gras ravioli with *fumet de morille*.

🕐 Closed Wed.–Thurs. & Nov.
🅲 🅲 AE, MC, V

## CANNES

### 🏨 CARLTON INTERCONTINENTAL
### $$$$$ ⓞⓞⓞⓞⓞ
58 La Croisette
TEL 04 93 06 40 06
ichotelsgroup.com

This luxury hotel with a private beach and a terrace where film moguls make deals during the Cannes festival provides a cinematic backdrop to anyone's French vacation.

ⓘ 295 + 18 suites 🅿 🅿 🅢
🅲 🅷 🅲 All major cards

## CAP D'ANTIBES

### 🏨 DU CAP-EDEN ROC
### $$$$$ ⓞⓞⓞⓞⓞ
Boulevard Kennedy
TEL 04 93 61 39 01
hotel-du-cap-eden-roc.com

Favored by Cannes film stars, this is the last word in luxury, especially the 1930s terrace and the pool hewn out of the rocks where Zelda Fitzgerald used to swim. Tennis is another option, whenever you get tired of filmstar-gazing.

📶 121 + 9 suites 🅿 🕑 Closed Nov.–March 🚫 🏊 📺
🈴 All major cards

## HAUT-DE-CAGNES

### 🍴 JOSY-JO
$$$
4 Place Planastel
TEL 04 93 20 68 76
restaurant-josyjo.com
This classy bistro is located in the old town and features rustic decor and a huge fireplace. Superb ingredients simply cooked, such as peppers marinated in olive oil, and *petits farcis* (stuffed vegetables).

🕑 Closed Sun. & Dec. 🚫 🈴 AE, MC, V

## ÎLE DE PORQUEROLLES

### 🏨 LA MAS DU 🍴 LANGOUSTIER
$$$$ ☉☉☉
Île de Porquerolles
TEL 04 94 58 30 09
FAX 04 94 58 36 02
langoustier.com
A luxury island hotel on a rocky position overlooking the sea, with a one-Michelin-star restaurant. Meals served in the garden. *Demi-pension* only.

📶 44 + 5 suites 🕑 Closed Oct.– April 🈴 All major cards

## JUAN-LES-PINS

### 🏨 DES MIMOSAS
$$ ☉☉☉
Rue Pauline
TEL 04 93 61 04 16
FAX 04 92 93 06 46
hotelmimosas.com
This quiet, 19th-century house with large modern rooms, many with bal-

---

conies, and a shady garden makes for an ideal escape on the French Riviera. No restaurant.

📶 34 🅿 🕑 Closed Oct.–late April 🚫 🏊 🈴 AE, MC, V

## MARSEILLE

### 🍴 LE MOLE PASSEDAT
$$–$$$
1 Esplanade de j4
TEL 04 91 19 17 80
FAX 04 92 93 06 46
lemole-passedat.com
Try this rooftop bistro and café at the Musée des Civilisations de l'Europe et de la Méditerranée for chic Mediterranean cuisine from celebrated chef Gérald Passedat. Enjoy stunning views of city and sea.

🕑 Closed Tues. & Sun. p.m.
🈴 All major cards

---

🏨 Hotel  🍴 Restaurant  📶 No. of Guest Rooms  💺 No. of Seats  🅿 Parking  🚇 Metro  🕑 Closed  🛗 Elevator

# MONACO: MONTE CARLO

## 🏢 HERMITAGE
## 🍴 $$$$$ ✪✪✪✪

Square Beaumarchais
TEL 00 377 98 06 40 00
FAX 00 377 98 06 59 70
hotelhermitagemontecarlo.com

A luxurious belle epoque palace with a huge, glass-domed winter garden, opulent restaurant, and terrace of cool marble. The perfect place for a winter weekend or a luxury break from the heat of summer in the south of France.

🛈 209 + 18 suites 🅿 🕃
🌊 🟥 🕃 All major cards

## 🍴 LOUIS XV
### $$$$$

Hôtel de Paris, Place du Casino
TEL 00 377 98 06 88 64
fax 00 377 98 06 59 07
alain-ducasse.com

Monaco's most famous and expensive restaurant, a prestigous Michelin three-star establishment presided over by the celebrated Alain Ducasse. If you need to look at the prices, don't go. Typical dishes might be Provençal vegetables with black truffles, or pigeon with *foie gras de canard.*

🕒 Closed Tues., Wed. (except D mid-July–late Aug.), 2 weeks Feb., & Dec. 🕃 All major cards

# MOUGINS

## 🍴 LE MOULIN DE MOUGINS
### $$$$$

Avenue Notre-Dame-de-Vie
TEL 04 93 75 78 24
moulindemougins.com

This restaurant with its sculpture-filled garden, founded by Roger Vergé—the chef celebrated for his "cuisine of the sun"—is now run with equal panache by Erwan Louaisil.

🕒 Closed Mon.–Tues. Oct.–April
🕃 All major cards

# NICE

## SOMETHING SPECIAL

## 🏢 NÉGRESCO
### $$$$–$$$$$ ✪✪✪✪✪

37 Promenade des Anglais
TEL 04 93 16 64 00
hotel-negresco-nice.com

The most famous and expensive hotel in Nice. This magnificent belle epoque building on the Promenade des Anglais has sumptuous furnishings and impeccable service. As grand as it gets—look for the vast Baccarat chandelier.

🛈 134 + 18 suites 🅿 🕃 🕃 🟥
🕃 All major cards

## 🏢 BEAU RIVAGE
### $$$–$$$$ ✪✪✪✪

24 Rue St.-François-de-Paule
TEL 04 92 47 82 82
FAX 04 92 47 82 83
hotelnicebeaurivage.com

Ideally located on the edge of the old town and with some views over the sea, this superbly renovated large hotel has its own private beach club. It was here that Matisse stayed on his first few visits to Nice.

🛈 118 🕃 🕃 🕃 All major cards

## 🏢 HI-HOTEL
### $$$

Avenue des Fleurs
TEL 04 97 07 26 26
FAX 04 97 07 26 27
hi-hotel.net

A boutique hotel with postmodern design and informal service offers themed guest rooms for music lovers, computer freaks, and movie fans.

⬟ All major cards

### 🏨 LA PÉROUSE
**$$–$$$$ ✪✪✪**

11 Quai Rauba-Capéu
TEL 04 93 62 34 63
hotel-la-perouse.com

For a sea view that won't break the bank, a flowery terrace and a garden restaurant, La Pérouse is the place to stay in Nice.

ℹ️ 64 🅿 ❄ 🏊 🖥
⬟ All major cards

### 🍴 LA MÉRENDA
**$$$**

4 Rue Raoul Bosio
lamerenda.net

This tiny bistro is famous for its traditional Niçois dishes: stockfish, beignets, stuffed sardines, beef daube. No phone, no booking, no cards. This is old-school dining out in the city by the sea. Get there early to secure yourself or your party a table.

🕐 Closed Sat.–Sun. ❄
⬟ No credit cards

### 🍴 LE COMPTOIR
**$$**

20 Rue St.-François-de-Paule
TEL 04 93 92 08 80
le-comptoir-2-nicole-restaurant-nice
.com

This 1930s-style bar/restaurant is particularly convenient for late-night dining or for a light meal after the opera. The fare is always good, the crowd is always entertaining.

⬟ AE, MC, V

### 🍴 LE SAFARI
**$$**

1 Cours Saleya
TEL 04 93 80 18 44

restaurantsafari.fr

A big café with Mediterranean blue shutters, close to the market on Cours Saleya. Great for alfresco dining. Try the deep rich calamari, daube, or *bagna cauda,* a hot anchovy dip with raw vegetables.

⬟ All major cards

## ST.-JEAN-CAP-FERRAT

### 🏨 GRAND HÔTEL DU
### 🍴 CAP-FERRAT
**$$$$$ ✪✪✪✪✪**

Boulevard du Général-de-Gaulle
TEL 04 93 76 50 50
FAX 04 93 76 04 52
grand-hotel-cap-ferrat.com

One of the Riviera's legendary grand hotels, secluded in its own tropical gardens overlooking the sea, with a private funicular down to a terrace and the seawater pool. Magnificent interior furnishings and a Michelin one-star restaurant. Tennis is always a fun way to spend the afternoon at the Grand Hôtel.

ℹ️ 44 + 9 suites 🅿 ❄
⬟ All major cards

## ST.-PAUL-DE-VENCE

### SOMETHING SPECIAL

### 🏨 LA COLOMBE
### 🍴 D'OR
**$$$–$$$$ ✪✪✪**

Place des Ormeaux/Place de Gaulle
TEL 04 93 32 80 02
FAX 04 93 32 77 70
la-colombe-dor.com

Dine on the terrace at this celebrity-haunted hotel-restaurant amid a priceless collection of art donated as payment for meals and rooms by Picasso, Calder, Braque, and more. Try the serving of 15 hors d'oeuvres and the soufflés. Reserve rooms in advance.

🛏 16 + 10 suites ⏰ Closed Nov.– late Dec. 🅰 All major cards

## 🛏 LE ST.-PAUL
🍴 $$$–$$$$ ✦✦✦✦
86 Rue Grande
TEL 04 93 32 65 25
lesaintpaul.com
A secluded, exquisitely furnished 16th-century townhouse within the village walls, with its own very high-standard restaurant.

🛏 15 + 3 suites ⏰ Closed Jan.
🅰 🅰 All major cards

## ST.-TROPEZ

## 🛏 LE BYBLOS
🍴 $$$$$ ✦✦✦✦✦
Avenue Paul-Signac
TEL 04 94 56 68 00
FAX 04 94 56 68 01
byblos.com
The famous hotel where Mick Jagger married Bianca amid a scrum of paparazzi; Le Byblos is designed like a village with sumptuous Moroccan decor, a nightclub, and restaurants.

🛏 86 + 11 suites 🅿 ⏰ Closed Nov.–March 🅰 🅰 🅰
🅰 All major cards

## 🛏 VILLA MARIE
$$$$$
Chemin Val Rian, Ramatuelle
TEL 04 94 97 40 22
fax 04 94 97 37 55
saint-tropez.villamarie.fr
Luxurious hotel in soft terra-cotta shades overlooking the bay of Pampelonne, with its own spa, pool with waterfall, and terrace restaurant.

⏰ Closed Oct.–April 🅿 🅰
🅰 🅰 All major cards

## 🛏 LE YACA
$$$$–$$$$$ ✦✦✦✦
1 Boulevard d'Aumale
TEL 04 94 55 81 00
FAX 04 94 97 58 50
hotel-le-yaca.fr
An old Provençal house in the town center, favored by Signac and Colette, built around a swimming pool and a sumptuous garden.

🛏 27 ⏰ Closed mid-Oct.–April
🅰 🅰 🅰 All major cards

## 🛏 LA PONCHE
$$$$ ✦✦✦✦
Place Révelin
TEL 04 94 97 02 53
FAX 04 94 97 78 61
laponche.com
A very charming ensemble of former fishermen's cottages located behind the port, complete with stylish, surprisingly large guest rooms.

🛏 13 + 5 suites ⏰ Closed Nov.–mid-Feb. 🅰 🅰 All major cards

## 🍴 CAFÉ SÉNÉQUIER
$$
Quai Jean-Jaurès
TEL 04 94 97 00 90
senequier.com
A favorite café on the port; pricey but good for evening aperitifs and the local French sport of watching celebrities on yachts drink theirs.

🅰 No credit cards

## VILLEFRANCHE-SUR-MER

## 🍴 LA MÈRE GERMAINE
$$$
8 Quai Courbet
TEL 04 93 01 71 39
meregermaine.com
A traditional Vieux Port restaurant with a modern take on southern

classics—bouillabaisse milkshake, anyone? Inventive dishes, good local wine list, and one Michelin star. This place has a rich history, which the owners might tell you about, if you're not dining at one of their rush hours.

🕐 Closed Nov.–Dec. 🔷 AE, MC, V

## PROVENCE

## AIX-EN-PROVENCE

### 🏨 PIGONNET
**$$$–$$$$** ○○○○
5 Avenue du Pigonnet
TEL 04 42 59 02 90
FAX 04 42 59 47 77
hotelpigonnet.com

A Provençal country house in its own park, charmingly embellished in the 1920s. Plus restaurant.

🛈 52 🅿 🕐 Closed Tues. Nov.–March 🔷 🏊 🔽
🔷 All major cards

### 🍴 LES DEUX GARÇONS
$
Cours Mirabeau
TEL 04 42 26 00 51
les2garcons.fr

A classic terrace café on the Cours Mirabeau; a favorite with artists and intellectuals since the 18th century.

🔷 🔷 All major cards

## APT

### 🍴 AUBERGE DU LUBÉRON
**$$–$$$$**
17 Quai Léon Sagy
TEL 04 90 74 12 50
rive-droite-apt.fr

Typical Provençal food in a peaceful atmosphere, with a terrace and garden. Try the duck foie gras with fruit *confits;* Lubéron lamb with

### PRICES

**HOTELS**
An indication of the cost of a double room in the high season is given by **$** signs.

| | |
|---|---|
| **$$$$$** | Over $800 |
| **$$$$** | $500–$800 |
| **$$$** | $300–$500 |
| **$$** | $150–$300 |
| **$** | Under $150 |

**RESTAURANTS**
An indication of the cost of a three-course meal without drinks is given by $ signs.

| | |
|---|---|
| **$$$$$** | Over $300 |
| **$$$$** | $200–$300 |
| **$$$** | $100–$200 |
| **$$** | $70–$100 |
| **$** | Under $70 |

*aubergine confits.* Reservations essential. Rooms are also available.

🕐 Closed Sun. in winter, Mon. (except D in season), & Dec. 23–Jan. 15 🔷 All major cards

## ARLES

### 🏨 LE MAS DE PEINT
**$$$$** ○○○○
Le Sambuc
TEL 04 90 97 20 62
FAX 04 90 97 22 20
masdepeint.com

Converted stables attached to an old Camargue farmhouse. Exquisite rooms have wooden ceilings, white linen furnishings, and antiques. Homegrown vegetables served.

🛈 8 + 2 suites 🅿 🕐 Closed early Jan.–March 🔷 🏊
🔷 All major cards

## 🏨 GRAND HÔTEL NORD PINUS
**$$$–$$$$$** ⊙⊙⊙⊙

14 Place du Forum
TEL 04 90 93 44 44
nord-pinus.com

Although brought up-to-date, this luxury hotel has kept its individuality. Traditional Provençal furniture. Popular with bullfighters at festival time.

ⓘ 25 🅿 ⊕ Closed mid-Nov.–mid-Feb. 🅢 Rooms 🅢 All major cards

## 🏨 HOTEL JULES CESAR
**$$**

14 Place du Forum
TEL 04 90 52 52 52
hotel-julescesar.fr

This hotel, long a grand Arlesian institution, is located in a 17th-century convent around a floral garden cloister, and has been newly renovated by designer Christian Lacroix, a son of Arles himself. The hotel has its own restaurant.

ⓘ 50 🖼 🅢 All major cards

## 🍴 LA GUEULE DU LOUP
**$$$**

39 Rue des Arènes
TEL 04 90 96 96 69
restaurant-lagueuleduloup.fr

A wood-beamed restaurant above the kitchen serves Midi classics with an original twist like the *charlotte d'agneau* with eggplant and red pepper coulis, or tart of turnips with foie gras and guinea fowl with pears. It is popular, so reserve.

⊕ Closed Jan., Sun., & Mon. L

# AVIGNON

## 🏨 LA MIRANDE
🍴 **$$$$$** ⊙⊙⊙⊙

4 Place Amirande
TEL 04 90 14 20 20
la-mirande.fr

An 18th-century hotel situated close to the Palais des Papes, with luxurious rooms and tasteful furnishings. The Michelin one-star restaurant offers Provençal specialties such as flavorsome Lubéron lamb.

ⓘ 19 🅿 🅢
🅢 All major cards

## 🏨 L'EUROPE
🍴 **$$–$$$$$** ⊙⊙⊙⊙⊙

12 Place Crillon
TEL 04 90 14 76 76
heurope.com

Avignon's top hotel—even the Emperor Napoleon stayed here. The grand entrance to this 16th-century mansion leads onto the peaceful terrace with a fountain. The one-Michelin-star restaurant, **La Vieille Fontaine,** lives up to the splendor of the establishment. Try zucchini flowers stuffed with artichoke or roast sea bream with tomato tart.

ⓘ 44 + 3 suites 🅿 ⊕ Restaurant closed Sun.–Mon. & 2 weeks in Aug. 🅢 🅢 All major cards

## 🍴 RESTAURANT CHRISTIAN ETIENNE
**$$$$**

10 Rue de Mons
TEL 04 90 86 16 50
restaurantsevin.fr

Fourteenth-century frescoed mansion with terrace, next to the Palais des Papes, serves luxury versions of local ingredients with emphasis on vegetables; try clam and asparagus gratin, or carrot sorbet.

⊕ Closed Sun.–Mon. 🅢 AE, CB, MC, V

# CHÂTEAUNEUF-DU-PAPE

## 🏨 LA SOMMELLERIE
**$** ⊙⊙⊙

Route de Roquemaure

TEL 04 90 83 50 00
FAX 04 90 83 51 85
la-sommellerie.fr
A charming 17th-century *bergerie* situated among the famous vineyards and now a delightful small hotel.
🛈 14 🕒 Closed Jan., Sat. L, Sun. D, & Mon. Nov.–March
🏧 All major cards

## GARGAS

### 🏨 LA COQUILLADE
### 🍴 $$$–$$$$
Gargas
TEL 04 90 74 71 71
FAX 04 90 74 71 72
coquillade.fr
A wine domaine and hotel—a hillside hamlet with panoramic views over the Luberon, surrounded by vineyards. Two restaurants (**Le Gourmet,** now with one Michelin star), cellar, chic high-tech rooms, artworks, and ecologically designed gardens.
🛈 14 🅿 🕒 Closed Jan.–mid-March 🏊 🏧 AE, MC, V

## GIGONDAS

### 🍴 LES FLORETS
### $–$$$
TEL 04 90 65 85 01
hotel-lesflorets.com
An attractive, quiet restaurant with Provençal decor and a terrace. Choices include monkfish braised with orange butter, and lamb on a bed of eggplant. Rooms available.
🅿 🕒 Closed Wed. & Jan.–March
🏧 All major cards

## GORDES

### 🏨 LA FERME DE LA HUPPE
### $–$$
Route d'Apt Les Pourquiers
TEL 04 90 72 12 25

## PRICES

**HOTELS**
An indication of the cost of a double room in the high season is given by $ signs.

| | |
|---|---|
| $$$$$ | Over $800 |
| $$$$ | $500–$800 |
| $$$ | $300–$500 |
| $$ | $150–$300 |
| $ | Under $150 |

**RESTAURANTS**
An indication of the cost of a three-course meal without drinks is given by $ signs.

| | |
|---|---|
| $$$$$ | Over $300 |
| $$$$ | $200–$300 |
| $$$ | $100–$200 |
| $$ | $70–$100 |
| $ | Under $70 |

lafermedelahuppe.com
Located in peaceful Lubéron countryside, this beautiful 18th-century farm with an inner courtyard has been renovated in Provençal style.
🛈 8 🅿 🕒 Closed Nov.–March 🛌 Some rooms 🏊 🏧 AE, MC, V

### 🍴 LE MAS TOURTERON
### $$$
Chemin St.-Blaise, Les Imberts
TEL 04 90 72 00 16
FAX 04 90 72 09 81
An old Provençal *mas* (farmhouse) with a walled garden serving light, fresh, and imaginative cuisine using seasonal products.
🕒 Closed Dec.–Feb.
🏧 All major cards

🏨 Hotel 🍴 Restaurant 🛈 No. of Guest Rooms 🛌 No. of Seats 🅿 Parking 🚇 Metro 🕒 Closed 🛗 Elevator

## LES BAUX-DE PROVENCE

### 🏨 LA BENVENGUDO
**$$ ✪✪✪**
1 mile/2 km S of Les Baux
TEL 04 90 54 32 54
FAX 04 90 54 42 58
benvengudo.fr
Tucked beneath the Alpilles hills, a manor-hotel with an elegant garden. The lounge and dining room are in Provençal style; some rooms have private terraces. Tennis is available.
🛈 20 + 3 suites 🅿 🕐 Closed Nov.–Feb. 🅰 Some rooms
🌊 🅰 AE, MC, V

### 🍽 OUSTAU DE BAUMANIÈRE
**$$$$–$$$$$**
TEL 04 90 54 33 07
Route d'Arles
baumaniere.com/gastronomie /loustau-de-bauman
A Michelin two-star restaurant in an elegantly furnished 16th-century building, famous for its *gigot d'agneau en croûte* and truffle ravioli.
🕐 Closed Jan.–Feb. & Tues. D– Thurs. L Nov.–March
🅰 All major cards

## MOUSTIERS-STE.-MARIE

### 🍽 LES SANTONS
**$$$–$$$$**
Place de l'Église
TEL 04 92 74 66 48
A tiny restaurant, located near the Gorges du Verdon, famous far and wide around these parts for its delicious chicken in lavender honey. This is authentic southern chicken, French-style.
🕐 Closed mid-Nov.–mid-Feb., Mon. 🅰 All major cards

## ORANGE

### 🍽🏨 AUBERGE DE L'ORANGERIE
**$$**
4 Place de l'Ormeau, Piolenc
TEL 04 90 29 59 88
FAX 04 90 29 67 74
This 18th-century auberge with a charming stone-walled courtyard provides a traditional atmosphere for inventive cuisine, such as langoustine with truffle sauce and osso buco. Rooms are available.
🕐 Closed Sun. D 🅰 AE, MC, V

## SAINTES-MARIES-DE-LA-MER

### 🏨 LE MAS DE LA FOUQUE
**$$$$ ✪✪✪✪**
Route du Petit Rhône
TEL 04 90 97 81 02
masdelafouque.com
A traditional Camargue hotel. Large rooms with tiled floors and wooden beams have private terraces overlooking the lagoon and park.
🛈 14 🅿 🕐 Closed Jan. 🅰 🌊
🅰 All major cards

## LANGUEDOC-ROUSSILLON

## BOUZIGUES

### 🍽🏨 LA CÔTE BLEUE
**$$–$$$**
Avenue Louis-Tudesq
TEL 04 67 78 30 87
la-cote-bleue.fr
A large family restaurant overlooking the Bassin de Thau, which is the best place to sample the vast variety of shellfish found here: Mussels and langoustines are excellent, and do try the tiny sweet Bouzigues oysters. Rooms are also available.

🔆 Closed Wed. out of season, end of Nov., & Feb. holidays 🏊 🅂 AE, MC, V

## CARCASSONNE

### 🏨 CITÉ
**$$$$-$$$$$** ✪✪✪✪
Place de l'Église
TEL 04 68 71 98 71
hoteldelacite.com
A grand neo-Gothic hotel built into the ramparts of the old city, with its own garden and two restaurants.
ⓘ 55 + 6 suites 🅿 🔆 Closed Dec. & mid-March 🏊
🅂 All major cards

### 🍴 BRASSERIE LE DONJON
**$**
2 Rue Porte d'Aude
TEL 04 68 25 95 72
FAX 04 68 25 06 60
brasserie-donjon.fr
An elegant eatery in the midst of the old walled city serving such traditional dishes as cassoulet and foie gras.
🔆 Closed Sun. D Nov.–March
🅂 All major cards

## COLLIOURE

### 🏨 CASA PARAÏL
**$-$$$** ✪✪✪
Impasse des Palmiers
TEL 04 68 82 05 81
FAX 04 68 82 52 10
hotel-casa-pairal.com
A 19th-century Catalan villa set in a shady garden with palm trees and fountains—a peaceful haven in the town center. No restaurant.
ⓘ 28 🅿 🏊 🅂
🅂 All major cards

### 🏨 LES TEMPLIERS
### 🍴 **$** ✪✪
12 Quai de l'Amirauté
TEL 04 68 98 31 10
FAX 04 68 98 01 24
hotel-templiers.com
A hotel and restaurant in the old town near the harbor. Great seafood with Collioure wine. The hotel is famous for the artists who stayed here, including Matisse and Braque; it retains its authentic atmosphere.
ⓘ 21 + 50 annex 🔆 Closed early Jan.–early Feb.; restaurant closed Sun. D & all Mon. in winter
🅂 AE, MC, V

## MOLITG-LES-BAINS

### 🏨 CHÂTEAU DE
### 🍴 RIELL
**$$$-$$$$** ✪✪✪✪

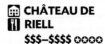

TEL 04 68 05 04 40
chateauderiell.com
A mock-Gothic château in the foothills of the Pyrenees with a view of Mont Canigou. Nearby spa. The restaurant serves Michel Guerard–style nouvelle cuisine. Tennis is available.

🛈 19 🅿 🕓 Closed Dec.–March
🏔 🍴 All major cards

## MONTPELLIER

### 🍴 LE JARDIN DES SENS
$$$$–$$$$$
11 Avenue St.-Lazare
TEL 04 99 58 38 38
FAX 04 99 58 38 39
jardindessens.com
A small, sophisticated, Michelin one-star restaurant with a garden in the middle of Montpellier, celebrated for its southern regional cooking.

🕓 Closed Mon. L, Wed. L, & Sun.
🍴 All major cards

## NÎMES

### 🍴 L'ENCLOS DE LA FONTAINE
$$$
Hôtel Imperator, Quai de la Fontaine
TEL 04 66 21 90 30
hotel-imperator.com
The restaurant of the Hôtel Imperator is favored by bullfighters at *féria* time. Try local specialties such as *brandade de morue* (creamy salt cod), *escabèche* (marinated fish), or sea bass with fennel compote.

🅿 🍴 🍴 All major cards

### 🍴 LE LISITA
$$$
2 Boulevard des Arenes
TEL 04 66 67 29 15
lelisita.com
Facing the Roman arena, an elegant restaurant with a tree-shaded ter-

race for stylish southern cuisine; local specialties include *brandade* (salt cod), roast pigeon, and strawberries in Cevennes honey.

🕓 Closed Sun.–Mon.
🍴 AE, MC, V

## PERPIGNAN

### 🍴 LE FRANCE
$$
Place de la Loge
TEL 04 68 51 61 71
This restaurant occupies one of Perpignan's finest Renaissance buildings in the old town, now converted with terrace dining for light Mediterranean-style cuisine.

🍴 MC, V

### 🍴 GARIANNE
$
15 Rue Frédéric Valette
TEL 04 68 67 07 44
Convenient for Perpignan's very modern train station, this deceptively simple bistro serves original seasonal dishes and exotic desserts. Try a little bit of everything with the degustation menu.

🕓 Closed Sun.–Mon. & Sat. L
🍴 CB, MC, V

## PORT VENDRES

### 🍴 LE BAR A HUITRES
$
Anse Gerbal, La Criée
TEL 04 68 98 46 00
cotecatalane.com
Traditional fish market installed in a swanky modern building; bar with view of port and sea for selection of oysters and tapas, and *plateaux de fruits de mer.*

🕓 Closed Mon. (except July–Aug.
🍴 All major cards

## SÈTE

### 🏨 GRAND HÔTEL
**$–$$ ❍❍❍**
17 Quai Maréchal de Lattre-de-
Tassigny
TEL 04 67 74 71 77
FAX 04 67 74 29 27
legrandhotelsete.com
A charming, classic belle epoque
hotel overlooking the Sète's pretty
Grand Canal.
ⓘ 45 🅿 🕐 Closed Dec.
🔆 Rooms 🀫 All major cards

▶ **CORSICA**

## BASTIA

### 🍴 LA CITADELLE
**$$–$$$**
6 Rue du Dragon
TEL 04 95 31 44 70
An old olive mill with a terrace
for alfresco dining with excellent
regional cuisine.
🕐 Closed Sun.–Mon. & mid-Dec.–
mid-Jan. 🔆 🀫 All major cards

## BONIFACIO

### 🏨 GENOVESE
**$$$$–$$$$$ ❍❍❍❍**
Haute Ville
TEL 04 95 73 12 34
hotel-genovese.com

The former Foreign Legion barracks
located in the old town has been
transformed into a modern luxury
hotel. No restaurant.
ⓘ 14 🅿 🕐 Closed Jan.–Feb.
🔆 🀫 🀫 AE, V

## CALVI

### 🏨 AUBERGE DE LA SIGNORIA
### 🍴 $$$–$$$$ ❍❍❍
Route de Forêt de Bonifato
TEL 04 95 65 93 00
FAX 04 95 65 38 77
hotel-la-signoria.com
A 17th-century house set peacefully in a park with pines, palms, and
orange trees to the south of Calvi. A
good restaurant with terrace where
you can dine by candlelight. Tennis.
ⓘ 20 🅿 🕐 Closed mid-Oct.–
April 🔆 Rooms 🀫 🀫 AE, MC, V

## PORTO-VECCHIO

### 🏨 GRAND HOTEL CALA ROSSA
### 🍴 $$$–$$$$$ ❍❍❍
TEL 04 95 71 61 51
FAX 04 95 71 60 11
cala-rossa.com
Located northeast of Porto-Vecchio,
this pleasant hotel with shady trees, a
flowery garden, and a terrace on the
beach also has a Michelin one-star
restaurant specializing in fish dishes.
ⓘ 49 🕐 Closed Nov.–March
🔆 🀫 All major cards

# SHOPPING

Shopping is one of the great pleasures of a visit to France. From the smallest streets to the grandest city boulevards, French stores offer delectable displays of pastries, chocolates, and all manner of sweetmeats. Ordinary practical products are often beautifully designed and can make excellent presents: Stationery stores *(papeteries)* offer wonderful little notebooks and files, and *drogueries* (not drugstores but hardware stores) are Aladdin's caves of intriguing kitchen utensils and charming pottery. Town centers are now often car-free, with supermarkets and hypermarkets on the outskirts. These are ideal for bulk food shopping, often have a good selection of wine, and are also useful for buying stamps, newspapers, and gas.

## Markets

Markets are the best way to shop in France. Most places have a weekly market, and in bigger cities they may even be daily. They usually start early in the morning and close at noon—if you want the pick of the produce, go early. The livestock section is not for the tenderhearted, as cages full of live ducks, geese, and chickens wait to be carried home for dinner. Look for local delicacies such as cheese, honey, olives, charcuterie, spices, herbs, and special breads and cakes.

France also has numerous flea markets (*marchés aux puces* or *brocantes*) selling secondhand goods, antiques, and local curios.

## Dégustations

*Dégustation* means "tasting." All over France, you will see signs inviting you to sample the local produce, particularly the wine. You are not obliged to buy, but it would be thought uncivil not to purchase at least one bottle.

## Opening Hours

Food stores, especially bakeries (*boulangeries*), open early, around 7 a.m. Small stores and big department stores (*grands magasins*) usually open at 9 a.m. Most stores close for lunch between noon and 2 or 3 p.m., staying open until 7 or 7:30 in the evening. Hypermarkets usually stay open all day until quite late. Many stores close on Mondays; food shops, and especially bakers, open on Sunday mornings, staying faithful to their tradition of serving the faithful.

## Payment

Supermarkets accept credit cards, but smaller stores often do not. Check the signs on the door before you go in. Some traders are reluctant to accept payment by American Express cards or traveler's checks.

## Exports

Most purchases include TVA (VAT or value-added tax) at a base rate running currently at 20 percent, and 10 percent for restaurants. Visitors from outside the EU may claim back TVA over a certain amount. Take your passport and ask the store for a completed *bordereau* (export sales invoice), which must be shown, together with the goods, to customs officers when you leave the country. TVA refunds are available by mail or electronically.

## What to Buy

The French are particularly good at luxuries such as lingerie, soap, cosmetics, perfume, chocolate, and delicious jam. Every region of France has its own special products that make irresistible souvenirs. Often these are gastronomic delights such as honey, herbs, cookies, foie gras, wine, brandies, or local liqueurs. Look, too, for local pottery, baskets, and fabrics.

The following is a list of regional products, with a selection of especially good places to buy in each region.

## ▨ NORTHERN FRANCE

## Champagne

The big houses are in Reims or Épernay and can be toured (see sidebar pp. 140 & 472). To buy champagne, the following stores have good selections:
**La Vinocave** 45 place Drouet, Reims 51100, tel 03 26 40 60 07
**Le Vintage** 3 cours Anatole France, Reims 51100, tel 03 26 40 40 00, levintage-reims.fr

## Cheese

**Philippe Olivier** 43–45 rue Thiers, Boulogne-sur-Mer 62200, tel 03 21 31 94 74, philippeolivier.fr. Famous cheese store with hundreds of different cheeses.

## Chocolate

**Chocolaterie de Beussent** 66 route de Desvres, Beussent 62170, tel 03 21 86 17 62, choco-france.com. Handmade.
**Chocolaterie Jean Trogneux** 1 rue Delambre, Amiens 80000, tel 03 22 71 17 17. Handmade chocolates and macarons.
**La Chocolaterie Thibaut** Zone Artisanale, rue Max-Menu, Pierry 51530, tel 03 26 51 58 04, chocolaterie -thibaut.com. Handmade chocolates,

including chocolate champagne corks filled with *marc de Champagne*.

## Enamelware

**Emaux Saint Jean l'Aigle** rue de la Chiers, Herserange-Longwy 54400, tel 03 82 24 58 20
**Société des Faienceries et Émaux de Longwy** 3 rue Acacias, Longwy 54400, tel 09 62 27 59 42

## Foie Gras

**Jean Lutz** 5 rue du Chaudron, Strasbourg, tel 03 88 32 00 64
**Traiteur Vincent** 11 rue des Boulangers, Colmar, tel 03 89 41 32 05

## Glass

**Cristal Daum** Vannes-le-Chatel, near Toul, tel 03 83 25 41 01
**Jardin de Cristal** rue de la Liberté, Vannes-le-Chatel, near Toul, tel 09 62 09 99 61
**Terres d'Est** 1 rue de la Faiencerie, Niderviller 57565, tel 03 87 23 80 04. Crystal products.

## Markets

| | |
|---|---|
| Amiens | Wed. & Sat. |
| Beauvais | Wed. & Sat. |
| Boulogne-sur-Mer | Wed. & Sat. |
| Calais | Wed., Thurs., & Sat. |
| Colmar | Thurs. & Sat. |
| Langres | Fri. |
| Le Touquet | Mon.–Thurs. & Sat. |
| Lille | daily |
| Metz | Wed.–Thurs. & Sat. |
| Nancy | Tues.–Sat. |
| Reims | daily |
| Strasbourg | Mon.–Sat. |
| Troyes | Sat. |

## ▨ NORMANDY & BRITTANY

## Benedictine

**Palais Bénédictine** 110 rue Alexandre-Le-Grand, Fecamp 76400, tel 02

35 10 26 10, benedictine.com. Try the taste of Benedictine liqueur.

## Calvados

**Christian Drouin Distilleries des Fiefs Ste.-Anne,** Coudray-Rabut 14130, tel 02 31 64 30 05, calvados-drouin.com

**Pierre Huet** Manoir la Brière des Fontaines, Cambremer 14170, tel 02 31 63 01 09

## Cheese

**Fromagerie Graindorge** 42 rue Général-Lectere, tel 02 31 48 20 00, Livarot 14140, graindorge.fr. Livarot cheese.

**Fromagerie Réaux** 1 rue des Planquettes, Lessay 50430, tel 02 33 46 41 33, reaux.fr. High-quality AOC Camembert. Open Mon.–Fri. Visits by appointment.

**Domaine de St.-Hippolyte** St.-Martin-de-la-Lisiuex 14100, tel 02 31 31 30 68, domaine-saint-hippolyte.fr. Dairy farm. Open daily May–Sept.

Several museums also offer sales and tastings, including the Musée du Fromage, Livarot; the Musée du Fromage, Vimoutiers; and La Ferme Président, the cheese museum of Camembert.

## Cider

**La Ferme de Beuvron** Beuvron-en-Auge 14430, tel 02 31 79 29 19. Cheese, Calvados, and cider.

**Route du Cidre, Pays d'Auge** For info about this route through cider country: tel 02 31 27 90 30, calvados-tourisme.com.

## Clothes

**Coopérative Maritime** Guilvinec 29730, tel 02 98 58 10 31. Breton fishermen's sweaters and other gear.

## Cookies

**Biscuiterie** 8 rue Gen de Gaulle, Pont-Aven 29930, tel 02 98 09 14 20, biscuiteriedepontaven.fr

## Faience

**Faïencerie HB Henriot** 16 rue Haute, Quimper 29337, tel 02 98 90 09 36, henriot-quimper.com

## Lace

**Musée des Beaux-Arts et de la Dentelle** Cour Carrée de la Dentelle, Alençon 61000, tel 02 33 32 40 07. Alençon lace.

## Mustard & Other Food Specialties

**Épicerie Claude Olivier** 16 rue St.-Jacques, Dieppe 76200, tel 02 35 84 22 55, olivierdieppe.com

## Sea Salt

**Les Salines de Guerande** Pradel 44350, tel 02 40 62 01 25

**La Salorge de Guérande** Buy from roadside stands amid the salt marshes south of Guérande.

## Markets

| | |
|---|---|
| Bayeux | Wed. & Sat. |
| Brest | daily |
| Caen | Fri. & Sun. |
| Concarneau | Mon. & Fri. |
| Dieppe | Tues., Thurs., & Sat. |
| Dinan | Thurs. |
| Honfleur | Sat. |
| Lorient | Sat. |
| Quimper | daily |
| Rennes | Tues.–Sun. |
| Rouen | Thurs.–Sun. |
| St.-Malo | Mon.–Sat. |
| Trouville-sur-Mer | Wed. & Sun. |
| Vannes | Wed. & Sat. |

**Apple fair** Ste.-Opportune-la-Mare (north of Pont Audemer). First Sunday of October.

**Camembert fair** South of Lisieux, last Sun. in July.
**Cider fair** Caudebec-en-Caux. September.

# ■ LOIRE VALLEY

## Baskets
**Coopérative de Vannerie de Villaines** 1 rue de la Cheneillère, Villaines-les-Rochers 37190, tel 02 47 45 43 03, vannerie.com

## Charcuterie
**Charcuterie Hardouin** Virage Gastronomique, Vouvray 37210, tel 02 47 40 40 40, hardouin.com

## Chocolates, Cookies & Patisserie
**Benoit Chocolats** 1 rue des Lices, Angers 49000, tel 02 41 88 94 52, chocolats-benoit.com.
**La Chocolaterie Royale** 53 rue Royale, Orléans 45000, tel 02 38 53 93 43, lachocolaterieroyale.com
**La Petite Marquise** 22 rue des Lices, Angers 49000, tel 02 41 87 43 01

## Faience
**Faïencerie de Gien** place de la Victoire, Gien 45500, tel 02 38 05 21 05, gien.com
**Faïenceries du Bourg-Joly** 16 rue Carnot, Malicorne-sur-Sarthe 72270, tel 02 43 94 80 10, malicorne.com. Since 1747.

## Wine & Spirits
Local *maisons du vin* will give information on tastings and on producers for direct sales (vinsvaldeloire.fr).
**Château de Montcontour** 40 rue Carnot, Vouvray 37210, tel 03 80 22 35 47, vins-vouvray.com
**Distillerie Cointreau** St.-Barthélemy-d'Anjou 49124, tel 02 41 31 50 50, carre-cointreau.fr. Distillery tour.

**Maison du Vin de l'Anjou** 5 bis place Kennedy, Angers 49100, tel 02 41 88 81 13
**Maison des Vin de Bourgueil** Bourgueil 37140, tel 02 47 97 92 20, vinbourgueil.com

## Markets
| | |
|---|---|
| Amboise | Fri. & Sun. |
| Angers | daily |
| Blois | Tues., Thurs., & Sat. |
| Bourges | Thurs.–Sun. |
| Chinon | Thurs. |
| Nantes | daily |
| Orléans | Tues.–Sun. |
| Saumur | Sat. |
| Tours | daily |

# ■ CENTRAL FRANCE & THE ALPS

## Charcuterie
**Charcuterie Raillard** 4 rue Monge, Beaune 21200, tel 03 80 22 23 04
**Charcuterie Reynon** 13 rue des Archers, Lyon 69000, tel 04 78 37 39 08, reynonlyon.com

## Cheese
**Abbaye Notre-Dame de Cîteaux** Cîteaux 21700, tel 03 80 61 34 28. Still produced by monks.
**Les Caves Societé** Roquefort-sur-Soulzon 12250, tel 05 65 58 54 38. Tours of caves where cheese ages.
**Coopérative Fromagerie d'Arbois** rue des Fosses, Arbois 39600, tel 03 84 66 09 71
**Fromagerie Berthaut** place Champ-de-Foire, Époisses 21460, tel 03 80 96 44 44
**Fromagerie René Richard** Les Halles, 102 cours Lafayette, Lyon 69000, tel 04 78 62 30 78

## Chocolate
**Le Chocolatier d'Annecy** 4 place St.-François-de-Sales, Annecy 74000, tel 04 50 45 12 08

Pâtisserie-Chocolaterie Bernachon
42 cours Franklin-Roosevelt, Lyon
69006, tel 04 78 24 37 98

## Montélimar Nougat
**Nougat Chabert et Guillot** 1 rue André Ducatz, Montélimar 26200, tel
04 75 00 64 84

## Mustard
**Grey-Poupon Maille** 32 rue de la Liberté, Dijon 21000, tel 03 80 30 41 02

## Olives
**Coopérative Agricole du Nyonsais**
place Olivier-de-Serres, Nyons 26110,
tel 04 75 26 95 00, vignolis.fr

## Pain d'Épices
**Mulot & Petitjean** 13 place Bossuet,
Dijon 21000, tel 03 80 30 07 10, mulot
petitjean.com

## Silk
**Atelier d'impression Brochier de
Soierie** 33 rue Romarin, Lyon 69001,
tel 04 72 07 97 83, brochiersoieries
.com/atelier
**Le Carre de Soie** 21 rue de la Charite
Lyon 69002, tel 04 78 37 14 24. Designer head scarves and fabrics.

## Wine
*Beaujolais*
**Le Hameau du Vin** Romanèche-Thorins 71570, tel 03 85 35 22 22, hameau
duvin.com. Wine museum & shop.
**Les Routes des Vins Beaujolais**
Villefranche-sur-Saône 69400, tel 04
74 07 27 40, villefranche-beaujolais.fr

*Burgundy*
**Marché aux Vins** 7 rue l'Hotel Dieu,
Beaune 21200, tel 03 80 25 08 20.
Tasting ($$$$$).
**Le Vigneron** 6 rue d'Alsace, Beaune
21200, tel 03 80 22 68 21. Wine accessories.

*Cassis*
**Cassis Boudier** 14 rue de Cluj, Dijon
21007, tel 03 80 74 33 33

*Chablis*
**La Chablisienne** 8 boulevard Pasteur,
Chablis 89800, tel 03 86 42 89 89

*Chartreuse*
**Les Caves de la Chartreuse** 10 boulevard Edgar-Kofler, Voiron 38500, tel
04 76 05 81 77

*Jura*
**Societé de Viticulture du Jura** 455
rue du Colonel de Casteljau RI, Lonsle-Saunier 39016, tel 03 84 35 14 02

*Mâcon*
**Maison du Vin** 484 avenue Maréchal
de Lattre-de-Tassigny, Mâcon 71000,
tel 03 85 22 91 11
**Syndicat Viticole de Pouilly** 2 rue des
Écoles, Pouilly-sur-Loire 58150, tel 03
86 39 06 83

## Markets
| | |
|---|---|
| Aubusson | Sat. |
| Autun | Wed., Fri., & Sun. |
| Auxerre | Tues. & Fri. |
| Beaune | Wed. & Sat. |
| Besançon | Tues., Fri., & Sun. |
| Bourg-en-Bresse | Wed. & Sat. |
| Chablis | Sun. |
| Chambéry | Sat. |
| Clermont-Ferrand | Mon.–Sat. |
| Dijon | Tues., Fri., & Sat. |
| Grenoble | Tues.–Sun. |
| Le Puy-en-Velay | Sat. |
| Louhans | Mon. (Bresse poultry) |
| Lyon | Tues.–Sun. |
| Nyons | Thurs. |
| Vichy | Wed. |

## ■ SOUTHWEST FRANCE

## Basque Berets
**Musée du Beret** place St. Roch, Nay
64800, tel 05 59 61 91 70

## Basque Linen
**Jean Vier Basque Linen**
25 rue Mazagran, Biarritz 64200,
tel 05 59 85 20 55

## Bayonne Ham
**Maison Montauzer** 17 rue de la
Salie, Bayonne 64100, tel 05 59 59
07 68, montauzer.fr
**Pierre d'Ibaïalde** 41 rue des Corde-
liers, Bayonne 64100, tel 05 59 25 65
30, pierre-ibaialde.com

## Chocolate &
## Basque Caramels
**Chocolaterie Cazenave** 19 rue du
Port-Neuf, Bayonne 64100, tel 05 59
59 03 16
**Atelier du Chocolat** 1 rue Poste, Bi-
arritz 64200, tel 05 59 24 47 05

## Makhila
**Ainciart Bergara** Larressore 64480,
tel 05 59 93 03 05. Traditional
Basque walking sticks in wood, often
silver-tipped.

## Porcelain
**Royal Limoges Magasin (factory
shop)** 15 rue Victor Duray, Limoges
87000, royal-limoges.fr. See limoges
-tourisme.com for more porcelain
shops, tel 05 55 33 27 30.

## Truffles, Foie Gras & Confits
**Aux Armes du Périgord** 1 rue de la
Liberté, Sarlat-la-Canéda 24200, tel
05 53 59 14 27
**Conserverie Godard** Gourdon
46300, tel 05 65 41 03 97
**La Ferme de Turnac** Domme 24150,
tel 05 53 28 10 84
**Le Gers Gourmet** 32400 Saint Mont,
tel 05 62 69 62 89
**Pebeyre** 66 rue Frédéric-Suisse,
Cahors 46000, tel 05 65 22 24 80
**Pierre Champion** 21 rue Taillefer,
Périgueux 24004, tel 05 53 03 90 29

## Wine & Spirits
For a good selection of Bordeaux
wines try:
**L'Intendant** 2 allée de Tourny, Bordeaux 33000, tel 05 56 48 01 29,
intendant.com
**La Vinothèque** 8 cours du 30 Juillet,
Bordeaux 33000, tel 05 57 10 41 41,
vinotheque-bordeaux.com

*Maisons du Vin*
**Maison des Sauternes** place de la
Mairie, Sauternes 33210, tel 05 56 76
69 83
**Maison des Vins de Graves** 61 cours
Maréchal Foch, Podensac 33720, tel
05 56 27 09 25
**Maison de Vins de Bergerac** 2 place
du Dr. Cayla, Bergerac 24100, tel 05
53 63 57 55
**Maison du Tourisme et du Vin** La Ver-
rerie, Pauillac 33250, tel 05 56 59 03 08
**Maison du Vin des Côtes de Blaye**
11 cours Vauban, Blaye 33390, tel 05
57 42 91 19
**Maison du Vin des Côtes de Bourg**
place de l'Éperon, Bourg 33710, tel 05
57 94 80 20
**Maison du Vin de St.-Émilion** place
Pierre, Meyrat, St.-Émilion 33330, tel
05 57 55 50 55
**Syndicat Interprofessionel du Vin de
Cahors** place F. Mitterand, tel 05 65
23 63 09

*Armagnac*
**Janneau Fils** avenue de la Gare, Con-
dom 32100, tel 05 62 28 24 77
**Jean-Gabriel Cénac** Domaine de
Laubuchon, Manciet 32370, tel 05
62 08 50 29

*Cognac*
**Cognac Otard** Château de Cognac,
127 boulevard Denfert-Rochereau,
Cognac 16101, tel 05 45 36 88 86
**Rémy Martin** 20 rue de la Société
Vinicole, Cognac 16100, tel 05 45 35
76 66, remymartin.com

## Markets

| | |
|---|---|
| Auch | Thurs. & Sat. |
| Bayonne | Mon.–Sat. |
| Bergerac | Wed. & Sat. |
| Biarritz | Mon.–Sat. |
| Bordeaux | Mon.–Sat. |
| Brantôme | Fri. |
| Cahors | Wed. |
| Lalbenque (truffle) | Tues. (Dec.–March) |
| Pauillac | Sat. |
| Périgueux | Wed. & Sat. |
| St.-Émilion | Sun. |
| St.-Jean-de-Luz | Tues. & Fri. |
| Sarlat-la-Canéda | Wed. & Sat. |

## ■ SOUTH OF FRANCE & CORSICA

### Anchovies

**Société Roque** 17 route d'Argelès, Collioure 66190, tel 04 68 82 04 99

### Charcuterie

**La Maison du Saucisson d'Arles** 3 avenue de la République, St.-Martin-de-Crau 13310, tel 04 90 47 30 40

### Espadrilles & Catalan Fabrics

**Maison Quinta** 3 rue des Grands Fabriques, 04 68 34 41 62, toiles-du-soleil .com

**Les Toiles du Soleil** Le Village, St.-Laurent-de-Cerdans 66260, tel 04 68 68 47 26

### Glassware

**Verrerie de Biot** chemin des Combes, Biot 06410, tel 04 93 65 03 00

### Herbs

**L'Herbier en Provence** Montée la Castre, St.-Paul de Vence 06570, tel 04 93 32 91 51

### Olives & Olive Oil

**Alziari** 14 rue St.-François-de-Paule, Nice 06000, tel 04 93 85 76 92

**Moulin de la Brague** 2 route de Châteauneuf, Opio 06650, tel 04 93 77 23 03

### Perfume

**Parfumerie Fragonard** 20 boulevard Fragonard, Grasse 06130, tel 04 93 36 44 65

**Parfumerie Galimard** 73 route de Cannes, Grasse, tel 04 93 09 20 00

**Parfumerie Molinard** 60 boulevard Victor-Hugo, Grasse 06130, tel 04 93 36 01 62

### Pottery

**Galerie Madoura** rue Suzanne Georges Ramiè, Vallauris 06220, tel 04 93 68 32 58

**Moustiers-Ste.-Marie** Many potteries along route de Riez, Moustiers-Ste.-Marie 06430

**Syndicat des Potiers** avenue Jean Gerbino, Vallauris 06220, tel 04 93 64 88 30

### Provençal Fabrics

**Souleîado** 5 rue Joseph-Vernet, Avignon 84000 (also in other locations including Nîmes & St.-Remy-de-Provence), tel 04 90 86 32 05, souleiado.com

### Santons

**Arterra** 15 rue du Petit Puits, Marseille, tel 04 91 91 03 31. Christmas crib figurines.

### Wine

**Cave Terres d'Avignon** 457 avenue Aristide Briand, Morières-les-Avignon 84310, tel 04 90 22 65 62, terresdavignon.com

**Caves des Vins de Fitou** Fitou 11510, tel 04 68 45 71 41

**Domaine Tempier** 1802 chemin des Fanges, Le Plan du Castellet 83330, tel 04 94 90 21 65, domainetempier .com

**Maison de la Truffe et du Vin du Luberon** place de l'Horloge, Ménerbes 84560, tel 04 90 72 38 37
**Vignerons de Beaumes-de-Venise** quartier Ravel, Beaumes-de-Venise 84190, tel 04 90 12 41 00
**Vignerons Catalans en Roussillon** 1870 avenue Julien Panchot, tel 04 68 85 04 51
**Les Vins du Palais**, 68 avenue General Leclerc, Narbonne 11100, tel 04 68 45 67 85

### Corsican Wine
**Vins de Corse** rue César Campinchi, Grandes Bastia 20200, tel 09 95 31 24 94

## Markets

| | |
|---|---|
| Aix-en-Provence | Tues., Thurs., & Sat. |
| Apt | Sat. |
| Arles | Wed. & Sat. |
| Avignon | Tues.–Sun. |
| Cannes | daily |
| Carpentras | Fri. |
| Céret | Sat. |
| Hyères | Sat. |
| L'Isle-sur-la-Sorgue | Thurs. & Sun. |
| Marseille | Fish market daily a.m., general & flea markets Tues.–Sun. |
| Montpellier | daily |
| Nice | Tues.–Sun., flea market Mon. |
| Orange | Thurs. |
| Perpignan | daily |
| St.-Rémy-de-Provence | Wed. |
| St.-Tropez | Tues. & Sat. |
| Tarascon | Tues. |

# ACTIVITIES

Almost every possible kind of leisure activity can be pursued in France, and your preference may influence the regions you choose to visit. Most towns have excellent public swimming pools and sports facilities. The cities offer more worldly entertainments, from casinos to opera, and from nightclubs to local feast days. Within each region, we have indicated the best places or contacts for activities of particular interest, and listed the main festivals and events during the year. Below is a list of national numbers to contact for specific activities, some of which also have regional contacts. Local tourist offices will provide further information.

## Canoeing & Kayaking

**Fédération Française du Canoë-Kayak** 87 quai de la Marne, Joinville-le-Pont 94340, tel 01 48 89 33 22, ffck .org.

## Cycling

**Cycling tours in Provence** cyclo mundo.com. Guided and self-guided tours.
**Fédération Française du Cyclo-Tourisme** 12 rue Louis Bertrand, Ivry-sur-Seine 94207, tel 01 56 20 88 88, ffct .org

## Golf

**Fédération Française du Golf** Levallois, tel 01 41 49 77 00, ffgolf.org. For all courses in France.

## Horseback Riding

**Comité National de Tourisme Équestre** Tel 02 54 94 46 80, tourisme -equestre.fr. For information on local riding centers.

## Mountain Climbing

**Club Alpin Français** 24 avenue Laumiere, 75019 Paris, tel 01 53 72 87 00, ffcam.fr. In mountain regions there are local clubs.
**Fédération Française de la Montagne et de l'Escalade** 8 quai de la Marne, Paris 75019, tel 01 40 18 75 50, ffme.fr

## Sailing

**Fédération Française de Voile** 17 rue Henri Bocquillon, Paris 75015, tel 01 40 60 37 00, ffvoile.fr

## Skiing

**Écoles de Ski Français** 6 allée des Mitaillères, Meylan 38246, tel 04 76 90 67 36, esf.net
**Fédération Française de Ski** 50 rue des Marquisats, Annecy 74011, tel 04 50 51 40 34, ffs.fr

## Underwater Sports

**Fédération Française d'Études et de Sports Sous-Marins** 24 quai de la Rive-Neuve, Marseille 13284, tel 04 91 33 99 31, ffessm.fr

## Walking

**Fédération Française de la Randonnée Pédestre** 64 rue de Dessous des Berges, Paris 75013, tel 01 44 89 93 90, ffrandonnee.fr

## Waterskiing

**Fédération Française du Ski Nautique** 9–11 rue du Borrego, Paris 75020, tel 01 53 20 19 19, ffsnw.fr

## Tours & Organized Sightseeing

The **Caisse Nationale des Monuments Historiques et des Sites** publishes a map of historic routes *(tel 01 44 61 20 00, monuments-nationaux.fr).* Routes include cathedrals, parks and gardens, and castles, as well as specific historic routes. For information on private historical buildings, contact **Demeure Historique** *(tel 01 55 42 60 00, demeure-historique.org).*

For tours by bus, contact local information offices. Many sights offer guided tours, but are often only in French and can be lengthy.

## ■ NORTHERN FRANCE

### Alsace Wine Route
**Maison des Vins d'Alsace** 12 avenue de la Foire aux Vins, Colmar 68012, tel 03 89 20 16 20, vinalsace.com

### Champagne Tours
Most big champagne houses have their cellars in Reims or Épernay and can be toured. Some of the château vineyards also have tours. It is always advisable to call or email first. In Épernay you can visit a museum (archeo champagne.epernay.fr/en/home).

**Lanson** 66 rue de Courlancy, Reims 51100, tel 03 26 78 50 50, lanson. com. By appointment.
**Moët & Chandon** 20 avenue de Champagne, Épernay 51200, tel 03 26 51 20 20, moet.com. $$$$$.
**Mumm** 29 rue de Champ de Mars, Reims 51100, tel 03 26 49 59 70, mumm.com. Tours in several languages, tasting. $$$$$.
**Piper-Heidsieck** 12 allée du Vignoble, Reims 51100, tel 03 26 84 43 00, piper-heidsieck.com
**Taittinger** 9 place St.-Nicaise, Reims 51100, tel 03 26 85 45 35, taittinger .com. Tours in French, English, and German. $$$$$.
**Veuve Clicquot** 1 place des Droits de l'Homme, Reims 51100, tel 03 26 89 53 90, veuve-clicquot.com

### Main Events
*Sunday before Easter*
**Coulommiers** Wine & cheese fair
*May*
**Amiens** Carnival
*June*
**Chantilly** Horse races
*July*
**Boulogne-sur-Mer** Fish festival
**Douai** Festival of giants
*August*
**Cambrai** Festival of giants
**Locon** Garlic fair
**Maroilles** Fête de la Flamiche (leek tart)
**Wimereux** Mussel festival *September*
**Lille** Grand flea market & mussel festival *(braderie)*
*October*
**Neuilly-St.-Front** Apple fair
**St.-Augustin** Apple & cider festival

## ■ NORMANDY & BRITTANY

### Boat Trips
**Seine Estuary** Promenade en Mer, quai des Passagers, Honfleur, tel 06 71 64 50 46, promenade-en-bateau -honfleur.fr
**Les Sept Îles** Perros-Guirec, tel 02 96 91 10 00, armor-decouverte.fr
**Tourisme et Loîsirs Maritimes** Le Havre, tel 06 16 80 24 10, visiteduport -lehavre.fr

### Cycling
**Bretagne Cyclisme**
bretagne-cyclisme.com
**Ligue de Basse-Normandie**
basse-normandie.ffct.org.

### Golf
**Ligue de Golf de Bretagne** Rennes, tel 02 99 31 68 80

### Horseback Riding
**Domain Equestre** Tel 02 31 28 04 28, cabourg-equitation.com

**Haras du Pin (National Stud)** Orne, tel
02 31 84 61 87, chevalnormandie.com

## Normandy Landings
**Bayeux Tourist Office** Tel 02 31 51 28
28, bayeux-bessin-tourisme.com
**Boat Tours** bessin-normandie.com
**Normandy Guide** normandy-guide
.com. Tours in English.
**Normandy Landings** normandie
memoire.com
**Normandy Tourism**
normandie-tourisme.fr
**Private D-Day Tour** d-daytours.com
**Les Vedettes de Normandie** Tel
02 31 43 86 12, lesvedettesde
normandie.fr. Orne canal boat tours.

## Oyster Route
**Huitres de Normandie** Tel 02 97 42
04 66, huitres-normandie.com

## Sea Fishing
**Trouville** Tel 02 31 65 23 30

## Thalassotherapy (Seawater Treatment)
**Institut de Thalassotherapie**
Arzon 56640, tel 02 97 53 49 00,
thalasso-thermale-atlantique.com
**Pornic Phytomer** Pornic 44210, tel
02 40 82 21 21, thalassopornic.com
**Thalassa Dinard** Dinard 35800, tel
02 99 16 78 10, noveltdinard.com
**Thermes Marin de St.-Malo** St.-
Malo 35400, tel 02 99 40 75 75,
thalassotherapy.com

## Walking
Tel 06 33 49 52 45
haute-normandie.ffrandonnee.fr
Tel 02 97 40 85 88
bretagne.ffrandonnee.fr

## Main Events
### Normandy
*May*
**Coutances** Jazz festival
**Mont St.-Michel** Spring festival

**Rouen** Joan of Arc festival
*June*
**Balleroy** Hot-air balloon meeting
**D-Day beaches** June 6
*July*
**Le Havre** International regatta
**Mont St.-Michel** Pilgrimage across
the sands
*August*
**Cabourg** William the Conqueror pro-
cession
**Carteret** Festival of the Sea
**Deauville** Grand Prix, horse race
*September*
**Lessay** Holy Cross fair
**Lisieux** St. Thérèse festival
*September–October*
**Haras du Pin** Horse trials

### Brittany
*May*
**Tréguier** Pardon of St. Yves
*July*
**Locronan** Petite (every year) or
Grande Troménie (every six years,
next in 2025)
**Rennes** Les Tombées de la Nuit
**Vannes** Jazz festival
*August*
**Carnac** Menhir festival
**Concarneau** Festival of Blue Nets
**Erquy** Festival of the Sea
**Lorient** Interceltic Festival
**Ste.-Anne-la-Palud** Grand Pardon
*September*
**Carnac** Pardon of St.-Cornély

## ■ LOIRE VALLEY

## Ballooning
**France Montgolfières** 24 rue Nationale, Montrichard 41400, tel 03 80
97 38 61, franceballoons.com

## Canoeing & Kayaking
**Ligue Pays de la Loire de Canoë-
Kayak** 75 ave du Lac de Maine,
Angers 49000, tel 02 41 73 86 10
canoekayakpaysdelaloire.fr

## Cruises

**Bateaux Nantais** quai de la Motte Rouge, Nantes, tel 02 40 14 51 14, bateaux-nantais.fr

## Main Events

Most large châteaus have son et lumière (sound and light) shows.

*February*
**Angers** Honey fair
**Saumur** Wine festival

*May*
**Orléans** Joan of Arc festival
**Saumur** International Horse Show

*May–June*
**Chambord** Festival de Chambord

*July*
**Amboise** Festival
**Chinon** Medieval market
**Doué La Fontaine** Rose festival
**Tours** Garlic and basil festival *August*
**Rochefort-sur-Loire**
Anjou folk festival
**Vouvray** Wine fair

*October*
**Azay-le-Rideau** Apple fair
**Bourgeuil** Chestnut fair

## ■ CENTRAL FRANCE & THE ALPS

## Ballooning

**Air Escargot** Remigny 71150, tel 03 85 87 12 30, air-escargot.com

## Canals/Boating

**France Fluviale**, Vermenton, tel 03 86 81 54 55 bourgogne-fluviale.com

## Food & Wine Lessons & Tours

**Burgundy on a Plate** Tel 03 80 39 09 88, burgundyonaplate.com. Gourmet tours with winemakers.
**Caves de l'Abbaye** 28 rue Sylvestre Chauvelot, Beaune, tel 03 80 21 52 98, caves-abbaye-beaune.com. Gourmet tasting lunches with wine and complementary food.

**École des Vins de Bourgogne** Beaune, tel 03 80 26 35 10 ecoledesvins-bourgogne.com

## Rock Climbing

**Club Alpin Français Savoie** club-alpin-savoie.org
**French Alpine Federation Club** clubalpin-rhone-alpes.com

## Silk Farm

**Ma Magnanerie** Lieu-dit Les Mazes, Vallon-Pont-d'Arc 07150, tel 04 75 88 01 27, mamagnarerie.com. Restored silk farm *(magnanerie)* and museum.

## Skiing

**Bureau Info Montagne, Maison de Tourisme**, 3 rue Raoul Blanchard, Grenoble 38019, tel 04 76 42 45 90, infos-montagne.com france-montagnes.com

## Steam Trains

**Chemin de Fer du Haut-Rhône** Maison d'Accueil, Montalieu Vercieu 38390, tel 04 78 81 84 30, cft-hr.com

## Walking

**Comité de la Côte-d'Or** tel 03 80 41 48 62, cotedor-randonnee.com
**Comité de Saône-et-Loire** Tournus, tel 03 85 09 15 08
**Comité de l'Yonne** Auxerre, tel 03 45 02 75 91

## Main Events

*Sunday before Palm Sunday*
**Nuits St.-George** Wine auction
*Maundy Thursday*
**Le Puy-en-Velay** Penitents procession by torchlight
*June*
**Villefranche-sur-Saône** Midsummer's night festivities
*July*
**Arbois** Wine festival
**Gannat** World folklore festival
**Le Puy-en-Velay** Marian procession

**Vienne** Jazz festival
*September*
**Mont Brouilly** Annual wine producers pilgrimage
*September–December*
Grape harvest
*October*
**Dijon** Annual gastronomic fair
*November*
**Beaune** Hospice wine auction
**Bourg-en-Bresse** Gastronomic fair
*December*
**Chablis** Wine festival
**Lyon** Festival of Light

## ■ SOUTHWEST FRANCE

**Périgord Tourisme** *(tel 05 53 35 50 24, dordogne-perigord-tourisme.fr)* offers information on horseback riding, kayaking, golf, and fishing.

### Boat Trips on the Lot River
**Comité Départemental du Tourisme** 107 quai Cavaignac, Cahors 46001, tel 05 65 35 07 09, tourisme-lot.com

### Gambling
**Casino de Biarritz** 1 avenue Édouard V11, Biarritz 64201, tel 05 59 22 77 77
**Casino La Rochelle** allée du Mail, La Rochelle 17000, tel 05 46 34 12 75, lucienbarriere.com

### Golf
**Golf de Biarritz** 2 avenue Edith Cavell, 64200 Biarritz, tel 05 59 03 71 80, golf-biarritz.com

### Skiing & Mountain Climbing in the Pyrenees
Tel 05 62 56 70 00, lespyrenees.net, tourisme-hautes-pyrenees.com

### Surfing
**Fédération Française de Surf** Plage Nord, boulevard Front de Mer, Hossegor 40150, tel 05 58 43 55 88, surfingfrance.com

**L'Ecole de Glisse** tel 05 56 03 27 60, lacanau.ucpa.com
**Lacanau Surf Club** tel 05 56 26 38 84, surflacanau.com

### Tennis
**Biarritz Olympique** Parc des Sports, Biarritz, tel 05 59 01 64 64, bo-pb.com

### Thalassotherapy
**Institut Louison-Bobet** 11 rue Louison-Bobet, Biarritz 64200, tel 05 59 41 30 00, thalasso-thermale.com
**Les Thermes Marins** 80 rue de Madrid, Biarritz 64200, tel 05 59 23 01 22, biarritz-thalasso.com

### Walking
**Randonnée Dordogne** Périgueux, tel 05 53 51 70 30, rando.cg24.fr

### Wine Courses
**École du Vin** Château Loudenne, Médoc, St. Yzans, tel 05 56 48 18 62, medoc-bordeaux.com

### Main Events
*June*
**St.-Jean-de-Luz** Fête de St.-Jean; Basque torchlight procession
*August*
**Arcachon** Festival of the Sea
**Gujan-Mestras** Oyster fair
**Marciac** Jazz festival
*September*
**Rocamadour** Torchlit Festival of the Assumption
**St.-Émilion** Grape harvest festival
*October*
**Nontron** Chestnut fair

## ■ SOUTH OF FRANCE & ■ CORSICA

### Casinos
**Le Casino** place du Casino, Monte Carlo, Monaco, tel 00 377 98 06 25 25, montecarlocacsinos.com

**Casino Ruhl**, Promenade des Anglais, Nice, tel 04 97 03 12 22

## Cycling
**Cycling Tours in Provence** cyclomundo.com

## Horseback Riding
**Centre Équestre de la Ville de Marseille** 33 Traverse Carthage, Marseille, tel 04 91 73 72 94
**Comité Regional d'Équitation Occitanie**, equitation-occitanie.fr
**Languedoc-Roussillon** 14 rue des Logis, Loupian, Mèze, tel 04 67 43 61 11

## River Fishing
**Fédération Inter-départmentale de Peche et Pisciculture** 19 avenue Noël Franchini, Ajaccio 20000, tel 04 95 23 13 32, federationpeche.fr

## Sailing & Windsurfing
**Cannes Station de Voile** Port du Mourre Rouge, Cannes 06400, tel 04 92 18 88 88
**Nautique 2000** Port Gallice, Juan-les-Pins 06160, tel 04 93 61 20 01
**Station Voile** place de la République, Port Bacarès, tel 04 68 86 16 56, portbarcares.com

## Scuba Diving
**Federation Française d'Études et de Sports Sous-Marins** 24 quai Rive-Neuve, Marseille 13284, tel 04 91 33 99 31, ffessm.fr

## Skiing
**Font Romeu Pyrénées** Office de Tourisme, tel 04 68 30 68 30, font-romeu.fr
**Isola 2000 Alpes-Maritimes** Office de Tourisme, tel 04 93 23 15 15 isola2000.com

## Walking
**Comité Départmental de la Randonnée Pédestre** 4 avenue de Verdun, Cagnes-sur-Mer, tel 04 93 20 74 73, cdrp06.org
**Corsica** randonnee-corse.com

## Main Events
### Côte d'Azur
*February*
**Menton** Lemon Festival (Procession of the Golden Fruit)
*Shrove Tuesday*
**Nice** Carnival (2 weeks)
*May*
**Cannes** International Film Festival
**Monaco** Formula One Grand Prix
*July*
**Juan-les-Pins–Antibes** World Jazz Festival
**Nice** Jazz festival

### Provence
*May*
**Stes.-Maries-de-la-Mer** Le Pelerinage (Romany Pilgrimage)
*Whitsun*
**Nîmes** Feria (Whitsun Festival)
*June*
**Tarascon** Fête de la Tarasque
*July*
**Aix-en-Provence** International Festival of Opera & Music
**Arles** Feria bullfight season begins
**Les Rencontres d'Arles** photography festival

### Languedoc–Roussillon
*Good Friday*
**Perpignan** Procession des Pénitents de la Sanch
*July*
**Carcassonne** Embrasement de la Cité
**Montpellier** Dance festival
**Prades** Pablo Casals music festival
*September*
**Perpignan** Visa pour l'Image, Festival of Photojournalism

### Corsica
*Good Friday*
**Sarténe** Procession du Catenacciu

# LANGUAGE GUIDE

## Useful Words & Phrases

### General
Yes *Oui*
No *Non*
Excuse me *Excusez-moi*
Hello *Bonjour*
Hi *Salut*
Please *S'il vous plaît*
Thank you (very much) *Merci (beaucoup)*
You're welcome *De rien*
Have a good day! *Bonne journée!*
OK *D'accord*
Goodbye *Au revoir*
Good night *Bonsoir*
Here *ici*
There *là*
Today *aujourd'hui*
Yesterday *hier*
Tomorrow *demain*
Now *maintenant*
Later *plus tard*
Right away *tout de suite*
This morning *ce matin*
This afternoon *cet après-midi*
This evening *ce soir*
Do you speak English? *Parlez-vous anglais?*
I am American *Je suis Américain* (man); *je suis Américaine* (woman)
I don't understand *Je ne comprends pas*
Please speak more slowly *Parlez plus lentement, s'il vous plaît*
Where is...? *Où est...?*
I don't know *Je ne sais pas*
No problem *Ce n'est pas grave*
That's it *C'est ça*
Here it is *Voici*
There it is *Voilà*
What is your name? *Comment vous-appelez-vous?*

My name is... *Je m'appelle...*
Let's go *On y va*
At what time? *À quelle heure?*
When? *Quand?*
What time is it? *Quelle heure est-il?*

### In the Hotel
Do you have...? *Avez-vous...?*
a single room *une chambre simple*
a double room *une chambre double*
with/without bathroom/shower *avec/sans salle de bain/douche*

### Help
I need a doctor/dentist *J'ai besoin d'un médecin/dentiste*
Can you help me? *Pouvez-vous m'aider?*
Where is the hospital? *Où est l'hôpital?*
Where is the police station? *Où est le commissariat?*

### Shopping
I'd like... *Je voudrais...*
How much is it? *C'est combien?*
Do you take credit cards? *Est-ce que vous acceptez les cartes de crédit?*
Size (clothes) *la taille*
Size (shoes) *la pointure*
Cheap *bon marché*
Expensive *cher*
Have you got...? *Avez vous...?*
I'll take it *Je le prends*
Anything else? *Avec ça?*
Enough *assez*
Too much *trop*
Bill *la note*

### Shops
bakery *la boulangerie*
bookshop *la librairie*
chemist *la pharmacie*

delicatessen *la charcuterie/le traiteur*
department store *le grand magasin*
fishmonger *la poissonnerie*
grocery *l'alimentation/l'épicerie*
junk shop *la brocante*
library *la bibliothèque*
supermarket *le supermarché*
tobacconist *le tabac*

## At a Restaurant
I'd like to order *Je voudrais commander*
Is service included? *Est-ce que le service est compris?*
I am on a diet *Je suis au régime*

## Sightseeing
visitor information office *office de tourisme* or *le syndicat d'initiative*

open *ouvert*
closed *fermé*
every day *tous les jours*
all year round *toute l'année*
all day long *toute la journée*
free *gratuit/libre*
abbey *l'abbaye* (f)
castle *le château*
church *l'église* (f)
museum *le musée*
staircase *l'escalier* (m)
tower *la tour* (La Tour Eiffel)
tour (walk or drive) *le tour*
town *la ville*
old town *la vieille ville*
Town Hall *Hôtel de Ville /la mairie*

# MENU READER

See regional food sections for
recommended regional dishes.

*le petit déjeuner* breakfast
*le déjeuner* lunch
*le dîner* dinner
*menu à prix fixe* meal at set price
*le plat principal* main course
*carte des vins* wine list
*l'addition* the bill

## *Les boissons* drinks

*café* coffee
*déca/décaffeiné* decaffeinated coffee
*express/noir* espresso/black
*filtre* American filtered coffee
*thé* tea
*le lait* milk
*eau minérale* mineral water
*gazeux* fizzy
*limonade* fizzy lemon drink
*citron pressé* fresh lemon juice served
    with sugar
*bière* beer
*la carafe/le pichet* pitcher of tap water
    or wine
*la demi-carafe* half liter
*vin de maison* house wine
*vin de pays* local wine
*digestif* after-dinner drink

## *Le repas* the meal

*le pain* bread
*le poivre* pepper
*le sel* salt
*le sucre* sugar
*le potage* soup

## Meat dishes

*l'agneau* lamb
*le bifteck* steak
*saignant* rare
*bien cuit* well done
*entrecôte* rib steak
*faux-filet* sirloin steak

*blanquette* stew of veal, lamb, or chicken
    with creamy egg sauce
*boeuf à la mode* beef in red wine with
    carrots & onions
*bourguignonne* cooked in red wine,
    onions & mushrooms
*le canard* duck
*la carbonnade* stew of beef in beer
*le carré d'agneau* rack of lamb
*le cassoulet* stew of beans, sausages,
    pork, or duck
*le confit* duck or goose preserved in its
    own fat
*le côte d'agneau* lamb chop
*le dinde* turkey
*le faisan* pheasant
*farci* stuffed
*le foie de veau* calf's liver
*le foie gras* liver of force-fed duck or
    goose
*le jambon* ham
*le lapin* rabbit
*le magret de canard* breast of duck
*l'oie* goose
*le porc* pork
*le pot-au-feu* casserole of beef &
    vegetables
*le poulet* chicken
*les rognons* kidneys
*rôti* roast
*le sanglier* wild boar
*la saucisse* fresh sausage
*le saucisson* salami
*le veau* veal

## Fish dishes

*l'anchois* anchovy
*l'anguille* eel
*la barbue* brill
*la bouillabaisse* fish soup
*le cabillaud* cod
*le coquillage* shellfish
*la coquille St.-Jacques* scallop
*la crevette* shrimp
*l'encornet* squid

*le flétan* halibut
*les fruits de mer* seafood
*le homard* lobster
*l'huître* oyster
*la lotte* monkfish
*la moule* mussel
*le saumon* salmon
*le thon* tuna
*la truite* trout

## Sauces

*américaine* white wine, tomatoes, butter
  & Cognac
*bearnaise* egg, butter, wine, & herbs
*forestière* mushrooms & bacon
*hollandaise* egg, butter & lemon
*meunière* butter, lemon & parsley
*meurette* red wine sauce
*Mornay* cream, egg & cheese
*Provençal* usually tomatoes, garlic &
  olive oil

## *Légumes* vegetables

*l'artichaut* artichoke
*les asperges* asparagus
*l'aubergine* eggplant
*l'avocat* avocado
*le champignon* mushroom
*le cornichon* gherkin
*la courgette* zucchini

*le chou* cabbage
*le chou-fleur* cauliflower
*les crudités* raw vegetables
*les épinards* spinach
*les haricots verts* green beans
*les lentilles* lentils
*le maïs* corn
*l'oignon* onion
*le pois* pea
*le poivron* bell pepper
*les pommes de terre* potatoes
*les pommes frites* french fries
*la salade verte* green salad

## Fruits

*la cerise* cherry
*le citron* lemon
*le citron vert* lime
*la fraise* strawberry
*la framboise* raspberry
*le pamplemousse* grapefruit
*la pêche* peach
*la poire* pear
*la pomme* apple
*le raisin* grape

## Snacks

*le croque-monsieur* ham & cheese toasted
  sandwich
*le yaourt* yogurt

# INDEX

# ILLUSTRATIONS CREDITS

National Geographic
## TRAVELER
# France
FIFTH EDITION

Since 1888, the National Geographic Society has funded more than 14,000 research, conservation, education, and storytelling projects around the world. National Geographic Partners distributes a portion of the funds it receives from your purchase to National Geographic Society to support programs including the conservation of animals and their habitats.

National Geographic Partners, LLC
1145 17th Street NW
Washington, DC 20036-4688 USA

Get closer to National Geographic Explorers and photographers, and connect with our global community. Join us today at nationalgeographic.org/joinus

For rights or permissions inquiries, please contact National Geographic Books Subsidiary Rights: bookrights@natgeo.com

Fifth edition edited by White Star s.r.l. Licensee of National Geographic Partners, LLC. Update by Justin Kavanaghr Layout by Bianco Tangerine, Turin

Map illustrations drawn by Chris Orr Associates, Southampton, England. Cutaway illustrations drawn by Maltings Partnership, Derby, England.

The information in this book has been carefully checked and to the best of our knowledge is accurate. However, details are subject to change, and the publisher cannot be responsible for such changes, or for errors or omissions. Assessments of sites, hotels, and restaurants are based on the author's subjective opinions, which do not necessarily reflect the publisher's opinion.

ISBN: 978-8-8544-2061-8

Printed in Malaysia
24/VIVA/1